IN
GOD
WE
TRUST

The Book
for Veterans
& Active Duty

NEW LIFE STUDY TESTAMENT
with complete
TOPICAL STUDY OUTLINES
also
WORD LIST
TOPICAL VERSE FINDER
HAPPENINGS IN THE GOSPELS

Translated by
Gleason H. Ledyard

WinePress Publishing  Mukilteo, WA 98275

To order additional copies of *IN GOD WE TRUST* contact:

WinePress Publishing
PO Box 1406
Mukilteo, WA 98275

(800) 326-4674

— Quantity discounts available —

This book is dedicated to those men and women who
sacrificially serve in the Armed Forces of America

*"The soldier, above all others, is
required to perform the highest act
of religious teaching — sacrifice."*

*General Douglas MacArthur,
July 14, 1935, Washington D.C.*

Dedication

In God We Trust is dedicated to Steve Pry, a soldier who was faithful to the end. He served with the 101st Airborne Division (Viet Nam, May, 1969 to July, 1970). Complications from a long battle with cancer resulted in Steve's death in December of 1995, but not before he had the opportunity to share his faith with many veterans. From the time that he was told he had a lethal form of cancer, Steve set about to make use of every waking moment to tell other veterans and soldiers about the goodness of God. He planted many "salvation seeds" of Jesus Christ in the hearts of those with whom he came in contact. His warm smile radiated the peace of God and it rubbed off on everyone around him. Right to the end, in the typical style of a true soldier, Steve Pry never complained about his condition. He has finally arrived at his permanent duty assignment...in the loving arms of Jesus Christ.

Acknowledgements

WinePress Publishing wishes to thank Dr. Frank Crealock, and his wife Barbara, for their support and dedication in making this book possible. We are grateful for these dear friends who saw the vision, and responded with their time and resources to further the message of our Lord Jesus Christ. May the seeds of these words bear much fruit for the glory of the Kingdom of God.

Table of Contents

Introduction

War is something shared by many. The reactions to war are also commonly shared among the soldiers, sailors and airmen who fought in it.

This book is for soldiers and veterans—the ones willing to make the ultimate sacrifice for their country. There are many truths and experiences in this section of *In God We Trust*. If you served in the armed forces, you will easily recognize them. Some of these experiences may be a mirror image of your own life. If you find it so, be encouraged. Identifying them is the first sign that you are on the right road.

After serving as a captain in the U.S. Air Force (as a medical doctor and flight surgeon) during the Korean War, I made several observations over the years about the impacting stress our veterans have lived with.

Military personnel often require emergency treatment for physical wounds sustained in combat. These wounds are visable and eventually heal, leaving only scars that serve as a reminder of the trauma. However, the emotional wounds of war are not always visable, nor identifiable. *Trauma of the soul* can be hidden for months or years, only to surface at unexpected times in the future. The sheer unpredictability of the symptoms and reactions caused by war time stress has wreaked havoc over the generations. Many veterans I have talked with manifest major distress from these invisible wounds. Although there is a general opinion that war stress is incurable, I believe help and healing is possible when the problem is first identified by the veteran, and then submitted to an Almighty God for His finishing touch.

Frank W. Crealock, M.D.
Seattle, Washington

Experiences from Different Wars

Note: The following short composites are war experiences from several different wars where American forces were involved. They all are true stories.

"I am young, I am twenty years old; yet I know nothing of life but despair, death, fear...What do they expect of us if a time ever comes when the war is over? Through the years our business has been killing — it was our first calling in life. Our knowledge of life is limited to death. What will happen afterwards? And what shall come out of us?"

"All Quiet On The Western Front"
Erich Maria Remarque

World War II

Honor, Glory and Battle Dreams

Twenty-two years after his last combat experience in World War II, America's best known hero, Audie Murphy, still slept with the lights on and a loaded .45 caliber pistol by his bed. He couldn't bring himself to ask for help concerning his war stress. After all, he had won The Congressional Medal of Honor. Mr. Murphy was not the only veteran in WW II to experience delayed wartime stress.

The World War II generation: A tough, uncomplaining people, children of the Depression generation who went off to war in 1941 to wage a victorious defense of freedom for humanity. They were irrepressible in their pursuit of the American Dream, and entered the combat theaters with a sense of honor and glory that the world had never before seen. The following is an actual account of one veteran's life after the war.

"My unit had it's baptism of fire in North Africa. I survived 39 months of sustained combat, and never got hit. Coming home I went back to work at the plant but things weren't right. At night I was having severe 'battle dreams,' and in the daytime I would go through periods of partial amnesia. I couldn't even remember my own name.

Since I didn't get wounded I kept my mouth shut about these things, figuring that only the guys who got hit had any problems. Besides, it wasn't too popular to admit that the war had caused any mental problems. I wanted to fit back in and be normal again so I joined a veteran club, not so much for the friendship, but for the opportunity to drink my problems away in the familiar environment of soldiers.

There was another veteran in our town who couldn't hide his problems, and I tried my best not to end up like him. The last thing I wanted anyone to say is, 'He was in the war, that's why he's that way.'"

(The people in town turned away and acted as if they had never noticed this veteran's odd behavior. After all, he wasn't quite there anymore.)

"There were times when I knew that I was out of control, and I would have to take time off work. I was staying up all hours of the night, afraid to go to sleep because of a dream I kept having. By daybreak I would be so exhausted that I couldn't even get in my car to drive.

During those days off I retreated to my own little "foxhole," a small, dimly lit room that was filled with some old relics I brought home from the war. There I would spend time with my demons, and they would torment my mind through the memories of what I had seen and experienced in Africa. Nobody at work ever knew of my problems because I covered it up so well. I never wanted anyone to think I was crazy because of the war."

The aftermath of World War II:

- Nearly 300,000 soldiers died in the war. Some 800,000 saw combat.
- Over 12,000 were listed as missing in action at the end of the war.
- Fully 37.5 percent of all casualties were "mental."
- By 1945 there were 111,000 neuropsychiatric casualties from the war.

The psychiatric discharge rate was 250 percent higher than World War I.

IN GOD WE TRUST

Korea

Mud, Cold and Terror

In November we moved within about ten miles of the Yalu River, right at the top of Korea. I was on a forward observer's post and saw thousands of Chinese soldiers fill the valley below. As I reported the figures to the command over the field telephone, they refused to believe me. "Yes," I said, "thousands, sir!" Frustrated, I slammed the phone down and watched in horror as the sea of life moved straight for us. The Chinese wanted the Yalu real bad. They pushed us back, slaughtered us, and that bit of war was one of the worst defeats in history. We kept falling back and regrouping, and each time we regrouped, the group was smaller. We had no choice but to fall back because we had no reinforcements or resupply. It wasn't like when I fought in Vietnam years later; we couldn't call in artillery or airstrikes at the drop of a hat.

We were just out there to face the waves of charging soldiers with what guts we had, and the little bit of weaponry that we could pack on our backs. Ultimately I was alone and became separated from my friends. Armed only with an Ml Garand rifle and a few clips of ammo, I evaded the enemy for three days, trying to get back to our lines. There was only snow, ice, slush, mud, cold and terror as I made my way carefully past all the North Koreans and Chinese who permeated the frozen hillsides.

Even though we got a few parades when we arrived back to the States, America wasn't sure if the war was over or not. It just sort of wound down with nothing to end it except a cease-fire with no side winning. We soldiers knew that we had fought hard, but since there was no victory and just a stalemate, we became a part of America that was put on hold to see "what would happen next" in Korea.

I was discharged and went silently back to my job. I was as confused as everyone else about the "police action." Not much was mentioned about it after that. At times I would feel some bitterness begin to rise up inside me about the war, and how we soldiers were ignored for our efforts. The best way for me to control any bad feelings and resentments was to work hard during the days and drink a lot at night. My wife and I became regulars at several taverns and dance halls, but my drinking became a threat to our marriage. When I would get drunk I would either become remorseful or belligerent. I would end up crying in my beer, or pick out the biggest drunk in the place and call him outside to fight. I just had too much pent up frustration that I had to release somehow.

The aftermath of the Korean war:

- 33,629 soldiers were killed.

- 103,284 were wounded.

- Of the 198,380 who saw combat, 24.2 percent were emotional casualties.

IN GOD WE TRUST

"We should like for you, our brothers, to know something of the trouble we went through in Asia. At that time we were completely overwhelmed, the burden was more than we could bear, in fact we told ourselves that this was the end. Yet we believe now that we had this sense of impending disaster so that we might learn to trust, not in ourselves, but in God who can raise the dead. It was God who kept us from such deadly perils, and it is he who still keeps us."

2 Corinthians 1:8-10

Viet Nam

Caught in the Middle

On a chilly day in February of 1963, I stood in front of the U.S. Army recruitment station, staring through the window at a life-size cardboard cutout of a soldier. This was not a photograph of just any ordinary soldier — he was a paratrooper! Tall, clean shaven, and the most rugged-looking man I had ever seen in a military uniform. I was sold. That's all it took for me to sign up for three years.

I was excited and didn't care what kind of job I got, as long as I could jump from airplanes, go to war and win some medals. I thought this was my doorway to being important — someone who could earn the respect of his family and countrymen.

After jump school I was assigned to the 82nd Airborne Division at Fort Bragg, North Carolina. However, I faced an unexpected problem — there was no war.

One day I met a man who arrived from duty in Okinawa, where he served with the 173rd Airborne Brigade. While there he was sent several times on temporary duty to a place called Vietnam. He saw combat as a door gunner on a helicopter. I knew right away that I wanted to go to Okinawa to get into the action. After a couple of weeks of paperwork, I was granted a transfer.

My new unit spent the next year jungle training on Okinawa, Taiwan, and various rain islands in the South China Sea. I did not get an opportunity to see any action until May of 1965. At that time President Johnson helped my dreams become a reality when he ordered my unit's deployment into South Vietnam. I was part of the first regular army combat forces to begin escalating the "10,000 day" war. My war had finally come, and the next eleven months changed my life forever.

Almost Home

It was two o'clock in the morning and the temperature hovered in the mid-90s. We had turned in our weapons and equipment the previous day, and were confined to a tiny barbed wire compound at the airbase. For at least some of us the war was over. Our one year tour of duty was complete, and it was our last night in Vietnam. We looked forward to boarding a jetliner to leave this living hell, forever. After drinking dozens of beers, we each scrounged for a place to sleep. I managed to find a mattress inside a small building made of corrugated tin and scrap wood, and settled in to relax for the next four hours before our plane would leave. Not long after lying down, I was on the edge of slipping into a drunken stupor when a frightening, but familiar, sound blasted me into consciousness. Incoming mortar explosions violently rocked the small compound.

Instinctively, I threw the mattress over me as the air-bursting explosions ripped through the fenced-in compound around me. Pounding my fists into the ground, I yelled out angrily to a faraway enemy gun crew, "You're not going to get me now! I'm going home! You're not getting me now!"

As suddenly as it had begun, the explosions ceased. I could hear the wounded crying out, and someone screaming to a dead friend, ordering him to get up. I ran to a wounded soldier nearby. His stomach was gashed open. I quickly ripped off my shirt and applied it to the wound, and shouted for a medic to assist me.

Seven teenage soldiers died that morning in a tiny compound ten thousand miles from home. After spending one year in the hell of the Vietnam war, this was their reward. How unjust it seemed. Later I wasn't so sure who the lucky ones were....we or they. We who lived that night may have come home physically, but a large part of our souls were left behind. The dead wouldn't have the memories, the nightmares, or people spitting on them when they finally got home.

War Is Not A John Wayne Movie

After I got home I could not forget the war. In my mind the same people kept dying over and over. The pain and fear of failure was standing on me like a giant in lead boots. I had been a good soldier, and had done what my country had asked me to do. Now I felt I had become an outcast for participating in an unpopular war. I felt blamed, as if I had done something wrong, when I was only doing what I was told to do, which is any soldier's obligation. This is not the way I had imagined my homecoming. Nobody wanted to hear about my experiences in

Vietnam. It seemed as though the entire country just wanted to forget the whole sorry mess. Students were rioting, brothers were fighting and quarreling with each other about the right and wrong of it, and I felt caught in the middle.

I found my way to escape. I began to drink a lot of alcohol and take drugs in heavy dosages. The alcohol and drugs gave me an acceptable excuse to behave in a reactive and inappropriate way. It was behavior that I couldn't control, and happened mostly during social experiences. The drugs and alcohol helped me sleep at night without too many nightmares of Vietnam. They also helped numb my emotions so that I could make it through each day without breaking down and crying uncontrollably about what my life had come to.

The war never ended for me, it only changed locations. My life seemed to be one mental ambush after another after I arrived home. Even though I wasn't afraid of losing my life, as I was in Vietnam, I lived in fear of unknown surprises that would be thrown at me in normal civilian situations. I dreaded to think of how I would react. I didn't want people to think I was crazy, so I just took more drugs and alcohol to cover up any social slips I might make.

Sometimes I would remember and feel sad about the thoughts and ideals I used to have before the war. It felt as though I had been deceived by the older generation. They led me to believe that war was an honor to participate in, and that it was something that every young man needed to do to prove his manhood. I had to hold myself back because I knew that if I allowed myself to get angry I would blow up, and would probably keep on blowing up until everything, including myself, was gone.

At one time I had great dreams of being a war hero. When I was young I would visualize myself marching down the main street of my little hometown in an army uniform, a chest full of decorations, and the whole town cheering me on. I used to fantasize about being in the movies. I would be John Wayne leading a heroic charge against a machine gun nest, and then the words, "The End" would flash across the screen as a man and woman embraced with an American flag flying over the background.

After the war I sat alone many nights drinking from another bottle, and downing a few more drugs trying to get it all straight in my mind. The next day I would wipe the tears from my eyes, and go out and try to do the impossible...be a normal person again. No, war was not what I expected.

Chuck Dean

The aftermath of the Viet Nam War:

- More Viet Nam veterans have committed suicide since the war officially ended in 1975 than were killed in the war itself—by nearly three times.

- The divorce rate among Viet Nam veterans is in the 90 percentile.

- One third of all prisoners in American prisons are veterans of Viet Nam.

- Today more than 800,000 veterans of Viet Nam suffer from symptoms of post-traumatic stress, and neurological disorders.

- More than 40 percent of all Viet Nam veterans were exposed to the defoliant, Agent Orange, which is now causing cancer, tumors, and birth defects (in their offspring) in thousands of veterans. The governnment is denying many of the claims for fear that it will cost too much money to properly treat all the sufferers. Some 12 million gallons of the poison was dumped on the troops while serving there.

Latin America

Shattered Dreams

In October of 1983, under heavy anti-aircraft and small arms fire, I made the combat parachute assault on the island of Grenada to free the medical students trapped there. I was wounded the second day while pulling another troop out under fire. Two days later, after personally killing several Cubans in combat, I was wounded again through the chest. This ended my military career. By this time I was beginning to question quite a few things that the military had me doing. Perhaps the bullets slowed me down long enough to think about it.

For security reasons I cannot mention other Latin American countries in which I served. I had planned to make a career of the military until my wounds got me retired. The first few years

14

on active duty I held onto all the beliefs of patriotism and noble ideals that drive most professional soldiers. But when I started working for Special Operations things began to change.

In the early 80s, another "advisor" and I had our troops out on a training combat patrol. While we were "practice" patrolling, my point man walked us into an actual ambush. Everything went off at once, and it sounded like the whole world had exploded. My other team member (advisor) was wounded and down. Several others were dead, and the rest of the training platoon had taken off in escape, leaving me and my wounded team member alone. The only thing I thought of doing was to charge the ambush as I was trained, and I guess I went a little crazy. Thirteen guerrillas had ambushed us, and I eliminated all of them within a few minutes. I was wounded and couldn't get a chopper down through the jungle to pull us out, so I carried my wounded buddy two kilometers to a pickup point.

I was very angry that the "indigenous" platoon had run off and left us for dead. I didn't trust anyone the rest of my tour down there. I still have trouble trusting people.

I was medically discharged after spending many months in the hospital. Because so many of my operations south of the border were classified it took me the next six years to get my medical records declassified in order to get the proper care I needed. By this time I knew I had been deceived by the military, and bitterness set in with a vengeance. My physical condition got worse because of it, and my distrust for the government mounted.

I had been brought up in a church believing that human life was sacred, and now I was faced with the fact that I violated that belief; I had taken another human's life. The thought left me confused. I really didn't know what God thought about me killing people, and I wasn't sure that He would ever forgive me. My life has become an array of shattered dreams. If I did all those things for "God, duty, and country," then why had I been rejected like this?

The aftermath of the Grenada Invasion:

- Duration: October 23 to November 21, 1983.

- 45 Americans dead, 175 wounded. 0 missing. Enemy deaths, unknown.

- Other Central America statistics are still classified by the U.S. Government.

The Gulf War

"I Don't Feel Like a Hero"

"Dear Dad,
I've personally blown up five Iraqi tanks in the air sorties I've flown over here. Dad, I know there were people inside those tanks, but I can't afford to think about that right now and still do my job. I know that when I get home I'll have to face it — I'll have to deal with the things I'm having to do in war. I'm not looking forward to that."

A U.S. pilot, Kuwait liberation, 1991

Incredibly, the ground war was over in 100 hours. Buzzards spun in patient circles overhead and wild dogs scavenged through the sand of the Iraqi desert. I'll never forget the detail I pulled burying the bodies of the enemy to keep the critters from getting them. It was a lonely and thankless task.

IN GOD WE TRUST

We searched each body for identification and placed it, with any photos, money and other personal effects, into plastic bags and hung them as best we could on sticks or under rocks on the carefully indicated graves. Then we wrapped each soldier in whatever we had, (usually a blanket or the chemical protection suit that each Republican Guard soldier owned), and laid him to rest.

This war has been called a war where "smart weapons attacked and destroyed dumb targets," and thousands of Iraqis gave up and surrendered. We lost so very few, and it was a war where everyone on the winning side was a hero. Our homecoming was quite a celebration. But, I don't feel like I did anything to deserve a hero's welcome.

I have had trouble sleeping since I got home, and sirens and noises keep me on edge. I hear a fire truck go by now and I want to look for shelter, thinking that something's going to explode nearby.

Even though we didn't fight too much over there I still think I've got some nerve problems. I don't dare tell anyone about it though because I'm afraid they will laugh at me, or tell me, "You don't deserve to have a problem. Remember, you won and we gave you a parade when you got home."

The aftermath of America's Gulf War:

- 105 Soldiers were killed.

- 21 were taken as POWS.

- Preliminary surveys are indicating that 54 percent of all the combat troops suffered significant psychological distress.

- 19 percent are suffering moderate or severe family readjustment problems.

- The divorce rate is already climbing so much that there aren't enough divorce attorneys in the vicinity of active U.S. military posts to handle the demand for divorces. The divorce rate increased at these bases 60 percent over a one-year period.

- To this date all the repercussions of the chemical exposure that the Gulf veterans suffered is unknown. Many are reporting birth defects in their offspring. The list of symptoms as a result of exposure to chemicals and other toxins is still growing.

IN GOD WE TRUST

Diseases of the Soul

"War is like a cancer in all of us. It quietly eats us up after awhile. We can only stuff our past experiences inside us for so long before they begin to eat their way to the surface. I'd like to talk to someone about these things, but I don't think there's anyone interested in talking about hell. For us the war never ended, but no one else can see that. To me that is the biggest let down of all. We struggled hard to survive, then we found out that nobody wanted to hear about the war and our problems, or where we had been. Coming home was hell."

A Veteran of the Vietnam War.

The Forgotten Warrior

War affects our lives in a unique way. It generates a sense of anxiety that can destroy our peace of mind, and it can create fears that wake us in the night and intrude on our thoughts during the day. It can break our ability to concentrate while we work and play. War's effects can turn small problems into huge issues. For the survivors, the ravages of war have a profound impact on their lives, robbing them of their personal sense of control and security. War creates a tremendous amount of stress.

21

IN GOD WE TRUST

If it goes unrecognized and unmanaged, this stress can severely damage a person's mental and physical health.

Throughout history the general costs tallied from war are things like lost territory, number of cities destroyed, and governments toppled. Little interest is shown about the aftershock soldiers go through. Rarely are their stressful reactions understood. Millions of individual soldiers around the world continue to be in need of emotional and psychological help because of their wartime experiences; this is the "human factor" of war. Unfortunately, this always seems to be the last casualty remembered when counting the costs of wars.

As long as there have been wars, there has been stress for the participants. It's a history that until recently has been hidden from view, and poorly documented. It has not been easy to record how the individual soldier felt after combat. War experiences are generally held in quiet confidentiality by most soldiers, and have been a puzzling secret kept from those who were not there to experience it. For years these experiences have been a mystery for war historians who have not themselves had war experience.

Within the great and special "secret" of war exists the darkest corner of all, war's essential feature: *combat*. Only the individual soldier, who has lived through it, can really tell with accuracy what it is like to survive the emotionally rigorous circumstances that arise from the field of combat. It is likewise, extremely difficult for soldiers to relate these experiences to anyone who was not there, making therapy and remedies from the professional community almost impossible. Unless the therapist is himself an ex-soldier with relative experiences, he will usually find the veteran unwilling to open himself up to significant treatment.

Traditionally society has had no answers for the soldier's "strange" reactions to life after war. They generally put him in a hopeless category, and with a degree of pity, try to forget that he is there.

Most soldiers have had to find their own remedies, and adopt their own devices to cope with the "diseases of the soul." The time has come to look beyond some of these coping mindsets and discover some lasting solutions to these "diseases."

Unseen Wounds

We veterans can watch our physical wounds heal up, but the scars on the flesh only remind us of our former pain and suffering that came during the war. With time the flesh wounds heal and don't bother us much anymore, but the wounds in our minds are the ones no one can see but us, and they afflict our souls as well.

Stress

The American Heritage Dictionary says stress is, "A mentally or emotionally disruptive or upsetting condition occurring in response to adverse external influences, and capable of affecting physical health, usually characterized by increased heart rate, a rise in blood pressure, muscular tension, irritability, and depression."

Stress is a personal response that our bodies and minds go through in order to meet the demands of different life situations. If these situations go beyond the range of normal human experiences (and war trauma is certainly something beyond that range), then we become particularly vulnerable to having severe symptoms of what is known as post-traumatic stress (commonly called PTS). PTS is NOT a mental illness, it is a reaction to the extreme stress we encountered during war. It becomes especially apparent when we find ourselves being unable to completely adjust to civilian life upon returning home.

Effects On Our Lives

When we suffer with PTS our lives are interfered with, and our ability to lead meaningful and productive lives is significantly hindered. Veterans with this "disease of the soul" may have serious problems identifying with others. They may feel so alienated that they are led into repeated destructive and self-destructive symptoms and behaviors — including committing relational suicide (destroying personal relationships with other people who have become close).

Carrying The Burden

PTS is a burden carried around inside the hearts and minds of most soldiers who survive the hard life of wartime experiences.

Soldiers are people trained and conditioned to survive constant life-threatening situations. However, our adjustment back to normal social (civilian) life has been difficult. PTS is the chief cause of this difficulty. Nearly every situation we face in "normal" life becomes a matter of survival for us. "Normal" people do not understand our responses, because sometimes we react in a survival combat mode to "get the job done." We have done and seen things in war that made returning to normal life practically unobtainable.

Do You Have PTS?

When I discovered that I may have a problem which stemmed from my war experiences, I began to search for simple explanations. I found that there were some basic indicators of PTS that told me that what I was experiencing were stress reactions, and that I was not really going crazy. Many veterans have the following PTS reactions:

- Sudden memories of the stressful event—flashbacks. These flashbacks may last from minutes to hours and may occur months or years after the trauma.

- Nightmares, or war dreams, causing fear-induced reactions while asleep. Also veterans may react intensely to loud noises when awake.

- Some avoid being around people as much as they can, which seriously affects their relationships with others, especially their family. It is hard for some to feel emotions the way others seem to. Even if they can identify their feelings, they have difficulty expressing them. Many times people think veterans are cold, and even aloof.

What happened to me:

- Since I thought that I had failed while serving in Viet Nam I didn't want to accept too many responsibilities when I got home. I was afraid that I would fail in those things too. I lacked the confidence to succeed.

- For years after the war I would become startled and react in a very exaggerated way. Sometimes I would find myself reverting to the way I behaved in a war time situation, which made the response inappropriate for the present circumstance. I was always on guard and hyper-alert to the point of irritating those around me.

- There were times in the war that I was overwhelmed with extreme fear. After coming home I would find myself having panic attacks at times when I was under pressure. Sometimes I would get dizzy, my breathing would increase, and often I would even get nauseated during these attacks.

It wasn't until I began to recognize and sort these things out, that I finally was able to control myself. I encourage you to study these reactions (PTS symptoms), and ask God to give you understanding and relief from the stress that he can bring.

PTS Symptoms

There are a number of primary PTS responses that soldiers and veterans exhibit as a result of wartime experiences. Here are some signs and clues that tell us that we may be suffering from PTS. Ask yourself the following questions:

Depression

Do you often feel helpless, worthless and rejected? Do you usually feel insecure? Do you not deserve to feel good?

Anger

Are you unable to identify the things that make you angry? Is your anger unexplainable or inappropriate? Do you take your anger out on loved ones close to you?

Guilt

Do you regularly wonder why you survived when others more worthy died? Do you get into hopeless fights? Do you try to sabotage any successful venture that you may be involved in?

Jumpy and nervous

Are you startled by cans popping, fireworks and loud noises? Are you uncomfortable when people walk closely behind you, or sit behind you?

Sleep disturbances

Do you try to stay awake because you are in fear of the dreams you may have? Do you take drugs or alcohol to assist in keeping you awake or making you sleep?

Numbed emotions

Do you have trouble feeling love? Do you find it hard to get close to your wife or other loved ones? Does the sight of death not affect you? Are you unable to talk about how you feel?

Isolated and closed down

Do you have difficulty talking about your war experiences because you are sure that nobody else could ever understand what you went through? Do you have few friends?

Substance abuse

Do you use alcohol or drugs regularly? Do they numb your painful memories, or relieve guilt? Do others think that you rely upon liquor or drugs too much?

IN GOD WE TRUST

If you answered "yes" to some of these questions you may be suffering from PTS.

(Note: — A few of these delayed stress responses may sound familiar to you. But if you are like me, I never wanted to admit it. Sometimes we may want to deny that the war bothered us when it actually did. This is a common denial response among soldiers because we have been trained to be "tough," and never admit our weaknesses. Admitting that the war affected you is not confessing weakness. It is being honest, and that is the first step in recovery.)

Warning Signs of PTS

Stress affects everyone differently. What might indicate negative stress in one person might just be a personality trait in another. In most cases there are warning signs that indicate a need for active stress management. Check off the signs that relate to you:

- persistent fatigue

- inability to concentrate

- flashes of anger—lashing out at friends and family for no apparent reason

- changes in eating and sleeping habits

- increased use of alcohol, drugs, tobacco, etc.

- prolonged tension headaches, lower back aches, stomach problems or other physical problems

- prolonged feelings of depression, guilt, anxiety and helplessness

These are just some of the ways that PTS may be affecting your life. The emotional and psychological stress of war does not go away simply by leaving it unattended.

Wounds of this type do not go away with time, or just by leaving them alone. They need to be addressed, and you cannot do it alone. If you were wounded physically during combat you would allow a medic to attend to the wound, wouldn't you? This is really no different. You need to call for help and allow others to look at the "wounds" and start the healing process.

First Aid For Stress

Just as stress affects everyone differently, each person finds different ways to cope with it. Here are some ways to help you manage negative stress in your life:

Talk it out. You're not alone in this. There are other veterans and soldiers who have experienced similar events in their lives and are feeling some of the same anxieties. Seek them out and listen to them and their personal stories. When you are ready, you also need to tell them about your experiences. By sharing experiences, you will find a genuine relief from PTS. And remember, it isn't necessary for the "listener" to be a trained professional. A lot of inner relief can happen by simply talking to someone — someone who is willing to listen and care. Getting together with other veterans for the purpose of having a support group is very important. Talking to men and women who have been through a war experience is very healing.

If you don't talk about the experience and try to hold your feelings inside, you will repress the bad memories without resolving the issues. This can lead to some very unsatisfactory results. You may be unexpectedly "triggered" at an inopportune moment. Then the memory could flood in and command a situation, taking you out of control.

You can only hold your feelings inside, or try to forget about them for so long before they explode into fits of rage, violence or self-destructive activities. Like physical wounds, psychological and emotional wounds have to be cleaned out before they can heal.

The best way to cleanse them is by talking about and sharing your pain, sorrow and terror. An excellent way to let it out is to attend a "rap" group (a support group) of peers, where veterans and soldiers meet regularly and help each other regain control of their lives. There is a certain sense of security that comes from knowing that every man (or woman) attending the group has probably done similar things during their wartime experiences. This will help you be honest with yourself — perhaps for the first time since the war. Talking it out helps cleanse the wound.

Try physical activity. Release the tension of stress by developing a regular routine of exercise. If you have a physical disability, consult a physician to determine what kind of exercise is right for you.

Avoid self-medication. Drugs and alcohol may seem to remove stress temporarily. However, in the long run they generally create problems, or behavior, that compounds the stress. Even caffeine and nicotine, agents that artificially create stress-like reactions in your body, can have a negative effect on your ability to control the sources of anxiety in your life.

It is important to note that these are merely suggested methods of coping with PTS. Many veterans and soldiers have found that permanent healing, which goes beyond coping, is possible by developing a personal spiritual relationship with God.

QUICK REFERENCE

Things to Remember:

- Post-traumatic stress is a reaction to events that go beyond the range of normal human experiences, and is **not** a mental illness.

- Unattended stress can damage you both physically and mentally.

Things to do:

- Talk it out.

- Try physical exercise.

- Avoid self-medication.

- Join a support group comprised of other soldiers or veterans

- Develop a personal spiritual relationship with God.

Forgiveness

I was a speaker at a national Viet Nam veteran's conference a couple of years ago. My topic was anger management. The subject of anger took my talk in a direction that I never expected. During the question and answer period, someone expressed his hatred for a notable movie star who opposed the Viet Nam war.

I suddenly decided to ask for a show of hands of all those who had never forgiven this celebrity. Nearly every man in the room shot his hand into the air; some even held up both hands at once. None wanted to forgive and forget.

Uncertain what kind of reaction would come, I cautiously broke some news to them. I announced that I had decided to forgive this person. I went on to say that I realized there was nothing I could accomplish by keeping hatred for her stored up inside me. I chose to let her go.

I went on to tell them how I felt that if I continued not to forgive her, then I was having a relationship with her that I didn't want to have. The unforgiveness locked me to this person and I had no control over it. By thinking of her, and holding onto the anger and hatred, I was creating my own prison of bondage. Consequently my fellow veterans attending saw too that they wanted to be free from this person, an object of hatred for so many years. As a group we made a vow to God to relinquish all our harsh feelings towards her.

Many men were set free that day from the trap of unforgiveness. Their lives, I have since heard, have taken on new wholeness. Some have made giant steps forward in their healing from war stress since that day. It all began with simply forgiving a person they actively disliked in their past.

One particular Marine veteran who came to the conference in a wheelchair was set free. Every veteran attending witnessed a genuine miracle that day. This vet had been hit with a 50 caliber machine gun bullet, and was paralyzed from the waist down since the war. By a simple act of faith, he forgave this famous (or infamous) person and his paralysis left. He stood and walked away from his wheelchair that day. Harboring bitterness and unforgiveness was the one thing that was keeping him bound to a life without walking.

Welcome To A New Life

I have been cursed with most of the "diseases of the soul" symptoms. I have suffered with post-traumatic stress, and through it seen the dark side of life. Since my war experiences I have lived as a wild man, hiding in the woods. I have been a drug user and dealer. I have trusted nobody, carrying a gun wherever I went. I have had three marriages, and lived with hate in my heart for even those I loved. However, I now have a new life. Peace and love are no longer foreign to me, and I can once again trust people and authority. My PTS immediately began to go into remission when I accepted Jesus Christ as my personal Savior in 1986.

That may sound overly simplistic, but it was a pivotal time for the most profound change in my life—for the better. Allow me to explain. It was 20 years after I came home from the war in Viet Nam that I found another battle going on. A battle for my soul. Facing an existence of drugs, constant turmoil and trouble with the law, a friend led me in a prayer of confession and surrender to God. In that prayer I asked Jesus Christ to be my Savior, and as 2 Corinthians 5:17 says, "Behold, a new creature was born."

Let me ask you, have you found the peace and forgiveness that only Jesus Christ can give? If you haven't, the Bible says that if you would believe that Jesus Christ came to die for the sins of men and women, and ask Jesus to be your Savior from sins, to take control of your life and live for Him, you will have eternal life.

IN GOD WE TRUST

How can we know God personally?

For many people, the words "God" and "personal" don't go together. They may believe God exists, but they see him as a concept or a distant force. But God is not an impersonal power in heaven. He is a person. He wants to be involved in our lives and to have a personal relationship with us. In fact, God came to earth and lived as a man. That man was Jesus.

Jesus came to earth to show us what God is like. By feeding the hungry, healing the lame, and touching lepers, Jesus showed us how to love and be compassionate.

Jesus also came to identify with us, to experience our pain. He faced temptation, hostile crowds, and a crooked judicial system. No matter what your pain, Jesus understands. He's been there and can deliver you from it.

But most important of all, Jesus came to earth to die in our place. "No greater love is there than when a man dies for his friends." [John 15:13] He took the penalty for our sins, making it possible for us to be forgiven and to know God personally. The cross was like a bridge between us and heaven. Now, through Christ, we can know God.

But knowing God personally does not result just from learning about him or by behaving a certain way. The Bible says that we must be "born again" [John 3:3], radically changed from the inside out. And this happens by faith.

First, every person must recognize what stands in the way of a relationship with God — sin. Romans 3:23 says "that all have sinned; all fall short of God's glorious ideal." And Romans 6:23 adds, "The wages of sin is death, but the free gift of God is eternal life through Jesus Christ our Lord."

Here's how it happens. First you must recognize your sin and understand that it is wrong. Then you should tell God that you are depending on his work to remove that sin, and ask him to empower you to live for him, rather than yourself. There's no special language or form. Just talk to God. That's what prayer is — talking to God in your own words. He'll understand. Tell him about your sins, ask him to forgive you, invite him to come into your heart and change your life. It's that simple.

The New Testament in the next section has been included especially for you. It has answers to critical questions, and is God's very own word to you.

Welcome home!

Chuck Dean, 1996

IN GOD WE TRUST

Key verses in the Bible to read when stress symptoms hit:

Depression:

"And we know that God causes all things to work together for good to those who love God, to those who are called according to His purpose." Romans 8:28

Guilt:

"But if we confess our sins to Him, He can be depended on to forgive us and to cleanse us from every wrong. [And it is perfectly proper for God to do this for us because Christ died to wash away our sins.]" 1 John 1:9

Anxiety:

"For this reason I say to you, do not be anxious for your life, as to what you shall eat, or what you shall drink; nor for your body, as to what you shall put on. Is not life more than food, and the body more than clothing?" Matthew 6:25

Anger:

"I am leaving you with a gift — peace of mind and heart! And the peace I give isn't fragile like the peace of the world. So don't be troubled or afraid." John 14:27

Fear:

"What can we ever say to such wonderful things as these? If God is on our side who can be against us? Since He did not spare even His own Son for us but gave Him up for us all, won't He also surely give us everything else?" Romans 8:31-32

Bitterness and unforgiveness:

"For if you forgive men when they sin against you, your heavenly Father will also forgive you. But if you do not forgive men their sins, your Father will not forgive your sins." Matthew 6:14, 15

Battlefield Baptisms

Army — Kuwait

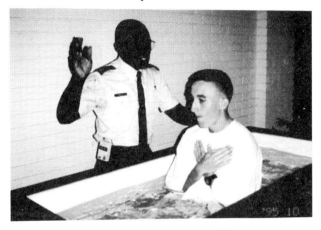

Army paratroopers — Vietnam

IN GOD WE TRUST

Battlefield Baptisms

Marines — Vietnam

RESOURCES

AUGA (America Under God Again) Ministries
Contact - Marvin Sprouse (U.S. Army)
PO Box 468 X
Sheffield, TX 79781
(915) 836-4316

AUGA ministers through various media forms across America. Speakers are available for veteran conferences and seminars.

Bob Boardman (U.S. Marine Corps)
1708 NE 120th
Seattle, Washington 98125
(206) 362-1122

Bob Boardman served with the First Marine Division in three battles in the Pacific during WW II. Wounded twice and awarded the Silver Star for action on Okinawa, he is the chaplain of the Marine Corps Tanker Association, and the Washington State chapter of the 1st Marine Division.

Canaan Land Ministries.
Contact - Mac Gober (U.S. Navy)
PO Box 310
Autaugaville, Alabama 36003-0310
(205) 365-2200

This is a 70 acre-camp where young men can get their GED, learn a trade, and discover how the Word of God can be applied to their daily living. There are veterans on staff.

IN GOD WE TRUST

Campus Crusade For Christ, Military Ministries
Contact - Steve Taylor (U.S. Navy)
6060 Jefferson Ave. Suite #6012
Newport News, Virginia 23605
(804) 247-7502
MilMin@AOL.Com

CBN National Counseling Center
Virginia Beach, Virginia 23463
24-hour, toll-free prayer line (800) 759-0700

Christian Military Fellowship
Contact - Bob Flynn (U.S. Navy)
3677 South Huron, Suite 101
Englewood, Colorado 80110
(800) 798-7875
cmfhdqtrs@AOL.Com

CMF is a Christ-centered, nondenominational peer ministry to military people, with a special emphasis to the enlisted ranks. *CMF* functions in cooperation with command sponsored chapel programs, chaplains, local churches and Christian organizations.

City of Refuge
Contact - Burt Stigen (Dept. Of Defense)
5899 Highway #3112
Vinton, Louisiana 70668
(318) 589-6404

City of Refuge is a Christ-centered transitional veterans shelter. It is a place for spiritual and physical restoration; providing housing, food, clothing and Christian guidance for veterans who are in transition. *City of Refuge* has weekly Bible studies and support meetings that teach veterans how to stand on their own through the power of Christ. It has one of the only color guards in America comprised of homeless veterans.

Crossfire International
Contact - Paul Hughes (U.S. Army)
PO Box 535
Sharon, Tennessee 38255
(901) 456-2571
(800) 246-1481

Crossfire International is a ministry designed to reach America for Christ and to restore the true spirit of patriotism through God's divine precepts. *Crossfire* works with veterans and their families to help renew respect and honor.

IN GOD WE TRUST

Firebase Hope
Contact - Ben Webster
8484 S. Mt. Hope Road
PO Box 627
Carson City, Michigan 48811
(517) 584-6201

Firebase Hope is a temporary shelter for homeless and troubled veterans. It provides Christ-centered rehabilitation counseling for substance abuse and post-traumatic stress. Job skills training is also available. Point Man Ministries also provides support group meetings for vets and immediate family.

Full Gospel Chaplaincy Churches
Contact - U.S. Army Colonel (Ret) Jim Ammerman
2721 Whitewood Drive
Dallas, Texas 75233
(214-333-2085

FGCC is a unique coalition of independent, nondenominational Full Gospel ministers who serve as chaplains around the world. Many associate *FGCC* chaplains serve in the active duty Armed Forces of America.

Jesus People Ministries
Contact - Reverend Rodney Hamilton (U.S. Marine Corps)
377 S. 600 W.
Layton, Utah 84041
(801) 544-7550

A Christ-centered outreach especially to veterans who are in transition.

LZ Dustoff
Contact - Lee Craig (U.S. Army)
PO Box 990112
Redding, California 96099
(916) 243-8387

LZ Dustoff is a Christian-based storefront ministry that serves the veteran community through support groups, career advisory, food banks and other physical assistance programs affiliated with *Point Man International Ministries.*

National Conference of Viet Nam Veteran Ministers
Contact - Father Phil Salois (U.S. Army)
PO Box 2965
Attleboro, Massachusetts 02703-0965
(508) 222-7313 (Hotline for veterans and families)

NCVNVM is a national network of professional ministers who served in Viet Nam. Many went into ordained ministry after the war. Some members served as chaplains during the war. *NCVNVM* focuses on the spiritual healing of its members and the formation of a pastoral plan to foster spiritual healing for the Vietnam veteran and his or her family. Its mission also includes being a prophetic voice to the American church community, our government, and the American people about the devastation war creates in its sons and daughters.

The Navigators U.S. Military Ministry
Contact - Don Hankins
5525 N. Union Blvd. Suite 201
Colorado Springs, Colorado 80918
(719) 594-2541 (719) 598-9325
http://www.n-gate.com/navmm/

IN GOD WE TRUST

Officer's Christian Fellowship
Contact - Donna Brooks
PO Box 1177
Englewood, Colorado 80150-1177
(800) 424-1984

Pastor Den Slattery (U.S. Marine Corps/U.S. Army)
224 Davis Street
Marcellus, Michigan 49067
(616) 646-2049

Point Man International Ministries
Contact - Del Wantland (U.S. Army)
PO Box 339
Sheridan, Michigan 48884
(800) 877-VETS

Point Man International Ministries is a Christian outreach to all veterans, with group meetings, one-on-one biblical guidance sessions, conferences, campouts, and other activities. Local "outposts" and "home fronts" offer aid to veterans, wives, and families nationwide.

Recon Ministries (Point Man International Ministries)
Contact - Skip Edlund
3590 Roundbottom Road, Suite #172467
Cincinnati, Ohio 45244-3000
(800) 445-1732 (#F172467)

Reverend John Steer (U.S. Army)
75 Holmes Road
Charlotte, Arkansas 72522
(501) 799-8111

John Steer served with the 173rd Airborne in Viet Nam, and was awarded the Silver Star for action on Hill 875 Dak To, South Viet Nam in 1967. John is a dynamic speaker and singer. He ministers to veterans of all wars, and is the chaplain for three national veteran organizations.

Rock Church Military Ministries
Contact - Pastor Paul Tribus (U.S. Marine Corps)
          Jimmy Hargrove   (U.S. Marine Corps)
99 Sherwood Mall
Newport News, VA 23602
(804) 874-3255

Vets For Christ
Contact - Wes Keith (U.S. Marine Corps)
PO Box 1132
Searcy, Arkansas 72145
(501) 268-6297

Vets For Christ is a ministry that reaches out to veterans for the purpose of showing them Christ's love. *Vets For Christ* actively promotes veterans' spiritual, emotional, and physical needs to the community.

IN GOD WE TRUST

Vets For Christ
Contact - Danny Daniels (U.S. Marine Corps)
38891 Mission Blvd.
Fremont, California 94536
(510) 797-7689

Danny Daniels travels extensively speaking to churches and veteran organizations about the hope of Christ. He is the pastor of Mission Way Baptist Church in Fremont, California, and hosts a popular radio show called "Profiles on the Winning Edge."

Vets With a Mission
Contact - Bill Kimball (U.S. Army)
PO Box 9112
South Lake Tahoe, California 96158
(916) 542-2868
FAX (916) 542-2400 E-Mail: vwamlink@sierra.net.

Vets With a Mission is dedicated to the ministry of reconciliation given in 2 Corinthians 5:18-20. The primary purpose and focus of *Vets With a Mission* is to provide opportunities for Viet Nam veterans to return to present-day Viet Nam to heal and reconcile, not only on a personal level, but on a humanitarian level as well between two peoples who shared so much common suffering.

Victory For Veterans Ministries
Contact - Earl Rollyson (U.S. Army)
1305 W. Royalton Road
Broadview Heights, Ohio 44147
(216) 582-3858

Victory For Veterans is a veterans-for-veterans organization that specializes in ministering to hospitalized veterans. The organization conducts regular Christ-centered support groups in the VA hospital system, and counsels veterans and their families who are contemplating VA medical help.

Viet Nam Veterans Restoration Foundation & Ministry
Contact - Dave Litteral (U.S. Army)
2926 Spantown Road
Arrington, Tennessee
(615) 395-7504

VVRFM is a Christ-centered ministry for Viet Nam veterans, and all others who were affected by the Viet Nam War. The ministry addresses physical needs while building trust to then minister on a spiritual level to those veterans who are still walking in conflict. Veteran support meetings, for fellowship and to learn about the Word of God, are available.

IN GOD WE TRUST

Welcome Home Vet Center
Contact - Ron & Marva Crecelius (U.S. Army)
309 E. First Street
Newberg, Oregon 97132
(503) 538-7755

Welcome Home Vet Center is a drop-in center for veterans and the general community. It hosts an extensive library of Christian reading materials, audio and video tapes, and conducts weekly Bible studies to help veterans become grounded in the Lord. Affiliated with *Point Man International Ministries.*

Welcome Home Ministries
Contact - Jack Ernest (U.S. Marine Corps)
PO Box 184
Richmond, Ohio 43944
(614) 765-4959

Welcome Home reaches out to veterans and Christian churches alike with the purpose of restoration of the past wounds of war. *Welcome Home* provides conferences and seminars for sharing God's love. This organization organizes and conducts missionary trips to Viet Nam on a regular basis. Many orphanages and hospitals in Viet Nam have received assistance and help from the veterans who make up the ministry teams.

Words For Living Ministries, Inc.
Contact - Tom C. McKenney (U.S. Marine Corps)
PO Box 413
Marion, Kentucky 42064
(502) 965-5060

A teaching and personal ministry focusing on emotional healing using the Scriptures. Missions and Bible-based retreats.

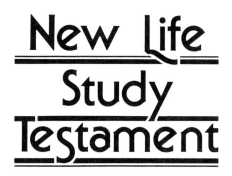

New Life Study Testament

Translated by

Gleason H. Ledyard

with complete

TOPICAL STUDY OUTLINES

also

WORD LIST
TOPICAL VERSE FINDER
HAPPENINGS IN THE GOSPELS

Christian Literature International

P.O. BOX 777 CANBY, OREGON 97013

THIS IS THE BOOK OF LIFE

From the beginning to the end of these Writings, they tell of the life of Jesus. He said, "I am the Way and the Truth and the Life. No one can go to the Father except by Me." New Life has come to many, many people who have read or heard the Word of God and have put their trust in Jesus Christ, the Son of God.

God's Written Word is as much alive today as when it was written many hundreds of years ago. Through the years, sinful men have tried to destroy It, but this living Book can never be destroyed. "Heaven and earth will pass away, but My words will not pass away."

Those early men of God wrote in a different language than we use today. When a translation is done from one language to another, it is hard to make the second language say what the first language said. Every part of the New Testament is important and should say what the Holy Spirit said to those early men of God who wrote it down. For many hundreds of years people could not have a copy for themselves because the Bible was not printed. After it was printed, only rich people could buy one. For over 350 years the King James Bible has been in print and now many people own a copy. Since about 1900 many different Versions have been printed in the English language.

The New Testament has many hundreds of quotations taken from the Old Testament. Many of these references are given in this Version so they can be read and studied in the Old Testament. The New Testament is made up of 27 different Books or Writings.

The reason for this Version of the New Testament is to take difficult words that are found in most Versions of the Bible and put them into words or phrases that are easy to understand. About 850 different words have been used in this Version.

The New Testament does not only tell of the life of Jesus, but it tells how to be saved from the punishment of sin. It shows the way to heaven. It tells how to live in peace and happiness. The promises God has made to all people are in it. GOD'S WRITTEN WORD IS THE GREATEST OF ALL BOOKS.

Gleason H. Ledyard

THE BOOKS OF THE NEW TESTAMENT

Part II

STUDY HELPS

MATTHEW

The Families Jesus Came Through
[Luke 3:23-38]

1 These are the families through which Jesus Christ came. He came through David and Abraham. ²Abraham was the father of Isaac. Isaac was the father of Jacob. Jacob was the father of Judah and his brothers. ³Judah was the father of Perez and Zerah. Their mother was Tamar. Perez was the father of Hezron. Hezron was the father of Aram. ⁴Aram was the father of Amminadab. Amminadab was the father of Nahshon. Nahshon was the father of Salmon. ⁵Salmon was the father of Boaz. The mother of Boaz was Rahab. Boaz was the father of Obed. The mother of Obed was Ruth. Obed was the father of Jesse. ⁶Jesse was the father of David the king.

King David was the father of Solomon. His mother had been the wife of Uriah. ⁷Solomon was the father of Rehoboam. Rehoboam was the father of Abijah. Abijah was the father of Asa. ⁸Asa was the father of Jehoshaphat. Jehoshaphat was the father of Joram. Joram was the father of Uzziah. ⁹Uzziah was the father of Jotham. Jotham was the father of Ahaz. Ahaz was the father of Hezekiah. ¹⁰Hezekiah was the father of Manasseh. Manasseh was the father of Amon. Amon was the father of Josiah. ¹¹Josiah was the father of Jeconiah and his brothers at the time the people were taken to Babylon.

¹²After they were taken to the city of Babylon, Jeconiah was the father of Shealtiel. Shealtiel was the father of Zerubbabel. ¹³Zerubbabel was the father of Abiud. Abiud was the father of Eliakim. Eliakim was the father of Azor. ¹⁴Azor was the father of Zadok. Zadok was the father of Achim. Achim was the father of Eliud. ¹⁵Eliud was the father of Eleazar. Eleazar was the father of Matthan. Matthan was the father of Jacob. ¹⁶Jacob was the father of Joseph. Joseph was the husband of Mary. She was the mother of Jesus Who is called the Christ. ¹⁷So the number of families from Abraham to David was fourteen. The number of families from David to the time the people were taken to Babylon was fourteen. The number of families after they were taken to Babylon to the birth of Jesus Christ was fourteen.

The Birth Of Jesus [Luke 2:1-7]

18The birth of Jesus Christ was like this: Mary His mother had been promised in marriage to Joseph. Before they were married, it was learned that she was to have a baby by the Holy Spirit. 19Joseph was her promised husband. He was a good man and did not want to make it hard for Mary in front of people. He thought it would be good to break the promised marriage without people knowing it. 20While he was thinking about this, an angel of the Lord came to him in a dream. The angel said, "Joseph, son of David, do not be afraid to take Mary as your wife. She is to become a mother by the Holy Spirit. 21A Son will be born to her. You will give Him the name Jesus because He will save His people from the punishment of their sins."

22This happened as the Lord said it would happen through the early preacher. 23He said, "The young woman, who has never had a man, will give birth to a Son. They will give Him the name Immanuel. This means God with us." (Isaiah 7:14)

24Joseph awoke from his sleep. He did what the angel of the Lord told him to do. He took Mary as his wife. 25But he did not have her, as a husband has a wife, until she gave birth to a Son. Joseph gave Him the name Jesus.

Men Who Learned From The Stars Visit The Young Child Jesus

2 Jesus was born in the town of Bethlehem in the country of Judea. It was the time when Herod was king of that part of the country. Soon after Jesus was born, some wise men who learned things from stars came to Jerusalem from the East. 2They asked, "Where is the King of the Jews Who has been born. We have seen His star in the East. We have come to worship Him."

3King Herod heard this. He and all the people of Jerusalem were worried. 4He called together all the religious leaders of the Jews and the teachers of the Law. Herod asked them where Christ was to be born. 5They said to him, "In Bethlehem of Judea. The early preacher wrote, 6'You, Bethlehem of Judah, are not the least of the leaders of Judah. Out of you will come a King Who will lead My people, the Jews.' " (Micah 5:2)

7Then Herod had a secret meeting with the men who learned things from stars. He asked them about what time the star had been seen. 8He sent them to Bethlehem and said, "Go and find the young Child. When you find Him, let me know. Then I can go and worship Him also."

9After the king had spoken, they went on their way. The star they had seen in the East went before them. It came and stopped over the place where the young Child was. 10When they saw the star, they were filled with much joy.

11They went into the house and found the young Child with Mary, His mother. Then they got down before Him and worshiped Him. They opened their bags of riches and gave Him gifts of gold and perfume and spices. 12Then God spoke to them in a dream. He told them not to go back to Herod. So they went to their own country by another road.

Joseph Goes To Egypt

13When they had gone, an angel of the Lord came to Joseph in a dream. He said, "Get up. Take the young Child and His mother to the country of Egypt. Go as fast as you can! Stay there until you hear from me. Herod is going to look for the young Child to kill Him." 14During the night he got up and left with the young Child and His mother for Egypt. 15He stayed there until Herod died. This happened as the Lord had said through an early preacher, "I called My Son out of Egypt." (Hosea 11:1)

Herod Had All The Young Boys Killed

16Herod learned that the wise men had fooled him. He was very angry. He sent men to kill all the young boys two years old and under in Bethlehem and in all the country near by. He decided to do this from what he had heard from the wise men as to the time when the star was seen. 17Then it happened as the early preacher Jeremiah said it would happen. 18He said, "The sound of crying and much sorrow was heard in Ramah. Rachel was crying for her children. She would not be comforted because they were dead." (Jeremiah 31:15)

Joseph Goes From Egypt To Nazareth [Luke 2:39-40]

19After Herod died, an angel of the Lord came to Joseph in a dream while he was in Egypt. 20He said, "Get up. Take the young Child and His mother and go into the land of the Jews. Those who tried to kill the young Child are dead." 21Joseph got up. He took the young Child and His mother and came into the land of the Jews. 22Joseph heard that Archelaus was the king of the country of Judea. Herod, the father of Archelaus, had died. Joseph was afraid to go there. God told him in a dream to go to the country of Galilee and he went. 23Joseph stayed in a town called Nazareth. It happened as the early preachers said it would happen. They said, "Jesus will be called a Nazarene."

John The Baptist Makes The Way Ready For Jesus [Mark 1:1-8; Luke 3:1-18; John 1:15-28]

3 In those days John the Baptist came preaching in the desert in the country of Judea. 2He said, "Be sorry for your sins and turn from them! The holy nation of heaven is near." 3The early preacher Isaiah spoke of this man. He said, "Listen! His voice calls out in the desert! 'Make the way ready for the Lord. Make the road straight for Him!'" (Isaiah 40:3)

4John wore clothes made of hair from camels. He had a leather belt around him. His food was locusts and wild honey.

5Then the people of Jerusalem and of all the country of Judea and those from near the Jordan River went to him. 6Those who told of their sins were baptized by him in the Jordan River. 7He saw many proud religious law-keepers and other people of the religious group who believe no one will be raised from the dead. They were coming to him to be baptized. He said to them, "You family of snakes! Who told you how to keep from God's anger that is coming? 8Do something to show me that your hearts are changed. 9Do not think you can say to yourselves, 'We have Abraham as our father.' For I tell you, God can make children for Abraham out of these stones.

10"Even now the ax is on the root of the trees. Every tree that does not give good fruit is cut down and thrown into the fire. 11For sure, I baptize with water those who are sorry for their sins and turn from them. The One Who comes after me will baptize you with the Holy Spirit and with fire. He is greater than I. I am not good enough to take off His shoes. 12He comes ready to clean the grain. He will gather the grain in and clean it all. The clean grain He will put into a building. He will burn that which is no good with a fire that cannot be put out."

The Baptism Of Jesus [Mark 1:9-11; Luke 3:21-22; John 1:29-34]

13Jesus came from Galilee. He went to John at the Jordan River to be baptized by him. 14John tried to stop Him. He said, "I need to be baptized by You. Do You come to me?" [15]Jesus said to him, "Let it be done now. We should do what is right." John agreed and baptized Jesus. [16]When Jesus came up out of the water, the heavens opened. He saw the Spirit of God coming down and resting on Jesus like a dove. [17]A voice was heard from heaven. It said, "This is My much-loved Son. I am very happy with Him."

Jesus Was Tempted [Mark 1:12-13; Luke 4:1-13]

4 Jesus was led by the Holy Spirit to a desert. There He was tempted by the devil. [2]Jesus went without food for forty days and forty nights. After that He was hungry. [3]The devil came tempting Him and said, "If You are the Son of God, tell these stones to be made into bread." [4]But Jesus said, "It is written, 'Man is not to live on bread only. Man is to live by every word that God speaks.' " (Deuteronomy 8:3)

[5]Then the devil took Jesus up to Jerusalem, the holy city. He had Jesus stand on the highest part of the house of God. [6]The devil said to Him, "If You are the Son of God, throw Yourself down. It is written, 'He has told His angels to look after You. In their hands they will hold You up. Then Your foot will not hit against a stone.' " (Psalm 91:11-12) [7]Jesus said to the devil, "It is written also, 'You must not tempt the Lord your God.' " (Deuteronomy 6:16)

[8]Again the devil took Jesus to a very high mountain. He had Jesus look at all the nations of the world to see how great they were. [9]He said to Jesus, "I will give You all these nations if You will get down at my feet and worship me." [10]Jesus said to the devil, "Get away, Satan. It is written, 'You must worship the Lord your God. You must obey Him only.' " (Deuteronomy 6:13) [11]Then the devil went away from Jesus. Angels came and cared for Him.

Jesus Preaches In Galilee [Mark 1:14-15; Luke 4:14-15]

[12]When Jesus heard that John the Baptist had been put in prison, He went to the country of Galilee. [13]He left Nazareth and went to live in the city of Capernaum. It is by the lake in the land of Zebulon and Naphtali. [14]This happened as the early preacher Isaiah said it would happen. He said, [15]"The land of Zebulon and Naphtali is along the road to the lake. It is on the other side of the Jordan River in Galilee. These people are not Jews. [16]The people who sat in darkness saw a great light. Light did shine on those in the land who were near death." (Isaiah 9:1-2) [17]From that time on, Jesus went about preaching. He said, "Be sorry for your sins and turn from them. The holy nation of heaven is near."

Jesus Calls Peter And Andrew [Mark 1:16-20; Luke 5:1-11]

[18]Jesus was walking by the Sea of Galilee. He saw two brothers. They were Simon (his other name was Peter) and Andrew, his brother. They were putting a net into the sea for they were fishermen. [19]Jesus said to them, "Follow Me. I will make you fish for men!" [20]At once they left their nets and followed Him.

[21]Going from there, Jesus saw two other brothers. They were James and John, the sons of Zebedee. They were sitting in a boat with their father, mending their nets. Jesus called them. [22]At once they left the boat and their father and followed Jesus.

Jesus Keeps On Preaching In Galilee [Mark 1:35-39; Luke 4:42-44]

[23]Jesus went over all Galilee. He taught in their places of worship and preached the Good News of the holy nation. He healed all kinds of sickness and disease among the people. [24]The news about Him went over all

the country of Syria. They brought all the sick people to Him with many kinds of diseases and pains. They brought to Him those who had demons. They brought those who at times lose the use of their minds. They brought those who could not use their hands and legs. He healed them. 25Many people followed Him from Galilee and Judea. They followed Him from the cities of Decapolis and Jerusalem. They followed Him from Judea and from the other side of the Jordan River.

Jesus Teaches On The Mountain
[Luke 6:20-49]

5 Jesus saw many people. He went up on the mountain and sat down. His followers came to Him. 2He began to teach them, saying, 3"Those who know there is nothing good in themselves are happy, because the holy nation of heaven is theirs. 4Those who have sorrow are happy, because they will be comforted. 5Those who have no pride in their hearts are happy, because the earth will be given to them. 6Those who are hungry and thirsty to be right with God are happy, because they will be filled. 7Those who show loving-kindness are happy, because they will have loving-kindness shown to them. 8Those who have a pure heart are happy, because they will see God. 9Those who make peace are happy, because they will be called the sons of God. 10Those who have it very hard for doing right are happy, because the holy nation of heaven is theirs. 11You are happy when people act and talk in a bad way to you and make it very hard for you and tell bad things and lies about you because you trust in Me. 12Be glad and full of joy because your pay will be much in heaven. They made it very hard for the early preachers who lived a long time before you.

Jesus Teaches About Salt And Light

13"You are the salt of the earth. If salt loses its taste, how can it be made to taste like salt again? It is no good. It is thrown away and people walk on it. 14You are the light of the world. You cannot hide a city that is on a mountain. 15Men do not light a lamp and put it under a basket. They put it on a table so it gives light to all in the house. 16Let your light shine in front of men. Then they will see the good things you do and will honor your Father Who is in heaven.

Jesus Teaches About The Law

17"Do not think that I have come to do away with the Law of Moses or the writings of the early preachers. I have not come to do away with them but to complete them. 18I tell you, as long as heaven and earth last, not one small mark or part of a word will pass away of the Law of Moses until it has all been done. 19Anyone who breaks even the least of the Law of Moses and teaches people not to do what it says, will be called the least in the holy nation of heaven. He who obeys and teaches others to obey what the Law of Moses says, will be called great in the holy nation of heaven. 20I tell you, unless you are more right with God than the teachers of the Law and the proud religious law-keepers, you will never get into the holy nation of heaven.

Jesus Teaches About Anger And Killing

21"You have heard that men were told long ago, 'You must not kill another person. If someone does kill, he will be guilty and will be punished for his wrong-doing.' 22But I tell you that whoever is angry with his brother will be guilty and have to suffer for his wrong-doing. Whoever says to his brother, 'You have no brains,' will have to stand in front of the court. Whoever says, 'You fool,' will be sent to the fire of hell. ²³If you take your gift to the altar and remember your brother has something against you, ²⁴leave your gift on the altar. Go and make right what is wrong between you and him. Then come back and give your gift. ²⁵Agree with the one who is against you while you are talking together, or he might take you to court. The court will hand you over to the police. You will be put in prison. ²⁶For sure, I tell you, you will not be let out of prison until you have paid every piece of money of the fine.

Jesus Teaches About Husband And Wife

²⁷"You have heard that it was said long ago, 'You must not do sex sins.' ²⁸But I tell you, anyone who even looks at a woman with a sinful desire of wanting her has already sinned in his heart. ²⁹If your right eye is the reason you sin, take it out and throw it away. It is better to lose one part of your body than for your whole body to be thrown into hell. ³⁰If your right hand is the reason you sin, cut it off and throw it away. It is better to lose one part of your body than for your whole body to go to hell.

Jesus Teaches About Marriage

³¹"It has been said, 'Whoever wants to divorce his wife should have it put in writing, telling her he is leaving her.' ³²But I tell you, whoever divorces his wife except if she has not been faithful to him, makes her guilty of a sex sin. Whoever marries a woman who has been divorced is guilty of a sex sin.

Jesus Teaches About What To Say

³³"You have heard that it was said long ago, 'You must not make a promise you cannot keep. You must carry out your promises to the Lord.' ³⁴I tell you, do not use strong words when you make a promise. Do not promise by heaven. It is the place where God is. ³⁵Do not promise by earth. It is where He rests His feet. Do not promise by Jerusalem. It is the city of the great King. ³⁶Do not promise by your head. You are not able to make one hair white or black. ³⁷Let your yes be YES. Let your no be NO. Anything more than this comes from the devil.

Jesus Teaches About Fighting

³⁸"You have heard that it has been said, 'An eye for an eye and a tooth for a tooth.' ³⁹But I tell you, do not fight with the man who wants to fight. Whoever hits you on the right side of the face, turn so he can hit the other side also. ⁴⁰If any person takes you to court to get your shirt, give him your coat also. ⁴¹Whoever makes you walk a short way, go with him twice as far. ⁴²Give to any person who asks you for something. Do not say no to the man who wants to use something of yours.

Jesus Teaches About Loving Those Who Hate You

⁴³"You have heard that it has been said, 'You must love your neighbor and hate those who hate you.' ⁴⁴But I tell you, love those who hate you. (*Respect and give thanks for those who say bad things to you. Do good to those who hate you.) Pray for those who do bad things to you and who make it hard for you. ⁴⁵Then you may be the sons of your Father Who is in heaven. His sun shines on bad people and on good people. He sends rain on those who are right with God and on those who are not right with God. ⁴⁶If you love those who love you, what pay can you expect from that? Do not even the tax gatherers do that? ⁴⁷If you say hello only to the people you like, are you

doing any more than others? The people who do not know God do that much. ⁴⁸You must be perfect as your Father in heaven is perfect.

Jesus Teaches On The Mountain About Helping Others

6 "Be sure you do not do good things in front of others just to be seen by them. If you do, you have no pay from your Father in heaven. ²When you give to the poor, do not be as those who pretend to be someone they are not. They blow a horn in the places of worship and in the streets so people may respect them. For sure, I tell you, they have all the pay they are going to get. ³When you give, do not let your left hand know what your right hand gives. ⁴Your giving should be in secret. Then your Father Who sees in secret will pay you.

Jesus Teaches About Prayer

⁵"When you pray, do not be as those who pretend to be someone they are not. They love to stand and pray in the places of worship or in the streets so people can see them. For sure, I tell you, they have all the pay they are going to get. ⁶When you pray, go into a room by yourself. After you have shut the door, pray to your Father Who is in secret. Then your Father Who sees in secret will pay you. ⁷When you pray, do not say the same thing over and over again making long prayers like the people who do not know God. They think they are heard because their prayers are long. ⁸Do not be like them. Your Father knows what you need before you ask Him.

⁹"Pray like this: 'Our Father in heaven, Your name is holy. ¹⁰May Your holy nation come. What You want done, may it be done on earth as it is in heaven. ¹¹Give us the bread we need today. ¹²Forgive us our sins as we forgive those who sin against us.

¹³'Do not let us be tempted, but keep us from sin. Your nation is holy. You have power and shining greatness forever. Let it be so.'

Jesus Teaches About Forgiveness

¹⁴"If you forgive people their sins, your Father in heaven will forgive your sins also. ¹⁵If you do not forgive people their sins, your Father will not forgive your sins.

Jesus Teaches About Not Eating So You Can Pray Better

¹⁶"When you go without food so you can pray better, do not be as those who pretend to be someone they are not. They make themselves look sad so people will see they are going without food. For sure, I tell you, they have all the pay they are going to get. ¹⁷When you go without food so you can pray better, put oil on your head and wash your face. ¹⁸Then nobody knows you are going without food. Then your Father Who sees in secret will pay you.

Jesus Teaches About Having Riches

¹⁹"Do not gather together for yourself riches of this earth. They will be eaten by bugs and become rusted. Men can break in and steal them. ²⁰Gather together riches in heaven where they will not be eaten by bugs or become rusted. Men cannot break in and steal them. ²¹For wherever your riches are, your heart will be there also. ²²The eye is the light of the body. If your eye is good, your whole body will be full of light. ²³If your eye is bad, your whole body will be dark. If the light in you is dark, how dark it will be! ²⁴No one can have two bosses. He will hate the one and love the other. Or he will listen to the one and work against the other. You cannot have both God and riches as your boss at the same time.

Jesus Teaches About Cares Of Life

²⁵"I tell you this: Do not worry about your life. Do not worry about what you are going to eat and drink. Do not worry about what you are going to wear. Is not life more important than food? Is not the body more important than clothes? ²⁶Look at the birds in the sky. They do not plant seeds. They do not gather grain. They do not put grain into a building to keep. Yet your Father in heaven feeds them! Are you not more important than the birds? ²⁷Which of you can make himself a little taller by worrying? ²⁸Why should you worry about clothes? Think how the flowers grow. They do not work or make cloth. ²⁹But I tell you that Solomon in all his greatness was not dressed as well as one of these flowers. ³⁰God clothes the grass of the field. It lives today and is burned in the stove tomorrow. How much more will He give you clothes? You have so little faith! ³¹Do not worry. Do not keep saying, 'What will we eat?' or, 'What will we drink?' or, 'What will we wear?' ³²The people who do not know God are looking for all these things. Your Father in heaven knows you need all these things. ³³First of all, look for the holy nation of God. Be right with Him. All these other things will be given to you also. ³⁴Do not worry about tomorrow. Tomorrow will have its own worries. The troubles we have in a day are enough for one day.

Jesus Teaches On The Mountain About Saying What Is Wrong In Others

7 "Do not say what is wrong in other people's lives. Then other people will not say what is wrong in your life. ²You will be guilty of the same things you find in others. When you say what is wrong in others, your words will be used to say what is wrong in you. ³Why do you look at the small piece of wood in your brother's eye, and do not see the big piece of wood in your own eye? ⁴How can you say to your brother, 'Let me take that small piece of wood out of your eye,' when there is a big piece of wood in your own eye? ⁵You who pretend to be someone you are not, first take the big piece of wood out of your own eye. Then you can see better to take the small piece of wood out of your brother's eye.

⁶"Do not give that which belongs to God to dogs. Do not throw your pearls in front of pigs. They will break them under their feet. Then they will turn and tear you to pieces.

Jesus Teaches About Prayer

⁷"Ask, and what you are asking for will be given to you. Look, and what you are looking for you will find. Knock, and the door you are knocking on will be opened to you. ⁸Everyone who asks receives what he asks for. Everyone who looks finds what he is looking for. Everyone who knocks has the door opened to him. ⁹What man among you would give his son a stone if he should ask for bread? ¹⁰Or if he asks for a fish, would he give him a snake? ¹¹You are bad and you know how to give good things to your children. How much more will your Father in heaven give good things to those who ask Him?

Jesus Teaches About Others

¹²"Do for other people whatever you would like to have them do for you. This is what the Jewish Law and the early preachers said.

Jesus Teaches About Two Roads

¹³"Go in through the narrow door. The door is wide and the road is easy that leads to hell. Many people are going through that door. ¹⁴But the door is narrow and the road is hard that leads to life that lasts forever. Few people are finding it.

Jesus Teaches About False Teachers

15"Watch out for false teachers. They come to you dressed as if they were sheep. On the inside they are hungry wolves. 16You will know them by their fruit. Do men pick grapes from thorns? Do men pick figs from thistles? 17It is true, every good tree has good fruit. Every bad tree has bad fruit. 18A good tree cannot have bad fruit. A bad tree cannot have good fruit. 19Every tree that does not have good fruit is cut down and thrown into the fire. 20So you will know them by their fruit. 21Not everyone who says to me, 'Lord, Lord,' will go into the holy nation of heaven. The one who does the things My Father in heaven wants him to do will go into the holy nation of heaven. 22Many people will say to Me on that day, 'Lord, Lord, did we not preach in Your Name? Did we not put out demons in Your Name? Did we not do many powerful works in Your Name?' 23Then I will say to them in plain words, 'I never knew you. Go away from Me, you who do wrong!'

Jesus Teaches About Houses Built On Rock Or Sand

24"Whoever hears these words of Mine and does them, will be like a wise man who built his house on rock. 25The rain came down. The water came up. The wind blew and hit the house. The house did not fall because it was built on rock. 26Whoever hears these words of Mine and does not do them, will be like a foolish man who built his house on sand. 27The rain came down. The water came up. The wind blew and hit the house. The house fell and broke apart." 28Then Jesus finished talking. The people were surprised and wondered about His teaching. 29He was teaching them as One Who has the right and the power to teach. He did not teach as the teachers of the Law.

The Healing Of A Man With A Bad Skin Disease [Mark 1:40-45; Luke 5:12-16]

8 Jesus came down from the mountain. Many people followed Him. 2A man with a bad skin disease came and got down before Him and worshiped Him. He said, "Lord, if You will, You can heal me!" 3Then Jesus put His hand on him and said, "I will. You are healed!" At once the man was healed. 4Jesus said to him, "Go now, but tell no one. Let the religious leader see you. Give the gift in worship that Moses told you to give. This will show them you have been healed." (Leviticus 13:49)

Healing Of The Captain's Helper Boy [Luke 7:1-10]

5Jesus came to the city of Capernaum. A captain of the army came to Him. He asked for help, 6saying, "Lord, my helper boy is sick in bed. He is not able to move his body. He is in much pain." 7Jesus said to the captain, "I will come and heal him." 8The captain said, "Lord, I am not good enough for You to come to my house. Only speak the word, and My helper boy will be healed. 9I am a man who works for someone else and I have men working under me. I say to this man, 'Go!' and he goes. I say to another, 'Come!' and he comes. I say to my servant, 'Do this!' and he does it."

10When Jesus heard this, He was surprised and wondered about it. He said to those who followed Him, "For sure, I tell you, I have not found so much faith in the Jewish nation. 11I say to you, many people will come from the east and from the west. They will sit down with Abraham and with Isaac and with Jacob in the holy nation of heaven. 12But those who should have belonged to the holy nation of heaven will be thrown out into outer darkness, where there will be crying and grinding of teeth."

[13]Jesus said to the captain, "Go your way. It is done for you even as you had faith to believe." The helper boy was healed at that time.

Peter's Mother-in-law Healed [Mark 1:29-31; Luke 4:38-39]

[14]Jesus came to Peter's house. He saw Peter's wife's mother in bed. She was very sick. [15]He touched her hand and the sickness left her. She got up and cared for Jesus.

Many People Are Healed [Mark 1:32-34; Luke 4:40-41]

[16]That evening they brought to Jesus many people who had demons in them. The demons were put out when Jesus spoke to them. All the sick people were healed. [17]It happened as the early preacher Isaiah said it would happen. He said, "He took on Himself our sickness and carried away our diseases." (Isaiah 53:4)

Testing Some Followers [Luke 9:57-62]

[18]Jesus saw many people and told them to go to the other side of the lake. [19]A teacher of the Law came to Jesus. He said, "Lord, I will follow You wherever You go." [20]Jesus said to him, "Foxes have holes. Birds have nests. But the Son of Man has no place to lay His head." [21]Another of His followers said to Him, "Lord, let me go first and bury my father." [22]Jesus said to him, "Follow Me. Let the people who are dead bury their own dead."

The Wind And Waves Obey Jesus [Mark 4:35-41; Luke 8:22-25]

[23]Jesus got into a boat. His followers followed Him. [24]At once a bad storm came over the lake. The waves were covering the boat. Jesus was sleeping. [25]His followers went to Him and called, "Help us, Lord, or we will die!" [26]He said to them, "Why are you afraid? You have so little faith!" Then He stood up. He spoke sharp words to the wind and the waves. Then the wind stopped blowing. [27]The men were surprised and wondered about it. They said, "What kind of a man is He? Even the winds and the waves obey Him."

Demons Ask Jesus To Let Them Live In Pigs [Mark 5:1-20; Luke 8:26-39]

[28]Jesus came to the other side of the lake into the country of the Gadarenes. Two men came to Him from among the graves. They had demons in them and were very wild men. They were so bad that no one would go near them. [29]They called out, saying, "What do You want of us, You Son of God? Have You come here to make us suffer before it is our time to suffer?" [30]A long way from there many pigs were eating. [31]The demons begged Jesus, saying, "If You put us out, send us into the pigs." [32]Jesus said to the demons, "Go!" They came out of the men and went into the pigs. At once the pigs ran down the mountain side. They fell into the water and died. [33]The men who cared for the pigs ran fast into the city and told everything. They told what happened to the men who had the demons. [34]Every person in the city came to meet Jesus. When they saw Jesus, they asked Him to leave their country.

The Healing Of A Man Who Could Not Move His Body [Mark 2:1-12; Luke 5:17-26]

9 Jesus got into a boat. He crossed over to the other side and came into His own city. [2]They took a man to Him who was on his bed. This man was not able to move his body. Jesus saw their faith. He said, "Son, take hope. Your sins are forgiven." ³Some of the teachers of the Law said to themselves, "This man speaks as if He is God, but He is not!" ⁴Jesus knew what they were thinking. He said, "Why do you think bad thoughts in your hearts? ⁵Which is easier to say, 'Your sins are forgiven,' or to say, 'Get up and walk?' ⁶But this is to show you that the Son of Man has power on earth to forgive sins." He said to the sick man, "Get up! Take your bed and go home." ⁷He got up and went to his home. ⁸All the people saw this. They were surprised and wondered about it. Then they gave thanks to God because He had given such power to men.

Jesus Calls Matthew [Mark 2:13-17; Luke 5:27-32]

⁹As Jesus went from there, He saw a man called Matthew. Matthew was sitting at his work gathering taxes. Jesus said to him, "Follow Me." Matthew got up and followed Jesus. ¹⁰Jesus ate in Matthew's house. Many men who gathered taxes and many who were sinners came to Matthew's house and sat down with Jesus and His followers. ¹¹The proud religious law-keepers saw this. They said to the followers of Jesus, "Why does your Teacher eat with men who gather taxes and with sinners?" ¹²Jesus heard them and said, "People who are well do not need a doctor. ¹³But go and understand these words, 'I want loving-kindness and not a gift to be given.' (Hosea 6:6) For I have not come to call good people. I have come to call those who are sinners."

Jesus Teaches About Going Without Food So You Can Pray Better [Mark 2:18-22; Luke 5:33-35]

¹⁴Then the followers of John the Baptist came to Jesus. They asked, "Why do we and the proud religious law-keepers many times go without food so we can pray better? But Your followers never go without food so they can pray better." ¹⁵Jesus said, "Can the friends at a wedding be sorry when the man just married is with them? But the days will come when the man just married will be taken from them. Then they will not eat food so they can pray better.

¹⁶"No one sews a piece of new cloth on an old coat, because if the new piece pulls away, it makes the hole bigger. ¹⁷Men do not put new wine into old skin bags. If they did, the skins would break and the wine would run out. The bags would be no good. They put new wine into new skin bags and both can be used."

Two Healed Through Faith [Mark 5:21-43; Luke 8:40-56]

¹⁸While Jesus talked to them, a leader of the people came and got down before Him, and worshiped Him. He said, "My daughter has just died. But come, lay Your hand on her and she will live." ¹⁹Jesus got up and followed him. His followers went also.

²⁰Just then a woman who had been sick with a flow of blood for twelve years came from behind. She touched the bottom of His coat. ²¹She said to herself, "If I only touch the bottom of His coat, I will be healed." ²²Then Jesus turned around. He saw her and said, "Daughter, take hope! Your faith has healed you." At once the woman was healed.

²³Jesus came into the leader's house. He saw the people playing music and making much noise. ²⁴He said to them, "Go now! For the girl is not dead, but is sleeping." But they laughed at Him. ²⁵He sent the people outside. Then He went in and took the girl's hand. She was raised up. ²⁶News of this went out into all the country.

The Healing Of Two Blind Men

27Jesus went on from there. Two blind men followed Him. They called out, "Take pity on us, Son of David." 28Jesus went into the house. The blind men came to Him. Then Jesus said to them, "Do you have faith that I can do this?" They said to Him, "Yes, Sir!" 29Then Jesus put His hands on their eyes and said, "You will have what you want because you have faith." 30Their eyes were opened. Jesus told them to tell no one. 31But when they had gone, they told about Him everywhere in the country.

32As they went on their way, a man who had a demon and could not talk was brought to Jesus. 33When the demon was put out of him, the man was able to talk. Many people were surprised and wondered about it. They said, "We have never seen anything in the nation of the Jews like this." 34But the proud religious law-keepers said, "He puts out demons by the help of the leader of the demons."

35Jesus went on to all the towns and cities. He taught in their places of worship. He preached the Good News of the holy nation of God. He healed every sickness and disease the people had. 36As He saw many people, He had loving-pity on them. They were troubled and were walking around everywhere. They were like sheep without a shepherd. 37Then He said to His followers, "There is much grain ready to gather. But the workmen are few. 38Pray then to the Lord Who is the Owner of the grain fields that He will send workmen to gather His grain."

Jesus Calls Twelve Followers And Sends Them Out [Mark 6:7-13; Luke 9:1-6]

10 Jesus called His twelve followers to Him. He gave them power to put out demons and to heal all kinds of sickness and disease. 2These are the names of the twelve followers. There were Simon who was called Peter, and Andrew his brother, and James and John who were the sons of Zebedee. 3There were Philip and Bartholomew and Thomas. There was Matthew, the man who gathered taxes. There were James the son of Alphaeus, and Thaddaeus, and 4Simon the Canaanite. There was Judas Iscariot who handed Jesus over to be killed.

5Jesus sent out these twelve followers. He told them to go, saying, "Stay away from people who are not Jews. And do not go to any town in the country of Samaria. 6But go to the Jewish people who are lost. 7As you go, preach. Say, 'The holy nation of heaven is near.' 8Heal the sick and those with bad skin diseases. Raise the dead. Put out demons. You have received much, now give much. 9Do not take gold or silver or brass money with you. 10Do not take a bag of things for the trip. Do not take two coats or shoes or a walking stick. A workman should receive his food and what he needs.

11"When you come to a city or town, find a home that is respected and stay there until you leave. 12As you go into a house, tell them you hope good comes to them. 13And if the house is respected, give them your good wishes. If it is not respected, let your good wishes come back to you. 14Whoever does not receive you or does not listen to what you say, as you leave that house or city, shake off the dust from your feet. 15For sure, I tell you, it will be easier for the land of Sodom and Gomorrha on the day men stand before God and are told they are guilty, than for that city.

16"I am sending you out like sheep with wolves all around you. Be wise like snakes and gentle like doves. 17But look out for men. They will take you up to their courts and they will hurt you in their places of worship. [18]They will take you in front of the leaders of the people and of the kings because of Me. You will tell them and the people who do not know God about Me. [19]When you are put into their hands, do not worry what you will say or how you will say it. The words will be given you when the time comes. [20]It will not be you who will speak the words. The Spirit of your Father will speak through you.

[21]"A brother will hand over a brother to be put to death. A father will hand over his child to be put to death. Children will hand over their parents to be put to death. [22]You will be hated by all people because of Me. But he who stays true to the end will be saved. [23]When they make it hard for you in one town, go to another. For sure, I tell you, before you have gone through the Jewish cities, the Son of Man will come.

[24]"A follower is not greater than his teacher. A servant who is owned by someone is not greater than his owner. [25]A follower should be happy to be as his teacher, and a servant who is owned by someone should be happy to be as his owner. If they have called the head of the house Satan, how much more will they speak against those of the house. [26]Then do not be afraid of them. For nothing is covered up that will not be brought out into the light. There is nothing hid that will not be made known. [27]You tell in the light what I tell you in the dark. You must speak with a loud voice from the roofs of houses what you have heard. [28]Do not be afraid of them who kill the body. They are not able to kill the soul. But fear Him Who is able to destroy both soul and body in hell. [29]Are not two small birds sold for a very small piece of money? And yet not one of the birds falls to the earth without your Father knowing it. [30]God knows how many hairs you have on your head. [31]So do not be afraid. You are more important than many small birds.

[32]"Whoever makes Me known in front of men, I will make him known to My Father in heaven. [33]But whoever does not make Me known in front of men and acts as if he does not know Me, I will not make him known to My Father in heaven.

[34]"Do not think I came to bring peace on the earth. I did not come to bring peace, but a sword. [35]I came to turn a man against his father. I came to turn a daughter against her mother. I came to turn a daughter-in-law against her mother-in-law. [36]A man will be hated by his own family.

Giving Up Things Of This Earth
[*Luke 14:25-35*]

[37]"He who loves his father and mother more than Me is not good enough for Me. He who loves son or daughter more than Me is not good enough for Me. [38]He who does not take his cross and follow Me is not good enough for Me. [39]He who wants to keep his life will have it taken away from him. He who loses his life because of Me will have it given back to him.

[40]"Whoever receives you, receives Me. Whoever receives Me, receives Him Who sent Me. [41]Whoever receives a preacher who speaks for God because he is a preacher, will get the pay of a preacher who speaks for God. Whoever receives a man right with God, because he is a man right with God, will get the pay of a man right with God. [42]For sure, I tell you, anyone who gives a cup of cold water to one of these little ones because he follows Me, will not lose his pay."

John The Baptist Asks About Jesus
[*Luke 7:18-23*]

11 When Jesus finished telling His twelve followers what to do, He went away from there to teach and preach in their towns.

²When John the Baptist was in prison, he heard what Jesus was doing. He sent his followers. ³They asked, "Are You the One Who was to come, or should we look for another?" ⁴Jesus said to them, "Go and tell John what you see and hear. ⁵The blind are made to see. Those who could not walk are walking. Those who have had bad skin diseases are healed. Those who could not hear are hearing. The dead are raised up to life and the Good News is preached to poor people. ⁶He is happy who is not ashamed of Me and does not turn away because of Me."

Jesus Tells About John The Baptist
[Luke 7:24-35]

⁷As the followers of John the Baptist went away, Jesus began to tell the people about John. He said, "What did you go out to see in the desert? A small tree shaking in the wind? ⁸But what did you go out to see? A man dressed in good clothes? Those who are dressed in good clothes are in the houses of kings. ⁹What did you go out to see? One who speaks for God? Yes, I tell you, he is more than one who speaks for God. ¹⁰This is the man the Holy Writings spoke of when they said, 'See! I will send My helper to carry news ahead of You. He will make Your way ready for You!' (Malachi 3:1) ¹¹For sure, I tell you, of those born of women, there is no one greater than John the Baptist. Yet the least in the holy nation of heaven is greater than he. ¹²From the days of John the Baptist until now, the holy nation of heaven has suffered very much. Fighting men try to take it. ¹³All the early preachers and the Law told about it until the time of John. ¹⁴And if you will believe it, he is Elijah who was to come. (Malachi 4:5) ¹⁵You have ears, then listen!

Jesus Speaks Against Cities In Galilee

¹⁶"What are the people of this day like? They are like children playing in the center of town where people gather. They call to their friends. ¹⁷They say, 'We played music for you, but you did not dance. We showed sorrow in front of you, but you did not show sorrow.' ¹⁸John came and did not eat or drink. They said, 'He has a demon.' ¹⁹Then the Son of Man came and ate and drank. They said, 'See! He eats too much and likes wine. He is a friend of men who gather taxes and of sinners!' But wisdom shows itself to be right by what it does."

²⁰Then He began to say strong words against the cities where most of His powerful works were done. He spoke to them because they were not sorry for their sins and did not turn from them. ²¹"It is bad for you, city of Chorazin! It is bad for you, town of Bethsaida! For if the powerful works which were done in you had been done in the cities of Tyre and Sidon, they would have turned from their sins long ago. They would have shown their sorrow by putting on clothes made from hair and would have sat in ashes. ²²I tell you, it will be better for Tyre and Sidon on the day men stand before God and are told they are guilty, than for you.

²³"And Capernaum, are you to be lifted up into heaven? You will be taken down to hell. If the powerful works which were done in you had been done in the city of Sodom, it would be here to this day. ²⁴But I say to you that it will be better for the land of Sodom on the day men stand before God and are told they are guilty, than for you."

Jesus Prays To His Father

²⁵At that time Jesus said, "Thank you, Father, Lord of heaven and

earth, because You hid these things from the wise and from those who have much learning. You have shown them to little children. ²⁶Yes, Father, it was good in Your sight. ²⁷"Everything has been given to Me by My Father. No one knows the Son but the Father. No one knows the Father but the Son, and those to whom the Son wants to make the Father known.

Jesus Calls People To Follow Him

²⁸"Come to Me, all of you who work and have heavy loads. I will give you rest. ²⁹Follow My teachings and learn from Me. I am gentle and do not have pride. You will have rest for your souls. ³⁰For My way of carrying a load is easy and My load is not heavy."

Jesus Teaches About The Day Of Rest [Mark 2:23-28; Luke 6:1-5]

12 At that time Jesus walked through the grain fields on the Day of Rest. His followers were hungry and began to pick off grain to eat. ²The proud religious law-keepers saw this. They said to Jesus, "See! Your followers do what the Law says not to do on the Day of Rest." ³He said to them, "Have you not read what David did when he and his men were hungry? ⁴He went into the house of God and ate the special bread used in worship which was against the Law for him or those with him to eat! Only the Jewish religious leaders were to eat that special bread. ⁵Have you not read in the Law how the religious leaders do that which is not right to do on the Day of Rest, and yet they are not guilty? ⁶I tell you that Someone greater than the house of God is here. ⁷If you had understood what the words mean, 'I want loving-kindness and not a gift to be given,' (Hosea 6:6) you would not say a person is guilty who has done no wrong. ⁸For the Son of Man is Lord of the Day of Rest."

Jesus Heals On The Day Of Rest [Mark 3:1-6; Luke 6:6-11]

⁹From there Jesus went into their place of worship. ¹⁰A man was there with a dried-up hand. The proud religious law-keepers asked Jesus, "Does the Law say it is right to heal on the Day of Rest?" They wanted something to say against Him. ¹¹He said to them, "If one of you has a sheep which falls into a hole on the Day of Rest, will you not take hold of it and pull it out? ¹²How much better is a man than a sheep! So it is right to do good on the Day of Rest." ¹³Then He said to the man, "Put out your hand." He held it out and it was made as well as the other. ¹⁴The proud religious law-keepers went out and made plans against Him. They planned how they might kill Him.

Jesus Heals Many People [Mark 3:7-12; Luke 6:17-19]

¹⁵Jesus knew this and went away from there. Many people followed Him and He healed all of them. ¹⁶He told them to tell no one of Him. ¹⁷It happened as the early preacher Isaiah said it would happen, saying, ¹⁸"See! My Servant Whom I have chosen! My much Loved, in Whom My soul is well pleased! I will put My Spirit in Him. He will say to the nations what is right from wrong. ¹⁹He will not fight or speak with a loud voice. No man will hear His voice in the streets. ²⁰He will not break a broken branch. He will not put out a little fire until He makes things right. ²¹In His name the nations will have hope." (Isaiah 42:2-4)

A Nation That Cannot Stand [Mark 3:22-30; Luke 11:14-23]

²²Then they brought to Him a man who had a demon. He was blind and could not speak. Jesus healed him and he could talk and see. ²³All the people were surprised and said, "Can

this Man be the Son of David?" 24But when the proud religious law-keepers heard it, they said, "This Man puts out demons only by Satan, the leader of demons."

25Jesus knew their thoughts and said to them, "Every nation divided into groups that fight each other is going to be destroyed. Every city or family divided into groups that fight each other will not stand. 26If the devil puts out the devil, he is divided against himself. How will his nation stand? 27If I put out demons by Satan, by whom do your followers put them out? So your followers will say if you are guilty. 28But if I put out demons by the Spirit of God, then the holy nation of God is come to you. 29How can anyone go into a strong man's house and take away his things, unless he ties up the strong man first? Only then can he take things from his house.

The Sin That Cannot Be Forgiven

30"Whoever is not with Me is against Me. Whoever is not gathering with Me is sending everywhere. 31I tell you, every sin and every bad word men speak against God will be forgiven, but bad words spoken against the Holy Spirit will not be forgiven. 32Whoever speaks a word against the Son of Man will be forgiven, but whoever speaks against the Holy Spirit will not be forgiven in this life or in the life to come.

The Sin Of Saying Bad Things

33"A good tree gives good fruit. A bad tree gives bad fruit. A tree is known by its fruit. 34You family of snakes! How can you say good things when you are sinful? The mouth speaks what the heart is full of. 35A good man will speak good things because of the good in him. A bad man will speak bad things because of the sin in him. 36I say to you, on the day men stand before God, they will

have to give an answer for every word they have spoken that was not important. 37For it is by your words that you will not be guilty and it is by your words that you will be guilty."

Jesus Tells About Jonah [Luke 11:29-32]

38Then some of the teachers of the Law and the proud religious law-keepers said to Jesus, "Teacher, we would like to have you do something special for us to see." 39He said to them, "The sinful people of this day look for something special to see. There will be nothing special to see but the powerful works of the early preacher Jonah. 40Jonah was three days and three nights in the stomach of a big fish. The Son of Man will be three days and three nights in the grave also. 41The men of the city of Ninevah will stand up with the people of this day on the day men stand before God. Those men will say these people are guilty because the men of Ninevah were sorry for their sins and turned from them when Jonah preached. And see, Someone greater than Jonah is here!

42"The Queen of the South will stand up with the people of this day on the day men stand before God. She will say that these people are guilty because she came from the ends of the earth to listen to the wise sayings of Solomon. And see, Someone greater than Solomon is here!

A Person Filled With Bad Or Good [Luke 11:24-26]

43"When a demon is gone out of a man, it goes through dry places to find rest. It finds none. 44Then it says, 'I will go back into my house from which I came.' When it goes back, it sees that it is empty. But it sees that the house has been cleaned and looks good. 45Then it goes out and comes back bringing with it seven demons more sinful than itself. They go in and live there. In the end that man is worse than at first. It will be like this with the sinful people of this day."

The New Kind Of Family [Mark 3:31-35; Luke 8:19-21]

⁴⁶While Jesus was still talking to the people, His mother and His brothers came and stood outside. They wanted to talk to Him. ⁴⁷Someone said to Him, "Your mother and brothers are outside and want to talk to you." ⁴⁸Jesus said, "Who is My mother? And who are My brothers?" ⁴⁹He put out His hand to His followers and said, "See, these are My mother and My brothers! ⁵⁰Whoever does what My father in heaven wants him to do is My brother and My sister and My mother."

Jesus Teaches With Picture-stories [Mark 4:1-34; Luke 8:4-18]

13 That same day Jesus went out of the house and sat down by the shore of the lake. ²Then He got in a boat and sat down because so many people had gathered around Him. Many people were standing on the shore.

The Picture-story Of The Man Who Planted Seeds

³Jesus taught them many things by using picture-stories. He said, "A man went out to plant seeds. ⁴As he planted the seeds, some fell by the side of the road. The birds came and ate the seeds. ⁵Some seeds fell between rocks. The seeds came up at once because there was so little ground. ⁶When the sun was high in the sky, they dried up and died because they had no root. ⁷Some seeds fell among thorns. The thorns grew and did not give the seeds room to grow. ⁸Some seeds fell on good

ground and gave much grain. Some gave one hundred times as much grain. Some gave sixty times as much grain. Some gave thirty times as much grain. ⁹You have ears, then listen."

Why Jesus Used Picture-stories

¹⁰The followers of Jesus came to Him and said, "Why do You speak to them in picture-stories?" ¹¹He said to the followers, "You were given the secrets about the holy nation of heaven. The secrets were not given to the others. ¹²He who has will have more given to him. He will have even more than enough. But he who has little will have even that taken away from him.

¹³"This is why I speak to them in picture-stories. They have eyes but they do not see. They have ears but they do not hear and they do not understand. ¹⁴It happened in their lives as Isaiah said it would happen. He said, 'You hear and hear but do not understand. You look and look but do not see. ¹⁵The hearts of these people have become fat. They hear very little with their ears. They have closed their eyes. If they did not do this, they would see with their eyes and hear with their ears and understand with their hearts. Then they would be changed in their ways, and I would heal them.' (Isaiah 6:9-10) ¹⁶But how great are your eyes because they see. How great are your ears because they hear. ¹⁷For sure, I tell you, that many early preachers and men right with God have wanted to see the things you see, but they did not see them. They wanted to hear the things you hear, but they did not hear them.

Jesus Tells About The Man Who Planted Seeds

¹⁸"Listen to the picture-story of the man who planted seeds in the ground. ¹⁹When anyone hears the

Word about the holy nation and does not understand it, the devil comes and takes away what was put in his heart. He is like the seed that fell by the side of the road. 20The seed which fell between rocks is like the person who receives the Word with joy as soon as he hears it. 21Its root is not deep and it does not last long. When troubles and suffering come because of the Word, he gives up and falls away. 22The seed which fell among thorns is like the person who hears the Word but the cares of this life, and the love for money let the thorns come up and do not give the seed room to grow and give grain. 23The seed which fell on good ground is like the one who hears the Word and understands it. He gives much grain. Some seed gives one hundred times as much grain. Some gives sixty times as much grain. Some gives thirty times as much grain."

The Picture-story Of The Good Seed And The Weed Seed

24Jesus told them another picture-story. He said, "The holy nation of heaven is like a man who planted good seed in his field. 25During the night someone who hated him came and planted weed seed with the good seed in his field and went away. 26When the good seed started to grow and give grain, weeds came up also. 27"The men came who worked for the man who planted the seed. They said to him, 'Sir, did you not plant good seed in your field? Why does it have weeds also?' 28The man who planted the seed said, 'Someone who hates me has done this.' The workmen asked him, 'Should we go and pull the weeds out from among the good grain?' 29He said, 'No, because if you pull out the weeds, the good grain will come up also. 30Let them grow together until the time to gather the grain. Then I will say to the workmen, "Gather the weeds first and put them together to be burned. Then gather the good grain into my building." ' "

The Picture-story Of The Mustard Seed

31Jesus told them another picture-story. He said, "The holy nation of heaven is like mustard seed which a man planted in his field. 32It is the smallest of seeds. But when it is full-grown, it is larger than the grain of the fields and it becomes a tree. The birds of the sky come and stay in its branches."

The Picture-story Of The Yeast

33Jesus gave them another picture-story. He said, "The holy nation of heaven is like yeast that a woman put into three pails of flour until it had become much more than at first."

34Jesus told all these things using picture-stories to the many people. He did not speak to them without using picture-stories. 35It happened as the early preacher said it would happen, "I will open My mouth in picture-stories. I will tell things which have been kept secret from the beginning of the world." (Psalm 78:2)

Jesus Tells About The Weed Seed

36After Jesus sent the people away, He went into the house. His followers came to Him and said, "Tell us what You mean by the picture-story of the weeds in the field." 37Jesus said, "He Who plants the good seed is the Son of Man. 38The field is the world. The good seed are the children of the holy nation. The weeds are the children of the devil. 39The devil is the one who got in and planted the weeds. The time to gather is the end of the world. The men who gather are the angels. 40As the weeds are gathered together and burned in the fire, so will it be in the end of the world. 41The Son of Man will send His angels. They will gather out of His holy nation all things that cause people to sin and those who do sin. 42They will put them into a stove of fire. There will be loud crying and grinding of teeth. 43Then the ones right with God will shine as the sun in the holy nation of their Father. You have ears, then listen!"

The Picture-stories Of The Gold Buried In The Field And Of Buying A Pearl

44"The holy nation of heaven is like a box of riches buried in a field. A man found it and then hid it again. In his joy he goes and sells all that he has and buys that field.

45"Again, the holy nation of heaven is like a man who buys and sells. He is looking for good pearls. 46When he finds one good pearl worth much money, he goes and sells all that he has and buys it.

The Picture-story Of The Fish Net

47"The holy nation of heaven is like a big net which was let down into the sea. It gathered fish of every kind. 48When it was full, they took it to the shore. They sat down and put the good fish into pails. They threw the bad fish away. 49It will be like this in the end of the world. Angels will come and take the sinful people from among those who are right with God. 50They will put the sinful people into a stove of fire where there will be loud crying and grinding of teeth."

51Jesus asked them, "Have you understood all these picture-stories?" They said, "Yes, Lord!" 52He said to them, "Every teacher of the Law who has become a follower of the holy nation of heaven is like a man who owns his house. He takes new and old riches from his house."

They Do Not Believe In Jesus In Nazareth [Mark 6:1-6]

53When Jesus had finished these picture-stories, He went away from there. 54He came to His own town and taught them in their places of worship. They were surprised and wondered, saying, "Where did this Man get this wisdom? How can He do these powerful works? 55Is not this the son of the man who makes things from wood? Is not Mary His mother? Are not James and Joseph and Simon and Judas His brothers? 56And are not all His sisters here? Then where did He get all these things?" 57And they were ashamed of Him and turned away because of Him. Jesus said to them, "One who speaks for God is shown no respect in his own town and in his own house."

58He did not do many powerful works there because they did not put their trust in Him.

John The Baptist Is Put In Prison [Mark 6:14-20; Luke 3:18-20]

14 At that time King Herod heard much about Jesus. 2He said to his helpers, "This must be John the Baptist. He has risen from the dead. That is why these powerful works are done by him." 3For Herod had taken John and put him in prison. It was because of Herodias, the wife of his brother Philip. 4For John had said to him, "It is against the Law for you to have her." 5He would have killed John but he was afraid of the people. The people thought John was one who spoke for God.

John The Baptist Is Killed [Mark 6:21-29; Luke 9:7-9]

6On Herod's birthday the daughter of Herodias danced in front of them. Herod was made happy by her. 7He promised he would give her anything she asked. 8Because her mother told her to do it, she said, "Give me the head of John the Baptist on a plate." 9The king was sorry. But he said for it to be given because he had promised and because of those who were eating with him. 10He sent to the prison and had John's head cut off. [11]It was brought in on a plate and given to the girl. She brought it to her mother. [12]Then the followers of John came and took his body and buried it. They went and told Jesus.

The Feeding Of The Five Thousand
[Mark 6:30-44; Luke 9:10-17; John 6:1-14]

[13]When Jesus heard that John had been killed, He went from there by boat to a desert. He wanted to be alone. When the people knew it, they followed after Him by land from the cities. [14]When He got out of the boat, He saw many people. He had loving-pity for them and healed those who were sick.

[15]When it was evening, His followers came to Him. They said, "This is a desert. The day is past. Send the people away so they may go into the towns and buy food for themselves." [16]Jesus said to them, "They do not have to go away. Give them something to eat." [17]They said to Him, "We have only five loaves of bread and two fish." [18]Jesus said, "Bring them to Me." [19]He told the people to sit down on the grass. Then He took the five loaves of bread and two fish. He looked up to heaven and gave thanks. He broke the loaves in pieces and gave them to His followers. The followers gave them to the people. [20]They all ate and were filled. They picked up twelve baskets full of pieces of bread and fish after the people were finished eating. [21]About five thousand men ate. Women and children ate also.

Jesus Walks On The Water [Mark 6:45-52; John 6:15-21]

[22]At once Jesus had His followers get into the boat. He told them to go ahead of Him to the other side while He sent the people away. [23]After He had sent them away, He went up the mountain by Himself to pray. When

evening came, He was there alone. [24]By this time the boat was far from land and was being thrown around by the waves. The wind was strong against them.

[25]Just before the light of day, Jesus went to them walking on the water. [26]When the followers saw Him walking on the water, they were afraid. They said, "It is a spirit." They cried out with fear. [27]At once Jesus spoke to them and said, "Take hope. It is I. Do not be afraid!"

[28]Peter said to Jesus, "If it is You, Lord, tell me to come to You on the water." [29]Jesus said, "Come!" Peter got out of the boat and walked on the water to Jesus. [30]But when he saw the strong wind, he was afraid. He began to go down in the water. He cried out, "Lord, save me!" [31]At once Jesus put out His hand and took hold of him. Jesus said to Peter, "You have so little faith! Why did you doubt?"

[32]When Jesus and Peter got into the boat, the wind stopped blowing. [33]Those in the boat worshiped Jesus. They said, "For sure, You are the Son of God!"

People Are Healed At Gennesaret
[Mark 6:53-56]

[34]When they had gone over to the other side, they came to the land of Gennesaret. [35]When the men of that land saw it was Jesus, they sent word into all the country around. They brought all who were sick to Jesus. [36]They begged Him that they might touch the bottom of His coat. As many as touched the bottom of His coat were healed.

Jesus Speaks Sharp Words To The Leaders [Mark 7:1-23]

15 Some of the teachers of the Law and the proud religious law-keepers from Jerusalem came to Jesus. They asked, [2]"Why do Your followers not obey the teaching that was given to them by our fathers?

They do not wash their hands before they eat." [3]Jesus said to them, "Why do you break the Law of God by trying to keep their teaching? [4]For God said, 'Show respect to your father and mother.' (Exodus 20:12) And, 'He who says bad things against his father or mother will be put to death.' (Exodus 21:17) [5]But you say that if a man says to his parents that anything he has, that might have been of help to them, is already given to God, [6]he does not have to show respect by helping his father and mother. You are putting aside the Word of God to keep their teaching. [7]You who pretend to be someone you are not, Isaiah told about you. He said, [8]'These people show respect to Me with their mouth, but their heart is far from Me. [9]Their worship of Me is worth nothing. They teach what men have made up.' "(Isaiah 29:13)

[10]Jesus called the people to Him and said to them, "Listen and understand this! [11]It is not what goes into a man's mouth that makes his mind and heart sinful. It is what comes out of a man's mouth that makes him sinful."

[12]His followers came to Him. They said, "Did You know the proud religious law-keepers were ashamed and turned away because of You when they heard this?" [13]He said, "Every plant that My Father in heaven did not plant will be pulled up by the roots. [14]Let them alone. They are blind leaders of the blind. If one blind man leads another blind man, they will both fall into a hole."

[15]Then Peter said to Jesus, "Tell us this picture-story so we can understand it." [16]Jesus said, "Do you not understand yet? [17]Do you not understand that whatever goes into the mouth goes into the stomach and then out of the body? [18]But whatever comes from the mouth has come out of the heart. These things make the man unclean inside. [19]For out of the heart come bad thoughts, killing other people, sex sins of a married person, sex sins of a person not married, stealing, lying, speaking against God. [20]These are the things that make the man unclean inside. It does not make a man sinful to eat with hands that have not been washed."

Jesus Puts A Demon Out Of A Girl
[Mark 7:24-30]

[21]Jesus went from there to the cities of Tyre and Sidon. [22]A woman came from the land of Canaan. She cried out to Jesus and said, "Take pity on me, Lord, Son of David! My daughter has a demon and is much troubled." [23]But Jesus did not speak a word to her. His followers kept asking, saying, "Send her away for she keeps calling us." [24]He said, "I was sent only to the Jewish people who are lost." [25]Then she came and got down before Jesus and worshiped Him. She said, "Lord, help me!" [26]But He said, "It is not right to take children's food and throw it to the dogs." [27]She said, "Yes, Lord, but even the dogs eat the pieces that fall from the table of their owners." [28]Jesus said to her, "Woman, you have much faith. You will have what you asked for." Her daughter was healed at that very time.

Jesus Heals All Who Come To Him

[29]Jesus went from there and came to the Sea of Galilee. Then He went up the mountain and sat down. [30]Many people came to Him. They brought with them those who were not able to walk. They brought those who were not able to see. They brought those who were not able to hear or speak and many others. Then they put them at the feet of Jesus and He healed them. [31]All the people wondered. They saw how those who could not speak were now talking. They saw how those who could not walk were now walking. They saw how those who could not see were

now seeing, and they gave thanks to the God of the Jews.

The Feeding Of The Four Thousand
[Mark 8:1-9]

32 Then Jesus called His followers to Him. He said, "I pity these people because they have been with Me three days and they have no food. I do not want to send them home without food. They might get too weak as they go." 33 The followers said to Jesus, "Where can we get enough bread to feed them all in this desert?" 34 Jesus said to them, "How many loaves of bread do you have?" They said, "Seven loaves and a few small fish." 35 He told the people to sit down on the ground. 36 Then He took the seven loaves of bread and the fish and gave thanks. He broke them and gave them to His followers. The followers gave them to the people. 37 They all ate and were filled. They picked up seven baskets full of pieces of bread and fish after the people finished eating. 38 Four thousand men ate. Women and children ate also. 39 After this Jesus sent the people away. Then He got into a boat and came to a place called Magadan.

Jesus Speaks Sharp Words To The Proud Religious Law-keepers [Mark 8:10-13]

16 The proud religious law-keepers and a religious group of people who believe no one will be raised from the dead came to Jesus. They asked Him to show something special from heaven. They wanted to trap Jesus. 2 (He said to them, "In the evening you say, 'The weather will be good tomorrow because the sky is red.' 3 And in the morning you say, 'We will have a storm today because the sky is red and the clouds are low.' You understand the things you see in the sky, but you cannot understand the special things you see these days!) 4 The sinful people of this day go after

something special to see. There will be nothing special for them to see but the early preacher Jonah." Then He went away from them.

Jesus Shows That The Teaching Of The Proud Religious Law-keepers Is Wrong [Mark 8:14-21]

5 The followers came to the other side of the lake. They remembered they had forgotten to bring bread. 6 Jesus said to them, "See! Have nothing to do with the yeast of the proud religious law-keepers and the religious group of people who believe no one will be raised from the dead." 7 They started to think about it' among themselves and said, "He said this because we forgot to bring bread." 8 Jesus knew this and said, "You have very little faith! Why are you talking among yourselves about not bringing bread? 9 Do you not yet understand or remember the five loaves of bread that fed five thousand men? And how many baskets full were gathered up? 10 Or do you not even remember the seven loaves of bread that fed the four thousand men? And how many baskets full were gathered up? 11 Why is it that you do not see that I was not talking to you about bread? I was talking to you about keeping away from the yeast of the proud religious law-keepers and the religious group of people who believe no one will be raised from the dead." 12 Then they understood that it was not the yeast of bread that He was talking about. But He was talking about the teaching of the proud religious law-keepers and of the other religious group of people.

Peter Says Jesus Is The Christ [Mark 8:27-30; Luke 9:18-20]

13 Jesus came into the country of Caesarea Philippi. He asked His followers, "Who do people say that I, the Son of Man, am?" 14 They said,

"Some say You are John the Baptist and some say Elijah and others say Jeremiah or one of the early preachers."

[15]He said to them, "But who do you say that I am?" [16]Simon Peter said, "You are the Christ, the Son of the living God."

[17]Jesus said to him, "Simon, son of Jonah, you are happy because you did not learn this from man. My Father in heaven has shown you this.

[18]"And I tell you that you are Peter. On this rock I will build My church. The powers of hell will not be able to have power over My church. [19]I will give you the keys of the holy nation of heaven. Whatever you do not allow on earth will not have been allowed in heaven. Whatever you allow on earth will have been allowed in heaven." [20]Then with strong words He told His followers to tell no one that He was the Christ.

Jesus Tells Of His Death For The First Time [Mark 8:31-38; Luke 9:21-27]

[21]From that time on Jesus began to tell His followers that He had to go to Jerusalem and suffer many things. These hard things would come from the leaders and from the head religious leaders of the Jews and from the teachers of the Law. He told them He would be killed and three days later He would be raised from the dead. [22]Peter took Jesus away from the others and spoke sharp words to Him. He said, "Never, Lord! This must not happen to You!" [23]Then Jesus turned to Peter and said, "Get behind Me, Satan! You are standing in My way. You are not thinking how God thinks. You are thinking how man thinks."

Giving Up Riches

[24]Jesus said to His followers, "If anyone wants to be My follower, he must forget about himself. He must take up his cross and follow Me. [25]If anyone wants to keep his life safe, he will lose it. If anyone gives up his life because of Me, he will save it. [26]For what does a man have if he gets all the world and loses his own soul? What can a man give to buy back his soul? [27]The Son of Man will come in the greatness of His Father with His angels. Then He will give to every man his pay as he has worked. [28]For sure, I tell you, there are some standing here that will not die until they see the Son of Man coming as King."

A Look At What Jesus Will Be Like [Mark 9:1-13; Luke 9:28-36]

17 Six days later Jesus took with Him Peter and James and his brother John. He led them up to a high mountain by themselves. [2]He was changed in looks before them. His face was as bright as the sun. His clothes looked as white as light. [3]Moses and Elijah were seen talking with Jesus. [4]Then Peter said to Jesus, "Lord, it is good for us to be here. If You will let us, we will build three altars here. One will be for You and one for Moses and one for Elijah."

[5]While Peter was speaking, a bright cloud came over them. A voice from the cloud said, "This is My much-loved Son, I am very happy with Him. Listen to Him!" [6]When the followers heard this, they got down on the ground on their faces and were very much afraid. [7]Jesus came and put His hand on them. He said, "Get up! Do not be afraid." [8]When they looked up, they saw no one there but Jesus only. [9]As they came down from the mountain, Jesus told them in strong words, saying, "Do not tell anyone what you have seen until the Son of Man is raised from the dead."

The Followers Ask About Elijah

[10]The followers asked Jesus, "Then why do the teachers of the Law say

that Elijah must come first?" ¹¹He said, "For sure, Elijah will come first and get things ready. ¹²But I tell you, Elijah has already come and they did not know him. They did to him whatever they wanted to do. In the same way the Son of Man will suffer from them also." ¹³Then the followers understood He was talking about John the Baptist.

A Boy With A Demon Is Healed
[Mark 9:14-29; Luke 9:37-42]

¹⁴When they came to many people, a man came up to Jesus and got on his knees. He said, ¹⁵"Lord, have pity on my son. He is very sick and at times loses the use of his mind. Many times he falls into the fire or into the water. ¹⁶I took him to Your followers but they were not able to heal him."

¹⁷Then Jesus said, "You people of this day have no faith and you are going the wrong way. How long must I be with you? How long must I put up with you? Bring him here to Me." ¹⁸Jesus spoke sharp words to the demon and the demon came out of him. At once the boy was healed.

¹⁹The followers came to Jesus when He was alone. They said, "Why were we not able to put the demon out?" ²⁰Jesus said to them, "Because you have so little faith. For sure, I tell you, if you have faith as a mustard seed, you will say to this mountain, 'Move from here to over there,' and it would move over. You will be able to do anything. ²¹ But this kind of demon does not go out but by prayer and by going without food so you can pray better."

Jesus Tells Of His Death The Second Time
[Mark 9:30-32; Luke 9:43-45]

²²While they were still in Galilee, Jesus said to the followers, "The Son of Man will be handed over to men. ²³They will kill Him, but He will be raised from the dead three days later." The followers were very sad.

Tax Money For The House Of God

²⁴They came to the city of Capernaum. Those who gathered the tax for the house of God came to Peter. They said, "Does not your Teacher pay tax money for the house of God?" ²⁵Peter said, "Yes." When Peter came into the house, Jesus spoke to him first. He said, "What do you think, Simon? From whom do the kings of this earth get their money or taxes, from their own people or from those of another country?" ²⁶Peter said to Him, "From those of another country." Then Jesus said, "Then their own people do not pay taxes. ²⁷But so we will not make them to be troubled, go down to the lake and throw in a hook. Take the first fish that comes up. In its mouth you will find a piece of money. Take that and pay the tax for Me and yourself."

Jesus Teaches About The Faith Of A Child
[Mark 9:33-50; Luke 9:46-50]

18 At that time the followers came to Jesus. They said, "Who is the greatest in the holy nation of heaven?" ²Jesus took a little child and put him among them. ³He said, "For sure, I tell you, unless you have a change of heart and become like a little child, you will not get into the holy nation of heaven. ⁴Whoever is without pride as this little child is the greatest in the holy nation of heaven. ⁵Whoever receives a little child because of Me receives Me. ⁶But whoever is the reason for one of these little children who believe in Me to fall into sin, it would be better for him to have a large rock put around his neck and to be thrown into the sea.

⁷"It is bad for the world because of that which makes people sin. Men will be tempted to sin. But it is bad for the one who is the reason for someone to sin. ⁸If your hand or your foot is the reason you sin, cut it off

and throw it away. It is better for you to go into life without a hand or a foot, than to have two hands or two feet and to be thrown into the fire of hell. [9]If your eye is the reason you sin, take it out and throw it away. It is better for you to go into life with one eye, than to have two eyes and be thrown into the fire of hell. [10]Be sure you do not hate one of these little children. I tell you, they have angels who are always looking into the face of My Father in heaven.

The Lost Sheep

[11] "For the Son of Man has come to save that which was lost. [12]What do you think about this? A man has one hundred sheep and one of them is lost. Will he not leave the ninety-nine and go to the mountains to look for that one lost sheep? [13]If he finds it, for sure, I tell you, he will have more joy over that one, than over the ninety-nine that were not lost. [14]I tell you, My Father in heaven does not want one of these little children to be lost.

What To Do With A Brother Who Sins Against You

[15]"If your brother sins against you, go and tell him what he did without other people hearing it. If he listens to you, you have won your brother back again. [16]But if he will not listen to you, take one or two other people with you. Every word may be remembered by the two or three who heard. [17]If he will not listen to them, tell the trouble to the church. If he does not listen to the church, think of him as a person who is as bad as one who does not know God and a person who gathers taxes. [18]"For sure, I tell you, whatever you do not allow on earth will not have been allowed in heaven. Whatever you allow on earth will have been allowed in heaven. [19]Again I tell you this: If two of you agree on earth about anything you pray for, it will be done for you by My Father in heaven. [20]For where two or three are gathered together in My name, there I am with them."

True Forgiveness

[21]Then Peter came to Jesus and said, "Lord, how many times may my brother sin against me and I forgive him, up to seven times?" [22]Jesus said to him, "I tell you, not seven times but seventy times seven! [23]"The holy nation of heaven is like a king who wanted to find out how much money his servants owed him. [24]As he began, one of the servants was brought to him who owed him very much money. [25]He could pay nothing that he owed. So the king spoke the word that he and his wife and his children and all that he had should be sold to pay what he owed. [26]The servant got down on his face in front of the king. He said, 'Give me time, and I will pay you all the money.' [27]Then the king took pity on his servant and let him go. He told him he did not have to pay the money back.

[28]"But that servant went out and found one of the other servants who owed him very little money. He took hold of his neck and said, 'Pay me the money you owe me!' [29]The other servant got down at his feet and said, 'Give me time, and I will pay you all the money.' [30]But he would not. He had him put in prison until he could pay the money.

[31]"When his other servants saw what had happened, they were very sorry. They came and told the king all that was done. [32]Then the king called for the first one. He said, 'You bad servant! I forgave you. I said that you would not have to pay back any of the money you owed me because you asked me. [33]Should you not have had pity on the other servant, even as I had pity on you?' [34]The king was very angry. He

handed him over to men who would beat and hurt him until he paid all the money he owed. 35So will My Father in heaven do to you, if each one of you does not forgive his brother from his heart."

What Jesus Taught About Marriage And Divorce [Mark 10:1-12]

19 When Jesus had finished talking, He went from the country of Galilee. He came to the part of the country of Judea which is on the other side of the Jordan River. 2Many people followed Him and He healed them there.

3The proud religious law-keepers came to Jesus. They tried to trap Him by saying, "Does the Law say a man can divorce his wife for any reason?" 4He said to them, "Have you not read that He Who made them in the first place made them man and woman? 5It says, 'For this reason a man will leave his father and his mother and will live with his wife. The two will become one.' 6So they are no longer two but one. Let no man divide what God has put together."

7The proud religious law-keepers said to Jesus, "Then why did the Law of Moses allow a man to divorce his wife if he put it down in writing and gave it to her?" 8Jesus said to them, "Because of your hard hearts Moses allowed you to divorce your wives. It was not like that from the beginning. 9And I say to you, whoever divorces his wife, except for sex sins, and marries another, is guilty of sex sins in marriage. Whoever marries her that is divorced is guilty of sex sins in marriage."

10His followers said to Him, "If that is the way of a man with his wife, it is better not to be married." 11But Jesus said to them, "Not all men are able to do this, but only those to whom it has been given. 12For there are some men who from birth will never be able to have children. There are some men who have been made

so by men. There are some men who have had themselves made that way because of the holy nation of heaven. The one who is able to do this, let him do it."

Jesus Gives Thanks For Little Children [Mark 10:13-16; Luke 18:15-17]

13Then little children were brought to Him that He might put His hands on them and pray for them. The followers spoke sharp words to them. 14But Jesus said, "Let the little children come to Me. Do not stop them. The holy nation of heaven is made up of ones like these." 15He put His hands on them and went away.

Jesus Teaches About Keeping The Law [Mark 10:17-31; Luke 18:18-30]

16A man came to Jesus and asked, "Good Teacher, what good work must I do to have life that lasts forever?" 17Jesus said to him, "Why are you asking Me about what is good? There is only One Who is good. If you want to have life that lasts forever, you must obey the Laws." 18The man said to Him, "What kind of laws?" Jesus said, "You must not kill another person. You must not be guilty of sex sins. You must not steal. You must not lie. 19Show respect to your father and your mother. And love your neighbor as you love yourself." 20The young man said to Jesus, "I have obeyed all these Laws. What more should I do?" 21Jesus said to him, "If you want to be perfect, go and sell everything you have and give the money to poor people. Then you will have riches in heaven. Come and follow Me." 22When the young man heard these words, he went away sad for he had many riches.

The Danger Of Riches

23Jesus said to His followers, "For sure, I tell you, it will be hard for a rich man to get into the holy nation of heaven. 24Again I tell you, it is easier for a camel to go through the eye of a needle than for a rich man to get into the holy nation of heaven." 25When His followers heard this, they could not understand it. They said, "Then who can be saved from the punishment of sin?" 26Jesus looked at them and said, "This cannot be done by men. But with God all things can be done."

27Then Peter said to Him, "We have given up everything and have followed You. Then what will we have?" 28Jesus said to them, "For sure, I tell you, when all the earth will be new and the Son of Man will sit on His throne in His shining greatness, you who have followed Me will also sit on twelve thrones, and judge the twelve family groups of the Jewish nation. 29Everyone who has given up houses or brothers or sisters or father or mother or wife or children or lands because of Me, will get a hundred times more. And you will get life that lasts forever. 30Many who are first will be last. Many who are last will be first.

The Picture-story Of The Workmen In The Grape Field

20 "For the holy nation of heaven is like the owner of a grape field. He went out early in the morning to hire workmen to work in his grape field. 2He promised to give them a day's pay and then sent them to his grape field. 3Later in the morning he went to the center of the town where people gather. He saw men standing there doing nothing. 4He said to them, 'You go to my grape field and work also. Whatever is right, I will pay you.' And they went. 5Again he went out about noon and at three o'clock and did the same thing. 6About five o'clock he went out and still found others doing nothing. He asked them, 'Why do

you stand here all day and do nothing?' 7They said to him, 'Because no one has hired us.' He said, 'Go to my grape field and work. Whatever is right, I will pay you.'

8"When evening came, the owner of the grape field said to the boss of the workmen, 'Call the workmen. Give them their pay. Start with the last ones hired and go on to the first ones hired.' 9The workmen who had been hired at five o'clock came up. Each one of them got a day's pay for his work. 10When the workmen who had been hired the first thing in the morning came, they thought they would get more. But each one got a day's pay. 11After they received it, they talked against the owner. 12They said, 'The last workmen hired have only worked one hour. You have given to them the same as to us. We have worked hard through the heat of the day.' 13But he said to one of them, 'Friend, I am doing you no wrong. Did you not agree with me when I promised to pay you a day's pay? 14Take your pay and go. I want to give the last ones hired the same as I have given you. 15Do I not have the right to do what I want to do with my own money? Does your eye make you want more because I am good?' 16So those who are last will be first and the first will be last."

Jesus Tells Of His Death The Third Time [Mark 10:32-34; Luke 18:31-34]

17As Jesus was going up to Jerusalem, He talked also to the twelve followers by the side of the road. He said, 18"Listen! We are going up to Jerusalem. The Son of Man will be handed over to the religious leaders and to the teachers of the Law. They will say that He must be put to death. 19They will hand Him over to people who do not know God. They will make fun of Him and will beat Him. They will nail Him to a cross. Three days later He will be raised to life."

The Mother Of James And John Asks Jesus Something Hard [Mark 10:35-45]

²⁰The mother of Zebedee's children (James and John) came to Jesus with her sons. She got down on her knees before Jesus to ask something of Him. ²¹He said to her, "What do you want?" She said, "Say that my two sons may sit, one at Your right side and one at Your left side, when You are King." ²²Jesus said to her, "You do not know what you are asking. Are you able to take the suffering that I am about to take? (*Are you able to be baptized with the baptism that I am baptized with?)" They said, "Yes, we are able." ²³He said to them, "You will suffer as I will suffer. But the places at My right side and at My left side are not Mine to give. Whoever My Father says will have those places."

²⁴The other ten followers heard this. They were angry with the two brothers. ²⁵Jesus called them to Him and said, "You know how the kings of the nations show their power to the people. Important leaders use their power over the people. ²⁶It must not be that way with you. But whoever wants to be great among you, let him care for you. ²⁷Whoever wants to be first among you must be as one who is owned by you and cares for you. ²⁸For the Son of Man came not to be cared for. He came to care for others. He came to give His life so that many could be bought by His blood and made free from the punishment of sin."

The Healing Of The Blind Men [Mark 10:46-52; Luke 18:35-43]

²⁹As they went away from the city of Jericho, many people followed Him. ³⁰Two blind men were sitting by the side of the road. They called out when they heard that Jesus was going by. They said, "Lord, take pity on us, Son of David!" ³¹Many people spoke sharp words to them. They told the blind men not to call out. But they called all the more, "Lord! Take pity on us, Son of David!" ³²Jesus stopped and called them. He asked, "What do you want Me to do for you?" ³³The blind men said to Jesus, "Lord, we want our eyes opened!" ³⁴Jesus had loving-pity for them, He put His hands on their eyes. At once they could see, and they followed Jesus.

The Last Time Jesus Goes Into Jerusalem [Mark 11:1-11; Luke 19:29-44; John 12:12-19]

21 They were near Jerusalem and had come to the town of Bethphage at the Mount of Olives. Jesus sent two followers on ahead. ²He said to them, "Go to the town over there. You will find a donkey tied and her young with her. Let them loose and bring them to Me. ³If anyone says something to you, say, 'The Lord needs them.' He will send them at once."

⁴It happened as the early preacher said it would happen, saying, ⁵"Say to the people in Jerusalem, 'See! Your King is coming to you. He is gentle. He is riding on a young donkey.'" (Zechariah 9:9; Isaiah 62:11) ⁶The followers went and did as Jesus told them. ⁷They brought the donkey and her young one. They put their clothes on the donkey and Jesus sat on them. ⁸Many people put their coats down on the road. Other people cut branches from the trees and put them along the way. ⁹The people who went in front and those who followed Jesus called out, "Greatest One! The Son of David! Great and honored is He Who comes in the name of the Lord! Greatest One in the highest heaven."

¹⁰When Jesus came into Jerusalem, all the people of the city were troubled. They said, "Who is this?" ¹¹Many people said, "This is Jesus, the One Who speaks for God from

the town of Nazareth in the country of Galilee."

Jesus Stops The Buying And The Selling In The House Of God [Mark 11:15-19; Luke 19:45-48; John 2:13-17]

¹²Then Jesus went into the house of God and made all those leave who were buying and selling there. He turned over the tables of the men who changed money. He turned over the seats of those who sold doves. ¹³He said to them, "It is written, 'My house is to be called a house of prayer.' You have made it a place of robbers." (Isaiah 56:7; Jeremiah 7:11)

¹⁴The blind and those who could not walk came to Jesus in the house of God and He healed them. ¹⁵The religious leaders of the Jews and the teachers of the Law saw the great things He did. They heard the children calling in the house of God and saying, "Greatest One! Son of David!" The leaders were very angry. ¹⁶They said to Jesus, "Do you hear what these children are saying?" Jesus said to them, "Yes, have you not read the writings, 'Even little children and babies will honor Him'?" ¹⁷Jesus left them and went out of the city to the town of Bethany. He stayed there that night.

The Fig Tree Dries Up [Mark 11:20-26]

¹⁸In the morning as He was coming back to the city, He was hungry. ¹⁹He saw a fig tree by the side of the road and went to it. There was nothing on it but leaves. He said to the tree, "No fruit will ever grow on you again." At once the fig tree dried up. ²⁰The followers saw it and were surprised and wondered. They said, "How did the fig tree dry up so fast?" ²¹Jesus said to them, "For sure, I tell you this: If you have faith and do not doubt, you will not only be able to do what was done to the fig tree. You will also be able to say to this mountain, 'Move from here and be thrown into the sea,' and it will be done. ²²All things you ask for in prayer, you will receive if you have faith."

They Ask Jesus Who Gave Him The Power To Do These Things [Mark 11:27-33; Luke 20:1-8]

²³Jesus came into the house of God. The religious leaders and the other leaders of the people came up to Him as He was teaching. They said, "By what right and power are You doing these things? Who gave You the right and the power to do them?" ²⁴Jesus said to them, "I will ask you one thing also. If you tell Me, then I will tell you by what right and power I do these things. ²⁵Was the baptism of John from heaven or from men?" They thought among themselves, "If we say, 'From heaven,' then He will say, 'Then why did you not believe him?' ²⁶But if we say, 'From men,' we are afraid of the people, because they all think John was one who spoke for God." ²⁷They said to Jesus, "We do not know." He said to them, "Then I will not tell you by what right and power I do these things.

The Picture-story Of The Two Sons

²⁸"What do you think about this? There was a man who had two sons. He came to the first son and said, 'My son, go to my grape field and work today.' ²⁹He said, 'I will go.' But he did not go. ³⁰The father came to the second son and asked the same thing. The son said, 'No, I will not go.' Later he was sorry and went. ³¹Which one of the two sons did what his father wanted?" They said to Jesus, "The second son." Jesus said to them, "For sure, I tell you this: Tax gatherers and women who sell the use of their bodies will get into the holy nation of heaven before you.

³²For John came to you preaching about being right with God. You did not believe him. But tax gatherers and women who sell the use of their bodies did believe him. When you saw this, you were not sorry for your sins and did not turn from them and believe him.

The Picture-story Of The Grape Field [*Mark 12:1-12; Luke 20:9-18*]

³³"Listen to another picture-story. A man who owned land planted grapes in a field and put a fence around it. He made a place for making wine. He built a tower to look over the grape field. He let farmers rent it and then he went into another country. ³⁴The time came for gathering the grapes. He sent his servants to the farmers to get the grapes. ³⁵The farmers took his servants and hit one. They killed another and threw stones at another. ³⁶Again he sent other servants. He sent more than the first time. The farmers did the same to those servants. ³⁷After this he sent his son to them. He said to himself, 'They will respect my son.' ³⁸When the farmers saw the son, they said to themselves, 'This is the one who will get everything when the owner dies. Let us kill him and we will get it all.' ³⁹They took him and threw him out of the grape field and killed him. ⁴⁰When the owner of the grape field comes, what will he do to those farmers?" ⁴¹They said to Him, "He will put those bad men to death. Then he will rent the grape field to other farmers who will give him the grapes when they are ready." ⁴²Jesus said to them, "Have you not read in the Holy Writings, 'The Stone that was put aside by the workman has become the most important Stone in the building? The Lord has done this. We think it is great!' (Psalm 118:22-23) ⁴³I say to you, because of this, the holy nation of God will be taken from you. It will be given to a nation

that will give fruit. ⁴⁴Whoever falls on this Stone will be broken. And on the one it falls, it will make him like dust."

⁴⁵When the religious leaders and the proud religious law-keepers heard this picture-story, they knew He spoke of them. ⁴⁶When they tried to put their hands on Him, they were afraid of the many people. The people thought He was One Who spoke for God.

The Picture-story Of The Marriage Supper

22 Again Jesus spoke to them in picture-stories. He said, ²"The holy nation of heaven is like a king who gave a wedding supper for his son. ³He sent his servants to tell the people, who had been asked, to come to the supper. But the people did not want to come.

⁴"He sent other servants, saying to them, 'Tell those who have been asked to come, "See! My supper is ready. My cows and fat calves are killed. Everything is ready. Come to the wedding supper!" ' ⁵But they did not listen and went on working. One went to his farm. Another went to his store. ⁶The others took hold of his servants, and hurt them and killed them.

⁷"When the king heard this, he was very angry. He sent his soldiers to put those to death who had killed his servants. He burned their city. ⁸Then he said to his servants, 'The wedding supper is ready. Those who were asked to come to the supper were not good enough. ⁹Go out into the roads and as many people as you can find, ask them to come to the wedding supper.'

¹⁰"The servants went out into the roads and brought all they could find, both bad and good. The wedding supper room was full of people. ¹¹The king came in to see those who had come. He saw one man who did not have on wedding

supper clothes. [12]He said to him, 'Friend, how did you get in here without wedding supper clothes?' The man could not speak! [13]Then the king said to his servants, 'Tie his hands and feet, and throw him out into the darkness. In that place there will be loud crying and grinding of teeth.' [14]For many are called but few are chosen."

The Proud Religious Law-keepers Try To Trap Jesus [Mark 12:13-17; Luke 20:19-26]

[15]Then the proud religious law-keepers got together to think how they could trap Jesus in His talk. [16]They sent their followers to Jesus with some of King Herod's men. They asked, "Teacher, we know that You are true. We know that You are teaching the truth about God. We know You are not afraid of what men think or say about You. [17]Tell us what You think of this. Is it right to pay taxes to Caesar, or not?" [18]Jesus knew their sinful thoughts and said, "You pretend to be someone you are not! Why do you try to trap Me? [19]Show Me a piece of money." They brought Him a piece. [20]Jesus said to them, "Whose picture is this? Whose name is on it?" [21]They said to Him, "Caesar's." Then He said to them, "Pay to Caesar the things that belong to Caesar. Pay to God the things that belong to God." [22]When they heard this, they were surprised and wondered about it. Then they went away from Him.

They Ask About Being Raised From The Dead [Mark 12:18-27; Luke 20:27-40]

[23]The same day some people from the religious group who believe no one will be raised from the dead came to Jesus. They asked, [24]"Teacher, Moses said, 'If a man should die without having children, then his brother must marry his wife. He should have children for his brother.' (Deuteronomy 25:5) [25]There were seven brothers with us. The first was married but died before he had any children. The second brother then married the first brother's wife. [26]The second brother died and the same with the third and on to the seventh. [27]Then the woman died also. [28]When people are raised from the dead, whose wife will she be of the seven? They all had her for a wife."

[29]Jesus said to them, "You are wrong because you do not know the Holy Writings or the power of God. [30]After people are raised from the dead, they do not marry. They are like the angels in heaven. [31]Have you not read what God said to you about those who are raised from the dead? He said, [32]'I am the God of Abraham and the God of Isaac and the God of Jacob.' He is not the God of the dead but of the living!" (Exodus 3:6) [33]When the people heard this, they were surprised and wondered about His teaching.

The Great Law [Mark 12:28-34]

[34]The proud religious law-keepers got together when they heard that the religious group of people who believe no one will be raised from the dead were not able to talk anymore to Jesus. [35]A proud religious law-keeper who knew the Law tried to trap Jesus. He said, [36]"Teacher, which one is the greatest of the Laws?" [37]Jesus said to him, " 'You must love the Lord your God with all your heart and with all your soul and with all your mind.' [38]This is the first and greatest of the Laws. [39]The second is like it, 'You must love your neighbor as you love yourself.' [40]All the Laws and the writings of the early preachers depend on these two most important Laws."

[41]The proud religious law-keepers were gathered together. Then Jesus asked, [42]"What do you think about the Christ? Whose Son is He?" They

said to Him, "The Son of David." [43]Jesus said to them, "Then how is it that David, being led by the Holy Spirit, calls Him 'Lord'? He said, [44]'The Lord said to my Lord, "Sit at My right side until I make those who hate you a place to rest Your feet." ' (Psalm 110:1) [45]If David calls Him 'Lord,' then how can He be the Son of David?" [46]No one could answer a word, and after that day no one asked Him anything.

The Teachers Of The Law And The Proud Religious Law-keepers [Mark 12:38-40; Luke 20:45-47]

23 Then Jesus talked to the many people and to His followers. [2]He said, "The teachers of the Law and the proud religious law-keepers have put themselves in Moses' place as teachers. [3]Do what they tell you to do and keep on doing it. But do not follow what they do. They preach but do not obey their own preaching. [4]They make heavy loads and put them on the shoulders of men. But they will not help lift them with a finger. [5]Everything they do, they do to be seen of men. They have words from the Holy Writings written in large letters on their left arm and forehead and they make wide trimming for their clothes. [6]They like to have the important places at big suppers and the best seats in the Jewish places of worship. [7]They like to have people show respect to them as they stand in the center of town where people gather. They like to be called teacher.

[8]"But you are not to be called teacher. There is only one Teacher, and all of you are brothers. [9]Do not call any man here on earth your father. There is only one Father and He is in heaven. [10]You are not to be called leader. There is only one Leader and He is Christ.

[11]"He who is greatest among you will be the one to care for you. [12]The person who thinks he is important

will find out how little he is worth. The person who is not trying to honor himself will be made important.

Jesus Speaks Sharp Words To The Proud Religious Law-keepers

[13]"It is bad for you, teachers of the Law and proud religious law-keepers, you who pretend to be someone you are not! You keep men from going into the holy nation of heaven. You are not going in yourselves, and you do not allow those to go in who are about to go in. [14]It is bad for you, teachers of the Law and proud religious law-keepers, you who pretend to be someone you are not! (You take houses from poor women whose husbands have died. Then you try to cover it up by making long prayers. You will be punished all the more because of this.) [15]It is bad for you, teachers of the Law and proud religious law-keepers, you who pretend to be someone you are not! You go over land and sea to win one follower. When you have him, you make him twice as much a child of hell as you are.

[16]"It is bad for you, blind leaders! You say, 'Whoever makes a promise by the house of God, his promise is worth nothing. But whoever makes a promise by the gold of the house of God, then his promise has to be kept.' [17]You fools and blind men! Which is greater, the gold or the house of God that makes the gold holy? [18]You say, 'Whoever will promise by the altar, his promise does not have to be kept. But whoever makes a promise by the gift on the altar, then his promise has to be kept.' [19]You fools and blind men! Which is greater, the gift, or the altar that makes the gift holy? [20]Whoever makes a promise by the altar, promises by it and by everything on it. [21]Whoever makes a promise by the house of God, promises by it and by

Him Who is in it. [22]Whoever makes a promise by heaven, promises by the throne of God and by Him Who sits there.

[23]"It is bad for you, teachers of the Law and proud religious law-keepers, you who pretend to be someone you are not! You give one-tenth part of your spices, and have not done the most important things of the Law, such as thinking what is right and wrong, and having pity and faith. These you should have done and still have done the other things also. [24]You blind leaders, you take a small bug out of your cup but you swallow a camel!

[25]"It is bad for you, teachers of the Law and proud religious law-keepers, you who pretend to be someone you are not! You clean the outside of the cup and plate, but leave the inside full of strong bad desires and are not able to keep from doing sinful things. [26]You blind proud religious law-keepers! Clean the inside of the cup and plate, then the outside will be clean also.

[27]"It is bad for you, teachers of the Law and proud religious law-keepers, you who pretend to be someone you are not! You are like graves that have been made white and look beautiful on the outside. But inside you are full of the bones of dead men and of every sinful thing. [28]As men look at you, you seem to be good and right but inside you are full of sin. You pretend to be someone you are not.

[29]"It is bad for you, teachers of the Law and proud religious law-keepers, you who pretend to be someone you are not! You make buildings for the graves of the early preachers, and you make the graves beautiful of those who are right with God. [30]You say, 'If we had lived in the days of our early fathers, we would not have helped kill the early preachers.' [31]In this way, you are showing that you are the sons of those who killed the early preachers.

[32]You might as well finish what your early fathers did. [33]You snakes! You family of snakes! How can you be kept from hell?

[34]"Because of this, I am going to keep on sending to you men who speak for God and wise men and teachers of the Law. Some of them you will kill and nail to a cross. Some of them you will beat in your places of worship. You will make it very hard for them as they go from city to city. [35]Because of this, you will be guilty of the blood of all those right with God on the earth. It will be from the blood of Abel who was right with God to the blood of Zachariah son of Barachias. He was the one you killed between the house of God and the altar. [36]For sure, I tell you, all these things will come on the people of this day.

Jesus Sorrows Over Jerusalem

[37]"O Jerusalem, Jerusalem! You kill the men who speak for God and throw stones at those who were sent to you. How many times I wanted to gather your children around Me, as a chicken gathers her young ones under her wings. But you would not let Me. [38]See! Your house is empty. [39]I say to you, you will not see Me again until you will say, 'Great is He Who comes in the name of the Lord!' "

Jesus Tells Of The House Of God
[Mark 13:1-37; Luke 21:5-36]

24 Jesus went out of the house of God. On the way His followers came to Him to show Him the buildings of the house of God. [2]Jesus said to them, "Do you see all these things? For sure, I tell you, all these stones will be thrown down. Not one will be left standing on another."

Jesus Teaches On The Mount Of Olives

[3]Jesus sat on the Mount of Olives. The followers came to Him when He

was alone and said, "Tell us, when will this happen? What can we look for to show us of Your coming and of the end of the world?"

4 Jesus said to them, "Be careful that no one leads you the wrong way. 5 Many people will come using My name. They will say, 'I am Christ.' They will fool many people and will turn them to the wrong way. 6 You will hear of wars and lots of talk about wars, but do not be afraid. These things must happen, but it is not the end yet. 7 Nations will have wars with other nations. Countries will fight against countries. There will be no food for people. The earth will shake and break apart in different places. 8 These things are the beginning of sorrows and pains.

9 "Then they will hand you over to be hurt. They will kill you. You will be hated by all the world because of My name. 10 Many people will give up and turn away at this time. People will hand over each other. They will hate each other. 11 Many false religious teachers will come. They will fool many people and will turn them to the wrong way. 12 Because of people breaking the laws and sin being everywhere, the love in the hearts of many people will become cold. 13 But the one who stays true to the end will be saved.

14 "This Good News about the holy nation of God must be preached over all the earth. It must be told to all nations and then the end will come.

Days Of Trouble And Pain And Sorrow

15 "You will see a very sinful man-made god standing in the house of God in Jerusalem. It was spoken of by the early preacher Daniel. (Daniel 9:27; 12:11) The one who reads this should understand it. 16 Then those in the country of Judea should run to the mountains. 17 The man who is on the top of his house should not come down to take anything out of his house. 18 The man who is in the field should not go back to get his coat. 19 It will be hard for a woman who will soon be a mother. It will be hard for the ones feeding babies in those days! 20 Pray that you will not have to go in the winter or on the Day of Rest. 21 In those days there will be very much trouble and pain and sorrow. It has never been this bad from the beginning of the world and never will be again. 22 If the time had not been made short, no life would have been saved. Because of God's people, the time will be made short.

The False Religious Teachers

23 "If anyone says to you, 'See! Here is the Christ!' or 'There He is!' do not believe it. 24 People who say they are Christ and false preachers will come. They will do special things for people to see. They will do great things, so that if it can be done, God's people will be fooled to believe something wrong. 25 Listen! I have told you before it comes. 26 If they tell you, 'See! He is in the desert,' do not go to see. Or if they say, 'See! He is in the inside room,' do not believe them. 27 The Son of Man will come as fast as lightning goes across the sky from east to west. 28 Birds gather wherever there is a dead body.

Jesus Will Come Again In His Shining Greatness

29 "As soon as those days of trouble and pain and sorrow are over, the sun will get dark. The moon will not give light. The stars will fall from the sky. The powers in the heavens will be shaken. 30 Then something special will be seen in the sky telling of the Son of Man. All nations of the earth will have sorrow. They will see the Son of Man coming in the clouds of the sky with power and shining greatness. 31 He will send His angels with the loud sound of a horn. They will gather together God's people

from the four winds. They will come from one end of the sky to the other.

The Picture-story Of The Fig Tree

³²"Now learn something from the fig tree. When the branch begins to grow and puts out its leaves, you know that summer is near. ³³In the same way, when you see all these things happen, you know the Son of Man is near, even at the door. ³⁴For sure, I tell you, the people of this day will not pass away before all these things have happened.

No One Knows When Jesus Will Come Again

³⁵"Heaven and earth will pass away, but My words will not pass away. ³⁶But no one knows the day or the hour. No! Not even the angels in heaven know. The Son does not know. Only the Father knows.

³⁷"When the Son of Man comes, it will be the same as when Noah lived. ³⁸In the days before the flood, people were eating and drinking. They were marrying and being given in marriage. This kept on until the day Noah went into the large boat. ³⁹They did not know what was happening until the flood came and the water carried them all away. It will be like this when the Son of Man comes.

⁴⁰"Two men will be working in a field. One will be taken and the other will be left. ⁴¹Two women will be grinding grain. One will be taken and the other will be left.

⁴²"Because of this, watch! You do not know on what day your Lord is coming. ⁴³But understand this: If the owner of a house had known when the robber was coming, he would have watched. He would not have allowed his house to have been broken into. ⁴⁴You must be ready also. The Son of Man is coming at a time when you do not think He will come.

Faithful Servants And Servants Who Are Not Faithful

⁴⁵"Who is the faithful and wise servant whom his owner has made boss over the other servants? He is to have food ready for them at the right time. ⁴⁶That servant is happy who is doing what his owner wants him to do when he comes back. ⁴⁷For sure, I tell you, he will make him boss over all that he has. ⁴⁸But if that servant is bad, he will think, 'The owner will not come soon.' ⁴⁹He will beat the others. He will eat and drink with those who are drunk. ⁵⁰The owner will come on a day and at an hour when the servant is not looking for him. ⁵¹The owner will punish the servant and will give him his place with those who pretend to be someone they are not. There will be loud crying and grinding of teeth.

The Picture-story Of Ten Young Women

25 "At that time the holy nation of heaven will be like ten women who have never had men. They took their lamps and went out to meet the man soon to be married. ²Five of them were wise and five were foolish. ³The foolish women took their lamps but did not take oil with them. ⁴The wise women took oil in a jar with their lamps. ⁵They all went to sleep because the man to be married did not come for a long time.

⁶"At twelve o'clock in the night there was a loud call, 'See! The man soon to be married is coming! Go out to meet him!' ⁷Then all the women got up and made their lamps brighter. ⁸The foolish women said to the wise women, 'Give us some of your oil because our lamps are going out.' ⁹But the wise women said, 'No! There will not be enough for us and you. Go to the store and buy oil for yourselves.' ¹⁰While they were gone to buy oil, the man soon to be married came. Those who were ready

went in with him to the marriage. The door was shut.

11"Later the foolish women came. They said, 'Sir, Sir, open the door for us!' 12But he said to them, 'For sure, I tell you, I do not know you!' 13So watch! You do not know what day or what hour the Son of Man is coming.

The Picture-story Of The Ten Servants And The Money

14"For the holy nation of heaven is like a man who was going to a country far away. He called together the servants he owned and gave them his money to use. 15He gave to one servant five pieces of money worth much. He gave to another servant two pieces of money worth much. He gave to another servant one piece of money worth much. He gave to each one as he was able to use it. Then he went on his trip. 16The servant who had the five pieces of money went out to the stores and traded until he made five more pieces. 17The servant who had two pieces of money did the same thing. He made two more pieces. 18The servants who had received the one piece of money went and hid the money in a hole in the ground. He hid his owner's money.

19"After a long time the owner of those servants came back. He wanted to know what had been done with his money. 20The one who had received the five pieces of money worth much came and handed him five pieces more. He said, 'Sir, you gave me five pieces of money. See! I used it and made five more pieces.' 21His owner said to him, 'You have done well. You are a good and faithful servant. You have been faithful over a few things. I will put many things in your care. Come and share my joy.' 22The one who received two pieces of money worth much came also. He said, 'Sir, you gave me two pieces of money. See! I used it and made two more pieces.' 23His owner said to him, 'You have done well. You are a

good and faithful servant. You have been faithful over a few things. I will put many things in your care. Come and share my joy.' 24The one who had received one piece of money worth much came. He said, 'Sir, I know that you are a hard man. You gather grain where you have not planted. You take up where you have not spread out. 25I was afraid and I hid your money in the ground. See! Here is your money.' 26His owner said to him, 'You bad and lazy servant. You knew that I gather grain where I have not planted. You knew that I take up where I have not spread out. 27You should have taken my money to the bank. When I came back, I could have had my own money and what the bank paid for using it. 28Take the one piece of money from him. Give it to the one who has ten pieces of money.' 29For the man who has will have more given to him. He will have more than enough. The man who has nothing, even what he has will be taken away. 30Throw the bad servant out into the darkness. There will be loud crying and grinding of teeth.

The Sheep And The Goats

31"When the Son of Man comes in His shining greatness, He will sit down on His throne of greatness. All the angels will be with Him. 32All the nations of the earth will be gathered before Him. He will divide them from each other as a shepherd divides the sheep from the goats. 33He will put the sheep on His right side, but the goats He will put on His left side.

34"Then the King will say to those on His right side, 'Come, you who have been called by My Father. Come into the holy nation that has been made ready for you before the world was made. 35For I was hungry and you gave Me food to eat. I was thirsty and you gave Me water to drink. I was a stranger and you gave Me a room. 36I had no clothes and you gave Me clothes to wear. I was sick and you cared for Me. I was in prison and you came to see Me.' ³⁷"Then those that are right with God will say, 'Lord, when did we see You hungry and feed You? When did we see You thirsty and give You a drink? ³⁸When did we see You a stranger and give You a room? When did we see You had no clothes and we gave You clothes? ³⁹And when did we see You sick or in prison and we came to You?' ⁴⁰Then the King will say, 'For sure, I tell you, because you did it to one of the least of My brothers, you have done it to Me.'

⁴¹"Then the King will say to those on His left side, 'Go away from Me! You are guilty! Go into the fire that lasts forever. It has been made ready for the devil and his angels. ⁴²For I was hungry but you did not give Me food to eat. I was thirsty but you did not give Me water to drink. ⁴³I was a stranger but you did not give Me a room. I had no clothes but you did not give Me clothes. I was sick and in prison but you did not come to see Me.'

⁴⁴"Then they will ask, 'Lord, when did we see You hungry or thirsty or a stranger? When did we see You without clothes or sick or in prison and did not care for You?' ⁴⁵Then He will say to them, 'For sure, I tell you, because you did not do it to one of the least of these, you did not do it to Me.' ⁴⁶These will go to the place where they will be punished forever. But those right with God will have life that lasts forever."

Jesus Tells Of His Death The Fourth Time [Mark 14:1-2; Luke 22:1-6]

26 When Jesus had finished all this teaching, He said to His followers, ²"You know that the special religious supper to remember how the Jews left Egypt is in two

days. The Son of Man will be handed over to be nailed to a cross."

³The religious leaders and the leaders of the people gathered at the house of the head religious leader. His name was Caiaphas. ⁴They talked together how they might trap Jesus and kill Him. ⁵But they said, "This must not happen on the day of the special supper. The people would be against it. They would make much trouble."

Mary Of Bethany Puts Special Perfume On Jesus [Mark 14:3-9; John 12:1-11]

⁶Jesus was in the town of Bethany in the house of Simon. Simon had a very bad skin disease. ⁷A woman came with a jar of perfume. She had given much money for this. As Jesus ate, she poured the perfume on His head. ⁸When the followers saw it, they were angry. They said, "Why was this wasted? ⁹This perfume could have been sold for much money and given to poor people."

¹⁰Jesus knew what they were saying. He said to them, "Why are you giving this woman trouble? She has done a good thing to Me. ¹¹You will have poor people with you all the time. But you will not have Me with you all the time. ¹²She put this perfume on My body to make it ready for the grave. ¹³For sure, I tell you, wherever this Good News is preached in all the world, this woman will be remembered for what she has done."

Judas Hands Jesus Over To Be Killed [Mark 14:10-11]

¹⁴Judas Iscariot was one of the twelve followers. He went to the religious leaders of the Jews. ¹⁵He said, "What will you pay me if I hand Jesus over to you?" They promised to

pay him thirty pieces of silver. [16]From that time on Judas looked for a way to hand Jesus over to them.

Getting Ready For The Special Supper [Mark 14:12-16; Luke 22:7-13]

[17]On the first day of the supper of bread without yeast the followers came to Jesus. They said, "What place do You want us to make ready for You to eat the supper of the special religious gathering to remember how the Jews left Egypt?" [18]He said, "Go into the city to a certain man and say to him, 'The Teacher says, "My time is near. I will eat the special supper at your house with My followers." ' " [19]The followers did as Jesus told them. They made things ready for this special supper.

The Last Special Supper [Mark 14:17-21; Luke 22:14-18; John 13:21-35]

[20]When evening came, Jesus sat with the twelve followers. [21]As they were eating, Jesus said, "For sure, I tell you, one of you will hand Me over." [22]They were very sad. They said to Him one after the other, "Lord, is it I?" [23]He said, "The one who will hand Me over is the one who has just put his hand with Mine in the dish. [24]The Son of Man is going away as it is written of Him. It is bad for that man who hands the Son of Man over! It would have been better if he had not been born!" [25]Judas was the one who was handing Jesus over. He said, "Teacher, am I the one?" Jesus said to him, "You have said it."

The First Lord's Supper [Mark 14:22-26; Luke 22:19-20]

[26]As they were eating, Jesus took a loaf of bread. He gave thanks and broke it in pieces. He gave it to His followers and said, "Take, eat, this is My body." [27]Then He took the cup and gave thanks. He gave it to them and said, "You must all drink from it. [28]This is My blood of the New Way of Worship which is given for many. It is given so the sins of many can be forgiven. [29]I tell you that I will not drink of the fruit of the vine again until that day when I will drink it new with you in the holy nation of My Father." [30]After they sang a song they went out to the Mount of Olives.

Jesus Tells How Peter Will Lie About Him [Mark 14:27-31; Luke 22:31-34; John 13:36-38]

[31]Jesus said to them, "All of you will be ashamed of Me and leave Me tonight. For it is written, 'I will kill the shepherd and the sheep of the flock will be spread everywhere.' (Zechariah 13:7) [32]After I am raised from the dead, I will go before you to the country of Galilee."

[33]Peter said to Jesus, "Even if all men give up and turn away because of You, I will never." [34]Jesus said to him, "For sure, I tell you, before a rooster crows this night, you will say three times you do not know Me." [35]Peter said to Him, "Even if I have to die with You, I will never say I do not know You." And all the followers said the same thing.

Jesus Prays In Gethsemane [Mark 14:32-42; Luke 22:39-46]

[36]Jesus came with them to a place called Gethsemane. He said to them, "You sit here while I go over there to pray." [37]He took Peter and the two sons of Zebedee with Him. He began to have much sorrow and a heavy heart. [38]Then He said to them, "My soul is very sad. My soul is so full of sorrow I am ready to die. You stay here and watch with Me."

[39]He went on a little farther and got down with His face on the ground. He prayed, "My Father, if it can be done, take away what is

before Me. Even so, not what I want but what You want."

40 Then He came to the followers and found them sleeping. He said to Peter, "Were you not able to watch with Me one hour? 41 Watch and pray so that you will not be tempted. Man's spirit is willing, but the body does not have the power to do it."

42 He went away again the second time. He prayed, saying, "My Father, if this must happen to Me, may whatever You want be done." 43 He came and found them asleep again. Their eyes were heavy. 44 He went away from them the third time and prayed the same prayer.

45 Then He came to His followers and asked them, "Are you still sleeping and getting your rest? As I speak, the time has come when the Son of Man will be handed over to sinners. 46 Get up and let us go. See! The man who will hand Me over is near."

Jesus Handed Over To Sinners [Mark 14:43-52; Luke 22:47-51; John 18:1-11]

47 Judas, one of the twelve followers, came while Jesus was talking. He came with many others who had swords and sticks. They came from the religious leaders of the Jews and the leaders of the people. 48 The man who handed Jesus over gave the men something to look for. He said, "The One I kiss is the One you want. Take Him!" 49 At once Judas went up to Jesus and said, "Hello, Teacher," and kissed Him. 50 Jesus said to him, "Friend, do what you came to do." Then they came and put their hands on Jesus and took Him.

51 One of those with Jesus took his sword. He hit the servant who was owned by the religious leader and cut off his ear. 52 Jesus said to him, "Put your sword back where it belongs. Everyone who uses a sword will die with a sword. 53 Do you not think that I can pray to My Father? At once

He would send Me more than 70,000 angels. 54 If I did, how could it happen as the Holy Writings said it would happen? It must be this way."

55 Then Jesus said to the many people, "Have you come with swords and sticks to take Me as if I were a robber? I have been with you every day teaching in the house of God. You never put your hands on Me then. 56 But this has happened as the early preachers said in the Holy Writings it would happen." Then all the followers left Him and ran away.

Jesus Stands In Front Of The Religious Leaders [Mark 14:53-54; Luke 22:52-54; John 18:19-24]

57 Those who had taken Jesus led Him away to Caiaphas. He was the head religious leader. The teachers of the Law and the other leaders were gathered there. 58 But Peter followed Him a long way behind while going to the house of the head religious leader. Then he went in and sat with the helpers to see what would happen.

59 The religious leaders and the other leaders and all the court were looking for false things to say against Jesus. They wanted some reason to kill Him. 60 They found none, but many came and told false things about Him. At last two came to the front. 61 They said, "This Man said, 'I am able to destroy the house of God and build it again in three days.' "

62 Then the head religious leader stood up. He said to Jesus, "Have You nothing to say? What about the things these men are saying against You?" 63 Jesus said nothing. Then the head religious leader said to Him, "In the name of the living God, I tell You to say the truth. Tell us if You are the Christ, the Son of God." 64 Jesus said to him, "What you said is true. I say to you, from now on you will see the Son of Man seated on the right hand of the All-powerful God. You will see Him coming on the clouds of the sky."

⁶⁵Then the head religious leader tore his clothes apart. He said, "He has spoken as if He were God! Do we need other people to speak against Him yet? You have heard Him speak as if He were God! ⁶⁶What do you think?" They said, "He is guilty of death!"

⁶⁷Then they spit on His face. They hit Him with their hands. Others beat Him. ⁶⁸They said, "Tell us, Christ, You Who can tell what is going to happen, who hit You?"

Peter Said He Did Not Know Jesus
[*Mark 14:66-72; Luke 22:55-62; John 18:15-18; 25-27*]

⁶⁹Peter sat outside in the yard. A young servant-girl came to him. She said, "You were also with Jesus Who is from the country of Galilee!" ⁷⁰But Peter lied in front of all of them, saying, "I do not know what you are talking about." ⁷¹After he had gone out, another young servant-girl saw him. She said to those standing around, "This man was with Jesus of Nazareth." ⁷²Again he lied and swore, "I do not know this Man!" ⁷³After a little while some of the people standing around came up to Peter and said, "For sure, you are one of them. You talk like they do." ⁷⁴Then he began to say bad words and swear. He said, "I do not know the Man!" At once a rooster crowed.

⁷⁵Peter remembered the words Jesus had said to him, "Before a rooster crows, you will say three times you do not know Me." Peter went outside and cried with loud cries.

Jesus Stands In Front Of Pilate [*Mark 15:1-5; Luke 23:1-5; John 18:28-37*]

27 Early in the morning all the head religious leaders of the Jews and the leaders of the people gathered together and talked about how they could put Jesus to death. ²They tied Him and took Him away.

Then they handed Him over to Pilate who was the leader of the country.

Judas Kills Himself

³Then Judas was sorry he had handed Jesus over when he saw that Jesus was going to be killed. He took back the thirty pieces of silver and gave it to the head religious leaders and the other leaders. ⁴He said, "I have sinned because I handed over a Man Who has done no wrong." And they said, "What is that to us? That is your own doing." ⁵He threw the money down in the house of God and went outside. Then he went away and killed himself by hanging from a rope.

⁶The head religious leaders took the money. They said, "It is against the Law to put this money in the house of God. This money has bought blood." ⁷They talked about what to do with the money. Then they decided to buy land to bury strangers in. ⁸Because of this, that land is called the Field of Blood to this day. ⁹It happened as the early preacher Jeremiah said it would happen. He said, "And they took the thirty pieces of silver which was the price the Jews said they would pay for Him. ¹⁰And they bought land to bury strangers in, as the Lord told me." (Zechariah 11:12-13)

¹¹Then Jesus stood in front of the leader of the country. The leader asked Jesus, "Are You the King of the Jews?" Jesus said to him, "What you say is true." ¹²When the head religious leaders and the other leaders spoke against Him, He said nothing. ¹³Then Pilate said to Him, "Do You not hear all these things they are saying against You?" ¹⁴Jesus did not say a word. The leader was much surprised and wondered about it.

Jesus Or Barabbas Is To Go Free

¹⁵At the special supper each year the leader of the country would

always let one person who was in prison go free. It would be the one the people wanted. [16]They had a man who was known by all the people whose name was Barabbas. [17]When they were gathered together, Pilate said to them, "Whom do you want me to let go free? Should it be Barabbas or Jesus Who is called Christ?" [18]For the leader of the country knew the religious leaders had given Jesus over to him because they were jealous.

[19]While Pilate was sitting in the place where he judges, his wife sent him this word, "Have nothing to do with that good Man. I have been troubled today in a dream about Him."

[20]The head religious leaders and the other leaders talked the many people into asking for Barabbas to go free and for Jesus to be put to death. [21]The leader of the country said to them, "Which one of the two do you want me to let go free?" They said, "Barabbas." [22]Pilate said to them, "Then what am I to do with Jesus Who is called Christ?" They all said to him, "Nail Him to a cross!" [23]Then Pilate said, "Why, what bad thing has He done?" But they cried out all the more, "Nail Him to a cross!"

[24]Pilate saw that he could do nothing. The people were making loud calls and there was much pushing around. He took water and washed his hands in front of the many people. He said, "I am not guilty of the blood of this good Man. This is your own doing." [25]Then all the people said, "Let His blood be on us and on our children!" [26]Pilate let Barabbas go free but he had men whip Jesus. Then he handed Him over to be nailed to a cross.

The Crown Of Thorns [*Mark 15:15-21; John 19:1-5*]

[27]Then the soldiers of Pilate took Jesus into a large room. A big group of soldiers gathered around Him.

[28]They took off His clothes and put a purple coat on Him. [29]They put a crown of thorns on His head. They put a stick in His right hand. They got on their knees before Him and made fun of Him. They said, "Hello, King of the Jews!" [30]They spit on Him. They took a stick and hit Him on the head. [31]After they had made fun of Him, they took the coat off and put His own clothes on Him. Then they led Him away to be nailed to a cross. [32]As they were on the way, they came to a man called Simon from the country of Cyrene. They made him carry the cross for Jesus.

Jesus On The Cross [*Mark 15:22-26; Luke 23:26-38; John 19:17-22*]

[33]They came to a place called Golgotha. This name means the place of a skull. [34]They gave Him wine with something in it to take away the pain. After tasting it, He took no more. [35]When they had nailed Him to the cross, they divided His clothes by drawing names. It happened as the early preacher said it would happen. He said, "They divided My clothes among them by drawing names to see who would get My coat." (Psalm 22:18) [36]Then they sat down and watched Him. [37]Over His head they put in writing what they had against Him, THIS IS JESUS THE KING OF THE JEWS.

The Two Robbers [*Mark 15:27-32; Luke 23:39-43*]

[38]They nailed two robbers to crosses beside Him. One was on His right side. The other was on His left side. [39]Those who walked by shook their heads and laughed at Him. [40]They said, "You are the One Who could destroy the house of God and build it up again in three days. Now save Yourself. If You are the Son of God, come down from the cross." [41]The head religious leaders and

the teachers of the Law and the other leaders made fun of Him also. They said, [42]"He saved others but He cannot save Himself. If He is the King of the Jews, let Him come down from the cross. Then we will believe in Him. [43]He trusts God. Let God save Him now, if God cares for Him. He has said, 'I am the Son of God.'" [44]And the robbers who were nailed to crosses beside Him made fun of Him the same way also.

The Death Of Jesus [Mark 15:33-36; Luke 23:44-49; John 19:28-37]

[45]From noon until three o'clock it was dark over all the land. [46]About three o'clock Jesus cried with a loud voice, "My God, My God, why have You left Me alone?" [47]When some of those who stood by heard that, they said, "This Man is calling for Elijah." [48]At once one of them ran and took a sponge and filled it with sour wine. He put it on a stick and gave it to Him to drink. [49]The others said, "Let Him alone. Let us see if Elijah will come and save Him." [50]Then Jesus gave another loud cry and gave up His spirit and died.

The Powerful Works At The Time Of His Death [Mark 15:37-39]

[51]At once the curtain in the house of God was torn in two from top to bottom. The earth shook and the rocks fell apart. [52]Graves were opened. Bodies of many of God's people who were dead were raised. [53]After Jesus was raised from the grave, these arose from their graves and went into Jerusalem, the Holy City. These were seen by many people. [54]The captain of the soldiers and those with him who were watching Jesus, saw all the things that were happening. They saw the earth shake and they were very much afraid. They said, "For sure, this Man was the Son of God."

The Women At The Cross

[55]Many women were looking on from far away. These had followed Jesus from the country of Galilee. They had cared for Him. [56]Among them was Mary Magdalene and Mary the mother of James and Joseph and the mother of Zebedee's sons.

The Grave Of Jesus [Mark 15:42-47; Luke 23:50-56; John 19:38-42]

[57]When it was evening, a rich man came from the city of Arimathea. His name was Joseph. He was a follower of Jesus also. [58]He went to Pilate and asked for the body of Jesus. Then Pilate said that the body should be given to him. [59]Joseph took the body and put clean linen cloth around it. [60]He laid it in his own new grave. This grave had been cut out in the side of a rock. He pushed a big stone over the door of the grave and went away. [61]Mary Magdalene and the other Mary stayed there. They were sitting near the grave. [62]The next day, the day after Jesus was killed, the head religious leaders and the proud religious law-keepers gathered together in front of Pilate. [63]They said, "Sir, we remember what that Man Who fooled people said when He was living, 'After three days I am to rise from the dead.' [64]Speak the word to have the grave watched for three days. Then His followers cannot come at night and take Him away and say to the people, 'He has been raised from the dead.' The last mistake would be worse than the first." [65]Pilate said to them, "Take the soldiers. Go and watch the grave." [66]Then they went and made the soldiers stand by the grave. They put a lock on the big stone door.

Jesus Is Raised From The Dead [Mark 16:1-8; Luke 24:1-12; John 20:1-18]

28 The Day of Rest was over. The sun was coming up on the first day of the week. Mary Magdalene and the other Mary came to see the grave. ²At once the earth shook and an angel of the Lord came down from heaven. He came and pushed back the stone from the door and sat on it. ³His face was bright like lightning. His clothes were white as snow. ⁴The soldiers were shaking with fear and became as dead men.

⁵The angel said to the women, "Do not be afraid. I know you are looking for Jesus Who was nailed to the cross. ⁶He is not here! He has risen from the dead as He said He would. Come and see the place where the Lord lay. ⁷Run fast and tell His followers that He is risen from the dead. He is going before you to the country of Galilee. You will see Him there as I have told you." ⁸They went away from the grave in a hurry. They were afraid and yet had much joy. They ran to tell the news to His followers.

⁹As they went to tell the followers, Jesus met them and said hello to them. They came and held His feet and worshiped Him. ¹⁰Then Jesus said to them, "Do not be afraid. Go and tell My followers to go to Galilee. They will see Me there."

¹¹While they were on their way, some of the soldiers who were to watch the grave came into the city.

They told the head religious leaders everything that had happened. ¹²The soldiers gathered together with the other leaders and talked about what to do. The leaders gave much money to the soldiers. ¹³They said, "Tell the people, 'His followers came at night and took His body while we were sleeping.' ¹⁴We will see that you do not get into trouble over this if Pilate hears about it." ¹⁵They took the money and did as they were told. This story was told among the Jews and is still told today.

Jesus Sends His Followers To Teach
[*Mark 16:15-18; Luke 24:44-49; John 20:21-23*]

¹⁶Then the eleven followers went to Galilee. They went to the mountain where Jesus had told them to go. ¹⁷When they saw Jesus, they worshiped Him. But some did not believe. ¹⁸Jesus came and said to them, "All power has been given to Me in heaven and on earth. ¹⁹Go and make followers of all the nations. Baptize them in the name of the Father and of the Son and of the Holy Spirit. ²⁰Teach them to do all the things I have told you. And I am with you always, even to the end of the world."

MARK

John The Baptist Makes The Way Ready For The Coming Of Jesus [Matthew 3:1-12; Luke 3:1-18; John 1:15-28]

1 The Good News of Jesus Christ, the Son of God, ²begins with the words of the early preachers: "Listen! I will send My helper to carry the news ahead of you. He will make the way ready. ³His voice calls out in the desert, 'Make the way ready for the Lord. Make the road straight for Him!' " (Isaiah 40:3)

⁴John the Baptist preached in the desert. He preached that people should be baptized because they were sorry for their sins and turned from them. And they would be forgiven. ⁵People from over all the country of Judea and from Jerusalem came to him. They told of their sins and were baptized by John in the Jordan River.

⁶John wore clothes made of hair from camels. He had a leather belt around him. His food was locusts and wild honey. ⁷He preached, saying, "One is coming after me Who is greater than I. I am not good enough to get down and help Him take off His shoes. ⁸I have baptized you with water. But He will baptize you with the Holy Spirit."

The Baptism Of Jesus [Matthew 3:13-17; Luke 3:21-22; John 1:29-34]

⁹Jesus came to the Jordan River from the town of Nazareth in the country of Galilee. He was baptized by John. ¹⁰As soon as Jesus came up out of the water, He saw heaven open up. The Holy Spirit came down on Him like a dove. ¹¹A voice came from heaven and said, "You are My much-loved Son. I am very happy with You."

Jesus Was Tempted [Matthew 4:1-11; Luke 4:1-13]

¹²At once the Holy Spirit sent Jesus to a desert. ¹³He was tempted by Satan for forty days there. He was with wild animals but angels took care of Him.

Jesus Preaches In Galilee [Matthew 4:12-17; Luke 4:14-15]

¹⁴After John the Baptist was put in prison, Jesus came to the country of Galilee. He preached the Good News of God. ¹⁵He said, "The time has come. The holy nation of God is near. Be sorry for your sins, turn from them, and believe the Good News."

Jesus Calls Simon And Andrew [Matthew 4:18-22; Luke 5:1-11]

¹⁶Jesus was walking by the Sea of Galilee. He saw Simon and his brother Andrew putting a net into the sea. They were fishermen. ¹⁷Jesus said to them, "Follow Me. I will make you fish for men!" ¹⁸At once they left their nets and followed Him.

Jesus Calls James And John

19Jesus went on a little farther. He saw James and his brother John who were sons of Zebedee. They were in a boat mending their nets. 20Jesus called them and they left their father Zebedee. He was in the boat with men who were working for him.

Jesus Heals A Man With A Demon [Luke 4:31-37]

21Jesus and His followers went to the city of Capernaum on the Day of Rest. They went to the Jewish place of worship where Jesus taught the people. 22The people were surprised and wondered about His teaching. He taught them as One Who had the right and the power to teach and not as the teachers of the Law.

23There was a man in the Jewish place of worship who had a demon. The demon cried out, 24"What do You want of us, Jesus of Nazareth? Have You come to destroy us? I know Who You are. You are the Holy One of God." 25Jesus spoke sharp words to the demon and said, "Do not talk! Come out of the man!" 26The demon threw the man down and gave a loud cry. Then he came out of him. 27The people were all surprised and wondered. They asked each other, "What is this? Is this a new teaching? He speaks with power even to the demons and they obey Him!" 28At once the news about Jesus went through all the country around Galilee.

Peter's Mother-in-law Healed [Matthew 8:14-15; Luke 4:38-39]

29Jesus and His followers came out of the Jewish place of worship. Then they went to the house of Simon and Andrew. James and John went with them. 30They told Jesus about Simon's mother-in-law who was in bed, very sick. 31He went and took her by the hand and raised her up. At once her sickness was gone. She got up and cared for them.

Jesus Heals In Galilee [Matthew 8:16-17; Luke 4:40-41]

32In the evening as the sun went down, the people took all who were sick to Jesus. They took those who had demons to Him. 33All the town gathered at the door. 34Jesus healed those who were sick of many kinds of diseases. He put out many demons. Jesus would not allow the demons to speak because they knew Who He was.

Jesus Keeps On Preaching In Galilee [Matthew 4:23-25; Luke 4:42-44]

35In the morning before the sun was up, Jesus went to a place where He could be alone. He prayed there. 36Simon and the others looked for Jesus. 37They found Him and said, "All the people are looking for You." 38Jesus said to the followers, "Let us go to the towns near here so I can preach there also. That is why I came." 39He went through Galilee. He preached in their places of worship and put out demons.

Jesus Heals A Man With A Bad Skin Disease [Matthew 8:1-4; Luke 5:12-16]

40A man came to Jesus with a bad skin disease. This man got down on his knees and begged Jesus, saying, "If You want to, You can heal me." 41Jesus put His hand on him with loving-pity. He said, "I want to. Be healed." 42At once the disease was gone and the man was healed. 43Jesus spoke strong words to the man before He sent him away. 44He said to him, "Tell no one about this. Go and let the religious leader of the Jews see you. Give the gifts Moses has told you to give when a man is healed of a disease. Let the leaders know you have been healed." ⁴⁵But the man went out and talked about it everywhere. After this Jesus could not go to any town if people knew He was there. He had to stay in the desert. People came to Him from everywhere.

Jesus Heals A Man Who Was Let Down Through The Roof Of A House [Matthew 9:1-8; Luke 5:17-26]

2 After some days Jesus went back to the city of Capernaum. Then news got around that He was home. ²Soon many people gathered there. There was no more room, not even at the door. He spoke the Word of God to them. ³Four men came to Jesus carrying a man who could not move his body. ⁴These men could not get near Jesus because of so many people. They made a hole in the roof of the house over where Jesus stood. Then they let down the bed with the sick man on it.

⁵When Jesus saw their faith, He said to the sick man, "Son, your sins are forgiven." ⁶Some teachers of the Law were sitting there. They thought to themselves, ⁷"Why does this Man talk like this? He is speaking as if He is God! Who can forgive sins? Only One can forgive sins and that is God!"

⁸At once Jesus knew the teachers of the Law were thinking this. He said to them, "Why do you think this in your hearts? ⁹Which is easier to say to the sick man, 'Your sins are forgiven,' or to say, 'Get up, take your bed, and start to walk?' ¹⁰I am doing this so you may know the Son of Man has power on earth to forgive sins." He said to the sick man who could not move his body, ¹¹"I say to you, 'Get up. Take your bed and go to your home.' " ¹²At once the sick man got up and took his bed and went away. Everybody saw him. They were all surprised and wondered about it. They thanked God,

saying, "We have never seen anything like this!"

Jesus Calls Matthew [Matthew 9:9-13; Luke 5:27-32]

¹³Jesus walked along the seashore again. Many people came together and He taught them. ¹⁴He walked farther and saw Levi (Matthew) the son of Alphaeus. Levi was sitting at his work gathering taxes. Jesus said to him, "Follow Me." Levi got up and followed Him.

Jesus Eats With Tax Gatherers And Sinners

¹⁵Jesus ate in Levi's house. Many men who gather taxes and others who were sinners came and sat down with Jesus and His followers. There were many following Him. ¹⁶The teachers of the Law and the proud religious law-keepers saw Jesus eat with men who gather taxes and others who were sinners. They said to His followers, "Why does He eat and drink with men who gather taxes and with sinners?" ¹⁷Jesus heard it and said to them, "People who are well do not need a doctor. Only those who are sick need a doctor. I have not come to call those who are right with God. I have come to call those who are sinners."

Jesus Teaches About Going Without Food So You Can Pray Better [Matthew 9:14-17; Luke 5:33-35]

¹⁸The followers of John and the proud religious law-keepers were not eating food so they could pray better. Some people came to Jesus and said, "Why do the followers of John and the proud religious law-keepers go without food so they can pray better, but Your followers do not?" ¹⁹Jesus said to them, "Can the friends at a wedding go without food when the man just married is with them? As

long as they have him with them, they will not go without food. [20]The days will come when the man just married will be taken from them. Then they will not eat food so they can pray better. [21]No man sews a piece of new cloth on an old coat. If it comes off, it will make the hole bigger. [22]No man puts new wine into old skin bags. The skin would break and the wine would run out. The bags would be no good. New wine must be put into new skin bags."

Jesus Teaches About The Day Of Rest [Matthew 12:1-8; Luke 6:1-5]

[23]At that time Jesus walked through the grain fields on the Day of Rest. As they went, His followers began to take some of the grain. [24]The proud religious law-keepers said to Jesus, "See! Why are they doing what the Law says should not be done on the Day of Rest?" [25]He said to them, "Have you not read what David did when he and his men were hungry? [26]He went into the house of God when Abiathar was head religious leader of the Jews. He ate the special bread used in the religious worship. The Law says only the Jewish religious leaders may eat that. David gave some to those who were with him also." [27]Jesus said to them, "The Day of Rest was made for the good of man. Man was not made for the Day of Rest. [28]The Son of Man is Lord of the Day of Rest also."

Jesus Heals On The Day Of Rest [Matthew 12:9-14; Luke 6:6-11]

3 Jesus went into the Jewish place of worship again. A man was there with a dried-up hand. [2]The proud religious law-keepers watched Jesus to see if He would heal the man on the Day of Rest. They wanted to have something to say against Jesus. [3]Jesus said to the man with the dried-up hand, "Stand up." [4]Then Jesus said to the proud religious law-keepers, "Does the Law say to do good on the Day of Rest or to do bad, to save life or to kill?" But they said nothing. [5]Jesus looked around at them with anger. He was sad because of their hard hearts. Then He said to the man, "Put out your hand." He put it out and his hand was healed. It was as good as the other. [6]The proud religious law-keepers went out and made plans with the followers of King Herod how they might kill Jesus.

Jesus Heals By The Shore Of The Sea [Matthew 12:15-21; Luke 6:17-19]

[7]Jesus went with His followers to the sea. Many people followed Him from the countries of Galilee and Judea. [8]They followed from Jerusalem and from the country of Idumea. They came from the other side of the Jordan River and from the cities of Tyre and Sidon. Many people heard all that Jesus was doing and came to Him. [9]He told His followers to have a small boat ready for Him because so many people might push Him down. [10]He had healed so many that the sick people were pushing in on Him. They were trying to put their hands on Him. [11]When demons saw Him, they got down at His feet and cried out, "You are the Son of God!" [12]He spoke strong words that the demons should tell no one Who He was.

Jesus Calls His Twelve Followers [Matthew 10:1-4; Luke 6:12-16]

[13]He went up on a mountain and called those He wanted. They followed Him. [14]He picked out twelve followers to be with Him so He might send them out to preach. [15]They would have the right and the power to heal diseases and to put out demons. [16]Jesus gave Simon another name, Peter. [17]James and John were brothers. They were the sons of Zebedee. He named them Boanerges,

which means, The Sons of Thunder.
[18] The others were Andrew, Philip,
Bartholomew, Matthew, Thomas,
James the son of Alphaeus, Thaddaeus, Simon the Canaanite, [19] and
Judas Iscariot. Judas was the one who
handed Jesus over to be killed.

The Family Of Jesus Holds Him Back

[20] When Jesus came into a house,
many people gathered around Him
again. Jesus and His followers could
not even eat. [21] When His family
heard of it, they went to take Him.
They said, "He must be crazy."

A Nation That Cannot Stand [Matthew 12:22-37; Luke 11:14-23]

[22] Teachers of the Law came down
from Jerusalem. They said, "Jesus has
Satan in Him. This Man puts out
demons by the king of demons."
[23] Jesus called them to Him and spoke
to them in picture-stories. He said,
"How can the devil put out the devil?
[24] A nation cannot last if it is divided
against itself. [25] A family cannot last
if it is divided against itself. [26] If the
devil fights against himself and is
divided, he cannot last. He will come
to an end. [27] No man can go into a
strong man's house and take away
his things, unless he ties up the strong
man first. Only then can he take
things from his house. [28] For sure, I
tell you, all sins will be forgiven
people, and bad things they speak
against God. [29] But if anyone speaks
bad things against the Holy Spirit, he
will never be forgiven. He is guilty of
a sin that lasts forever." [30] Jesus told
them this because they said, "He has
a demon."

The New Kind Of Family [Matthew 12:46-50; Luke 8:19-21]

[31] Then His mother and brothers
came and stood outside. They sent
for Jesus. [32] Many people were sitting
around Him. They said, "See! Your
mother and brothers are outside
looking for You." [33] He said to them,
"Who is My mother or My brothers?" [34] He turned to those sitting
around Him and said, "See! My
mother and My brothers! [35] Whoever
does what My Father wants is My
brother and My sister and My
mother."

The Picture-story Of The Man Who Planted Seed [Matthew 13:1-52; Luke 8:4-18]

4 Jesus began to teach by the seashore again. Many people gathered around Him. There were so
many He had to get into a boat and
sit down. The people were on the
shore. [2] He taught them many things
by using picture-stories. As He
taught, He said, [3] "Listen! A man
went out to plant seed. [4] As he planted the seed, some fell by the side of
the road. Birds came and ate them.
[5] Some seed fell among rocks. It came
up at once because there was so little
ground. [6] But it dried up when the sun
was high in the sky because it had no
root. [7] Some seed fell among thorns.
The thorns grew and did not give the
seed room to grow. This seed gave no
grain. [8] Some seed fell on good
ground. It came up and grew and
gave much grain. Some gave thirty
times as much grain. Some gave sixty
times as much grain. Some gave one
hundred times as much grain." [9] He
said to them, "You have ears, then
listen!" [10] Those who were with Jesus
and the twelve followers came to
Him when He was alone. They asked
about the picture-story. [11] He said to
them, "You were given the secrets
about the holy nation of God.
Everything is told in picture-stories
to those who are outside the holy
nation of God. [12] They see, but do not
know what it means. They hear, but
do not understand. If they did, they

might turn to God and have their sins forgiven." (Isaiah 6:9-10)

Jesus Tells About The Man Who Planted The Seed

¹³Jesus said to them, "Do you not understand this picture-story? Then how will you understand any of the picture-stories? ¹⁴What the man plants is the Word of God. ¹⁵Those by the side of the road are the ones who hear the Word. As soon as they hear it, the devil comes and takes away the Word that is planted in their hearts. ¹⁶The seed that fell among rocks is like people who receive the Word with joy when they hear it. ¹⁷Their roots are not deep so they live only a short time. When sorrow and trouble come because of the Word, they give up and fall away. ¹⁸The seed that was planted among thorns is like some people who listen to the Word. ¹⁹But the cares of this life let thorns come up. A love for riches and always wanting other things let thorns grow. These things do not give the Word room to grow so it does not give grain. ²⁰The seed that fell on good ground is like people who hear the Word and understand it. They give much grain. Some give thirty times as much grain. Some give sixty times as much grain. Some give one hundred times as much grain."

The Picture-story Of The Lamp

²¹He said to them, "Is a lamp to be put under a pail or under a bed? Should it not be put on a table? ²²Everything that is hidden will be brought into the light. Everything that is a secret will be made known. ²³You have ears, then listen!"

²⁴Jesus said to them, "Be careful what you listen to. The same amount you give will be given to you, and even more. ²⁵He who has, to him will be given. To him who does not have,

even the little he has will be taken from him."

The Picture-story Of The Grain

²⁶He said, "The holy nation of God is like a man who plants seed in the ground. ²⁷He goes to sleep every night and gets up every day. The seed grows, but he does not know how. ²⁸The earth gives fruit by itself. The leaf comes first and then the young grain can be seen. And last, the grain is ready to gather. ²⁹As soon as the grain is ready, he cuts it. The time of gathering the grain has come."

The Picture-story Of The Mustard Seed

³⁰Jesus said, "In what way can we show what the holy nation of God is like? Or what picture-story can we use to help you understand? ³¹It is like a grain of mustard seed that is planted in the ground. It is the smallest of all seeds. ³²After it is put in the ground, it grows and becomes the largest of the spices. It puts out long branches so birds of the sky can live in it." ³³As they were able to understand, He spoke the Word to them by using many picture-stories. ³⁴Jesus helped His followers understand everything when He was alone with them.

The Wind And Waves Obey Jesus
[Matthew 8:23-27; Luke 8:22-25]

³⁵It was evening of that same day. Jesus said to them, "Let us go over to the other side." ³⁶After sending the people away, they took Jesus with them in a boat. It was the same boat He used when He taught them. Other little boats went along with them. ³⁷A bad wind storm came up. The waves were coming over the side of the boat. It was filling up with water. ³⁸Jesus was in the back part of the boat sleeping on a pillow. They woke

Him up, crying out, "Teacher, do You not care that we are about to die?" 39He got up and spoke sharp words to the wind. He said to the sea, "Be quiet! Be still." At once the wind stopped blowing. There were no more waves. 40He said to His followers, "Why are you so full of fear? Do you not have faith?" 41They were very much afraid and said to each other, "Who is this? Even the wind and waves obey Him!"

Demons Ask Jesus To Let Them Live In Pigs [Matthew 8:28-34; Luke 8:26-39]

5 Jesus and His followers came to the other side of the sea to the country of the Gerasenes. 2He got out of the boat. At once a man came to Him from among the graves. This man had a demon. 3He lived among the graves. No man could tie him, even with chains. 4Many times he had been tied with chains on his feet. He had broken the chains as well as the irons from his hands and legs. No man was strong enough to keep him tied. 5Night and day he was among the graves and in the mountains. He would cry out and cut himself with stones.

6When the man with the demon saw Jesus a long way off, he ran and worshiped Him. 7The man spoke with a loud voice and said, "What do You want with me, Jesus, Son of the Most High God? I ask You, in the name of God, do not hurt me!" 8At the same time, Jesus was saying, "Come out of the man, you demon!" 9Jesus asked the demon, "What is your name?" He said, "My name is Many, for there are many of us." 10The demons asked Jesus not to send them out of the country. 11There were many pigs feeding on the mountain side. 12The demons asked Him saying, "Send us to the pigs that we may go into them." 13Then Jesus let them do what they wanted to do. So they went into the pigs. The pigs

ran fast down the side of the mountain and into the sea and died. There were about 2000. 14The men who cared for the pigs ran fast to the town and out to the country telling what had been done. People came to see what had happened. 15They came to Jesus and saw the man who had had the demons. He was sitting with clothes on and in his right mind. The men were afraid. 16Those who had seen it told what had happened to the man who had had the demons. They told what had happened to the pigs. 17Then they asked Jesus to leave their country.

18Jesus got into the boat. The man who had had the demons asked to go with Him. 19Jesus would not let him go but said to him, "Go home to your own people. Tell them what great things the Lord has done for you. Tell them how He had pity on you." 20The man went his way and told everyone in the land of Decapolis what great things Jesus had done for him. All the people were surprised and wondered.

Two Were Healed Through Faith [Matthew 9:18-26; Luke 8:40-56]

21Then Jesus went over to the other side of the sea by boat. Many people gathered around Him. He stayed by the seashore. 22Jairus was one of the leaders of the Jewish place of worship. As Jairus came to Jesus, he got down at His feet. 23He cried out to Jesus and said, "My little daughter is almost dead. Come and put your hand on her that she may be healed and live." 24Jesus went with him. Many people followed and pushed around Jesus.

25A woman had been sick for twelve years with a flow of blood. 26She had suffered much because of having many doctors. She had spent all the money she had. She had received no help, but became worse. 27She heard about Jesus and went among the people who were following Him. She touched His coat. ²⁸For she said to herself, "If I can only touch His coat, I will be healed." ²⁹At once the flow of blood stopped. She felt in her body that she was healed of her sickness.

³⁰At the same time Jesus knew that power had gone from Him. He turned and said to the people following Him, "Who touched My coat?" ³¹His followers said to Him, "You see the many people pushing on every side. Why do You ask, 'Who touched My coat?' " ³²He looked around to see who had done it. ³³The woman was filled with fear when she knew what had happened to her. She came and got down before Jesus and told Him the truth. ³⁴He said to her, "Daughter, your faith has healed you. Go in peace and be free from your sickness."

³⁵While Jesus spoke, men came from the house of the leader of the place of worship. They said, "Your daughter is dead. Why trouble the Teacher anymore?" ³⁶Jesus heard this. He said to the leader of the Jewish place of worship, "Do not be afraid, just believe." ³⁷He allowed no one to go with Him but Peter and James and John, the brother of James. ³⁸They came to the house where the leader of the place of worship lived. Jesus found many people making much noise and crying. ³⁹He went in and asked them, "Why is there so much noise and crying? The girl is not dead. She is sleeping."

⁴⁰They laughed at Jesus. But He sent them all out of the room. Then He took the girl's father and mother and those who were with Him. They went into the room where the girl was. ⁴¹He took the girl by the hand and said, "Little girl, I say to you, get up!" ⁴²At once the girl got up and walked. She was twelve years old. They were very much surprised and wondered about it. ⁴³He spoke sharp words to them that they should not

tell anyone. He told them to give her something to eat.

Jesus Visits His Own Town, Nazareth [Matthew 13:53-58]

6 Jesus went from the house of Jairus and came to His home town. His followers came after Him. ²On the Day of Rest He began to teach in the Jewish place of worship. Many people heard Him. They were surprised and wondered, saying, "Where did this Man get all this? What wisdom is this that has been given to Him? How can He do these powerful works with His hands? ³Is He not a Man Who makes things from wood? Is He not the Son of Mary and the brother of James and Joses and Judas and Simon? Do not His sisters live here with us?" The people were ashamed of Him and turned away from Him. ⁴Jesus said to them, "One who speaks for God is respected everywhere but in his own country and among his own family and in his own house."

⁵So Jesus could do no powerful works there. But He did put His hands on a few sick people and healed them. ⁶He wondered because they had no faith. But He went around to the towns and taught as He went.

Jesus Calls Twelve Followers And Sends Them Out [Matthew 10:1-42; Luke 9:1-6]

⁷Jesus called the twelve followers to Him and began to send them out two by two. He gave them power over demons. ⁸He told them to take nothing along with them but a walking stick. They were not to take a bag or food or money in their belts. ⁹They were to wear shoes. They were not to take two coats.

¹⁰He said to them, "Whatever house you go into, stay there until you leave that town. ¹¹Whoever does

not take you in or listen to you, when you leave there, shake the dust off your feet. By doing that, you will speak against them. For sure, I tell you, it will be easier for the cities of Sodom and Gomorrha on the day men stand before God and are told they are guilty than for that city."

¹²Then they left. They preached that men should be sorry for their sins and turn from them. ¹³They put out many demons. They poured oil on many people that were sick and healed them.

John The Baptist Is Put In Prison
[Matthew 14:1-5; Luke 3:18-20]

¹⁴King Herod heard about Jesus because everyone was talking about Him. Some people said, "John the Baptist has been raised from the dead. That is why he is doing such powerful works." ¹⁵Other people said, "He is Elijah." Others said, "He is one who speaks for God like one of the early preachers." ¹⁶When Herod heard this, he said, "It is John the Baptist, whose head I cut off. He has been raised from the dead." ¹⁷For Herod had sent men to take John and put him into prison. He did this because of his wife, Herodias. She had been the wife of his brother Philip. ¹⁸John the Baptist had said to Herod, "It is wrong for you to have your brother's wife." ¹⁹Herodias became angry with him. She wanted to have John the Baptist killed but she could not. ²⁰Herod was afraid of John. He knew he was a good man and right with God, and he kept John from being hurt or killed. He liked to listen to John preach. But when he did, he became troubled.

John The Baptist Is Killed [Matthew 14:6-12; Luke 9:7-9]

²¹Then Herodias found a way to have John killed. Herod gave a big supper on his birthday. He asked the leaders of the country and army captains and the leaders of Galilee to come. ²²The daughter of Herodias came in and danced before them. This made Herod and his friends happy. The king said to the girl, "Ask me for whatever you want and I will give it to you." ²³Then he made a promise to her, "Whatever you ask for, I will give it to you. I will give you even half of my nation." ²⁴She went to her mother and asked, "What should I ask for?" The mother answered, "I want the head of John the Baptist." ²⁵At once the girl went to Herod. She said, "I want you to give me the head of John the Baptist on a plate now."

²⁶Herod was very sorry. He had to do it because of his promise and because of those who ate with him. ²⁷At once he sent one of his soldiers and told him to bring the head of John the Baptist. The soldier went to the prison and cut off John's head. ²⁸He took John's head in on a plate and gave it to the girl. The girl gave it to her mother. ²⁹John's followers heard this. They went and took his body and buried it.

The Feeding Of The Five Thousand
[Matthew 14:13-21; Luke 9:10-17; John 6:1-14]

³⁰The followers of Jesus came back to Him. They told Jesus all they had done and taught. ³¹He said to them, "Come away from the people. Be by yourselves and rest." There were many people coming and going. They had had no time even to eat. ³²They went by themselves in a boat to a desert. ³³Many people saw them leave and knew who they were. People ran fast from all the cities and got there first. ³⁴When Jesus got out of the boat, He saw many people gathered together. He had loving-pity for them. They were like sheep without a shepherd. He began to teach them many things.

³⁵The day was almost gone. The followers of Jesus came to Him. They

said, "This is a desert. It is getting late. ³⁶Tell the people to go to the towns and villages and buy food for themselves." ³⁷He said to them, "Give them something to eat." They said to Him, "Are we to go and buy many loaves of bread and give it to them?" ³⁸He said to them, "How many loaves of bread do you have here? Go and see." When they knew, they said, "Five loaves of bread and two fish." ³⁹Then He told them to have all the people sit down together in groups on the green grass. ⁴⁰They sat down in groups of fifty people and in groups of one hundred people. ⁴¹Jesus took the five loaves of bread and two fish. He looked up to heaven and gave thanks. He broke the loaves in pieces and gave them to the followers to set before the people. He divided the two fish among them all. ⁴²They all ate and were filled. ⁴³After that the followers picked up twelve baskets full of pieces of bread and fish. ⁴⁴About five thousand men ate the bread.

Jesus Walks On The Water [Matthew 14:22-33; John 6:15-21]

⁴⁵At once Jesus had His followers get into the boat and go ahead of Him to the other side to the town of Bethsaida. He sent the people away. ⁴⁶When they were all gone, He went up to the mountain to pray. ⁴⁷It was evening. The boat was half way across the sea. Jesus was alone on the land. ⁴⁸He saw His followers were in trouble. The wind was against them. They were working very hard rowing the boat. About three o'clock in the morning Jesus came to them walking on the sea. He would have gone past them. ⁴⁹When the followers saw Him walking on the water, they thought it was a spirit and cried out with fear. ⁵⁰For they all saw Him and were afraid. At once Jesus talked to them. He said, "Take hope. It is I, do not be afraid." ⁵¹He came over to them and got into the boat. The wind stopped.

They were very much surprised and wondered about it. ⁵²They had not learned what they should have learned from the loaves because their hearts were hard.

People Are Healed At Gennesaret [Matthew 14:34-36]

⁵³Then they crossed the sea and came to the land of Gennesaret and went to shore. ⁵⁴When Jesus got out of the boat, the people knew Him at once. ⁵⁵They ran through all the country bringing people who were sick on their beds to Jesus. ⁵⁶Wherever He went, they would lay the sick people in the streets in the center of town where people gather. They begged Him that they might touch the bottom of His coat. Everyone who did was healed. This happened in the towns and in the cities and in the country where He went.

Jesus Speaks Sharp Words To The Leaders [Matthew 15:1-20]

7 The proud religious law-keepers and some of the teachers of the Law had come from Jerusalem. They gathered around Jesus. ²They had seen some of His followers eat bread without washing their hands. ³The proud religious law-keepers and all the Jews never eat until they wash their hands. They keep the teaching that was given to them by their early fathers. ⁴When they come from the stores, they never eat until they wash. There are many other teachings they keep. Some are the washing of cups and pots and pans in a special way.

⁵Then the proud religious law-keepers and the teachers of the Law asked Jesus, "Why do Your followers not obey the teaching given to them by their early fathers? They eat bread without washing their hands." ⁶He said to them, "Isaiah told about you who pretend to be someone you are not. Isaiah wrote, 'This people honor

Me with their lips, but their hearts are far from Me. [7]Their worship of Me is worth nothing. They teach what men say must be done.' (Isaiah 29:13) [8]You put away the Laws of God and obey the laws made by men."

[9]Jesus said to them, "You put away the Laws of God but keep your own teaching. [10]Moses said, 'Respect your father and mother.' (Exodus 20:12) 'He who says bad things against his father and mother will be put to death!' (Exodus 21:17) [11]But you say that it is right if a man does not help his father and mother because he says he has given to God what he could have given to them. [12]You are not making him do anything for his father and mother. [13]You are putting away the Word of God to keep your own teaching. You are doing many other things like this."

[14]Jesus called the people to Him again. He said, "Listen to Me, all of you, and understand this. [15]It is not what goes into a man's mouth from the outside that makes his mind and heart sinful. It is what comes out from the inside that makes him sinful. [16]You have ears, then listen!"

[17]He went into the house away from all the people. His followers began to ask about the picture-story. [18]He said to them, "Do you not understand yet? Do you not understand that whatever goes into a man cannot make him sinful? [19]It does not go into his heart, but into his stomach and then on out of his body." In this way, He was saying that all food is clean. [20]He said, "Whatever comes out of a man is what makes the man sinful. [21]From the inside, out of the heart of men .come bad thoughts, sex sins of a married person, sex sins of a person not married, killing other people, [22]stealing, wanting something that belongs to someone else, doing wrong, lying, having a desire for sex sins, having a mind that is always looking for sin, speaking against God, thinking you are better than you are and doing foolish things. [23]All these bad things come from the inside and make the man sinful."

Jesus Puts A Demon Out Of A Girl
[Matthew 15:21-28]

[24]Jesus went from their towns and cities to the cities of Tyre and Sidon. He went into a house and wanted to stay there without people knowing where He was. But He could not hide Himself. [25]A woman who had a daughter with a demon heard of Him. She came and got down at His feet. [26]The woman was not a Jew. She was from the country of Syrophenicia. She asked Jesus if He would put the demon out of her daughter. [27]Jesus said to her, "Let the children have what they want first. It is wrong to take children's food and throw it to the dogs." [28]She said to Him, "Yes, Lord, but even the dogs eat the pieces that fall from the children's table." [29]He said to her, "Because of what you have said, go your way. The demon is gone out of your daughter." [30]So she went to her house and found the demon was gone and her daughter was lying on the bed.

Jesus Heals The Man Who Could Not Hear Or Speak Well

[31]Then Jesus left the cities of Tyre and Sidon. He came back to the Sea of Galilee by way of the land of Decapolis. [32]They took a man to Him who could not hear or speak well. They asked Jesus to put His hand on him. [33]Jesus took him away from the other people. He put His fingers into the man's ears. He spit and put His finger on the man's tongue. [34]Then Jesus looked up to heaven and breathed deep within. He said to the man, "Be opened!" [35]At once his ears were opened. His tongue was made loose and he spoke as other people. [36]Then Jesus told them they should

tell no one. The more He told them this, the more they told what He had done. 37They were very much surprised and wondered about it. They said, "He has done all things well. He makes those who could not hear so they can hear. He makes those who could not speak so they can speak."

The Feeding Of The Four Thousand
[Matthew 15:32-39]

8 In those days many people were gathered together. They had nothing to eat. Jesus called His followers to Him and said, 2"I pity these people because they have been with Me three days and have nothing to eat. 3If I send them home without food, they may be too weak as they go. Many of them have come a long way."

4His followers said to Him, "Where can anyone get enough bread for them here in this desert?" 5He asked them, "How many loaves of bread do you have?" They said, "Seven." 6Then He told the people to sit down on the ground. Jesus took the seven loaves of bread and gave thanks to God. He broke the loaves and gave them to His followers to give to the people. The followers gave the bread to them. 7They had a few small fish also. He gave thanks to God and told the followers to give the fish to them. 8They all ate and were filled. They picked up seven baskets full of pieces of bread and fish after the people were finished eating. 9About four thousand ate. Then Jesus sent the people away.

The Proud Religious Law-keepers Ask For Something Special To See
[Matthew 16:1-4]

10At once Jesus got in a boat with His followers and came to the country of Dalmanutha. 11The proud religious law-keepers came and began to ask Him for something special to see from heaven. They wanted to trap Jesus. 12He breathed deep within and said, "Why do the people of this day look for something special to see? For sure, I tell you, the people of this day will have nothing special to see from heaven." 13Then He left them. He got in the boat and went to the other side of the sea.

Jesus Shows That The Teaching Of The Proud Religious Law-keepers Is Wrong [Matthew 16:5-12]

14The followers had forgotten to take bread, only one loaf was in the boat. 15He said to them, "Look out! Have nothing to do with the yeast of the proud religious law-keepers and of Herod." 16They talked about it among themselves. They said, "He said this because we forgot to bring bread." 17Jesus knew what they were thinking. He said to them, "Why are you talking among yourselves about forgetting to bring bread? Do you not understand? Is it not plain to you? Are your hearts still hard? 18You have eyes, do you not see? You have ears, do you not hear? Do you not remember? 19When I divided the five loaves of bread among the five thousand, how many baskets full of pieces did you pick up?" They said, "Twelve." 20"When I divided the seven loaves of bread among the four thousand, how many baskets full of pieces did you pick up?" They said, "Seven." 21Then He asked, "Why do you not understand yet?"

Jesus Heals A Blind Man

22Then they came to the town of Bethsaida. Some people brought a blind man to Jesus. They asked if He would touch him. 23He took the blind man by the hand out of town. Then He spit on the eyes of the blind man and put His hands on him. He asked, "Do you see anything?" 24The blind man looked up and said, "I see some men. They look like trees, walking." 25Jesus put His hands on the man's eyes again and told him to look up. Then he was healed and saw everything well. ²⁶Jesus sent him to his home and said, "Do not go into the town, * or tell it to anyone there."

Peter Says Jesus Is The Christ
[Matthew 16:13-20; Luke 9:18-20]

²⁷Jesus and His followers went from there to the towns of Caesarea Philippi. As they went, He asked His followers, "Who do people say that I am?" ²⁸They answered, "Some say John the Baptist and some say Elijah and others say one of the early preachers." ²⁹He said to them, "But who do you say that I am?" Peter said, "You are the Christ." ³⁰He told them with strong words that they should tell no one about Him.

Jesus Tells Of His Death For The First Time [Matthew 16:21-28; Luke 9:21-27]

³¹He began to teach them that the Son of Man must suffer many things. He told them that the leaders and the religious leaders of the Jews and the teachers of the Law would have nothing to do with Him. He told them He would be killed and three days later He would be raised from the dead.

³²He had said this in plain words. Peter took Him away from the others and began to speak sharp words to Him. ³³Jesus turned around. He looked at His followers and spoke sharp words to Peter. He said, "Get behind Me, Satan! Your thoughts are not thoughts from God but from men."

Giving Up Self And One's Own Desires

³⁴Jesus called the people and His followers to Him. He said to them, "If anyone wants to be My follower, he must give up himself and his own desires. He must take up his cross and follow Me. ³⁵If anyone wants to keep his own life safe, he will lose it. If anyone gives up his life because of Me and because of the Good News, he will save it. ³⁶For what does a man have if he gets all the world and loses his own soul? ³⁷What can a man give to buy back his soul? ³⁸Whoever is ashamed of Me and My Words among the sinful people of this day, the Son of Man will be ashamed of him when He comes in the shining greatness of His Father and His holy angels."

A Look At What Jesus Will Be Like
[Matthew 17:1-13; Luke 9:28-36]

9 Jesus said to them, "For sure I tell you, some standing here will not die until they see the holy nation of God come with power!"

²Six days later Jesus took Peter and James and John with Him. He led them up to a high mountain by themselves. Jesus was changed as they looked at Him. ³His clothes did shine. They were as white as snow. No one on earth could clean them so white. ⁴Moses and Elijah were seen talking to Jesus.

⁵Peter said to Jesus, "Teacher, it is good for us to be here. Let us make three altars. One will be for You and one for Moses and one for Elijah." ⁶Peter did not know what to say. They were very much afraid.

⁷A cloud came over them and a voice from the cloud said, "This is My much-loved Son. Listen to Him." ⁸At once they looked around but saw no one there but Jesus.

⁹They came down from the mountain. Then Jesus said with strong words that they should tell no one what they had seen. They should wait until the Son of Man had risen from the dead. ¹⁰So they kept those words to themselves, talking to each other about what He meant by being raised from the dead.

¹¹They asked Jesus, "Why do the teachers of the Law say that Elijah

must come first?" [12]He said to them, "For sure, Elijah will come first and get things ready. Is it not written that the Son of Man must suffer many things and that men will have nothing to do with Him? (Isaiah 53:3) [13]But I say to you, Elijah has already come. They did to him whatever they wanted to do. It is written that they would."

A Boy With A Demon Is Healed
[Matthew 17:14-21; Luke 9:37-42]

[14]When Jesus came back to His followers, He saw many people standing around them. The teachers of the Law were arguing with them. [15]The people saw Jesus and were surprised and ran to say hello to Him. [16]Jesus asked the teachers of the Law, "What are you arguing about with them?" [17]One of the people said, "Teacher, I brought my son to You. He has a demon in him and cannot talk. [18]Wherever the demon takes him, it throws him down. Spit runs from his mouth. He grinds his teeth. He is getting weaker. I asked Your followers to put the demon out but they could not."
[19]He said, "You people of this day have no faith. How long must I be with you? How long must I put up with you? Bring the boy to Me." [20]They brought the boy to Jesus. The demon saw Jesus and at once held the boy in his power. The boy fell to the ground with spit running from his mouth. [21]Jesus asked the boy's father, "How long has he been like this?" The father said, "From the time he was a child. [22]Many times it throws him into the fire and into the water to kill him. If You can do anything to help us, take pity on us!" [23]Jesus said to him, "Why do you ask Me that? The one who has faith can do all things." [24]At once the father cried out. He said with tears in his eyes, "Lord, I have faith. Help my weak faith to be stronger!" [25]Jesus saw that many people were gathering together

in a hurry. He spoke sharp words to the demon. He said, "Demon! You who cannot speak or hear, I say to you, come out of him! Do not ever go into him again." [26]The demon gave a cry. It threw the boy down and came out of him. The boy was so much like a dead man that people said, "He is dead!" [27]But Jesus took him by the hand and helped him and he stood up.
[28]When Jesus went into the house, His followers asked Him when He was alone, "Why could we not put out the demon?" [29]He said to them, "The only way this kind of demon is put out is by prayer and by going without food so you can pray better."

Jesus Tells Of His Death The Second Time
[Matthew 17:22-23; Luke 9:43-45]

[30]From there Jesus and His followers went through the country of Galilee. He did not want anyone to know where He was. [31]He taught His followers, saying, "The Son of Man will be handed over to men. They will kill Him. Three days after He is killed, He will be raised from the dead." [32]They did not understand what He said and were afraid to ask Him.

Jesus Teaches About The Faith Of A Child
[Matthew 18:1-35; Luke 9:46-50]

[33]They came to the city of Capernaum and were in the house. Jesus asked His followers, "What were you arguing about along the road?" [34]They did not answer. They had been arguing along the road about who was the greatest. [35]Jesus sat down and called the followers to Him. He said, "If anyone wants to be first, he must be last of all. He will be the one to care for all."
[36]Jesus took a child and stood it among them. Then He took the child

up in His arms and said to the followers, 37"Whoever receives one of these little children in My name, receives Me. Whoever will receive Me, receives not Me, but Him Who sent Me."

Jesus Speaks Sharp Words Against The Followers

38John said to Him, "Teacher, we saw someone putting out demons in Your name. We told him to stop because he was not following us." 39Jesus said, "Do not stop him. No one who does a powerful work in My name can say anything bad about Me soon after. 40The person who is not against us is for us. 41For sure, I tell you, whoever gives you a cup of water to drink in My name because you belong to Christ will not lose his pay from God. 42Whoever is the reason for one of these little ones who believes in Me to sin, it would be better for him to have a large stone put around his neck and to be thrown into the sea. 43If your hand is the reason you fall into sin, cut it off. It is better to go into life without a hand, than to have two hands and go into the fire of hell that cannot be put out. *44There is where their worm never dies and the fire cannot be put out. 45If your foot is the reason you fall into sin, cut it off. It is better to go into life with only one foot, than to have two feet and go into the fire of hell that cannot be put out. 46*There is where their worm never dies and the fire cannot be put out. 47If your eye is the reason you fall into sin, take it out. It is better to go into the holy nation of God with only one eye, than to have two eyes and be thrown into the fire of hell. 48There is where their worm never dies and the fire is never put out.

49"Everyone will be made cleaner and stronger with fire. 50Salt is good. But if salt loses its taste, how can it be made to taste like salt again? Have salt in yourselves and be at peace with each other."

Jesus Teaches About Divorce [Matthew 19:1-12]

10 Jesus went away from the city of Capernaum. He came to the country of Judea and to the other side of the Jordan River. Again the people gathered around Him. He began to teach them as He had been doing. 2The proud religious law-keepers came to Him. They tried to trap Him and asked, "Does the Law say a man can divorce his wife?" 3He said to them, "What did the Law of Moses say?" 4They said, "Moses allowed a man to divorce his wife, if he put it in writing and gave it to her." 5Jesus said to them, "Because of your hard hearts, Moses gave you this Law. 6From the beginning of the world, God made them man and woman. 7Because of this, a man is to leave his father and mother and is to live with his wife. 8The two will become one. So they are no longer two, but one. 9Let no man divide what God has put together."

10In the house the followers asked Jesus about this again. 11He said to them, "Whoever divorces his wife and marries another is not faithful to her and is guilty of a sex sin. 12If a woman divorces her husband and marries another, she is not faithful to her husband and is guilty of a sex sin."

Jesus Gives Thanks For Little Children [Matthew 19:13-15; Luke 18:15-17]

13They brought little children to Jesus that He might put His hand on them. The followers spoke sharp words to those who brought them. 14Jesus saw this and was angry with the followers. He said, "Let the little children come to Me. Do not stop them. The holy nation of God is made up of ones like these. [15]For sure, I tell you, whoever does not receive the holy nation of God as a little child does not go into it." [16]He took the children in His arms. He put His hands on them and prayed that good would come to them.

Jesus Teaches About Keeping The Law [Matthew 19:16-30; Luke 18:18-30]

[17]Jesus was going on His way. A man ran to Him and got down on his knees. He said, "Good Teacher, what must I do to have life that lasts forever?" [18]Jesus said to him, "Why do you call Me good? There is only One Who is good. That is God. [19]You know the Laws, 'Do not be guilty of sex sins in marriage. Do not kill another person. Do not take things from people in wrong ways. Do not steal. Do not lie. Respect your father and mother.' " [20]The man said to Jesus, "Teacher, I have obeyed all these Laws since I was a boy." [21]Jesus looked at him with love and said, "There is one thing for you to do yet. Go and sell everything you have and give the money to poor people. You will have riches in heaven. Then come and follow Me." [22]When the man heard these words, he was sad. He walked away with sorrow because he had many riches here on earth.

The Danger Of Riches

[23]Jesus looked around Him. He said to His followers, "How hard it is for rich people to get into the holy nation of God!" [24]The followers were surprised and wondered about His words. But Jesus said to them again, "Children! How hard it is for those who put their trust in riches to get into the holy nation of God! [25]It is easier for a camel to go through the eye of a needle than for a rich man to go to heaven." [26]They were very surprised and

wondered, saying to themselves, "Then who can be saved from the punishment of sin?" [27]Jesus looked at them and said, "This cannot be done by men but God can do anything."

[28]Then Peter began to say to Him, "We have given up everything we had and have followed You." [29]Jesus said, "For sure, I tell you, there are those who have given up houses or brothers or sisters or father or mother or wife or children or lands because of Me, and the Good News. [30]They will get back one hundred times as much now at this time in houses and brothers and sisters and mothers and children and lands. Along with this, they will have very much trouble. And they will have life that lasts forever in the world to come. [31]Many who are first will be last. Many who are last will be first."

Jesus Tells Of His Death The Third Time [Matthew 20:17-19; Luke 18:31-34]

[32]They were on their way to Jerusalem. Jesus walked in front of them. Those who followed were surprised and afraid. Then Jesus took the twelve followers by themselves. He told them what would happen to Him. [33]He said, "Listen, we are going to Jerusalem. The Son of Man will be handed over to the religious leaders of the Jews and to the teachers of the Law. They will say that He must be put to death. They will hand Him over to the people who are not Jews. [34]They will make fun of Him and will beat Him. They will spit on Him and will kill Him. But three days later He will be raised from the dead."

James and John Ask Jesus Something Hard [Matthew 20:20-28]

[35]James and John, the sons of Zebedee, came to Jesus. They said, "Teacher, we would like to have You do for us whatever we ask You." [36]He said to them, "What would you like

to have Me do for you?" [37]They said to Him, "Let one of us sit by Your right side and the other by Your left side when You receive Your great honor in heaven." [38]Jesus said to them, "You do not know what you ask. Can you take the suffering I am about to take? Can you be baptized with the baptism that I am baptized with?" [39]They said to Him, "Yes, we can." Jesus said to them, "You will, for sure, suffer the way I will suffer. You will be baptized with the baptism that I am baptized with. [40]But to sit on My right side or on My left side is not for Me to give. It will be given to those for whom it has been made ready." [41]The other ten followers heard it. They were angry with James and John. [42]Jesus called them to Him and said, "You know that those who are made leaders over the nations show their power to the people. Important leaders use their power over the people. [43]It must not be that way with you. Whoever wants to be great among you, let him care for you. [44]Whoever wants to be first among you, must be the one who is owned and cares for all. [45]For the Son of Man did not come to be cared for. He came to care for others. He came to give His life so that many could be bought by His blood and be made free from sin."

Healing Of The Blind Man [*Matthew 20:29-34; Luke 18:35-43*]

[46]Then they came to the city of Jericho. When He was leaving the city with His followers and many people, a blind man was sitting by the road. He was asking people for food or money as they passed by. His name was Bartimaeus, the son of Timaeus. [47]He heard that Jesus of Nazareth was passing by. He began to speak with a loud voice, saying, "Jesus, Son of David, take pity on me!" [48]Many people spoke sharp words to the blind man telling him not to call out like that. But he spoke

all the more. He said, "Son of David, take pity on me." [49]Jesus stopped and told them to call the blind man. They called to him and said, "Take hope! Stand up, He is calling for you!" [50]As he jumped up, he threw off his coat and came to Jesus. [51]Jesus said to him, "What do you want Me to do for you?" The blind man said to Him, "Lord, I want to see!" [52]Jesus said, "Go! Your faith has healed you." At once he could see and he followed Jesus down the road.

The Last Time Jesus Goes To Jerusalem [*Matthew 21:1-11; Luke 19:29-44; John 12:12-19*]

11 Jesus and His followers were near Jerusalem at the Mount of Olives. They were in the towns of Bethphage and Bethany. Jesus sent two of His followers on ahead. [2]He said to them, "Go into the town over there. As soon as you get there, you will find a young donkey tied. No man has ever sat on it. Let the donkey loose and bring it here. [3]If anyone asks you, 'Why are you doing that?' say, 'The Lord needs it. He will send it back again soon.' "

[4]The two followers went on their way. They found the young donkey tied by the door where two streets crossed. They took the rope off its neck. [5]Some men were standing there. They said to the two followers, "Why are you taking the rope off that young donkey?" [6]The two followers told them what Jesus had said and the men let them take the donkey. [7]They brought it to Jesus and put their coats over it. Jesus sat on the donkey. [8]Many people put their clothes down on the road. Others cut branches off the trees and put them down on the road. [9]Those who went in front and those who followed spoke with loud voices, "Greatest One! Great and honored is He Who comes in the name of the Lord! [10]Great is the coming holy nation of our father David. It will

come in the name of the Lord, Greatest One in the highest heaven."
¹¹Jesus came to Jerusalem and went into the house of God. He looked around at everything. Then He went with the twelve followers to the town of Bethany because it was late.

The Fig Tree With No Fruit

¹²They came from Bethany the next morning. Jesus was hungry. ¹³Along the road He saw a fig tree with leaves on it. He went over to see if it had any fruit. He saw nothing but leaves. It was not the right time for figs. ¹⁴Jesus said to the tree, "Let no one ever again eat fruit from you." His followers heard Him say it.

Jesus Stops The Buying And The Selling In The House Of God [Matthew 21:12-17; Luke 19:45-48; John 2:13-17]

¹⁵Then they came to Jerusalem. Jesus went into the house of God. He began to make the people leave who were selling and buying in the house of God. He turned over the tables of the men who changed money. He turned over the seats of those who sold doves. ¹⁶He would not allow anyone to carry a pot or pan through the house of God. ¹⁷He taught them saying, "Is it not written, 'My house is to be called a house of prayer for all the nations'? You have made it a place of robbers."

¹⁸The teachers of the Law and the religious leaders of the Jews heard it. They tried to find some way to put Jesus to death. But they were afraid of Him because all the people were surprised and wondered about His teaching. ¹⁹When evening came, Jesus and His followers went out of the city.

The Fig Tree Dries Up [Matthew 21:18-22]

²⁰In the morning they passed by the fig tree. They saw it was dried up from the roots. ²¹Peter remembered what had happened the day before and said to Jesus, "Teacher, see! The fig tree which You spoke to has dried up!" ²²Jesus said to them, "Have faith in God. ²³For sure, I tell you, a person may say to this mountain, 'Move from here into the sea.' And if he does not doubt, but believes that what he says will be done, it will happen. ²⁴Because of this, I say to you, whatever you ask for when you pray, have faith that you will receive it. Then you will get it. ²⁵When you stand to pray, if you have anything against anyone, forgive him. Then your Father in heaven will forgive your sins also. ²⁶ If you do not forgive them their sins, your Father in heaven will not forgive your sins."

²⁷They came again to Jerusalem. Jesus was walking around in the house of God. The religious leaders and the teachers of the Law and other leaders came to Him. ²⁸They asked, "How do You have the right and the power to do these things? Who gave You the right and the power to do them?" ²⁹Jesus said to them, "I will ask you one thing also. If you tell Me, then I will tell you by what right and power I do these things. ³⁰Was the baptism of John from heaven or from men? Tell Me." ³¹They talked among themselves. They said, "If we say from heaven, He will say, 'Why did you not believe him?' ³²But how can we say, 'From men'?" They were afraid of the people because everyone believed that John was one who spoke for God. ³³So they said, "We do not know." Then Jesus said, "Then I will not tell you by what right and power I do these things."

The Picture-story Of The Grape Field [Matthew 21:33-46; Luke 20:9-18]

12 Jesus began to teach them by using picture-stories, saying, "There was a man who planted grapes in a field. He put a fence around it and made a place for making wine. He built a tower to look over the field. Then he let farmers rent it and went into another country. ²"The time came for gathering the grapes. He sent his servant to the farmers to get some of the grapes. ³The farmers took him and beat him. They sent him back with nothing. ⁴The owner sent another servant. The farmers threw stones at him and hit him on the head and did other bad things to him. ⁵Again the owner sent another servant. The farmers killed that one. Many other servants were sent. They beat some and they killed others.

⁶"He had a much-loved son to send yet. So last of all he sent him to them, saying, 'They will respect my son.' ⁷The farmers said to themselves, 'This is the one who will get everything when the owner dies. Let us kill him and we will get everything.' ⁸They took him and killed him. They threw his body outside the field. ⁹What will the owner of the field do? He will come and kill the farmers. He will give the field to other farmers.

¹⁰"Have you not read what the Holy Writings say? 'The Stone that was put aside by the workmen has become the most important Stone in the corner of the building. ¹¹The Lord has done this. It is great in our eyes.'" (Psalm 118:22-23) ¹²The leaders wanted to take Him but they were afraid of the people. They knew He had told the picture-story against them. They left Him and went away.

They Try To Trap Jesus [Matthew 22:15-22; Luke 20:19-26]

¹³Some of the proud religious law-keepers and Herod's men were sent to trap Jesus in His talk. ¹⁴They came to Him and said, "Teacher, we know You are true. We know You are not afraid of what men think or say about You. You teach the way of God in truth. Is it right to pay taxes to Caesar or not? ¹⁵Should we pay or not pay?" Jesus knew how they pretended to be someone they were not. He said to them, "Why do you try to trap Me? Bring Me a small piece of money so I may look at it." ¹⁶They brought Him one. He asked them, "Whose picture is this? Whose name is on it?" They answered, "Caesar's." ¹⁷Then Jesus said to them, "Pay to Caesar the things that belong to Caesar. Pay to God the things that belong to God." They were surprised and wondered at Him.

They Ask About Being Raised From The Dead [Matthew 22:23-33; Luke 20:27-40]

¹⁸Some people from the religious group who believe no one will be raised from the dead came to Jesus. They asked Him, ¹⁹"Teacher, Moses gave us a Law. It said, 'If a man's brother dies and leaves his wife behind, but no children, then his brother should marry his wife and raise children for his brother.' (Deuteronomy 25:5) ²⁰There were seven brothers. The first was married. He died before he had any children. ²¹The second married her and died. He had no children. The same happened with the third. ²²All seven had her for a wife. All died without children. Last of all the woman died. ²³When people are raised from the dead, whose wife will she be? All seven had her for a wife." ²⁴Jesus said to them, "Is this not the reason you are wrong, because you do not know the Holy Writings or the power of God? ²⁵When people are raised from the dead, they do not marry and are not given in marriage. They are like angels in heaven. ²⁶As for the dead being raised, have you not read in the book of Moses how God spoke to him in the burning bush? He said, 'I am the God of Abraham and the God of Isaac and the God of Jacob.' (Exodus 3:2-6) ²⁷He is not the God of the dead, He is

the God of the living. So you are very much wrong."

The Great Law [Matthew 22:34-40]

²⁸Then one of the teachers of the Law heard them arguing. He thought Jesus had spoken well. He asked Him, "Which Law is the greatest of all?" ²⁹Jesus said to him, "The greatest Law is this, 'Listen, Jewish people, The Lord our God is one Lord! ³⁰You must love the Lord your God with all your heart and with all your soul and with all your mind and with all your strength.' (Deuteronomy 6:4-5) This is the first Law.

³¹"The second Law is this: 'You must love your neighbor as yourself.' (Leviticus 19:18) No other Law is greater than these."

³²Then the teacher of the Law said, "Teacher, You have told the truth. There is one God. There is no other God but Him. ³³A man should love Him with all his heart and with all his understanding. He should love Him with all his soul and with all his strength and love his neighbor as himself. This is more important than to bring animals to be burned on the altar or to give God other gifts on the altar in worship." ³⁴Jesus saw he had spoken with understanding. He said to him, "You are not far from the holy nation of God." After that no one thought they could ask Him anything.

Jesus Asks The Proud Religious Law-keepers About The Christ [Matthew 22:41-46; Luke 20:41-44]

³⁵Jesus was in the house of God teaching. He asked, "How do the teachers of the Law say that Christ is the Son of David? ³⁶For David himself, led by the Holy Spirit, said, 'The Lord said to my Lord, sit at my right side until I make those who hate You a place to rest Your feet.' (Psalm 110:1) ³⁷David himself calls Him

Lord. Then how can He be his son?" Many people were glad to hear Him.

False Teachers [Matthew 23:1-36; Luke 20:45-47]

³⁸Jesus taught them, saying, "Look out for the teachers of the Law. They like to walk around in long coats. They like to have the respect of men as they stand in the center of town where people gather. ³⁹They like to have the important seats in the places of worship and the important places at big suppers. ⁴⁰They take houses from poor women whose husbands have died. They cover up the bad they do by saying long prayers. They will be punished all the more."

The Woman Whose Husband Had Died Gave All She Had [Luke 21:1-4]

⁴¹Jesus sat near the money box in the house of God. He watched the people putting in money. Many of them were rich and gave much money. ⁴²A poor woman whose husband had died came by and gave two very small pieces of money. ⁴³Jesus called His followers to Him. He said, "For sure, I tell you, this poor woman whose husband has died has given more money than all the others. ⁴⁴They all gave of that which was more than they needed for their own living. She is poor and yet she gave all she had, even what she needed for her own living."

Jesus Tells Of The House Of God [Matthew 24:1-51; Luke 21:5-36]

13 Jesus went out of the house of God. One of His followers said to Him, "Teacher, look at the big stones and these great buildings!" ²Jesus said, "Do you see these great buildings? All these stones will be thrown down. Not one will be left standing on another."

Jesus Teaches On The Mount Of Olives

³Jesus sat down on the Mount of Olives at a place where He could see the house of God. Peter and James and John and Andrew came to Him. They asked without anyone else hearing, ⁴"Tell us when this will be. What are we to look for when these things are to happen?"

What To Look For Before Jesus Returns

⁵Jesus began to say to them, "Be careful that no one leads you the wrong way. ⁶Many people will come using My name. They will say, 'I am Christ.' They will turn many to the wrong way. ⁷When you hear of wars and much talk about wars, do not be surprised. These things have to happen. But the end is not yet. ⁸Nations will have wars with other nations. Countries will fight against countries. The earth will shake and break apart in different places. There will be no food for people. There will be much trouble. These things are the beginning of much sorrow and pain.

It Will Be Hard For Those Who Believe

⁹"Watch out for yourselves. They will take you to the courts. In the places of worship they will beat you. You will be taken in front of the leaders of the people and in front of kings because of Me. You will be there to tell them about Me. ¹⁰The Good News must first be preached to all the nations. ¹¹"When you are put into their hands, do not be afraid of what you are to say or how you are to say it. Whatever is given to you to say at that time, say it. It will not be you who speaks, but the Holy Spirit. ¹²A brother will hand over a brother to death. A father will hand over his son. Children will turn against their

parents and have them put to death. ¹³You will be hated by all people because of Me. But he who stays true to the end will be saved.

Days Of Trouble And Pain And Sorrow

¹⁴"You will see a very sinful man-made god standing in the house of God where it has no right to stand. Then those in the country of Judea should run to the mountains. It was spoken of by the early preacher Daniel. (Daniel 9:27; 12:11) The one who reads this should understand. ¹⁵He that is on the top of the house should not take the time to get anything out of his house. ¹⁶He that is in the field should not go back to get his coat. ¹⁷It will be hard for women who will soon be mothers. It will be hard for those feeding babies in those days! ¹⁸Pray that it will not be during the winter. ¹⁹In those days there will be much trouble and pain and sorrow. It has never been this bad from the beginning of time and never will be again. ²⁰If the Lord had not made those days short, no life would have been saved. Because of God's people whom He has chosen, He made the days short.

The False Religious Teachers

²¹"If anyone says to you, 'See! Here is the Christ,' or, 'There He is!' do not believe it. ²²Some will come who will say they are Christ. False preachers will come. These people will do special things for people to see. They will do surprising things, so that if it can be, God's people will be led to believe something wrong. ²³See! I have told you about these things before they happen.

Jesus Will Come Again In His Greatness

²⁴"After those days of much trouble and pain and sorrow are

over, the sun will get dark. The moon will not give light. 25The stars will fall from the sky. The powers in the heavens will be shaken. 26Then they will see the Son of Man coming in the clouds with great power and shining greatness. 27He will send His angels. They will gather together God's people from the four winds. They will come from one end of the earth to the other end of heaven.

28"Now learn something from the fig tree. When the branch begins to grow and puts out its leaves, you know summer is near. 29In the same way, when you see all these things happen, you know the Son of Man is near. He is even at the door. 30For sure, I tell you, the people of this day will not pass away before all these things have happened.

31"Heaven and earth will pass away, but My Words will not pass away. 32But no one knows the day or the hour. No! Not even the angels in heaven know. The Son does not know. Only the Father knows.

33"Be careful! Watch and pray. You do not know when it will happen. 34The coming of the Son of Man is as a man who went from his house to a far country. He gave each one of his servants some work to do. He told the one standing at the door to watch. 35In the same way, you are to watch also! You do not know when the Owner of the house will be coming. It may be in the evening or in the night or when the sun comes up or in the morning. 36He may come when you are not looking for Him and find you sleeping. 37What I say to you, I say to all. Watch!"

They Look For A Way To Put Jesus To Death [Matthew 26:1-5; Luke 22:1-6]

14 It was now two days before the supper of the special religious gathering to remember how the Jews left Egypt and the supper of bread without yeast. The religious leaders and the teachers of the Law tried to trap Jesus. They tried to take Him so they could put Him to death. 2These men said, "This must not happen on the day of the special supper. The people would be against it and make much trouble."

Mary Of Bethany Puts Special Perfume On Jesus [Matthew 26:6-13; John 12:1-11]

3Jesus was in the town of Bethany eating in the house of Simon. Simon was a man with a very bad skin disease. A woman came with a jar of special perfume. She had given much money for this. She broke the jar and poured the special perfume on the head of Jesus. 4Some of them were angry. They said, "Why was this special perfume wasted? 5This perfume could have been sold for much money and given to poor people." They spoke against her.

6Jesus said, "Let her alone. Why are you giving her trouble? She has done a good thing to Me. 7You will have poor people with you all the time. Whenever you want, you can do something good for them. You will not have Me all the time. 8She did what she could. She put this perfume on My body to make Me ready for the grave. 9For sure, I tell you, wherever this Good News is preached in all the world, this woman will be remembered for what she has done."

Judas Hands Jesus Over To Be Killed [Matthew 26:14-16]

10Judas Iscariot was one of the twelve followers. He went to the head religious leaders of the Jews to talk about how he might hand Jesus over to them. 11When the leaders heard it, they were glad. They promised to give Judas money. Then he looked for a way to hand Jesus over.

Getting Ready For The Special Supper [*Matthew 26:17-19; Luke 22:7-13*]

¹²The first day of the supper of bread without yeast was the day to kill an animal. It was for the special religious gathering to remember how the Jews left Egypt. His followers said to Jesus, "What place do You want us to make ready for You to eat this special supper?" ¹³Jesus sent two of His followers on ahead and said to them, "Go into the city. There a man will meet you carrying a jar of water. Follow him. ¹⁴He will go into a house. You say to the owner of the house, 'The Teacher asks, "Where is the room you keep for friends, where I can eat this special supper with My followers?" ' ¹⁵He will take you to a large room on the second floor with everything on it. Make it ready for us."

¹⁶The followers went from there and came into the city. They found everything as Jesus had said. They made things ready for the special supper.

¹⁷In the evening He came with the twelve followers. ¹⁸They sat at the table and ate. Jesus said, "For sure, I tell you, one of you will hand Me over to be killed. He is eating with Me." ¹⁹They were very sad. They said to Him one after the other, "Is it I?" ²⁰He said to them, "It is one of the twelve followers. It is the one who is putting his hand with mine into the same dish. ²¹The Son of Man is going away as it is written of Him. But it will be bad for that man who hands the Son of Man over to be killed! It would have been better if he had not been born!"

The First Lord's Supper [*Matthew 26:26-30; Luke 22:19-20*]

²²As they were eating, Jesus took a loaf of bread. He gave thanks and broke it in pieces. He gave it to them and said, "Take, eat, this is My body." ²³Then He took the cup and gave thanks. He gave it to them and they all drank from it. ²⁴He said to them, "This is My blood of the New Way of Worship which is given for many. ²⁵For sure, I tell you, that I will not drink of the fruit of the vine until that day when I drink it new in the holy nation of God." ²⁶After they sang a song, they went out to the Mount of Olives.

Jesus Tells How Peter Will Lie About Him [*Matthew 26:31-35; Luke 22:31-34; John 13:36-38*]

²⁷Jesus said to them, "All of you will be ashamed of Me and leave Me tonight. For it is written, 'I will kill the shepherd and the sheep of the flock will spread everywhere.' (Zechariah 13:7) ²⁸After I am raised from the dead, I will go before you into the country of Galilee." ²⁹Peter said to Him, "Even if all men are ashamed of You and leave You, I never will." ³⁰Jesus said to him, "For sure, I tell you, that today, even tonight, before a rooster crows two times, you will say three times you do not know Me." ³¹Peter spoke with strong words, "Even if I have to die with You, I will never say that I do not know You." All the followers said the same thing.

Jesus Prays In Gethsemane [*Matthew 26:36-46; Luke 22:39-46*]

³²They came to a place called Gethsemane. Jesus said to His followers, "You sit here while I pray." ³³He took Peter and James and John with Him. He began to have much sorrow and a heavy heart. ³⁴He said to them, "My soul is very sad. My soul is so full of sorrow I am ready to die. You stay here and watch." ³⁵He went a little farther and got down with His face on the ground. He prayed that this time of suffering might pass from Him if it could. ³⁶He said, "Father, You can do all things.

Take away what must happen to Me. Even so, not what I want, but what You want."

37Then Jesus came to the followers and found them sleeping. He said to Peter, "Simon, are you sleeping? Were you not able to watch one hour? 38Watch and pray so that you will not be tempted. Man's spirit wants to do this, but the body does not have the power to do it."

39Again Jesus went away and prayed saying the same words. 40He came back and found them sleeping again. Their eyes were heavy. They did not know what to say to Him. 41He came the third time and said to them, "Are you still sleeping and resting? It is enough! Listen, the time has come when the Son of Man will be handed over to sinners. 42Get up and let us go. See! The man who will hand Me over to the head religious leader is near."

Jesus Handed Over To Sinners [*Matthew 26:47-56; Luke 22:47-51; John 18:1-11*]

43At once, while Jesus was talking, Judas came. He was one of the twelve followers. He came with many other men who had swords and sticks. They came from the head religious leaders of the Jews and the teachers of the Law and the leaders of the people. 44The man who was going to hand Jesus over gave the men something to look for. He said, "The Man I kiss is the One. Take hold of Him and take Him away."

45At once Judas went straight to Jesus and said, "Teacher!" and kissed Him. 46Then they put their hands on Him and took Him.

47One of the followers of Jesus who stood watching took his sword. He hit the workman owned by the head religious leader and cut off his ear. 48Jesus said to them, "Have you come with swords and sticks to take Me as if I were a robber? 49I have been with you every day teaching in the house of God. You never took hold of Me. But this has happened as the Holy Writings said it would happen." 50Then all His followers left Him and ran away.

51A young man was following Him with only a piece of cloth around his body. They put their hands on the young man. 52Leaving the cloth behind, he ran away with no clothes on.

Jesus Stands In Front Of The Head Religious Leaders [*Matthew 26:57-58; Luke 22:52-54; John 18:19-24*]

53They led Jesus away to the head religious leader. All the religious leaders and other leaders and the teachers of the Law were gathered there. 54But Peter followed a long way behind as they went to the house of the head religious leader. He sat with the helpers and got warm by the fire.

Jesus Stands In Front Of The Court [*Matthew 26:59-68*]

55The religious leaders and all the court were looking for something against Jesus. They wanted to find something so they could kill Him. But they could find nothing. 56Many came and told false things about Him, but their words did not agree. 57Some got up and said false things against Him. They said, 58"We have heard Him say, 'I will destroy the house of God that was made with hands. In three days I will build another that is not made with hands.'" 59Even these who spoke against Him were not able to agree.

60The head religious leader stood up in front of the people. He asked Jesus, "Have You nothing to say? What about the things these men are saying against You?" 61Jesus said nothing. Again the head religious leader asked Him, "Are You the Christ, the Son of the Holy One?" 62Jesus said, "I am! And you will see the Son of Man seated on the right side of the All-powerful God. You will see Him coming again in the clouds of the sky."

63Then the head religious leader tore his clothes apart. He said, "Do we need other people to speak against Him? 64You have heard Him speak as if He were God! What do you think?" They all said He was guilty of death. 65Some began to spit on Him. They covered Jesus' face, and they hit Him. They said, "Tell us what is going to happen." Soldiers hit Him with their hands.

Peter Said He Did Not Know Jesus

66Peter was outside in the yard. One of the servant-girls of the head religious leader came. 67She saw Peter getting warm. She looked at him and said, "You were with Jesus of Nazareth." 68Peter lied, saying, "I do not know Jesus and do not understand what you are talking about." As he went out, a rooster crowed.

69The servant-girl saw him again. She said to the people standing around, "This man is one of them." 70He lied again saying that he did not know Jesus. Later, those who stood around said to Peter again, "For sure you are one of them. You are from the country of Galilee. You talk like they do." 71He began to say strong words and to swear. He said, "I do not know the Man you are talking about!"

72At once a rooster crowed the second time. Peter remembered what Jesus had said to him, "Before a rooster crows two times, you will say three times you do not know Me." When he thought about it, he cried.

Jesus Before Pilate [Matthew 27:1-2, 11-14; Luke 23:1-5; John 18:28-37]

15 Early in the morning the head religious leaders of the Jews and other leaders and the teachers of the Law and all the court gathered together to talk about Jesus. Then they tied up Jesus and led Him away. They handed Him over to Pilate. 2Pilate asked Jesus, "Are You the King of the Jews?" He said to Pilate, "What you say is true."

3The religious leaders spoke many things against Him. Jesus did not say a word. 4Pilate asked Him again, "Have You nothing to say? Listen to the things they are saying against You!" 5Jesus did not say a word. Pilate was much surprised and wondered about it.

Jesus Or Barabbas Is To Go Free [Matthew 27:15-26; Luke 23:17-25; John 18:38-40]

6Each year at the special supper Pilate would let one person who was in prison go free. It would be the one the people asked for. 7The name of one of those in prison was Barabbas. He, together with others, had killed people while working against the leaders of the country. 8All the people went to Pilate and asked him to do as he had done before. 9Pilate said, "Do you want me to let the King of the Jews go free?" 10He knew the religious leaders had handed Jesus over to him because they were jealous. 11The religious leaders talked the people into thinking that Pilate should let Barabbas go free. 12Pilate said to them again, "What do you want me to do with the Man you call the King of the Jews?" 13They spoke with loud voices again, "Nail Him to a cross." 14Then Pilate said to them, "Why? What bad thing has He done?" They spoke with loud voices all the more, "Nail Him to a cross!"

The Crown Of Thorns [Matthew 27:27-32; John 19:1-5]

15Pilate wanted to please the people. He gave Barabbas to them and had Jesus beaten. Then he handed Him over to be nailed to a cross. [16]The soldiers led Jesus away to a large room in the court. They called all the soldiers together. [17]The soldiers put a purple coat on Him. They put a crown of thorns on His head, [18]and said to Him, "Hello, King of the Jews!" [19]They hit Him on the head with a stick and spit on Him. They got down on their knees and worshiped Him. [20]After they had made fun of Him, they took the purple coat off of Him and put His own clothes back on Him. Then they led Him away to be nailed to a cross.

[21]They came to a man called Simon who was coming from the country of Cyrene. He was the father of Alexander and Rufus. They made Simon carry the cross of Jesus.

Jesus On The Cross [Matthew 27:33-37; Luke 23:26-38; John 19:17-22]

[22]They led Jesus to a place called Golgotha. This name means the place of the skull. [23]They gave Him wine with something in it to take away the pain, but He would not drink it. [24]When they had nailed Jesus to the cross, they divided His clothes by drawing names to see what each man should take. [25]It was about nine o'clock in the morning when they nailed Him to the cross. [26]Over Jesus' head they put in writing what they had against Him, THE KING OF THE JEWS.

The Two Robbers [Matthew 27:38-44; Luke 23:39-43]

[27]They nailed two robbers on crosses beside Jesus. One was on His right side and the other was on His left side. [28]*It happened as the Holy Writings said it would happen, "They thought of Him as One Who broke the Law." (Isaiah 53:12) [29]Those who walked by shook their heads and laughed at Jesus. They said, "You were the One Who could destroy the house of God and build it again in three days. [30]Save Yourself and come down from the cross." [31]The head religious leaders and the teachers of the Law made fun of Him also. They said to each other, "He saved others but He cannot save Himself. [32]Let Christ, the King of the Jews, come down from the cross. We want to see it and then we will believe." Those who were on the crosses beside Jesus spoke bad things to Him.

The Death Of Jesus [Matthew 27:45-50; Luke 23:44-49; John 19:28-37]

[33]From noon until three o'clock it was dark over all the land. [34]At three o'clock Jesus cried with a loud voice, "My God, My God, why have You left Me alone?"

[35]When some of those who stood by heard that, they said, "Listen! He is calling for Elijah." [36]One of them ran and took a sponge and filled it with sour wine. He put it on a stick and gave it to Him to drink. He said, "Let Him alone. Let us see if Elijah will come and take Him down."

The Powerful Works At The Time Of His Death [Matthew 27:51-54]

[37]Then Jesus gave a loud cry. He gave up His spirit and died. [38]The curtain in the house of God was torn in two from top to bottom.

[39]The captain of the soldiers was looking at Jesus when He cried out. He saw Him die and said, "For sure, this Man was the Son of God."

The Women At The Cross [Matthew 27:55-56; John 19:25-27]

[40]Women were looking on from far away. Among them was Mary Magdalene and Mary the mother of the younger James and of Joses, and Salome. [41]These cared for Him when He was in the country of Galilee. There were many other women there who had followed Him to Jerusalem.

The Grave Of Jesus [Matthew 27:57-66; Luke 23:50-56; John 19:38-42]

⁴²It was the day to get ready for the Day of Rest and it was now evening. ⁴³Joseph, who was from the city of Arimathea, was an important man in the court. He was looking for the holy nation of God. Without being afraid, he went to Pilate and asked for the body of Jesus. ⁴⁴Pilate was surprised and wondered if Jesus was dead so soon. He called the captain of the soldiers and asked if Jesus was already dead. ⁴⁵After the captain said that Jesus was dead, Pilate let Joseph take the body. ⁴⁶Joseph took the body of Jesus down from the cross. He put the linen cloth he had bought around the body. Then he laid the body in a grave which had been cut out in the side of a rock. He pushed a stone over to cover the door of the grave. ⁴⁷Mary Magdalene and Mary the mother of Joses saw where He was laid.

Jesus Is Raised From The Dead [Matthew 28:1-10; Luke 24:1-12; John 20:1-18]

16 The Day of Rest was over. Mary Magdalene and Mary the mother of James, and Salome bought spices. They wanted to put the spices on Jesus' body. ²Very early in the morning on the first day of the week, they came to the grave. The sun had come up. ³They said to themselves, "Who will roll the stone away from the door of the grave for us?" ⁴But when they looked, they saw the very large stone had been rolled away.

⁵They went into the grave. There they saw a young man with a long white coat sitting on the right side. They were afraid. ⁶He said, "Do not be afraid. You are looking for Jesus of Nazareth Who was nailed to a cross. He is risen! He is not here! See, here is the place where they laid Him. ⁷Go and tell His followers and Peter

that He is going ahead of you into Galilee. You will see Him there as He told you." ⁸They ran from the grave shaking and were surprised. They did not say anything to anyone because they were afraid.

The Followers Of Jesus Do Not Believe He Was Raised From The Dead [Luke 24:13-43; John 20:24-29]

⁹(*It was early on the first day of the week when Jesus was raised from the dead. Mary Magdalene saw Him first. He had put seven demons out of her. ¹⁰She went and told His followers. They were crying because of much sorrow. ¹¹But they did not believe her when she said she had seen Him alive.

¹²After that He was seen again by two of His followers as they walked into the country. He did not look like He had looked before to these two people. ¹³They went and told it to the others. The others did not believe them.

¹⁴Later He was seen by the eleven followers as they were eating. He spoke to them with sharp words because they did not believe and their hearts were hard. And they did not believe the others who had seen Him since He had been raised from the dead.

Jesus Sends His Followers To Preach [Matthew 28:16-20; Luke 24:44-49; John 20:21-23]

¹⁵He said to them, "You are to go to all the world and preach the Good News to every person. ¹⁶He who puts his trust in Me and is baptized will be saved from the punishment of sin. But he who does not put his trust in Me is guilty and will be punished forever. ¹⁷These special powerful works will be done by those who have put their trust in Me. In My name they will put out demons. They will speak with languages they have never learned. ¹⁸They will pick up

snakes. If they drink any poison, it will not hurt them. They will put their hands on the sick and they will be healed."

¹⁹After Jesus had talked to them, He was taken up into heaven. He sat down on the right side of God.

²⁰The followers went from there and preached everywhere. The Lord worked with them. The Lord showed that the Word of God was true by the special works they had power to do.)

LUKE

Luke Writes To Theophilus

1 Many people have written about the things that have happened among us. ²Those who saw everything from the first and helped teach the Good News have passed these things on to us. ³Dear Theophilus, I have looked with care into these things from the beginning. I have decided it would be good to write them to you one after the other the way they happened. ⁴Then you can be sure you know the truth about the things you have been taught.

An Angel Tells Of The Birth Of John The Baptist

⁵When Herod was king of the country of Judea, there was a Jewish religious leader named Zacharias. He worked for Abijah. His wife was of the family group of Aaron. Her name was Elizabeth. ⁶They were right with God and obeyed the Jewish Law and did what the Lord said to do. ⁷They had no children because Elizabeth was not able to have a child. Both of them were older people.

⁸Zacharias was doing his work as a religious leader for God. ⁹The religious leaders were given certain kinds of work to do. Zacharias was chosen to go to the house of God to burn special perfume. ¹⁰Many people stood outside praying during the time the special perfume was burning.

¹¹Zacharias saw an angel of the Lord standing on the right side of the altar where the special perfume was burning. ¹²When he saw the angel, Zacharias was troubled and afraid. ¹³The angel said to him, "Zacharias, do not be afraid. Your prayer has been heard. Your wife Elizabeth will give birth to a son. You are to name him John. ¹⁴You will be glad and have much joy. Many people will be happy because he is born. ¹⁵He will be great in the sight of the Lord and will never drink wine or any strong drink. Even from his birth, he will be filled with the Holy Spirit. ¹⁶Many of the Jews will be turned to the Lord their God by him. ¹⁷He will be the one to go in the spirit and power of Elijah before Christ comes. He will turn the hearts of the fathers back to their children. He will teach those who do not obey to be right with God. He will get people ready for the Lord." (Malachi 4:5-6)

Zacharias Does Not Believe The Angel

¹⁸Zacharias said to the angel, "How can I know this for sure? I am

old and my wife is old also." [19]The angel said to him, "My name is Gabriel. I stand near God. He sent me to talk to you and bring to you this good news. [20]See! You will not be able to talk until the day this happens. It is because you did not believe my words. What I said will happen at the right time."

[21]The people outside were waiting. They were surprised and wondered why Zacharias stayed so long in the house of God. [22]When he came out, he could not talk to them. They knew he had seen something special from God while he was in the house of God. He tried to talk to them with his hands but could say nothing. [23]When his days of working in the house of God were over, he went to his home.

The Lord Did What He Promised

[24]Some time later Elizabeth knew she was to become a mother. She kept herself hidden for five months. She said, [25]"This is what the Lord has done for me. He has looked on me and has taken away my shame from among men."

Gabriel Speaks To Mary

[26]Six months after Elizabeth knew she was to become a mother, Gabriel was sent from God to Nazareth. Nazareth was a town in the country of Galilee. [27]He went to a woman who had never had a man. Her name was Mary. She was promised in marriage to a man named Joseph. Joseph was of the family of David. [28]The angel came to her and said, "You are honored very much. You are a favored woman. The Lord is with you. *You are chosen from among many women."

[29]When she saw the angel, she was troubled at his words. She thought about what had been said. [30]The angel said to her, "Mary, do not be afraid. You have found favor with God. [31]See! You are to become a mother and have a Son. You are to give Him the name Jesus. [32]He will be great. He will be called the Son of the Most High. The Lord God will give Him the place where His early father David sat. [33]He will be King over the family of Jacob forever and His nation will have no end."

[34]Mary said to the angel, "How can this happen? I have never had a man." [35]The angel said to her, "The Holy Spirit will come on you. The power of the Most High will cover you. The holy Child you give birth to will be called the Son of God.

[36]"See, your cousin Elizabeth, as old as she is, is going to give birth to a child. She was not able to have children before, but now she is in her sixth month. [37]For God can do all things." [38]Then Mary said, "I am willing to be used of the Lord. Let it happen to me as you have said." Then the angel went away from her.

Mary Visits Elizabeth

[39]At once Mary went from there to a town in the hill country of Judea. [40]She went to the house of Zacharias to see Elizabeth. [41]When Elizabeth heard Mary speak, the baby moved in her body. At the same time Elizabeth was filled with the Holy Spirit. [42]Elizabeth spoke in a loud voice, "You are honored among women! Your Child is honored! [43]Why has this happened to me? Why has the mother of my Lord come to me? [44]As soon as I heard your voice, the baby in my body moved for joy. [45]You are happy because you believed. Everything will happen as the Lord told you it would happen."

Mary's Song Of Thanks

[46]Then Mary said, "My heart sings with thanks for my Lord. [47]And my spirit is happy in God, the One Who saves from the punishment of sin. [48]The Lord has looked on me, the one

He owns and the one who is not important. But from now on all people will honor me. ⁴⁹He Who is powerful has done great things for me. His name is holy. ⁵⁰The loving-pity of the Lord is given to the people of all times who honor Him. ⁵¹He has done powerful works with His arm. He has divided from each other those who have pride in their hearts. ⁵²He has taken kings down from their thrones. He has put those who are in a place that is not important to a place that is important. ⁵³He has filled those who are hungry with good things. He has sent the rich people away with nothing. ⁵⁴He has helped the Jews who are the people He owns. This was done to remember His loving-pity. ⁵⁵He promised He would do this to our early fathers and to Abraham and to his family forever." ⁵⁶Mary stayed with Elizabeth about three months. Then she went to her own home.

The Birth Of John The Baptist

⁵⁷When the time came, Elizabeth gave birth to a son. ⁵⁸Her neighbors and family heard how the Lord had shown loving-pity to her. They were happy for her. ⁵⁹On the eighth day they did the religious act of the Jews on the child. They named him Zacharias, after his father. ⁶⁰But his mother said, "No! His name is John." ⁶¹They said to her, "No one in your family has that name."

⁶²Then they talked to his father with their hands to find out what he would name the child. ⁶³He asked for something to write on. He wrote, "His name is John." They were all surprised and wondered about it. ⁶⁴Zacharias was able to talk from that time on and he gave thanks to God.

⁶⁵All those who lived near them were afraid. The news of what had happened was told through all the hill country of Judea. ⁶⁶And all who heard those words remembered them

and said, "What is this child going to be?" For the hand of the Lord was on him.

Zacharias' Song Of Thanks To God

⁶⁷Zacharias, the father of John, was filled with the Holy Spirit. He told what was going to happen, saying, ⁶⁸"Let us thank the Lord God of the Jews. He has bought His people and made them free. ⁶⁹He has raised up One from the family of David Who saves people from the punishment of their sins. ⁷⁰His holy early preachers told us this long ago. ⁷¹God told us that we should be saved from those who hate us and from all those who work against us. ⁷²He would show loving-pity to our early fathers. He would remember His holy promise. ⁷³God promised this to our early father Abraham. ⁷⁴He promised that we would be saved from those who hate us and that we might worship Him without being afraid. ⁷⁵We can be holy and right with God all the days of our life.

⁷⁶"And you, my son, will be the one who speaks for the Most High. For you will go before the Lord to make the way ready for Him. ⁷⁷You will tell His people how to be saved from the punishment of sin by being forgiven of their sins. ⁷⁸Because the heart of our God is full of loving-pity for us, a light from heaven will shine on us. ⁷⁹It will give light to those who live in darkness and are under the shadow of death. It will lead our feet in the way of peace."

⁸⁰The child grew and became strong in spirit. He lived in a desert until the day he started to preach to the Jews.

The Birth Of Jesus [Matthew 1:18-25]

2 In those days Caesar Augustus sent out word that the name of every person in the Roman nation must be written in the books of the nation. [2]This first writing took place while Quirinius was leader of Syria.

[3]So all the people went to their own cities to have their names written in the books of the nation. [4]Joseph went up from the town of Nazareth in the country of Galilee to the town of Bethlehem. It was known as the city of David. He went there because he was from the family of David. [5]Joseph went to have his and Mary's names written in the books of the nation. Mary was his promised wife and soon to become a mother.

[6]While they were there in Bethlehem, the time came for Mary to give birth to her baby. [7]Her first son was born. She put cloth around Him and laid Him in a place where cattle are fed. There was no room for them in the place where people stay for the night.

The Shepherds Learn Of The Birth Of Jesus

[8]In the same country there were shepherds in the fields. They were watching their flocks of sheep at night. [9]The angel of the Lord came to them. The shining greatness of the Lord shone around them. They were very much afraid. [10]The angel said to them, "Do not be afraid. See! I bring you good news of great joy which is for all people. [11]Today, One Who saves from the punishment of sin has been born in the city of David. He is Christ the Lord. [12]There will be something special for you to see. This is the way you will know Him. You will find the Baby with cloth around Him, lying in a place where cattle are fed."

[13]At once many angels from heaven were seen, along with the angel, giving thanks to God. They were saying, [14]"Greatness and honor to our God in the highest heaven and peace on earth among men who please Him."

The Shepherds Go To Bethlehem

[15]The angels went from the shepherds back to heaven. The shepherds said to each other, "Let us go to Bethlehem and see what has happened. The Lord has told us about this." [16]They went fast and found Mary and Joseph. They found the Baby lying in a place where cattle are fed. [17]When they saw the Child, they told what the angel said about Him. [18]All who heard it were surprised at what the shepherds told them. [19]But Mary hid all these words in her heart. She thought about them much. [20]The shepherds went back full of joy. They thanked God for all they had heard and seen. It happened as the angel had told them.

Jesus Taken To The House Of God

[21]When eight days were over, they did the religious act of the Jews on the Child. He was named Jesus. This name was given to Him by the angel when Mary was told He was to be born. [22]When the days were over for her to be made pure as it was written in the Law of Moses, they took Jesus to Jerusalem to give Him to the Lord. [23]It is written in the Law of the Lord, "The first boy child born of a woman will be called holy to the Lord." [24]They were to give a gift of two doves or two young birds on the altar in worship to the Lord. This was written in the Law of the Lord.

Simeon's Song Of Thanks

[25]There was a man in Jerusalem by the name of Simeon. He was a good man and very religious. He was looking for the time when the Jewish nation would be saved. The Holy Spirit was on him. [26]The Holy Spirit made it known to Simeon that he would not die before he had seen God's Chosen One. [27]He came to the

house of God being led by the Holy Spirit. The parents took Jesus to the house of God. They came to do what the Law said must be done. 28Then Simeon took Jesus in his arms. He gave honor to Him and thanked God, saying,

29"Lord, now let me die in peace, as You have said. 30My eyes have seen the One Who will save men from the punishment of their sins. 31You have made Him ready in the sight of all nations. 32He will be a light to shine on the people who are not Jews. He will be the shining greatness of Your people the Jews." 33Joseph and the mother of Jesus were surprised and wondered about these words which were said about Jesus. 34Simeon honored them and said to Mary the mother of Jesus, "See! This Child will make many people fall and many people rise in the Jewish nation. He will be spoken against. 35A sword will cut through your soul. By this the thoughts of many hearts will be understood."

Anna Gives Thanks For Jesus

36Anna was a woman who spoke God's Word. She was the daughter of Phanuel of the family group of Asher. Anna was many years old. She had lived with her husband seven years after she was married. 37Her husband had died and she had lived without a husband eighty-four years. Yet she did not go away from the house of God. She worked for God day and night, praying and going without food so she could pray better. 38At that time she came and gave thanks to God. She told the people in Jerusalem about Jesus. They were looking for the One to save them from the punishment of their sins and to set them free.

They Return To Nazareth [Matthew 2:19-23]

39When Joseph and Mary had done everything the Law said to do, they went back to Nazareth in Galilee. 40The Child grew and became strong in spirit. He was filled with wisdom and the loving-favor of God was on Him.

41His parents went to Jerusalem every year for the special religious gathering to remember how the Jews left Egypt. 42When He was twelve years old, they went up to Jerusalem as they had done before. 43When the days of the special supper were over, they started back to their town. But the boy Jesus was still in Jerusalem. His parents did not know it. 44They thought Jesus was with the others of the group. They walked for one day. Then they looked for Him among their family and friends.

45When they could not find Jesus, they turned back to Jerusalem to look for Him. 46Three days later they found Him in the house of God. He was sitting among the teachers. He was hearing what they said and asking questions. 47All those who heard Him were surprised and wondered about His understanding and at what He said. 48When His parents saw Him, they were surprised. His mother said to Him, "My Son, why have You done this to us? See! Your father and I have had much sorrow looking for You." 49He said to them, "Why were you looking for Me? Do you not know that I must be in My Father's house?" 50They did not understand the things He said to them.

51He went with them to Nazareth and obeyed them. But His mother kept all these words in her heart. 52Jesus grew strong in mind and body. He grew in favor with God and men.

John The Baptist Makes The Way Ready For Jesus [Matthew 3:1-12; Mark 1:1-8; John 1:15-28]

3 Tiberius Caesar had been leader for fifteen years. Pontius Pilate was leader of the country of

Judea. Herod was the leader of the country of Galilee. His brother Philip was the leader of the countries of Ituraea and Trachonitis. Lysanias was the leader of the country of Abilene. [2]Annas and Caiaphas were the head religious leaders.

The Word of God came to John the Baptist, the son of Zacharias. John was in the desert. [3]He went into all the country around the Jordan River. He preached that people should be baptized because they were sorry for their sins and had turned from them, and they would be forgiven. [4]The early preacher Isaiah wrote these words: "His voice calls out in the desert. 'Make the way ready for the Lord. Make the road straight for Him! [5]Every valley will be filled and every mountain and hill will be brought down. The turns in the road will be made straight and the rough places will be made smooth. [6]And all men will see God saving people from the punishment of their sins.' " (Isaiah 40:3-5)

[7]John said to the people who came to be baptized by him, "You family of snakes! Who told you how to keep from the anger of God that is coming? [8]Do something to let me see that you have turned from your sins. Do not begin to say to yourselves, 'We have Abraham as our father.' I tell you, God can make children for Abraham out of these stones. [9]Even now the ax is on the root of the trees. Every tree that does not give good fruit is cut down and thrown into the fire." [10]The people asked him, "Then what should we do?" [11]He answered them, "If you have two coats, give one to him who has none. If you have food, you must share some."

[12]Tax gatherers came to be baptized also. They asked him, "Teacher, what are we to do?" [13]He said to them, "Do not take more money from people than you should." [14]Also soldiers asked him, "What are we to do?" He answered them, "Take no money from anyone by using your own strength. Do not lie about anyone. Be happy with the pay you get."

[15]The people were looking for something to happen. They were thinking in their hearts about John the Baptist. They wondered if he might be the Christ. [16]But John said to all of them, "I baptize you with water. There is One coming Who is greater than I. I am not good enough to get down and help Him take off His shoes. He will baptize you with the Holy Spirit and with fire. [17]He comes ready to clean the grain. He will gather the grain and clean it all. He will put the clean grain into a building. But He will burn that which is no good with a fire that cannot be put out."

John The Baptist Is Put In Prison
[Matthew 14:1-5; Mark 6:14-20]

[18]John spoke much more as he preached the Good News to the people. [19]He had also spoken sharp words to Herod the leader because of Herodias. She was his brother Philip's wife. And John spoke to Herod about all the wrongs he had done. [20]To all these, Herod added another sin by putting John in prison.

The Baptism Of Jesus [Matthew 3:13-17; Mark 1:9-11; John 1:29-34]

[21]When all the people were being baptized, Jesus was baptized also. As He prayed, the heaven opened. [22]The Holy Spirit came down on Him in a body like a dove. A voice came from heaven and said, "You are My much-loved Son. I am very happy with You."

The Family Of Jesus Through Mary
[Matthew 1:1-17]

[23]Jesus was about thirty years old when He began His work. People thought Jesus was the son of Joseph, the son of Heli. [24]Heli was the son of

Matthat. Matthat was the son of Levi. Levi was the son of Melchi. Melchi was the son of Jannai. Jannai was the son of Joseph. ²⁵Joseph was the son of Mattathias. Mattathias was the son of Amos. Amos was the son of Nahum. Nahum was the son of Esli. Esli was the son of Naggai. ²⁶Naggai was the son of Maath. Maath was the son of Mattathias. Mattathias was the son of Semein. Semein was the son of Joseck. Joseck was the son of Juda. ²⁷Juda was the son of Johanan. Johanan was the son of Rhesa. Rhesa was the son of Zerubbabel. Zerubbabel was the son of Salathiel. Salathiel was the son of Neri. ²⁸Neri was the son of Melchi. Melchi was the son of Addi. Addi was the son of Cosam. Cosam was the son of Elmadam. Elmadam was the son of Er. ²⁹Er was the son of Joshua. Joshua was the son of Eliezer. Eliezer was the son of Jorim. Jorim was the son of Matthat. Matthat was the son of Levi. ³⁰Levi was the son of Simeon. Simeon was the son of Judah. Judah was the son of Joseph. Joseph was the son of Janam. Janam was the son of Eliakim. ³¹Eliakim was the son of Melea. Melea was the son of Menna. Menna was the son of Mattatha. Mattatha was the son of Nathan. Nathan was the son of David. ³²David was the son of Jesse. Jesse was the son of Obed. Obed was the son of Boaz. Boaz was the son of Salmon. Salmon was the son of Nahshon. ³³Nahshon was the son of Amminadab. Amminadab was the son of Admin. Admin was the son of Hezron. Hezron was the son of Perez. Perez was the son of Judah. ³⁴Judah was the son of Jacob. Jacob was the son of Isaac. Isaac was the son of Abraham. Abraham was the son of Terah. Terah was the son of Nahor. ³⁵Nahor was the son of Serug. Serug was the son of Ragau. Ragau was the son of Peleg. Peleg was the son of Eber. Eber was the son of Shelah. ³⁶Shelah was the son of Cainan. Cainan was the son of

Arphaxad. Arphaxad was the son of Shem. Shem was the son of Noah. Noah was the son of Lamech. ³⁷Lamech was the son of Methuselah. Methuselah was the son of Enoch. Enoch was the son of Jared. Jared was the son of Mahalaleel. Mahalaleel was the son of Cainan. ³⁸Cainan was the son of Enos. Enos was the son of Seth. Seth was the son of Adam. Adam was the son of God.

Jesus Was Tempted [Matthew 4:1-11; Mark 1:12-13]

4 Jesus was full of the Holy Spirit when He returned from the Jordan River. Then He was led by the Holy Spirit to a desert. ²He was tempted by the devil for forty days and He ate nothing during that time. After that He was hungry. ³The devil said to Him, "If You are the Son of God, tell this stone to be made into bread." ⁴Jesus said to him, "It is written, 'Man is not to live by bread alone.' " (Deuteronomy 8:3) ⁵The devil took Jesus up on a high mountain. He had Jesus look at all the nations of the world at one time. ⁶The devil said to Jesus, "I will give You all this power and greatness. It has been given to me. I can give it to anyone I want to. ⁷If You will worship me, all this will be Yours." ⁸Jesus said to the devil, "Get behind Me, Satan! For it is written, 'You must worship the Lord your God. You must obey Him only.' " (Deuteronomy 6:13) ⁹Then the devil took Jesus up to Jerusalem. He had Jesus stand on the highest part of the house of God. The devil said to Jesus, "If You are the Son of God, throw Yourself down from here. ¹⁰For it is written, 'He has told His angels to care for You and to keep You. ¹¹In their hands they will hold You up. Then Your foot will not hit against a stone.' " (Psalm 91:11-12) ¹²Jesus said to the devil, "It is written, 'You must not tempt the Lord your God.' " (Deuteronomy 6:16) ¹³When the devil finished tempting Jesus in every way, he went away from Jesus for awhile.

Jesus Preaches In Galilee [Matthew 4:12-17; Mark 1:14-15]

¹⁴Jesus went back to Galilee in the power of the Holy Spirit. People talked about Him so much that He was well-known through all the country. ¹⁵Jesus taught in their places of worship and was honored by all people.

In Nazareth They Do Not Believe In Jesus

¹⁶Jesus came to Nazareth where He had grown up. As He had done before, He went into the Jewish place of worship on the Day of Rest. Then He stood up to read. ¹⁷Someone handed Him the book of the early preacher Isaiah. He opened it and found the place where it was written, ¹⁸"The Spirit of the Lord is on Me. He has put His hand on Me to preach the Good News to poor people. He has sent Me to heal those with a sad heart. He has sent Me to tell those who are being held that they can go free. He has sent Me to make the blind to see and to free those who are held because of trouble. ¹⁹He sent Me to tell of the time when men can receive favor with the Lord." (Isaiah 61:1-2)

²⁰Jesus closed the book. Then He gave it back to the leader and sat down. All those in the Jewish place of worship kept their eyes on Him. ²¹Then He began to say to them, "The Holy Writings you have just heard have been completed today."

²²They all spoke well of Jesus and agreed with the words He spoke. They said, "Is not this the son of Joseph?" ²³He said to them, "I wonder if you will tell this old saying to Me, 'Doctor, heal Yourself. What You did in the city of Capernaum, do

in Your own country!' " ²⁴He said, "A man who speaks for God is not respected in his own country. ²⁵It is true that there were many women whose husbands had died in the Jewish land when Elijah lived. For three and a half years there was no rain and there was very little food in the land. ²⁶Elijah was sent to none of them, but he was sent to a woman in the city of Zarephath in the land of Sidon. This woman's husband had died. ²⁷There were many people in the Jewish land who had a bad skin disease when the early preacher Elisha lived. None of them was healed. But Naaman from the country of Syria was healed."

²⁸All those in the Jewish place of worship were angry when they heard His words. ²⁹They got up and took Jesus out of town to the top of a high hill. They wanted to throw Him over the side. ³⁰But Jesus got away from among them and went on His way.

Jesus Heals A Man With A Demon [Mark 1:21-28]

³¹Jesus went down to Capernaum in Galilee. He taught them on the Days of Rest. ³²The people were surprised and wondered about His teaching. His words had power. ³³A man in the Jewish place of worship had a demon. He cried with a loud voice, ³⁴"What do You want of us, Jesus of Nazareth? I know Who You are. You are the Holy One of God." ³⁵Jesus spoke sharp words to the demon and said, "Do not talk! Come out of him!" When the demon had thrown the man down, he came out without hurting the man.

³⁶The people were all surprised. They asked each other, "What kind of word is this? He speaks to the demons with power and they come out!" ³⁷The news about Jesus went through all the country.

Peter's Mother-in-law Healed [Matthew 8:14-15; Mark 1:29-31]

38Jesus went away from the Jewish place of worship and went into Simon's house. Simon's mother-in-law was in bed, very sick. They asked Jesus to help her. 39He stood by her and told the disease to leave. It went from her. At once she got up and cared for them.

Jesus Heals In Galilee [Matthew 8:16-17; Mark 1:32-34]

40As the sun went down, the people took all that were sick with many kinds of disease to Jesus. He put His hands on all of them and they were healed. 41Also demons came out of many people. The demons cried out and said, "You are Christ, the Son of God." Jesus spoke strong words to them and would not let them speak. They knew He was the Christ.

Jesus Keeps On Preaching In Galilee [Matthew 4:23-25; Mark 1:35-39]

42In the morning He went out to a desert. The people looked for Him. When they found Him, they were trying to keep Him from going away from them. 43He said to them, "I must preach about the holy nation of God in other cities also. This is why I was sent." 44And He kept on preaching in the Jewish places of worship in Galilee.

Jesus Calls Simon And James And John [Matthew 4:18-22; Mark 1:16-20]

5 While Jesus was standing by the lake of Gennesaret, many people pushed to get near Him. They wanted to hear the Word of God. 2Jesus saw two boats on the shore.

The fishermen were not there because they were washing their nets. 3Jesus got into a boat which belonged to Simon. Jesus asked him to push it out a little way from land. Then He sat down and taught the people from the boat.

4When He had finished speaking, He said to Simon, "Push out into the deep water. Let down your nets for some fish." 5Simon said to Him, "Teacher, we have worked all night and we have caught nothing. But because You told me to, I will let the net down." 6When they had done this, they caught so many fish, their net started to break. 7They called to their friends working in the other boat to come and help them. They came and both boats were so full of fish they began to sink. 8When Simon Peter saw it, he got down at the feet of Jesus. He said, "Go away from me, Lord, because I am a sinful man." 9He and all those with him were surprised and wondered about the many fish. 10James and John, the sons of Zebedee, were surprised also. They were working together with Simon. Then Jesus said to Simon, "Do not be afraid. From now on you will fish for men." 11When they came to land with their boats, they left everything and followed Jesus.

Jesus Heals A Man With A Bad Skin Disease [Matthew 8:1-4; Mark 1:40-45]

12While Jesus was in one of the towns, a man came to Him with a bad skin disease over all his body. When he saw Jesus, he got down on his face before Him. He begged Him, saying, "Lord, if You are willing, You can heal me." 13Jesus put His hand on him and said, "I will, be healed." At once the disease went away from him. 14Then Jesus told him to tell no one. He said, "Go and let the religious leader of the Jews see you. Give the gift on the altar in worship that Moses told you to give when a man is healed of a disease. This will show the leaders you have been healed." [15] The news about Jesus went out all the more. Many people came to hear Him and to be healed of their diseases. [16] Then He went away by Himself to pray in a desert.

Jesus Heals A Man Let Down Through The Roof Of A House

[17] On one of the days while Jesus was teaching, some proud religious law-keepers and teachers of the Law were sitting by Him. They had come from every town in the countries of Galilee and Judea and from Jerusalem. The power of the Lord was there to heal them. [18] Some men took a man who was not able to move his body to Jesus. He was carried on a bed. They looked for a way to take the man into the house where Jesus was. [19] But they could not find a way to take him in because of so many people. They made a hole in the roof over where Jesus stood. Then they let the bed with the sick man on it down before Jesus. [20] When Jesus saw their faith, He said to the man, "Friend, your sins are forgiven."

[21] The teachers of the Law and the proud religious law-keepers thought to themselves, "Who is this Man Who speaks as if He is God? Who can forgive sins but God only?" [22] Jesus knew what they were thinking. He said to them, "Why do you think this way in your hearts? [23] Which is easier to say, 'Your sins are forgiven,' or, 'Get up and walk'?

[24] "So that you may know the Son of Man has the right and the power on earth to forgive sins," He said to the man who could not move his body, "I say to you, get up. Take your bed and go to your home." [25] At once the sick man got up in front of them. He took his bed and went to his home thanking God. [26] All those who were there were surprised and gave thanks to God, saying, "We have seen very special things today."

Jesus Calls Matthew [Matthew 9:9-13; Mark 2:13-17]

[27] After this Jesus went out and saw a man who gathered taxes. His name was Levi (Matthew). Levi was sitting at his work. Jesus said to him, "Follow Me." [28] Levi got up, left everything and followed Jesus. [29] Levi made a big supper for Jesus in his house. Many men who gathered taxes and other people sat down with them. [30] The teachers of the Law and the proud religious law-keepers talked against the followers of Jesus. They said, "Why do You eat and drink with men who gather taxes and with sinners?" [31] Jesus said to them, "People who are well do not need a doctor. Only those who are sick need a doctor. [32] I have not come to call good people. I have come to call sinners to be sorry for their sins and to turn from them."

Jesus Teaches About Going Without Food So You Can Pray Better [Matthew 9:14-17; Mark 2:18-22]

[33] They asked Jesus, "Why do the followers of John and of the proud religious law-keepers go without food so they can pray better, but Your followers keep on eating and drinking?" [34] Jesus answered them, "Can the friends at a wedding be sorry when the man just married is with them? [35] The days will come when the man just married will be taken from them. Then they will not eat food so they can pray better in those days."

The Picture-story Of The Cloth And The Bags

[36] Then Jesus told them a picture-story. He said, "No one sews a piece of cloth from a new coat on an old coat. If he does, the new coat will have a hole. The new piece and the old coat will not be the same. [37] No man puts new wine into old skin

bags. If they did, the skins would break and the wine would run out. The bags would be no good. 38New wine must be put into new bags and both are kept safe. 39No one wants new wine after drinking old wine. He says, 'The old wine is better.' "

Jesus Teaches About The Day Of Rest [Matthew 12:1-8; Mark 2:23-28]

6 On the next Day of Rest Jesus was walking through the grain fields. His followers picked grain. They rubbed it in their hands and ate it. 2Some of the proud religious law-keepers said to them, "Why are you doing what the Law says should not be done on the Day of Rest?" 3Jesus answered them, "Have you not read what David did when he and his men were hungry? 4He went into the house of God and ate the special bread used in the religious worship. He gave some to those who were with him also. The Law says only the religious leaders may eat that bread. 5The Son of Man is Lord of the Day of Rest also."

Jesus Heals On The Day Of Rest [Matthew 12:9-14; Mark 3:1-6]

6On another Day of Rest Jesus went into the Jewish place of worship and taught. A man with a dried-up hand was there. 7The teachers of the Law and the proud religious law-keepers watched to see if He would heal on the Day of Rest. They wanted to have something to say against Him. 8Jesus knew what they were thinking. He said to the man with the dried-up hand, "Stand up and come here." The man stood up and went to Jesus. 9Then Jesus said to them, "I will ask you one thing. Does the Law say to do good on the Day of Rest or to do bad? To save life or to kill?" 10Jesus looked around at them all and said to the man, "Put out your hand." He put it out and his hand was healed. It was as good as

his other hand. 11The teachers of the Law and the proud religious law-keepers were filled with anger. They talked with each other about what they might do to Jesus.

Jesus Calls His Twelve Followers [Matthew 10:1-4; Mark 3:13-19]

12One day Jesus went up on a mountain to pray. He prayed all night to God. 13In the morning He called His followers to Him. He chose twelve of them and called them missionaries. 14There were Simon, whom He also named Peter, and his brother Andrew. There were James and John, Philip and Bartholomew, 15Matthew and Thomas. There were James the son of Alphaeus, and Simon the Canaanite. 16There were Judas, who was the brother of James, and Judas Iscariot who would hand Jesus over to be killed.

Jesus Heals Many People [Matthew 12:15-21; Mark 3:7-12]

17Then Jesus came down and stood on a plain with many of His followers. Many people came from the country of Judea and from Jerusalem and from the cities of Tyre and Sidon. They came to hear Him and to be healed of their diseases. 18Those who were troubled with demons came and were healed. 19All the people tried to put their hands on Jesus. Power came from Him and He healed them all.

Jesus Teaches On The Mountain [Matthew 5:1-7:29]

20He looked at His followers and said, "Those of you who are poor are happy, because the holy nation of God is yours. 21Those of you who are hungry now are happy, because you will be filled. Those of you who have sorrow now are happy, because you will laugh. 22You are happy when men hate you and do not want you around and put shame on you because you trust in Me. 23Be glad in that day. Be full of joy for your pay is much in heaven. Their fathers did these things to the early preachers.

24"It is bad for you who are rich. You are receiving all that you will get. 25It is bad for you that are full. You will be hungry. It is bad for you who laugh now. You will have sorrow and you will cry. 26It is bad for you when everyone speaks well of you. In the same way, their fathers spoke well of the false teachers.

Jesus Teaches What The Law Says About Love

27"I say to you who hear Me, love those who work against you. Do good to those who hate you. 28Respect and give thanks for those who try to bring bad to you. Pray for those who make it very hard for you. 29Whoever hits you on one side of the face, turn so he can hit the other side also. Whoever takes your coat, give him your shirt also. 30Give to any person who asks you for something. If a person takes something from you, do not ask for it back. 31Do for other people what you would like to have them do for you.

32"If you love those who love you, what pay can you expect from that? Sinners also love those who love them. 33If you do good to those who do good to you, what pay can you expect from that? Sinners also do good to those who do good to them. 34If you let people use your things and expect to get something back, what pay can you expect from that? Even sinners let sinners use things and they expect to get something back. 35But love those who hate you. Do good to them. Let them use your things and do not expect something back. Your pay will be much. You will be the children of the Most High. He is kind to those who are not thankful and to those who are full of sin.

Jesus Teaches About Finding Bad In Others

36"You must have loving-kindness just as your Father has loving-kindness. 37Do not say what is wrong in other people's lives. Then other people will not say what is wrong in your life. Do not say someone is guilty. Then other people will not say you are guilty. Forgive other people and other people will forgive you. 38"Give, and it will be given to you. You will have more than enough. It can be pushed down and shaken together and it will still run over as it is given to you. The way you give to others is the way you will receive in return."

39Jesus used a picture-story as He spoke to them. He said, "Can one blind man lead another blind man? Will they not fall into the ditch together? 40The follower is not more important than his teacher. But everyone who learns well will be like his teacher.

Jesus Teaches About Saying What Is Wrong In Others

41"Why do you look at the small piece of wood in your brother's eye and do not see the big piece of wood in your own eye? 42How can you say to your brother, 'Let me take that small piece of wood out of your eye,' when you do not see the big piece of wood in your own eye? You pretend to be someone you are not. First, take the big piece of wood out of your own eye. Then you can see better to take the small piece of wood out of your brother's eye.

Jesus Teaches About False Teachers

43"A good tree cannot have bad fruit. A bad tree cannot have good fruit. 44For every tree is known by its own fruit. Men do not gather figs from thorns. They do not gather grapes from thistles. 45Good comes from a good man because of the riches he has in his heart. Sin comes from a sinful man because of the sin he has in his heart. The mouth speaks of what the heart is full of.

Jesus Teaches About Houses Built On Rock And Sand

46"And why do you call Me, 'Lord, Lord,' but do not do what I say? 47Whoever comes to Me and hears and does what I say, I will show you who he is like. 48He is like a man who built a house. He dug deep to put the building on rock. When the water came up and the river beat against the house, the building could not be shaken because it was built on rock. 49But he who hears and does not do what I say, is like a man who built a house on nothing but earth. The water beat against the house. At once it fell and was destroyed."

The Healing Of The Captain's Helper [Matthew 8:5-13]

7 When Jesus had finished teaching the people, He went back to Capernaum. 2A captain of the army had a servant that he thought much of. This servant was very sick and was about to die. 3When the captain heard of Jesus, he sent some Jewish leaders to Him. They were to ask if He would come and heal this servant. 4They came to Jesus and begged Him, saying, "The man is respected and should have this done for him. 5He loves our nation and has built our Jewish place of worship."

6Jesus went with them. When He was not far from the house, the captain told some friends to tell this to Jesus, "Lord, do not take the time to come to my house, because I am not good enough. 7And I am not good enough to come to You. But just say the word and my servant will be healed. 8For I am a man who works for someone else also, and I

have soldiers who work for me. I say to this man, 'Go!' and he goes. I say to another, 'Come!' and he comes. I say to my workman, 'Do this!' and he does it."

9Jesus was surprised when He heard this. He turned to the people following Him and said, "I tell you, I have not found so much faith even in the Jewish nation." 10Those who had been sent went back to the captain's house and found the servant well again.

The Son Of A Woman Whose Husband Had Died Was Raised From The Dead

11The next day Jesus went to a city called Nain. His followers and many other people went with Him. 12When they came near the city gate, a dead man was being carried out. He was the only son of a woman whose husband had died. Many people of the city were with her. 13When the Lord saw her, He had loving-pity for her and said, "Do not cry." 14He went and put His hand on the box in which the dead man was carried. The men who were carrying it, stopped. Jesus said, "Young man, I say to you, get up!" 15The man who was dead sat up and began to talk. Then Jesus gave him to his mother. 16Everyone was afraid and they gave thanks to God. They said, "A great Man Who speaks for God has come among us! God has cared for His people!" 17The news about Jesus went through all the country of Judea and over all the land.

John The Baptist Asks About Jesus [Matthew 11:1-6]

18The followers of John the Baptist told him about all these things. 19John called two of his followers and sent them to Jesus to ask, "Are You the One Who is to come? Or are we to look for another?" 20The men came to Jesus and said, "John the

Baptist sent us to ask You, 'Are You the One Who is to come? Or are we to look for another?' "

21 At that time Jesus was healing many people of all kinds of sickness and disease and was putting out demons. Many that were blind were able to see. 22 Jesus said to John's followers, "Go back to John the Baptist and tell him what you have seen and heard. Tell him the blind are made to see. Those who could not walk, are walking. Those with a bad skin disease are healed. Those who could not hear, are hearing. The dead are raised to life and poor people have the Good News preached to them. 23 The person who is not ashamed of Me and does not turn away from Me is happy."

Jesus Tells About John The Baptist
[Matthew 11:7-19]

24 As John's followers were going away, Jesus began to tell the people about John the Baptist. He said, "Why did you go out to the desert? Did you go out to see a small tree moving in the wind? 25 What did you go out to see? A man dressed in good clothes? Those who are dressed in good clothes are in the houses of kings. 26 But what did you go to see? One who speaks for God? Yes, I tell you, he is more than one who speaks for God. 27 This is the man the Holy Writings spoke of when they said, 'See! I will send My helper to carry news ahead of You. He will make Your way ready for You!' (Malachi 3:1; Isaiah 40:3)

28 "I tell you, of those born of women, there is no one greater than John the Baptist. The least in the holy nation of God is greater than he."

29 All the people who heard Jesus and those who gathered taxes showed they knew God was right and were baptized by John. 30 But the proud religious law-keepers and the men who knew the Law would not listen. They would not be baptized

by John and they did not receive what God had for them.

31 Then the Lord said, "What are the people of this day like? 32 They are like children playing in front of stores. They call to their friends, 'We have played music for you, but you did not dance. We have had sorrow for you, but you did not have sorrow.' 33 John the Baptist did not come eating bread or drinking wine and you say, 'He has a demon.' 34 The Son of Man came eating and drinking and you say, 'See! He likes food and wine. He is a friend of men who gather taxes and of sinners!' 35 Wisdom is shown to be right by those who are wise."

A Woman Puts Special Perfume On The Feet Of Jesus

36 One of the proud religious law-keepers wanted Jesus to eat with him. Jesus went to his house and sat down to eat. 37 There was a woman in the city who was a sinner. She knew Jesus was eating in the house of the proud religious law-keeper. She brought a jar of special perfume. 38 Then she stood behind Him by His feet and cried. Her tears wet His feet and she dried them with her hair. She kissed His feet and put the special perfume on them.

39 The proud religious law-keeper who had asked Jesus to eat with him saw this. He said to himself, "If this Man were One Who speaks for God, He would know who and what kind of a woman put her hands on Him. She is a sinner." 40 Jesus said to him, "I have something to say to you, Simon." And Simon said, "Teacher, say it."

41 "There were two men who owed a certain man some money. The one man owed 500 pieces of silver money. The other man owed 50 pieces of silver money. 42 Neither one of them had any money, so he told them they did not have to pay him back. Tell Me, which one would love

him the most?" ⁴³Simon said, "I think it would be the one who owed the most." And Jesus said to him, "You have said the right thing."

⁴⁴He turned to the woman and said to Simon, "Do you see this woman? I came into your house and you gave Me no water to wash My feet. She washed My feet with her tears and dried them with the hairs of her head. ⁴⁵You gave me no kiss, but this woman has kissed my feet from the time I came in. ⁴⁶You did not put even oil on My head but this woman has put special perfume on My feet. ⁴⁷I tell you, her many sins are forgiven because she loves much. But the one who has little to be forgiven, loves only a little."

⁴⁸Then He said to the woman, "Your sins are forgiven." ⁴⁹Those who were eating with Him began to say to themselves, "Who is this Man Who even forgives sins?" ⁵⁰He said to the woman, "Your faith has saved you from the punishment of sin. Go in peace."

Jesus Teaches In Galilee

8 After this Jesus went to all the cities and towns preaching and telling the Good News about the holy nation of God. The twelve followers were with Him. ²Some women who had been healed of demons and diseases were with Him. Mary Magdalene, who had had seven demons put out of her, was one of them. ³Joanna, the wife of Chuza who was one of Herod's helpers, was another one. Susanna and many others also cared for Jesus by using what they had.

The Picture-story Of The Man Who Planted Seed [Matthew 13:1-52; Mark 4:1-34]

⁴Many people came together from every town to Jesus. He told them a picture-story.
⁵"A man went out to plant seed. As he planted the seed, some fell by the side of the road. They were walked on and birds came and ate them. ⁶Some seed fell between rocks. As soon as they started to grow, they dried up because they had no water. ⁷Some seed fell among thorns. The thorns grew and did not give the seed room to grow. ⁸Some seed fell on good ground. They grew and gave one hundred times as much grain." When Jesus had finished saying this, He cried out, "You have ears, then listen!"

⁹His followers asked Him what this picture-story meant. ¹⁰Jesus said, "You were given the secrets about the holy nation of God. Others are told picture-stories. As they look, they do not see. As they hear, they do not understand.

Jesus Tells About The Man Who Planted Seed

¹¹"This is what the picture-story means. The seed is the Word of God. ¹²Those by the side of the road hear the Word. Then the devil comes and takes the Word from their hearts. He does not want them to believe and be saved from the punishment of sin. ¹³Those which fell among rocks receive the Word with joy. These have no root. For awhile they believe, but when they are tempted they give up. ¹⁴Those which fell among thorns hear the Word but go their own way. The cares of this life let the thorns grow. A love for money lets the thorns grow also. And the fun of this life lets the thorns grow. Their grain never becomes full-grown. ¹⁵But those which fell on good ground have heard the Word. They keep it in a good and true heart and they keep on giving good grain.

The Picture-story Of The Lamp

¹⁶"No man lights a lamp and puts it under a pail or under a bed. He puts it on a table so all who come into the

room may see it. 17Nothing is secret but what will be known. Anything that is hidden will be brought into the light. 18Be careful how you listen! Whoever has, to him will be given. Whoever does not have, even the little he has will be taken from him."

The New Kind Of Family [Matthew 12:46-50; Mark 3:31-35]

19The mother of Jesus and His brothers came to Him. They could not get near Him because of so many people. 20Someone said to Jesus, "Your mother and brothers are standing outside. They want to see You." 21Jesus said to them, "My mother and brothers are these who hear the Word of God and do it."

The Wind And Waves Obey Jesus [Matthew 8:23-27; Mark 4:35-41]

22On one of those days Jesus and His followers got into a boat. Jesus said to them, "Let us go over to the other side of the lake." Then they pushed out into the water. 23As they were going, Jesus fell asleep. A wind storm came over the lake. The boat was filling with water and they were in danger. 24The followers came to awake Jesus. They said, "Teacher! Teacher! We are going to die!" Then Jesus got up and spoke sharp words to the wind and the high waves. The wind stopped blowing and there were no more waves. 25He said to them, "Where is your faith?" The followers were surprised and afraid. They said to each other, "What kind of a man is He? He speaks to the wind and the waves and they obey Him."

Demons Ask Jesus To Let Them Live In Pigs [Matthew 8:28-34; Mark 5:1-20]

26They came to the land of the Gadarenes, which is on the other side of the country of Galilee. 27As Jesus stepped out on land, a man met Him who had come from the city. This man had demons in him. For a long time he had worn no clothes. He did not live in a house, but lived among the graves. 28When he saw Jesus, he got down before Him and cried with a loud voice, "What do You want with me, Jesus, Son of the Most High? I beg of You not to hurt me!" 29For Jesus had spoken to the demon to come out of the man. Many times the demon had taken hold of him. The man had to be tied with chains. But he would break the chains and be taken by the demon into the desert.

30Jesus asked him, "What is your name?" And the demon answered, "Many," because many demons had gone into him. 31The demons asked Jesus not to send them to the hole without a bottom in the earth. 32There were many pigs feeding on the side of the mountain. The demons begged Jesus to let them go into the pigs. Jesus said they could. 33The demons came out of the man and went into the pigs. Then the many pigs ran down the side of the mountain into the water and died.

34The men who cared for the pigs ran fast and told what had happened in the town and in the country. 35People came to see what had happened. They came to Jesus and saw the man from whom the demons had been sent. He was sitting at the feet of Jesus with clothes on and had the right use of his mind. The people were afraid. 36Those who had seen it told how the man who had had the demons was healed. 37Then all the people of the country of the Gadarenes begged Jesus to go away from them. They were very much afraid. Jesus got into the boat and went back to the other side.

38The man out of whom the demons had gone begged to go with Jesus. But Jesus sent him away and said, 39"Go back to your house and tell everything God has done for you." He went back and told all the people of the city what great things Jesus had done for him.

Two Were Healed Through Faith
[Matthew 9:18-26; Mark 5:21-43]

⁴⁰Many people were glad to see Jesus when He got back. They were waiting for Him. ⁴¹A man named Jairus was a leader of the Jewish place of worship. As he came to Jesus, he got down at His feet. He asked Jesus if He would come to his house. ⁴²He had only one daughter and she was dying. This girl was about twelve years old. As Jesus went, the people pushed Him from every side.

⁴³A woman had been sick for twelve years with a flow of blood. *(She had spent all the money she had on doctors.) But she could not be healed by anyone. ⁴⁴She came behind Jesus and touched the bottom of His coat. At once the flow of blood stopped. ⁴⁵Jesus said, "Who touched Me?" Everyone said that they had not touched Him. Peter said, "Teacher, so many people are pushing You from every side and You say, 'Who touched Me?'" ⁴⁶Then Jesus said, "Someone touched Me because I know power has gone from Me." ⁴⁷When the woman saw she could not hide it, she came shaking. She got down before Jesus. Then she told Jesus in front of all the people why she had touched Him. She told how she was healed at once. ⁴⁸Jesus said to her, "Daughter, your faith has healed you. Go in peace."

⁴⁹While Jesus was yet talking, a man came from the house of the leader of the place of worship. This man said to Jairus, "Your daughter is dead. Do not make the Teacher use anymore of His time." ⁵⁰Jesus heard it and said to Jairus, "Do not be afraid, only believe. She will be made well." ⁵¹Jesus went into the house. He let only Peter and James and John and the father and mother of the girl go in with Him. ⁵²Everyone was crying and full of sorrow because of her. Jesus said, "Do not cry. She is not dead, but is sleeping." ⁵³Then they laughed at Jesus because they knew she was dead. ⁵⁴Jesus sent them all out. He took the girl by the hand and said, "Child, get up!" ⁵⁵Her spirit came back and she got up at once. Jesus told them to bring her food. ⁵⁶Her parents were surprised and wondered about it. Then Jesus told them they should tell no one what had happened.

Jesus Sends His Twelve Followers Out [Matthew 10:1-42; Mark 6:7-13]

9 Jesus called His twelve followers to Him. He gave them the right and the power over all demons and to heal diseases. ²He sent them to preach about the holy nation of God and to heal the sick. ³Then He said to them, "Take nothing along for the trip. Do not take a walking stick or a bag or bread or money. Do not take two coats. ⁴Whatever house you go into, stay there until you are ready to go on. ⁵If anyone will not take you in, as you leave that city, shake its dust off your feet. That will speak against them."

⁶They went out, going from town to town. They preached the Good News and healed the sick everywhere.

John The Baptist Is Killed

⁷Now Herod the leader heard of all that had been done by Jesus. He was troubled because some people said that John the Baptist had been raised from the dead. ⁸Some people said that Elijah had come back. Others thought one of the early preachers had been raised from the dead. ⁹Then Herod said, "I had John's head cut off. But who is this Man that I hear these things about?" He wanted to see Jesus.

The Feeding Of The Five Thousand
[Matthew 14:13-21; Mark 6:30-44; John 6:1-14]

¹⁰The twelve followers came back. They told Jesus what they had done.

Jesus took them to a desert near the town of Bethsaida. There they could be alone. [11]When the people knew where Jesus was, they followed Him. Jesus was happy to see them and talked to them about the holy nation of God. He healed all who were sick.

[12]When the day was about over, the twelve followers came to Jesus. They said, "Send these many people away so they can go to the towns and country near here. There they can find a place to sleep and get food. We are here in a desert." [13]But Jesus said to them, "Give them something to eat." They said, "We have only five loaves of bread and two fish. Are we to go and buy food for all these people?" [14]There were about five thousand men. Jesus said to His followers, "Have them sit down in groups of fifty people." [15]They did as He told them. They made all of the people sit down. [16]As Jesus took the five loaves of bread and two fish, He looked up to heaven and gave thanks. He broke them in pieces and gave them to His followers to give to the people. [17]They all ate and were filled. They picked up twelve baskets full of pieces of bread and fish after the people finished eating.

Peter Says Jesus Is The Christ [Matthew 16:13-20; Mark 8:27-30]

[18]While Jesus was praying alone, His followers were with Him. Jesus asked them, "Who do people say that I am?" [19]They said, "John the Baptist, but some say Elijah. Others say that one of the early preachers has been raised from the dead." [20]Jesus said to them, "But who do you say that I am?" Peter said, "You are the Christ of God."

Jesus Tells Of His Death For The First Time [Matthew 16:21-28; Mark 8:31-38]

[21]Then Jesus spoke to them and told them to tell no one. [22]He said,

"The Son of Man must suffer many things. The leaders and the religious leaders and the teachers of the Law will have nothing to do with Him. He must be killed and be raised from the dead three days later."

Giving Up Self And One's Own Desires

[23]Then Jesus said to them all, "If anyone wants to follow Me, he must give up himself and his own desires. He must take up his cross everyday and follow Me. [24]If anyone wants to keep his own life safe, he must lose it. If anyone gives up his life because of Me, he will save it. [25]For what does a man have if he gets all the world and loses or gives up his life? [26]Whoever is ashamed of Me and My Words, the Son of Man will be ashamed of him when He comes in His own shining greatness and of the Father's and of the holy angels. [27]I tell you the truth, some standing here will not die until they see the holy nation of God."

A Look At What Jesus Will Be Like [Matthew 17:1-13; Mark 9:1-13]

[28]About eight days after Jesus had said these things, He took Peter and James and John with Him. They went up on a mountain to pray. [29]As Jesus prayed, He was changed in looks before them. His clothes became white and shining bright. [30]Two men talked with Jesus. They were Moses and Elijah. [31]They looked like the shining greatness of heaven as they talked about His death in Jerusalem which was soon to happen.

[32]But Peter and those with him had gone to sleep. When they woke up, they saw His shining greatness and the two men who stood with Him. [33]As the two men went from Jesus, Peter said to Him, "Teacher, it is good for us to be here. Let us build three altars. One will be for You. One will be for Moses. One will be for Elijah." He did not know what he

was saying. 34While he was talking, a cloud came over them. They were afraid as the cloud came in around them.

35A voice came out of the cloud, saying, "This is My Son, the One I have chosen. Listen to Him!" 36When the voice was gone, Jesus was standing there alone. From that time on, they kept these things to themselves. They told no one what they had seen.

A Boy With A Demon Is Healed
[Matthew 17:14-21; Mark 9:14-29]

37The next day they came down from the mountain and many people met Jesus. 38A man from among the people cried out, "Teacher, I beg of You to look at my son. He is my only child. 39See, a demon takes him and makes him cry out. It takes hold of him and makes him shake. Spit runs from his mouth. He has marks on his body from being hurt. The demon does not want to go from him. 40I begged Your followers to put the demon out, but they could not."

41Then Jesus said, "You people of this day do not have faith. You turn from what is right! How long must I be with you? How long must I put up with you? Bring your son to Me." 42While the boy was coming, the demon threw him down and made him lose the use of his mind for awhile. Jesus spoke sharp words to the demon. He healed the child and gave him back to his father.

Jesus Tells Of His Death The Second Time [Matthew 17:22-23; Mark 9:30-32]

43They were all surprised at the great power of God. They all were thinking about the special things Jesus had done. And Jesus said to His followers, 44"Remember these words. For the Son of Man will be given over into the hands of men." 45They did not understand these words because it was hid from them. They did not

know what Jesus meant and were afraid to ask Him.

Jesus Teaches About The Faith Of A Child [Matthew 18:1-35; Mark 9:33-50]

46The followers argued among themselves about which of them would be the greatest. 47Jesus knew what they were thinking. He put a child beside Him. 48He said to the followers, "Whoever receives this child in My name, receives Me. Whoever receives Me, receives Him Who sent Me. The one who is least among you is the one who is great."

The Sharp Words Against The Followers

49John said, "Teacher, we saw someone putting out demons in Your name. We told him to stop because he was not following us." 50Jesus said to him, "Do not stop him. He who is not against us is for us."

Jesus And His Followers Leave Galilee

51It was about time for Jesus to be taken up into heaven. He turned toward Jerusalem and was sure that nothing would stop Him from going. 52He sent men on ahead of Him. They came to a town in Samaria. There they got things ready for Jesus. 53The people did not want Him there because they knew He was on His way to Jerusalem. 54James and John, His followers, saw this. They said, "Lord, do You want us to speak so fire will come down from heaven and burn them up as Elijah did?" 55Jesus turned and spoke sharp words to them. *(He said, "You do not know what kind of spirit you have. 56The Son of Man did not come to destroy men's lives. He came to save them from the punishment of sin." They went on their way to another town.)

The Testing Of Some Followers
[Matthew 8:18-22]

[57] As they were going on their way, a man said to Jesus, "Lord, I will follow You wherever You go." [58] Jesus said to him, "Foxes have holes. Birds of the sky have nests. The Son of Man has no place to put His head." [59] He said to another, "Follow Me." But the man said, "Lord, let me go first and bury my father." [60] Jesus said to him, "Let the people who are dead bury their own dead. You go and preach about the holy nation of God." [61] And another one said, "Lord, I will follow You, but first let me go and say good-by to those at home." [62] Jesus said to him, "Anyone who puts his hand on a plow and looks back at the things behind is of no use in the holy nation of God."

Seventy Are Sent Out

10 After this the Lord chose seventy others. He sent them out two together to every city and place where He would be going later. [2] Jesus said to them, "There is much grain ready to gather. But the workmen are few. Pray then to the Lord Who is the Owner of the grain fields that He will send workmen to gather His grain. [3] Go on your way. Listen! I send you out like lambs among wolves. [4] Take no money. Do not take a bag or shoes. Speak to no one along the way. [5] When you go into a house, say that you hope peace will come to them. [6] If a man who loves peace lives there, your good wishes will come to him. If your good wishes are not received, they will come back to you. [7] Stay in the same house. Eat and drink what they give you. The workman should have his pay. Do not move from house to house.

[8] "Whenever a city receives you, eat the things that are put before you there. [9] Heal the sick. Say to them, 'The holy nation of God is near.' [10] Whatever city does not receive you, go into its streets and say, [11] 'Even the dust of your city that is on our feet we are cleaning off against you. But understand this, the holy nation of God has come near you!' [12] I tell you, on the day men stand before God, it will be easier for the city of Sodom than for that city.

[13] "It is bad for you, city of Chorazin! It is bad for you, town of Bethsaida! For if the powerful works which were done in you had been done in the cities of Tyre and Sidon they would have turned from their sins long ago. They would have shown their sorrow by putting on clothes made from hair and would have sat in ashes. [14] It will be better for Tyre and Sidon on the day men stand before God and be told they are guilty than for you. [15] And you, Capernaum, are you to be lifted up into heaven? You will be taken down to hell. [16] Whoever listens to you, listens to Me. Whoever has nothing to do with you, has nothing to do with Me. Whoever has nothing to do with Me, has nothing to do with the One Who sent Me."

The Seventy Came Back

[17] The seventy came back full of joy. They said, "Lord, even the demons obeyed us when we used Your name." [18] Jesus said to them, "I saw Satan fall from heaven like lightning. [19] Listen! I have given you power to walk on snakes. I have given you power over small animals with a sting of poison. I have given you power over all the power of the one who works against you. Nothing will hurt you. [20] Even so, you should not be happy because the demons obey you but be happy because your names are written in heaven."

The Joy Of The Holy Spirit

[21] At this time Jesus was full of the joy of the Holy Spirit. He said, "I

thank You, Father, Lord of heaven and earth. You have kept these things hid from the wise and from those who have much learning. You have shown them to little children. Yes, Father, it was what you wanted done.

22 "Everything has been given to Me by My Father. No one knows the Son but the Father. No one knows the Father but the Son and the Son makes the Father known to those He chooses."

23 Then He turned to His followers and said without anyone else hearing, "Happy are those who see what you see! 24 I tell you, many early preachers and kings have wanted to see the things you are seeing, but they did not see them. They have wanted to hear the things you are hearing, but they did not hear them."

Jesus Talks To The Man Who Knew The Law

25 A man stood up who knew the Law and tried to trap Jesus. He said, "Teacher, what must I do to have life that lasts forever?" 26 Jesus said to him, "What is written in the Law? What does the Law say?" 27 The man said, "You must love the Lord your God with all your heart. You must love Him with all your soul. You must love Him with all your strength. You must love Him with all your mind. You must love your neighbor as you love yourself." 28 Jesus said to him, "You have said the right thing. Do this and you will have life." 29 The man tried to make himself look good. He asked Jesus, "Who is my neighbor?"

The Picture-story Of The Good Samaritan

30 Jesus said, "A man was going down from Jerusalem to the city of Jericho. Robbers came out after him. They took his clothes off and beat him. Then they went away, leaving him almost dead. 31 A religious leader was walking down that road and saw the man. But he went by on the other side. 32 In the same way, a man from the family group of Levi was walking down that road. When he saw the man who was hurt, he came near to him but kept on going on the other side of the road. 33 Then a man from the country of Samaria came by. He went up to the man. As he saw him, he had loving-pity on him. 34 He got down and put oil and wine on the places where he was hurt and put cloth around them. Then the man from Samaria put this man on his own donkey. He took him to a place where people stay for the night and cared for him. 35 The next day the man from Samaria was ready to leave. He gave the owner of that place two pieces of money to care for him. He said to him, 'Take care of this man. If you use more than this, I will give it to you when I come again.'

36 "Which of these three do you think was a neighbor to the man who was beaten by the robbers?" 37 The man who knew the Law said, "The one who showed loving-pity on him." Then Jesus said, "Go and do the same."

Mary And Martha Care For Jesus

38 As they went on their way, they came to a town where a woman named Martha lived. She cared for Jesus in her home. 39 Martha had a sister named Mary. Mary sat at the feet of Jesus and listened to all He said. 40 Martha was working hard getting the supper ready. She came to Jesus and said, "Do You see that my sister is not helping me? Tell her to help me." 41 Jesus said to her, "Martha, Martha, you are worried and troubled about many things. 42 Only a few things are important, even just one. Mary has chosen the good thing. It will not be taken away from her."

Jesus Teaches His Followers To Pray

11 Jesus had been praying. One of His followers said to Him, "Lord, teach us to pray as John the Baptist taught his followers." ²Jesus said to them, "When you pray, say, 'Our Father in heaven, Your name is holy. May Your holy nation come. *What You want done, may it be done on earth as it is in heaven. ³Give us the bread we need everyday. ⁴Forgive us our sins, as we forgive those who sin against us. Do not let us be tempted.' "

A Picture-story About How To Ask

⁵Jesus said to them, "If any of you have a friend and go to him in the night and say, 'Friend, give me three loaves of bread. ⁶A friend of mine is on a trip and has stopped at my house. I have no food to give him.' ⁷The man inside the house will say, 'Do not trouble me. The door is shut. My children and I are in bed. I cannot get up and give you bread.' ⁸I say to you, he may not get up and give him bread because he is a friend. Yet, if he keeps on asking, he will get up and give him as much as he needs. ⁹I say to you, ask, and what you ask for will be given to you. Look, and what you are looking for you will find. Knock, and the door you are knocking on will be opened to you. ¹⁰For everyone who asks, will receive what he asks for. Everyone who looks, will find what he is looking for. Everyone who knocks, will have the door opened to him.

¹¹"Would any of you fathers give your son a stone if he asked for bread? Or would you give a snake if he asked for a fish? ¹²Or if he asked for an egg, would you give him a small animal with a sting of poison? ¹³You are sinful and you know how to give good things to your children. How much more will your Father in heaven give the Holy Spirit to those who ask Him?"

A Nation That Cannot Stand
[*Matthew 12:22-37; Mark 3:22-30*]

¹⁴Jesus was putting a demon out of a man who could not speak. When the demon was gone, the man could speak. All the people were surprised and wondered about it. ¹⁵Some of them said, "He puts out demons through Satan, the king of demons." ¹⁶Others tried to trap Jesus. They asked for something special to see from heaven. ¹⁷But He knew their thoughts and said to them, "Every nation divided into groups that fight each other will be destroyed. Every family divided into groups that fight each other will not stand. ¹⁸If Satan is divided against himself, how will his nation stand? And yet you say I put out demons through Satan! ¹⁹If I put out demons through Satan, by whose help do your sons put them out? Your own sons will say if you are guilty or not. ²⁰But if I put out demons by the power of God, then the holy nation of God has come to you.

²¹"When a strong man watches his house and is ready to fight, his things are safe. ²²When a stronger man comes along, he wins the fight. He takes away all the things to fight with that the man of the house had put his trust in. Then the stronger man takes anything he wants from the house. ²³Whoever is not with Me is against Me. Whoever does not gather with Me is sending them everywhere.

²⁴"When a demon is gone out of a man, it goes through dry places to find rest. If it finds none, it says, 'I will go back to my house I came from.' ²⁵When the demon comes back, it finds the house cleaned and looking good. ²⁶Then the demon goes out and comes back bringing seven demons worse than itself. They go in and live there. In the end that man is worse than at the first."

²⁷As Jesus was talking, a woman of the group said with a loud voice, "The woman is happy who gave You

birth and who fed You." ²⁸But He said, "Yes, but those who hear the Word of God and obey it are happy."

Jesus Tells About Jonah [Matthew 12:38-42]

²⁹When the people were gathered near Jesus, He said, "The people of this day are sinful. They are looking for something special to see. They will get nothing special to see, except what Jonah the early preacher did. ³⁰As Jonah was something special to the people of the city of Ninevah, the Son of Man will be to the people of this day also. ³¹The queen of the south will stand up on the day men stand before God. She will say the people of this day are guilty because she came from the ends of the earth to listen to the wise sayings of Solomon. And look, Someone greater than Solomon is here! ³²The men of Ninevah will stand up on the day men stand before God. They will say the people of this day are guilty because the men of Ninevah were sorry for their sins and turned from them when Jonah preached. And look, Someone greater than Jonah is here!

Jesus Teaches About Light

³³"No man lights a lamp and then hides it under a pail. He puts the light on a table so those who come in can see it. ³⁴The eye is the light of the body. When your eye is good, your whole body is full of light. When your eye is sinful, your whole body is full of darkness. ³⁵Be careful that the light in you is not dark. ³⁶If your whole body is full of light, with no dark part, then it will shine. It will be as a lamp that gives light."

Jesus Speaks Sharp Words To The Proud Religious Law-keeper

³⁷As Jesus was talking, a proud religious law-keeper asked Him to eat with him. Jesus went to the man's house and took His place at the table. ³⁸The proud religious law-keeper was surprised and wondered why Jesus had not washed before He ate. ³⁹But the Lord said to him, "You proud religious law-keepers make the outside of the cup and plate clean, but inside you are full of stealing and sinning. ⁴⁰You are foolish. Did not He that made the outside make the inside also? ⁴¹Give yourself as a gift and then you will be clean.

⁴²"It is bad for you, proud religious law-keepers! You give one-tenth part of your spices. But you give no thought to what is right and to the love of God. You should do both of these.

⁴³"It is bad for you, proud religious law-keepers! For you like to have important seats in the places of worship. You like to have people speak good-sounding words to you as you are in the center of town where people gather. ⁴⁴It is bad for you, teachers of the Law and proud religious law-keepers and you who pretend to be someone you are not! For you are like graves that are hidden. Men walk on graves without knowing they are there."

Jesus Speaks Sharp Words To The Men Who Knew The Law

⁴⁵One of the men who knew the Law said to Jesus, "Teacher, You are making us look bad when You speak like this." ⁴⁶Jesus said, "It is bad for you also, you men who know the Law! For you put heavy loads on the shoulders of men. But you will not even put your finger on one of these loads to help them. ⁴⁷It is bad for you! For you make beautiful buildings for the graves of the early preachers your fathers killed. ⁴⁸You are saying what your fathers did was good, because they killed the early preachers and you are making their graves.

⁴⁹"For this reason the wisdom of

God has said, 'I will send them early preachers and missionaries. Some they will kill and some they will make it very hard for.' ⁵⁰The blood of all the early preachers from the beginning of the world is on the people of this day. ⁵¹It will be from the blood of Abel to the blood of Zacharias, the one who died between the altar and the house of God. For sure, I tell you, the people of this day will be guilty for this.

⁵²"It is bad for you men who know the Law! For you have locked the door to the house of learning. You are not going in yourselves and you do not allow those to go in who are about to go in."

⁵³As Jesus went away from there, the teachers of the Law and the proud religious law-keepers were very angry and tried to make Him say many things. ⁵⁴They planned against Jesus and tried to trap Him with something He might say.

Jesus Teaches His Followers And Thousands Of Other People

12 At that time thousands of people gathered together. There were so many that they walked on each other. Jesus spoke to His twelve followers first, saying, "Look out! Have nothing to do with the yeast of the proud religious law-keepers which is pretending to be something it is not. ²For there is nothing covered up that will not be seen. There is nothing hidden that will not be known. ³What you have said in the dark will be heard in the light. What you have said in a low voice in a closed room will be spoken with a loud voice from the top of houses.

⁴"I say to you, My friends, do not be afraid of those who kill the body and then can do no more. ⁵I will tell you the one to be afraid of. Be afraid of Him Who has power to put you into hell after He has killed you. Yes, I say to you, be afraid of Him!

⁶"Are not five small birds sold for two small pieces of money? God does not forget even one of the birds. ⁷God knows how many hairs you have on your head. Do not be afraid. You are worth more than many small birds.

⁸"Also, I tell you, everyone who makes Me known to men, the Son of Man will make him known to the angels of God. ⁹But whoever acts as if he does not know Me and does not make Me known to men, he will not be spoken of to the angels of God.

The Sin That Cannot Be Forgiven

¹⁰"Whoever speaks a word against the Son of Man will be forgiven. Whoever speaks against the Holy Spirit will not be forgiven. ¹¹When they take you to the places of worship and to the courts and to the leaders of the country, do not be worried about what you should say or how to say it. ¹²The Holy Spirit will tell you what you should say at that time."

¹³One of the people said to Jesus, "Teacher, tell my brother to divide the riches that our father left us." ¹⁴Jesus said to him, "Friend, who has told Me to say who should get what?" ¹⁵Then Jesus said to them all, "Watch yourselves! Keep from wanting all kinds of things you should not have. A man's life is not made up of things, even if he has many riches."

The Picture-story Of The Rich Fool

¹⁶Then He told them a picture-story, saying, "The fields of a rich man gave much grain. ¹⁷The rich man thought to himself, 'What will I do? I have no place to put the grain.' ¹⁸Then he said, 'I know what I will do. I will take down my grain building and I will build a bigger one. I will put all my grain and other things I own into it. ¹⁹And I will say to my soul, "Soul, you have many good things put away in your

building. It will be all you need for many years to come. Now rest and eat and drink and have lots of fun." ' ²⁰But God said to him, 'You fool! Tonight your soul will be taken from you. Then who will have all the things you have put away?' ²¹It is the same with a man who puts away riches for himself and does not have the riches of God."

Jesus Teaches About The Cares Of This Life

²²Jesus said to His followers, "Because of this, I say to you, do not worry about your life, what you are going to eat. Do not worry about your body, what you are going to wear. ²³Life is worth more than food. The body is worth more than clothes. ²⁴Look at the birds. They do not plant seeds. They do not gather grain. They have no grain buildings for keeping grain. Yet God feeds them. Are you not worth more than the birds?

²⁵"Which of you can make yourself a little taller by worrying? ²⁶If you cannot do that which is so little, why do you worry about other things? ²⁷Think how the flowers grow. They do not work or make cloth. Yet, I tell you, that King Solomon in all his greatness was not dressed as well as one of these flowers. ²⁸God puts these clothes on the grass of the field. The grass is in the field today and put into the fire tomorrow. How much more would He want to give you clothing? You have so little faith! ²⁹Do not give so much thought to what you will eat or drink. Do not be worried about it. ³⁰For all the nations of the world go after these things. Your Father knows you need these things. ³¹Instead, go after the holy nation of God. Then all these other things will be given to you. ³²Do not be afraid, little flock. Your Father wants to give you the holy nation of God. ³³Sell what you have and give the money to poor people. Have money-bags for

yourselves that will never wear out. These money-bags are riches in heaven that will always be there. No robber can take them and no bugs can eat them there. ³⁴Your heart will be wherever your riches are.

Jesus Says To Watch And Be Ready For His Second Coming

³⁵"Be ready and dressed. Have your lights burning. ³⁶Be like men who are waiting for their owner to come home from a wedding supper. When he comes and knocks on the door, they will open it for him at once. ³⁷Those servants are happy when their owner finds them watching when he comes. For sure, I tell you, he will be dressed and ready to care for them. He will have them seated at the table. ³⁸The owner might come late at night or early in the morning. Those servants are happy if their owner finds them watching whenever he comes. ³⁹But understand this, that if the owner of a house had known when the robber was coming, he would have been watching. He would not have allowed his house to be broken into. ⁴⁰You must be ready also. The Son of Man is coming at a time when you do not think He will come."

Faithful Servants And Servants Who Are Not Faithful

⁴¹Peter said, "Lord, are You telling this picture-story to us or to all the people?" ⁴²The Lord said, "Who is the faithful and wise servant his owner made boss over the others? He is the one who is to have food ready at the right time. ⁴³That servant is happy who is doing his work when the owner comes. ⁴⁴For sure, I tell you, he will make him boss over all he has.

⁴⁵"But what if that servant says to himself, 'The owner will not be coming soon,' and then beats the other servants and eats and drinks

and gets drunk? 46The owner of that servant will come on a day and at an hour when he is not looking for him. He will cut him in pieces and will put him with those who do not believe.

47"The servant who knew what the owner wanted done, but did not get ready for him, or did not do what he wanted done, will be beaten many times. 48But the servant who did not know what his owner wanted done, but did things that would be reason to be beaten, will be beaten only a few times. The man who receives much will have to give much. If much is given to a man to take care of, men will expect to get more from him.

Men Are Divided When They Follow Christ

49"I have come to bring fire down to the earth. I wish it were already started! 50I have a baptism to go through. How troubled I am until it is over! 51Do you think I came to bring peace on the earth? I tell you, no! I came to divide. 52From now on there will be five in one house divided. Three will be against two and two will be against three. 53The father will be against the son. The son will be against the father. The mother will be against the daughter. The daughter will be against the mother. The mother-in-law will be against the daughter-in-law. The daughter-in-law will be against the mother-in-law."

54Then Jesus also said to the people, "When you see a cloud coming in the west, you say at once, 'It is going to rain.' And it does. 55When you see the wind blow from the south, you say, 'It will be a hot day.' And it is. 56You who pretend to be someone you are not, you know all about the sky and the earth. But why do you not know what is happening these days? 57Why do you not know for yourselves what is right? 58When a person says you are

wrong and takes you to court, try to make it right with him as you go, or he will take you to the head of the court. Then he will take you to the police and you will be put in prison. 59I tell you, you will not be let out of prison until you have paid the last piece of money of the fine."

Everyone Should Be Sorry For Their Sins And Turn From Them

13 At this time some people came to Jesus. They told Him that Pilate had killed some people from the country of Galilee. It was while they were giving gifts of animals on the altar in worship to God. 2Pilate put their blood together with the blood of the animals. Jesus said to them, "What about these people from Galilee? Were they worse sinners than all the other people from Galilee because they suffered these things? 3No, I tell you. But unless you are sorry for your sins and turn from them, you too will all die. 4What about those eighteen men who were killed when the high building in Siloam fell on them? Do you think they were the worst sinners living in Jerusalem? 5No, I tell you. But unless you are sorry for your sins and turn from them, you too will all die."

The Picture-story Of The Fig Tree Which Had No Fruit

6Then He told them this picture-story: "A man had a fig tree in his grape field. He looked for fruit on it but found none. 7He said to his servant, 'See! For three years I have been coming here looking for fruit on this fig tree. I never find any. Cut it down. Why does it even waste the ground?' 8The servant said, 'Sir! Leave it here one more year. I will dig around it and put plant food on it. 9It may be that it will give fruit next year. If it does not, then cut it down.'"

Jesus Heals On The Day Of Rest

¹⁰Jesus was teaching in one of the Jewish places of worship on the Day of Rest. ¹¹A woman was there who had suffered for eighteen years because of a demon. She was not able to stand up straight. ¹²Jesus saw her and said, "Woman, you are now free from your trouble!" ¹³Then He put His hand on her. At once she stood up straight and gave thanks to God.

¹⁴The leader of the Jewish place of worship was angry because Jesus healed on the Day of Rest. The leader said to the people, "There are six days in which work should be done. Come on those days and get healed. Do not come to be healed on the Day of Rest." ¹⁵The Lord said to him, "You pretend to be someone you are not! Do not each of you let his cow or his donkey out and lead them to water on the Day of Rest? ¹⁶Should not this Jewish woman be made free from this trouble on the Day of Rest? She has been chained by Satan for eighteen years." ¹⁷When He said this, all those who were against Him were ashamed. All the many people were glad for the great things being done by Him.

¹⁸Then Jesus asked, "What is the holy nation of God like? What can I use to show you? ¹⁹It is like a mustard seed which a man took and planted in his field. It grew and became a tree. The birds of the sky stayed in its branches." ²⁰Again Jesus said, "What can I use to show you what the holy nation of God is like? ²¹It is like yeast that a woman put into three pails of flour until it was all full of yeast."

Jesus Teaches On The Way To Jerusalem

²²Jesus taught the people as He went through the cities and towns on His way to Jerusalem. ²³Someone asked Jesus, "Lord, will only a few people be saved from the punishment of sin?" Jesus said to them, ²⁴"Work hard to go in through the narrow door. I tell you, many will try to go in but will not be able to go in. ²⁵The owner of the house will get up and shut the door. You who are on the outside will knock on the door and say, 'Lord, let us in.' Then He will say, 'I do not know you.' ²⁶Then you will say, 'We ate and drank with You when You taught in our streets.' ²⁷But He will say, 'I tell you, I do not know you. Go away from Me. You are sinful.'

²⁸"There will be loud crying and grinding of teeth when you see Abraham and Isaac and Jacob and all the early preachers in the holy nation of God, but you will be put out. ²⁹Those who sit at the table in the holy nation of God will come from the east and west and from the north and south. ³⁰Listen! Some are last who will be first. Some are first who will be last."

³¹That same day some of the proud religious law-keepers came to Jesus. They said, "Go away from here! Herod wants to kill You." ³²Jesus said to them, "Go and tell that fox, 'See. I put out demons and heal the sick. I will do these things today and tomorrow. And the third day My work will be finished.' ³³But I must go on My way today and tomorrow and the day after. One who speaks for God cannot die except at Jerusalem.

Jesus Sorrows Over Jerusalem

³⁴"Jerusalem, Jerusalem, you kill the early preachers and throw stones on those sent to you. How many times I wanted to gather your children around me, as a bird gathers her young under her wings, but you would not let Me. ³⁵See! Your house is empty. And I tell you, you will not see Me again until the time comes when you will say, 'Great and honored is the One Who comes in the name of the Lord.' "

Another Man Healed On The Day Of Rest

14 On the Day of Rest Jesus went into the house of one of the leaders of the proud religious law-keepers to eat. They all watched Jesus to see what He would do. ²A man who had very large arms and legs because of a sickness was put before Jesus. ³Jesus asked the teachers of the Law and the proud religious law-keepers, "Does the Law say it is right to heal on the Day of Rest, or not?" ⁴They did not answer. Jesus took hold of the man and healed him and sent him away. ⁵Then Jesus said to the leaders, "If one of you had a cow or donkey that fell into a hole, would you not go at once and pull it out on the Day of Rest?" ⁶And they were not able to answer His questions.

Jesus Teaches About How To Live With Others

⁷Jesus had been watching those who were asked to come to supper. They were all trying to get the important seats. He told them a picture-story, saying, ⁸"When you are asked by someone to a wedding supper, do not take the important seat. Someone more important than you may have been asked to come also. ⁹The one who asked both of you to come may say to you, 'The important seat is for this man.' Then you will be ashamed as you take the last place. ¹⁰But when you are asked to come to the table, sit down on the last seat. Then the one who asked you may come and say to you, 'Friend, go to a more important place.' Then you will be shown respect in front of all who are at the table with you. ¹¹Whoever makes himself look more important than he is will find out how little he is worth. Whoever does not try to honor himself will be made important."

¹²Then Jesus said to the man who asked Him to eat in his house, "When you have a supper, do not ask your friends or your brothers or your family or your rich neighbors. They will ask you to come to their place for a supper. That way you will be paid back for what you have done. ¹³When you have a supper, ask poor people. Ask those who cannot walk and those who are blind. ¹⁴You will be happy if you do this. They cannot pay you back. You will get your pay when the people who are right with God are raised from the dead."

¹⁵When one of those eating at the table with Jesus heard this, he said, "Everyone is happy who will eat in the holy nation of God."

The Picture-story Of The Big Supper
[Matthew 22:1-14]

¹⁶Then Jesus said to the leader of the proud religious law-keepers, "There was a man who was giving a big supper. He asked many people to come to eat. ¹⁷When it was about time to eat, he sent one of the servants he owned to tell those he had asked, saying, 'Come, everything is ready now.' ¹⁸They all gave different reasons why they could not come. The first said, 'I have bought some land and I must go and see it. Do not expect me to come.' ¹⁹Another one said, 'I have bought ten oxen to use for working in my fields. I must go and try them out. Do not expect me to come.' ²⁰And another one said, 'I have just been married and I cannot come.'

²¹"The servant went back to his owner and told him these things. Then his owner became angry. He said to his servant, 'Hurry into the streets and narrow roads of the city and bring poor people here. Bring those whose bodies are diseased. Bring those who cannot walk and those who are blind.' ²²The servant came back and said, 'Sir, what you

told me to do has been done. But there are still some empty places.' [23] Then the owner said to his servant, 'Go out along the roads leading away from the city and into the fields. Tell them they must come. Do this so my house will be filled. [24] I tell you, not one of those I had asked will eat of my supper.' "

Giving Up Things Of This Earth
[Matthew 10:37-39]

[25] Many people followed Jesus. Then He turned around and said to them, [26] "If any man comes to Me and does not have much more love for Me than for his father and mother, wife and children, brothers and sisters, and even his own life, he cannot be My follower. [27] If he does not carry his cross and follow Me, he cannot be My follower.

[28] "If one of you wanted to build a large building, you would sit down first and think of how much money it would take to build it. You would see if you had enough money to finish it, [29] or when the base of the building is finished, you might see that you do not have enough money to finish it. Then all who would see it would make fun of you. [30] They would say, 'This man began to build and was not able to finish.'

[31] "What if a king is going to war with another king? Will he not sit down first and decide if he is able to go with 10,000 men against the other king who is coming with 20,000 men? [32] Or, he will send a soldier to the other king while he is still a long way off. He will ask what can be done to have peace. [33] In the same way, whoever does not give up all that he has, cannot be My follower.

[34] "Salt is good. But if salt has lost its taste, how can it be made to taste like salt again? [35] It is no good for the field or the waste place. Men throw it away. You have ears, then listen!"

The Picture-story Of The Lost Sheep

15 All the men who gathered taxes and sinners were coming to hear Jesus. [2] The proud religious law-keepers and the teachers of the Law began to speak against Him. They said, "This man receives sinners and eats with them."

[3] Then Jesus told them a picture-story, saying, [4] "What if one of you had one hundred sheep and you lost one of them? Would you not leave the ninety-nine in the country and go back and look for the one which was lost until you find it? [5] When you find it, you are happy as you carry it back on your shoulders. [6] Then you would go to your house and call your friends and neighbors. You would say to them, 'Be happy with me because I have found my sheep that was lost.' [7] I tell you, there will be more joy in heaven because of one sinner who is sorry for his sins and turns from them, than for ninety-nine people right with God who do not have sins to be sorry for.

The Picture-story Of The Lost Piece Of Money

[8] "What if a woman has ten silver pieces of money and loses one of them? Does she not light a lamp and sweep the floor and look until she finds it? [9] When she finds it, she calls her friends and neighbors together. She says to them, 'Be happy with me. I have found the piece of money I had lost.' [10] I tell you, it is the same way among the angels of God. If one sinner is sorry for his sins and turns from them, the angels are very happy."

The Picture-story Of The Foolish Son Who Spent All His Money

[11] And Jesus said, "There was a man who had two sons. [12] The younger son said to his father,

'Father, let me have the part of the family riches that will be coming to me.' Then the father divided all that he owned between his two sons. [13]Soon after that the younger son took all that had been given to him and went to another country far away. There he spent all he had on wild and foolish living. [14]When all his money was spent, he was hungry. There was no food in the land. [15]He went to work for a man in this far away country. His work was to feed pigs. [16]He was so hungry he was ready to eat the outside part of the ears of the corn the pigs ate because no one gave him anything.

[17]"He began to think about what he had done. He said to himself, 'My father pays many men who work for him. They have all the food they want and more than enough. I am about dead because I am so hungry. [18]I will get up and go to my father. I will say to him, "Father, I have sinned against heaven and against you. [19]I am not good enough to be called your son. But may I be as one of the workmen you pay to work?" '

[20]"The son got up and went to his father. While he was yet a long way off, his father saw him. The father was full of loving-pity for him. He ran and threw his arms around him and kissed him. [21]The son said to him, 'Father, I have sinned against heaven and against you. I am not good enough to be called your son.' [22]But the father said to the workmen he owned, 'Hurry! Get the best coat and put it on him. Put a ring on his hand and shoes on his feet. [23]Bring the calf that is fat and kill it. Let us eat and be glad. [24]For my son was dead and now he is alive again. He was lost and now he is found. Let us eat and have a good time.'

[25]"The older son was out in the field. As he was coming near the house, he heard music and dancing. [26]He called one of the helper boys and asked what was happening. [27]The helper boy answered, 'Your brother has come back and your father has killed the fat calf. Your brother is in the house and is well.' [28]The older brother was angry and would not go into the house. His father went outside and asked him to come in. [29]The older son said to his father, 'All these many years I have worked for you. I have always obeyed what you said. But you never gave me a young goat so I could have a supper and a good time with my friends. [30]But as soon as this son of yours came back, you killed the fat calf. And yet he wasted your money with bad women.'

[31]"The father said to him, 'My son, you are with me all the time. All that I have is yours. [32]It is right and good that we should have a good time and be glad. Your brother was dead and now he is alive again. He was lost and now he is found.' "

The Picture-story Of The Boss Who Stole

16 Jesus said to His followers, "There was a rich man who put a boss over his houses and lands. Someone told him that his boss was not using his riches in a right way. [2]The rich man sent for the boss and said, 'What is this I hear about you? Tell me what you have done with my things. You are not to be the boss of my houses and lands anymore.'

[3]"The boss said to himself, 'What will I do now? The owner of the houses and lands is taking my work away from me. I cannot dig in the ground for a living. I am too proud to ask for help. [4]I know what I will do. I will make it so that when I lose this work I will be able to go to the homes of my friends.'

[5]"He sent for the people who owed the rich man. He asked the first one, 'How much do you owe the owner?' [6]The first man said, 'One hundred barrels of oil.' The boss said to him, 'Take your bill. Sit down at once and change it to fifty.' [7]He asked another

one, 'How much do you owe?' He said, 'One hundred bags of wheat.' He said to him, 'Take your bill and change it to eighty.' [8]Then the rich man said that this sinful boss had been wise to plan for himself for the days ahead. For the people of the world are wiser in their day than the children of light.

[9]"I tell you, make friends for yourselves by using the riches of the world that are so often used in wrong ways. So when riches are a thing of the past, friends may receive you into a home that will be forever. [10]He that is faithful with little things is faithful with big things also. He that is not honest with little things is not honest with big things. [11]If you have not been faithful with riches of this world, who will trust you with true riches? [12]If you have not been faithful in that which belongs to another person, who will give you things to have as your own? [13]No workman can have two bosses. He will hate the one and love the other. Or, he will be faithful to one and not faithful to the other. You cannot be faithful to God and to riches at the same time."

Jesus Teaches That The Law Is Not Finished

[14]The proud religious law-keepers heard all these things. They loved money so they made fun of Jesus. [15]Jesus said to them, "You are the kind of people who make yourselves look good before other people. God knows your hearts. What men think is good is hated in the eyes of God. [16]Until John came, you had the writings of the Law and of the early preachers. From that time until now the Good News of the holy nation of God has been preached. Everyone is pushing his way in. [17]But it is easier for heaven and earth to pass away than for one small part of a word in the Law to be of no more use.

[18]"Whoever divorces his wife and marries another woman is not faithful in marriage and is guilty of sex sins.

The Rich Man And The Man Who Begged For Food

[19]"There was a rich man who dressed in purple linen clothes everyday. He lived like a king would live with the best of food. [20]There was a poor man named Lazarus who had many bad sores. He was put by the door of the rich man. [21]He wanted the pieces of food that fell from the table of the rich man. Even dogs came and licked his sores.

[22]"The poor man who asked for food died. He was taken by the angels into the arms of Abraham. The rich man died also and was buried. [23]In hell the rich man was in much pain. He looked up and saw Abraham far away and Lazarus beside him. [24]He cried out and said, 'Father Abraham, take pity on me. Send Lazarus. Let him put the end of his finger in water and cool my tongue. I am in much pain in this fire.' [25]Abraham said, 'My son, do not forget that when you were living you had your good things. Lazarus had bad things. Now he is well cared for. You are in pain. [26]And more than all this, there is a big deep place between us. No one from here can go there even if he wanted to go. No one can come from there.'

[27]"Then the rich man said, 'Father, then I beg you to send Lazarus to my father's house. [28]I have five brothers. Let him tell them of these things, or they will come to this place of much pain also.' [29]Abraham said, 'They have the Writings of Moses and of the early preachers. Let them hear what they say.' [30]But the rich man said, 'No, Father Abraham. If someone goes to them from the dead, they will be sorry for their sins and turn from them.' [31]Abraham said to him, 'If they do not listen to Moses and to the early preachers, they will not

listen even if someone is raised from the dead.' "

Jesus Teaches About Forgiving

17 Jesus said to His followers, "For sure, things will come that will make people sin. But it is bad for the person who makes someone else sin. ²It would be better for him to have a large rock put around his neck and be thrown into the sea, than that he should be the reason one of these little ones sin.

³"Watch yourselves! If your brother sins, speak sharp words to him. If he is sorry and turns from his sin, forgive him. ⁴What if he sins against you seven times in one day? If he comes to you and says he is sorry and turns from his sin, forgive him."

⁵The missionaries said to the Lord, "Give us more faith." ⁶The Lord said, "If your faith was as a mustard seed, you could say to this tree, 'Be pulled out of the ground and planted in the sea,' and it would obey you.

Jesus Teaches About Being Faithful

⁷"What if you owned a servant who was working in the field or taking care of sheep? Would you say to him when he came in from his work, 'Come and sit down to eat?' ⁸No, instead you would say, 'Get my supper ready. Dress yourself and care for me until I am through eating and drinking. Then you can eat and drink.' ⁹Does the servant get thanks for doing what he was told to do? I am sure he does not. ¹⁰It is the same with you also. When you do everything you have been told to do, you must say, 'We are not any special servants. We have done only what we should have done.' "

Jesus Heals Ten Men With A Bad Skin Disease

¹¹Jesus went on His way to Jerusalem. He was passing between the countries of Samaria and Galilee. ¹²As He was going into one of the towns, ten men with a bad skin disease came to Him. They stood a little way off. ¹³They called to Him, "Jesus! Teacher! Take pity on us!" ¹⁴When Jesus saw them, He said, "Go and show yourselves to the religious leaders." As they went, they were healed. ¹⁵One of them turned back when he saw he was healed. He thanked God with a loud voice. ¹⁶He got down on his face at the feet of Jesus and thanked Him. He was from the country of Samaria. ¹⁷Jesus asked, "Were there not ten men who were healed? Where are the other nine? ¹⁸Is this stranger from another country the only one who turned back to give thanks to God?" ¹⁹Then Jesus said to him, "Get up and go on your way. Your trust in God has healed you."

Jesus Teaches About The Holy Nation Of God

²⁰The proud religious law-keepers asked when the holy nation of God would come. Jesus said to them, "The holy nation of God is not coming in such a way that can be seen with the eyes. ²¹It will not be said, 'See, here it is!' or, 'There it is!' For the holy nation of God is in you."

Jesus Tells Of His Second Coming

²²Jesus said to His followers, "The time will come when you will wish you could see the Son of Man for one day. But you will not be able to. ²³They will say to you, 'He is here,' or, 'He is there,' but do not follow them. ²⁴When the Son of Man comes, He will be as lightning that shines from one part of the sky to the other. ²⁵But before that, He must suffer many hard things. The people of this day will have nothing to do with Him.

²⁶"As it was in the time of Noah, so will it be when the Son of Man comes

back. [27]People ate and drank. They married and were given in marriage. They did these things until the day Noah went into the large boat. Then the flood came and killed all the people on earth. [28]It was the same in the time of Lot. People ate and drank. They bought and sold. They planted and built. [29]But the day Lot left the city of Sodom, fire and sulphur came down from heaven like rain. It killed all the people of Sodom.

[30]"It will be the same on the day when the Son of Man comes again. [31]In that day the man who is on top of a house should not come down to take his things out of the house. In the same way, the man who is in the field should not go back to his house. [32]Remember Lot's wife!

[33]"He who wants to keep his life will have it taken away from him. He who loses his life will have it given back to him. [34]I tell you, on that night there will be two men in the same bed. One of them will be taken. The other will be left. [35]Two women will be grinding grain together. One of them will be taken. The other will be left. [36]*Two men will be working in a field. One will be taken. The other will be left."

[37]Then they asked Jesus, "Where will this happen?" He said to them, "Birds also gather where there is a dead body."

The Picture-story Of The Woman Whose Husband Had Died

18 Jesus told them a picture-story to show that men should always pray and not give up. [2]He said, "There was a man in one of the cities who was head of the court. His work was to say if a person was guilty or not. This man was not afraid of God. He did not respect any man. [3]In that city there was a woman whose husband had died. She kept coming to him and saying, 'Help me! There is someone who is working against me.' [4]For awhile he would not help her. Then he began to think, 'I am not afraid of God and I do not respect any man. [5]But I will see that this woman whose husband has died gets her rights because I get tired of her coming all the time.' "

[6]Then the Lord said, "Listen to the words of the sinful man who is head of the court. [7]Will not God make the things that are right come to His chosen people who cry day and night to Him? Will He wait a long time to help them? [8]I tell you, He will be quick to help them. But when the Son of Man comes, will He find faith on the earth?"

The Picture-story Of The Proud Religious Law-keepers And The Tax-Gatherers

[9]Jesus told another picture-story to some people who trusted in themselves and thought they were right with God. These people did not think well of other men. [10]Jesus said, "Two men went up to the house of God to pray. One of them was a proud religious law-keeper. The other was a man who gathered taxes. [11]The proud religious law-keeper stood and prayed to himself like this, 'God, I thank You that I am not like other men. I am not like those who steal. I am not like those who do things that are wrong. I am not like those who do sex sins. I am not like even this tax-gatherer. [12]I go without food two times a week so I can pray better. I give one-tenth part of the money I earn.' [13]But the man who gathered taxes stood a long way off. He would not even lift his eyes to heaven. But he hit himself on his chest and said, 'God, have pity on me! I am a sinner!' [14]I tell you, this man went back to his house forgiven, and not the other man. For whoever makes himself look more important than he is will find out how little he is worth. Whoever does not try to honor himself will be made important.

Jesus Gives Thanks For Little Children [*Matthew 19:13-15; Mark 10:13-16*]

15 People took their little children to Jesus so He could put His hand on them. When His followers saw it, they spoke sharp words to the people. 16 Jesus called the followers to Him and said, "Let the little children come to Me. Do not try to stop them. The holy nation of God is made up of ones like these. 17 For sure, I tell you, whoever does not receive the holy nation of God as a child will not go into the holy nation."

Jesus Teaches About Keeping The Law [*Matthew 19:16-30; Mark 10:17-31*]

18 A leader of the people asked Jesus, "Good Teacher, what must I do to have life that lasts forever?" 19 Jesus said to him, "Why do you call Me good? There is only One Who is good. That is God. 20 You know the Laws. You must not do any sex sins. You must not kill another person. You must not steal. You must not tell a lie about someone else. Respect your father and your mother." 21 The leader said, "I have obeyed all these Laws since I was a boy."

22 When Jesus heard this, He said to the leader of the people, "There is still one thing you need to do. Sell everything you have. Give the money to poor people. Then you will have riches in heaven. Come and follow Me." 23 When the leader heard this, he was very sad because he had many riches. 24 When Jesus saw that he was very sad, He said, "It is hard for those with riches to go into the holy nation of God! 25 It is easier for a camel to go through the eye of a needle than for a rich man to go into the holy nation of God."

26 Those who heard this, said, "Then who can be saved from the punishment of sin?" 27 Jesus said, "God can do things men cannot do."

28 Then Peter said, "See, we have left everything and have followed You." 29 Jesus said to them, "For sure, I tell you, anyone who has left his house or parents or brothers or wife or children because of the holy nation of God 30 will receive much more now. In the time to come he will have life that lasts forever."

Jesus Tells Of His Death The Third Time [*Matthew 20:17-19; Mark 10:32-34*]

31 Then Jesus took the twelve followers to one side and said, "See! We are going up to Jerusalem. All the things the early preachers wrote about the Son of Man are going to happen. 32 He will be given over to the people who are not Jews. He will be made fun of. He will be hurt. He will be spit on. 33 They will beat Him and kill Him. After three days He will be raised again."

34 The followers did not understand these words. The meaning of these words was hidden from them. They did not know what He said.

Healing Of The Blind Man [*Matthew 20:29-34; Mark 10:46-52*]

35 Jesus was coming near Jericho. A blind man was sitting by the side of the road, begging. 36 He heard many people going by and asked what was happening. 37 They told him that Jesus of Nazareth was going by. 38 Then he cried out and said, "Jesus, Son of David, have pity on me." 39 The people spoke sharp words to him and told him not to call out. But he cried out all the more, "Son of David, have pity on me."

40 Jesus stopped and told the people to bring the blind man to Him. When the man was near, Jesus asked, 41 "What do you want Me to do for you?" He answered, "Lord, I want to see." 42 Jesus said to him, "Then see! Your faith has healed you." 43 At once he could see. He followed Jesus and

gave thanks to God. All the people gave thanks to God when they saw it.

The Changed Life Of Zaccheus

19 Jesus went on to the city of Jericho and was passing through it. ²There was a rich man named Zaccheus. He was a leader of those who gathered taxes. ³Zaccheus wanted to see Jesus but he could not because so many people were there and he was a short man. ⁴He ran ahead and got up into a sycamore tree to see Him. Jesus was going by that way.

⁵When Jesus came to the place, He looked up and saw Zaccheus. He said, "Zaccheus, come down at once. I must stay in your house today." ⁶At once he came down and was glad to have Jesus come to his house. ⁷When the people saw it, they began to complain among themselves. They said, "He is going to stay with a man who is known to be a sinner."

⁸Zaccheus stood up and said to the Lord, "Lord, see! Half of what I own I will give to poor people. And if I have taken money from anyone in a wrong way, I will pay him back four times as much." ⁹Jesus said to him, "Today, a person has been saved in this house. This man is a Jew also. ¹⁰For the Son of Man came to look for and to save from the punishment of sin those who are lost."

The Picture-story Of The Ten Servants And The Money

¹¹As they heard these things, Jesus told them a picture-story. Because He was near Jerusalem, they thought the holy nation of God would come at once. ¹²So Jesus said, "A leader of a country went to another country far away. A nation was to be given to him, then he would return home. ¹³He called ten of the servants he owned. He gave them ten pieces of money and said to them, 'Put this money to use until I return.' ¹⁴But

other men in his country hated him. They sent men after him to tell him they did not want him as their king. ¹⁵After he had been given the other nation, he returned as king. He asked for his servants who had received the money to come to him. He wanted to know how much more they had after putting it to use. ¹⁶The first one came and said, 'Lord, the piece of money you gave me has made ten more pieces of money.' ¹⁷He said to him, 'You are a good servant. You have been faithful in using a little. Now you will be leader over ten cities.'

¹⁸"The second man came to him and said, 'Lord, the piece of money you gave me has made five more pieces of money.' ¹⁹He said to him, 'You are to be leader over five cities.'

²⁰"Another one came saying, 'Lord, look! Here is your piece of money. I have kept it hid in a piece of cloth. ²¹I was afraid of you. You are a hard man. You take what you have not put down. You gather where you have not planted.' ²²The king said to him, 'By the words from your own mouth I must say that you are guilty. You are a sinful servant. You knew I was a hard man. You knew I take what I have not put down. You knew I gather where I have not planted. ²³Why did you not put my money in the bank? Then when I came back I could have had my own money and what the bank paid for using it.'

²⁴"Then he said to those who were standing by, 'Take the piece of money from him and give it to the one who has ten pieces of money.' ²⁵And they said to him, 'Lord, he already has ten pieces of money.' "

²⁶Jesus said, "I tell you, he who has, to him will be given more. To him who does not have, even the little he has will be taken from him. ²⁷'Bring here those who hated me and did not want me to be their king and kill them in front of me.' " ²⁸When He had finished the picture-story, He went on ahead of them up to Jerusalem.

The Last Time Jesus Goes Into Jerusalem [Matthew 21:1-11; Mark 11:1-11; John 12:12-19]

29When Jesus was coming near the towns of Bethphage and Bethany by the Mount of Olives, He sent two of His followers on ahead. 30He said, "Go into the town ahead of you. There you will find a young donkey tied. No man has ever sat on it. Let it loose and bring it to Me. 31If anyone asks you, 'Why are you letting it loose?' say to him, 'Because the Lord needs it.' "

32Those who were sent found everything as Jesus had told them. 33As they were letting the young donkey loose, the owners said to them, "Why are you letting the young donkey loose?" 34They answered, "The Lord needs it." 35Then they brought it to Jesus. They put their coats on the donkey and they put Jesus on it.

36As Jesus was going, they put their coats down on the road. 37Jesus was near the city and ready to go down the Mount of Olives. The many people who were following Him began to sing with loud voices and give thanks for all the powerful works they had seen. 38They said, "Great and honored is the King Who comes in the name of the Lord. There is peace and greatness in the highest heaven."

39Some of the proud religious law-keepers who were in among the people said to Jesus, "Teacher, speak sharp words to Your followers." 40Jesus said to them, "I tell you that if these did not speak, the very stones would call out."

Jesus Cried As He Saw Jerusalem

41When Jesus came near the city, He cried as He saw it. 42He said, "If you had only known on this great day the things that make peace! But now they are hidden from your eyes. 43The time is coming when those who

hate you will dig earth and throw it up around you making a wall. They will shut you in from every side. 44They will destroy you and your children with you. There will not be one stone on another. It is because you did not know when God visited you."

Jesus Stops The Buying And Selling In The House Of God [Matthew 21:12-17; Mark 11:15-19; John 2:13-17]

45Jesus went into the house of God. He made those leave who were buying and selling there. 46He said to them, "It is written, 'My house is a house of prayer.' 'But you have made it a place of robbers.' " (Isaiah 56:7; Jeremiah 7:11)

47Jesus taught each day in the house of God. But the religious leaders and the teachers of the Law and other leaders of the people tried to think of some way they could kill Him. 48They could not find a way because the people were always near Him listening to Him teach.

They Ask Jesus Who Gave Him The Power To Do These Things [Matthew 21:23-32; Mark 11:27-33]

20 As He was teaching and preaching the Good News, the religious leaders and the teachers of the Law and the elders came. 2They said to Him, "Tell us, by what right and power are You doing these things? Who gave You the right and the power?" 3Jesus said to them, "I will ask you one question also. You answer Me. 4Was the baptism of John from heaven or from men?"

5They said to themselves, "If we say, 'From heaven,' He will say, 'Then why did you not believe Him?' 6But if we say, 'From men,' then all the people will throw stones at us because they believe John was one who spoke for God." 7They said that they did not know where John's baptism came from. ⁸Jesus said to them, "And I will not tell you where I get the right and the power to do these things."

The Picture-story Of The Grape Field [Matthew 21:33-46; Mark 12:1-12]

⁹Jesus began to tell the people a picture-story, saying, "There was a man who planted a grape field. He rented it to farmers. Then he went to a country far away for a long time. ¹⁰At the time of gathering fruit he sent one of his servants to the farmers to get some of the fruit. But the farmers beat him and sent him away without fruit. ¹¹He sent another servant. The farmers beat him also. They made it very hard for him and sent him away without fruit. ¹²He sent a third servant. They hurt him and threw him out of the grape field. ¹³"Then the owner of the grape field said, 'What should I do? I will send my much-loved son. They might respect him.' ¹⁴The farmers saw the son. They said to themselves, 'This is the one who will get everything when the owner dies. Let us kill him, and we will get everything.' ¹⁵They put him out of the grape field and killed him. Now what will the owner of the grape field do to them? ¹⁶He will come and kill those farmers. Then he will rent the grape field to other farmers."

When they heard this, they said, "May this never be done!" ¹⁷Jesus looked at them and said, "What does this writing mean, 'The Stone that was put aside by the workman has become the most important Stone in the building'? (Psalm 118:22) ¹⁸Whoever falls on this Stone will be broken. And on the one it falls, it will make him like dust." (Isaiah 8:14-15)

They Try To Trap Jesus [Matthew 22:15-22; Mark 12:13-17]

¹⁹At this time the religious leaders and the teachers of the Law tried to take Jesus, but they were afraid of the people. These leaders knew Jesus had told this picture-story against them. ²⁰They watched Jesus and they sent men who pretended to be good people to watch Him. They wanted to trap Him in something He said. Then they could give Him over to the leader of the people who had the right and the power to say what to do with Him.

²¹These men who were sent asked Jesus, "Teacher, we know what You say and teach is right. We know You do not show more respect to one person than to another. We know You teach the truth about God. ²²Is it right for us to pay taxes to Caesar or not?" ²³Jesus knew they were trying to trap Him. He said, ²⁴"Show Me a piece of money. Whose picture is this? Whose name is on it?" And they said, "Caesar's." ²⁵Jesus said to them, "Pay to Caesar the things that belong to Caesar. Pay to God the things that belong to God." ²⁶They could find nothing wrong with what He taught. They were surprised and wondered about what He told the people, so they said nothing more.

They Ask About Being Raised From The Dead [Matthew 22:23-33; Mark 12:18-27]

²⁷Some people from the religious group who believe no one will be raised from the dead came to Jesus. They asked Him, ²⁸"Teacher, Moses wrote to us in the Law, 'If a man's brother dies and leaves a wife but no children, then his brother must marry her. He should have children for his brother who died.' (Deuteronomy 25:5) ²⁹There were seven brothers. The first had a wife but died without children. ³⁰The second brother took her for his wife. He died without children. ³¹The third brother took her for his wife. In the same way all seven took her for a wife. They all died without children. ³²Then the woman died also. ³³When

people are raised from the dead, whose wife will she be? All seven brothers had her for a wife."

34Jesus said to them, "People of this earth marry and are given in marriage. 35But those who have the right to have that life and are raised from the dead do not marry and are not given in marriage. 36They cannot die anymore. They are as the angels and are sons of God. They are children who have been raised from the dead. 37As for the dead being raised, even Moses spoke of that when he told of the burning bush. There he calls the Lord, the God of Abraham and the God of Isaac and the God of Jacob. 38For He is not the God of the dead. He is the God of the living. All live for Him."

39One of the teachers of the Law said, "Teacher, You have spoken well." 40After that they were afraid to ask Him anything.

Jesus Asks The Teachers Of The Law About The Christ [Matthew 22:41-46; Mark 12:35-37]

41Jesus said to them, "How do they say that Christ is the Son of David? 42For David himself said in the Book of Psalms, 'The Lord said to My Lord, "Sit at my right side 43until I make those who hate You a place to rest Your Feet." ' (Psalm 110:1) 44David calls Him, 'Lord!' Then how can He be his son?"

False Teachers [Matthew 23:1-36; Mark 12:38-40]

45All the people were listening. He said to His followers, 46"Look out for the teachers of the Law. They like to walk around in long coats. They like to have people speak words of respect to them in the center of town where people gather. They like the important seats in the places of worship. They like the important places at big suppers. 47They take houses from poor women whose husbands have died. They cover up their actions by making long prayers. They will be punished all the more."

A Woman Whose Husband Had Died Gave All She Had [Mark 12:41-44]

21 Jesus looked up and saw rich men putting their money into the money box in the house of God. 2He saw a poor woman whose husband had died. She put in two very small pieces of money. 3He said, "I tell you the truth, this poor woman has put in more than all of them. 4For they have put in a little of the money they had no need for. She is very poor and has put in all she had. She has put in what she needed for her own living."

Jesus Tells Of The House Of God [Matthew 24:1-51; Mark 13:11-37]

5Some people were talking about the house of God. They were saying that the stones were beautiful and that many gifts had been given. Jesus said, 6"As for these things you see, all these stones will be thrown down. Not one will be left on another." 7They asked Jesus, 'Teacher, when will this take place? What are we to look for to show us these things are about to happen?" 8He said, "Be careful that no one leads you the wrong way. For many people will come in My name. They will say, 'I am the Christ.' The time is near. Do not follow them. 9When you hear of wars and fighting in different places, do not be afraid. These things have to happen first, but the end is not yet."

10Then Jesus said to them, "Nations will have wars with other nations. Countries will fight against countries. 11The earth will shake and break apart in different places. There will be no food. There will be bad diseases among many people. Very special things will be seen in the sky that will make people much afraid.

¹²"But before all this happens, men will take hold of you and make it very hard for you. They will give you over to the places of worship and to the prisons. They will bring you in front of kings and the leaders of the people. This will all be done to you because of Me. ¹³This will be a time for you to tell about Me. ¹⁴Do not think about what you will say ahead of time. ¹⁵For I will give you wisdom in what to say and I will help you say it. Those who are against you will not be able to stop you or say you are wrong.

¹⁶"You will be handed over by your parents and your brothers and your family and your friends. They will kill some of you. ¹⁷All men will hate you because of Me. ¹⁸Yet not one hair of your head will be lost. ¹⁹But stay true and your souls will have life.

Days Of Trouble And Pain And Sorrow

²⁰"When you see armies all around Jerusalem, know that it will soon be destroyed. ²¹Those in the country of Judea must run to the mountains. Those in the city must leave at once. Those in the country must not go into the city. ²²People will be punished in these hard days. All things will happen as it is written.

²³"It will be hard for women who will soon be mothers. It will be hard for those feeding babies in those days. It will be very hard for the people in the land and anger will be brought down on them. ²⁴People will be killed by the sword. They will be held in prison by all nations. Jerusalem will be walked over by the people who are not Jews until their time is finished.

Jesus Will Come Again In His Shining Greatness

²⁵"There will be special things to look for in the sun and moon and stars. The nations of the earth will be troubled and will not know what to do. They will be troubled at the angry sea and waves. ²⁶The hearts of men will give up because of being afraid of what is coming on the earth. The powers of the heavens will be shaken. ²⁷Then they will see the Son of Man coming in the clouds with power and much greatness. ²⁸When these things begin to happen, lift up your heads because you have been bought by the blood of Christ and will soon be free."

The Picture-story Of The Fig Tree

²⁹Jesus told them a picture-story. He said, "Look at the fig tree and all the other trees. ³⁰When you see their leaves coming out, you know summer is near. ³¹In the same way, when you see these things happening, you will know the holy nation of God is near. ³²For sure, I tell you, that the people of this day will not die before all these things happen.

³³"Heaven and earth will pass away, but My Words will not pass away. ³⁴Watch yourselves! Do not let yourselves be loaded down with too much eating and strong drink. Do not be troubled with the cares of this life. If you do, that day will come on you without you knowing it. ³⁵It will come on all people over all the earth. ³⁶Be sure you watch. Pray all the time so that you may be able to keep from going through all these things that will happen and be able to stand before the Son of Man."

³⁷Everyday Jesus taught in the house of God. At night He went to the Mount of Olives and stayed there. ³⁸Early in the morning all the people came to the house of God to hear Him.

They Look For A Way To Put Jesus To Death

22 The time for the supper of bread without yeast was near. It was the special religious gathering to remember how the Jews left Egypt. [2]The religious leaders and the teachers of the Law looked for a way to kill Jesus. But they were afraid of the people.

[3]Then Satan came into the heart of Judas who was called Iscariot. He was one of the twelve followers. [4]Judas went away and talked with the religious leaders and the leaders of the people. He talked about how he might hand Jesus over to them. [5]They were glad and promised to pay him money. [6]Judas promised to do this and then looked for a way to hand Jesus over when there were no people around.

Getting Ready For The Special Supper [Matthew 26:17-19; Mark 14:12-16]

[7]The day of bread without yeast came. It was the day when the lamb had to be killed and given on the altar in worship in the house of God. It was the special religious gathering to remember how the Jews left Egypt. [8]Jesus sent Peter and John and said, "Go and get this special supper ready for us that we may eat." [9]They said to Him, "Where do You want us to get it ready?" [10]He answered, "See, when you go into the city, you will meet a man carrying a jar of water. Follow him into the house where he goes. [11]Say to the owner of the house, 'The Teacher asks you, "Where is the room you keep for friends where I may eat this special supper with My followers?" ' [12]He will take you to a large room on the second floor with everything in it. Make it ready for us."

[13]They went and found everything as Jesus had said. They got ready for the special supper.

The Last Special Supper [Matthew 26:20-25; Mark 14:17-21; John 13:21-35]

[14]When the time came, Jesus sat down with the twelve followers. [15]He said to them, "I have wanted very much to eat this special supper with you to remember how the Jews left Egypt. I have wanted to eat this with you before I suffer. [16]I say to you, I will not eat this special supper again until its true meaning is completed in the holy nation of God."

[17]Then Jesus took the cup and gave thanks. He said, "Take this and pass it to each one. [18]I say to you that I will not drink of the fruit of the vine until the holy nation of God comes."

The First Lord's Supper [Matthew 26:26-30; Mark 14:22-26]

[19]Then Jesus took bread and gave thanks and broke it in pieces. He gave it to them, saying, "This is My body which is given for you. Do this to remember Me." [20]In the same way, after they had finished the bread, He took the cup. He said, "This cup is My blood of the New Way of Worship which is given for you.

Jesus Tells Of The One Who Will Hand Him Over

[21]"See, the hand of the one who will give Me over to the leaders of the country is on the table with Me. [22]The Son of Man will be taken this way because it has been in God's plan. But it is bad for that man who hands Him over!" [23]They began to ask each other which of them would do this.

They Argue About Who Is The Greatest

[24]They started to argue among themselves about who was thought to be the greatest. [25]Jesus said to them, "The kings of the nations show their power to the people. Those who have power over the people are given names of honor. [26]But you will not be like that. Let the greatest among you be as the least. Let the leader be as the one who cares for others. [27]Who is

greater, the one who is eating at the table, or the one who is caring for him? Is it not the one who is eating at the table? But I am here with you as One Who cares for you.

The Followers Will Be Honored

28"You have stayed with Me through all the hard things that have come to Me. 29As My Father has given Me a holy nation, I will give you the right 30to eat and drink at My table in My holy nation. You will sit on thrones and judge the twelve family groups of the Jewish nation."

Jesus Tells How Peter Will Lie About Him [Matthew 26:31-35; Mark 14:27-31; John 13:36-38]

31The Lord said, "Simon, Simon, listen! Satan has wanted to have you. He will divide you as wheat is divided from that which is no good. 32But I have prayed for you. I have prayed that your faith will be strong and that you will not give up. When you return, you must help to make your brothers strong." 33Peter said to Jesus, "Lord, I am ready to go to prison and to die with You!" 34Jesus said, "I tell you, Peter, a rooster will not crow today before you will say three times that you do not know Me."

The Followers Are Told Of Trouble To Come

35Jesus said to them, "I sent you without money or bag or shoes. Did you need anything?" They said, "Nothing." 36Then He said to them, "But now whoever has a money-bag and a bag for food should take it. Whoever does not have a sword should sell his coat and buy one. 37I tell you, that what has been written about Me must happen. It says, 'He was among the wrong-doers.' What is told about Me must happen."

(Isaiah 53:12)

38They said, "Lord, look, we have two swords." He answered, "That is enough."

Jesus Prays In The Garden [Matthew 26:36-46; Mark 14:32-42]

39Jesus came out of the room. Then He went to the Mount of Olives as He had been doing. The followers went with Him. 40When He got there, He said to them, "Pray that you will not be tempted." 41He walked away from them about as far as a stone can be thrown. There He got down with His face on the ground and prayed. 42He said, "Father, if it can be done, take away what must happen to Me. Even so, not what I want, but what You want."

43An angel from heaven came and gave Him strength. 44His heart was much troubled and He prayed all the more. Water ran from His face like blood and fell to the ground.

45When Jesus got up after praying, He went back to the followers. He found them sleeping because of so much sorrow. 46He said to them, "Why are you sleeping? Get up and pray that you will not be tempted."

Jesus Is Handed Over To Sinners [Matthew 26:47-56; Mark 14:43-52; John 18:1-11]

47While Jesus was speaking, Judas came walking ahead of many people. He was one of the twelve followers. He came near to Jesus to kiss Him. 48But Jesus said to him, "Judas, are you handing over the Son of Man with a kiss?" 49Those around Jesus saw what was going to happen and asked, "Lord, should we fight with our swords?" 50One of them hit a servant who was owned by the head religious leader and cut off his right ear. 51Jesus said, "Stop! This is enough." And He put His hand on his ear and healed him.

Jesus Stands In Front Of The Religious Leaders [*Matthew 26:57-58; Mark 14:53-54; John 18:19-24*]

⁵²Jesus said to the religious leaders and the leaders of the house of God and the other leaders who came to Him, "Have you come with swords and sticks to take Me, as if I were a robber? ⁵³While I was with you everyday in the house of God, you never took hold of Me. But now is the time you are to come and you have come in the dark."

⁵⁴Then they led Jesus away to the house of the head religious leader. Peter followed a long way behind Him.

Peter Said He Did Not Know Jesus [*Matthew 26:69-75; Mark 14:66-72; John 18:15-18, 25-27*]

⁵⁵They built a fire in the yard and sat down. Peter sat down with them. ⁵⁶One of the servant-girls saw Peter as he sat by the fire and looked right at him. She said, "This man was with Jesus also." ⁵⁷Peter lied and said, "Woman, I do not know Him." ⁵⁸After awhile another person saw him and said, "You are one of them also." Peter said, "No, sir, I am not." ⁵⁹About an hour later another person said the same thing, "For sure, this man was with Jesus also because he is from Galilee." ⁶⁰But Peter said, "Sir, I do not know what you are saying." And at once, while he was talking, a rooster crowed. ⁶¹The Lord turned and looked at Peter. He remembered the Lord had said, "Before a rooster crows, you will say three times that you do not know Me." ⁶²Peter went outside and cried with a troubled heart.

⁶³Those who watched Jesus so He could not get away made fun of Him and beat Him. ⁶⁴They covered His eyes with a cloth and asked Him, "Tell us who hit You?" ⁶⁵They said many other bad things against Jesus.

⁶⁶When it was morning the leaders of the people and the religious leaders and the teachers of the Law got together. They took Jesus to the court of the religious leader. They said, ⁶⁷"Tell us if you are the Christ." He said to them, "If I tell you, you will not believe Me. ⁶⁸If I ask you something, you will not tell Me. ⁶⁹From now on, the Son of Man will be seated at the right hand of the All-powerful God." ⁷⁰They all said, "Then are You the Son of God?" He said, "You say that I am." ⁷¹Then they said, "What other word do we need against Him? We have heard Him say this with His own mouth."

Jesus Stands In Front Of Pilate [*Matthew 27:1-2, 11-14; Mark 15:1-5; John 18:28-37*]

23 Then all the many people got up and took Jesus to Pilate. ²They began to tell things against Him, saying, "We have found this Man leading the people of our nation in a wrong way. He has been telling them not to pay taxes to Caesar. He has been saying He is Christ, a King."

³Pilate asked Jesus, "Are You the King of the Jews?" He said, "What you said is true." ⁴Then Pilate said to the religious leaders and to the people, "I find nothing wrong in this Man." ⁵They became more angry. They said, "He makes trouble among the people. He has been teaching over all the country of Judea, starting in Galilee and now here."

Jesus Is Sent To Herod

⁶When Pilate heard the word, Galilee, he asked, "Is the Man from Galilee?" ⁷As soon as Pilate knew Jesus belonged in the country where Herod was king, he sent Him to Herod. Herod was in Jerusalem at that time also.

⁸Herod was very glad when he saw Jesus because he had wanted to see Him for a long time. He had heard many things about Him and had

hoped to see Him do some powerful work. [9]Herod talked to Jesus and asked many things. But Jesus said nothing. [10]The religious leaders and the teachers of the Law were standing there. They said many false things against Him.

[11]Then Herod and his soldiers were very bad to Jesus and made fun of Him. They put a beautiful coat on Him and sent Him back to Pilate. [12]That day Pilate and Herod became friends. Before that they had worked against each other.

[13]Pilate called the religious leaders and the leaders of the people and the people together. [14]He said to them, "You brought this Man to me as one that leads the people in the wrong way. I have asked Him about these things in front of you. I do not find Him guilty of the things you say against Him. [15]Herod found nothing wrong with Him because he sent Him back to us. There is no reason to have Him put to death. [16]I will punish Him and let Him go free."

Jesus Or Barabbas Is To Go Free [*Matthew 27:15-26; Mark 15:6-14; John 18:38-40*]

[17]*Every year at the time of the special supper, Pilate would let one person who was in prison go free. [18]They all cried out together with a loud voice, "Take this Man away! Let Barabbas go free." [19]Barabbas had killed some people and had made trouble against the leaders of the country. He had been put in prison.

[20]Pilate wanted to let Jesus go free so he talked to them again. [21]But they cried out, "Nail Him to a cross! Nail Him to a cross!" [22]Pilate said to them the third time, "Why, what bad thing has He done? I have found no reason to put Him to death. I will punish Him and let Him go free."

[23]But they kept on crying out with loud voices saying that He must be nailed to a cross. Their loud voices got what they wanted. [24]Then Pilate said that it should be done as they wanted. [25]Pilate let the man go free who had made trouble against the leaders of the country and who had killed people. He gave Jesus over to them to do with as they wanted.

Jesus On The Cross [*Matthew 27:33-37; Mark 15:22-26; John 19:17-22*]

[26]They led Jesus away. A man named Simon was coming in from the country of Cyrene and they made him carry the cross following behind Jesus.

[27]Many people followed Jesus. There were women who cried and had sorrow for Him. [28]Jesus turned to them and said, "Daughters of Jerusalem, do not cry for Me. Cry for yourselves and your children. [29]Listen! The days are coming when they will say, 'Those who have never had children are happy. Those whose bodies have never given birth are happy. Those who have never fed babies are happy.' [30]They will begin to say to the mountains, 'Fall on us.' They will say to the hills, 'Cover us.' [31]If they do these things to a green tree, what will they do when it is dry?"

[32]Two other men were led away with Jesus to be put to death also. These men had done things making them guilty of death. [33]When they came to the place called Calvary, they nailed Jesus to a cross. The other two men were nailed to crosses also. One was on the right side of Jesus and the other was on His left side. [34]Then Jesus said, "Father, forgive them. They do not know what they are doing." And they divided His clothes by drawing names.

[35]The people stood around looking on. The leaders were there with them making fun of Jesus. They said, "He saved others, let Him save Himself if He is the Christ, the Chosen One of God!" [36]The soldiers made fun of Him also. They put sour wine before Him. [37]They said, "If You are the King of the Jews, save Yourself."

[38]These words were written in the Greek and Latin and Hebrew languages above His head: "THIS IS THE KING OF THE JEWS."

The Two Robbers

[39]One of the men who was guilty of death who was on a cross beside Jesus spoke bad words to Him. He said, "If You are the Christ, save Yourself and us." [40]But the other man on a cross spoke sharp words to the one who made fun of Jesus. He said, "Are you not afraid of God? You are also guilty and will be punished. [41]We are suffering and we should, because of the wrong we have done. But this Man has done nothing wrong." [42]And he said to Jesus, "Lord, remember me when You come into Your holy nation." [43]Jesus said to him, "For sure, I tell you, today you will be with Me in Paradise."

The Death Of Jesus [Matthew 27:45-50; Mark 15:33-36; John 19:28-37]

[44]It was dark over all the earth from noon until three o'clock. [45]The sun did not shine. In the house of God the curtain was torn in two pieces. [46]Then Jesus cried out with a loud voice, "Father, into Your hands I give My spirit." When He said this, He died.

[47]When the soldier saw what had happened, he thanked God. He said, "For sure, He was a good man." [48]All the many people who came together to see the things that were done, went away beating themselves on their chests. [49]All His friends and the women who had come with Him from Galilee stood a long way off watching these things.

The Grave Of Jesus [Matthew 27:57-66; Mark 15:42-47; John 19:38-42]

[50]There was a man named Joseph who belonged to the court. He was a good man and one who did right. [51]This man did not agree with what the court did. He was from Arimathea, a city of the Jews. He was looking for the holy nation of God to come. [52]Joseph went to Pilate and asked for the body of Jesus.

[53]Then he took it down and put it in linen cloth. It was laid in a grave which had been cut out in the side of a rock. This grave had never been used.

[54]It was time to get ready for the Day of Rest which was about to begin. [55]The women who had come with Jesus from Galilee followed behind. They saw the grave and how His body was laid. [56]They went back and got some spices and perfumes ready. But they rested on the Day of Rest as the Law said to do.

Jesus Is Raised From The Dead [Matthew 28:1-10; Mark 16:1-8; John 20:1-18]

24 Early in the morning on the first day of the week, the women went to the grave taking the spices they had made ready. [2]They found the stone had been pushed away from the grave. [3]They went in but they did not find the body of the Lord Jesus.

[4]While they wondered about what had happened, they saw two men standing by them in shining clothes. [5]They were very much afraid and got down with their faces to the ground. The men said to them, "Why do you look for the living One among those who are dead? [6]He is not here. He is risen. Do you not remember what He said to you when He was yet in Galilee? [7]He said, 'The Son of Man must be given over into the hands of sinful men. He must be nailed to a cross. He will rise again three days later.' " [8]They remembered what He had said.

[9]When they came back from the grave, they told all these things to the eleven followers and to all the others.

[10]They were Mary Magdalene and Joanna and Mary the mother of James. Other women who were with them told these things to the followers also. [11]Their words sounded like foolish talk. The followers did not believe them. [12]But Peter got up and ran to the grave. He got down to look in and saw only the linen clothes. Then he went away, surprised about what had happened.

The Followers Of Jesus Do Not Believe He Is Risen [Mark 16:9-14; John 20:24-29]

[13]That same day two of His followers were going to the town of Emmaus. It was about a two-hour walk from Jerusalem. [14]They talked of all these things that had happened. [15]While they were talking together, Jesus Himself came and walked along with them. [16]Something kept their eyes from seeing Who He was.

[17]He said to them, "What are you talking about as you walk?" They stood still and looked sad. [18]One of them, whose name was Cleopas, said to Him, "Are you the only one visiting Jerusalem who has not heard of the things that have happened here these days?" [19]Jesus said to them, "What things?" They answered, "The things about Jesus of Nazareth. He was the great One Who spoke for God. He did powerful works and spoke powerful words in the sight of God and the people. [20]And the religious leaders and the leaders of the people gave Him over to be killed and nailed Him to a cross. [21]We were hoping He was the One Who was going to make the Jewish people free. But it was three days ago when these things happened.

[22]"Some of the women of our group have surprised us and made us wonder. They went to the grave early this morning. [23]They did not find His body. They came back saying they had seen angels in a special dream who said that He was alive. [24]Some of those who were with us went to the grave and found it as the women had said. But they did not see Him."

[25]Then Jesus said to them, "You foolish men. How slow you are to believe what the early preachers said. [26]Did not Christ have to go through these hard things to come into His shining greatness?" [27]Jesus kept on telling them what Moses and all the early preachers had said about Him in the Holy Writings.

[28]When they came to the town where they were going, Jesus acted as if He were going farther. [29]But they said to Him, "Stay with us. It will soon be evening. The day is about over." He went in to stay with them. [30]As He sat at the table with them, He took the bread and gave thanks and broke it. Then He gave it to them. [31]And their eyes were opened and they knew Him. Then He left them and could not be seen. [32]They said to each other, "Were not our hearts filled with joy when He talked to us on the road about what the Holy Writings said?"

[33]Then they got up at once and went back to Jerusalem. They found the eleven followers together and others with them. [34]They said, "For sure the Lord is risen and was seen by Simon." [35]Then they told what had happened on the road and how they came to know Him when He broke the bread.

Jesus Is Seen By The Other Ten Followers

[36]As they talked, Jesus Himself stood among them. He said, "May you have peace." [37]But they were afraid and full of fear. They thought they saw a spirit. [38]Jesus said to them, "Why are you afraid? Why do you have doubts in your hearts? [39]Look at My hands and My feet. See! It is I, Myself! Touch Me and see for yourself. A spirit does not have flesh and bones as I have." [40]When

Jesus had said this, He showed them His hands and feet.

⁴¹They still wondered. It was hard for them to believe it and yet it made them happy. Then He said to them, "Do you have anything here to eat?" ⁴²They gave Jesus a piece of fish that had been cooked and some honey. ⁴³He took it and ate it in front of them.

Jesus Sends His Followers To Teach
[Matthew 28:16-20; Mark 16:15-18; John 20:21-23]

⁴⁴Jesus said to them, "These are the things I told you while I was yet with you. All things written about Me in the Law of Moses and in the Books of the early preachers and in the Psalms must happen as they said they would happen." ⁴⁵Then He opened their minds to understand the Holy Writings. ⁴⁶He said to them, "It is written that Christ should suffer and be raised from the dead after three days.

⁴⁷It must be preached that men must be sorry for their sins and turn from them. Then they will be forgiven. This must be preached in His name to all nations beginning in Jerusalem. ⁴⁸You are to tell what you have seen. ⁴⁹See! I will send you what My Father promised. But you are to stay in Jerusalem until you have received power from above."

Jesus Goes To Be Beside His Father
[Mark 16:19-20]

⁵⁰Jesus led them out as far as Bethany. Then He lifted up His hands and prayed that good would come to them. ⁵¹And while He was praying that good would come to them, He went from them *(and was taken up to heaven and ⁵²they worshiped Him). Then they went back to Jerusalem with great joy. ⁵³They spent all their time in the house of God honoring and giving thanks to God.

JOHN

Christ Lived Before The World Was Made

1 The Word (Christ) was in the beginning. The Word was with God. The Word was God. ²He was with God in the beginning. ³He made all things. Nothing was made without Him making it. ⁴Life began by Him. His Life was the Light for men. ⁵The Light shines in the darkness. The darkness has never been able to put out the Light.

John The Baptist Tells Of The Coming Of Christ

⁶There was a man sent from God whose name was John. ⁷He came to tell what he knew about the Light so that all men might believe through him. ⁸John was not the Light, but he

was sent to tell about the Light.

⁹This true Light, coming into the world, gives light to every man. ¹⁰He came into the world. The world was made by Him, but it did not know Him. ¹¹He came to His own, but His own did not receive Him. ¹²He gave the right and the power to become children of God to those who received Him. He gave this to those who put their trust in His name. ¹³These children of God were not born of blood and of flesh and of man's desires, but they were born of God. ¹⁴Christ became human flesh and lived among us. We saw His shining greatness. This greatness is given only to a much-loved Son from His Father. He was full of loving-favor and truth.

John The Baptist Makes The Way Ready For Jesus Christ [Matthew 3:1-12; Mark 1:1-8; Luke 3:1-18]

¹⁵John told about Christ and said, "I have been telling you about this One. I said, 'He is coming after me. He is more important than I because He lived before me.'" ¹⁶From Him Who has so much we have all received loving-favor, one loving-favor after another. ¹⁷The Law was given through Moses, but loving-favor and truth came through Jesus Christ. ¹⁸The much-loved Son is beside the Father. No man has ever seen God. But Christ has made God known to us.

¹⁹The Jews sent their religious leaders and men from the family group of Levi to ask John, "Who are you?" ²⁰He told them without holding back any words, "I am not the Christ!" ²¹They asked him, "Then who are you? Are you Elijah?" He said, "I am not!" Then they asked, "Are you the special One Who was to come to speak for God?" John said, "No." ²²Then they asked him, "Who are you? We must tell those who sent us. What do you say about yourself?"

²³John said, "I am the voice of one crying in the desert. 'Make the road straight for the Lord,' as the early preacher Isaiah said." (Isaiah 40:3)

²⁴Those who had been sent were from the proud religious law-keepers. ²⁵They asked John again, "Then why do you baptize if you are not the Christ or Elijah or that special One Who was to come to speak for God?" ²⁶John answered, "I baptize with water. But there is One standing among you Whom you do not know. ²⁷He is the One Who is coming after me. I am not good enough to get down and help Him take off His shoes." ²⁸All this happened when John was baptizing in the town of Bethany. He was on the other side of the Jordan River.

The Baptism Of Jesus [Matthew 3:13-17; Mark 1:9-11; Luke 3:21-22]

²⁹The next day John the Baptist saw Jesus coming to him. He said, "See! The Lamb of God Who takes away the sin of the world! ³⁰I have been talking about Him. I said, 'One is coming after me Who is more important than I, because He lived before I was born.' ³¹I have not known Jesus but I have come to baptize with water so the Jews might know about Him."

³²Then John said, "I saw the Holy Spirit come down on Jesus as a dove from heaven. The Holy Spirit stayed on Him. ³³I did not know Him then. But God sent me to baptize with water. God said to me, 'The Holy Spirit will come down and stay on Him. He is the One Who baptizes with the Holy Spirit.' ³⁴I saw this happen. I am now saying that Jesus is the Son of God."

Jesus Calls Andrew And Peter

³⁵The next day John the Baptist was standing with two of his own followers. ³⁶Jesus walked by. John looked at Him and said, "See! The

Lamb of God." [37]John's two followers heard him say this and followed Jesus.

[38]Jesus turned around and saw them following. He said to them, "What are you looking for?" They answered, "Teacher, where are you staying?" [39]He said to them, "Come and see." They followed Him and saw where He lived. They stayed with Him that day. It was about four o'clock in the afternoon.

[40]Andrew, Simon Peter's brother, was one of the two who had heard John's words and had followed Jesus. [41]The first thing he did was to find his brother Simon. He said to him, "We have found the Christ!" [42]Andrew took Simon to Jesus. When Jesus saw Simon, He said, "You are Simon, the son of John. Your name will be Cephas." The name Cephas means Peter, or a rock.

Jesus Calls Philip And Nathanael

[43]The next day Jesus wanted to go to the country of Galilee. He found Philip and said to him, "Follow Me." [44]Philip was from the town of Bethsaida. Andrew and Peter were from this town also. [45]Philip found Nathanael and said to him, "We have found the One Moses wrote about in the Law. He is the One the early preachers wrote about. He is Jesus of Nazareth, the Son of Joseph." [46]Nathanael said, "Can anything good come out of the town of Nazareth?" Philip said, "Come and see."

[47]Jesus saw Nathanael coming to Him and said, "See! There is a true Jew. There is nothing false in him." [48]Nathanael said to Jesus, "How do You know me?" Jesus answered him, "Before Philip talked to you, I saw you under the fig tree." [49]Nathanael said to Him, "Teacher, You are the Son of God. You are the King of the Jews." [50]Jesus said to him, "Do you believe because I said I saw you under the fig tree? You will see greater things than that. [51]For sure, I tell you, you will see heaven opened and God's angels going up and coming down on the Son of Man."

The Powerful Work At The Wedding Of Cana

2 Three days later there was a wedding in the town of Cana in the country of Galilee. The mother of Jesus was there. [2]Jesus and His followers were asked to come to the wedding. [3]When the wine was all gone, the mother of Jesus said to Him, "They have no more wine." [4]Jesus said to her, "Woman, what is that to you and to Me. It is not time for Me to work yet." [5]His mother said to the helpers, "Do whatever He says."

[6]Six stone water jars were there. Each one held about one-half barrel of water. These water jars were used in the Jewish worship of washing. [7]Jesus said to the helpers, "Fill the jars with water." They filled them to the top. [8]Then He said, "Take some out and give it to the head man who is caring for the people." They took some to him. [9]The head man tasted the water that had become wine. He did not know where it came from but the helpers who took it to him knew. He called the man who had just been married. [10]The head man said to him, "Everyone puts out his best wine first. After people have had much to drink, he puts out the wine that is not so good. You have kept the good wine until now!"

[11]This was the first powerful work Jesus did. It was done in Cana of Galilee where He showed His power. His followers put their trust in Him. [12]After this He went down to the city of Capernaum. His mother and brothers and followers went with Him. They stayed there a few days.

Jesus Stops The Buying And The Selling In The House Of God

[13]It was time for the special religious gathering to remember how

the Jews left Egypt. Jesus went up to Jerusalem. [14]He went into the house of God and found cattle and sheep and doves being sold. Men were sitting there changing money. [15]Jesus made a whip of small ropes. He used it to make them all leave the house of God along with the sheep and cattle. He pushed their money off the tables and turned the tables over. [16]He said to those who sold doves, "Take these things out of here! You must not make My Father's house a place for buying and selling!" [17]Then His followers remembered that it was written in the Holy Writings, "I am jealous for the honor of Your house." (Psalm 69:9)

The Jews Ask For Something Special To See

[18]Then the Jews asked Him, "What can You do to show us You have the right and the power to do these things?" [19]Jesus answered them, "Destroy this house of God and in three days I will build it again." [20]Then the Jews said, "It took forty-six years to build this house of God. Will You build it up in three days?" [21]Jesus was speaking of His body as the house of God. [22]After Jesus had been raised from the dead, His followers remembered He said this. They believed the Holy Writings and what He had said.

[23]Jesus was in Jerusalem at the time of the special religious gathering to remember how the Jews left Egypt. Many people put their trust in Him when they saw the powerful works He did. [24]But Jesus did not trust them because He knew all men. [25]He did not need anyone to tell Him about man. He knew what was in man.

Nicodemus Asks Jesus About Life

3 There was a man named Nicodemus. He was a proud religious law-keeper and a leader of the Jews. [2]He came to Jesus at night and said, "Teacher, we know You have come from God to teach us. No one can do these powerful works You do unless God is with Him."

Jesus Tells Of The New Kind Of Birth

[3]Jesus said to him, "For sure, I tell you, unless a man is born again, he cannot see the holy nation of God." [4]Nicodemus said to Him, "How can a man be born when he is old? How can he get into his mother's body and be born the second time?" [5]Jesus answered, "For sure, I tell you, unless a man is born of water and of the Spirit of God, he cannot get into the holy nation of God. [6]Whatever is born of the flesh is flesh. Whatever is born of the Spirit is spirit.

[7]"Do not be surprised that I said to you, 'You must be born again.' [8]The wind blows where it wants to and you hear its sound. You do not know where it comes from or where it goes. It is the same with everyone who is born of the Spirit of God."

[9]Nicodemus said to Him, "How can this be?" [10]Jesus said, "Are you a teacher among the Jews and do not know these things? [11]For sure, I tell you, We are talking about things We know. We tell of what We have seen. Yet you do not take Our words to be true. [12]I tell you about things of the earth and you do not believe them. How will you believe if I tell you things about heaven?

[13]"No one has gone up into heaven except the One Who came down from heaven. That One is the Son of Man *Who is in heaven. [14]As Moses lifted up the snake in the desert, so the Son of Man must be lifted up. [15]Then whoever puts his trust in Him will have life that lasts forever. [16]For God so loved the world that He gave His only Son. Whoever puts his trust in God's Son will not be lost but will have life that lasts forever. [17]For God did not send His Son into the world to say it is guilty. He sent His Son so the world might be saved from the

punishment of sin by Him. [18]Whoever puts his trust in His Son is not guilty. Whoever does not put his trust in Him is guilty already. It is because he does not put his trust in the name of the only Son of God.

[19]"The Light has come into the world. And the Light is the test by which men are guilty or not. People love darkness more than the Light because the things they do are sinful. [20]Everyone who sins hates the Light. He stays away from the Light because his sin would be found out. [21]The man who does what is right comes to the Light. What he does will be seen because he has done what God wanted him to do."

Jesus Preaches In Judea

[22]After this, Jesus and His followers came into the country of Judea. He stayed with them there and baptized people.

John The Baptist Tells More About Jesus

[23]John was baptizing in the town of Aenon near Salim. There was much water there and people were coming to be baptized. [24]John had not been put in prison yet.

[25]Then some of the followers of John and a Jew started to argue about the religious washing of the Jewish worship. [26]They came to John and said to him, "Teacher, the One with you on the other side of the Jordan River is baptizing also. He is the One you told of. Everyone is going to Him."

[27]John said, "A man can receive nothing unless it has been given to him from heaven. [28]You heard the words that I said, 'I am not the Christ, but I have been sent before Him.' [29]The man who has just been married has the bride. The friend of the man just married stands at his side and listens to him. He has joy when he hears the voice of the man just married. I am full of this joy. [30]He must become more important. I must become less important.

[31]"He Who comes from above is above all. He who comes from the earth is of the earth and speaks of the earth. He Who comes from heaven is above all. [32]He tells of what He has seen and heard. But no one believes what He says. [33]Whoever receives His words proves that God is true. [34]He was sent by God and He speaks God's Word. God gives Him all of His Spirit. [35]The Father loves the Son and has given all things into His hand. [36]He who puts his trust in the Son has life that lasts forever. He who does not put his trust in the Son will not have life, but the anger of God is on him."

A Woman Of Samaria At The Well

4 Jesus knew the proud religious law-keepers had heard He was making and baptizing more followers than John. [2]Jesus did not baptize anyone Himself but His followers did. [3]Then Jesus went from the country of Judea to the country of Galilee. [4]He had to go through the country of Samaria. [5]So He came to a town in Samaria called Sychar. It was near the piece of ground that Jacob gave to his son Joseph. [6]Jacob's well was there. Jesus was tired from traveling so He sat down just as He was by the well. It was about noon.

[7]A woman of Samaria came to get water. Jesus said to her, "Give Me a drink." [8]His followers had gone to the town to buy food. [9]The woman of Samaria said to Him, "You are a Jew. I am of Samaria. Why do You ask me for a drink when the Jews have nothing to do with the people of Samaria?"

[10]Jesus said to her, "You do not know what God has to give. You do not know Who said to you, 'Give Me a drink.' If you knew, you would have asked Him. He would have given you living water." [11]The wo-

man said to Him, "Sir, the well is deep. You have nothing to get water with. Where will You get the living water? ¹²Are You greater than our early father Jacob? He gave us the well. He and his children and his cattle drank from it."

Jesus Tells Of The Living Water

¹³Jesus said to her, "Whoever drinks this water will be thirsty again. ¹⁴Whoever drinks the water that I will give him will never be thirsty. The water that I will give him will become in him a well of life that lasts forever."

¹⁵The woman said, "Sir, give me this water so I will never be thirsty. Then I will not have to come all this way for water."

The True Kind Of Worship

¹⁶Jesus said to her, "Go call your husband and come back." ¹⁷The woman said, "I have no husband." Jesus said, "You told the truth when you said, 'I have no husband.' ¹⁸You have had five husbands. The one you have now is not your husband. You told the truth."

¹⁹The woman said to Him, "Sir, I think You are a person Who speaks for God. ²⁰Our early fathers worshiped on this mountain. You Jews say Jerusalem is the place where men should worship."

²¹Jesus said to her, "Woman, believe Me. The time is coming when you will not worship the Father on this mountain or in Jerusalem. ²²You people do not know what you worship. We Jews know what we worship. It is through the Jews that men are saved from the punishment of their sins. ²³The time is coming, yes, it is here now, when the true worshipers will worship the Father in spirit and in truth. The Father wants that kind of worshipers. ²⁴God is Spirit. Those who worship Him must worship Him in spirit and in truth."

²⁵The woman said to Him, "I know the Jews are looking for One Who is coming. He is called the Christ. When He comes, He will tell us everything." ²⁶Jesus said to her, "I am the Christ, the One talking with you!"

²⁷Right then the followers came back and were surprised and wondered about finding Him talking with a woman. But no one said, "What do You want?" or, "Why are You talking with her?"

²⁸The woman left her water jar and went into the town. She said to the men, ²⁹"Come and see a Man Who told me everything I ever did! Can this be the Christ?" ³⁰They went out of town and came to Him.

Jesus Tells Them Of A New Kind Of Food

³¹During this time His followers were saying to Him, "Teacher, eat something." ³²He said, "I have food to eat that you do not know of." ³³The followers said to each other, "Has someone taken food to Him?" ³⁴Jesus said, "My food is to do what God wants Me to do and to finish His work. ³⁵Do you not say, 'It is four months yet until the time to gather grain'? Listen! I say to you, open your eyes and look at the fields. They are white now and waiting for the grain to be gathered in. ³⁶The one who gathers gets his pay. He gathers fruit that lasts forever. The one who plants and the one who gathers will have joy together. ³⁷These words are true, 'One man plants and another man gathers.' ³⁸I sent you to gather where you have not planted. Others have planted and you have come along to gather in their fruit."

The People of Samaria Believe In Jesus

³⁹Many people in that town of Samaria believed in Jesus because of what the woman said about Him.

She said, "He told me everything I ever did." [40]So the people of Samaria came to Him. They asked Him to stay with them. Jesus stayed there two days. [41]Many more people believed because of what He said. [42]They said to the woman, "Now we believe! It is no longer because of what you said about Jesus but we have heard Him ourselves. We know, for sure, that He is the Christ, the One Who saves men of this world from the punishment of their sins."

Jesus Goes To Galilee

[43]Two days later He went from there and came to the country of Galilee. [44]Jesus Himself said that no one who speaks for God is respected in his own country. [45]When He came to Galilee, the people there were glad. They had seen all the things He did in Jerusalem. It was at the time of the special religious gathering to remember how the Jews left Egypt. They had been there also.

Jesus Heals The Dying Boy In Capernaum

[46]Jesus came again to the town of Cana of Galilee where He had made water into wine. A man who worked with the king had a son who was sick in the city of Capernaum. [47]This man went to Jesus. He had heard that Jesus had come from the country of Judea to Galilee. The man asked Jesus if He would go to Capernaum and heal his son who was dying. [48]Then Jesus said to him, "Unless you see special things and powerful works done, you will not believe." [49]The man said to Him, "Sir, come with me before my son dies." [50]Jesus said to him, "Go your way. Your son will live." The man put his trust in what Jesus said and left.

[51]As he was on his way home, his servants met him. They said to him, "Your son is living!" [52]He asked them what time his boy began to get well. They said to him, "Yesterday at one o'clock the sickness left." [53]The father knew it was the time Jesus had said to him, "Your son will live." He and everyone in his house put their trust in Jesus. [54]This was the second powerful work that Jesus did after He came from the country of Judea to the country of Galilee.

Jesus Heals The Man At The Pool Of Bethesda

5 Some time later, there was a religious gathering of the Jews. Jesus went up to Jerusalem. [2]In Jerusalem there is a pool with five porches called Bethesda near the sheep gate. [3]Inside these porches lay many sick people. Some were blind. Some could not walk. Some could not move their bodies. [4]*An angel of the Lord came at certain times and made the water move. All of them were waiting for it to move. Whoever got in the water first after it was moving was healed of whatever sickness he had.

[5]A man was there who had been sick for thirty-eight years. [6]Jesus saw him lying there and knew the man had been sick a long time. Jesus said to him, "Would you like to be healed?" [7]The sick man said, "Sir, I have no one to put me in the pool when the water is moving. While I am coming, another one gets in first." [8]Jesus said to him, "Get up! Pick up your bed and walk." [9]At once the man was healed and picked up his bed and walked. This happened on the Day of Rest.

[10]The Jews said to the man who had been healed, "This is the Day of Rest. It is against the Law for you to carry your bed." [11]He said to them, "The Man Who healed me said to me, 'Pick up your bed and walk.' " [12]Then the Jews asked him, "What man said to you, 'Pick up your bed and walk'?" [13]The man who had been healed did not know Who He was. Jesus had gone away while many

people were there.

14Later Jesus found the man who had been healed in the house of God. He said to him, "Listen! You have been healed. Stop sinning or something worse will come to you." 15The man went away and told the Jews that it was Jesus Who had healed him.

The Jews Want To Kill Jesus

16Because Jesus did these things on the Day of Rest, the Jews made it very hard for Him. 17Jesus said to them, "My Father is still working all the time so I am working also." 18The Jews tried all the more to kill Him, not only because He had worked on the Day of Rest, but because He had also called God His Own Father. This made Him the same as God.

Jesus Tells How He Works

19Then Jesus said to them, "For sure, I tell you, the Son can do nothing by Himself. He does what He sees the Father doing. Whatever the Father does, the Son does also. 20The Father loves the Son and shows the Son everything He does. The Father will show Him greater works than these. They will surprise you. 21The Father raises up the dead and makes them live. The Son also gives life to anyone He chooses. 22The Father does not say who is guilty. He gives this to the Son to do. 23He does this so that all men will honor the Son as they honor the Father. He who does not honor the Son does not honor the Father Who sent Him.

24"For sure, I tell you, anyone who hears My Word and puts his trust in Him Who sent Me has life that lasts forever. He will not be guilty. He has already passed from death into life.

The Good People And The Sinful People Are Raised From The Dead

25"For sure, I tell you, the time is coming. Yes, the time is here when

the dead will hear the voice of the Son of God. Those who hear will live. 26The Father has life in Himself. He has given power to the Son to have life in Himself. 27God has given Him the right and the power to say if people are guilty, because He is the Son of Man. 28Do not be surprised at this. The time is coming when all who are in their graves will hear His voice. 29They will come out. Those who have done good will be raised again and will have new life. Those who have been sinful will be raised again and will be told they are guilty and will be punished.

Jesus Tells Of John And Of Himself

30"I can do nothing by Myself. I say who is guilty only as My Father tells Me. That way, what I say is right, because I am not trying to do what I want to do. I am doing what the Father, Who sent Me, wants Me to do. 31If I tell about Myself, My words are worth nothing. 32There is another One Who tells about Me. I know the words He says about Me are true.

33"You sent to John the Baptist and he told you the truth. 34I do not need words from men to say I am right. I say this that you might be saved from the punishment of sin. 35John the Baptist was a burning and shining light. You were willing for awhile to be glad in his light. 36I have something greater than John which tells of Me. I am doing works the Father has given Me to do and they are proving that the Father has sent Me. 37The Father has told of Me and has sent Me. You have never heard His voice. You have never seen Him. 38You do not have His word living in your hearts because you do not put your trust in the One He sent.

39"You do read the Holy Writings. You think you have life that lasts forever just because you read them. They do tell of Me. 40But you do not want to come to Me so you might have life. [41]I do not take any honor from men. [42]I know you and you do not have the love of God in your hearts. [43]I have come in the name of My Father. You do not receive Me. If another person comes in his own name, you will receive him. [44]How can you believe when you are always wanting honor from each other. And yet you do not look for the honor that comes from the only God.

[45]"Do not think that I will tell the Father you are guilty. The one who says you are guilty is Moses. You trust him. [46]If you had believed Moses, you would believe Me. For Moses wrote about Me. [47]If you do not believe what he wrote, how will you believe My Words?"

The Feeding Of The Five Thousand [*Matthew 14:13-21; Mark 6:30-44; Luke 9:10-17*]

6 After this Jesus went over to the other side of the sea of Galilee. It is sometimes called Tiberias. [2]Many people followed Him. They saw the powerful works He did on those who were sick. [3]Jesus went up on a mountain and sat down with His followers. [4]The special religious supper to remember how the Jews left Egypt was soon.

[5]Jesus looked up and saw many people coming to Him. He said to Philip, "Where can we buy bread to feed these people?" [6]He said this to see what Philip would say. Jesus knew what He would do. [7]Philip said to Him, "The money we have is not enough to buy bread to give each one a little."

[8]One of His followers was Andrew, Simon Peter's brother. He said to Jesus, [9]"There is a boy here who has five loaves of barley bread and two small fish. What is that for so many people?" [10]Jesus said, "Have the people sit down." There was much grass in that place. About five thousand men sat down.

[11]Jesus took the loaves and gave thanks. Then He gave the bread to those who were sitting down. The fish were given out the same way. The people had as much as they wanted. [12]When they were filled, Jesus said to His followers, "Gather up the pieces that are left. None will be wasted." [13]The followers gathered the pieces together. Twelve baskets were filled with pieces of barley bread. These were left after all the people had eaten.

[14]The people saw the powerful work Jesus had done. They said, "It is true! This is the One Who speaks for God Who is to come into the world."

Jesus Walks On The Water [*Matthew 14:22-33; Mark 6:45-52*]

[15]Jesus knew they were about to come and take Him to make Him king, so He went to the mountain by Himself. [16]When evening had come, His followers went down to the lake. [17]They got into a boat and started to cross the lake to go to the city of Capernaum. By this time it was dark. Jesus had not come back to them yet. [18]A strong wind was making high waves on the lake. [19]They were about half way across the lake when they saw Jesus walking on the water. As He got near the boat, they were afraid. [20]But Jesus called to them, "It is I. Do not be afraid." [21]They were glad to take Him into the boat. At once they got to the other side where they wanted to go.

Jesus Teaches Many People

[22]The next day the people on the other side of the lake saw no other boat there but the one His followers had been in. The people knew Jesus had not gone with His followers in the boat because they had gone alone. [23]There were other boats from Tiberias that had come near the place where they had eaten the bread after the Lord had given thanks. [24]The

people saw that Jesus and His followers were not there. They got into boats and went to Capernaum looking for Jesus.

²⁵The people found Him on the other side of the lake. They said to Him, "Teacher, when did You come here?" ²⁶Jesus said to them, "For sure, I tell you, you are not looking for Me because of the powerful works. You are looking for Me because you ate bread and were filled. ²⁷Do not work for food that does not last. Work for food that lasts forever. The Son of Man will give you that kind of food. God the Father has shown He will do this."

Jesus Teaches About Doing The Work Of God

²⁸Then the people said to Him, "What are the works God wants us to do?" ²⁹Jesus said to them, "This is the work of God, that you put your trust in the One He has sent." ³⁰They said to Him, "Can You show us some powerful work? Then we can see it and believe You. What will You do? ³¹Our early fathers ate bread that came from heaven in the desert. This happened as it is written, 'He gave them bread from heaven to eat.' " (Exodus 16:15)

Jesus Is The Bread Of Life

³²Then Jesus said to the people, "For sure, I tell you, it was not Moses who gave you bread from heaven. My Father gives you the true Bread from heaven. ³³The Bread of God is He Who comes down from heaven and gives life to the world." ³⁴They said to Him, "Sir, give us this Bread all the time."

³⁵Jesus said to them, "I am the Bread of Life. He who comes to Me will never be hungry. He who puts his trust in Me will never be thirsty. ³⁶I said to you that you have seen Me and yet you do not put your trust in Me. ³⁷All whom My Father has given

to Me will come to Me. I will never turn away anyone who comes to Me. ³⁸I came down from heaven. I did not come to do what I wanted to do. I came to do what My Father wanted Me to do. He is the One Who sent Me.

³⁹"The Father sent Me. He did not want Me to lose any of all those He gave Me. He wants Me to raise them to life on the last day. ⁴⁰He wants everyone who sees the Son to put his trust in Him and have life that lasts forever. I will raise that one up on the last day."

The Jews Do Not Like The Words Of Jesus

⁴¹The Jews talked among themselves against Him. They did not like it because He said, "I am the Bread that came down from heaven." ⁴²They asked each other, "Is not this Jesus, the son of Joseph? We know His father and mother. How can He say, 'I came down from heaven'?"

Jesus Keeps On Teaching About The Bread Of Life

⁴³Jesus said to them, "Do not talk among yourselves against Me. ⁴⁴The Father sent Me. No man can come to Me unless the Father gives him the desire to come to Me. Then I will raise him to life on the last day. ⁴⁵The early preachers wrote, 'They will all be taught of God.' (Isaiah 54:13) Everyone who listens to the Father and learns from Him comes to Me. ⁴⁶No one has seen the Father. I am the only One Who has seen Him. ⁴⁷For sure, I tell you, he who puts his trust in Me has life that lasts forever. ⁴⁸I am the Bread of Life. ⁴⁹Your early fathers ate bread that came from heaven in the desert. They died. ⁵⁰But this is the Bread that comes down from heaven. The one who eats it never dies. ⁵¹I am the Living Bread that came down from heaven. If anyone eats this Bread, he will live

forever. The Bread which I will give is My flesh. I will give this for the life of the world." ⁵²The Jews argued among themselves, saying, "How can this Man give us His flesh to eat?" ⁵³Jesus said to them, "For sure, I tell you, unless you eat the flesh of the Son of Man and drink His blood, you do not have life in you. ⁵⁴Whoever eats My flesh and drinks My blood has life that lasts forever. I will raise him up on the last day. ⁵⁵My flesh is true food and My blood is true drink. ⁵⁶Whoever eats My flesh and drinks My blood lives in Me and I live in him. ⁵⁷The living Father sent Me and I live because of Him. In the same way, the one who eats Me will live because of Me. ⁵⁸I am this Bread that came down from heaven. It is not like the bread that your early fathers ate and they died. Whoever eats this Bread will live forever." ⁵⁹Jesus said these things in the Jewish place of worship while He was teaching in the city of Capernaum.

The Troubled Followers Leave Jesus

⁶⁰After hearing this, many of His followers said, "This teaching is too hard! Who can listen to it?" ⁶¹Jesus knew His followers talked against what He had said. He said to them, "Does this trouble you? ⁶²Then what would you say if you saw the Son of Man going up where He was before? ⁶³It is the Spirit that gives life. The flesh is of no help. The words I speak to you are spirit and life. ⁶⁴But some of you do not believe." Jesus knew from the beginning who would not put their trust in Him. He knew who would hand Him over to the leaders of the country. ⁶⁵He said, "That is why I told you no one can come to Me unless the Father allows it." ⁶⁶From that time on, many of His followers turned back to their old ways of living. They would not go along with Him after that.

Peter Knows Who Jesus Is

⁶⁷Then Jesus said to the twelve followers, "Will you leave Me also?" ⁶⁸Simon Peter said to Him, "Lord, who else can we go to? You have words that give life that lasts forever. ⁶⁹We believe and know You are the Christ. You are the Son of the Living God." ⁷⁰Jesus said to them, "I chose you twelve as My followers. And one of you is a devil." ⁷¹He was speaking of Judas Iscariot, Simon's son, who was one of the twelve followers. He was ready to hand Jesus over to the leaders of the country.

The Brothers Of Jesus Argue With Him

7 Jesus did not stay in the country of Judea because the Jews were trying to kill Him. After this He went from place to place in the country of Galilee. ²A religious gathering of the Jews was near. This gathering was called the Supper of Tents. ³The brothers of Jesus said to Him, "Leave here and go to the country of Judea. Let your followers there see the things You do. ⁴If a person wants others to know what he is doing, he does things to be seen. Since You are doing such things, show Yourself to the world." ⁵Not even His brothers were putting their trust in Him.

⁶Jesus said to them, "My time has not yet come. But any time is good for you. ⁷The world cannot hate you but it hates Me. I speak against the world because of its sinful works. ⁸You go to the religious gathering. I am not going yet. My time has not yet come."

⁹Jesus told His brothers this and then stayed in Galilee. ¹⁰His brothers went to the religious gathering. He went later by Himself so He would not be seen there.

¹¹At the religious gathering the Jews were looking for Jesus. They were saying, "Where is He?" ¹²There

was much talk among the people about Him. Some said, "He is a good Man." Others said, "No, He leads the people in the wrong way." [13]No one spoke about Him in front of other people. They were afraid of the Jews.

Jesus Tells Where His Teaching Is From

[14]The religious gathering was half over when Jesus went to the house of God and taught. [15]The Jews were surprised and wondered, saying, "How can this Man know so much when He has never been to school?" [16]Jesus said to them, "What I teach is not Mine. It is from God Who sent Me. [17]If anyone will do what God wants, he will know if My teaching is from God, or if I am speaking of Myself. [18]The man who speaks of himself is looking for greatness for himself. But He Who is looking for the greatness of the One Who sent Him is true. There is nothing false in Him. [19]Did not Moses give you the Law? And yet not one of you keeps the Law. Why do you try to kill me?" [20]The people said, "You have a demon in You. Who is trying to kill You?" [21]Jesus said to them, "I did one work and you are surprised. [22]Moses gave you the religious act of becoming a Jew. (Yet it was not from Moses but from the early fathers.) You do this religious act on a man on the Day of Rest. [23]Now if you can do that, why are you angry with Me for healing a man on the Day of Rest? [24]Do not say a person is guilty by what you see. Be sure you know when you say what is right or wrong."

[25]Some of the people of Jerusalem said, "Is not this the Man the Jews want to kill? [26]But see! This Man is speaking out in the open. They are saying nothing to Him. Do the leaders know this is the true Christ? [27]We know where this Man came

from. When the Christ comes, no one will know where He comes from."

[28]Then Jesus spoke with a loud voice as He taught in the house of God. He said, "You know Me. You know where I came from. I have not come on My own. The One Who sent Me is true but you do not know Him. [29]I know Him because I am from Him and He sent Me."

[30]Then they wanted to take Jesus but no one put his hands on Him. His time had not yet come. [31]Many of the people believed in Him. They said, "When Christ comes, will He do more powerful works than this Man?"

[32]The proud religious law-keepers heard the people talking about Jesus. The religious leaders of the Jews and the proud religious law-keepers sent soldiers to take Him. [33]Jesus said to them, "I will be with you a little while yet. Then I will go back to Him Who sent Me. [34]You will look for Me but you will not find Me. Where I go, you cannot come."

[35]The Jews said to themselves, "Where can He go that we will not find Him? Will He go to our people who live among the Greeks and teach the Greeks? [36]What does He mean when He says, 'You will look for Me but you will not find Me, and where I go, you cannot come'?"

Jesus Promises To Give The Holy Spirit

[37]It was the last and great day of the religious gathering. Jesus stood up and spoke with a loud voice, "If anyone is thirsty, let him come to Me and drink. [38]The Holy Writings say that rivers of living water will flow from the heart of the one who puts his trust in Me." [39]Jesus said this about the Holy Spirit Who would come to those who put their trust in Him. The Holy Spirit had not yet been given. Jesus had not yet been raised to the place of honor.

The People Cannot Make Up Their Minds Who He Is

⁴⁰When many of the people heard His words, they said, "For sure, this is the One Who speaks for God." ⁴¹Others said, "He is the Christ!" Some said, "The Christ would not come from the country of Galilee, would He? ⁴²Do not the Holy Writings say that the Christ will come from the family of David? Will He not come from the town of Bethlehem where David lived?" ⁴³The people were divided in what they thought about Him. ⁴⁴Some of them wanted to take Him. But no one put their hands on Him.

⁴⁵The soldiers came back to the religious leaders of the Jews and to the proud religious law-keepers. They said to the soldiers, "Why did you not bring Him?" ⁴⁶The soldiers answered, "No man has ever spoken like this Man speaks." ⁴⁷The proud religious law-keepers said, "Have you been led the wrong way also? ⁴⁸Has anyone of the leaders or anyone from our group believed in Him? ⁴⁹As for all these people, they do not know the Law. They are guilty and will be punished by God."

⁵⁰(Nicodemus was one of the proud religious law-keepers. He had come to Jesus at another time.) Nicodemus said to them, ⁵¹"Our Law does not say a man is guilty before he has been in court and before we know what he has done." ⁵²They said to him, "Are you from Galilee also? Look into the Word of God yourself. You will see that no one who speaks for God comes from Galilee." ⁵³*Then everyone went home.

Jesus Speaks To The Teachers Of The Law And The Proud Religious Law-Keepers

8 *(Jesus went to the Mount of Olives. ²Early in the morning He went back to the house of God and all the people came to Him. He sat down and taught them.

³The teachers of the Law and the proud religious law-keepers came to Him. They brought a woman who had been caught doing a sex sin. They made her stand in front of them all. ⁴Then they said to Jesus, "Teacher, this woman was caught in the act of doing a sex sin. ⁵Moses told us in the Law to throw stones and kill a woman like this. What do You say about it?

⁶They were trying to set a trap to find something against Him. Jesus got down and began to write in the dust with His finger. ⁷They kept on asking Him. Then He stood up and said, "Anyone of you who is without sin can throw the first stone at her." ⁸Again He got down and wrote in the dust. ⁹When they heard what He said, they went away one by one, beginning with the older ones until they were all gone. Then Jesus was left alone with the woman.

¹⁰Jesus stood up and said to her, "Woman, where are those who spoke against you? Has no man said you are guilty?" ¹¹She said, "No one, Sir." Jesus said to her, "Neither do I say you are guilty. Go on your way and do not sin again.")

Jesus Teaches About The Light Of The World

¹²Jesus spoke to all the people, saying, "I am the Light of the world. Anyone who follows Me will not walk in darkness. He will have the Light of Life."

¹³The proud religious law-keepers said to Him, "You are talking about Yourself. What You say about Yourself is not true."

¹⁴Jesus said, "Even if I speak of Myself, what I am saying is true. I know where I came from and where I am going. You do not know where I came from or where I am going. ¹⁵You say as a man would say if people are guilty or not guilty. I am not saying anyone is guilty. ¹⁶But

even if I did, it would be true. I am not alone. The Father Who sent Me is with Me. ¹⁷It is written in your Law that when two men agree about something, it proves it is true. (Deuteronomy 19:15) ¹⁸I speak for Myself and the Father Who sent Me speaks for Me."

¹⁹The proud religious law-keepers asked Him, "Where is Your Father?" Jesus said, "You do not know Me or My Father. If you had known Me, you would have known My Father also."

²⁰Jesus spoke these words near the money box while He taught in the house of God. No one put his hands on Jesus because His time had not yet come.

Jesus Tells Of His Going Away

²¹Jesus spoke to the Jews again, saying, "I am going away. You will look for Me but you will die in your sins. Where I am going, you cannot come." ²²The Jews said, "Will He kill Himself because He said, 'Where I am going you cannot come'?"

²³He answered them, "You are from below. I am from above. You are of this world. I am not of this world. ²⁴That is why I said that you will die in your sins. If you do not believe that I am the Christ, you will die in your sins."

²⁵Then they said to Him, "Who are You?" Jesus answered, "The answer is the same as I told you from the beginning. ²⁶I have much to say about you. I must say if you are guilty. But He Who sent Me is true. I tell the world the things I have heard from Him."

²⁷They did not understand that Jesus was speaking to them about the Father. ²⁸Jesus said to them, "When you have lifted up the Son of Man, you will know that I am the Christ. I do nothing of Myself. I say these things as My Father has taught Me. ²⁹He that sent Me is with Me. The Father has not left Me alone. I always

do what He wants Me to do." ³⁰As Jesus said these things, many people put their trust in Him. ³¹He said to the Jews who believed, "If you keep and obey My Word, then you are My followers for sure. ³²You will know the truth and the truth will make you free."

Jesus Teaches What It Means To Be Free

³³They said to Jesus, "We are children of Abraham. We have never been servants to anyone. What do you mean when You say, 'You will be free'?" ³⁴Jesus answered them, "For sure, I tell you, everyone who sins is the servant of sin because sin has a hold on him. ³⁵And the servant does not belong in the house. The son belongs in the house. ³⁶So if the Son makes you free, you will be free for sure.

Jesus Asks The Jews About Their Father

³⁷"I know that you are the children of Abraham. But you want to kill Me because My Word is not in your hearts. ³⁸I speak of what I saw when I was with My Father. You do what you have seen your father do."

³⁹They said to Him, "Abraham is our father." Jesus said, "If you were children of Abraham, you would do what he did. ⁴⁰I am a Man Who has told you the truth as I heard it from God. Now you are trying to kill Me. Abraham never did anything like that. ⁴¹You are doing the works of your father." They said to Him, "We were born of parents who were faithful in marriage. We have one Father. He is God."

⁴²Jesus said to them, "If God were your father, you would love Me. I came from God. I did not come on My own, but God sent Me. ⁴³Why do you not understand what I say? It is because you do not want to hear My teaching. ⁴⁴The devil is your father.

You are from him. You want to do the sinful things your father, the devil, wants you to do. He has been a killer from the beginning. The devil has nothing to do with the truth. There is no truth in him. It is expected of the devil to lie, for he is a liar and the father of lies. 45I tell you the truth and that is why you do not put your trust in Me. 46Which one of you can say I am guilty of sin? If I tell you the truth, why do you not believe Me? 47Whoever is born of God listens to God's Word. You do not hear His Word because you are not born of God."

The Jews Say Jesus Has A Demon

48The Jews said to Jesus, "Are we not right when we say You are from the country of Samaria, and You have a demon?" 49Jesus said, "No, I do not have a demon. I honor My Father. You do not honor Me. 50I am not looking for honor for Myself. There is One Who is looking for it. He says what is right from wrong. 51For sure, I tell you, if anyone keeps My Word, that one will never die."

52Then the Jews said to Him, "Now we know You have a demon. Abraham died. The early preachers died. You say, 'If anyone keeps My Word, that one will never die.' 53Are you greater than our father Abraham? He died and the early preachers died. Who do You think You are?" 54Jesus said, "If I honor Myself, My honor would be worth nothing. My Father honors Me. You say He is your God. 55You have never known Him, but I know Him. If I said I did not know Him, I would be a liar like you. But I do know the Father and obey His Word. 56Your father Abraham was glad that he was to see My coming. He saw it and was happy."

57The Jews said to Jesus, "You are not even fifty years old. How could you have seen Abraham?" 58Jesus said to them, "For sure, I tell you, before Abraham was born, I was and am and always will be!"

59Then they picked up stones to throw at Him. *Jesus hid Himself and left the house of God.

Jesus Heals A Man Who Was Born Blind

9 As Jesus went on His way, He saw a man who had been born blind. 2His followers asked Him, "Teacher, whose sin made this man to be born blind? Was it the sin of this man or the sin of his parents?" 3Jesus answered, "The sin of this man or the sin of his parents did not make him to be born blind. He was born blind so the work of God would be seen in him. 4We must keep on doing the work of Him Who sent Me while it is day. Night is coming when no man can work. 5While I am in the world, I am the Light of the world."

6After Jesus had said this, He spit on the ground. He mixed it with dust and put that mud on the eyes of the blind man. 7Then Jesus said to him, "Go and wash in the pool of Siloam." (Siloam means Sent.) The man went away and washed. When he came back, he could see.

8Neighbors and others had seen him begging. They said, "Is not this the man who sat and begged?" 9Some said, "This is the one." Others said, "No, but he looks like him." But the man who had been blind said, "I am the man." 10They said to him, "How were your eyes opened?" 11He answered, "A Man called Jesus made mud and put it on my eyes. Then He said to me, 'Go and wash in the pool of Siloam.' I went and washed and I can see." 12Then they asked him, "Where is He?" He answered, "I do not know."

The Proud Religious Law-Keepers Are Troubled About This Healing

13They took the man who had been born blind to the proud religious law-keepers. [14]It was the Day of Rest when Jesus had made mud and opened his eyes. [15]Again the proud religious law-keepers asked the man who had been born blind how he had been made to see. He answered them, "Jesus put mud on my eyes. I washed and now I see!" [16]Some of the proud religious law-keepers said, "The Man Who did this is not from God because He worked on the Day of Rest." Others said, "How can a sinful man do powerful works?" They could not agree about Jesus. [17]They spoke again to the blind man, saying, "What do you say about Him since He opened your eyes?" He answered, "He is One Who speaks for God."

[18]The Jews did not believe this man had been blind and had been made to see. They called his parents [19]and asked them, "Is this your son? Do you say he was born blind? How does he see now?" [20]They answered, "We know this is our son and we know he was born blind. [21]But we do not know how it is that he can see now. We do not know who opened his eyes. He is old enough, ask him. He can tell you himself." [22]His parents said this because they were afraid of the Jews. The Jews had talked among themselves. They had agreed that the person who said that Jesus was the Christ would be put out of the Jewish place of worship. [23]That is why his parents said, "He is old enough, ask him."

[24]The proud religious law-keepers asked the man again, who had been blind, to come. They said to him, "Give thanks to God. We know this man is a sinner." [25]The man who had been blind said to them, "I do not know if He is a sinner or not. One thing I know. I was blind, but now I can see." [26]They asked him again, "What did He do to you? How did He open your eyes?" [27]He answered, "I have told you already. You did not listen. Why do you want to hear it again? Do you want to become His

followers also?"

[28]The proud religious law-keepers became angry at him and said, "You are a follower of Jesus. We are followers of Moses. [29]We know God spoke to Moses. We do not know where this Man is from." [30]The man said to them, "This is strange! You do not know where He came from and yet He opened my eyes. [31]We know that God does not listen to sinners. We know if anyone loves and worships God, and does what He wants, God listens to him. [32]From the beginning of the world no one has ever heard of anyone opening the eyes of a man born blind. [33]If this Man were not from God, He would not be able to do anything like this."

[34]They said to him, "You were born in sin. Are you trying to teach us?" Then they put him out of the place of worship.

Jesus Speaks Sharp Words To The Proud Religious Law-Keepers

[35]Jesus heard that the proud religious law-keepers had put the man who had been healed out of the place of worship. He found the man and said to him, "Do you put your trust in the Son of God?" [36]He said, "Who is He, Sir? Tell me so that I can put my trust in Him." [37]Jesus said to him, "You have seen Him. He is talking with you." [38]He said, "I do put my trust in You, Lord." Then he got down in front of Jesus and worshiped Him.

[39]Jesus said, "I came into this world to say what is right from wrong. I came so those who do not see might see, and those who do see might be made blind." [40]Some of the proud religious law-keepers who were with Him heard this. They said to Him, "Are we blind also?" [41]Jesus said to them, "If you were blind, you would not be guilty of sin. But because you say, 'We see,' you still are guilty of your sin.

The Shepherd And The Door

10 "For sure, I tell you, the man who goes into the sheep-pen some other way than through the door is one who steals and robs. ²The shepherd of the sheep goes in through the door. ³The one who watches the door opens it for him. The sheep listen to the voice of the shepherd. He calls his own sheep by name and he leads them out. ⁴When the shepherd walks ahead of them, they follow him because they know his voice. ⁵They will not follow someone they do not know because they do not know his voice. They will run away from him." ⁶Jesus told this picture-story to them. Yet they did not understand what He said.

Jesus Is The Door

⁷Again Jesus said to them, "For sure, I tell you, I am the Door of the sheep. ⁸All others who came ahead of Me are men who steal and rob. The sheep did not obey them. ⁹I am the Door. Anyone who goes in through Me will be saved from the punishment of sin. He will go in and out and find food. ¹⁰The robber comes only to steal and to kill and to destroy. I came so they might have life, a great full life.

Jesus Teaches About The Good Shepherd

¹¹"I am the Good Shepherd. The Good Shepherd gives His life for the sheep. ¹²One who is hired to watch the sheep is not the shepherd. He does not own the sheep. He sees the wolf coming and leaves the sheep. He runs away while the wolf gets the sheep and makes them run everywhere. ¹³The hired man runs away because he is hired. He does not care about the sheep.

¹⁴"I am the Good Shepherd. I know My sheep and My sheep know Me. ¹⁵I know My Father as My Father knows Me. I give My life for the sheep. ¹⁶I have other sheep which are not from this sheep-pen. I must bring them also. They will listen to My voice. Then there will be one flock with one shepherd.

¹⁷"For this reason My Father loves Me. It is because I give My life that I might take it back again. ¹⁸No one takes my life from Me. I give it by Myself. I have the right and the power to take it back again. My Father has given Me this right and power."

¹⁹Because of what He said, the Jews did not agree in their thinking. ²⁰Many of them said, "He has a demon and is crazy. Why listen to Him?" ²¹Others said, "A man who has a demon does not talk this way. Can a demon open the eyes of a blind man?"

Jesus Tells Who He Is

²²It was time for the religious gathering of remembering how the house of God was opened in Jerusalem. ²³It was winter and Jesus was there. He was walking in Solomon's porch in the house of God. ²⁴The Jews gathered around Him. They said, "How long are You going to keep us in doubt? If You are the Christ, tell us."

²⁵Jesus answered, "I told you and you do not believe. The works I do in My Father's name speak of Me. ²⁶You do not believe because you are not My sheep. ²⁷My sheep hear My voice and I know them. They follow Me. ²⁸I give them life that lasts forever. They will never be punished. No one is able to take them out of My hand. ²⁹My Father Who gave them to Me is greater than all. No one is able to take them out of My Father's hand. ³⁰My Father and I are one!"

Jesus Talks To Angry Men

³¹Again the Jews picked up stones to throw at Him. ³²Jesus said to them,

"Many good things have I shown you from My Father. For which of these things are you going to throw stones at Me?" [33]They said, "We are not going to throw stones at You for any good work. It is because of the way You talk against God. It is because You make Yourself to be God when You are only a man." [34]Jesus said to them, "Is it not written in your Law, 'I said, you are gods'? (Psalm 82:6) [35]The Holy Writings were given to them and God called them gods. (The Word of God cannot be put aside.) [36]But God has set Me apart for Himself. He sent Me into the world. Then how can you say that I am speaking against God because I said, 'I am the Son of God'? [37]If I am not doing the works of My Father, do not believe Me. [38]But if I do them, even if you do not believe Me, believe the works that I do. Then you will know the Father is in Me and I am in Him." [39]They tried again to take Him but He got out of their hands.

Jesus Goes To The Other Side Of The Jordan River

[40]Jesus went away to the other side of the Jordan River to the place where John was baptizing people. Jesus stayed there. [41]Many people came to Him and said, "John did no powerful work, but what John said about this Man is true." [42]Many people put their trust in Jesus there.

Jesus Hears About Lazarus

11 A man named Lazarus was sick. He lived in the town of Bethany with his sisters, Mary and Martha. [2]This was the Mary who put perfume on the Lord and dried His feet with her hair. It was her brother Lazarus who was sick. [3]The sisters sent word to Jesus, saying, "Lord, your friend is sick!" [4]When Jesus heard this, He said, "This sickness will not end in death. It has happened so that it will bring honor to God.

And the Son of God will be honored by it also."

Jesus Tells Of The Death Of Lazarus

[5]Jesus loved Martha and her sister and Lazarus. [6]But when He heard that Lazarus was sick, He stayed where He was two more days. [7]Then He said to His followers, "Let us go into the country of Judea again." [8]The followers said to Him, "Teacher, the Jews tried to throw stones at You to kill You not long ago. Are You going there again?" [9]Jesus said, "Are there not twelve hours in the day? If a man walks during the day, he will not fall. He sees the light of this world. [10]If a man walks during the night, he will fall. The light is not in him."

[11]After Jesus had said this, He spoke again and said, "Our friend Lazarus is sleeping. I will go and wake him up." [12]The followers said to Him, "If he is sleeping, he will get well." [13]But Jesus meant Lazarus was dead. They thought He meant Lazarus was resting in sleep. [14]Then Jesus said to them, "Lazarus is dead. [15]Because of you I am glad I was not there so that you may believe. Come, let us go to him."

[16]Thomas, who was called the Twin, said to the other followers, "Let us go also so we may die with Jesus."

Jesus Tells That The Grave Will Not Hold The Dead

[17]When Jesus got there, He heard that Lazarus had been in the grave four days. [18]Bethany was about one-half hour walk from Jerusalem. [19]Many Jews had come to Martha and Mary to give words of comfort about their brother.

[20]Martha heard that Jesus was coming and went to meet Him. Mary stayed in the house. [21]Martha said to Jesus, "Lord, if You had been here, my brother would not have died. [22]I

know even now God will give You whatever You ask." ²³Jesus said to her, "Your brother will rise again." ²⁴Martha said to Him, "I know that he will rise again when the dead are raised from the grave on the last day."

²⁵Jesus said to her, "I am the One Who raises the dead and gives them life. Anyone who puts his trust in Me will live again, even if he dies. ²⁶Anyone who lives and has put his trust in Me will never die. Do you believe this?" ²⁷She answered, "Yes, Lord, I believe that You are the Christ, the Son of God. You are the One Who was to come into the world."

Lazarus Is Raised From The Dead

²⁸After Martha said this, she went and called her sister Mary. She said without anyone else hearing, "The Teacher is here and has sent for you." ²⁹When Mary heard this, she got up and went to Him. ³⁰Jesus had not yet come into their town. He was still where Martha had met Him.

³¹The Jews had been in the house comforting Mary. They saw her get up and hurry out. They followed her and said, "She is going to the grave to cry there." ³²Mary went to the place where Jesus was. When she saw Him, she got down at His feet. She said to Him, "Lord, if You had been here, my brother would not have died." ³³Jesus saw her crying. The Jews who came with her were crying also. His heart was very sad and He was troubled. ³⁴He said, "Where did you lay Lazarus?" They said, "Lord, come and see." ³⁵Then Jesus cried. ³⁶The Jews said, "See how much He loved Lazarus." ³⁷Some of them said, "This Man opened the eyes of the blind man. Could He not have kept this man from dying?"

³⁸Jesus went to the grave with a sad heart. The grave was a hole in the side of a hill. A stone covered the door. ³⁹Jesus said, "Take the stone away." The dead man's sister, Martha, said to Him, "Lord, by now his body has a bad smell. He has been dead four days." ⁴⁰Jesus said to her, "Did I not say that if you would believe, you would see the shining greatness of God?"

⁴¹They took the stone away. Jesus looked up and said, "Father, I thank You for hearing Me. ⁴²I know You always hear Me. But I have said this for the people standing here, so they may believe You have sent Me."

⁴³When He had said this, He called with a loud voice, "Lazarus, come out!" ⁴⁴The man who had been dead came out. His hands and feet were tied in grave clothes. A white cloth was tied around his face. Jesus said to the people, "Take off the grave clothes and let him go!"

The Proud Religious Law-keepers Try To Think Of A Way To Kill Jesus

⁴⁵Many of the Jews who had come to visit Mary and had seen what Jesus had done put their trust in Him. ⁴⁶Some of them went to the proud religious law-keepers and told them what Jesus had done. ⁴⁷The religious leaders of the Jews and the proud religious law-keepers gathered a court together. They said, "What will we do? This Man is doing many powerful works. ⁴⁸If we let Him keep doing these things, all men will put their trust in Him. The Romans will come and take away the house of God and our nation." ⁴⁹Caiaphas was the head religious leader that year. He said to them, "You know nothing about this. ⁵⁰Do you not see it is better for one man to die for the people than for the whole nation to be destroyed?"

⁵¹Caiaphas did not think of these words himself. He spoke what God had said would happen. He was telling before it happened that Jesus must die for the nation. ⁵²He must die not only for the nation, but also to

bring together into one group the children of God who were living in many places.

53 From that day on they talked together about how they might kill Jesus. 54 For this reason Jesus did not walk out in the open among the Jews. He went to a town called Ephraim. It was near a desert. He stayed there with His followers.

The Proud Religious Law-keepers Look For Jesus

55 The special religious gathering to remember how the Jews left Egypt was soon. Many people from around the country came up to Jerusalem. They came to wash themselves in their religious worship before the special supper. 56 They looked for Jesus. They stood together in the house of God and asked each other, "What do you think? Will He come to the special supper?" 57 The religious leaders of the Jews and the proud religious law-keepers had said that if any man knew where Jesus was, he should tell them. They wanted to take Him.

Mary Of Bethany Puts Special Perfume On Jesus [Matthew 26:6-13; Mark 14:3-9]

12 It was six days before the special religious gathering to remember how the Jews left Egypt. Jesus came to Bethany where Lazarus lived. Jesus had raised Lazarus from the dead. 2 They made supper for Him. Martha put the food on the table. Lazarus was at the table with Him.

3 Mary took a jar of special perfume that cost much money and poured it on the feet of Jesus. She dried His feet with her hair. The house was filled with the smell of the special perfume.

4 Judas Iscariot was one of the followers. He was about to hand Jesus over to the leaders of the country. He said, 5 "Why was not this special perfume sold for much money and given to poor people?" 6 He did not say this because he cared for poor people. He said this because he was a robber. He carried the bag of money and would steal some of it for himself. 7 Jesus said, "Let her alone. She has kept it for the time when I will be buried. 8 You will always have poor people with you. You will not always have Me."

The Jews Talk About Having Lazarus Killed

9 Many Jews came to the place because they knew Jesus was there. They came not only to see Jesus, but to see Lazarus also. Jesus had raised Lazarus from the dead. 10 The religious leaders of the Jews talked together about having Lazarus killed also. 11 Because of Lazarus, many Jews were leaving their own religion. They were putting their trust in Jesus.

The Last Time Jesus Goes To Jerusalem [Matthew 21:1-11; Mark 11:1-11; Luke 19:29-44]

12 The next day many people were in Jerusalem for the religious gathering. They heard Jesus was coming. 13 They took branches of trees and went to meet Him. They spoke with a loud voice, "Greatest One! Great and honored is He Who comes in the name of the Lord, the King of the Jews!" 14 Jesus found a young donkey and sat on it. The Holy Writings say, 15 "Do not be afraid, people of Jerusalem. See! Your King comes sitting on a young donkey!" (Zechariah 9:9) 16 His followers did not understand what this meant at first. When Jesus had gone back to heaven to receive great honor, they remembered these things were written about Him. They remembered they had done this to Him.

17 The people who had been with Jesus when He had called Lazarus

from the grave kept telling of this powerful work to others. They had seen Lazarus raised from the dead. [18]Because of this the people went to meet Jesus. They had heard He had done this powerful work. [19]The proud religious law-keepers said among themselves, "Look, we are losing followers. Everyone is following Jesus!"

The Greek People Want To See Jesus

[20]Some Greek people had come to worship at the religious gathering. They were among the others who had come to worship. [21]These Greek people came to Philip. He was from the city of Bethsaida in the country of Galilee. They said to him, "Sir, we want to see Jesus!" [22]Philip went and told Andrew. Then Andrew and Philip told Jesus.

The Law Of Life

[23]Jesus said to them, "The hour is near for the Son of Man to be taken to heaven to receive great honor. [24]For sure, I tell you, unless a seed falls into the ground and dies, it will only be a seed. If it dies, it will give much grain. [25]Anyone who loves his life will lose it. Anyone who hates his life in this world will keep it forever. [26]If anyone wants to serve Me, he must follow Me. So where I am, the one who wants to serve Me will be there also. If anyone serves Me, My Father will honor him.

[27]"Now My soul is troubled. Should I say, 'Father, save Me from this time of trouble and pain'? No, this is why I came to this time. [28]Father, honor Your name!"

The People Hear The Voice Of God

Then a voice from heaven came, saying, "I have already honored My name. I will honor it again!" [29]The people heard the voice. Some who stood there said, "It was thunder."

Others said, "An angel spoke to Him." [30]Jesus said, "The voice did not come for Me, but it came to be a help to you.

Jesus Tells How He Will Die

[31]"Now this world is being told it is guilty. Now the leader of this world will be thrown out. [32]And when I am lifted up from the earth, I will attract all people toward Me." [33]He said this to tell the kind of death He was going to die.

[34]The people said to Him, "The Law of Moses says that the Christ is to live forever. Why do you say, 'The Son of Man must be lifted up'? Who is this Son of Man?"

[35]Jesus said to them, "The Light will be with you for a little while yet. Go on your way while you have the Light so you will not be in the dark. When a man is walking in the dark, he does not know where he is going. [36]While you have the Light, put your trust in the Light. Then you will be the sons of the Light." Jesus said these things and then went away. He hid Himself from them.

The People Do Not Believe

[37]Jesus had done many powerful works in front of them, but they did not put their trust in Him. [38]This happened as the words of the early preacher Isaiah said it would happen. He had said, "Lord, has anyone believed our preaching? Has the Lord shown His power to anyone?" [39]The reason they could not believe is written again in Isaiah. [40]It says, "He has blinded their eyes and made their hearts hard. Then they would not see with their eyes. They would not understand with their heart. They would not turn to Me. I could not heal them." (Isaiah 6:9-10) [41]This is what Isaiah said when he saw the shining greatness of Jesus and spoke of Him.

[42]Even among the leaders of the

people there were many who believed in Jesus. But because of the proud religious law-keepers, they did not tell about it. If they had, they would have been put out of the Jewish place of worship. ⁴³They loved to have the respect from men more than honor from God.

Jesus And His Father Are One

⁴⁴Then Jesus spoke with a loud voice, "Anyone who puts his trust in Me, puts his trust not only in Me, but in Him Who sent Me. ⁴⁵Anyone who sees Me, sees Him Who sent Me. ⁴⁶I came to the world to be a Light. Anyone who puts his trust in Me will not be in darkness. ⁴⁷If anyone hears My Words but does not believe them, I do not say he is guilty. I did not come to say the world is guilty. I came to save the world from the punishment of sin. ⁴⁸Anyone who does not receive Me and does not receive My teaching has One Who will say he is guilty. The Word that I have spoken will say he is guilty on the last day. ⁴⁹I have not spoken by My own power. The Father Who sent Me has told Me what to say and speak. ⁵⁰I know that His Word is life that lasts forever. I speak the things the Father has told Me to speak."

Jesus Washes The Feet Of His Followers

13 It was before the special religious gathering to remember how the Jews left Egypt. Jesus knew the time had come for Him to leave this world and go to the Father. He had loved His own who were in the world. He loved them to the end. ²He and His followers were having supper. Satan had put the thought into the heart of Judas Iscariot of handing Jesus over to the leaders of the country. ³Jesus knew the Father had put everything into His hands. He knew He had come from God and was going back to God. ⁴Jesus got up

from the supper and took off His coat. He picked up a cloth and put it around Him. ⁵Then He put water into a wash pan and began to wash the feet of His followers. He dried their feet with the cloth He had put around Himself.

Peter Speaks Out Against Jesus Washing His Feet

⁶Jesus came to Simon Peter. Peter said to Him, "Lord, are You going to wash my feet?" ⁷Jesus answered him, "You do not understand now what I am doing but you will later." ⁸Peter said to Him, "I will never let You wash my feet." Jesus said, "Unless I wash you, you will not be a part of Me." ⁹Simon Peter said to Him, "Lord, do not wash only my feet, but wash my hands and my head also." ¹⁰Jesus said to him, "Anyone who has washed his body needs only to wash his feet. Then he is clean all over. You are all clean except one." ¹¹Jesus knew who was going to hand Him over to the leaders. That is why He said, "You are all clean except one."

Jesus Tells Why He Washed Their Feet

¹²Jesus washed their feet and put on His coat. Then He sat down again and said to them, "Do you understand what I have done to you? ¹³You call Me Teacher and Lord. You are right because that is what I am. ¹⁴I am your Teacher and Lord. I have washed your feet. You should wash each other's feet also. ¹⁵I have done this to show you what should be done. You should do as I have done to you. ¹⁶For sure, I tell you, a workman who is owned by someone is not greater than his owner. One who is sent is not greater than the one who sent him. ¹⁷If you know these things, you will be happy if you do them.

¹⁸"I am not speaking about all of you. I know the ones I have chosen. What is written in the Holy Writings

must happen. It says, 'The man who eats bread with Me has turned against Me.' (Psalm 41:9) ¹⁹I tell you this now before it happens. After it happens, you will believe that I am Who I say I am, the Christ. ²⁰For sure, I tell you, he who receives the one I send out, receives Me. He who receives Me receives Him who sent Me."

The Last Special Supper - Jesus Tells Of The One Who Will Hand Him Over To The Leaders [Matthew 26:20-25; Mark 14:17-21; Luke 22:14-18]

²¹When Jesus had said this, He was troubled in heart. He told them in very plain words, saying, "For sure, I tell you, one of you is going to hand Me over to the leaders of the country."
²²The followers began to look at each other. They did not know which one He was speaking of. ²³One follower, whom Jesus loved, was beside Jesus. ²⁴Simon Peter got this follower to look his way. He wanted him to ask Jesus which one He was speaking of. ²⁵While close beside Jesus, he asked, "Lord, who is it?"
²⁶Jesus answered, "It is the one I give this piece of bread to after I have put it in the dish." Then He put the bread in the dish and gave it to Judas Iscariot, the son of Simon. ²⁷After Judas had eaten the piece of bread, Satan went into him. Jesus said to Judas, "What you are going to do, do in a hurry."
²⁸No one at the supper knew why Jesus had said this to Judas. ²⁹They thought it was because Judas carried the bag of money, and Jesus had said that Judas should buy what they needed for the religious gathering. Or they thought Judas should give something to poor people. ³⁰As soon as Judas had taken the piece of bread, he went out. It was night.

Love - The Greatest Law

³¹After Judas went out, Jesus said, "The Son of Man is now honored and God has been honored in Him. ³²If God is honored in Him, God will also honor Him in Himself right now. ³³Little children, I will be with you only a little while. You will look for Me. I say to you what I said to the Jews, 'Where I am going, you cannot come!' ³⁴I give you a new Law. You are to love each other. You must love each other as I have loved you. ³⁵If you love each other, all men will know you are My followers."

Jesus Tells How Peter Will Lie About Him [Matthew 26:31-35; Mark 14:27-31; Luke 22:31-34]

³⁶Simon Peter said to Jesus, "Lord, where are You going?" Jesus answered, "You cannot follow Me now where I am going. Later you will follow Me." ³⁷Peter said to Jesus, "Why can I not follow You now? I will die for You." ³⁸Jesus answered Peter, "Will you die for Me? For sure, I tell you, before a rooster crows, you will have said three times that you do not know Me."

Jesus Comforts His Followers

14 "Do not let your heart be troubled. You have put your trust in God, put your trust in Me also. ²There are many rooms in My Father's house. If it were not so, I would have told you. I am going away to make a place for you. ³After I go and make a place for you, I will come back and take you with Me. Then you may be where I am. ⁴You know where I am going and you know how to get there."
⁵Thomas said to Jesus, "Lord, we do not know where You are going. How can we know the way to get there?" ⁶Jesus said, "I am the Way and the Truth and the Life. No one

can go to the Father except by Me. [7]If you had known Me, you would know My Father also. From now on you know Him and have seen Him."

Jesus And His Father Are One

[8]Philip said to Jesus, "Lord, show us the Father. That is all we ask." [9]Jesus said to him, "Have I been with you all this time and you do not know Me yet? Whoever has seen Me, has seen the Father. How can you say, 'Show us the Father'? [10]Do you not believe that I am in the Father and that the Father is in Me? What I say to you, I do not say by My own power. The Father Who lives in Me does His work through Me. [11]"Believe Me that I am in the Father and that the Father is in Me. Or else believe Me because of the things I do. [12]For sure, I tell you, whoever puts his trust in Me can do the things I am doing. He will do even greater things than these because I am going to the Father. [13]Whatever you ask in My name, I will do it so the shining greatness of the Father may be seen in the Son. [14]Yes, if you ask anything in My name, I will do it.

[15]"If you love Me, you will do what I say. [16]Then I will ask My Father and He will give you another Helper. He will be with you forever. [17]He is the Spirit of Truth. The world cannot receive Him. It does not see Him or know Him. You know Him because He lives with you and will be in you.

Jesus Tells Of His Death

[18]"I will not leave you without help as children without parents. I will come to you. [19]In a little while the world will see Me no more. You will see Me. Because I live, you will live also. [20]When that day comes, you will know that I am in My Father. You will know that you are in Me. You will know that I am in you.

[21]The one who loves Me is the one who has My teaching and obeys it. My Father will love whoever loves Me. I will love him and will show Myself to him."

[22]The other Judas (not Iscariot) said to Him, "Why is it You are going to show Yourself to us followers and not to the world?" [23]Jesus said, "The one who loves Me will obey My teaching. My Father will love him. We will come to him and live with him. [24]The one who does not love Me does not obey My teaching. The teaching you are now hearing is not My teaching but it is from My Father Who sent Me.

[25]"I have told you these things while I am still with you. [26]The Helper is the Holy Spirit. The Father will send Him in My place. He will teach you everything and help you remember everything I have told you.

Jesus Gives His Followers Peace

[27]"I give you My peace and leave it with you. I do not give peace to you as the world gives. Do not let your hearts be troubled or afraid. [28]You heard Me say that I am going away. But I am coming back to you. If you love Me, you would be glad that I am going to the Father. The Father is greater than I. [29]I have told you this before it happens. Then when it does happen, you will believe. [30]"I will not talk much more with you. The leader of this world is coming. He has no power over Me. [31]I am doing what the Father told Me to do so the world may know I love the Father. Come, let us be on our way.

The Vine And The Branches

15 "I am the true Vine. My Father is the One Who cares for the Vine. [2]He takes away any branch in Me that does not give fruit. Any branch that gives fruit, He cuts it

back so it will give more fruit. ³You are made clean by the words I have spoken to you. ⁴Get your life from Me and I will live in you. No branch can give fruit by itself. It has to get life from the vine. You are able to give fruit only when you have life from Me. ⁵I am the Vine and you are the branches. Get your life from Me. Then I will live in you and you will give much fruit. You can do nothing without Me.

⁶"If anyone does not get his life from Me, he is cut off like a branch and dries up. Such branches are gathered and thrown into the fire and they are burned. ⁷If you get your life from Me and My Words live in you, ask whatever you want. It will be done for you.

⁸"When you give much fruit, My Father is honored. This shows you are My followers. ⁹I have loved you just as My Father has loved Me. Stay in My love. ¹⁰If you obey My teaching, you will live in My love. In this way, I have obeyed My Father's teaching and live in His love. ¹¹I have told you these things so My joy may be in you and your joy may be full.

¹²"This is what I tell you to do: Love each other just as I have loved you. ¹³No one can have greater love than to give his life for his friends. ¹⁴You are My friends if you do what I tell you. ¹⁵I do not call you servants that I own anymore. A servant does not know what his owner is doing. I call you friends, because I have told you everything I have heard from My Father. ¹⁶You have not chosen Me, I have chosen you. I have set you apart for the work of bringing in fruit. Your fruit should last. And whatever you ask the Father in My name, He will give it to you.

The Christian And The World

¹⁷"This is what I tell you to do: Love each other. ¹⁸If the world hates you, you know it hated Me before it hated you. ¹⁹If you

belonged to the world, the world would love you as its own. You do not belong to the world. I have chosen you out of the world and the world hates you. ²⁰Remember I said to you, 'A servant is not greater than his owner.' If they made it very hard for Me, they will make it very hard for you also. If they obeyed My teachings, they will obey your teachings also. ²¹They will do all these things to you because you belong to Me. They do not know My Father Who sent Me.

²²"I have come and have spoken to them so they are guilty of sin. But now they have no reason to give for keeping their sin any longer. ²³Whoever hates Me, hates My Father also. ²⁴I have done things among them which no one else has done so they are guilty of sin. But now they have seen these things and have hated Me and My Father. ²⁵This happened as their Law said it would happen, 'They hated Me without a reason.'

²⁶"The Helper (Holy Spirit) will tell about Me when He comes. I will send Him to you from the Father. He is the Spirit of Truth and comes from the Father. ²⁷You will also tell of Me because you have been with Me from the beginning.

Jesus Tells His Followers It Will Be Very Hard For Them

16 "I have told you these things so you will not be ashamed of Me and leave Me. ²They will put you out of the places of worship. The time will come when anyone who kills you will think he is helping God. ³They will do these things to you because they do not know the Father or Me.

⁴"When these things happen, you will remember I told you they would happen. That is why I am telling you about these things now. I did not tell you these things before, because I was with you. ⁵But now I am going to Him Who sent Me. Yet none of you asks Me, 'Where are You going?'

The Three Kinds Of Work Of The Holy Spirit

6"Your hearts are full of sorrow because I am telling you these things. 7I tell you the truth. It is better for you that I go away. If I do not go, the Helper will not come to you. If I go, I will send Him to you. 8When the Helper comes, He will show the world the truth about sin. He will show the world about being right with God. And He will show the world what it is to be guilty. 9He will show the world about sin, because they do not put their trust in Me. 10He will show the world about being right with God, because I go to My Father and you will see Me no more. 11He will show the world what it is to be guilty because the leader of this world (Satan) is guilty.

The Holy Spirit Will Give Honor To The Son

12"I still have many things to say to you. You are not strong enough to understand them now. 13The Holy Spirit is coming. He will lead you into all truth. He will not speak His Own words. He will speak what He hears. He will tell you of things to come. 14He will honor Me. He will receive what is Mine and will tell it to you. 15Everything the Father has is Mine. That is why I said to you, 'He will receive what is Mine and will tell it to you.'

Jesus Tells Of His Death

16"In a little while you will not see Me. Then in a little while you will see Me again." 17Some of His followers said to each other, "What is He trying to tell us when He says, 'In a little while you will not see Me, and in a little while you will see Me again,' and 'Because I go to My Father'?" 18So they said, "What is He trying to tell us by saying, 'A little while'? We do not know what He is talking about."

19Jesus knew they wanted to ask Him something. He said to them, "Are you asking each other why I said, 'In a little while you will not see Me, and in a little while you will see Me again'? 20For sure, I tell you, you will cry and have sorrow, but the world will have joy. You will have sorrow, but your sorrow will turn into joy. 21When a woman gives birth to a child, she has sorrow because her time has come. After the child is born, she forgets her pain. She is full of joy because a child has been born into the world. 22You are sad now. I will see you again and then your hearts will be full of joy. No one can take your joy from you.

Asking And Receiving

23"When the time comes that you see Me again, you will ask Me no question. For sure, I tell you, My Father will give you whatever you ask in My name. 24Until now you have not asked for anything in My name. Ask and you will receive. Then your joy will be full.

25"I have told you these things in picture-stories. The time is coming when I will not use picture-stories. I will talk about My Father in plain words. 26In that day you will ask in My name. I will not ask the Father for you 27because the Father loves you. He loves you because you love Me and believe that I came from the Father.

Jesus Tells Of His Going

28"I came from the Father and have come into the world. I am leaving the world and going to the Father." 29His followers said to Him, "Now You are talking in plain words. You are not using picture-stories. 30Now we are sure You know everything. You do not need anyone to tell You anything. Because of this we believe that You came from God."

[31]Jesus said to them, "Do you believe now? [32]The time is coming, yes, it is already here when you will be going your own way. Everyone will go to his own house and leave Me alone. Yet I am not alone because the Father is with Me. [33]I have told you these things so you may have peace in Me. In the world you will have much trouble. But take hope! I have power over the world!"

Jesus Prays For Himself

17 When Jesus had said these things, He looked up to heaven and said, "Father, the time has come! Honor Your Son so Your Son may honor You. [2]You have given Him power over all men. He is to give life that lasts forever to all You have given to Him. [3]This is life that lasts forever. It is to know You, the only true God, and to know Jesus Christ Whom You have sent. [4]I honored You on earth. I did the work You gave Me to do. [5]Now, Father, honor Me with the honor I had with You before the world was made.

Jesus Prays For His Followers

[6]"I have made Your name known to the people You have given Me from the world. They were Yours but You gave them to Me. They have obeyed Your Word. [7]Now they know that everything You have given Me came from You. [8]I gave them the Word which You gave Me. They received it. They know I came from You and they believe You sent Me.

[9]"I pray for them. I do not pray for the world. I pray for those You gave Me. They are Yours. [10]All that is Mine is Yours. All that is Yours is Mine. I have been honored through them. [11]I am no longer in the world. I am coming to You. But these are still in the world. Holy Father, keep those You have given to Me in the power of Your name. Then they will be one, even as We are One. [12]While I have been with them in the world, I have kept them in the power of Your name. I have kept watch over those You gave Me. Not one of them has been lost except the one who is going to be destroyed, which is the son of death. The Holy Writings said it would happen. (Psalm 41:9; John 6:70) [13]But now I come to You, Father. I say these things while I am in the world. In this way, My followers may have My joy in their hearts.

[14]"I have given Your Word to My followers. The world hated them because they do not belong to the world, even as I do not belong to the world. [15]I do not ask You to take them out of the world. I ask You to keep them from the devil. [16]My followers do not belong to the world just as I do not belong to the world. [17]Make them holy for Yourself by the truth. Your Word is truth. [18]As You sent Me into the world so I have sent them into the world also. [19]I set Myself apart to be holy for them. Then they may be made holy by the truth.

Jesus Prays For All Christians

[20]"I do not pray for these followers only. I pray for those who will put their trust in Me through the teaching they have heard. [21]May they all be as one, Father, as You are in Me and I am in You. May they belong to Us. Then the world will believe that You sent Me. [22]I gave them the honor You gave Me that they may be one as We are One. [23]I am in them and You are in Me so they may be one and be made perfect. Then the world may know that You sent Me and that You love them as You love Me.

[24]"Father, I want My followers You gave Me to be with Me where I am. Then they may see My shining greatness which You gave Me because You loved Me before the world was made. [25]Holy Father, the world has not known You. I have

known You. These have known You
sent Me. 26I have made Your name
known to them and will make it
known. So then the love You have
for Me may be in them and I may be
in them."

Jesus Handed Over To Sinners
[*Matthew 26:47-56; Mark 14:43-52;*
Luke 22:47-51]

18 When Jesus had said these
things, He went with His
followers across the small river
Kidron. He and His followers went to
a garden there. 2Judas, who was
handing Him over to the leaders,
knew the place also. Jesus and His
followers had met there many times.
3Judas led some soldiers and some
men who had been sent by the head
religious leaders of the Jews and the
proud religious law-keepers to the
garden. They carried lamps and
sticks that were burning and swords.
4Jesus knew what was going to
happen to Him. He went out and
asked them, "Who are you looking
for?" 5The soldiers answered Him,
"Jesus of Nazareth." Jesus said, "I am
Jesus." Judas, who was handing Him
over, was with them also.
6When He said to them, "I am
Jesus," they stepped back and fell to
the ground. 7He asked them again,
"Who are you looking for?" They
said again, "Jesus of Nazareth." 8He
said, "I have told you that I am Jesus.
If you are looking for Me, let these
men go their way." 9He said this so
the words He spoke might happen, "I
have not lost one of those You gave
Me."
10Simon Peter had a sword. He
took it and hit a servant who was
owned by the head religious leader
and cut off his right ear. The servant's name was Malchus. 11Then
Jesus said to Peter, "Put your sword
back where it belongs. Am I not to go
through what My Father has given
Me to go through?"

Jesus Stands In Front Of Annas

12Then the soldiers and their
captain and the men sent by the
Jewish religious leaders took Jesus
and tied Him. 13They took Him to
Annas first. He was the father-in-law
of Caiaphas. Caiaphas was the head
religious leader that year. 14Caiaphas
had talked to the Jews. He told them
it would be a good thing if one man
should die for the people.

Peter Lies About Jesus [*Matthew*
2:69-75; Mark 14:66-72; Luke 22:55-
62]

15Simon Peter and another follower came behind Jesus. This other
follower was known to the head
religious leader. He went with Jesus
to the head religious leader's house.
16Peter stood outside at the gate. The
other follower, who was known by
the head religious leader, went out
and talked to the servant-girl who
watched the gate. Then he took Peter
inside. 17The servant-girl who
watched the door said to Peter, "Are
you not a follower of this Man?" He
said, "I am not!" 18The servants who
were owned by someone and the
soldiers had made a fire because it
was cold. They were getting warm by
the fire. Peter was standing with
them getting warm.

Jesus Stands In Front Of Caiaphas
[*Matthew 26:57-58; Mark 14:53-54;*
Luke 22:52-54]

19The head religious leader of the
Jews asked Jesus about His followers.
He asked Jesus about His teaching.
20Jesus said, "I have spoken very
plain words to the world. I have
always taught in the Jewish place of
worship and in the house of God. It is
where the Jews go all the time. My
words have not been said in secret.
21Why do you ask Me? Ask those
who have heard what I said to them.

They know what I said."

22 Then one of the soldiers standing there hit Jesus with his hand. He said, "Is that how You talk to the head religious leaders?" 23 Jesus said, "If I said anything wrong, tell Me what was wrong. If I said what was right, why did you hit Me?" 24 Then Annas sent Jesus to Caiaphas, the head religious leader. Jesus was still tied up.

25 Simon Peter was standing there and getting warm. They said to him, "Are you not one of His followers also?" He lied and said he did not know Jesus and answered, "I am not!" 26 A servant who was owned by the head religious leader was there. He was of the family of the man whose ear Peter cut off. The man said, "Did I not see you in the garden with Him?" 27 Again Peter lied and said he did not know Jesus. At once a rooster crowed.

Jesus Stands In Front Of Pilate [Matthew 27:1-2, 11-14; Mark 15:1-5; Luke 23:1-5]

28 They led Jesus from Caiaphas into the court room. It was early in the morning. They did not go inside because their Law said if they did they would become dirty with sin. Then they would not be able to eat the religious supper to remember how the Jews left Egypt. 29 So Pilate came out to them. He asked, "What have you to say against the Man?" 30 The Jews said, "If He had not done wrong, we would not have brought Him to you."

31 Then Pilate said to them, "Take Him yourselves and give Him a trial by your Law." The Jews said to him, "It is against our Law to put anyone to death." 32 This happened as Jesus said it would happen. He had told what kind of death He would die.

33 Then Pilate went back into the court room. He called for Jesus and said to Him, "Are You the King of the Jews?" 34 Jesus said, "Do you ask Me this yourself, or did others say this to you about Me?" 35 Pilate said, "Do you think I am a Jew? Your own people and religious leaders have handed You over to me. What have You done?"

36 Jesus said, "My holy nation does not belong to this world. If My holy nation were of this world, My helpers would fight so I would not be handed over to the Jews. My holy nation is not of this world." 37 Pilate said to Him, "So You are a King?" Jesus said, "You are right when you say that I am a King. I was born for this reason. I came into the world for this reason. I came to speak about the truth. Everyone who is of the truth hears My voice."

Jesus Or Barabbas Is To Go Free [Matthew 27:15-26; Mark 15:6-14; Luke 23:17-25]

38 Pilate said to Jesus, "What is truth?" After Pilate said this, he went out again to the Jews. He said, "I do not find Him guilty. 39 But every year a man who is in prison is allowed to go free at the special religious gathering to remember how the Jews left Egypt. Do you want the King of the Jews to go free?" 40 Then they spoke with loud voices, "Not this Man, but Barabbas!" Now Barabbas was a robber.

The Crown Of Thorns [Matthew 27:27-32; Mark 15:15-21]

19 Then Pilate took Jesus and had Him beaten. 2 The soldiers put a crown of thorns on His head. They put a purple coat on Him. 3 Then they said, "Hello, King of the Jews!" and hit Him with their hands.

4 Pilate went out again and said to the people, "See, I bring Him out to you so you will know I do not find Him guilty." 5 Jesus came out. He had on the crown of thorns and a purple coat. Pilate said to the people, "See! This is the Man!"

Pilate Tries To Let Jesus Go Free

⁶The religious leaders and the soldiers saw Him. They spoke with loud voices, "Nail Him to a cross! Nail Him to a cross!" Pilate said, "Take Him yourselves and nail Him to a cross. As for me, I do not find Him guilty." ⁷The Jews said to Pilate, "We have a Law that says He should die because He has said He is the Son of God."

⁸When Pilate heard them say this, he was more afraid. ⁹He went into the court room again. He said to Jesus, "Where do You come from?" Jesus did not say a word. ¹⁰Pilate said, "Will You not speak to me? Do You not know that I have the right and the power to nail You to a cross? I have the right and the power to let You go free also." ¹¹Jesus said, "You would not have any right or power over Me if it were not given you from above. For this reason the one who handed Me over to you has the worse sin."

¹²When Pilate heard this, he wanted to let Jesus go free. But the Jews kept saying, "If you let this Man go free, you are not a friend of Caesar! Whoever makes himself as a king is working against Caesar." ¹³When Pilate heard this, he had Jesus brought in front of him. Pilate sat down at the place where men stand in front of him if they are thought to be guilty. The place is called the Stone Floor. ¹⁴It was the day to get ready for the special religious gathering to remember how the Jews left Egypt. It was about noon. Pilate said to the Jews, "See, your King!" ¹⁵They spoke with a loud voice, "Take Him away! Nail Him to a cross!" Pilate said to them, "Do you want me to nail your King to a cross?" The head religious leaders said, "We have no king but Caesar!" ¹⁶Then Pilate handed Him over to be nailed to a cross. They took Jesus and led Him away.

Jesus On The Cross [Matthew 27:33-37; Mark 15:22-26; Luke 23:26-38]

¹⁷Jesus carried His own cross to a hill called the Place of the Skull. ¹⁸There they nailed Him to the cross. With Him were two others. There was one on each side of Jesus. ¹⁹Then Pilate put a writing on the cross which said, JESUS OF NAZARETH, THE KING OF THE JEWS. ²⁰This was read by many of the Jews. The place where Jesus was nailed to the cross was near the city. The writing was written in the Hebrew and the Latin and the Greek languages. ²¹Then the head religious leaders of the Jews said to Pilate, "Do not write, 'The King of the Jews'! Write, 'He said, I am the King of the Jews.' " ²²Pilate said, "What I have written is to stay just as it is!"

They Divided His Clothes

²³The soldiers who nailed Jesus to the cross took His clothes and divided them in four parts, each soldier getting one part. But His coat which was not sewed was made in one piece. ²⁴They said to each other, "Let us not cut it up. Let us draw names to see whose it should be." This happened as the Holy Writings said it would happen, "They divided My clothes among them and they drew names for My coat." (Psalm 22:18) ²⁵This is what the soldiers did.

The Women At The Cross

The mother of Jesus and her sister Mary, the wife of Cleophas, were standing near the cross. Mary Magdalene was there also. ²⁶Jesus saw His mother and the follower whom He loved standing near. He said to His mother, "Woman, look at your son." ²⁷Then Jesus said to the follower, "Look at your mother." From that time the follower took her to his own house.

The Death Of Jesus [Matthew 27:45-50; Mark 15:33-36; Luke 23:44-49]

²⁸Jesus knew that everything was now finished. Everything happened as the Holy Writings said it would happen. He said, "I am thirsty." (Psalm 69:21) ²⁹There was a jar full of sour wine near. They filled a sponge and put it on a stick and put it to His mouth. ³⁰Jesus took the sour wine and said, "It is finished." He put His head down and gave up His spirit and died.

His Bones Were Not Broken

³¹This was the day before the special religious gathering to remember how the Jews left Egypt. The next day was the Day of Rest and the great day of the religious gathering. The Jews went to Pilate and asked to have the legs of the men broken. They wanted their bodies taken away so they would not be hanging on the crosses on the Day of Rest. ³²Then the soldiers came and broke the legs of the first man and of the other one who had been nailed to crosses beside Jesus. ³³They came to Jesus. They saw He was already dead so they did not break His legs. ³⁴But one of the soldiers pushed a spear into His side. Blood and water ran out.

³⁵The one who saw it is writing this and what he says is true. He knows he is telling the truth so you may believe. ³⁶These things happened as the Holy Writings said they would happen, "Not one of His bones will be broken." (Exodus 12:46) ³⁷And in another place the Holy Writings say, "They will look at Him Whose side they cut." (Zechariah 12:10)

The Grave Of Jesus [Matthew 27:57-66; Mark 15:42-47; Luke 23:50-56]

³⁸Joseph was from the town of Arimathea. He was a follower of Jesus but was afraid of the Jews. So

he worshiped without anyone knowing it. He asked Pilate if he could take away the body of Jesus. Pilate said he could. Then Joseph came and took it away. ³⁹Nicodemus came also. The first time he had come to Jesus had been at night. He brought with him a large box of spices. ⁴⁰Then they took the body of Jesus with the spices and put it in linen cloths. This was the way the Jews made a body ready for the grave.

⁴¹There was a garden near the place where He had been nailed to the cross. In the garden there was a new grave in the side of the hill. No one had ever been laid there. ⁴²This place was near by. Because it was the day the Jews got ready for the special religious gathering, they laid Jesus in it.

Jesus Is Raised From The Grave [Matthew 28:1-10; Mark 16:1-8; Luke 24:1-12]

20 It was the first day of the week. Mary Magdalene came to the grave early in the morning while it was still dark. She saw that the stone had been pushed away from the grave. ²She ran to Simon Peter and the other follower whom Jesus loved. She said to them, "They have taken the Lord out of the grave. We do not know where they have put Him."

³Then Peter and the other follower went to the grave. ⁴They ran but the other follower ran faster than Peter and came to the grave first. ⁵He got down and looked in and saw the linen cloths but did not go in. ⁶Then Simon Peter came and went into the grave. He saw the linen cloths lying there. ⁷The white cloth that had been around the head of Jesus was not lying with the other linen cloths. It was rolled up and lying apart by itself. ⁸Then the other follower, who had come first, went in also. He saw and believed. ⁹They still did not understand what the Holy Writings

meant when they said that He must rise again from the dead. [10]Then the followers went back again to their homes.

[11]Mary stood outside the grave crying. As she cried, she got down and looked inside the grave. [12]She saw two angels dressed in white clothes. They were sitting where the body of Jesus had lain. One angel was where His head had lain and one angel was where His feet had lain. [13]They said to her, "Woman, why are you crying?" She said to them, "Because they have taken away my Lord. I do not know where they have put Him."

[14]After saying this, she turned around and saw Jesus standing there. But she did not know that it was Jesus. [15]He said to her, "Woman, why are you crying? Who are you looking for?" She thought He was the man who cared for the garden. She said to Him, "Sir, if you have taken Jesus from here, tell me where you have put Him. I will take Him away." [16]Jesus said to her, "Mary!" She turned around and said to Him, "Teacher!" [17]Jesus said to her, "Do not hold on to Me. I have not yet gone up to My Father. But go to My brothers. Tell them that I will go up to My Father and your Father, and to My God and your God!" [18]Mary Magdalene went and told the followers that she had seen the Lord. She told them the things He had said to her.

Jesus Was Seen By His Followers - Thomas Was Not There

[19]It was evening of the first day of the week. The followers had gathered together with the doors locked because they were afraid of the Jews. Jesus came and stood among them. He said, "May you have peace." [20]When He had said this, He showed them His hands and His side. When the followers saw the Lord, they were filled with joy.

Jesus Sends His Followers To Preach [Matthew 28:16-20; Mark 16:15-18; Luke 24:44-49]

[21]Then Jesus said to them again, "May you have peace. As the Father has sent Me, I also am sending you." [22]When Jesus had said this, He breathed on them. He said, "Receive the Holy Spirit. [23]If you say that people are free of sins, they are free of them. If you say that people are not free of sins, they still have them."

Thomas Does Not Believe Jesus Is Raised From The Dead [Mark 16:9-14; Luke 24:13-43]

[24]Thomas was not with them when Jesus came. He was one of the twelve followers and was called the Twin. [25]The other followers told him, "We have seen the Lord!" He said to them, "I will not believe until I see the marks made by the nails in His hands. I will not believe until I put my finger into the marks of the nails. I will not believe until I put my hand into His side."

Jesus Was Seen Again By His Followers - Thomas Was There

[26]Eight days later the followers were again inside a house. Thomas was with them. The doors were locked. Jesus came and stood among them. He said, "May you have peace!" [27]He said to Thomas, "Put your finger into My hands. Put your hand into My side. Do not doubt, believe!" [28]Thomas said to Him, "My Lord and my God!" [29]Jesus said to him, "Thomas, because you have seen Me, you believe. Those are happy who have never seen Me and yet believe!"

[30]Jesus did many other powerful works in front of His followers. They are not written in this book. [31]But these are written so you may believe that Jesus is the Christ, the Son of God. When you put your trust in

Him, you will have life that lasts forever through His name.

The Risen Christ Talks To His Followers

21 After this, Jesus again showed Himself to His followers at the lake of Tiberias. It happened like this: ²Simon Peter and Thomas who was called the Twin and Nathanael from the town of Cana in the country of Galilee and the sons of Zebedee and two other followers were all together. ³Simon Peter said to them, "I am going fishing." The others said, "We will go with you." They went out and got into a boat. That night they caught no fish.

⁴Early in the morning Jesus stood on the shore of the lake. The followers did not know it was Jesus. ⁵Then Jesus said to them, "Children, do you have any fish?" They said, "No." ⁶He said to them, "Put your net over the right side of the boat. Then you will catch some fish." They put out the net. They were not able to pull it in because it was so full of fish.

⁷Then the follower whom Jesus loved said to Peter, "It is the Lord!" When Peter heard it was the Lord, he put on his fisherman's coat. (He had taken it off.) Then he jumped into the water. ⁸The other followers came in the boat. They were pulling the net with the fish. They were not far from land, only a little way out.

⁹When they came to land they saw fish and bread on a fire. ¹⁰Jesus said to them, "Bring some of the fish you have just caught." ¹¹Simon Peter went out and pulled the net to land. There were 153 big fish. The net was not broken even with so many.

¹²Jesus said to them, "Come and eat." Not one of the followers would ask, "Who are You?" They knew it was the Lord. ¹³Jesus came and took bread and fish and gave it to them. ¹⁴This was the third time Jesus had shown Himself to His followers after He had risen from the dead.

The Risen Christ Talks To Peter

¹⁵When they were finished eating, Jesus said to Simon Peter, "Simon, son of John, do you love Me more than these?" Peter answered Jesus, "Yes, Lord, You know that I love You." Jesus said to him, "Feed My lambs."

¹⁶Jesus said to Peter the second time, "Simon, son of John, do you love Me?" He answered Jesus, "Yes, Lord, You know that I love You." Jesus said to him, "Take care of My sheep."

¹⁷Jesus said to Peter the third time, "Simon, son of John, do you love Me?" Peter felt bad because Jesus asked him the third time, "Do you love Me?" He answered Jesus, "Lord, You know everything. You know I love You." Jesus said to him, "Feed My sheep. ¹⁸For sure, I tell you, when you were young, you put on your belt and went wherever you wanted to go. When you get old, you will put out your hands and someone else will put on your belt and take you away where you do not want to go." ¹⁹He said this to tell Peter what kind of death he would die to honor God. After Jesus said this, He said to Peter, "Follow Me."

Jesus Talks To That Other Follower

²⁰Peter turned around. He saw the follower whom Jesus loved, following. This one had been beside Jesus at the supper. This is the one who had asked Jesus, "Lord, who will hand You over?" ²¹Peter saw him and said to Jesus, "But Lord, what about this one?" ²²Jesus said, "If I want this one to wait until I come, what is that to you? You follow Me." ²³So the news spread among the followers that this follower would not die. But Jesus did

not say to him that he would not die. He said, "If I want him to wait until I come, what is that to you?"

John Tells That He Wrote This Book

24 This is the follower who is telling of these things and who has written them. We know that his word is true. 25 There are many other things which Jesus did also. If they were all written down, I do not think the world itself could hold the books that would be written.

ACTS

Luke Writes To Theophilus

1 Dear Theophilus, in my first writings I wrote about all the things Jesus did and taught from the beginning 2 until the day He went to heaven. He spoke to the missionaries through the Holy Spirit. He told those whom He had chosen what they should do. 3 After He had suffered much and then died, He showed Himself alive in many sure ways for forty days. He told them many things about the holy nation of God.

Jesus Speaks Before He Goes To Be With The Father

4 As they were gathered together with Him, He told them, "Do not leave Jerusalem. Wait for what the Father has promised. You heard Me speak of this. 5 For John the Baptist baptized with water but in a few days you will be baptized with the Holy Spirit."

6 Those who were with Him asked, "Lord, is this the time for You to give the nation back to the Jews?" 7 He said, "It is not for you to know the special days or the special times which the Father has put in His own power.

8 "But you will receive power when the Holy Spirit comes into your life. You will tell about Me in the city of Jerusalem and over all the countries of Judea and Samaria and to the ends of the earth."

Jesus Goes To Be With The Father

9 When Jesus had said this and while they were still looking at Him, He was taken up. A cloud carried Him away so they could not see Him. 10 They were still looking up to heaven, watching Him go. All at once two men dressed in white stood beside them. 11 They said, "You men of the country of Galilee, why do you stand looking up into heaven? This same Jesus Who was taken from you into heaven will return in the same way you saw Him go up into heaven."

Matthias Is Chosen To Take The Place Of Judas

12 The followers went back to Jerusalem from the Mount of Olives,

which is close to Jerusalem. [13]When they came into the city, they went up to a room on the second floor where they stayed. The followers were Peter and John, James and Andrew, Philip and Thomas, Bartholomew and Matthew, James the son of Alphaeus, Simon the Canaanite, and Judas the brother of James. [14]These all agreed as they prayed together. The women and Mary the mother of Jesus and His brothers were there.

[15]On one of those days Peter got up in front of the followers. (There were about 120 people there.) He said, [16]"Men and brothers, it happened as the Holy Writings said it would happen which the Holy Spirit spoke through David. They told about Judas who would hand Jesus over to those who wanted to take Him. [17]Judas was one of our group and had a part in our work. [18]This man bought a field with the money he received for his sin. And falling down head first, his body broke open and his insides ran out. [19]All the people of Jerusalem knew about this. They called the place Field of Blood. [20]For it is written in the Book of Psalms, 'Let his place of living be empty and let no one live there,' and, 'Let another person take over his work.' (Psalm 69:25; 109:8)

[21]"The man to take the place of Judas should be one of these men who walked along with us when the Lord Jesus was with us. [22]He must have been with Jesus from the day He was baptized by John to the day He was taken up from us. So one of these should be added to our group who will tell others that he saw Jesus raised from the dead."

[23]They brought two men in front of them. They were Joseph, also called Barsabbas Justus, and Matthias. [24]Then the followers prayed, saying, "Lord, You know the hearts of all men. Show us which of these two men You have chosen. [25]He is to take the place of Judas in this work

and be a missionary. Judas lost his place and went where he belonged because of sin." [26]Then they drew names and the name of Matthias was chosen. He became one with the eleven missionaries.

The Holy Spirit Comes On The Followers Of Jesus

2 The followers of Jesus were all together in one place fifty days after the special religious gathering to remember how the Jews left Egypt. [2]All at once there was a sound from heaven like a powerful wind. It filled the house where they were sitting. [3]Then they saw tongues which were divided that looked like fire. These came down on each one of them. [4]They were all filled with the Holy Spirit. Then they began to speak in other languages which the Holy Spirit made them able to speak.

[5]There were many religious Jews staying in Jerusalem. They were from every country of the world. [6]When they heard this strange sound, they gathered together. They all listened! It was hard for them to believe they were hearing words in their own language. [7]They were surprised and wondered about it. They said to each other, "Are not these Galileans who are speaking? [8]How is it that each one of us can hear his own language? [9]We are Parthians and Medes, Elamites and from the countries of Mesopotamia, Judea and Cappadocia, Pontus and in the countries of Asia, [10]Phrygia and Pamphylia, Egypt and the parts of Libya near Cyrene. Some have come from the city of Rome. Some are Jews by birth and others have become Jews. [11]Some are also men of the countries of Crete and Arabia. They are speaking of the powerful works of God to all of us in our own language!" [12]They were all surprised and wondered about this. They said to each other, "What can this mean?"

¹³But others laughed and made fun, saying, "These men are full of new wine."

Peter Preaches - What Joel Said Would Happen Has Happened

¹⁴Then Peter stood up with the eleven missionaries and spoke with a loud voice, "Men of the country of Judea and all of you who are living in Jerusalem, I want you to know what is happening. So listen to what I am going to say. ¹⁵These men are not drunk as you think. It is only nine o'clock in the morning. ¹⁶The early preacher Joel said this would happen. ¹⁷God says, 'In the last days I will send My Spirit on all men. Then your sons and daughters will speak God's Word. Your young men will see what God has given them to see. Your old men will dream dreams. ¹⁸Yes, on those I own, both men and women, I will send My Spirit in those days. They will speak God's Word. ¹⁹I will show powerful works in the sky above. There will be things to see in the earth below like blood and fire and clouds of smoke. ²⁰The sun will turn dark and the moon will turn to blood before the day of the Lord. His coming will be a great and special day. ²¹It will be that whoever calls on the name of the Lord will be saved from the punishment of sin.' (Joel 2:28-32)

Peter Preaches - Jesus Shows Who He Is By What He Did

²²"Jewish men, listen to what I have to say! You knew Jesus of the town of Nazareth by the powerful works He did. God worked through Jesus while He was with you. You all know this. ²³Jesus was handed over to sinful men. God knew this and planned for it to happen. You had sinful men take Him and nail Him to a cross. ²⁴But God raised Him up. He allowed Him to be set free from the pain of death. Death could not hold its power over Him.

Peter Preaches - Jesus Shows Who He Is By What He Said

²⁵"David said this about Him, 'I can see the Lord before me all the time. He is at my right side so that I do not need to be troubled. ²⁶I am glad and my tongue is full of joy. My body rests in hope. ²⁷You will not leave my soul in death. You will not allow Your Holy One to be destroyed. ²⁸You have shown me the ways of life. I will be full of joy when I see Your face.' (Psalm 16)

²⁹"Brothers, I can tell you in plain words that our early father David not only died but was buried. We know where his grave is today. ³⁰He was one who spoke for God. He knew God had made a promise to him. From his family Christ would come and take His place as King. ³¹He knew this before and spoke of Christ being raised from the dead. Christ's soul would not be left in hell. His body would not be destroyed. ³²Jesus is this One! God has raised Him up and we have all seen Him.

³³"This Jesus has been lifted up to God's right side. The Holy Spirit was promised by the Father. God has given Him to us. That is what you are seeing and hearing now! ³⁴It was not David who was taken up to heaven, because he said, 'The Lord said to my Lord, "Sit at My right side, ³⁵for those who hate You will be a place to rest Your feet." ' (Psalm 110:1) ³⁶The whole Jewish nation must know for sure that God has made this Jesus, Lord and Christ. He is the One you nailed to a cross!"

They Ask Peter What They Should Do

³⁷When the Jews heard this, their hearts were troubled. They said to Peter and to the other missionaries, "Brothers, what should we do?" ³⁸Peter said to them, "Be sorry for your sins and turn from them and be baptized in the name of Jesus Christ,

and your sins will be forgiven. You will receive the gift of the Holy Spirit. 39This promise is to you and your children. It is to all people everywhere. It is to as many as the Lord our God will call."

40He said many other things. He helped them understand that they should keep themselves from the sinful people of this day. 41Those who believed what he said were baptized. There were about 3,000 more followers added that day.

The First Church

42They were faithful in listening to the teaching of the missionaries. They worshiped and prayed and ate the Lord's supper together. 43Many .powerful works were done by the missionaries. Surprise and fear came on them all. 44All those who put their trust in Christ were together and shared what they owned. 45As anyone had need, they sold what they owned and shared with everyone. 46Day after day they went to the house of God together. In their houses they ate their food together. Their hearts were happy. 47They gave thanks to God and all the people respected them. The Lord added to the group each day those who were being saved from the punishment of sin.

Peter And John Heal A Man At The Gate Of The House Of God

3 Peter and John were going to the house of God about three o'clock. It was the time for prayer. 2Each day a certain man was carried to the Beautiful Gate of the house of God. This man had never been able to walk. He was there begging for money from those who were going in. 3He asked Peter and John for money when he saw them going in. 4Peter and John looked at him. Then Peter said, "Look at us!" 5The man who could not walk looked at them.

He thought he would get something from them. 6Peter said, "I have no money, but what I have I will give you! In the name of Jesus Christ of Nazareth, get up and walk!" 7Peter took the man by the right hand and lifted him up. At once his feet and the bones in his legs became strong. 8He jumped up on his feet and walked. Then he went into the house of God with them. He gave thanks to God as he walked.

9All the people saw him walking and giving thanks to God. 10They knew it was the man who had been sitting and begging at the Beautiful Gate. They were surprised he was walking. 11The man who was healed held on to Peter and John. All the people who were surprised gathered together around them in a place called Solomon's Porch.

Peter Preaches The Second Time

12When Peter saw this, he said to them, "Jewish men, why are you surprised at this? Why do you look at us as if we had made this man walk by our own power or holy lives? 13The God of our fathers, the God of Abraham and Isaac and Jacob, has done this. He has honored His Son Jesus. He is the One you handed over to Pilate. You turned your backs on Him after Pilate had decided to let Him go free. 14But you turned your backs against the Holy and Right One. Then you asked for a man who had killed someone to go free. 15You killed the very One Who made all life. But God raised Him from the dead. We saw Him alive. 16You see and know this man here. He has been made strong through faith in Jesus' name. Yes, it is faith in Christ that has made this man well and strong. This man is standing here in front of you all.

17"Brothers, I know you and your leaders did this without knowing what you were doing. 18In this way, God did what He said He would do through all the early preachers. He said that Christ must suffer many hard things. [19]But you must be sorry for your sins and turn from them. You must turn to God and have your sins taken away. Then many times your soul will receive new strength from the Lord. [20]He will send Jesus back to the world. He is the Christ Who long ago was chosen for you. [21]But for awhile He must stay in heaven until the time when all things are made right. God said these things would happen through His holy early preachers.

[22]"Moses said, 'The Lord God will raise up from among your brothers One Who speaks for God, as He raised me. You must listen to everything He says. [23]Everyone among the people who will not listen to that One Who speaks for God will be put to death.' (Deuteronomy 18:19) [24]All the early preachers who have spoken from Samuel until now have told of these days. [25]You are of the family of the early preachers and of the promise that God made with our early fathers. He said to Abraham, 'All the families of the earth will receive God's favor through your children.' [26]God has raised up His Son Jesus and has sent Him to you first to give God's favor to each of you who will turn away from his sinful ways."

Peter And John Are Put In Prison

4 The religious leaders and the leader of the house of God and some of the religious group who believe no one will be raised from the dead came to Peter and John while they were talking to the people. [2]They were angry because Peter and John had been teaching the people and preaching that Jesus had been raised from the dead. [3]So they took them and put them in prison until the next day because it was evening. [4]But many of those who heard what Peter and John said put their trust in Christ. The group of followers was now about 5,000 men.

Peter Speaks To The Religious Leader's Court

[5]The next day the leaders of the court and the leaders of the people and the teachers of the Law came together in Jerusalem. [6]Annas the head religious leader was there. Caiaphas and John and Alexander were there also and all who were in the family of the head religious leader. [7]They put the missionaries in front of them and asked, "By what power or in whose name have you done this?"

[8]Then Peter, having been filled with the Holy Spirit, said, "You who are leaders of the people, [9]are you asking us today about the good work we did to a man who needed help? Are you asking how he was healed? [10]You and all the Jews must know that it was by the name of Jesus Christ of Nazareth, the One you nailed to a cross and God raised from the dead. It is through Him that this man stands in front of you well and strong. [11]Christ is the Stone that was put aside by you workmen. But He has become the most important Stone in the building. (Psalm 118:22) [12]There is no way to be saved from the punishment of sin through anyone else. For there is no other name under heaven given to men by which we can be saved."

Peter And John Are Free To Go But Are Told Not To Preach

[13]They were surprised and wondered how easy it was for Peter and John to speak. They could tell they were men who had not gone to school. But they knew they had been with Jesus. [14]They were not able to argue about what Peter and John had said because the man who had been healed was standing with them.

[15]The religious leaders told Peter

and John to leave the court so the leaders could talk together. [16]They said, "What should we do with these men? Everyone living in Jerusalem knows a powerful work has been done by them. We cannot say that it did not happen. [17]Let us tell them with strong words that they must not speak again to anyone in this name. This will keep the news from going out among the people."

[18]Then they called them in and told them they must not speak or teach anymore in the name of Jesus. [19]Peter and John said, "If it is right to listen to you more than to God, you decide about that. [20]For we must tell what we have seen and heard."

[21]After they had spoken more sharp words to them, they let them go. They could not beat them because the people were giving thanks to God for what had happened. [22]The man on whom this powerful work of healing had been done was more than forty years old.

The Prayer Of The Young Church

[23]As soon as the missionaries were free to go, they went back to their own group. They told them everything the religious leaders had said. [24]When they heard it, they all prayed to God, saying, "Lord God, You made the heaven and the earth and the sea and everything that is in them. [25]You said through the Holy Spirit by the mouth of our father David, 'Why are the nations so shaken up and the people planning foolish things? [26]The kings of the earth stood in a line ready to fight, and the leaders were all against the Lord and against His Christ.' (Psalm 2:1-2) [27]You know that Herod and Pilate and the Jews and the people who are not Jews gathered together here against Jesus. He was Your Holy Son and the One You had chosen [28]to do everything You planned and said would happen. [29]And now, Lord, listen to their sharp words. Make it easy for your servants to preach Your Word with power. [30]May You heal and do powerful works and special things to see through the name of Jesus, Your Holy Son!"

The Christians Are Filled With The Holy Spirit

[31]When they had finished praying, the place where they were gathered was shaken. They were all filled with the Holy Spirit. It was easy for them to speak the Word of God.

The New Way Of Life

[32]The many followers acted and thought the same way. None of them said that any of their things were their own, but they shared all things. [33]The missionaries told with much power how Jesus was raised from the dead. God's favor was on them all. [34]No one was in need. All who owned houses or pieces of land sold them and brought the money from what was sold. [35]They gave it to the missionaries. It was divided to each one as he had need.

[36]Joseph was among them. The missionaries called him Barnabas. His name means Son of Comfort. He was from the family group of Levi and from the country of Cyprus. [37]He had some land which he sold and brought the money to the missionaries.

The Sin Of Ananias And Sapphira

5 A man by the name of Ananias and his wife, Sapphira, sold some land. [2]He kept back part of the money for himself. His wife knew it also. The other part he took to the missionaries. [3]Peter said to Ananias, "Why did you let Satan fill your heart? He made you lie to the Holy Spirit. You kept back part of the money you got from your land. [4]Was not the land yours before you sold it? After it was sold, you could have

done what you wanted to do with the money. Why did you allow your heart to do this? You have lied to God, not to men."

⁵When Ananias heard these words, he fell down dead. Much fear came on all those who heard what was done. ⁶The young men got up and covered his body and carried him out and buried him.

⁷About three hours later his wife came in. She did not know what had happened. ⁸Peter said to her, "Tell me, did you sell the land for this amount of money?" She said, "Yes." ⁹Then Peter said to her, "How could you two have talked together about lying to the Holy Spirit? See! Those who buried your husband are standing at the door and they will carry you out also." ¹⁰At once she fell down at his feet and died. When the young men came in, they found that she was dead. They took her out and buried her beside her husband. ¹¹Much fear came on all the church and on all who heard it.

The First Church Grows

¹²The missionaries did many powerful works among the people. They gathered together on Solomon's porch. ¹³No one from outside their own group came in with them because they were afraid. But those outside the church had respect for the followers. ¹⁴Many more men and women put their trust in Christ and were added to the group. ¹⁵They brought the sick people and laid them on the streets hoping that if Peter walked by, his shadow would fall on some of them. ¹⁶Many people went into Jerusalem from towns nearby. They took with them their sick people and all who were troubled with demons. All of them were healed.

The Missionaries Are Put In Prison

¹⁷The head religious leader heard this. Some of the religious group who believe no one will be raised from the dead also heard of the people being healed. They became very jealous. ¹⁸They took hold of the missionaries and put them in prison. ¹⁹An angel of the Lord opened the doors of the prison in the night and let them out. The angel said to them, ²⁰"Go, stand where you have been standing in the house of God. Keep on telling the people about this new life."

²¹When Peter and John heard this, they went in the house of God early in the morning and began to teach. When the head religious leader and those with him had come, they gathered the men of the court and the leaders of the Jews together. Then they sent to have the missionaries brought to them from the prison. ²²When the soldiers got there, they did not find them in prison. They went back and told the court. ²³The soldiers said, "We found the door of the prison locked and the soldiers watching the doors. When we opened the door, we found no one inside."

²⁴When the religious leaders and the leader of the house of God heard this, they were much troubled as to what might happen. ²⁵Then someone came and told them, "The men you put in prison are now standing in the house of God and teaching the people." ²⁶The leader of the house of God took his men and got them. They did not hurt the missionaries because they were afraid the people would throw stones at them.

²⁷They brought the missionaries in and made them stand in front of the court. The head religious leader said, ²⁸"We told you not to teach about Christ! See! You are spreading this teaching over all Jerusalem. Now you are making it look as if we are guilty of killing this Man."

The Missionaries Speak The Truth

²⁹Then Peter and the missionaries said, "We must obey God instead of

men! [30]The God of our early fathers raised up Jesus, the One you killed and nailed to a cross. [31]God raised this Man to His own right side as a leader and as the One Who saves from the punishment of sin. He makes it possible for the Jews to be sorry for their sins. Then they can turn from them and be forgiven. [32]We have seen these things and are telling about them. The Holy Spirit makes these things known also. God gives His Spirit to those who obey Him."

Gamaliel Speaks In Court

[33]The religious leaders became angry when they heard this. They planned to kill the missionaries. [34]Gamaliel was a man of the religious leaders' court. He was a proud religious law-keeper and a teacher of the Law. He was respected by all the people. He stood up and said that the missionaries should be sent outside for a short time.

[35]Then Gamaliel said to the court, "Jewish men, be careful what you plan to do with these men. [36]Remember that many years ago a man called Theudas made himself out to be someone great. He had about 400 followers. He was killed. His followers were divided and nothing came of his teaching. [37]After him, Judas of the country of Galilee gathered many followers. It was the time for every person to have his name written in the books of the nation. This Judas was killed also. All his followers were divided and went away. [38]I say to you now, stay away from these men and leave them alone. If this teaching and work is from men, it will come to nothing. [39]If it is from God, you will not be able to stop it. You may even find yourselves fighting against God."

[40]The court agreed with Gamaliel. So they called the missionaries in and beat them. They told them they must not speak in the name of Jesus. Then they were sent away.

[41]So the missionaries went away from the court happy that they could suffer shame because of His Name. [42]Every day in the house of God and in the homes, they kept teaching and preaching about Jesus Christ.

Church Leaders Are Chosen

6 In those days the group of followers was getting larger. Greek-speaking Jews in the group complained against the Jews living in the country around Jerusalem. The Greek-speaking Jews said that their women whose husbands had died were not taken care of when the food was given out each day. [2]So the twelve missionaries called a meeting of the many followers and said, "It is not right that we should give up preaching the Word of God to hand out food. [3]Brothers, choose from among you seven men who are respected and who are full of the Holy Spirit and wisdom. We will have them take care of this work. [4]Then we will use all of our time to pray and to teach the Word of God." [5]These words pleased all of them. They chose Stephen who was a man full of faith and full of the Holy Spirit. They also chose Philip, Prochorus, Nicanor, Timon, Parmenas and Nicholas of Antioch who had become a Jew. [6]These men were taken to the missionaries. After praying, the missionaries laid their hands on them.

[7]The Word of God spread further. The group of followers became much larger in Jerusalem. Many of the religious leaders believed in the faith of the Christians.

Stephen Is Brought In Front Of The Religious Leaders' Court

[8]Stephen was a man full of faith and power. He did many great things among the people. [9]But some men came from their place of worship

who were known as the Free people. They started to argue with Stephen. These men were from the countries of Cyrene and Alexandria and Cilicia and Asia. ¹⁰Stephen spoke with wisdom and power given by the Holy Spirit. They were not able to say anything against what he said. ¹¹So they told other men to say, "We have heard him say things against Moses and God." ¹²In this way they got the people talking against Stephen. The leaders of the people and the teachers of the Law came and took him to the religious leader's court. ¹³The people were told to lie and say, "This man keeps on talking against this place of worship and the Law of Moses. ¹⁴We have heard him say, 'Jesus of Nazareth is going to pull down this place. He is going to change what Moses taught us.'"

¹⁵The men sitting in the religious leader's court were looking at Stephen. They all saw that his face looked like the face of an angel.

Stephen Speaks About The God Of Abraham

7 The head religious leader asked Stephen, "Is this true?" ²Stephen said, "My brothers and fathers, listen to me. The great God showed Himself to our early father Abraham while he lived in the country of Mesopotamia. This was before he moved to the country of Haran. ³God said to him, 'Leave your family and this land where you were born. Go to a land that I will show you.' ⁴He went from the land of the Chaldeans and lived in Haran. After his father died, he came to this country where you now live. ⁵God did not give him any land to own, not even enough to put his feet on. But He promised that the land would be his and his children's after him. At that time he had no children. ⁶This is what God said, 'Your children's children will be living in a strange land. They will live there 400 years.

They will be made to work without pay and will suffer many hard things. ⁷I will say to that nation that it is guilty for holding them and making them work without pay. After that they will go free. They will leave that country and worship Me in this place.'

⁸"He made a promise with Abraham. It was kept by a religious act of becoming a Jew. Abraham had a son, Isaac. On the eighth day Abraham took Isaac and had this religious act done to him. Isaac was the father of Jacob. Jacob was the father of our twelve early fathers.

⁹"The sons of Jacob sold Joseph to people from the country of Egypt because they were jealous of him. But God was with Joseph. ¹⁰He helped him in all his troubles. He gave him wisdom and favor with Pharaoh, the king of Egypt. This king made Joseph leader over Egypt and over all the king's house.

¹¹"The time came when there was no food to eat in all the land of Egypt and Canaan. The people suffered much. Our early fathers were not able to get food. ¹²Then Jacob heard there was food in Egypt. He sent our early fathers there the first time. ¹³"The second time they went to the country of Egypt, Joseph made himself known to his brothers. The family of Joseph became known to Pharaoh. ¹⁴Joseph asked his father Jacob and all his family to come. There were seventy-five people in the family. ¹⁵Jacob moved down to Egypt and died there. Our early fathers died there also. ¹⁶They were brought back to the city of Shechem where they were buried. Abraham paid money for the grave from the sons of Hamor in Shechem.

Stephen Speaks About The God Of Moses

¹⁷"The promise God had given Abraham was about to happen. At this time many more of our people

were in the country of Egypt. [18]Then another man became king in Egypt. He was a king who did not know Joseph. [19]He was hard on our people and nation. He worked against our early fathers. He made them put their babies outside so they would die.

[20]"At that time Moses was born. He was beautiful in God's sight. He was fed in his father's house for three months. [21]Then he was put outside. Pharaoh's daughter took him and cared for him as her own son. [22]Moses was taught in all the wisdom of the Egyptians. He became a powerful man in words and in the things he did. [23]When he was forty years old, he thought he should visit his brothers, the Jews. [24]He saw one of the Jews being hurt. Moses helped the Jew and killed the man from Egypt. [25]He thought his people would understand. He thought they knew God would let them go free by his help. But the people did not understand.

[26]"The next day Moses came to some Jews who were fighting. He tried to get them to stop. Moses said to the Jews, 'Sirs, you are brothers. Why do you hurt each other?' [27]One was beating his neighbor. He pushed Moses away and said, 'Who made you a leader over us? Who said you could say who is guilty? [28]Do you want to kill me as you killed the man from Egypt yesterday?' [29]When Moses heard that, he went as fast as he could to the country of Midian where he was a stranger. While he was there, he became the father of two sons. [30]Forty years passed and Moses was near Mount Sinai where no people live. There he saw an angel in the fire of a burning bush. [31]He was surprised and wondered when he saw it. He went up close to see it better. Then he heard the voice of the Lord speak to him. [32]'I am the God of your fathers, the God of Abraham and of Isaac and of Jacob.' Moses shook! He was so afraid he did not look at the bush.

[33]"Then the Lord said to him, 'Take your shoes off your feet! The place where you are standing is holy ground. [34]I have seen My people suffer in the country of Egypt and I have heard their cries. I have come down to let them go free. So come now, I will send you back to Egypt.'

[35]"The people had put Moses aside. They said, 'Who made you a leader over us? Who said you are the one to say what is right or wrong?' But God made this man a leader. Moses was the one who brought them out of the country of Egypt. This was done by the help of the angel who was in the burning bush. [36]This man led them. He did powerful works in Egypt and at the Red Sea. For forty years he led them in the desert.

[37]"Moses said to the Jews, 'God will give you one who speaks for Him like me from among your brothers.' [38]This is the man who was with the Jewish nation in the desert. The angel talked to him on Mount Sinai. Moses told it to our early fathers. He also received the living Words of God to give to us.

[39]"Our early fathers would not listen to him. They did not obey him. In their hearts they wanted to go back to the country of Egypt. [40]They said to Aaron, 'Make us gods to go before us. We do not know what has happened to this Moses who led us out of Egypt.'

[41]"In those days they made a calf of gold. They put gifts down in front of their god in worship. They were happy with what they had made with their hands. [42]But God turned from them and let them worship the stars of heaven. This is written in the book of the early preachers, 'Nation of Jews, was it to Me you gave gifts of sheep and cattle on the altar for forty years in the desert? [43]No, you set up the tent to worship in to the god of Molock and the star of your god Rompha. You made gods to worship

them. I will carry you away to the other side of the country of Babylon.' (Amos 5:25-27)

The Place Of Worship And The House Of God

44 "Our early fathers had the tent to worship in. They used it in the desert. God told Moses to make it like the plan which he had seen. 45 This was received by our early fathers. They brought it here when they won the wars with the people who were not Jews. It was when Joshua was our leader. God made those people leave as our early fathers took the land. The tent was here until the time of David. 46 David pleased God and wanted to build a house for worship for the God of Jacob. 47 But Solomon was the one who built the house of God for Him. 48 But the Most High does not live in buildings made by hands. The early preacher said, 49 'Heaven is the place where I sit and the earth is the place where I rest My feet. What house will you build Me?' says the Lord. 'Or what is My place of rest? 50 Did not My hands make all these things?' (Isaiah 66:1-2)

The Jews Are Hurt

51 "You have hard hearts and ears that will not listen to me! You are always working against the Holy Spirit. Your early fathers did. You do too. 52 Which of the early preachers was not beaten and hurt by your early fathers? They killed those who told of the coming of the One Right with God. Now you have handed Him over and killed Him. 53 You had the Law given to you by angels. Yet you have not kept it.''

Stephen Is Killed

54 The Jews and religious leaders listened to Stephen. Then they became angry and began to grind their teeth at him. 55 He was filled with the Holy Spirit. As he looked up to heaven, he saw the shining greatness of God and Jesus standing at the right side of God. 56 He said, "See! I see heaven open and the Son of Man standing at the right side of God!'' 57 They cried out with loud voices. They put their hands over their ears and they all pushed on him. 58 Then they took him out of the city and threw stones at him. The men who were throwing the stones laid their coats down in front of a young man named Saul. 59 While they threw stones at Stephen, he prayed, "Lord Jesus, receive my spirit." 60 After that he fell on his knees and cried out with a loud voice, "Lord, do not hold this sin against them." When he had said this, he died.

It Is Hard For The Christians In Jerusalem

8 Saul thought it was all right that Stephen was killed. On that day people started to work very hard against the church in Jerusalem. All the followers, except the missionaries, were made to leave. They went to parts of the countries of Judea and Samaria. 2 Good men put Stephen in a grave. There was much sorrow because of him. 3 During this time Saul was making it very hard for the church. He went into every house of the followers of Jesus and took men and women and put them in prison.

Philip Preaches In Samaria

4 Those who had been made to go to other places preached the Word as they went. 5 Philip went down to a city in Samaria and preached about Christ. 6 The people all listened to what Philip said. As they listened, they watched him do powerful works. 7 There were many people who had demons in their bodies. The demons cried with loud voices when they went out of the people. Many of

the people could not move their bodies or arms and legs. They were all healed. ⁸There was much joy in that city.

Simon The Witchdoctor

⁹A man by the name of Simon had done witchcraft there. The people of Samaria were surprised at the things he did. He pretended that he was a great man. ¹⁰All the people watched and listened to him. They said, "This man must be that great power of God." ¹¹They kept running after him. For a long time he fooled them with his witchcraft.

¹²Philip told the Good News of the holy nation of God and of Jesus Christ. Both men and women put their trust in Christ and were baptized. ¹³Even Simon believed in Christ and was baptized. He went along with Philip everywhere. He was surprised when he saw the powerful works that were being done.

¹⁴The missionaries in Jerusalem heard that the people of Samaria had received the Word of God. They sent Peter and John to them. ¹⁵When Peter and John got there, they prayed that the new followers might receive the Holy Spirit. ¹⁶He had not yet come on any of them. They had been baptized in the name of the Lord Jesus only. ¹⁷They laid their hands on them and the followers received the Holy Spirit.

¹⁸When Simon saw that the Holy Spirit was given when the missionaries laid their hands on the people, he wanted to give money to the missionaries. ¹⁹He said, "Let me also have this power. Then I can give the Holy Spirit to anyone I lay my hands on." ²⁰Peter said to him, "May your money be destroyed with you because you thought you could buy the gift of God with money! ²¹You have no part or place in this work. Your heart is not right in God's sight. ²²You must be sorry for this sin of yours and turn from it. Pray to the Lord that He will forgive you for having such a thought in your heart. ²³I see that you are full of jealousy and chained by your sin." ²⁴Simon said, "Pray to the Lord for me that nothing you have said will come to me."

²⁵Peter and John went back to Jerusalem after telling what they had seen and heard. They had preached the Word of the Lord also. On the way they preached the Good News in many other towns in the country of Samaria.

Philip And The Man From Ethiopia

²⁶An angel of the Lord spoke to Philip saying, "Get up and go south. Take the road that goes down from Jerusalem to the country of Gaza. It goes through the desert." ²⁷Philip got up and went. A man from the country of Ethiopia had come to Jerusalem to worship. He had been made so he could not have children. He cared for all the riches that belonged to Candace who was Queen of Ethiopia. ²⁸As he was going back home, he was sitting in his wagon reading the Book of the early preacher Isaiah. ²⁹The Holy Spirit said to Philip, "Go over to that wagon and get on it." ³⁰Philip ran up to him. He saw that the man from Ethiopia was reading from the writings of the early preacher Isaiah and said, "Do you understand what you are reading?" ³¹The man from Ethiopia said, "How can I, unless someone teaches me?" Then he asked Philip to come up and sit beside him.

³²He was reading the part in the Holy Writings which says, "He was taken like a sheep to be put to death. A lamb does not make a sound while its wool is cut. So He made no sound. ³³No one listened to Him because of His shame. Who will tell the story of His day? For His life was taken away from the earth." (Isaiah 53:7-8) ³⁴The man from Ethiopia said to

Philip, "Who is the early preacher talking about, himself, or someone else?" 35So Philip started with this part of the Holy Writings and preached the Good News of Jesus to him.

36As they went on their way, they came to some water. The man from Ethiopia said, "See! Here is water. What is to stop me from being baptized?" 37*Philip said, "If you believe with all your heart, you may." The man said, "I believe that Jesus Christ is the Son of God." 38He stopped the wagon. Then both Philip and the man from Ethiopia went down into the water and Philip baptized him.

39When they came up out of the water, the Holy Spirit took Philip away. The man from Ethiopia did not see Philip again. He went on his way full of joy. 40Philip found himself at the city of Azotus. Then Philip went through all the towns as far as the city of Caesarea preaching the Good News at each place.

Saul Becomes A Christian

9 Saul was still talking much about how he would like to kill the followers of the Lord. He went to the head religious leader. 2He asked for letters to be written to the Jewish places of worship in the city of Damascus. The letters were to say that if he found any men or women following the Way of Christ he might bring them to Jerusalem in chains.

3He went on his way until he came near Damascus. All at once he saw a light from heaven shining around him. 4He fell to the ground. Then he heard a voice say, "Saul, Saul, why are you working so hard against Me?" 5Saul answered, "Who are You, Lord?" He said, "I am Jesus, the One Whom you are working against. You hurt yourself by trying to hurt Me." 6Saul was shaken and surprised. Then he said, "What do you want me to do, Lord?" The Lord said to him, "Get up! Go into the city and you will be told what to do."

7Those with Saul were not able to say anything. They heard a voice but saw no one. 8Saul got up from the ground. When he opened his eyes, he saw nothing. They took him by the hand and led him to Damascus. 9He could not see for three days. During that time he did not eat or drink.

10In Damascus there was a follower by the name of Ananias. The Lord showed him in a dream what He wanted him to see. He said, "Ananias!" And Ananias answered, "Yes, Lord, I am here." 11The Lord said, "Get up! Go over to Straight Street to Judas' house and ask for a man from the city of Tarsus. His name is Saul. You will find him praying there. 12Saul has seen a man called Ananias in a dream. He is to come and put his hands on Saul so he might see again."

13Ananias said, "But Lord, many people have told me about this man. He is the reason many of Your followers in Jerusalem have had to suffer much. 14He came here with the right and the power from the head religious leaders to put everyone in chains who call on Your name." 15The Lord said to him, "Go! This man is the one I have chosen to carry My name among the people who are not Jews and to their kings and to Jews. 16I will show him how much he will have to suffer because of Me."

Saul Is Baptized

17So Ananias went to that house. He put his hands on Saul and said, "Brother Saul, the Lord Jesus has sent me to you. You saw the Lord along the road as you came here. The Lord has sent me so you might be able to see again and be filled with the Holy Spirit." 18At once something like a covering fell from the eyes of Saul and he could see. He got up and was baptized. 19After that he ate some food and received strength. For some days he stayed with the followers in Damascus.

Saul Preaches The Good News

20 At once Saul began to preach in the Jewish places of worship that Jesus is the Son of God. 21 All who heard him were surprised and wondered. They said, "This is the man who beat and killed the followers in Jerusalem. He came here to tie the followers in chains and take them to the head religious leaders." 22 But Saul kept on growing in power. The Jews living in Damascus wondered about Saul's preaching. He was proving that Jesus was the Christ.

23 After some days the Jews talked together and made plans how they might kill Saul. 24 He heard of their plans. Day and night they watched for him at the city gates to kill him. 25 So the followers helped him get away at night. They let him down over the wall in a basket.

Saul Comes To Jerusalem

26 When Saul had come to Jerusalem, he tried to join the followers. But they were afraid of him. They did not believe he was a true follower of Jesus. 27 Then Barnabas took him to the missionaries. He told them that Saul had seen the Lord on the road. He told them also how the Lord had spoken to Saul and how he had preached without fear in Damascus in the name of Jesus. 28 After that he was with them going in and out of Jerusalem. 29 He preached without fear in the name of the Lord. He talked and argued with the Jews who spoke the Greek language. They kept trying to kill him. 30 When the followers heard this, they took him down to the city of Caesarea. From there they sent him to the city of Tarsus.

31 Then the church through all the countries of Judea and Galilee and Samaria had peace for awhile. The church was made strong and it was given comfort by the Holy Spirit. It honored the Lord. More people were added to the church.

Aeneas Is Healed

32 When Peter was visiting all parts of the country, he came to the faithful followers who were living in the city of Lydda. 33 A man there named Aeneas could not move his body. He had been in bed eight years. 34 Peter said to him, "Aeneas, Jesus Christ heals you. Get up and roll up your bed." He got up at once. 35 All the people who lived in Lydda and in the city of Sharon saw Aeneas and they turned to the Lord.

Dorcas Is Raised From The Dead

36 A woman who was a follower lived in the city of Joppa. Her name was Tabitha, or Dorcas. She did many good things and many acts of kindness. 37 One day she became sick and died. After they had washed her body, they laid her in a room on the second floor. 38 The city of Lydda was near Joppa. The followers heard that Peter was at Lydda and sent two men to ask him to come at once. 39 Peter went back with them. When he came, they took him to the room. All the women whose husbands had died were standing around crying. They were showing the clothes Dorcas had made while she was with them.

40 Peter made them all leave the room. Then he got down on his knees and prayed. He turned to her body and said, "Tabitha, get up!" She opened her eyes and looked at Peter and sat up. 41 He took her by the hand and lifted her up. Then he called in the faithful followers and the women whose husbands had died. He gave her to them, a living person.

42 News of this went through all Joppa. Many people put their trust in

the Lord. [43]After this, Peter stayed in Joppa many days in the house of Simon who worked with leather.

God Speaks To A Man Who Was Not A Jew

10 There was a man in the city of Caesarea by the name of Cornelius. He was a captain of an Italian group of the army. [2]He and his family were good people and honored God. He gave much money to the people and prayed always to God. [3]One afternoon about three o'clock he saw in a dream what God wanted him to see. An angel of God came to him and said, "Cornelius." [4]He was afraid as he looked at the angel. He said, "What is it, Lord?" The angel said, "Your prayers and your gifts of money have gone up to God. He has remembered them. [5]Send some men to the city of Joppa and ask Simon Peter to come here. [6]He is living with Simon, the man who works with leather. His house is by the seashore. He will tell you what you must do." [7]The angel left him. Then Cornelius called two of his servants and a religious soldier who took care of him. [8]He told what had happened. Then he sent them to Joppa.

Peter's Dream

[9]The next day they went on their way. About noon they were coming near the town. At this time Peter went up on the roof to pray. [10]He became very hungry and wanted something to eat. While they were getting food ready to eat, he saw in a dream things God wanted him to see. [11]He saw heaven opened and something like a large linen cloth being let down to earth by the four corners. [12]On the cloth were all kinds of four-footed animals and snakes of the earth and birds of the sky. [13]A voice came to him, "Get up, Peter, kill something and eat it." [14]Peter said, "No, Lord! I have never eaten anything that our Law says is unclean." [15]The voice said the second time, "What God has made clean you must not say is unclean." [16]This happened three times. Then it was taken back to heaven.

Cornelius' Men Find Peter

[17]Peter thought about the meaning of the dream. The men that Cornelius had sent came. They were standing by the gate asking about Simon's house. [18]They called to ask if Simon Peter was staying there. [19]Peter was still thinking about the dream when the Holy Spirit said to him, "See, three men are looking for you. [20]Get up. Go down and go with them. Do not doubt if you should go, because I sent them." [21]Peter went down to the men who had been sent by Cornelius. He said, "I am the one you are looking for. Why have you come?" [22]They said, "Cornelius sent us. He is a captain and a good man and he honors God. The whole Jewish nation can say this is true. An angel from God told him to send for you. He asks you to come to his house. He wants to hear what you have to say."

Peter Goes To Cornelius

[23]Peter asked them to come in and stay with him for the night. The next day he went with them. Some of the brothers from Joppa went along. [24]The next day they came to Caesarea. Cornelius was looking for them. He had gathered all his family and close friends at his house. [25]When Peter came, Cornelius got down at his feet and worshiped him. [26]But Peter raised him up and said, "Get up! I am just a man like you." [27]As Peter spoke with Cornelius, he went into the house and found a large group of people gathered together. [28]Peter said to them, "You know it is against our Law for a Jew to visit a

person of another nation. But God has shown me I should not say that any man is unclean. ²⁹For this reason I came as soon as you sent for me. But I want to ask you why you sent for me?"

³⁰Cornelius said, "Four days ago at three o'clock in the afternoon I was praying here in my house. All at once, I saw a man standing in front of me. He had on bright clothes. ³¹He said to me, 'Cornelius, God has heard your prayers and has remembered your gifts of love. ³²You must send to Joppa and ask Simon Peter to come here. He is staying at the house of Simon, the man who works with leather. His house is by the seashore.' ³³I sent for you at once. You have done well to come. We are all here and God is with us. We are ready to hear whatever the Lord has told you to say."

Peter Preached In Cornelius' House

³⁴Then Peter said, "I can see, for sure, that God does not respect one person more than another. ³⁵He is pleased with any man in any nation who honors Him and does what is right. ³⁶He has sent His Word to the Jews. He told them the Good News of peace through Jesus Christ. Jesus is Lord of all. ³⁷You know the story yourselves. It was told in all the country of Judea. It began in the country of Galilee after the preaching of John the Baptist. ³⁸God gave Jesus of Nazareth the Holy Spirit and power. He went around doing good and healing all who were troubled by the devil because God was with Him. ³⁹We have seen and heard everything He did in the land of the Jews and in Jerusalem. And yet they killed Him by nailing Him to a cross. ⁴⁰God raised Him to life on the third day and made Him to be seen. ⁴¹Not all the people saw Him but those who were chosen to see Him. We saw Him. We ate and drank with Him after He was raised from the dead.

⁴²He told us to preach to the people and tell them that God gave Christ the right to be the One Who says who is guilty of the living and the dead. ⁴³All the early preachers spoke of this. Everyone who puts his trust in Christ will have his sins forgiven through His name."

The Holy Spirit Comes To The Family Of Cornelius

⁴⁴While Peter was speaking, the Holy Spirit came on all who were hearing his words. ⁴⁵The Jewish followers who had come along with Peter were surprised and wondered because the gift of the Holy Spirit was also given to the people who were not Jews. ⁴⁶They heard them speak in special sounds and give thanks to God. Then Peter said, ⁴⁷"Will anyone say that these people may not be baptized? They have received the Holy Spirit just as we have." ⁴⁸He gave the word that they should be baptized in the name of the Lord. Then they asked Peter to stay with them for some days.

Peter Tells Why He Preached To The People Who Are Not Jews

11 The missionaries and followers who were in the country of Judea heard that the people who were not Jews also had received the Word of God. ²When Peter went up to Jerusalem, the Jewish followers argued with him. ³They said, "Why did you visit those people who are not Jews and eat with them?"

⁴Then Peter began to tell all that had happened from the beginning to the end. He said, ⁵"While I was praying in the city of Joppa, I saw in a dream something coming down from heaven. It was like a large linen cloth let down by the four corners until it came to me. ⁶As I looked at it, I saw four-footed animals and snakes of the earth and birds of the sky. ⁷I heard a voice saying to me, 'Get up,

Peter, kill something and eat it.' ⁸But I said, 'No, Lord! Nothing that is unclean has ever gone into my mouth.' ⁹The voice from heaven said the second time, 'What God has made clean you must not say is unclean.' ¹⁰This happened three times and then it was taken up again to heaven.

¹¹"Three men had already come to the house where I was staying. They had been sent to me from the city of Caesarea. ¹²The Holy Spirit told me to go with them and not doubt about going. These six men also went with me to this man's house. ¹³He told us how he had seen an angel in his own home. The angel had stood in front of him and said, 'Send men to Joppa to ask for Simon Peter. ¹⁴He will tell you and all your family how you can be saved from the punishment of sin.'

¹⁵"As I began to talk to them, the Holy Spirit came down on them just as He did on us at the beginning. ¹⁶Then I remembered the Lord had said, 'John baptized with water but you will be baptized with the Holy Spirit.' ¹⁷If God gave to them the same gift He gave to us when we put our trust in the Lord Jesus Christ, how could I stand against God?"

¹⁸When they heard these words, they said nothing more. They thanked God, saying, "Then God has given life also to the people who are not Jews. They have this new life by being sorry for their sins and turning from them."

The Followers Are Called Christians First In Antioch

¹⁹Those who went different places because of the trouble that started over Stephen had gone as far as the cities of Phoenicia and Cyprus and Antioch. They had preached the Word, but only to the Jews. ²⁰Some of the men from Cyprus and Cyrene returned to Antioch. They preached the Good News of Jesus Christ to the Greek people there. ²¹The Lord gave them power. Many people put their trust in the Lord and turned to Him.

²²The news of this came to the church in Jerusalem. They sent Barnabas to Antioch. ²³When he got there and saw how good God had been to them, he was full of joy. He told them to be true and faithful to the Lord. ²⁴Barnabas was a good man and full of the Holy Spirit and faith. And many people became followers of the Lord.

²⁵From there Barnabas went on to the city of Tarsus to look for Saul. ²⁶When he found Saul, he brought him back with him to Antioch. For a year they taught many people in the church. The followers were first called Christians in Antioch.

The Antioch Church Helps The Jerusalem Church

²⁷At that time some men who preached God's Word came to Antioch and told what was going to happen. They were from Jerusalem. ²⁸One of them was Agabus. The Holy Spirit told him to stand up and speak. He told them there would be very little food to eat over all the world. This happened when Claudius was leader of the country. ²⁹The Christians agreed that each one should give what money he could to help the Christians living in Judea. ³⁰They did this and sent it to the church leaders with Barnabas and Saul.

The King Makes It Hard For The Church

12 At that time King Herod used his power to make it hard for the Christians in the church. ²He killed James, the brother of John, with a sword. ³When he saw that it made the Jews happy, he took hold of Peter also. This was during the special religious gathering to remember how the Jews left Egypt. ⁴Herod took Peter and put him in prison and had sixteen soldiers watch him. After the special religious gathering was over, he planned to bring Peter out to the people.

Peter Goes Free

⁵So Peter was held in prison. But the church kept praying to God for him. ⁶The night before Herod was to bring him out for his trial, Peter was sleeping between two soldiers. He was tied with two chains. Soldiers stood by the door and watched the prison.

⁷All at once an angel of the Lord was seen standing beside him. A light shone in the building. The angel hit Peter on the side and said, "Get up!" Then the chains fell off his hands. ⁸The angel said, "Put on your belt and shoes!" He did. The angel said to Peter, "Put on your coat and follow me." ⁹Peter followed him out. He was not sure what was happening as the angel helped him. He thought it was a dream.

¹⁰They passed one soldier, then another one. They came to the big iron door that leads to the city and it opened by itself and they went through. As soon as they had gone up one street, the angel left him.

The Christians Find It Hard To Believe Peter Is Free

¹¹As Peter began to see what was happening, he said to himself, "Now I am sure the Lord has sent His angel and has taken me out of the hands of Herod. He has taken me also from all the things the Jews wanted to do to me." ¹²After thinking about all this, he went to Mary's house. She was the mother of John Mark. Many Christians were gathered there praying.

¹³When Peter knocked at the gate, a girl named Rhoda went to see who it was. ¹⁴She knew Peter's voice, but in her joy she forgot to open the gate. She ran in and told them that Peter

was standing outside the gate. ¹⁵They said to her, "You are crazy." But she said again that it was so. They kept saying, "It is his angel." ¹⁶Peter kept knocking. When they opened the gate and saw him, they were surprised and wondered about it. ¹⁷He raised his hand and told them not to talk but to listen to him. He told them how the Lord had brought him out of prison. He said, "Tell all these things to James and to the other Christian brothers." Then he went to another place.

The Death Of Herod

¹⁸In the morning the soldiers were very troubled about what had happened to Peter. ¹⁹Herod looked for him but could not find him. He asked the soldiers who watched the prison about Peter. Herod said that the soldiers must be killed because Peter got away. Then Herod went down from the country of Judea to the city of Caesarea to stay for awhile.

²⁰Herod was very angry with the people of the cities of Tyre and Sidon. They went to him and asked for peace to be made between them and the king. They asked this because their country got food from the king's country. The people made friends with Blastus, the king's helper. ²¹A day was set aside. On that day Herod put on purple clothes a king wears. He sat on his throne and spoke to the people. ²²They all started to speak with a loud voice, "This is the voice of a god, not of a man." ²³The angel of the Lord knocked him down because he did not give honor to God. He was eaten by worms and died.

²⁴The Word of God was heard by many people and went into more places. ²⁵Saul and Barnabas went back to Jerusalem after they had finished their work. They took John Mark with them.

Saul And Barnabas Are Called To Be Missionaries

13 In the church in the city of Antioch there were preachers and teachers. They were Barnabas, Simeon Niger, Lucius of the country of Cyrene, Manaen of Herod's family, and Saul. ²While they were worshiping the Lord and eating no food so they could pray better, the Holy Spirit said, "Let Barnabas and Saul be given to Me for the work I have called them to."

Paul And Barnabas Go To Antioch

³These preachers and teachers went without food during that time and prayed. Then they laid their hands on Barnabas and Saul and sent them away. ⁴They were sent by the Holy Spirit to the city of Seleucia. From there they went by ship to the island of Cyprus. ⁵When they went to shore at the city of Salamis, they preached the Word of God in the Jewish place of worship. John Mark was with them as their helper.

⁶They went over Cyprus as far as the city of Paphos. While there, they found a Jew who did witchcraft. He was a false preacher named Barjesus. ⁷Sergius Paulus was the leader of the country and a man who knew much. Barjesus was with Sergius Paulus. Sergius Paulus asked Barnabas and Saul to come to him so he might hear the Word of God. ⁸But Elymas (as he called himself), the man who did witchcraft, worked against Barnabas and Saul. He tried to keep the leader of the country from putting his trust in the Lord.

⁹Saul, whose other name was Paul, was full of the Holy Spirit. He looked at Elymas. ¹⁰Then Saul said, "You false preacher and trouble-maker! You son of the devil! You hate what is right! Will you always be turning people from the right ways of the Lord? ¹¹And now look! The hand of the Lord is on you. You will become blind. For a time you will not be able to see the sun." At once it became dark to Elymas, and he could not see. He asked people to take him by the hand to lead him from place to place.

¹²The leader of the country put his trust in the Lord because he saw what had happened. He was surprised and wondered about the teaching of the Lord. ¹³Paul and those with him went by ship from Paphos to the city of Perga in the country of Pamphylia. John Mark did not go with them but went back to Jerusalem.

Paul Preaches In Antioch

¹⁴From Perga they went on to the city of Antioch in the country of Pisidia. On the Day of Rest they went into the Jewish place of worship and sat down. ¹⁵After the leaders had read from the Jewish Law and the writings of the early preachers, they sent to them saying, "Brothers, if you have any word of comfort and help for the people, say it now." ¹⁶Paul got up. He raised his hand and said, "Jewish men and you who honor God, listen! ¹⁷The God of the Jews chose our early fathers and made them a great people during the time they lived in the land of Egypt. With a strong hand He took them out from there. ¹⁸For about forty years He took care of them in the desert. ¹⁹He destroyed the people of seven nations in the land of Canaan. Then he divided the land and gave it to them as their own. ²⁰For about 450 years he let them have special leaders. They had these leaders until the time of Samuel.

²¹"Then they wanted a king. God gave them Saul who was the son of Kish from the family group of Benjamin. He was king forty years. ²²When God took Saul as king from them, He made David to be their king. He said, 'David, Jesse's son, will please My heart. He will do all I want done.'

²³"From this man's family, God

gave to the Jews the One Who saves from the punishment of sin as He had promised. He is Jesus. 24Before Jesus came, John had preached to all the Jews that they should be baptized because they were sorry for their sins and turned from them. 25When John was near the end of his work, he asked, 'Who do you think I am? I am not the Christ. No, but He is coming later and I am not good enough to get down and help Him take off His shoes!'

26"Men and brothers, sons of the family of Abraham, and all of you who honor God, listen! This news of being able to be saved from the punishment of sin has been sent to you. 27The people of Jerusalem and their leaders did not know Him. They did not understand the words from the early preachers. These words were read to them every Day of Rest. But they did the very thing the early preachers had said they would do by handing Him over to die. 28They could find no reason that He should die, but they asked Pilate to have Him killed. 29When everything was done that had been written about Him, they took Him down from the cross and laid Him in a grave. 30But God raised Him from the dead. 31For many days He was seen by those who came up with Him from Galilee to Jerusalem. These are the ones who tell the people about Him.

32"We bring you the Good News about the promise made to our early fathers. 33God has finished this for us who are their children. He did this by raising Jesus from the dead. It is written in the second Psalm, 'You are My Son. I have given you life today.' (Psalm 2:7) 34God proved that Jesus was His Son by raising Him from the dead. He will never die again. He has said, 'I will finish the promises made to David.' (Isaiah 55:3)

35"In another Psalm He says, 'You will not allow Your Holy One to go back to dust!' (Psalm 16:10) 36David

was a good leader for the people of his day. He did what God wanted. Then he died and was put into a grave close to his father's grave. His body went back to dust. 37But God raised this One (Christ) to life. He did not go back to dust.

38"Men and brothers, listen to this. You may be forgiven of your sins by this One I am telling you about. 39Everyone who puts his trust in Christ will be made right with God. You will be made free from those things the Law of Moses could not make you free from. 40But look out! The writings of the early preachers tell of many things that you do not want to happen to you. 41'Listen, you who doubt and laugh at the truth will die. I will do a work during your days. It will be a work that you will not believe even if someone tells you about it.' " (Habakkuk 1:5)

42As Paul and Barnabas went out of the Jewish place of worship, the people asked them to talk about these things on the next Day of Rest. 43The people went from the place of worship. Many Jews and others who had become Jews followed Paul and Barnabas as they talked to the Jews. They told them to keep on trusting in the loving-favor of God.

Paul And Barnabas Go To The People Who Are Not Jews

44Almost all of the people of the town came to hear the Word of God on the next Day of Rest. 45The Jews were filled with jealousy when they saw so many people. They spoke against the things Paul said by saying he was wrong. They also spoke against God. 46Paul and Barnabas said to the people in plain words, "We must preach the Word of God to you first. But because you put it aside, you are not good enough for life that lasts forever. So we will go to the people who are not Jews. 47The Lord gave us a work to do. He said, 'You are to be a light to the people who are not Jews. You are to preach so that men over all the earth can be saved from the punishment of their sins.' " (Isaiah 49:6)

⁴⁸The people who were not Jews were glad when they heard this. They were thankful for the Word of God. Those who were chosen for life that lasts forever believed. ⁴⁹The Word of God was preached over all that land.

⁵⁰The Jews worked on the feelings of the women who were religious and respected. They worked on the leading men of the city also. They worked against Paul and Barnabas and made them leave their city. ⁵¹But Paul and Barnabas shook off the dust from their feet against them and went to the city of Iconium. ⁵²The missionaries were filled with joy and with the Holy Spirit.

Paul And Barnabas Preach In Iconium

14 In the city of Iconium, Paul and Barnabas went into the Jewish place of worship. They preached with power and many people became Christians. These people were Jews and Greeks. ²But the Jews who did not want to believe worked against those who were not Jews. They made them turn against the Christians. ³Paul and Barnabas stayed there a long time preaching with the strength the Lord gave. God helped them to do powerful works when they preached which showed He was with them. ⁴The people of the city were divided. Some were on the side of the Jews. Some were on the side of the missionaries. ⁵All the people and the leaders tried to hurt them and throw stones at them.

Paul And Barnabas Go To Lystra

⁶When Paul and Barnabas heard this, they got away and went to the cities of Lystra and Derbe in Lycaonia and to the country close by. ⁷They stayed there and kept on preaching the Good News. ⁸There was a man in Lystra who had never walked from the time he was born. ⁹This man listened as Paul spoke. Paul watched him. He saw that the man believed he could be healed. ¹⁰Calling to him with a loud voice, Paul said, "Stand up on your feet!" The man jumped up and walked around.

Paul And Barnabas Are Called Gods, Then Stoned

¹¹The people saw what Paul did. They called with loud voices in the language of the people of Lycaonia, "The gods have become like men and have come down to us." ¹²They said that Barnabas was Jupiter. Paul was called Mercury because he spoke more than Barnabas. ¹³The god of Jupiter was in a building near the gate leading into the city. The religious leader of that place brought cattle and flowers to the gate. He and many other people wanted to burn these as gifts in an act of worship to Paul and Barnabas.

¹⁴When Paul and Barnabas heard this, they ran among the people. They tore their clothes and cried out, ¹⁵"Why are you doing this? We are only men with feelings like yours. We preach the Good News that you should turn from these empty things to the living God. He made the heavens and the earth and the sea and everything in them. ¹⁶Long ago He allowed all people to live the way they wanted to. ¹⁷Even then God did not leave you without something to see of Him. He did good. He gave you rain from heaven and much food. He made you happy." ¹⁸Even with these words it was hard for Paul and Barnabas to keep the people from burning cattle in an act of worship to them.

¹⁹By this time some Jews from the cities of Antioch and Iconium came. They turned the minds of the people against Paul and Barnabas and told

them to throw stones at Paul. After they threw stones at him, they dragged him out of the city thinking he was dead.

Paul And Barnabas Preach To The Christians On Their Return Trip To Antioch

20 As the Christians gathered around Paul, he got up and went back into the city. The next day he went with Barnabas to Derbe. 21 In that city they preached the Good News and taught many people. Then they returned to the cities of Lystra and Iconium and Antioch. 22 In each city they helped the Christians to be strong and true to the faith. They told them, "We must suffer many hard things to get into the holy nation of God."

23 In every church they chose leaders for them. They went without food during that time so they could pray better. Paul and Barnabas prayed for the leaders, giving them over to the Lord in Whom they believed.

24 When they had gone through the city of Pisidia, they came to the city of Pamphylia. 25 Then they preached the Good News in the city of Perga. After this they went down to the city of Attalia. 26 From there they went by ship to Antioch where they had been given to the Lord for His work. The work of this trip was done.

27 When they got there, they called the church together. They told them everything God had done for them. They told how God had opened the door for the people who were not Jews to have faith. 28 They stayed there with the followers a long time.

A Meeting Of Church Leaders In Jerusalem

15 Some men came down from the country of Judea and started to teach the Christians. They said, "Unless you go through the religious act of becoming a Jew as Moses taught, you cannot be saved from the punishment of sin." 2 Paul and Barnabas argued with them. Then Paul and Barnabas and some other men were chosen to go up to Jerusalem. They were to talk to the missionaries and church leaders about this teaching. 3 The church sent them on their way. They went through the countries of Phoenicia and Samaria and told how those who were not Jews were turning to God. This made the Christians very happy.

4 When they got to Jerusalem, the church and the missionaries and the church leaders were glad to see them. Paul and Barnabas told them what God had done through them.

5 Some of the Christians there had been proud religious law-keepers. They got up and said, "Doing the religious act of becoming a Jew and keeping the Law of Moses are two things that must be done." 6 The missionaries and church leaders got together to talk about this. 7 After a long time of much talking, Peter got up and said to them, "Brothers, you know in the early days God was pleased to use me to preach the Good News to the people who are not Jews so they might put their trust in Christ. 8 God knows the hearts of all men. He showed them they were to have His loving-favor by giving them the Holy Spirit the same as He gave to us. 9 He has made no difference between them and us. They had their hearts made clean when they put their trust in Him also. 10 Why do you test God by putting too heavy a load on the back of the followers? It was too heavy for our fathers or for us to carry. 11 We believe it is by the loving-favor of the Lord Jesus that we are saved. They are saved from the punishment of sin the same way."

12 All those who were gathered together said nothing. They listened to Paul and Barnabas who told of the powerful works God had done

through them among the people who are not Jews.

God's Call Is Also For The People Who Are Not Jews

13When they finished speaking, James said, "Brothers, listen to me. 14Simon Peter has told how God first visited the people who are not Jews. He was getting a people for Himself. 15This agrees with what the early preacher said, 16'After this I will come back and build again the building of David that fell down. Yes, I will build it again from the stones that fell down. I will set it up again. 17Then all the nations may look for the Lord, even all the people who are not Jews who are called by My name. The Lord said this. He does all these things. 18God has made all His works known from the beginning of time.' (Amos 9:11-12)

The People Who Are Not Jews Are Not Under The Law

19"So we should not trouble these people who are not Jews who are turning to God. 20We should write to them that they should keep away from everything that is given to gods. They should keep away from sex sins and not eat blood or meat from animals that have been killed in ways against the Law. 21For the Law of Moses has been read in every city from the early days. It has been read in the Jewish places of worship on every Day of Rest."

22Then the missionaries and the church leaders and the whole church chose some men from among them. They were to be sent to the city of Antioch with Paul and Barnabas. They chose Judas Barsabbas and Silas. These men were leaders among the Christians.

23They sent them with this letter: "The missionaries and church leaders and Christians say hello to the brothers who are not Jews in Antioch and Syria and Cilicia. 24We have heard that some from our group have troubled you and have put doubt in your minds. They said that you must go through the religious act of becoming a Jew and you must keep the Law of Moses. We did not tell them to say these things. 25All of us have wanted to send men to you with our much-loved Paul and Barnabas. 26Their lives have been in danger for the name of our Lord Jesus Christ. 27So now we send Judas and Silas to you. They will tell you the same things. 28It pleased the Holy Spirit and us to ask you to do nothing more than these things that have to be done. 29You are to keep away from everything that is given to gods. Do not eat blood or meat from animals that have been killed in ways against the Law. Keep away from sex sins. If you keep yourselves free from these things you will do well. Goodby."

The Missionaries Go Back To Antioch

30When the meeting was finished, they went to Antioch. As soon as they gathered the people together, they gave them the letter. 31When they read it, they were glad for the comfort and strength it brought them. 32Judas and Silas were preachers also. They preached to the Christians and helped them to become stronger in the faith.

33They were there for some time. Then they were sent back in peace to the missionaries who had sent them. 34But Silas thought he should stay there. 35Paul and Barnabas stayed in Antioch. With the help of many others, they preached and taught the Word of God.

Paul Starts Out The Second Time

36After awhile, Paul said to Barnabas, "Let us go back and visit the Christians in every city where we have preached the Word of God. Let us see how they are doing." ³⁷Barnabas wanted to take John Mark with them. ³⁸Paul did not think it was good to take him because he had left them while they were in Pamphylia. He had not helped them in the work. ³⁹They argued so much that they left each other. Barnabas took John Mark with him and went by ship to the island of Cyprus. ⁴⁰Paul chose Silas. After the Christians asked for the Lord's favor to be on Paul and Silas, they went on their way. ⁴¹They went through Syria and Cilicia making the churches stronger in the faith.

Timothy Starts To Work With Paul

16 Paul went down to the cities of Derbe and Lystra. There was a follower there named Timothy. His mother was a Jewish Christian and his father was a Greek. ²The Christians in the city of Lystra and Iconium respected Timothy. ³Paul wanted Timothy to go with him as a missionary. He took him and had Timothy go through the religious act of becoming a Jew because of the Jews who were in those places. Every-one knew his father was a Greek. ⁴They went from city to city and told the Christians what the missionaries and the church leaders in Jerusalem had written for the Christians to do. ⁵The churches were made stronger in the faith. More people were added each day.

Paul Is Called To Macedonia In A Dream

⁶They went through the countries of Phrygia and Galatia. The Holy Spirit kept them from preaching the Word of God in the countries of Asia. ⁷When they came to the city of Mysia, they tried to go on to the city of Bithynia but the Holy Spirit would not let them go. ⁸From Mysia they went down to the city of Troas.

⁹That night Paul had a dream. A man was standing in front of him crying out, "Come over to the country of Macedonia and help us!" ¹⁰After he had seen this, we agreed that God told us to go to Macedonia to tell them the Good News.

Lydia, The First Christian In Europe

¹¹We took a ship from the city of Troas to the city of Samothracia. The next day we went to the city of Neapolis. ¹²From there we went to the city of Philippi. This was an important city in Macedonia. It was ruled by the leaders of the country of Rome. We stayed here for some days. ¹³On the Day of Rest we went outside the city to a place down by the river. We thought people would be gathering there for prayer. Some women came and we sat down and talked to them. ¹⁴One of the women who listened sold purple cloth. She was from the city of Thyatira. Her name was Lydia and she was a worshiper of God. The Lord opened her heart to hear what Paul said. ¹⁵When she and her family had been baptized, she said to us, "If you think I am faithful to the Lord, come and stay at my house." She kept on asking. Then we went with her.

A Girl Who Had A Demon Was Healed by Paul

¹⁶One day as we were going to the place to pray, we met a servant-girl who could tell what was going to happen in the future by a demon she had. Her owner made much money from her power. ¹⁷She followed Paul and us crying out, "These are servants of the Highest God. They are telling you how to be saved from the punishment of sin." ¹⁸She did this many days. Paul was troubled. Then he turned and said to the demon in her, "In the name of Jesus Christ, I speak to you. Come out of her!" At once it left her.

Paul and Silas In Jail

¹⁹The girl's owner saw that they could not make money with her anymore. Then they took hold of Paul and Silas and dragged them to the leaders. This happened in the center of town where people gather. ²⁰After they brought them in front of the leaders, they said, "These men are Jews and are making a lot of trouble in our city. ²¹They are teaching a religion that we Romans are not allowed to follow."

²²Many people had gathered around Paul and Silas. They were calling out things against them. The leaders had the clothes of Paul and Silas taken off and had them beaten with sticks. ²³After they had hit them many times, they put Paul and Silas in prison. The soldiers told the man who watched the prison to be sure to keep them from getting away. ²⁴Because of this, they were put in the inside room of the prison and their feet were put in pieces of wood that held them.

²⁵About midnight Paul and Silas were praying and singing songs of thanks to God. The other men in prison were listening to them. ²⁶All at once the earth started to shake. The stones under the prison shook and the doors opened. The chains fell off from everyone.

²⁷The man who watched the prison woke up. He saw the prison doors wide open and thought the men in prison had gotten away. At once he pulled out his sword to kill himself. ²⁸But Paul called to him, "Do not hurt yourself. We are all here!" ²⁹The man who watched the prison called for a light. Then he ran in and got down in front of Paul and Silas. He was shaking with fear. ³⁰As he took them outside, he said, "Sirs, what must I do to be saved?"

³¹They said, "Put your trust in the Lord Jesus Christ and you and your family will be saved from the punishment of sin."

³²Then Paul spoke the Word of God to him and his family. ³³It was late at night, but the man who watched the prison took Paul and Silas in and washed the places on their bodies where they were hurt. Right then he and his family were baptized. ³⁴He took Paul and Silas to his house and gave them food. He and all his family were full of joy for having put their trust in God.

Paul And Silas Are Allowed To Go Free

³⁵When it was day, the leaders sent a soldier to say, "Let these men go free." ³⁶The man who watched the prison told this to Paul. He said, "The leaders have sent word to let you go free. Come out now and go without any trouble."

³⁷Paul said, "No! They have beaten us in front of many people without a trial. We are Roman citizens and they have put us in prison. Now do they think they can send us away without anyone knowing? No! They must come themselves and take us out." ³⁸The soldiers told this to the leaders. Then the leaders were afraid when they heard that Paul and Silas were Roman citizens. ³⁹They went themselves and told Paul and Silas they were sorry. Then they took them out and asked them to leave their city. ⁴⁰Paul and Silas went to Lydia's house after they left the prison. They met with the Christians and gave them comfort. Then they went away from the city.

Paul And Silas Start A Church In Thessalonica

17 After Paul and Silas had gone through the cities of Amphipolis and Apollonia, they came to the city of Thessalonica. The Jews had a place of worship there. ²Paul went in as he always did. They gathered together each Day of Rest for three weeks and he taught them from the

Holy Writings. ³He showed them that Christ had to suffer and rise again from the dead. He said, "I preach this Jesus to you. He is the Christ." ⁴Some of them put their trust in Christ and followed Paul and Silas. There were many Greek people and some leading women who honored God among those who had become Christians.

The Jews Make It Hard For Paul And Silas

⁵The Jews who did not put their trust in Christ became jealous. They took along some sinful men from the center of town where people gather and brought them out on the street. These angry men started all the people in the city to cry out with loud voices. They went to the house of Jason hoping to find Paul and Silas there and bring them out to the people. ⁶But they did not find them there. Then they dragged Jason and some other Christians out in front of the leaders and cried out, "These men who have been making trouble over all the world have come here also. ⁷And Jason has taken them in. They say there is another King called Jesus. They are working against the laws made by Caesar."

⁸When the people and city leaders heard this, they were troubled. ⁹Then they made Jason and the others pay some money and let them go.

¹⁰At once the Christians sent Paul and Silas away at night to the city of Berea. When they got there, they went to the Jewish place of worship. ¹¹These Jews were more willing to understand than those in the city of Thessalonica. They were very glad to hear the Word of God, and they looked into the Holy Writings to see if those things were true. ¹²Many of them became Christians. Some of them were respected Greek women and men. ¹³The Jews of Thessalonica heard that Paul was preaching the Word of God in Berea. They went there and worked against the missionaries by talking to the people. ¹⁴At once the Christians sent Paul away to the seashore. But Silas and Timothy stayed there.

Paul Preaches On Mars' Hill In Athens

¹⁵Those who took Paul brought him to the city of Athens. Paul sent word with them that Silas and Timothy should come to him as soon as they could. Then they left. ¹⁶While Paul was waiting for Silas and Timothy in Athens, his spirit was troubled as he saw the whole city worshiping false gods. ¹⁷He talked to the Jews and other people who were worshiping in the Jewish place of worship. Every day he talked with people who gathered in the center of town.

¹⁸Some men from two different groups were arguing with Paul. The one group thought that men might as well get all the fun out of life that they can. The other group thought that wisdom alone makes men happy. Some of them said, "This man has lots of little things to talk about. They are not important. What is he trying to say?" Others said, "He preaches about strange gods." It was because he preached of Jesus and of His being raised from the dead.

¹⁹Then they took him to Mars' Hill and said, "We want to hear of this new teaching of yours. ²⁰Some of the things you are telling us are strange to our ears. We want to know what these things mean." ²¹The people of Athens and those visiting from far countries used all their time in talking or hearing some new thing.

²²Then Paul stood up on Mars' Hill and said, "Men of Athens, I see how very religious you are in every way. ²³As I was walking around and looking at the things you worship, I found an altar where you worship with the words written on it, TO THE GOD WHO IS NOT KNOWN.

You are worshiping Him without knowing Him. He is the One I will tell you about. 24"The God Who made the world and everything in it is the Lord of heaven and earth. He does not live in buildings made by hands. 25No one needs to care for Him as if He needed anything. He is the One who gives life and breath and everything to everyone. 26He made from one blood all nations who live on the earth. He set the times and places where they should live.

27"They were to look for God. Then they might feel after Him and find Him because He is not far from each one of us. 28It is in Him that we live and move and keep on living. Some of your own men have written, 'We are God's children.' 29If we are God's children, we should not think of Him as being like gold or silver or stone. Such gods made of gold or silver or stone are planned by men and are made by them.

30"God did not remember these times when people did not know better. But now He tells all men everywhere to be sorry for their sins and to turn from them. 31He has set a day when He will say in the right way if the people of the world are guilty. This will be done by Jesus Christ, the One He has chosen. God has proven this to all men by raising Jesus Christ from the dead."

32Some people laughed and made fun when they heard Paul speak of Christ being raised from the dead. Others said, "We want to listen to you again about this." 33So Paul went away from the people. 34Some people followed him and became Christians. One was Dionysius, a leader in the city. A woman named Damaris believed. And there were others also.

Paul Goes To Corinth

18 After that Paul went from the city of Athens and came to the city of Corinth. 2He met a Jew there named Aquila who was born in the country of Pontus. He had lived in the country of Italy a short time. His wife Priscilla was with him. Claudius, who was the leader of the country, had told all the Jews to leave Rome. Paul went to see Aquila and Priscilla. 3They made tents for a living. Paul did the same kind of work so he stayed with them and they worked together.

4Every Day of Rest he would go to the Jewish place of worship and teach both Jews and Greeks. 5Silas and Timothy came down from the country of Macedonia. Then Paul used all his time preaching to the Jews. He taught that Jesus was the Christ. 6But they worked against Paul and said bad things about him. He shook his clothes and said, "Whatever happens to you is your own doing. I am free from your guilt. From now on I will go to the people who are not Jews."

7Paul went from there and came to the house of a man named Titus Justus who worshiped God. His house was next to the Jewish place of worship. 8Crispus was the leader of the Jewish place of worship. He and his family believed in the Lord. Many of the people of Corinth who heard Paul became Christians and were baptized.

9Paul saw the Lord in a dream one night. He said to Paul, "Do not be afraid. Keep speaking. Do not close your mouth. 10I am with you. No one will hurt you. I have many people in this city who belong to Me." 11For a year and a half Paul stayed there and taught them the Word of God.

12Gallio was leader of the country of Greece. All the Jews worked against Paul and brought him in front of the court. 13They said, "This man is trying to get people to worship God against the Law." 14Paul was ready to speak, but Gallio said to the Jews, "If this were something bad or a wrong doing, I would listen to you. 15But because it is about words and names and your own Law, you will have to take care of it yourselves. I do not want to judge who is right or wrong in things like this." [16]And he sent them out of his court.

[17]Then all the Greek people took Sosthenes, the leader of the Jewish place of worship, and beat him in front of the court. But Gallio did not let this trouble him.

Paul Goes Back To Antioch

[18]Paul stayed in Corinth many days longer. Then he said goodby and left the followers. He went by ship to the country of Syria with Priscilla and Aquila going with him. In the city of Cenchrea he had his hair cut short because of a promise he had made to God. [19]They came to the city of Ephesus. Priscilla and Aquila stayed there. Paul went to the Jewish place of worship and argued with the Jews. [20]They wanted him to stay longer but he would not. [21]As he left them, he said, *("I must go to the special supper at Jerusalem.) I will return again to you if God wants me to." Then he got on a ship and left Ephesus. [22]He stopped in the city of Caesarea to say hello to the people in the church. Then he went down to the city of Antioch. [23]Paul stayed there for some time. Then he went from city to city through the countries of Galatia and Phrygia. In each place he helped the Christians become strong in the faith.

Aquila And Priscilla Help Apollos In Ephesus

[24]A Jew by the name of Apollos had come to Ephesus. He was from the city of Alexandria. He could talk to people about the Holy Writings very well. [25]He had been taught in the way of the Lord. And with a strong desire in his heart, he taught about Jesus. What he said was true, but he knew only about the baptism of John.

[26]He began to speak without fear in the Jewish place of worship. Aquila and Priscilla heard him. They took him to their house and taught him much more about the things of God. [27]Apollos wanted to cross over to Greece. The Christians wrote a letter to the followers there asking them to be good to him. When he got there, he was much help to those who had put their trust in Christ. [28]In front of everyone he proved with great power that the Jews were wrong. He showed from the Holy Writings that Jesus was the Christ.

Christians In Ephesus Are Filled With The Holy Spirit

19 While Apollos was in the city of Corinth, Paul went through the hill country to get to the city of Ephesus. He found a few followers there. [2]He asked them, "Did you receive the Holy Spirit when you put your trust in Christ?" They said, "No, we have not even heard that there is a Holy Spirit." [3]He asked them, "How were you baptized?" They answered, "The way John baptized." [4]Paul said, "John baptized those who were sorry for their sins and turned from them. He told the people to put their trust in Jesus Who was coming later."

[5]The people there were baptized in the name of the Lord Jesus when they heard this. [6]When Paul laid his hands on them, the Holy Spirit came on them. They started to talk in special sounds and to speak God's Word. [7]There were about twelve men.

Paul Preaches In A Place Of Worship And In A School In Ephesus

[8]For three months Paul went into the Jewish place of worship and spoke without fear. He taught them things about the holy nation of God. [9]Some let their hearts grow hard. They would not put their trust in

Christ. These spoke against the Christian religion in front of other people. Then Paul took the followers away from the others. He taught them each day in the school of Tyrannus. [10]He did this for two years. All the Jews and the Greeks in the countries of Asia heard the Word of the Lord.

Paul Does Powerful Works

[11]God used Paul to do powerful special works. [12]Pieces of cloth and parts of his clothes that had been next to his body were put on sick people. Then they were healed of their diseases and demons came out of them.

[13]There were Jews who went from city to city trying to put demons out of people. Some of these tried to use the name of the Lord Jesus on those who had demons. They said, "I speak to you in the name of Jesus, the One Paul preaches about." [14]A Jewish leader of the people by the name of Sceva had seven sons. These sons were trying to do this. [15]The demon said, "I know Jesus. I know about Paul. But who are you?" [16]Then the man with the demon jumped on the sons. He had power over them and beat them. They ran out of the house with no clothes on and they were hurt.

[17]All the Jews and Greeks living in Ephesus heard about it. Because of this all the people became afraid. And the name of the Lord Jesus was held in great honor. [18]Many Christians came and told of the wrong things they were doing. [19]Many of those who did witchcraft gathered their books together and burned them in front of everyone. These books were worth 50,000 pieces of silver money. [20]The Word of the Lord became well-known.

[21]After this, Paul thought he would go through the countries of Macedonia and Greece. Then he would go to Jerusalem. He said, "After I have been there, I must go to the city of Rome also." [22]He sent two of his helpers, Timothy and Erastus, to Macedonia. Paul stayed in the countries of Asia awhile longer.

The Meeting Of The Silver Workmen In Ephesus

[23]During that time there was much trouble about the Christians. [24]A man named Demetrius made small silver buildings for the worship of Diana. His workmen received much money for their work. [25]He called his workmen together and other men who made these small silver buildings. He said to them, "Men, you know we make much money from this work. [26]Now you hear that Paul has turned away many people in Ephesus as well as in Asia. He tells them that gods made with hands are not gods. [27]It could be that our work will not be respected. Not only that, the house of worship for the god of Diana will be worth nothing and her greatness will be destroyed. All the countries of Asia and the world worship her."

[28]They became angry when they heard this and cried out, "Great is Diana of Ephesus." [29]The whole city was filled with loud cries. They caught Gaius and Aristarchus. These two men from Macedonia were with Paul. They gathered around them at the meeting place in the city.

[30]Paul wanted to stand in front of all the people but his followers would not let him. [31]Some of the city leaders who were his friends told him not to go to the meeting. [32]All this time some were crying out one thing and some another. The meeting was all noise. Most of the people did not know why they had come together. [33]Then the Jews pushed Alexander to the front. Alexander held his hand up and was going to speak. [34]As soon as they saw he was a Jew, they cried out with a loud voice for two hours, "Great is Diana of Ephesus!"

³⁵One of the city leaders stopped the noise. He spoke, "Men of Ephesus, everyone knows our city is where the god of Diana is kept. That is the stone god that fell from the sky. ³⁶Everyone knows this is true, so you must not cry out or do anything foolish. ³⁷The men you brought here do not rob houses of worship or talk against our god. ³⁸If Demetrius and his workmen have something against anyone, we have special days for courts. Let them go to court. ³⁹If you want anything else, it should be done in another meeting. ⁴⁰We are in danger of being asked about this trouble today. There is no good reason we can give for this meeting." ⁴¹When he had said this, he told them to leave.

Paul Goes To Greece And Macedonia

20 When the noise had come to an end, Paul called the followers to him. He spoke words of comfort and then said goodby. He left to go to the country of Macedonia. ²As he went through those parts of the country, he spoke words of comfort and help to the Christians. Then he went on to the country of Greece. ³He stayed there three months. As he was about to get on a ship for the country of Syria, he learned that the Jews had made a plan to take him. He changed his plans and went back through Macedonia. ⁴Some men were going along with him. They were Sopater of the city of Berea, Aristarchus and Secundus of the city of Thessalonica, Gaius of the city of Derbe, and Timothy and Tychicus and Trophimus of the countries of Asia. ⁵They went on to the city of Troas and waited there for us. ⁶After the supper of bread without yeast we got on a ship in the city of Philippi. We met these men at Troas. It took five days to get there and we stayed one week.

Eutychus Falls From A Building While Paul Preaches

⁷On the first day of the week we met together to eat the Lord's supper. Paul talked to them. He thought he would leave the next day, so he kept on talking until twelve o'clock at night. ⁸There were many lights in the room on the third floor where we had our meeting. ⁹A young man named Eutychus sat in the window. As Paul kept on preaching, this man started to go to sleep. At last he went to sleep. He fell from the third floor to the ground and was picked up dead. ¹⁰Paul went down and stood over him. Then he took him in his arms and said, "Do not be worried. He is alive!" ¹¹Paul went up again to the meeting and ate with them. He talked with them until the sun came up. Then he left. ¹²They were happy they could take the young man home alive.

Paul Goes From The City Of Troas To Miletus

¹³We went on ahead by ship to the city of Assos. There we were to pick up Paul. He had planned it that way. He wanted to walk by land that far. ¹⁴We got to Assos and met him there. We picked him up and went on to the city of Mitylene. ¹⁵The next day we went by ship to a place beside the island of Chios. The next day we crossed over to the island of Samos. Then the next day we came to the city of Miletus. ¹⁶Paul planned to pass by the city of Ephesus so he would not lose more time in Asia. He wanted to be in Jerusalem if he could be on the day to remember how the Holy Spirit came on the church.

Paul Meets With The Leaders Of The Church Of Ephesus

¹⁷From Miletus he sent word to Ephesus. He asked the leaders of the

church to come to him. ¹⁸When they got there, he said to them, "From the first day that I came to Asia you have seen what my life has been like. ¹⁹I worked for the Lord without pride. Because of the trouble the Jews gave me, I have had many tears. ²⁰I always told you everything that would be a help to you. I taught you in open meetings and from house to house. ²¹I preached to the Jews and to the Greeks. I told them to turn from their sin to God and to put their trust in our Lord Jesus Christ.

²²"As you see, I am on my way to Jerusalem. The Holy Spirit makes me go. I do not know what will happen to me there. ²³But in every city I have been, the Holy Spirit tells me that trouble and chains will be waiting for me there. ²⁴But I am not worried about this. I do not think of my life as worth much, but I do want to finish the work the Lord Jesus gave me to do. My work is to preach the Good News of God's loving-favor.

²⁵"All of you have heard me preach the Good News. I am sure that none of you will ever see my face again. ²⁶I tell you this day that I am clean and free from the blood of all men. ²⁷I told you all the truth about God. ²⁸Keep a careful watch over yourselves and over the church. The Holy Spirit has made you its leaders. Feed and care for the church of God. He bought it with His own blood.

²⁹"Yes, I know that when I am gone, hungry wolves will come in among you. They will try to destroy the church. ³⁰Also men from your own group will begin to teach things that are not true. They will get men to follow them. ³¹I say again, keep watching! Remember that for three years I taught everyone of you night and day, even with tears.

³²"And now, my brothers, I give you over to God and His word of love. It is able to make you strong and to give you what you are to have, along with all those who are set apart for God. ³³I have not tried to get anyone's money or clothes. ³⁴You all know that these hands worked for what I needed and for what those with me needed. ³⁵In every way I showed you that by working hard like this we can help those who are weak. We must remember what the Lord Jesus said, 'We are more happy when we give than when we receive.' "

³⁶As he finished talking, he got down on his knees and prayed with them all. ³⁷They cried and put their arms around Paul and kissed him. ³⁸What made them sad most of all was because he said that they would never see his face again. Then they went with him to the ship.

Paul Goes From Miletus To Tyre

21 After we left them, we got on a ship and came straight down to the island of Cos. The next day we came to the island of Rhodes and from there to the city of Patara. ²There we found a ship that was going over to the country of Phoenicia. We got on it and went along. ³We saw the island of Cyprus to our left but went on to the country of Syria. We came to land at the city of Tyre. The ship was to leave its load of freight there.

⁴We looked for the Christians and stayed with them seven days. The Christians had been told by the Holy Spirit to tell Paul not to go to Jerusalem. ⁵When our time was up, we left there and went on our way. All of them with their wives and children went with us out of town. They got down on their knees on shore and prayed. ⁶After we said goodby, we got on the ship and they went back to their houses.

Paul Goes From Tyre To Jerusalem

⁷The same ship took us from Tyre to the city of Ptolemais. We stayed with the Christians there one day. ⁸The next day we left and came to the

city of Caesarea. We went to the house of Philip and stayed with him. He was a preacher who goes from town to town and was one of the seven church leaders. [9]Philip had four daughters who were not married. They spoke the Word of God.

[10]While we were there a few days, a man who speaks for God named Agabus came down from the country of Judea. [11]He came to see us. Then he took Paul's belt and used it to tie his own feet and hands. He said, "This is what the Holy Spirit says, 'The Jews at Jerusalem will tie the man who owns this belt. Then they will hand him over to the people who are not Jews.' "

[12]When we heard this, we and all the people living there begged Paul not to go up to Jerusalem. [13]Then Paul said, "What do you mean by crying and breaking my heart? I am ready to be put in chains in Jerusalem. I am also ready to die for the name of the Lord Jesus." [14]Paul would not listen to us. So we stopped begging him and said, "May whatever God wants be done."

Paul Is In Jerusalem

[15]After this, we got ready and started up to Jerusalem. [16]Some of the followers in Caesarea went with us. They took us to Mnason's house. He was one of the first followers from Cyprus. We stayed with him.

[17]When we got to Jerusalem, the Christians were glad to see us. [18]The next day we went with Paul to see James. All the church leaders came also. [19]After saying hello to them, Paul told of what God had done through his work for the people who were not Jews.

[20]When they heard this, they thanked the Lord. Then they said to him, "You see, brother, how many thousands of Christians there are among the Jews. They all obey the Law of Moses. [21]They have heard

about you. They have heard you teach the Jews who live among people who are not Jews. They have heard you teach them to break away from the Law of Moses. They say you are telling them not to do the religious act of becoming a Jew and not to follow old religious ways of worship. [22]What should we do about it? They will hear that you have come. [23]You must do what we tell you. We have four men with us who have made a promise to God. [24]Take these four men and go through the religious worship of washing with them. You pay to have their hair cut off. Then everybody will know what they have heard about you is not true. They will know you are careful to obey the Law of Moses. [25]As for the people who are not Jews, we wrote to them. We said that they must keep away from everything that has been given to gods. They must not eat blood or meat from animals that have been killed in ways against the Law. They must keep away from sex sins."

[26]The next day Paul took the men. He went through the religious worship of washing with them. They went into the house of God to tell when their religious worship of washing would be finished. Then the gift for each one of them would be given as an act of worship.

[27]The seven days were almost finished. Jews from the countries of Asia saw Paul in the house of God. They made the people turn against him. Then they took hold of him. [28]They cried out, "You who are Jews, help us! This is the man who is teaching against our people and our Law and this house of God. Also he has brought Greek people into the house of God. This has made this holy place unclean." [29]They had seen him before in the city with Trophimus who was from the city of Ephesus. They thought Paul had brought him into the house of God also.

30All the people in the city were crying out with loud voices. The people pushed and moved together. They took Paul and dragged him out of the house of God. Then the doors were shut. 31They were getting ready to kill him. The captain of the soldiers heard there was trouble over all Jerusalem. 32At once the captain called his soldiers and they ran down to the people. When the people saw the captain and his soldiers, they stopped beating Paul.

Paul Is Tied With Chains

33The captain came and took hold of Paul. He told his soldiers to tie Paul with two chains. Then he asked who he was and what he had done. 34Some of the people called out one thing and some another. The captain was not able to find out what had happened. He told his men to take Paul into the soldiers' building. 35The people cried out so loud and pushed so hard that Paul had to be carried up the steps by the soldiers. 36All the people kept pushing and calling out, "Kill him!"

37Paul was brought into the soldiers' building. He said to the captain, "May I say something to you?" The captain said, "Can you speak the Greek language? 38Are you not the man from the country of Egypt who made trouble against our country? That man led 4,000 fighting men into the desert." 39Paul said, "No! I am a Jew and a citizen of a large city. I am from Tarsus in the country of Cilicia. I ask you to let me speak to the people." 40The captain told Paul to speak. So Paul stood on the steps and held up his hand. When there was no more noise, he spoke to them in the language of the Jews.

Paul Tells Of The Work He Did Before He Was A Christian

22 Paul said, "Brothers and fathers, listen to what I have to say to you." 2When they heard him speak to them in their own language, they stopped making noise. Then he said,

3"I am a Jew. I was born in the city of Tarsus in the country of Cilicia. When I was a young man, I lived here in Jerusalem. I went to Gamaliel's school and learned all about the Law of our early fathers. I worked hard for God as you all do today. 4"I worked hard and killed men and women who believed as I believe today. I put them in chains and sent them to prison. 5The head religious leader and the leaders of the people can tell you this is true. I got letters from them to take to our Jewish brothers in the city of Damascus. I was going there to put the Christians in chains and bring them to Jerusalem where they would be beaten.

The Change In Paul's Life On The Damascus Road

6"I was near Damascus. All at once, about noon, I saw a bright light from heaven shining around me. 7I fell to the ground. A voice said to me, 'Saul, Saul, why do you work so hard against Me?' 8I said, 'Who are You, Lord?' He said to me, 'I am Jesus of Nazareth, the One you are working against.' 9Those who were with me saw the light. But they did not hear Him speaking to me. 10I asked, 'Lord, what should I do?' The Lord said to me, 'Get up! Go to Damascus. You will be told what to do there.'

11"I could not see because of the bright light. Those who were with me had to lead me by the hand until we came to Damascus. 12Ananias lived there. He obeyed the Law and was respected by all the Jews. 13He came and stood near me and said, 'Brother Saul, receive your sight.' At once I was able to see him. 14Then Ananias said, 'The God of our fathers chose you to know what He wants done. He chose you to see Jesus Christ, the One Right with God, and to hear His voice. [15]You are to tell all men what you have seen and heard. [16]What are you waiting for? Get up! Be baptized. Have your sins washed away by calling on His name.'

Paul Is Called To Work With The People Who Are Not Jews

[17]"I came back to Jerusalem. When I was praying in the house of God, I had a dream. [18]I saw Him as He said to me, 'Get out of Jerusalem! They will not listen to you when you tell them about Me!' [19]I said, 'Lord, they know I took Christians out of every Jewish place of worship. I had them beaten and put in prison. [20]Also when Stephen was killed, I stood there and watched them throw stones at him. Those who threw the stones had me watch their coats.' [21]The Lord said to me, 'Go! I will send you far away to the people who are not Jews.' " [22]They listened to him until he said that. Then they all cried out with loud voices, "Kill him! Take such a man from the earth! He should not live!" [23]They kept on calling out. Then they pulled off their coats and threw dust in the air.

Paul Tells Who He Is

[24]The captain told them to bring Paul into the soldiers' building. He told his soldiers to find out from Paul, by beating him, why the people were crying out against him. [25]As they tied him up, Paul said to the soldier, "Does the law say that you can beat a Roman citizen when no one has said he is guilty?" [26]When the soldier heard this, he told it to the captain. He said, "Listen! What are you doing? This man is a Roman citizen." [27]The captain came and asked Paul, "Tell me, are you a Roman citizen?" Paul said, "Yes!" [28]The captain said, "I had to pay a lot of money to be a citizen." Paul said, "But I was born a Roman." [29]Those who were going to

beat him left him at once. The captain was also afraid when he heard that Paul was a Roman citizen because he had him tied.

Paul Stands In Front Of The Religious Leaders' Court

[30]The next day they took off the chains that were holding Paul. The captain wanted to know why the Jews wanted to kill him. So the captain told the head religious leaders to gather for their court. They brought Paul and put him in front of them.

Paul Speaks To The Religious Leaders' Court

23 Paul looked straight at the court and said, "Brother Jews, I have lived for God with a heart that has said I am not guilty to this day." [2]Then Ananias, the head religious leader, told those standing near him to hit him on the mouth. [3]Paul said, "God will hit you, you white-washed wall! Do you sit there and say I am guilty by the Law when you break the Law by having me hit?"

[4]Those standing near said, "Do you talk like that to God's head religious leader?" [5]Paul said, "Brother Jews, I did not know that he was God's head religious leader. I know the Holy Writings say, 'You must not speak against the leader of your people.' " (Exodus 22:28)

[6]Paul saw that part of the court was made up of the religious group who believe no one is raised from the dead. The other part were proud religious law-keepers. Then he cried out, "Brother Jews, I am a proud religious law-keeper and from a family of proud religious law-keepers. I have been brought in front of this court because of the hope of being raised from the dead."

[7]When they heard this, both religious groups started to argue and the people of the court were divided

in what they thought. ⁸The one religious group believes that no one is raised from the dead. Also, they do not believe in angels or spirits. But the other religious group, the proud religious law-keepers, believe that people are raised from the dead and that there are angels and spirits. ⁹The courtroom was filled with noise. Some of the teachers of the Law working with the proud religious law-keepers stood up and said, "We find nothing wrong with this man. What if an angel or spirit has spoken to him?"

¹⁰They argued all the more. Then the captain was afraid they would pull Paul to pieces. He told his men to get Paul out of there and take him back to the soldiers' building. ¹¹The next night the Lord came to Paul and said, "Paul, do not be afraid! You will tell about Me in the city of Rome the same as you have told about Me in Jerusalem."

The Plan To Kill Paul

¹²In the morning some of the Jews gathered together and made a plan to kill Paul. They promised each other that they would not eat or drink until they had killed him. ¹³There were more than forty of them who had made this promise. ¹⁴These people came to the head religious leader and to the leaders of the people and said, "We have made a promise not to eat any food until we have killed Paul. ¹⁵We ask you and the court to have the captain bring Paul down to you tomorrow. It will look as if you want to ask him some things. Before he gets near you, we will be waiting to kill him."

¹⁶Paul's nephew heard about the plan. He went to the soldiers' building and told Paul. ¹⁷Paul called one of the soldiers and said, "Take this young man to the captain. He has something to tell him." ¹⁸The soldiers brought the young man to the captain and said, "Paul asked me to bring this young man to you. He has something to tell you." ¹⁹The captain took him by the hand and they walked over where they could be alone. He said, "What is it that you have to tell me?" ²⁰The young man said, "The Jews have made a plan to ask you to bring Paul to the courtroom tomorrow. It would look as if they were going to ask him some things. ²¹Do not let them talk you into it. More than forty men are waiting in secret to kill him. They have promised each other not to eat or drink anything until they have killed him. They are all waiting for you to say the word." ²²The captain told the young man to go. He said, "Do not tell anyone you have told me this."

Paul Is Sent To Felix In Caesarea

²³Then the captain called two soldiers and said, "Get 200 men ready to go to the city of Caesarea by nine o'clock tonight. Also have seventy men ride on horses and 200 men carry spears. ²⁴Get horses ready for Paul to ride. Take him to Felix, the leader of the people."

²⁵He wrote a letter which said, ²⁶"Claudius Lysias says hello to Felix, the best leader of the people. ²⁷This man Paul was taken by the Jews. He was about to be killed by them. But I came along with my soldiers and kept him from being killed. I did this when I learned that he was a Roman citizen. ²⁸I wanted to know what they had against him. So I took him to the religious leaders' court. ²⁹I learned they were holding him because of something about their Law. There was no reason for him to be killed or to be put in prison. ³⁰I was told that the Jews had a plan to kill this man. At once I sent him to you. I told the Jews who wanted to kill him to tell you what they have against him. Goodby."

³¹The soldiers took Paul as they were told. They brought him during

the night to Antipatris. [32]The next day they went back to their building in Jerusalem. The men riding horses went on with Paul. [33]When they came to Caesarea, they gave the letter to the leader of the people. They also handed Paul over to him. [34]After he read the letter, he asked what part of the country Paul was from. He was told that Paul was from the city of Cilicia. [35]He said, "I will listen to all of this when the men come who want to kill you." He had Paul kept in King Herod's building.

Paul Stands In Front Of Felix

24 Five days later Ananias came to the city of Caesarea. He was the head religious leader. Some other religious leaders and a man whose name was Tertullus came also. This man worked in courts and knew all about the laws. He told Felix what the Jews had against Paul. [2]They brought in Paul. Then Tertullus started to tell what the Jews had against him, saying,

"Most respected Felix, because of you, we are living in peace. Wrong-doings have been made right in this nation. [3]In every way and in every place, we thank you for all of this. [4]We do not want to keep you here too long. I ask you to listen to our few words. You are known to be kind in this way. [5]We have found this man to be a troublemaker among all the Jews in the world. He is a leader of a religious group called the Nazarenes. [6]He even tried to make the house of God unclean by taking people into it who were not Jews. But we took hold of him. We could have said he was guilty by our Law. [7]*But Lysias, the captain, came and took him out of our hands. [8]He told those who wanted to kill him to tell you what they had against him. When you ask him these things, you will be able to learn everything we have against him." [9]The Jews agreed to what he said against Paul.

Paul Speaks For Himself The First Time

[10]Then Felix, the leader of the people, told Paul to speak. Paul said, "I know that you have been a leader of this nation for many years. I am happy to be able to speak for myself. [11]Not more than twelve days ago I went up to Jerusalem to worship. You can find out about this yourself. [12]I did not argue with anyone in the house of God or in the Jewish places of worship or in the city. I was not making trouble. [13]They cannot prove any of these things they say against me.

[14]"I will say this, I worship the God of our fathers in the new Way. They say it is a false way. But I believe everything that has been written in the Law and by the early preachers. [15]I trust God for the same things they are looking for. I am looking for the dead to rise, both those right with God and the sinful. [16]I always try to live so my own heart tells me I am not guilty before God or man.

[17]"After a few years I came to bring gifts of money to the people of my country (Jerusalem). [18]Some Jews from the countries of Asia found me in the house of God after I had gone through the worship of washing. There were no people around me and there was no noise or fighting. [19]They should be here if they have anything against me. [20]Or let these men tell what wrong they found in me as I stood in front of their court, [21]unless it was the words I cried out as I stood in front of them. I said, 'I have been brought in front of this court because of the hope of being raised from the dead.' "

Felix Waits For Lysias To Come

[22]Felix knew about the Christian religion. He stopped the court, saying, "When Lysias the captain comes down, I will decide about this." [23]He told the soldier to watch

Paul, but to let him come and go as much as he wanted to. Paul's friends were to be able to come and care for him.

Paul Speaks For Himself The Second Time

24 Some days later Felix came again. His Jewish wife Drusilla was with him. He sent for Paul and heard him talk about faith in Christ Jesus. 25 Paul spoke about being right with God. He spoke about being the boss over our own desires. He spoke about standing before One Who will tell us if we are guilty. When Felix heard this, he became afraid and said, "Go now. I will send for you when it is a better time." 26 He was hoping that Paul would give him money so he could go free. For that reason he kept sending for Paul and talking to him.

27 After two years Porcius Festus became leader of the people instead of Felix. Felix wanted to please the Jews so he kept Paul in prison.

Paul Stands In Front Of Festus

25 Three days after Festus had become leader in the country, he went from the city of Caesarea to Jerusalem. 2 The head religious leaders and the leaders of the Jews told Festus what they had against Paul. 3 They asked Festus for a favor. They wanted Paul to be brought to Jerusalem because they had plans to kill him on the way. 4 Festus told them that Paul was to be kept in Caesarea and that he would be going there soon. 5 Festus said, "If Paul has done anything wrong, let your leaders go along with me and say what they have against him."

6 After staying with them about ten days, Festus went down to Caesarea. The next day he sat in the courtroom and asked for Paul to be brought in. 7 Paul came into the courtroom. The Jews who had come down from Jerusalem stood around him. They said many bad things against him. But they could not prove any of the things they said. 8 Paul spoke for himself, saying, "I have done nothing wrong against the Law of the Jews or against the house of God or against Caesar."

9 Festus was hoping to get the respect of the Jews. He asked Paul, "Will you go to the court in Jerusalem and let me say if you are guilty or not about these things?" 10 Paul said, "I am standing in front of Caesar's court where I should be told I am right or wrong. I have done no wrong to the Jews. You know that. 11 If I have done wrong and should die, I am not trying to keep from dying. But if these things they say against me are not true, no one can give me over to them. I ask to be taken to Caesar." 12 Festus talked to the leaders of the court. Then he said to Paul, "You have asked to be taken to Caesar. You will go to him."

Festus Tells King Agrippa About Paul

13 After a few days, King Agrippa and his wife, Bernice, came down to Caesarea. They went to Festus to say hello to him. 14 They stayed there a few days. Festus told them about Paul. He said, "There is a man here who was left in prison by Felix. 15 When I was at Jerusalem, the head religious leaders and the leaders of the people told me about him and asked me to say that he is guilty. 16 I told them it was against the Roman law to hand over a man to be put to death before he stood face to face with those who had something against him and could speak for himself. 17 When they came here, I took my seat in the courtroom at once. I had the man brought in. 18 When the others spoke, they had nothing against him that I thought they had. 19 They did not agree with him about their own religion, and

they argued about someone called Jesus. He had died but Paul kept saying He was alive. 20I did not know what to do. Then I asked him if he would go on trial about these things at Jerusalem. 21But Paul asked to go on trial in front of Caesar. I said that he should be kept in prison until he could be sent to Caesar." 22Agrippa said to Festus, "I would like to hear this man." Festus said, "Tomorrow you will hear him."

Paul Stands In Front Of King Agrippa

23The next day Agrippa and Bernice came into the courtroom. They were dressed to show their greatness as king and queen. Army leaders and leading men of the city came in with them. Festus had Paul brought in.

24Festus said, "King Agrippa and all of you who are here with us, you see this man. All of the Jews both here and at Jerusalem are saying that Paul should be put to death. 25I have heard nothing against him that would be reason to put him to death. But he asked for a trial in front of Caesar. I have agreed to send Paul to him. 26When I write to Caesar, I have nothing to say against him. For this reason, I brought him in front of you all and in front of you, King Agrippa. After we ask him questions, I may have something to write about. 27It is foolish for me to send a man up for trial without writing what is against him."

Paul Speaks To King Agrippa

26 Agrippa said to Paul, "You may now speak for yourself." Paul lifted his hand and started to talk, 2"King Agrippa, the Jews have said many things against me. I am happy to be able to tell you my side of the story. 3You know all about the Jewish ways and problems. So I ask you to listen to me until I have finished.

4"All the Jews know about my life from the time I was a boy until now. I lived among my own people in Jerusalem. 5If they would tell what they know, they would say that I lived the life of a proud religious law-keeper. I was in the group of proud religious law-keepers who tried to obey every law.

6"And now I am on trial here because I trust the promise God made to our fathers. 7This promise is what our twelve family groups of the Jewish nation hope to see happen. They worship God day and night. King Agrippa, it is because of this hope that they are saying things against me. 8Why do you think it is hard to believe that God raises people from the dead?

9"I used to think I should work hard against the name of Jesus of Nazareth. 10I did that in Jerusalem. I put many of the followers in prison. The head religious leaders gave me the right and the power to do it. Then when the followers were killed, I said it was all right. 11I beat them and tried to make them speak against God in all the Jewish places of worship. In my fight against them, I kept going after them even into cities in other countries.

12"When I was going to Damascus to do this, I had the right and the power from the head religious leaders to make it hard for the followers. 13I was on the road at noon. King Agrippa, I saw a light from heaven brighter than the sun. It was shining around me and the men with me. 14We all fell to the ground. Then I heard a voice speaking to me in the Jewish language, 'Saul, Saul, why are you working so hard against Me? You hurt yourself by trying to hurt Me.' 15I said, 'Who are You, Lord?' And He said, 'I am Jesus, the One you are working against. 16Get up. Stand on your feet. I have chosen you to work for Me. You will tell what you have seen and you will say what I want you to say. This is the reason I have allowed you to see Me. [17]I will keep you safe from the Jews and from the people who are not Jews. I am sending you to these people. [18]You are to open their eyes. You are to turn them from darkness to light. You are to turn them from the power of Satan to the power of God. In this way, they may have their sins forgiven. They may have what is given to them, along with all those who are set apart for God by having faith in Me.'

[19]"King Agrippa, I obeyed what I saw from heaven. [20]First I told what I saw to those in Damascus and then in Jerusalem. I told it through all the country of Judea. I even preached to the people who are not Jews that they should be sorry for their sins and turn from them to God. I told them they should do things to show they are sorry for their sins.

[21]"That is why the Jews took hold of me in the house of God and tried to kill me. [22]God has helped me. To this day I have told these things to the people who are well-known and to those not known. I have told only what the early preachers and Moses said would happen. [23]It was that Christ must suffer and be the first to rise from the dead. He would give light to the Jews and to the other nations."

[24]As Paul was speaking for himself, Festus cried out in a loud voice, "Paul, you are crazy! All your learning keeps you from thinking right!" [25]Paul said, "Most respected Festus, I am not crazy. I am speaking the truth! [26]The king knows about all this. I am free to speak to him in plain words. Nothing I have said is new to him. These things happened where everyone saw them. [27]King Agrippa, do you believe the writings of the early preachers? I know that you believe them."

[28]Then Agrippa said to Paul, "In this short time you have almost proven to me that I should become a Christian!" [29]Paul said, "My prayer to God is that you and all who hear me today would be a Christian as I am, only not have these chains!" [30]King Agrippa and Festus and Bernice and those who sat with them got up. [31]As they left the courtroom, they said to each other, "This man has done nothing for which he should be kept in prison or be put to death." [32]Agrippa told Festus, "This man could go free if he had not asked to be sent to Caesar."

Paul Is Sent To Rome

27 It was decided that we should go to the country of Italy by ship. Then they put Paul and some other men in chains. Julius, a captain of Caesar's army, was to watch them. [2]We went on a ship that was from the city of Adramyttian. It was going to stop at the towns along the seashore of Asia. Aristarchus was with us. He was a man from the city of Thessalonica in the country of Macedonia. [3]The next day we stopped in the city of Sidon. Julius was kind to Paul. He let him visit friends who cared for him.

[4]After leaving Sidon we were blown by the wind along the south side of the island of Cyprus. The wind was against us. [5]We crossed the sea along the countries of Cilicia and Pamphylia and got to the city of Myra in the country of Lycia. [6]The captain found a ship from the city of Alexandria that was going to the country of Italy. He put us on it. [7]For many days the ship did not move fast. It was hard to get to the city of Cnidus. The wind would not let us go on. So we went along the south shore of the island of Crete and passed the end of the island called Salome. [8]The wind was against us, and we did not sail very fast. Then we came to a place called Fair Havens. It was near the city of Lasea.

[9]Much time had been lost. To keep going that late in the year would

mean danger. Paul spoke with strong words, 10"Sirs, it looks to me as if this ship and its freight will be lost. We are in danger of being lost also."

11The captain of the soldiers listened to what the captain of the ship said and not to what Paul said. 12It was not a good place to spend the winter. Most of those on the ship wanted to go on and try to get to Phoenix. Crete was a good place to tie up the ship. They wanted to spend the winter there. 13When a south wind started to blow, they thought their plan was right. They pulled up the anchor and went close to the shore of Crete.

14Later a bad wind storm came down from the land. It was called a northeaster. 15The ship was stopped by the wind. After awhile we gave up and let it go with the wind. 16We went behind a small island called Claudia. It was hard work but we were able to make the ship's boat safe. 17They pulled it up and tied ropes around it and the ship. They were afraid of going on the Syrtis sands. So they took the sail down and let the ship go with the wind.

18The storm was so bad the high waves were beating against the ship. The next day the men threw some of the freight over into the sea. 19On the third day, with their own hands, they threw part of the sails and ropes into the sea. 20We did not see the sun or stars for many days. A very bad storm kept beating against us. We lost all hope of being saved.

Paul Shows His Faith

21No one had eaten for a long time. Then Paul stood up and said to them, "Men, you should have listened to me and not left Crete. You would not have had this trouble and loss. 22But now I want you to take hope. No one will lose his life. Only the ship will be lost. 23I belong to God and I work for Him. Last night an angel of God stood by me 24and said, 'Do not be afraid, Paul. You must stand in front of Caesar. God has given you the lives of all the men on this ship.' 25So take hope, men. I believe my God will do what He has told me. 26But the ship will be lost on some island."

27It was now the fourteenth night. We were going with the wind on the Adriatic Sea. At midnight the sailors thought land was near. 28They let down the lead weight and found the water was not very deep. After they had gone a little farther, they found there was not as much water. 29They were afraid we might be thrown against the rocks on the shore. So they put out four anchors from the back of the ship. Then they waited for morning to come.

30The sailors were thinking of leaving the ship. They let down a boat as if they were going to put out anchors from the front of the ship. 31But Paul said to the captain and the soldiers, "These men must stay on the ship or you cannot be safe!" 32Then the soldiers cut the ropes and let the boat fall into the sea.

33Just before the light of day came, Paul told all of them to eat. He said, "Today is the fourteenth day you have not eaten. 34You must eat. It will give you strength. Not one of you will lose a hair from your head."

35After he said this, he took some bread. He gave thanks to God in front of them all. He broke it in pieces and started to eat. 36They all were comforted. Each one ate some food. 37All together there were 276 of us on the ship. 38After they had eaten, they threw the wheat into the sea so the ship would not be as heavy.

39In the morning they could not see what land they were near. Later they could see a river. Near its mouth there was a shore of sand. They planned to run the ship onto the sand if they could. 40The anchors were cut loose and left in the sea. Then they took the ropes off that were holding the rudder. When they put up the sail, the wind took the ship toward shore. [41]But the ship hit a place where the water was low. It was made from where two seas meet. The front of the ship did not move but the back part broke in pieces by the high waves.

[42]The soldiers planned to kill the men in chains. They were afraid they would swim to shore and get away, [43]but the captain wanted to save Paul. He kept them from their plan. Calling out to those who could swim, he told them to jump into the sea and swim to shore. [44]The others should use wood or anything from the ship. In this way, they all got to shore without getting hurt.

The Powerful Work Of Paul

28 After we were safe on the island, we knew that it was Malta. [2]The people on the island were very kind to us. It was raining and cold. They made a fire so we could get warm. [3]Paul had gathered some wood. As he laid it on the fire, a snake came out because of the heat. It held fast to Paul's hand. [4]When the people of the island saw the snake holding to his hand, they said to each other, "This man is a killer. He was saved from the sea and yet it is not right for him to live." [5]Paul shook off the snake into the fire. He was not hurt in any way. [6]The people waited. They thought his hand would get large and he would fall over dead. After watching for a long time, they saw nothing happen to him. Then they changed their minds and said that Paul was a god.

The Father Of Publius Is Healed

[7]Publius was the head man of the island. He owned land around there. For three days he took us in and gave us everything we needed. [8]The father of Publius was sick with a stomach sickness. Paul went to see him. He prayed and laid his hands on him and the man was healed. [9]Because of this,

other people of the island who were sick came to Paul and were healed. [10]They had great respect for us. When we got into a ship to leave, they gave us everything we needed.

[11]We had stayed on the island three months. Then we left on a ship that had stayed there during the winter. It was from the city of Alexandria. This ship was called the Twin Brothers. [12]From there we went by ship around to the city of Rhegium. After a day a south wind started to blow. On the second day we came to the city of Puteoli. [14]We found some Christians there, and they asked us to stay with them. We were there seven days and then went on to the city of Rome. [15]When the Christians heard of our coming, they came to meet us. They came as far as the town of Appius and to a place to stay called the Three Stores. When Paul saw them, he thanked God and took courage.

Paul Tells Why And How He Has Come

[16]When we got to Rome, Paul was allowed to live where he wanted to. But a soldier was always by his side to watch him. [17]Three days later Paul asked the leaders of the Jews to come to him. When they had gathered together, he said, "Brothers, I have done nothing against our people or the way our early fathers lived. And yet, I was tied with chains in Jerusalem and handed over to the Romans. [18]I was put on trial, but they found no reason to put me to death. They would have let me go free. [19]But the Jews did not like this. So I had to ask to be sent to Caesar. It was not because I had anything against my people. [20]The reason I have asked you to come is to tell you this. It is because of the hope of the Jewish nation that I am tied in these chains."

[21]They said to Paul, "We have had no letters from Judea about you. No Jew who has come here has ever said

anything bad about you. 22We would like to hear from you what you believe. As for this new religion, all we know is that everyone is talking against it."

23They planned to meet him on a certain day. Many people came to the place where he stayed. He preached to them about the holy nation of God. He tried to get them to put their trust in Jesus Christ by preaching from the Law of Moses and from the writings of the early preachers. From morning until night he spoke to them. 24Some of them believed his teaching. Others did not believe.

25As they left, they did not agree with each other. Then Paul said, "The Holy Spirit spoke the truth to your early fathers through the early preacher Isaiah. 26He said, 'Go to these people and say, "You will hear and never understand, you will look and never see, 27because these people have hearts that have become fat. They do not hear well with their ears. They have closed their eyes so their eyes do not see and their ears do not hear and their minds do not understand and they do not turn to Me and let Me heal them." ' (Isaiah 6:9-10)

28"I want you to know that the Good News of God of knowing how to be saved from the punishment of sin has been sent to the people who are not Jews. And they will listen to it!" 29*After he had said these things, the Jews went away and argued with each other.

30Paul paid money to live in a house by himself for two years. He was happy for all who came to see him. 31He kept on preaching about the holy nation of God. He taught about the Lord Jesus Christ without fear. No one stopped him.

ROMANS

1 This letter is from Paul. I am a servant owned by Jesus Christ and a missionary chosen by God to preach His Good News. 2The Good News was promised long ago by God's early preachers in His Holy Writings. 3It tells of His Son, our Lord Jesus Christ, Who was born as a person in the flesh through the family of King David. 4The Holy Spirit proved by a powerful act that Jesus our Lord is the Son of God because He was raised from the dead. 5Jesus has given us His loving-favor and has made us His missionaries. We are to preach to the people of all nations that they should obey Him and put their trust in Him. 6You have been chosen to belong to Jesus Christ also. 7So I write to all of you in the city of Rome. God loves you and has chosen you to be set apart for Himself. May God our Father and the Lord Jesus Christ give you His loving-favor and peace.

Prayer Of Thanks

8First of all, I keep thanking my God, through Jesus Christ, for all of you. This is because the whole world knows of your faith in Christ. 9God knows how I work for Him. He knows how I preach with all my heart the Good News about His Son. He knows how I always pray for you. 10I pray that I might be able to visit you, if God wants me to. 11I want to see you so I can share some special gift of the Holy Spirit with you. It will make you strong. 12Both of us need help. I can help make your faith strong and you can do the same for me. We need each other.

Sinful Man

13Christian brothers, many times I have wanted to visit you. Something has kept me from going until now. I have wanted to lead some of you to Christ also, as I have done in other places where they did not know God. 14I must help the people who have had a chance to hear the Good News and those who have not. I must help those with much learning and those who have never learned from books. 15So I want to preach the Good News to you who live in Rome also.

16I am not ashamed of the Good News. It is the power of God. It is the way He saves men from the punishment of their sins if they put their trust in Him. It is for the Jew first and for all other people also. 17The Good News tells us we are made right with God by faith in Him. Then, by faith we live that new life through Him. The Holy Writings say, "A man right with God lives by faith." (Habakkuk 2:4)

The Sinful World

18We see the anger of God coming down from heaven against all the sins of men. These sinful men keep the truth from being known. 19Men know about God. He has made it plain to them. 20Men cannot say they do not know about God. From the beginning of the world, men could see what God is like through the things He has made. This shows His power that lasts forever. It shows that He is God. 21They did know God, but they did not honor Him as God. They were not thankful to Him and thought only of foolish things. Their foolish minds became dark. 22They said that they were wise, but they showed how foolish they were. 23They gave honor to false gods that looked like people who can die and to birds and animals and snakes. This honor belongs to God Who can never die.

24So God let them follow the desires of their sinful hearts. They did sinful things among themselves with their bodies. 25They traded the truth of God for a lie. They worshiped and cared for what God made instead of worshiping the God Who made it. He is the One Who is to receive honor and thanks forever. Let it be so.

26Because of this, God let them follow their sinful desires which lead to shame. Women used their bodies in ways God had not planned. 27In the same way, men left the right use of women's bodies. They did sex sins with other men. They received for themselves the punishment that was coming to them for their sin.

28Because they would not keep God in their thoughts anymore, He gave them up. Their minds were sinful and they wanted only to do things they should not do. 29They are full of everything that is sinful and want things that belong to others. They hate people and are jealous. They kill other people. They fight and lie. They do not like other people and talk against them. 30They talk about people, and they hate God. They are filled with pride and tell of all the good they do. They think of new ways to sin. They do not obey their parents. 31They are not able to understand. They do not do what they say they will do. They have no love and no loving-pity. 32They know God has said that all who do such things should die. But they keep on doing these things and are happy when others do them also.

All Men Are Sinners

2 So you can say nothing because you are guilty when you say someone else is guilty. While you say someone is guilty, you are doing the same things he does. ²We know that God will say those who do such things are guilty. ³Do you think God will punish others for doing wrong and let you keep sinning? ⁴Do you forget about His loving-kindness to you? Do you forget how long He is waiting for you? You know that God is kind. He is trying to get you to be sorry for your sins and turn from them. ⁵Because you are not sorry for your sins and will not turn from them, you will be punished even more on the day of God's anger. God will be right in saying you are guilty. ⁶He will give to every man what he should get for the things he has done. ⁷Those who keep on doing good and are looking for His greatness and honor will receive life that lasts forever. ⁸Those who love only themselves and do not obey the truth, but do what is wrong, will be punished by God. His anger will be on them. ⁹Every Jew and every person who is not a Jew who sins will suffer and have great sorrow. ¹⁰But God will give His greatness and honor and peace to all those who obey the truth. Both Jews and those who are not Jews will receive this. ¹¹God does not show favor to one man more than to another.

God Does What Is Right To All Men

¹²Those who have sinned without having the Law will be lost without the Law being used. Those who have the Law and have sinned will be told they are guilty by the Law. ¹³Just to hear the Law does not make a man right with God. The man right with God is the one who obeys the Law. ¹⁴The people who are not Jews do not have the Law. When they do what the Law tells them to do, even if they do not have the Law, it shows they know what they should do. ¹⁵They show that what the Law wants them to do is written in their hearts. Their own hearts tell them if they are guilty. ¹⁶There will be a day when God will say who is guilty because He knows the secret thoughts of men. He will do this through Jesus Christ. This is part of the Good News I preach.

¹⁷You are a Jew and think you are safe because of the Law. You tell others about how you know God. ¹⁸You know what He wants you to do. You understand how the Law works. You know right from wrong. ¹⁹You think you can lead a blind man. You think you can give light to those in darkness. ²⁰You think you can teach foolish people and children about God. You have in the Law the plan of truth and wisdom. ²¹You teach others. Why do you not teach yourselves? You tell others not to steal. Do you steal? ²²You say that no one should do sex sins. Do you do sex sins? You hate false gods. Do you rob the houses where they are kept? ²³You are proud of the Law. Do you take honor away from God when you do not obey the Law? ²⁴The Holy Writings say, "God's name is hated by the people who are not Jews because of you." (Isaiah 52:5)

²⁵Going through the religious act of becoming a Jew is worth something if you obey the Law. If you do not obey the Law, it is worth nothing to you. ²⁶If a person who is not a Jew, but has not gone through the act of becoming a Jew, and obeys the Law, God will think of him as a Jew. ²⁷You Jews have the Law but do not obey it. You have gone through the religious act also. At the same time those who are not Jews obey the Law even if they have not gone through the

religious act of becoming a Jew. In this way, these people show you are guilty. ²⁸A man is not a Jew just because he goes through the religious act of becoming a Jew. ²⁹The true Jew is one whose heart is right with God. The religious act of becoming a Jew must be done in the heart. That is the work of the Holy Spirit. The Law does not do that kind of work. The true Jew gets his thanks from God, not from men.

Jews Are Sinners Also

3 Do the Jews have anything that those who are not Jews do not have? What good does it do to go through the religious act of becoming a Jew? ²Yes, the Jews have much more in every way. First of all, God gave the Jews His Law. ³If some of them were not faithful, does it mean that God will not be faithful? ⁴No, not at all! God is always true even if every man lies. The Holy Writings say, "Speak the truth and you will not be proven guilty." (Psalm 51:4)

⁵If our sins show how right God is, what can we say? Is it wrong for God to punish us for it? (I am speaking as men do.) ⁶No, not at all! If it were wrong for God to punish us, how could He say what was right from wrong with the world? ⁷If my lies honor God by showing how true He is, why am I still being punished as a sinner? ⁸Why not say, "Let us sin that good will come from it." (Some people have said I talk like this!) They will be punished as they should be.

The Whole World Is Guilty Of Sin

⁹What about it then? Are we Jews better than the people who are not Jews? Not at all! I have already said that Jews and the people who are not Jews are all sinners. ¹⁰The Holy Writings say, "There is not one person who is right with God. No, not even one! ¹¹There is not one who

understands. There is not one who tries to find God." (Psalm 14:2) ¹²Everyone has turned away from God. They have all done wrong. Not one of them does what is good. No, not even one! ¹³Their mouth is like an open grave. They tell lies with their tongues. (Psalm 5:9; 140:3) Whatever they say is like the poison of snakes. ¹⁴Their mouths speak bad things against God. They say bad things about other people. (Psalm 10:7) ¹⁵They are quick to hurt and kill people. ¹⁶Wherever they go, they destroy and make people suffer. ¹⁷They know nothing about peace. (Isaiah 59:7-8) ¹⁸They do not honor God with love and fear." (Psalm 36:1)

¹⁹Now we know that the Law speaks to those who live under the Law. No one can say that he does not know what sin is. Yes, every person in the world stands guilty before God. ²⁰No person will be made right with God by doing what the Law says. The Law shows us how sinful we are.

²¹But now God has made another way to make men right with Himself. It is not by the Law. The Law and the early preachers tell about it. ²²Men become right with God by putting their trust in Jesus Christ. God will accept men if they come this way. All men are the same to God. ²³For all men have sinned and have missed the shining greatness of God. ²⁴Anyone can be made right with God by the free gift of His loving-favor. It is Jesus Christ Who bought them with His blood and made them free from their sins. ²⁵God gave Jesus Christ to the world. Men's sins can be forgiven through the blood of Christ when they put their trust in Him. God gave His Son Jesus Christ to show how right He is. Before this, God did not look on the sins that were done. ²⁶But now God proves that He is right in saving men from sin. He shows that He is the One Who has no sin. God makes anyone right with Himself

who puts his trust in Jesus.

27What then do we have to be proud of? Nothing at all! Why? Is it because men obey the Law? No! It is because men put their trust in Christ. 28This is what we have come to know. A man is made right with God by putting his trust in Christ. It is not by his doing what the Law says. 29Is God the God of the Jews only? Is He not the God of the people who are not Jews also? He is for sure. 30He is one God. He will make Jews and the people who are not Jews right with Himself if they put their trust in Christ. 31Does this mean that we do away with the Law when we put our trust in Christ? No, not at all. It means we know the Law is important.

Abraham Was Saved From Sin By His Trust In God

4 What about Abraham, our early father? What did he learn? 2If Abraham was made right with God by what he did, he would have had something to be proud of. But he could not be proud before God. 3The Holy Writings say, "Abraham put his trust in God and that made him right with God." (Genesis 15:6) 4If a man works, his pay is not a gift. It is something he has earned. 5If a man has not worked to be saved, but has put his trust in God Who saves men from the punishment of their sins, that man is made right with God because of his trust in God. 6David tells of this. He spoke of how happy the man is who puts his trust in God without working to be saved from the punishment of sin. 7"Those people are happy whose sinful acts are forgiven and whose sins are covered. 8Those people are happy whose sins the Lord will not remember." (Psalm 32:1-2)

9Is this happiness given to the Jews only? Or is it given also to the people who are not Jews? We say again,

"Abraham put his trust in God and that made him right with God." (Genesis 15:6) 10When did this happen? Was it before or after Abraham went through the religious act of becoming a Jew? It was before. 11He went through the religious act after he had put his trust in God. That religious act proved that his trust in God made him right with God even before he went through the religious act of becoming a Jew. In that way, it made him the early father of all those who believe. It showed that those who did not go through the religious act of becoming a Jew could be right with God. 12He is also the early father of all those who have gone through the religious act of becoming a Jew. It is not because they went through the act. It is because they put their trust in God the same as Abraham did before he went through the religious act of becoming a Jew. 13God promised to give the world to him and to all his family after him. He did not make this promise because Abraham obeyed the Law. He promised to give the world to Abraham because he put his trust in God. This made him right with God. 14If those who obey the Law are to get the world, then a person putting his trust in God means nothing. God's promise to Abraham would be worth nothing. 15God's anger comes on a man when he does not obey the Law. But if there were no Law, then no one could break it.

16So God's promise is given to us because we put our trust in Him. We can be sure of it. It is because of His loving-favor to us. It is for all the family of Abraham. It is for those who obey the Law. It is for those who put their trust in God as Abraham did. In this way, he is the father of all Christians. 17The Holy Writings say, "I have made you a father of many nations." This promise is good because of Who God is. He makes the dead live again. He speaks, and something is made out of nothing. [18]Abraham believed he would be the father of many nations. He had no reason to hope for this, but he had been told, "Your children will become many nations." (Genesis 15:5) [19]Abraham was about one hundred years old. His body was about dead, but his faith in God was not weak when he thought of his body. His faith was not weak when he thought of his wife Sarah being past the age of having children. [20]Abraham did not doubt God's promise. His faith in God was strong, and he gave thanks to God. [21]He was sure God was able to do what He had promised. [22]Abraham put his trust in God and was made right with Him. [23]The words, "He was made right with God," were not for Abraham only. [24]They were for us also. God will make us right with Himself the same way He did Abraham, if we put our trust in God Who raised Jesus our Lord from the dead. [25]Jesus died for our sins. He was raised from the dead to make us right with God.

The Joy Of Being Right With God

5 Now that we have been made right with God by putting our trust in Him, we have peace with Him. It is because of what our Lord Jesus Christ did for us. [2]By putting our trust in God, He has given us His loving-favor and has received us. We are happy for the hope we have of sharing the shining greatness of God. [3]We are glad for our troubles also. We know that troubles help us learn not to give up. [4]When we have learned not to give up, it shows we have stood the test. When we have stood the test, it gives us hope. [5]Hope never makes us ashamed because the love of God has come into our hearts through the Holy Spirit Who was given to us.

[6]We were weak and could not help ourselves. Then Christ came at the right time and gave His life for all sinners. [7]No one is willing to die for another person, but for a good man someone might be willing to die. [8]But God showed His love to us. While we were still sinners, Christ died for us. [9]Now that we have been saved from the punishment of sin by the blood of Christ, He will save us from God's anger also. [10]We hated God. But we were saved from the punishment of sin by the death of Christ. He has brought us back to God and we will be saved by His life. [11]Not only that, we give thanks to God through our Lord Jesus Christ. Through Him we have been brought back to God.

Adam And Christ

[12]This is what happened: Sin came into the world by one man, Adam. Sin brought death with it. Death spread to all men because all have sinned. [13]Sin was in the world before the Law was given. But sin is not held against a person when there is no Law. [14]And yet death had power over men from the time of Adam until the time of Moses. Even the power of death was over those who had not sinned in the same way Adam sinned. Adam was like the One Who was to come.

[15]God's free gift is not like the sin of Adam. Many people died because of the sin of this one man, Adam. But the loving-favor of God came to many people also. This gift came also by one Man Jesus Christ, God's Son. [16]The free gift of God is not like Adam's sin. God told Adam he was guilty because of his sin and through this one came sin and guilt. But the free gift makes men right with God. Through One, Christ, men's sins are forgiven. [17]The power of death was over all men because of the sin of one man, Adam. But many people will receive His loving-favor and the gift of being made right with God. They will have power in life by Jesus Christ.

[18]Through Adam's sin, death and hell came to all men. But another

Man, Christ, by His right act makes men free and gives them life. ¹⁹Adam did not obey God, and many people become sinners through him. Christ obeyed God and makes many people right with Himself.

God's Loving-favor Is Greater Than The Jewish Law

²⁰Sin spread when the Law was given. But where sin spread, God's loving-favor spread all the more. ²¹Sin had power that ended in death. Now, God's loving-favor has power to make men right with Himself. It gives life that lasts forever. Our Lord Jesus Christ did this for us.

Being Right With God

6 What does this mean? Are we to keep on sinning so that God will give us more of His loving-favor? ²No, not at all! We are dead to sin. How then can we keep on living in sin? ³All of us were baptized to show we belong to Christ. We were baptized first of all to show His death. ⁴We were buried in baptism as Christ was buried in death. As Christ was raised from the dead by the great power of God, so we will have new life also. ⁵If we have become one with Christ in His death, we will be one with Him in being raised from the dead to new life.

⁶We know that our old life, our old sinful self, was nailed to the cross with Christ. And so the power of sin that held us was destroyed. Sin is no longer our boss. ⁷When a man is dead, he is free from the power of sin. ⁸And if we have died with Christ, we believe we will live with Him also. ⁹We know that Christ was raised from the dead. He will never die again. Death has no more power over Him. ¹⁰He died once but now lives. He died to break the power of sin, and the life He now lives is for God. ¹¹You must do the same thing! Think of yourselves as dead to the power of sin. But now you have new life because of Jesus Christ our Lord. You are living this new life for God.

¹²So do not let sin have power over your body here on earth. You must not obey the body and let it do what it wants to do. ¹³Do not give any part of your body for sinful use. Instead, give yourself to God as a living person who has been raised from the dead. Give every part of your body to God to do what is right. ¹⁴Sin must not have power over you. You are not living by the Law. You have life because of God's loving-favor.

¹⁵What are we to do then? Are we to sin because we have God's loving-favor and are not living by the Law? No, not at all! ¹⁶Do you not know that when you give yourself as a servant to be owned by someone, that one becomes your owner? If you give yourself to sin, the end is death. If you give yourself to God, the end is being right with Him. ¹⁷At one time you were held by the power of sin. But now you obey with all your heart the teaching that was given to you. Thank God for this! ¹⁸You were made free from the power of sin. Being right with God has power over you now. ¹⁹I speak with words easy to understand because your human thinking is weak. At one time you gave yourselves over to the power of sin. You kept on sinning all the more. Now give yourselves over to being right with God. Set yourself apart for God-like living and to do His work.

²⁰When sin had power over your life, you were not right with God. ²¹What good did you get from the things you are ashamed of now? Those things bring death. ²²But now you are free from the power of sin. You have become a servant for God. Your life is set apart for God-like living. The end is life that lasts forever. ²³You get what is coming to you when you sin. It is death! But God's free gift is life that lasts forever. It is given to us by our Lord Jesus Christ.

The Law Shows What Sin Is

7 Christian brothers, I am sure you understand what I am going to say. You know all about the Law. The Law has power over a man as long as he lives. ²A married woman is joined by law to her husband as long as he lives. But if he dies, she is free from the law that joined her to him. ³If she marries another man while her husband is still alive, she is sinning by not being faithful in marriage. If her husband dies, she is free from the law that joined her to him. After that she can marry someone else. She does not sin if she marries another man.

⁴My Christian brothers, that is the way it is with you. You were under the power of the Law. But now you are dead to it because you are joined to another. You are joined to Christ Who was raised from the dead. This is so we may be what God wants us to be. Our lives are to give fruit for Him. ⁵When we lived to please our bodies, those sinful desires were pulling at us all the time. We always wanted to do what the Law said not to do. Living that kind of life brings death, ⁶but now we are free from the Law. We are dead to sin that once held us in its power. No longer do we follow the Law which is the old way. We now follow the new way, the way of the Spirit.

The Law And Sin

⁷Then what are we saying? Is the Law sinful? No, not at all! But it was the Law that showed me what sin is. I did not know it was sin to follow wrong desires, but the Law said, "You must not follow wrong desires." ⁸The Law made me know how much I was sinning. It showed me how I had a desire for all kinds of things. For without the Law, sin is dead. ⁹I was once alive. That was when I did not know what the Law said I had to do. Then I found that I had broken the Law. I knew I was a sinner. Death was mine because of the Law. ¹⁰The Law was supposed to give me new life. Instead, it gave me death. ¹¹Sin found a way to trap me by working through the Law. Then sin killed me by using the Law.

¹²The Law is holy. Each one of the Laws is holy and right and good. ¹³Then does it mean that the Law, which is good, brought death to me? No, not at all! It was sin that did it. Sin brought death to me by the Law that is good. In that way, sin was shown to be what it is. So because of the Law, sin becomes much more sinful.

The Two Kinds Of Men

¹⁴We know that the Law is right and good, but I am a person who does what is wrong and bad. I am not my own boss. Sin is my boss. ¹⁵I do not understand myself. I want to do what is right but I do not do it. Instead, I do the very thing I hate. ¹⁶When I do the thing I do not want to do, it shows me that the Law is right and good. ¹⁷So I am not doing it. Sin living in me is doing it. ¹⁸I know there is nothing good in me, that is, in my flesh. For I want to do good but I do not. ¹⁹I do not do the good I want to do. Instead, I am always doing the sinful things I do not want to do. ²⁰If I am always doing the very thing I do not want to do, it means I am no longer the one who does it. It is sin that lives in me. ²¹This has become my way of life: When I want to do what is right, I always do what is wrong. ²²My mind and heart agree with the Law of God. ²³But there is a different law at work deep inside of me that fights with my mind. This law of sin holds me in its power because sin is still in me. ²⁴There is no happiness in me! Who can set me free from my sinful old self? ²⁵God's Law has power over my mind, but sin still has power over my sinful old self. I thank God I can be free through Jesus Christ our Lord!

The Holy Spirit Makes Us Free

8 Now, because of this, those who belong to Christ will not suffer the punishment of sin. ²The power of the Holy Spirit has made me free from the power of sin and death. This power is mine because I belong to Christ Jesus. ³The Law could not make me free from the power of sin and death. It was weak because it had to work with weak human beings. But God sent His own Son. He came to earth in a body of flesh which could be tempted to sin as we in our bodies can be. He gave Himself to take away sin. By doing that, He took away the power sin had over us. ⁴In that way, Jesus did for us what the Law said had to be done. We do not do what our sinful old selves tell us to do anymore. Now we do what the Holy Spirit wants us to do. ⁵Those who let their sinful old selves tell them what to do live under that power of their sinful old selves. But those who let the Holy Spirit tell them what to do are under His power. ⁶If your sinful old self is the boss over your mind, it leads to death. But if the Holy Spirit is the boss over your mind, it leads to life and peace. ⁷The mind that thinks only of ways to please the sinful old self is fighting against God. It is not able to obey God's Laws. It never can. ⁸Those who do what their sinful old selves want to do cannot please God.

⁹But you are not doing what your sinful old selves want you to do. You are doing what the Holy Spirit tells you to do, if you have God's Spirit living in you. No one belongs to Christ if he does not have Christ's Spirit in him. ¹⁰If Christ is in you, your spirit lives because you are right with God, and yet your body is dead because of sin. ¹¹The Holy Spirit raised Jesus from the dead. If the same Holy Spirit lives in you, He will give life to your bodies in the same way.

¹²So then, Christian brothers, we are not to do what our sinful old selves want us to do. ¹³If you do what your sinful old selves want you to do, you will die in sin. But if, through the power of the Holy Spirit, you destroy those actions to which the body can be led, you will have life. ¹⁴All those who are led by the Holy Spirit are sons of God. ¹⁵You should not act like people who are owned by someone. They are always afraid. Instead, the Holy Spirit makes us His sons, and we can call to Him, "My Father." ¹⁶For the Holy Spirit speaks to us and tells our spirit that we are children of God. ¹⁷If we are children of God, we will receive everything He has promised us. We will share with Christ all the things God has given to Him. But we must share His suffering if we are to share His shining greatness.

Another Picture Of The Future

¹⁸I am sure that our suffering now cannot be compared to the shining greatness that He is going to give us. ¹⁹Everything that has been made in the world is waiting for the day when God will make His sons known. ²⁰Everything that has been made in the world is weak. It is not that the world wanted it to be that way. God allowed it to be that way. Yet there is hope. ²¹Everything that has been made in the world will be set free from the power that can destroy. These will become free just as the children of God become free. ²²We know that everything on the earth cries out with pain the same as a woman giving birth to a child. ²³We also cry inside ourselves, even we who have received the Holy Spirit. The Holy Spirit is the first of God's gifts to us. We are waiting to become His complete sons when our bodies are made free. ²⁴We were saved with this hope ahead of us. Now hope means we are waiting for something we do not have. How can a man

hope for something he already has?
[25]But if we hope for something we do
not yet see, we must learn how to
wait for it.

[26]In the same way, the Holy Spirit
helps us where we are weak. We do
not know how to pray or what we
should pray for, but the Holy Spirit
prays to God for us with sounds that
cannot be put into words. [27]God
knows the hearts of men. He knows
what the Holy Spirit is thinking. The
Holy Spirit prays for those who
belong to Christ the way God wants
Him to pray.

God Gives Us His Greatness

[28]We know that God makes all
things work together for the good of
those who love Him and are chosen
to be a part of His plan. [29]God knew
from the beginning who would put
their trust in Him. So He chose them
and made them to be like His Son.
Christ was first and all those who
belong to God are His brothers. [30]He
called to Himself also those He chose.
Those He called, He made right with
Himself. Then He shared His shining
greatness with those He made right
with Himself.

[31]What can we say about all these
things? Since God is for us, who can
be against us? [32]God did not keep His
own Son for Himself but gave Him
for us all. Then with His Son, will He
not give us all things? [33]Who can say
anything against the people God has
chosen? It is God Who says they are
right with Himself. [34]Who then can
say we are guilty? It was Christ Jesus
Who died. He was raised from the
dead. He is on the right side of God
praying to Him for us. [35]Who can
keep us away from the love of
Christ? Can trouble or problems?
Can suffering wrong from others or
no food? Can it be because of no
clothes or because of danger or war?
[36]The Holy Writings say, "Because of
belonging to Jesus, we are in danger
of being killed all day long. We are

thought of as sheep that are ready to
be killed." (Psalm 44:22) [37]But we
have power over all these things
through Jesus Who loves us so much.
[38]For I know that nothing can keep us
from the love of God. Death cannot!
Life cannot! Angels cannot! Leaders
cannot! Any other power cannot!
Hard things now or in the future
cannot! [39]The world above or the
world below cannot! Any other
living thing cannot keep us away
from the love of God which is ours
through Christ Jesus our Lord.

The People God Chose For Himself

9 I am telling the truth because I
belong to Christ. The Holy
Spirit tells my heart that I am not
lying. [2]I have much sorrow. The pain
in my heart never leaves. [3]I could
even wish that I might be kept from
being with Christ if that would help
my people to be saved from the
punishment of sin. They are of my
own flesh and blood. [4]They are Jews
and are the people God chose for
Himself. He shared His shining
greatness with them and gave them
His Law and a way to worship. They
have His promises. [5]The early
preachers came from this family.
Christ Himself was born of flesh
from this family and He is over all
things. May God be honored and
thanked forever. Let it be so.

[6]I am not saying that God did not
keep His promises. Not all the Jews
are people God chose for Himself.
[7]Not all of Abraham's family are
children of God. God told Abraham,
"Only the family of Isaac will be
called your family." (Genesis 21:9-
12) [8]This means that children born to
Abraham are not all children of God.
Only those that are born because of
God's promise to Abraham are His
children. [9]This was the promise God
made: "About this time next year I
will come, and Sarah will have a
son." (Genesis 18:10) [10]Not only this,
but there was Rebecca also. Rebecca

gave birth to two sons at the same time. Both of them were sons of Isaac. ¹¹Even before the two sons were born, we see God's plan of choosing. God could choose whom He wanted. It could not be changed because of anything the older son tried to do about it. It was before either one had done anything good or bad. ¹²Rebecca was told, "The older son will work for the younger son." ¹³The Holy Writings say, "I loved Jacob, but hated Esau." (Malachi 1:2)

¹⁴What about it then? Can we say that God is not fair? No, not at all! ¹⁵God said to Moses, "I will have loving-kindness and loving-pity for anyone I want to." (Exodus 33:19) ¹⁶These good things from God are not given to someone because he wants them or works to get them. They are given because of His loving-kindness. ¹⁷The Holy Writings say to Pharaoh, "I made you leader for this reason: I used you to show My power. I used you to make My name known over all the world." (Exodus 9:16) ¹⁸So God has loving-kindness for those He wants to. He makes some have hard hearts if He wants to.

¹⁹But you will ask me, "Why does God blame men for what they do? Who can go against what God wants?" ²⁰Who are you to talk back to God? A pot being made from clay does not talk to the man making it and say, "Why did you make me like this?" ²¹The man making the pots has the right to use the clay as he wants to. He can make two pots from the same piece of clay. One can have an important use. The other one can be of little use. ²²It may be that God wants to show His power and His anger against sin. He waits a long time on some men who are ready to be destroyed. ²³God also wanted to show His shining greatness to those He has given His loving-kindness. He made them ready for His shining greatness from the beginning. ²⁴We are the ones He chose. He did not only choose Jews. He also chose some from among the people who are not Jews. ²⁵In the Book of Hosea He says, "Those who are not My people, I will call, 'My people.' Those who are not loved, I will call, 'My loved ones.' " (Hosea 2:23) ²⁶"And where it said, 'You are not my people,' they will be called sons of the living God." (Hosea 1:10) ²⁷Isaiah says this about the Jews, "Even if there are as many Jews as the sand by the sea, only a few of them will be saved from the punishment of sin. ²⁸For the Lord will do on earth what He says in His Word. He will work fast when He says what will happen here." (Isaiah 10:22-23) ²⁹Isaiah said also, "If God had not left some of the Jews, we would have all been destroyed like the people who lived in the cities of Sodom and Gomorrah." (Isaiah 1:9)

The Jews And The Good News

³⁰What are we to say about these things? The people who are not Jews were not made right with God by the Law. They were made right with God because they put their trust in Him. ³¹The Jews tried to be right with God by obeying the Law, but they did not become right with God. ³²Why? Because they did not put their trust in God. They tried to be right with God by working for it. They tripped over the most important Stone (Christ). ³³The Holy Writings say, "See! I put in Jerusalem a Stone that people will trip over. It is a Rock that will make them fall. But the person who puts his trust in the Rock (Christ) will not be put to shame." (Isaiah 28:16)

The Jews Have Tried To Make Their Own Way

10 Christian brothers, the desire of my heart and my prayer to God is that the Jews might be saved from the punishment of sin. ²I know about them. They have a strong desire for God, but they do not know what they should about Him. ³They have not known how God makes men right with Himself. Instead, they have tried to make their own way. They have not become right with God because they have not done what God said to do. ⁴For Christ has put an end to the Law, so everyone who has put his trust in Christ is made right with God.

⁵Moses writes that the man who obeys the Law has to live by it. ⁶But when a man puts his trust in Christ, he is made right with God. You do not need to ask yourself, "Who will go up to heaven to bring Christ down?" ⁷And you do not need to ask, "Who will go below and bring Christ up from the dead?" ⁸This is what it says, "The Good News is near you. It is in your mouth and in your heart." (Deuteronomy 30:14) This Good News tells about putting your trust in Christ. This is what we preach to you. ⁹If you say with your mouth that Jesus is Lord, and believe in your heart that God raised Him from the dead, you will be saved from the punishment of sin. ¹⁰When we believe in our hearts, we are made right with God. We tell with our mouth how we were saved from the punishment of sin. ¹¹The Holy Writings say, "No one who puts his trust in Christ will ever be put to shame." (Isaiah 28:16) ¹²There is no difference between the Jews and the people who are not Jews. They are all the same to the Lord. And He is Lord over all of them. He gives of His greatness to all who call on Him for help. ¹³For everyone who calls on the name of the Lord will be saved from the punishment of sin.

¹⁴But how can they call on Him if they have not put their trust in Him? And how can they put their trust in Him if they have not heard of Him? And how can they hear of Him unless someone tells them? ¹⁵And how can someone tell them if he is not sent? The Holy Writings say, "The feet of those who bring the Good News are

beautiful." (Isaiah 52:7)

¹⁶But they have not all listened to the Good News. Isaiah says, "Lord, who believed what we told them?" (Isaiah 53:1) ¹⁷So then, faith comes to us by hearing the Good News. And the Good News comes by someone preaching it. ¹⁸And so I ask, "Did they not hear?" For sure they did. The Holy Writings say, "Their voice was heard over all the earth. The Good News was told to the ends of the earth." (Psalm 19:4) ¹⁹Again I ask, "Did the Jews not understand?" First of all, Moses says, "I will make you jealous of those who are not a nation. I will make you angry with a foolish nation of people who do not understand." (Deuteronomy 32:21) ²⁰Isaiah says even stronger words, "I have been found by men who did not look for Me. I have shown Myself to those who were not asking for Me." (Isaiah 65:1) ²¹This is what God says about the Jews, "All day long I held out my hand to a people who would not obey Me and who worked against Me." (Isaiah 65:2)

God's Loving-kindness For The Jews

11 I ask then, "Has God put His people, the Jews, aside?" No, not at all! I myself am a Jew. Abraham was my early father. I am from the family group of Benjamin. ²God has not put His people aside. He chose them from the beginning. Do you know what the Holy Writings say about Elijah? Do you know what Elijah said to God against the Jews? ³He said, "Lord, they have killed Your early preachers. They have destroyed the places where You are worshiped. I am the only one left. They are trying to kill me." ⁴But what did God say to him? God said, "I still have 7,000 men. None of them have worshiped the false god Baal." ⁵It is the same now. A few of the Jews are being chosen because of God's loving-favor. ⁶If they are saved from the punishment of sin because of

God's loving-favor, it is nothing men have done to earn it. If men had earned it, then His loving-favor would not be a free gift. 7This is the way it was. Many Jews did not get what they were looking for. Only those God chose received it. The hearts of the others were made hard. They could not understand it. 8The Holy Writings say this about them, "God gave them hearts and minds that want to sleep. He gave them eyes that could not see. To this very day He gave them ears that could not hear." (Isaiah 29:10) 9David said, "Let their table of food become a trap to hold them. Let it be a hole into which they fall and will suffer. 10Let their eyes be closed so they cannot see. Keep their backs from being straight always because of their troubles." (Psalm 69:23)

11I ask then, "Did the Jews fall so they would be lost forever?" No, not at all! It means the people who are not Jews are able to be saved from the punishment of sin because the Jews sinned by not putting their trust in Christ. This made the Jews jealous of those who are not Jews. 12The world received good things from God because of the sin of the Jews. Because the Jews did not receive God's free gift, the people who are not Jews received good things from Him. Think how much more the world will receive when the Jews finish God's plan by putting their trust in Christ!

The People Who Are Not Jews Can Be Saved Too

13I am speaking to you people who are not Jews. As long as I am a missionary to you, I want you to know how important my job is. 14I do this so it will make my own people, the Jews, jealous. Then it may be that some will be saved from the punishment of sin. 15Because the Jews have been put aside, many other people in the world have been saved

from the punishment of sin. Think what it will be like when they are also gathered in. It will be like the dead coming back to life!

16If the first loaf is holy, all the bread is holy. If the root is holy, all the branches are holy.

17But some of the branches (who are the Jews) were broken off. You who are not Jews were put in the place where the branches had been broken off. Now you are sharing the rich root of the olive tree. 18Do not be proud. Do not think you are better than the branches that were broken off. If you are proud, remember that you do not hold the root. It is the root that holds you. 19You may say, "Branches were broken off to make room for me." 20It is true. They were broken off because they did not put their trust in Christ. And you are there only because of your faith. Do not be proud. Instead, be afraid. 21God did not keep the first branches (who are the Jews) on the tree. Then watch, or He will not keep you on the tree. 22We see how kind God is. It shows how hard He is also. He is hard on those who fall away. But He is kind to you if you keep on trusting Him. If you do not, He will cut you off. 23If the Jews would put their trust in Christ, God would put them back into the tree. He has power to do that. 24You people who are not Jews were cut off from a wild olive tree. Instead of being there, you were put into a garden olive tree which is not the right place for you to grow. It would be easy for God to put the Jews back onto their own olive tree because they are the branches that belong there.

God's Loving-kindness To All

25Christian brothers, I want you to understand this truth which is no longer a secret. It will keep you from thinking you are so wise. Some Jews have become hard until the right amount of people who are not Jews come to God. [26] Then all the Jews will be saved, as the Holy Writings say, "The One Who saves from the punishment of sin will come out of Jerusalem. He will turn the Jews from doing sinful things." (Isaiah 59:20-21) [27] "And this is My promise to them when I take away their sins." (Isaiah 27:9)

[28] The Jews are fighting against the Good News. Because they hate the Good News, it has helped you who are not Jews. But God still loves the Jews because He has chosen them and because of His promise to their early fathers. [29] God does not change His mind when He chooses men and gives them His gifts. [30] At one time you did not obey God. But when the Jews did not receive God's gift, you did. It was because they did not obey. [31] The Jews will not obey now. God's loving-kindness to you will some day turn them to Him. Then the Jews may have His loving-kindness also. [32] God has said that all men have broken His Law. But He will show loving-kindness on all of them.

[33] God's riches are so great! The things He knows and His wisdom are so deep! No one can understand His thoughts. No one can understand His ways. [34] The Holy Writings say, "Who knows the mind of the Lord? Who is able to tell Him what to do?" (Isaiah 40:13-14) [35] "Who has given first to God, that God should pay him back?" (Job 35:7; 41:11) [36] Everything comes from Him. His power keeps all things together. All things are made for Him. May He be honored forever. Let it be so.

Our Bodies Are To Be A Living Gift

12 Christian brothers, I ask you from my heart to give your bodies to God because of His loving-kindness to us. Let your bodies be a living and holy gift given to God. He is pleased with this kind of gift. This is the true worship that you should give Him. [2] Do not act like the sinful people of the world. Let God change your life. First of all, let Him give you a new mind. Then you will know what God wants you to do. And the things you do will be good and pleasing and perfect.

God's Church And The Gifts He Uses

[3] God has given me His loving-favor. This helps me write these things to you. I ask each one of you not to think more of himself than he should think. Instead, think in the right way toward yourself by the faith God has given you. [4] Our bodies are made up of many parts. None of these parts have the same use. [5] There are many people who belong to Christ. And yet, we are one body which is Christ's. We are all different but we depend on each other. [6] We all have different gifts that God has given to us by His loving-favor. We are to use them. If someone has the gift of preaching the Good News, he should preach. He should use the faith God has given him. [7] If someone has the gift of helping others, then he should help. If someone has the gift of teaching, he should teach. [8] If someone has the gift of speaking words of comfort and help, he should speak. If someone has the gift of sharing what he has, he should give from a willing heart. If someone has the gift of leading other people, he should lead them. If someone has the gift of showing kindness to others, he should be happy as he does it.

Ways Christians Can Help Other Christians

[9] Be sure your love is true love. Hate what is sinful. Hold on to whatever is good. [10] Love each other as Christian brothers. Show respect for each other. [11] Do not be lazy but always work hard. Work for the Lord with a heart full of love for Him. [12] Be happy in your hope. Do

not give up when trouble comes. Do not let anything stop you from praying. [13]Share what you have with Christian brothers who are in need. Give meals and a place to stay to those who need it. [14]Pray and give thanks for those who make trouble for you. Yes, pray for them instead of talking against them. [15]Be happy with those who are happy. Be sad with those who are sad. [16]Live in peace with each other. Do not act or think with pride. Be happy to be with poor people. Keep yourself from thinking you are so wise. [17]When someone does something bad to you, do not pay him back with something bad. Try to do what all men know is right and good. [18]As much as you can, live in peace with all men. [19]Christian brothers, never pay back someone for the bad he has done to you. Let the anger of God take care of the other person. The Holy Writings say, "I will pay back to them what they should get, says the Lord." (Deuteronomy 32:35) [20]"If the one who hates you is hungry, feed him. If he is thirsty, give him water. If you do that, you will be making him more ashamed of himself." (Proverbs 25:21-22) [21]Do not let sin have power over you. Let good have power over sin!

Obey The Leaders Of The Land

13 Every person must obey the leaders of the land. There is no power given but from God, and all leaders are allowed by God. [2]The person who does not obey the leaders of the land is working against what God has done. Anyone who does that will be punished.

[3]Those who do right do not have to be afraid of the leaders. Those who do wrong are afraid of them. Do you want to be free from fear of them? Then do what is right. You will be respected instead. [4]Leaders are God's servants to help you. If you do wrong, you should be afraid.

They have the power to punish you. They work for God. They do what God wants done to those who do wrong. [5]You must obey the leaders of the land, not only to keep from God's anger, but so your own heart will have peace. [6]It is right for you to pay taxes because the leaders of the land are servants for God who care for these things. [7]Pay taxes to whom taxes are to be paid. Be afraid of those you should fear. Respect those you should respect.

How A Christian Should Live With His Neighbor

[8]Do not owe anyone anything, but love each other. Whoever loves his neighbor has done what the Law says to do. [9]The Law says, "You must not do any sex sin. You must not kill another person. You must not steal. You must not tell a lie about another person. You must not want something someone else has." The Law also says that these and many other Laws are brought together in one Law, "You must love your neighbor as yourself." [10]Anyone who loves his neighbor will do no wrong to him. You keep the Law with love.

[11]There is another reason for doing what is right. You know what time it is. It is time for you to wake up from your sleep. The time when we will be taken up to be with Christ is not as far off as when we first put our trust in Him. [12]Night is almost gone. Day is almost here. We must stop doing the sinful things that are done in the dark. We must put on all the things God gives us to fight with for the day. [13]We must act all the time as if it were day. Keep away from wild parties and do not be drunk. Keep yourself free from sex sins and bad actions. Do not fight or be jealous. [14]Let every part of you belong to the Lord Jesus Christ. Do not allow your weak thoughts to lead you into sinful actions.

Help Weak Christians

14 If there is someone whose faith is weak, be kind and receive him. Do not argue about what he thinks. ²One man believes he may eat everything. Another man with weak faith eats only vegetables. ³The man who eats everything should not think he is better than the one who eats only vegetables. The man who eats only vegetables should not say the other man is wrong, because God has received him. ⁴Who are you to tell another person's servant if he is right or wrong? It is to his owner that he does good or bad. The Lord is able to help him.

⁵One man thinks one day is more important than another. Another man thinks every day is the same. Every man must be sure in his own mind. ⁶The man who worships on a special day does it to honor the Lord. The man who eats meat does it to honor the Lord. He gives thanks to God for what he eats. The other man does not eat meat. In this way, he honors the Lord. He gives thanks to God also.

⁷No one lives for himself alone. No one dies for himself alone. ⁸If we live, it is for the Lord. If we die, it is for the Lord. If we live or die, we belong to the Lord. ⁹Christ died and lived again. This is why He is the Lord of the living and of the dead. ¹⁰Why do you try to say your Christian brother is right or wrong? Why do you hate your Christian brother? We will all stand before God to be judged by Him. ¹¹The Holy Writings say, "As I live, says the Lord, every knee will get down before Me. And every tongue will say that I am God." ¹²Everyone of us will give an answer to God about himself.

Your Christian Brother

¹³So you should stop saying that you think other people are wrong. Instead, decide to live so that your Christian brother will not have a reason to trip or fall into sin because of you. ¹⁴Christ has made me know that everything in itself is clean. But if a person thinks something is not clean, then to him it is not clean. ¹⁵If your Christian brother is hurt because of some foods you eat, then you are no longer living by love. Do not destroy the man for whom Christ died by the food you eat. ¹⁶Do not let what is good for you be talked about as bad. ¹⁷For the holy nation of God is not food and drink. It is being right with God. It is peace and joy given by the Holy Spirit. ¹⁸If you follow Christ in these things, God will be happy with you. Men will think well of you also.

¹⁹Work for the things that make peace and help each other become stronger Christians. ²⁰Do not destroy what God has done just because of some food. All food is good to eat. But it is wrong to eat anything that will make someone fall into sin. ²¹Do not eat meat or drink wine or do anything else if it would make your Christian brother fall into sin. ²²Keep the faith you have between yourself and God. A man is happy if he knows he is doing right. ²³But if he has doubts about the food he eats, God says he is guilty when he eats it. It is because he is eating without faith. Anything that is not done in faith is sin.

Live To Please Your Neighbor

15 We who have strong faith should help those who are weak. We should not live to please ourselves. ²Each of us should live to please his neighbor. This will help him grow in faith. ³Even Christ did not please Himself. The Holy Writings say, "The sharp words spoken against you fell on Me." (Psalm 69:9) ⁴Everything that was written in the Holy Writings long ago was written to teach us. By not giving up, God's Word gives us strength and hope.

⁵Now the God Who helps you not to give up and gives you strength will help you think so you can please each other as Christ Jesus did. ⁶Then all of you together can thank the God and Father of our Lord Jesus Christ.

The Good News Is For The People Who Are Not Jews

⁷Receive each other as Christ received you. This will honor God. ⁸Christ came to help the Jews. This proved that God had told the truth to their early fathers. This proved that God would do what He promised. ⁹This was done so the people who are not Jews can thank God for His loving-kindness. The Holy Writings say, "This is why I will give thanks to you among the people who are not Jews. I will sing to Your name." (Psalm 18:49) ¹⁰It says also, "You who are not Jews, be happy with His people, the Jews." (Deuteronomy 32:43) ¹¹And, "Honor and give thanks to the Lord, you who are not Jews. Let everyone honor Him." (Psalm 117:1) ¹²And Isaiah says, "There will be One from the family of Jesse Who will be a leader over the people who are not Jews. Their hope will be in Him." (Isaiah 11:10) ¹³Our hope comes from God. May He fill you with joy and peace because of your trust in Him. May your hope grow stronger by the power of the Holy Spirit.

Paul's Reason For Visiting

¹⁴I am sure you are wise in all things and full of much good. You are able to help and teach each other. ¹⁵I have written to you with strong words about some things. I have written so you would remember. God helped me write like this. ¹⁶I am able to write these things because God made me a missionary to the people who are not Jews. I work as a servant of Jesus Christ. I preach the

Good News of God so the people who are not Jews may be as a gift to God. The Holy Spirit will set them apart so God will be pleased with them. ¹⁷I have reason to be proud of my work for God. It is because I belong to Christ Jesus. ¹⁸I can only speak of what Christ has done through me. I have helped the people who are not Jews to obey Him. I have done it by words and by living with them. ¹⁹God showed them His power through me. The Holy Spirit did powerful works through me in front of them. From Jerusalem to the country of Illyricum I have preached the Good News of Christ. ²⁰It is my desire to preach the Good News where it has never been preached. I want to preach only where Christ is not known. ²¹The Holy Writings say, "Those who have never known about Him will see. And those who have never heard about Him will understand." (Isaiah 52:15)

Paul Hopes To Visit The Christians In Rome

²²This is why I have been kept many times from coming to you. ²³But now I am finished with my work here. I have been wanting to come and visit you for many years. ²⁴I hope I can now. I am making plans to go to the country of Spain. On my way there I will stop and visit you. After I have had the joy of visiting you for awhile, you can help me on my way again. ²⁵But now I am going to Jerusalem to hand the Christians the gift of money. ²⁶The churches in the countries of Macedonia and Greece have decided to give money to help some of the poor Christians in Jerusalem. ²⁷They wanted to do it. They should help them in this way because they owe much to the Christians in Jerusalem. The Jews shared the Good News with the people who are not Jews. For this reason, they should share what they

can with the Jews. [28]I will hand this gift of money to them. Then I will stop to see you on my way to the country of Spain. [29]I know that when I come to you, Christ will give me much good to share with you.

[30]I ask you from my heart, Christian brothers, to pray much for me. I ask this in the name of our Lord Jesus Christ. [31]Pray that God will keep me safe from the people in the country of Judea who are not Christians. Pray also that the work I am to do for the Christians in Jerusalem will help them. [32]Then I will be coming to you if God wants me to come. I will be full of joy, and together we can have some rest. [33]May our God Who gives us peace, be with you all. Let it be so.

Paul Says Hello To Many Friends

16 I want to let you know about our Christian sister Phoebe. She is a helper in the church in the city of Cenchrea. [2]The Christians should receive her as a sister who belongs to the Lord. Help her any way you can. She has helped many people and has helped me also.

[3]Say hello to Prisca and Aquila. They worked with me for Christ. [4]They almost died for me. I am thankful for them. All the churches that were started among the people who are not Jews are thankful for them also. [5]Say hello to the church that worships in their house. Say hello to Epaenetus, my much-loved friend. He was the first Christian in the countries of Asia. [6]Say hello to Mary. She worked hard for you. [7]Say hello to Andronicus and Junias. They are from my family and were in prison with me. They put their trust in Christ before I did. They have been respected missionaries. [8]Say hello to Ampliatus. He is a much-loved Christian brother. [9]Say hello to Urbanus. He worked with us for Christ. Say hello to Stachys, my much-loved friend. [10]Say hello to

Apelles. He proved he was faithful to Christ. Say hello to all the family of Aristobulus. [11]Say hello to Herodian. He is one of my family. Say hello to the Christians in the family of Narcissus. [12]Say hello to Tryphaena and Tryphosa and Persis. They are all much-loved workmen for the Lord. [13]Say hello to Rufus and his mother. She was like a mother to me. Rufus is a good Christian. [14]Say hello to Asyncritus and Phlegon and Hermes and Patrobas and Hermas and all the Christians with them. [15]Say hello to Philologus and Julia and Nereus and his sister and Olympas and all the Christians with them. [16]Say hello to each other with a kiss of holy love. All the churches here say hello to you.

Watch Out For Trouble-makers

[17]I ask you, Christian brothers, watch out for those who make trouble and start fights. Keep your eye on those who work against the teaching you received. Keep away from them. [18]Men like that are not working for our Lord Jesus Christ. They are chained to their own desires. With soft words they say things people want to hear. People are fooled by them. [19]Everyone knows you have obeyed the teaching you received. I am happy with you because of this. But I want you to be wise about good things and pure about sinful things. [20]God, Who is our peace, will soon crush Satan under your feet. May the loving-favor of our Lord Jesus be yours.

[21]Timothy, my helper, says hello to you. Lucius and Jason and Sosipater from my family say hello also. [22]I, Tertius, who am writing this letter for Paul, say hello to you as a Christian brother. [23]Gaius is the man taking care of me. The church meets here in his house. He says hello to you. Erastus, the man who takes care of the money for the city, says hello and Quartus does also. He is a

Christian brother. 24*May you have loving-favor from our Lord Jesus Christ. Let it be so.

25We give honor to God. He is able to make you strong as I preach from the Holy Writings about Jesus Christ. It was a secret hidden from the beginning of the world. 26But now it is for us to know. The early preachers wrote about it. God says it is to be preached to all the people of the world so men can put their trust in God and obey Him.

27May God, Who only is wise, be honored forever through our Lord Jesus Christ. Let it be so.

1 CORINTHIANS

1 This letter is from Paul. I have been chosen by God to be a missionary of Jesus Christ. Sosthenes, a Christian brother, writes also. 2I write to God's church in the city of Corinth. I write to those who belong to Christ Jesus and to those who are set apart by Him and made holy. I write to all the Christians everywhere who call on the name of Jesus Christ. He is our Lord and their Lord also. 3May you have loving-favor and peace from God our Father and from the Lord Jesus Christ.

Paul Gives Thanks For Their Faith

4I am thankful to God all the time for you. I am thankful for the loving-favor God has given to you because you belong to Christ Jesus. 5He has made your lives rich in every way. Now you have power to speak for Him. He gave you good understanding. 6This shows that what I told you about Christ and what He could do for you has been done in your lives. 7You have the gifts of the Holy Spirit that you need while you wait for the Lord Jesus Christ to come again. 8Christ will keep you strong until He comes again. No blame will be held against you. 9God is faithful. He chose you to be joined together with His Son, Jesus Christ our Lord.

The Church In Corinth Is Divided

10Christian brothers, I ask you with all my heart in the name of the Lord Jesus Christ to agree among yourselves. Do not be divided into little groups. Think and act as if you all had the same mind. 11My Christian brothers, I have heard from some of Chloe's family that you are arguing among yourselves. 12I hear that some of you are saying, "I am a follower of Paul," and "I am a follower of Apollos," and "I am a follower of Peter," and "I am a follower of Christ." 13Has Christ been divided? Was Paul put on a cross to die for your sins? Were you baptized in the name of Paul? 14I am thankful to God that I baptized Crispus and Gaius only. 15No one can say that you were baptized in the name of Paul. 16I remember I did baptize the family of Stephanas, but I do not remember baptizing any others.

¹⁷Christ did not send me to baptize. He sent me to preach the Good News. I did not use big sounding words when I preached. If I had, the power of the cross of Christ would be taken away.

Christ Is The Power And Wisdom Of God

¹⁸Preaching about the cross sounds foolish to those who are dying in sin. But it is the power of God to those of us who are being saved from the punishment of sin. ¹⁹The Holy Writings say, "I will destroy the wisdom of the wise people. I will put aside the learning of those who think they know a lot." ²⁰Where is the man who is wise? Where is the man who thinks he knows a lot? Where is the man who thinks he has all the answers? God has made the wisdom of this world look foolish. ²¹In His wisdom, He did not allow man to come to know Him through the wisdom of this world. It pleased God to save men from the punishment of their sins through preaching the Good News. This preaching sounds foolish. ²²The Jews are looking for something special to see. The Greek people are looking for the answer in wisdom. ²³But we preach that Christ died on a cross to save them from their sins. These words are hard for the Jews to listen to. The Greek people think it is foolish. ²⁴Christ is the power and wisdom of God to those who are chosen to be saved from the punishment of sin for both Jews and Greeks. ²⁵God's plan looked foolish to men, but it is wiser than the best plans of men. God's plan which may look weak is stronger than the strongest plans of men.

God's Wisdom - Human Wisdom

²⁶Christian brothers, think who you were when the Lord called you. Not many of you were wise or powerful or born into the family of leaders of a country. ²⁷But God has chosen what the world calls foolish to shame the wise. He has chosen what the world calls weak to shame what is strong. ²⁸God has chosen what is weak and foolish of the world, what is hated and not known, to destroy the things the world trusts in. ²⁹In that way, no man can be proud as he stands before God. ³⁰God Himself made the way so you can have new life through Christ Jesus. God gave us Christ to be our wisdom. Christ made us right with God and set us apart for God and made us holy. Christ bought us with His blood and made us free from our sins. ³¹It is as the Holy Writings say, "If anyone is going to be proud of anything, he should be proud of the Lord."

Paul Received The Good News From God

2 Christian brothers, when I came to you, I did not preach the secrets of God with big sounding words or make it sound as if I were so wise. ²I made up my mind that while I was with you I would speak of nothing except Jesus Christ and of His death on the cross. ³When I was with you, I was weak. I was afraid and I shook. ⁴What I had to say when I preached was not in big sounding words of man's wisdom. But it was given in the power of the Holy Spirit. ⁵In this way, you do not have faith in Christ because of the wisdom of men. You have faith in Christ because of the power of God.

True Wisdom Comes From God

⁶We speak wisdom to full-grown Christians. This wisdom is not from this world or from the leaders of today. They die and their wisdom dies with them. ⁷What we preach is God's wisdom. It was a secret until now. God planned for us to have this honor before the world began. ⁸None

of the world leaders understood this wisdom. If they had, they would not have put Christ up on a cross to die. He is the Lord of shining greatness. 9The Holy Writings say, "No eye has ever seen or no ear has ever heard or no mind has ever thought of the wonderful things God has made ready for those who love Him." (Isaiah 64:4; 65:17) 10God has shown these things to us through His Holy Spirit. It is the Holy Spirit Who looks into all things, even the secrets of God, and shows them to us. 11Who can know the things about a man, except a man's own spirit that is in him? It is the same with God. Who can understand Him except the Holy Spirit? 12We have not received the spirit of the world. God has given us His Holy Spirit that we may know about the things given to us by Him. 13We speak about these things also. We do not use words of man's wisdom. We use words given to us by the Holy Spirit. We use these words to tell what the Holy Spirit wants to say to those who put their trust in Him. 14But the person who is not a Christian does not understand these words from the Holy Spirit. He thinks they are foolish. He cannot understand them because he does not have the Holy Spirit to help him understand. 15The full-grown Christian understands all things, and yet he is not understood. 16For who has the thoughts of the Lord? Who can tell Him what to do? But we have the thoughts of Christ.

3 Christian brothers, I could not speak to you as to full-grown Christians. I spoke to you as men who have not obeyed the things you have been taught. I spoke to you as if you were baby Christians. 2My teaching was as if I were giving you milk to drink. I could not give you meat because you were not ready for it. Even yet you are not able to have anything but milk. 3You still live as men who are not Christians. When you are jealous and fight with each other, you are still living in sin and acting like sinful men in the world. 4When one says, "I am a follower of Paul," and another says, "I am a follower of Apollos," does not this sound like the talk of baby Christians? 5Who is Apollos? Who is Paul? We are only servants owned by God. He gave us gifts to preach His Word. And because of that, you put your trust in Christ. 6I planted the seed. Apollos watered it, but it was God Who kept it growing. 7This shows that the one who plants or the one who waters is not the important one. God is the important One. He makes it grow. 8The one who plants and the one who waters are alike. Each one will get his own pay. 9For we work together with God. You are God's field.

You are God's building also. 10Through God's loving-favor to me, I laid the stones on which the building was to be built. I did it like one who knew what he was doing. Now another person is building on it. Each person who builds must be careful how he builds on it. 11Jesus Christ is the Stone on which other stones for the building must be laid. It can be only Christ. 12Now if a man builds on the Stone with gold or silver or beautiful stones, or if he builds with wood or grass or straw, 13each man's work will become known. There will be a day when it will be tested by fire. The fire will show what kind of work it is. 14If a man builds on work that lasts, he will receive his pay. 15If his work is burned up, he will lose it. Yet he himself will be saved as if he were going through a fire.

16Do you not know that you are a house of God and that the Holy Spirit lives in you? 17If any man destroys the house of God, God will destroy him. God's house is holy. You are the place where He lives.

18Do not fool yourself. If anyone thinks he knows a lot about the things of this world, he had better become a fool. Then he may become wise. ¹⁹The wisdom of this world is foolish to God. The Holy Writings say, "He is the One Who gets them in a trap when they use their own wisdom." (Job 5:13) ²⁰They also say, "The Lord knows how the wise man thinks. His thinking is worth nothing." (Psalm 94:11) ²¹As a Christian, do not be proud of men and of what they can do. All things belong to you. ²²Paul and Apollos and Peter belong to you. The world and life and death belong to you. Things now and things to come belong to you. ²³You belong to Christ, and Christ belongs to God.

Servants Of Christ

4 Think of us as servants who are owned by Christ. It is our job to share the secrets of God. ²A servant must be faithful to his owner. This is expected of him. ³It is not the most important thing to me what you or any other people think of me. Even what I think of myself does not mean much. ⁴As for me, my heart tells me I am not guilty of anything. But that does not prove I am free from guilt. It is the Lord Who looks into my life and says what is wrong. ⁵Do not be quick to say who is right or wrong. Wait until the Lord comes. He will bring into the light the things that are hidden in men's hearts. He will show why men have done these things. Every man will receive from God the thanks he should have.

⁶Christian brothers, I have used Apollos and myself to show you what I am talking about. This is to help you so you will not think more of men than what God's Word will allow. Never think more of one of God's servants than another. ⁷Who made you better than your brother? Or what do you have that has not been given to you? If God has given you everything, why do you have pride? Why do you act as if He did not give it to you? ⁸You are full. You

are rich. You live like kings and we do not. I wish you were kings and we could be leaders with you. ⁹I think that God has made a show of us missionaries. We are the last and the least among men. We are like men waiting to be put to death. The whole world, men and angels alike, are watching us. ¹⁰We are thought of as fools because of Christ. But you are thought of as wise Christians! We are weak. You are strong. People respect you. They have no respect for us. ¹¹To this hour we are hungry and thirsty, and our clothes are worn out. People hurt us. We have no homes. ¹²We work with our hands to make a living. We speak kind words to those who speak against us. When people hurt us, we say nothing. ¹³When people say bad things about us, we answer with kind words. People think of us as dirt that is worth nothing and as the worst thing on earth to this very day.

Follow Paul's Way Of Life

¹⁴I do not write these things to shame you. I am doing this to help you know what you should do. You are my much-loved children. ¹⁵You may have 10,000 Christian teachers. But remember, I am the only father you have. You became Christians when I preached the Good News to you. ¹⁶So I ask you with all my heart to follow the way I live. ¹⁷For this reason I have sent Timothy to you. He is my much-loved child and a faithful Christian. He will tell you how I act as a Christian. This is the kind of life I teach in the churches wherever I go.

¹⁸Some of you are full of pride. You think that I am not coming to visit you. ¹⁹If the Lord wants me to, I will come soon. I will find out when I come if these proud people have God's power, or if they just use a lot of big words. ²⁰The holy nation of God is not made up of words. It is made up of power. ²¹What do you

want? Do you want me to come with a stick to whip you? Or do you want me to come with love and a gentle spirit?

Sin In The Church

5 Someone has told me about a sex sin among you. It is so bad that even the people who do not know God would not do it. I have been told that one of the men is living with his father's wife as if she were his wife. ²Instead of being sorry, you are proud of yourselves. The man who is living like that should be sent away from you. ³I am far from you. Even if I am not there, my spirit is with you. I have already said that the man is guilty of this sin. I am saying this as if I were there with you. ⁴Call a meeting of the church. I will be with you in spirit. In the name of the Lord Jesus Christ, and by His power, ⁵hand this person over to the devil. His body is to be destroyed so his spirit may be saved on the day the Lord comes again.

⁶It is not good for you to be proud of the way things are going in your church. You know a little yeast makes the whole loaf of bread rise. ⁷Clean out the old yeast. Then you will be new bread with none of the old yeast in you. The Jews killed lambs when they left Egypt. Christ is our lamb. He has already been killed as a gift on the altar to God for us. ⁸Bread with yeast in it is like being full of sin and hate. Let us eat this supper together with bread that has no yeast in it. This bread is pure and true.

⁹I told you in my letter not to keep on being with people who do any kind of sex sins. ¹⁰I was not talking about people doing sex sins who are bad people of this world. I was not talking about people of this world who always want to get more or or those who get things in a wrong way or those who worship false gods. To get away from people like that you would have to leave this world! ¹¹What I wrote was that you should not keep on being with a person who calls himself a Christian if he does any kind of sex sins. You should not even eat with a person who says he is a Christian but always wants to get more of everything or uses bad language or who gets drunk or gets things in a wrong way. ¹²It is not for me to say if those outside the church are guilty. You are to say if those who belong to the church are guilty. ¹³God will say if those outside the church are guilty. So you must put that sinful person out of your church.

Going To Court Against Christians

6 Why do you go to court when you have something against another Christian? You are asking people who are not Christians to judge who is guilty. You should go to those who belong to Christ and ask them. ²Did you not know that those who belong to Christ will someday judge this world? If you judge the people of the world as guilty, are you not able to do this in small things? ³Did you not know that we are to judge angels? So you should be able to take care of your problem here in this world without any trouble.

⁴When you have things to decide about this life, why do you go to men in courts who are not even Christians? ⁵You should be ashamed! Is it true that there is not one person wise enough in your church to decide who is right when people argue? ⁶Instead, one Christian takes another Christian to court. And that court is made up of people who are not Christians! ⁷This shows you are wrong when you have to go to court against each other. Would it not be better to let someone do something against you that is wrong? Would it not be better to let them rob you? ⁸Instead, you rob and do wrong to other Christians.

The Body Is To Be Holy

⁹Do you not know that sinful men will have no place in the holy nation of God? Do not be fooled. A person who does sex sins, or who worships false gods, or who is not faithful in marriage, or men who act like women, or people who do sex sins with their own sex, will have no place in the holy nation of God. ¹⁰Also those who steal, or those who always want to get more of everything, or who get drunk, or who say bad things about others, or take things that are not theirs, will have no place in the holy nation of God. ¹¹Some of you were like that. But now your sins are washed away. You were set apart for God-like living to do His work. You were made right with God through our Lord Jesus Christ by the Spirit of our God.

¹²I am allowed to do all things, but not everything is good for me to do! Even if I am free to do all things, I will not do them if I think it would be hard for me to stop when I know I should. ¹³Food was meant for the stomach. The stomach needs food, but God will bring to an end both food and the stomach. The body was not meant for sex sins. It was meant to work for the Lord. The Lord is for our body. ¹⁴God raised the Lord from death. He will raise us from death by His power also.

The Body Belongs To The Lord

¹⁵Do you not know that your bodies are a part of Christ Himself? Am I to take a part of Christ and make it a part of a woman who sells the use of her body? No! Never! ¹⁶Do you not know that a man who joins himself to a woman who sells the use of her body becomes a part of her? The Holy Writings say, "The two will become one." ¹⁷But if you join yourself to the Lord, you are one with Him in spirit.

¹⁸Have nothing to do with sex sins! Any other sin that a man does, does not hurt his own body. But the man who does a sex sin sins against his own body. ¹⁹Do you not know that your body is a house of God where the Holy Spirit lives? God gave you His Holy Spirit. Now you belong to God. You do not belong to yourselves. ²⁰God bought you with a great price. So honor God with your body. You belong to Him.

How A Husband And Wife Should Live

7 You asked me some questions in your letter. This is my answer. It is good if a man does not get married. ²But because of being tempted to sex sins, each man should get married and have his own wife. Each woman should get married and have her own husband. ³The husband should please his wife as a husband. The wife should please her husband as a wife. ⁴The wife is not the boss of her own body. It belongs to the husband. And in the same way, the husband is not the boss of his own body. It belongs to the wife.

⁵Do not keep from each other that which belongs to each other in marriage unless you agree for awhile so you can use your time to pray. Then come together again or the devil will tempt you to do that which you know you should not do.

⁶This is what I think. I am not saying you must do it. ⁷I wish everyone were as I am, but each has his own gift from God. One has one gift. Another has another gift.

⁸This is what I say to those who are not married and to women whose husbands have died. It is good if you do not get married. I am not married. ⁹But if you are not able to keep from doing that which you know is wrong, get married. It is better to get married than to have such strong sex desires.

¹⁰I have this to say to those who are married. These words are from the Lord. A wife should not leave her

husband, [11]but if she does leave him, she should not get married to another man. It would be better for her to go back to her husband. The husband should not divorce his wife. [12]I have this to say. These words are not from the Lord. If a Christian husband has a wife who is not a Christian, and she wants to live with him, he must not divorce her. [13]If a Christian wife has a husband who is not a Christian, and he wants to live with her, she must not divorce him. [14]The husband who is not a Christian is set apart from the sin of the world because of his Christian wife. The wife who is not a Christian is set apart from the sin of the world because of her Christian husband. In this way, the lives of the children are not unclean because of sin, they are clean. [15]If the one who is not a Christian wants to leave, let that one go. The Christian husband or wife should not try to make the other one stay. God wants you to live in peace. [16]Christian wife, how do you know you will not help your husband to become a Christian? Or Christian husband, how do you know you will not help your wife to become a Christian?

Stay As You Were When God Chose You

[17]Everyone should live the life the Lord gave to him. He should live as he was when he became a Christian. This is what I teach in all the churches. [18]If a man became a Christian after he had gone through the religious act of becoming a Jew, he should do nothing about it. If a man became a Christian before, he should not go through the religious act of becoming a Jew. [19]If it is done or not done, it means nothing. What is important is to obey God's Word. [20]Everyone should stay the same way he was when he became a Christian. [21]Were you a servant who was owned by someone when you became a Christian? Do not worry

about it. But if you are able to become free, do that. [22]A servant who is owned by someone and who has become a Christian is the Lord's free man. A free man who has become a Christian is a servant owned by Christ. [23]He paid a great price for you when He bought you. Do not let yourselves become servants owned by men. [24]Christian brothers, each one should stay as he was when he became a Christian.

[25]I have no word from the Lord about women or men who have never been married. I will tell you what I think. You can trust me because the Lord has given me His loving-kindness. [26]I think, because of the troubles that are coming, it is a good thing for a person not to get married. [27]Are you married to a wife? Do not try to get a divorce. If you are not married, do not look for a wife. [28]If you do get married, you have not sinned. If a woman who is not married gets married, it is no sin. But being married will add problems. I would like to have you free from such problems.

[29]I mean this, Christian brothers. The time is very short. A married man should use his time as if he did not have a wife. [30]Those who have sorrow should keep on working as if they had no sorrow. Those who have joy should keep on working as if there was no time for joy. Those who buy should have no time to get joy from what they have. [31]While you live in this world, live as if the world has no hold on you. The way of this world will soon be gone.

[32]I want you to be free from the cares of this world. The man who is not married can spend his time working for the Lord and pleasing Him. [33]The man who is married cares for the things of the world. He wants to please his wife. [34]Married women and women who have never been married are different. The woman who has never been married can spend her time working for the Lord.

She wants to please the Lord with her body and spirit. The woman who is married cares for the things of the world. She wants to please her husband. 35I am saying these things to help you. I am not trying to keep you from getting married. I want you to do what is best. You should work for Him without other things taking your time.

36If a man and woman expect to get married, and he thinks his desires to marry her are getting too strong, and she is getting older, they should get married. It is no sin. 37But if a man has the power to keep from getting married and knows in his mind that he should not, he is wise if he does not get married. 38The man who gets married does well, but the man who does not get married does better.

39A wife is not free as long as her husband lives. If her husband dies, she is free to marry anyone she wants, if he is a Christian. 40I think she will be much more happy if she does not get married again. This is what I think. I believe it is what the Holy Spirit is saying.

Food Given To False Gods

8 I want to write about food that has been given as a gift in worship to a false god. We all know something about it. Knowing about it makes one feel important. But love makes one strong. 2The person who thinks he knows all the answers still has a lot to learn. 3But if he loves God, he is known by God also.

4What about food that has been given as a gift to a false god in worship? Is it right? We know that a false god is not a god at all. There is only one God! There is no other. 5Men have thought there are many such gods and lords in the sky and on the earth. 6But we know there is only one God. He is the Father. All things are from Him. He made us for Himself. There is one Lord. He is Jesus Christ. He made all things. He

keeps us alive.

7Not all men know this. They have given food as a gift in worship to a god as if the god were alive. Some men have done this all their lives. If they eat such food, their hearts tell them it is wrong. 8Food will not bring us near to God. We are no worse if we do not eat it, or we are no better if we eat it. 9Since you are free to do as you please, be careful that this does not hurt a weak Christian. 10A Christian who is weak may see you eat food in a place where it has been given as a gift to false gods in worship. Since he sees you eat it, he will eat it also. 11You may make the weak Christian fall into sin by what you have done. Remember, he is a Christian brother for whom Christ died. 12When you sin against a weak Christian by making him do what is wrong, you sin against Christ. 13So then, if eating meat makes my Christian brother trip and fall, I will never eat it again. I do not want to make my Christian brother sin.

A Missionary's Rights

9 Am I not a missionary? Am I not free? Have I not seen Jesus our Lord? Are you not Christians because of the work I have done for the Lord? 2Other people may not think of me as a missionary, but you do. It proves I am a missionary because you are Christians now. 3When people ask questions about me, I say this: 4Do we not have the right to have food and drink when we are working for the Lord? 5Do we not have the right to take a Christian wife along with us? The other missionaries do. The Lord's brothers do and Peter does. 6Are Barnabas and I the only ones who should keep working for a living so we can preach?

7Have you ever heard of a soldier who goes to war and pays for what he needs himself? Have you ever heard of a man planting a field of grapes and not eating some of the fruit? Have you ever heard of a farmer who feeds cattle and does not drink some of the milk? 8These things are not just what men think are right to do. God's Law speaks about this. 9God gave Moses the Law. It says, "When the cow is made to walk on the grain to break it open, do not stop it from eating some." (Deuteronomy 25:4) Does God care about the cow? 10Did not God speak about this because of us. For sure, this was written for us. The man who gets the fields ready and the man who gathers in the grain should expect some of the grain. 11We have planted God's Word among you. Is it too much to expect you to give us what we need to live each day? 12If other people have the right to expect this from you, do we not have more right? But we have not asked this of you. We have suffered many things. We did this so the Good News of Christ would not be held back.

13You must know that those who work in the house of God get their food there. Those who work at the altar in the house of God get a part of the food that is given there. 14The Lord has said also that those who preach the Good News should get their living from those who hear it.

15I have not used any of these things. I am not writing now to get anything. I would rather die than lose the joy of preaching to you without you paying me. 16I cannot be proud because I preach the Good News. I have been told to do it. It would be bad for me if I do not preach the Good News. 17If I do this because I want to, I will get my pay. If I do not want to do it, I am still expected to do it. 18Then what is my pay? It is when I preach the Good News without you paying me. I do not ask you to pay me as I could.

Learning To Get Along

19No man has any hold on me, but I have made myself a workman owned by all. I do this so I might lead more people to Christ. 20I became as a Jew to the Jews so I might lead them to Christ. There are some who live by obeying the Jewish Law. I became as one who lives by obeying the Jewish Law so I might lead them to Christ. 21There are some who live by not obeying the Jewish law. I became as one who lives by not obeying the Jewish law so I might lead them to Christ. This does not mean that I do not obey God's Law. I obey the teachings of Christ. 22Some are weak. I have become weak so I might lead them to Christ. I have become like every person so in every way I might lead some to Christ. 23Everything I do, I do to get the Good News to men. I want to have a part in this work.

Live A Life That Pleases Christ

24You know that only one person gets a prize for being in a race even if many people run. You must run so you will win the prize. 25Everyone who runs in a race does many things so his body will be strong. He does it to get a prize that will soon be worth nothing, but we work for a prize that will last forever. 26In the same way, I run straight for the place at the end of the race. I fight to win. I do not beat the air. 27I keep working over my body. I make it obey me. I do this because I am afraid that after I have preached the Good News to others, I myself might be put aside.

The Danger Of Worshiping False Gods

10 Christian brothers, I want you to know what happened to our early fathers. They all walked from the country of Egypt under the cloud that showed them the way, and they all passed through the waters of the Red Sea. 2They were all baptized in the cloud and in the sea as they followed Moses. 3All of them ate the same holy food. 4They all drank the same holy drink. They drank from a

holy Rock that went along with them. That holy Rock was Christ. [5]Even then most of them did not please God. He destroyed them in the desert.

[6]These things show us something. They teach us not to want things that are bad for us like those people did. [7]We must not worship false gods as some of them did. The Holy Writings tell us, "The people sat down to eat and drink. Then they got up to play." (Exodus 32:6) [8]We must not do sex sins as some of them did. In one day 23,000 died. [9]We must not test the Lord as some of them did. They were destroyed by snakes. [10]We must not complain against God as some of them did. That is why they were destroyed.

[11]All these things happened to show us something. They were written to teach us that the end of the world is near. [12]So watch yourself! The person who thinks he can stand against sin had better watch that he does not fall into sin. [13]You have never been tempted to sin in any different way than other people. God is faithful. He will not allow you to be tempted more than you can take. But when you are tempted, He will make a way for you to keep from falling into sin.

Teaching About The Lord's Supper

[14]My dear friends, keep away from the worship of false gods. [15]I am speaking to you who are able to understand. See if what I am saying is true. [16]When we give thanks for the fruit of the vine at the Lord's supper, are we not sharing in the blood of Christ? The bread we eat at the Lord's supper, are we not sharing in the body of Christ? [17]There is one bread, and many of us Christians make up the body of Christ. All of us eat from that bread.

[18]Look at the Jews. They ate the animals that were brought to God as gifts in worship and put on the altar.

Did this not show they were sharing with God? [19]What do I mean? Am I saying that a false god or the food brought to it in worship is worth anything? [20]No, not at all! I am saying that the people who do not know God bring gifts of animals in worship. But they have given them to demons, not to God. You do not want to have any share with demons. [21]You cannot drink from the cup of the Lord and from the cup of demons. You cannot eat at the Lord's table and at the demon's table. [22]Are we trying to make the Lord jealous? Do we think we are stronger than the Lord?

[23]We are allowed to do anything, but not everything is good for us to do. We are allowed to do anything, but not all things help us grow strong as Christians. [24]Do not work only for your own good. Think of what you can do for others. [25]Eat any meat that is sold in the stores. Ask no questions about it. Then your heart will not say it is wrong. [26]The Holy Writings say, "The earth and everything in it belongs to the Lord." [27]If a person who is not a Christian wants you to eat with him, and you want to go, eat anything that is on the table. Ask no questions about the food. Then your heart will not say it is wrong. [28]But if someone says, "This meat has been given as a gift to false gods in worship," do not eat it. In that way, it will not hurt the faith of the one who told you and his heart will have peace. [29]How the other person feels is important. We are not free to do things that will hurt another person. [30]If I can give thanks to God for my food, why should anyone say that I am wrong about eating food I can give thanks for? [31]So if you eat or drink or whatever you do, do everything to honor God. [32]Do nothing that would make trouble for a Greek or for a Jew or for the church of God. [33]I want to please everyone in all that I do. I am not thinking of myself. I want to do what is best for

them so they may be saved from the punishment of sin.

11 Follow my way of thinking as I follow Christ.

How Christian Women Should Live

[2]I think you have done well because you always remember me and have followed the things I taught you. [3]I want you to know that Christ is the head of every man. The husband is the head of his wife. God is the head of Christ. [4]If any man prays or preaches with his head covered, he does not give honor to Christ. [5]Every woman who prays or preaches without her head covered does not respect her head. It is the same as if she had her hair cut off. [6]If a woman does not cover her head, she might as well cut off her hair also. If a woman is ashamed to have her hair cut off, she should cover her head. [7]Man is made like God and His shining greatness. For this reason a man should not have his head covered when he prays or preaches, but the woman respects the man. [8]Man was not made from woman. Woman was made from man, [9]and man was not made for woman. Woman was made for man. [10]For this reason a woman should have a covering on her head. This shows she respects man. This is for the angels to see also. [11]In God's plan women need men and men need women. [12]Woman was made from man, but man is born of woman. God made all things.

[13]Think this over yourselves. Does it look right for a woman to pray with no covering on her head? [14]Have we not already learned that it is a shame for a man to have long hair? [15]But a woman can be proud to have long hair. Her hair is given to her for a covering. [16]If anyone wants to argue about this, my answer is that this is what we teach, and all the churches agree with me.

How The Lord's Supper Should Be Eaten

[17]While writing about these things, let me tell you what I think. Nothing good is coming from your meeting together. [18]First of all, I hear that when you meet together in the church you are divided into groups and you argue. I almost believe this is true. [19]For there must be different groups among you. In that way, those who are right will be seen from those who are wrong. [20]When you gather together for your meetings, it is not to eat the Lord's supper. [21]Each one is in a hurry to eat his own food first. He does not wait for others. In this way, one does not get enough food and drink. Others get too much and get drunk. [22]You have your own homes to eat and drink in. Or do you hate the church of God and shame those who are poor? What am I to say to you? Am I to say you are right? No! I cannot say you are right in this.

The Meaning Of The Lord's Supper

[23]I have given you the teaching I received from the Lord. The night Jesus was handed over to the soldiers, He took bread. [24]When He had given thanks, He broke it and said, "Take this bread and eat it. This is My body which is broken for you. Do this to remember Me."

[25]In the same way after supper, He took the cup. He said, "This cup is the New Way of Worship made between God and you by My blood. Whenever you drink it, do it to remember Me."

[26]Every time you eat this bread and drink from this cup you are telling of the Lord's death until He comes again. [27]Anyone who eats the bread or drinks from the cup, if his spirit is not right with the Lord, will be guilty of sinning against the body and the blood of the Lord. [28]This is why a man should look into his own heart

and life before eating the bread and drinking from the cup. ²⁹Anyone who eats the bread and drinks from the cup, if his spirit is not right with the Lord, will be guilty as he eats and drinks. He does not understand the meaning of the Lord's body. ³⁰This is why some of you are sick and weak, and some have died. ³¹But if we would look into our own lives and see if we are guilty, then God would not have to say we are guilty. ³²When we are guilty, we are punished by the Lord so we will not be told we are guilty with the rest of the world.

³³Christian brothers, when you come together to eat, wait for each other. ³⁴If anyone is hungry, he should eat at home. Then he will not be guilty as you meet together. I will talk about the other things when I come.

The Gifts Of The Holy Spirit

12 Christian brothers, I want you to know about the gifts of the Holy Spirit. You need to understand the truth about this. ²You know that before you were Christians you were led to worship false gods. None of these gods could speak. ³So I tell you that no one speaking by the help of the Holy Spirit can say that he hates Jesus. No one can say, "Jesus is Lord," except by the help of the Holy Spirit.

The Kinds Of Gifts

⁴There are different kinds of gifts. But it is the same Holy Spirit Who gives them. ⁵There are different kinds of work to be done for Him. But the work is for the same Lord. ⁶There are different ways of doing His work. But it is the same God who uses all these ways in all people. ⁷The Holy Spirit works in each person in one way or another for the good of all. ⁸One person is given the gift of teaching words of wisdom. Another person is given the gift of teaching what he has learned and knows. These gifts are by the same Holy Spirit. ⁹One person receives the gift of faith. Another person receives the gifts of healing. These gifts are given by the same Holy Spirit. ¹⁰One person is given the gift of doing powerful works. Another person is given the gift of speaking God's Word. Another person is given the gift of telling the difference between the Holy Spirit and false spirits. Another person is given the gift of speaking in special sounds. Another person is given the gift of telling what these special sounds mean. ¹¹But it is the same Holy Spirit, the Spirit of God, Who does all these things. He gives to each person as He wants to give.

Our Body Is Like The Body Of Christ

¹²Our own body has many parts. When all these many parts are put together, they are only one body. The body of Christ is like this. ¹³It is the same way with us. Jews or those who are not Jews, men who are owned by someone or men who are free to do what they want to do, have all been baptized into the one body by the same Holy Spirit. We have all received the one Spirit.

¹⁴The body is not one part, but many parts. ¹⁵If the foot should say, "I am not a part of the body because I am not a hand," that would not stop it from being a part of the body. ¹⁶If the ear should say, "I am not a part of the body because I am not an eye," that would not stop it from being a part of the body. ¹⁷If the whole body were an eye how would it hear? If the whole body were an ear, how would it smell? ¹⁸But God has put all the parts into the body just as He wants to have them. ¹⁹If all the parts were the same, it could not be a body. ²⁰But now there are many parts, but one body.

²¹The eye cannot say to the hand, "I do not need you." Or the head

cannot say to the feet, "I do not need you." [22]Some of the parts we think are weak and not important are very important. [23]We take good care of and cover with clothes the parts of the body that look less important. The parts which do not look beautiful have an important work to do. [24]The parts that can be seen do not need as much care. God has made the body so more care is given to the parts that need it most. [25]This is so the body will not be divided into parts. All the parts care for each other. [26]If one part of the body suffers, all the other parts suffer with it. If one part is given special care, the other parts are happy.

The Body Of Christ

[27]You are all a part of the body of Christ. [28]God has chosen different ones in the church to do His work. First, there are missionaries. Second, there are preachers or those who speak for God. And third, there are teachers. He has also chosen those who do powerful works and those who have the gifts of healing. And He has chosen those who help others who are in need and those who are able to lead others in work and those who speak in special sounds. [29]Are they all missionaries? No. Are they all preachers or those who speak for God? No. Do they all do powerful works? No. [30]Do they all have the gifts of healing? No. Do they all speak in special sounds? No. Are they all able to tell what the special sounds mean? No. [31]But from your heart you should want the best gifts. Now I will show you even a better way.

Love - The Greatest Of All

13 I may be able to speak the languages of men and even of angels, but if I do not have love, it will sound like noise. [2]If I have the gift of speaking God's Word and if I understand all secrets, but do not have love, I am nothing. If I know all things and if I have the gift of faith so I can move mountains, but do not have love, I am nothing. [3]If I give everything I have to feed poor people and if I give my body to be burned, but do not have love, it will not help me.

[4]Love does not give up. Love is kind. Love is not jealous. Love does not put itself up as being important. Love has no pride. [5]Love does not do the wrong thing. Love never thinks of itself. Love does not get angry. Love does not remember the suffering that comes from being hurt by someone. [6]Love is not happy with sin. Love is happy with the truth. [7]Love takes everything that comes without giving up. Love believes all things. Love hopes for all things. Love keeps on in all things.

[8]Love never comes to an end. The gift of speaking God's Word will come to an end. The gift of speaking in special sounds will be stopped. The gift of understanding will come to an end. [9]For we only know a part now, and we speak only a part. [10]When everything is perfect, then we will not need these gifts that are not perfect. [11]When I was a child, I spoke like a child. I thought like a child. I understood like a child. Now I am a man. I do not act like a child anymore. [12]Now that which we see is as if we were looking in a broken mirror. But then we will see everything. Now I know only a part. But then I will know everything in a perfect way. That is how God knows me right now. [13]And now we have these three: faith and hope and love, but the greatest of these is love.

Speaking In Special Sounds Is Not The Greatest Gift

14 You should want to have this love. You should want the gifts of the Holy Spirit and most of all to be able to speak God's Word. [2]The man who speaks in special sounds speaks to God. He is not speaking to men. No one understands. He is speaking secret things through the power of the Holy Spirit. [3]The man who speaks God's Word speaks to men. It helps them to learn and understand. It gives them comfort. [4]The man who speaks in special sounds receives strength. The man who speaks God's Word gives strength to the church. [5]I wish all of you spoke in special sounds. But more than that, I wish all of you spoke God's Word. The one who speaks God's Word has a more important gift than the one who speaks in special sounds. But if he can tell what he is speaking, the church will be helped. [6]Christian brothers, if I come to you speaking in special sounds, what good is it to you? But if I tell you something God has shown me or something I have learned or what God's Word says will happen in the future or teach you God's Word, it will be for your good. [7]There are things on which people play music. If strange sounds are made on these, how will others know which one is played. [8]If a horn does not make a good sound, how will men know they are to get ready to fight? [9]It is the same if you speak to a person in special sounds. How will he know what you say? Your sounds will be lost in the air. [10]There are many languages in the world. All of them have meaning to the people who understand them. [11]But if I do not understand the language someone uses to speak to me, the man who speaks is a stranger to me. I am a stranger to him. [12]Since you want gifts from the Holy Spirit, ask for those that will build up the whole church. [13]So the man who speaks in special sounds should pray for the gift to be able to tell what they mean.

[14]If I pray in special sounds, my spirit is doing the praying. My mind does not understand. [15]What should I do? I will pray with my spirit and I will pray with my mind also. I will sing with my spirit and I will sing with my mind also. [16]If you honor and give thanks to God with your spirit in sounds nobody understands, how can others honor and give thanks also if they do not know what you are saying? [17]You are honoring and giving thanks to God, but it is not helping other people.

[18]I thank God that I speak in special sounds more than all of you. [19]But in a meeting of the church, it is better if I say five words that others can understand and be helped by than 10,000 words in special sounds.

[20]Christian brothers, do not be like children in your thinking. Be full-grown, but be like children in not knowing how to sin. [21]God says in the Holy Writings, "I will speak to My people. I will speak through men from other lands in other languages. Even then My people will not listen to Me." (Isaiah 28:11-12) [22]So then speaking in special sounds is for those who do not believe. It is not for those who believe. But speaking God's Word is for those who believe. It is not for those who do not believe.

[23]If some people who are not Christians come to your church meeting while all the people are speaking in special sounds, they will think you are crazy. [24]But if a man who is not a Christian comes to your church meeting while you are all speaking God's Word, he will understand that he is a sinner by what he hears. He will know he is guilty. [25]The secrets of his heart will be brought into the open. He will get on his knees and worship God. He will say, "For sure, God is here with you!"

[26]What am I saying, Christian brothers? When you meet together for worship, some of you have a song to sing. Some of you want to teach and some have special words from God. Some of you speak in special

sounds and some of you tell what they mean. Everything should be done to help those who are meeting together to grow strong as Christians. 27No more than two or three people should speak in special sounds. Only one should speak at a time. Someone must tell the meaning of the special sounds. 28If no one is there who can tell the meaning of the special sounds, he should not speak in the church. He should speak only to himself and to God. 29Two or three should speak God's Word. The other people should listen and decide if they are speaking right. 30If someone sitting in the meeting gets some special word from God, the one who is speaking should stop. 31All of you can speak God's Word, but only one person at a time. In that way, all of you can learn and be helped. 32Men who speak God's Word are able to stop when they should. 33God does not want everyone speaking at the same time in church meetings. He wants peace. All the churches of God's people worship this way.

34Women should not be allowed to speak in church meetings. They are to obey this teaching. The Law says this also. 35If they want to find out about something, they should ask their husbands at home. It is a shame for a woman to speak in a church meeting.

36Did the Word of God come from you Christians in the city of Corinth? Or are you the only people who received it? 37Some of you may think you have the gift of speaking God's Word or some other gift from the Holy Spirit. If you do, you should know that what I am writing to you is what God has told us we must obey. 38If any man does not listen to this, have nothing to do with him.

39So then, my Christian brothers, you should want to speak God's Word. Do not stop anyone from speaking in special sounds. 40All things should be done in the right way, one after the other.

Jesus Christ Was Raised From The Dead

15 Christian brothers, I want to tell the Good News to you again. It is the same as I preached to you before. You received it and your faith has been made strong by it. 2This is what I preached to you. You are saved from the punishment of sin by the Good News if you keep hold of it, unless your faith was worth nothing.

3First of all, I taught you what I had received. It was this: Christ died for our sins as the Holy Writings said He would. (Isaiah 53:5-12) 4Christ was buried. He was raised from the dead three days later as the Holy Writings said He would. (Psalm 16:9-10) 5Christ was seen by Peter. After that, the twelve followers saw Him. 6After that, more than 500 of His followers saw Him at one time. Most of them are still here, but some have died. 7After that, James saw Christ. Then all the missionaries saw Him. 8Last of all, Christ showed Himself to me as if I had been born too late. 9For I am the least important of all the missionaries. I should not be called a missionary because I made it so hard for God's church. 10I am different now. It is all because of what God did for me by His loving-favor. His loving-favor was not wasted. I worked harder than all the other missionaries. But it was not I who worked. It was God's loving-favor working through me. 11It makes no difference how you heard the Good News. It could have been through me or other missionaries or through me. The important thing is this: We preached the Good News to you and you believed it.

We Will Be Raised From The Dead Also

12We preached to you that Christ has been raised from the dead. But some of you say that people are not raised from the dead. Why do you say this? 13If the dead are not raised, then Christ was not raised from the dead. 14If Christ was not raised from the dead, then what we preach to you is worth nothing. Your faith in Christ is worth nothing. 15That makes us all liars because we said that God raised Christ from the dead. But God did not raise Christ from the dead if the dead do not come to life again. 16If the dead are not raised, then not even Christ was raised from the dead. 17If Christ was not raised from the dead, your faith is worth nothing and you are still living in your sins. 18Then the Christians who have already died are lost in sin. 19If we have hope in Christ in this life only, we are more sad than anyone else.

20But it is true! Christ has been raised from the dead! He was the first One to be raised from the dead and all those who are in graves will follow. 21Death came because of a man, Adam. Being raised from the dead also came because of a Man, Christ. 22All men will die as Adam died. But all those who belong to Christ will be raised to new life. 23This is the way it is: Christ was raised from the dead first. Then all those who belong to Christ will be raised from the dead when He comes again. 24Next, at the end of the world, Christ will give His holy nation over to God the Father. Christ will have destroyed every nation and power. 25Christ must be King until He has destroyed all those who hate Him and work against Him. 26The last thing that will be destroyed is death. 27The Holy Writings say that God has put all things under Christ's feet except Himself. 28When Christ is over all things, He will put Himself under God Who put all things under Christ. And God will be over all things.

29What good will it do people if they are baptized for the dead? If the dead are not raised, why are people baptized for them? 30Why are we also in danger every hour? 31I say this, Christian brothers, I have joy in what Jesus Christ our Lord has done for you. That is why I face death every day. 32As men look at it, what good has it done for me in the city of Ephesus to fight with men who act like wild animals? If the dead are not raised, we might as well be like those who say, "Let us eat and drink, for tomorrow we die."

33Do not let anyone fool you. Bad people can make those who want to live good become bad. 34Keep your minds awake! Stop sinning. Some do not know God at all. I say this to your shame.

The Body That Will Be Raised

35Someone will say, "How are the dead raised? What kind of bodies will they have?" 36What a foolish question! When you plant a seed, it must die before it starts new life. 37When you put it in the earth, you are not planting the body which it will become. You put in only a seed. 38It is God Who gives it a body just as He wants it to have. Each kind of seed becomes a different kind of body.

39All flesh is not the same. Men have one kind of flesh. Animals have another kind. Fish have another kind, and birds have another kind. 40There are bodies in the heavens. There are bodies on earth. Their greatness is not the same. 41The sun has its greatness. The moon has its greatness. Stars have their greatness. One star is different from another star in greatness.

42It is the same with people who are raised from the dead. The body will turn back to dust when it is put in a grave. When the body is raised from the grave, it will never die. 43It has no greatness when it is put in a grave, but it is raised with shining greatness. It is weak when it is put in a grave, but it is raised with power. 44It is a human body when it dies, but it is a God-like body when it is raised from the dead. There are human bodies and there are God-like bodies. 45The Holy Writings say, "The first man, Adam, became a living soul." But the last Adam (Christ) is a life-giving Spirit.

46We have these human bodies first. Then we are given God-like bodies that are ready for heaven. 47Adam was the first man. He was made from the dust of the earth. Christ was the second man. He came down from heaven. 48All men of the earth are made like Adam. But those who belong to Christ will have a body like the body of Christ Who came from heaven. 49Now, our bodies are like Adam's body. But in heaven, our bodies will be like the body of Christ.

50Christian brothers, our bodies which are made of flesh and blood will not go into the holy nation of God. That which dies can have no part in that which will never die. 51For sure, I am telling you a secret. We will not all die, but we will all be changed. 52In a very short time, no longer than it takes for the eye to close and open, the Christians who have died will be raised. It will happen when the last horn sounds. The dead will be raised never to die again. Then the rest of us who are alive will be changed. 53Our human bodies made from dust must be changed into a body that cannot be destroyed. Our human bodies that can die must be changed into bodies that will never die. 54When this that can be destroyed has been changed into that which cannot be destroyed, and when this that does die has been changed into that which cannot die, then it will happen as the Holy Writings said it would happen. They said, "Death has no more power over life." (Isaiah 25:8) 55O death, where is your power? O death, where are your pains? 56The pain in death is sin. Sin has power over those under the Law. 57But God is the One Who gives us power over sin through Jesus Christ our Lord. We give thanks to Him for this.

58So then, Christian brothers, because of all this, be strong. Do not allow anyone to change your mind. Always do your work well for the Lord. You know that whatever you do for Him will not be wasted.

Gifts For The Poor

16 I want to tell you what to do about the money you are gathering for the Christians. Do the same as I told the churches in the country of Galatia to do. 2On the first day of every week each of you should put aside some of your money. Give a certain part of what you have earned. Keep it there because I do not want money gathered when I come. 3When I get there, I will give letters to the men you want to send. They will take your gift to Jerusalem. 4If I can go, they can go with me.

Plans For A Visit

5I want to visit you after I have gone through the country of Macedonia for I am going through there. 6I may be staying with you and even spend the winter with you. Then you can send me on my way to the next place. 7I do not want to stop now. I want to spend some time with you when I can stay longer, if that is what the Lord wants. 8I will stay in the city of Ephesus until the special day to remember how the Holy Spirit came on the church. 9A wide door has been opened to me here to preach the Good News. But there are many who work against me.

10If Timothy comes, receive him and help him so he will not be afraid. He is working for the Lord as I am. 11Everyone should respect him. Send him on his way to me in peace. I expect to see him and some of the other Christians soon. 12I wanted brother Apollos to go with the other

Christians to visit you. But he is not sure he should go now. He will come when he can. [13]Watch and keep awake! Stand true to the Lord. Keep on acting like men and be strong. [14]Everything you do should be done in love.

[15]You know that the family of Stephanas were the first Christians in the country of Greece. They are working for the Lord in helping His people. [16]I ask you to listen to leaders like these and work with them as well as others like them. [17]I am happy that Stephanas and Fortunatus and Achaicus came here. They have helped me and you would have also if you had been here. [18]They have made me happy. They would have made you happy also. Show them you are thankful for their help.

[19]The churches in the countries of Asia say hello. Aquila and Priscilla and the Christians who meet in their house say hello with Christian love. [20]All the Christians here say hello to you. Say hello to each other with a kiss of holy love. [21]I, Paul, am writing the last part of this letter with my own hand. [22]If anyone does not love the Lord, let him be kept from being with Christ. The Lord is coming soon! [23]May you have the loving-favor of our Lord Jesus. [24]I love you all through Christ Jesus. Let it be so.

2 CORINTHIANS

1 This letter is from Paul. I have been chosen by God to be a missionary for Jesus Christ. Timothy is here with me and is writing to you also. We are writing to God's church in the city of Corinth and to all of God's people in the country of Greece. [2]May you have loving-favor and peace from God our Father and the Lord Jesus Christ.

[3]We give thanks to the God and Father of our Lord Jesus Christ. He is our Father Who shows us loving-kindness and our God Who gives us comfort. [4]He gives us comfort in all our troubles. Then we can comfort other people who have the same troubles. We give the same kind of comfort God gives us. [5]As we have suffered much for Christ and have shared in His pain, we also share His great comfort.

[6]But if we are in trouble, it is for your good. And it is so you will be saved from the punishment of sin. If God comforts us, it is for your good also. You too will be given strength not to give up when you have the same kind of trouble we have. [7]Our hope for you is the same all the time. We know you are sharing our troubles. And so you will share the comfort we receive.

[8]We want you to know, Christian brothers, of the trouble we had in the countries of Asia. The load was so heavy we did not have the strength to keep going. At times we did not think we could live. [9]We thought we would die. This happened so we would not put our trust in ourselves, but in God Who raises the dead. [10]Yes, God kept us from what looked like sure death and He is keeping us. As we trust Him, He will keep us in the future. [11]You also help us by praying for us.

Many people thank God for His favor to us. This is an answer to the prayers of many people.

Paul Wants To Visit Corinth

¹²I am happy to say this. Whatever we did in this world, and for sure when we were with you, we were honest and had pure desires. We did not trust in human wisdom. Our power came from God's loving-favor. ¹³We write to you only what we know you can understand. I hope you will understand everything. ¹⁴When the Lord Jesus comes again, you can be as proud of us as we will be proud of you. Right now you do not understand us very well.

¹⁵It was because of this, I wanted to visit you first. In that way, you would be helped two times. ¹⁶I wanted to stop to visit you on my way to the country of Macedonia. I would stop again as I came from there. Then you could help me on my way to the country of Judea. ¹⁷Yes, I changed my mind. Does that show that I change my mind a lot? Do I plan things as people of the world who say yes when they mean no? You know I am not like that! ¹⁸As God is true, my yes means yes. I am not the kind of person who says one thing and means another. ¹⁹Timothy and Silvanus and I have preached to you about Jesus Christ, the Son of God. In Him there is no yes and no. In Him is yes. ²⁰Jesus says yes to all of God's many promises. It is through Jesus that we say, "Let it be so," when we give thanks to God. ²¹God is the One Who makes our faith and your faith strong in Christ. He has set us apart for Himself. ²²He has put His mark on us to show we belong to Him. His Spirit is in our hearts to prove this.

²³I call on God to look into my heart. The reason I did not come to the city of Corinth was because I did not want my strong words to hurt you. ²⁴We are not the boss of your faith but we are working with you to make you happy. Your faith is strong.

2 As I thought about it, I decided I would not come to you again. It would only make you sad. ²If I make you sad, who is going to make me happy? How can you make me happy if I make you sad? ³That is why I wrote that letter to you. I did not want to visit you and be made sad by the very ones who should be making me happy. I am sure when I am happy, you are happy also. ⁴I wrote you with a troubled heart. Tears were coming from my eyes. I did not want to make you sad. I wanted you to know how much I loved you.

Forgiving A Christian

⁵If someone among you has brought sorrow, he has not made me as sad as he has all of you. I say this so I may not make it hard for you. ⁶Most of you have punished him. That is enough for such a person. ⁷Now you should forgive him and comfort him. If you do not, he will be so sad that he will want to give up. ⁸I ask you to show him you do love him. ⁹This is why I wrote to you. I wanted to test you to see if you were willing to obey in all things. ¹⁰If you forgive a man, I forgive him also. If I have forgiven anything, I have done it because of you. Christ sees me as I forgive. ¹¹We forgive so that Satan will not win. We know how he works!

¹²When I arrived in the city of Troas, the Lord opened the door for me to preach the Good News of Christ. ¹³I was worried because I could not find our brother Titus. After saying good-by, I went on my way to the country of Macedonia. ¹⁴We thank God for the power Christ has given us. He leads us and makes us win in everything. He speaks through us wherever we go. The

Good News is like a sweet smell to those who hear it. 15We are a sweet smell of Christ that reaches up to God. It reaches out to those who are being saved from the punishment of sin and to those who are still lost in sin. 16It is the smell of death to those who are lost in sin. It is the smell of life to those who are being saved from the punishment of sin. Who is able for such a work? 17We are not like others. They preach God's Word to make money. We are men of truth and have been sent by God. We speak God's Word with Christ's power. All the time God sees us.

The Old And The New Way

3 Are we making it sound as if we think we are so important? Other people write letters about themselves. Do we need to write such a letter to you? 2You are our letter. You are written in our hearts. You are known and read by all men. 3You are as a letter from Christ written by us. You are not written as other letters are written with ink on pieces of stone. You are written in human hearts by the Spirit of the living God.

4We can say these things because of our faith in God through Christ. 5We know we are not able in ourselves to do any of this work. God makes us able to do these things. 6God is the One Who made us preachers of a New Way of Worship. This New Way of Worship is not of the Law. It is of the Holy Spirit. The Law brings death, but the Holy Spirit gives life.

7The Law of Moses was written on stone and it brought death. But God's shining greatness was seen when it was given. When Moses took it to the Jews, they could not look at his face because of the bright light. But that bright light in his face began to pass away. 8The new way of life through the Holy Spirit comes with much more shining greatness. 9If the Law of Moses, that leads to death, came in

shining greatness, how much greater and brighter is the light that makes us right with God? 10The Law of Moses came with shining greatness long ago. But that light is no longer bright. The shining greatness of the New Way of Worship that brings us life is so much brighter. 11The shining light that came with the Law of Moses soon passed away. But the new way of life is much brighter. It will never pass away.

12We speak without fear because our trust is in Christ. 13We are not like Moses. He put a covering over his face so the Jews would not see that the bright light was passing away. 14Their minds were not able to understand. Even to this day when the Law is read, there is a covering over their minds. They do not see that Christ is the only One Who can take the covering away. 15Yes, to this very day, there is a covering over their hearts whenever the Law of Moses is read. 16But whenever a man turns to the Lord, the covering is taken away. 17The heart is free where the Spirit of the Lord is. The Lord is the Spirit. 18All of us, with no covering on our faces, show the shining greatness of the Lord as in a mirror. All the time we are being changed to look like Him, with more and more of His shining greatness. This change is from the Lord Who is the Spirit.

Paul Is Faithful In Preaching The Good News

4 Through God's loving-kindness, He has given us this job to do. So we do not give up. 2We have put away all things that are done in secret and in shame. We do not play with the Word of God or use it in a false way. Because we are telling the truth, we want men's hearts to listen to us. God knows our desires. 3If the Good News we preach is hidden, it is hidden to those who are lost in sin. 4The eyes of those who do not believe are made blind by Satan who is the god of this world. He does not want the light of the Good News to shine in their hearts. This Good News shines as the shining greatness of Christ. Christ is as God is. 5We do not preach about ourselves. We preach Christ Jesus the Lord. We are your servants because of Jesus. 6It was God Who said, "The light will shine in darkness." (Genesis 1:3) He is the One Who made His light shine in our hearts. This brings us the light of knowing God's shining greatness which is seen in Christ's face.

7We have this light from God in our human bodies. This shows that the power is from God. It is not from ourselves. 8We are pressed on every side, but we still have room to move. We are often in much trouble, but we never give up. 9People make it very hard for us, but we are not left alone. We are knocked down, but we are not destroyed. 10We carry marks on our bodies that show the death of Jesus. This is how Jesus makes His life seen in our bodies. 11Every day of our life we face death because of Jesus. In this way, His life is seen in our bodies. 12Death is working in us because we work for the Lord, but His life is working in you.

13The Holy Writings say, "I believed, so I spoke." (Psalm 116:10) We have the same kind of faith as David had. We also believe, so we speak. 14We know that God raised the Lord Jesus from the dead. He will raise us up also. God will take us to Himself and He will take you. 15These things happened for your good. As more people receive God's favor, they will give thanks for the shining greatness of God.

Life Now - Life In Heaven

16This is the reason we do not give up. Our human body is wearing out. But our spirits are getting stronger every day. 17The little troubles we suffer now for a short time are making us ready for the great things God is going to give us forever. 18We do not look at the things that can be seen. We look at the things that cannot be seen. The things that can be seen will come to an end. But the things that cannot be seen will last forever.

Our Weak Human Bodies

5 Our body is like a house we live in here on earth. When it is destroyed, we know that God has another body for us in heaven. The new one will not be made by human hands as a house is made. This body will last forever. 2Right now we cry inside ourselves because we wish we could have our new body which we will have in heaven. 3We will not be without a body. We will live in a new body. 4While we are in this body, we cry inside ourselves because things are hard for us. It is not that we want to die. Instead, we want to live in our new bodies. We want this dying body to be changed into a living body that lasts forever. 5It is God Who has made us ready for this change. He has given us His Spirit to show us what He has for us.

6We are sure of this. We know that while we are at home in this body we are not with the Lord. 7Our life is lived by faith. We do not live by what we see in front of us. 8We are sure we will be glad to be free of these bodies. It will be good to be at home with the Lord. 9So if we stay here on earth or go home to Him, we always want to please Him. 10For all of us must stand before Christ when He says who is guilty or not guilty. Each one will receive pay for what he has done. He will be paid for the good or the bad done while he lived in this body.

11Because of this, we know the fear of God. So we try to get men to put their trust in Christ. God knows us. I hope that your hearts know me well also. 12We do not want to sound as if we think we are so important. Instead, we are making it easy for you to be proud of us. In that way, you will be able to tell them about us. They always talk about the way people look, but do not care about their hearts. 13Are we crazy to talk like this? It is all because of what God has done. If we are using our minds well, it is for you. 14For the love of Christ puts us into action. We are sure that Christ died for everyone. So, because of that, everyone has a part in His death. 15Christ died for everyone so that they would live for Him. They should not live to please themselves but for Christ Who died on a cross and was raised from the dead for them.

16So from now on, we do not think about what people are like by looking at them. We even thought about Christ that way one time. But we do not think of Him that way anymore. 17For if a man belongs to Christ, he is a new person. The old life is gone. New life has begun. 18All this comes from God. He is the One Who brought us to Himself when we hated Him. He did this through Christ. Then He gave us the work of bringing others to Him. 19God was in Christ. He was working through Christ to bring the whole world back to Himself. God no longer held men's sins against them. And He gave us the work of telling and showing men this.

20We are Christ's missionaries. God is speaking to you through us. We are speaking for Christ and we ask you from our hearts to turn from your sins and come to God. 21Christ never sinned but God put our sin on Him. Then we are made right with God because of what Christ has done for us.

Our Job To Do

6 We are working together with God. We ask you from our hearts not to receive God's loving-favor and then waste it. 2The Holy Writings say, "I heard you at the right time. I helped you on that day to be saved from the punishment of sin. Now is the right time! See! Now is the day to be saved." (Isaiah 49:8) 3We do not want to put anything in the way that would keep people from God. We do not want to be blamed. 4Everything we do shows we are God's servants. We have had to wait and suffer. We have needed things. We have been in many hard places and have had many troubles. 5We have been beaten. We have been put in prison. We have been in fights. We have worked hard. We have stayed awake watching. We have gone without food. 6We have been pure. We have known what to do. We have suffered long. We have been kind. The Holy Spirit has worked in us. We have had true love. 7We have spoken the truth. We have God's power. We have the right kind of sword in the right hand and the right kind of covering in the left hand to fight with. 8Some men respect us and some do not. Some men speak bad against us and some thank us. They say we lie, but we speak the truth. 9Some men act as if they do not know us. And yet we are known by everyone. They act as if we were dead, but we are alive. They try to hurt and destroy us, but they are not able to kill us. 10We are full of sorrow and yet we are always happy. We are poor and yet we make many people rich. We have nothing and yet we have everything.

11We have spoken to you who are in the city of Corinth with plain words. Our hearts are wide open. 12Our hearts are not closed to you. But you have closed your hearts to us. 13I am speaking to you now as if you were my own children. Open your hearts wide to us! That will pay us back for what we have done for you.

14Do not be joined together with those who do not belong to Christ.

How can that which is good get along with that which is bad? How can light be in the same place with darkness? [15]How can Christ get along with the devil? How can one who has put his trust in Christ get along with one who has not put his trust in Christ? [16]How can the house of God get along with false gods? We are the house of the living God. God has said, "I will live in them and will walk among them. I will be their God and they will be my people." (Leviticus 26:12) [17]The Lord has said, "So come out from among them. Do not be joined to them. Touch nothing that is sinful. And I will receive you. [18]I will be a Father to you. You will be My sons and daughters, says the All-powerful God." (Isaiah 52:11)

7 Since we have these great promises, dear friends, let us turn away from every sin of the body or of the spirit. Let us honor God with love and fear by giving ourselves to Him in every way.

His Love For The Corinthians

[2]Receive us into your hearts. We have done no wrong to anyone. We have not led anyone in the wrong way. We have not used anyone for our good. [3]I do not say this to tell you that you are wrong. As I have said before, you have a place in our hearts and always will. If we live or die, we will be together. [4]I trust you and am proud of you. You give me much comfort and joy even when I suffer.

[5]When we arrived in the country of Macedonia, we had no rest. We had all kinds of trouble. There was fighting all around us. Our hearts were afraid. [6]But God gives comfort to those whose hearts are heavy. He gave us comfort when Titus came. [7]Not only did his coming comfort us, but the comfort you had given him made me happy also. He told us how much you wanted to see us. He said

that you were sad because of my trouble and that you wanted to help me. This made me happy.

[8]I am not sorry now if my letter made you sad. I know it made you sad, but it was only for awhile. [9]I am happy now. It is not because you were hurt by my letter, but because it turned you from sin to God. God used it and you were not hurt by what we did. [10]The sorrow that God uses makes people sorry for their sin and leads them to turn from sin so they can be saved from the punishment of sin. We should be happy for that kind of sorrow, but the sorrow of this world brings death. [11]See how this sorrow God allowed you to have has worked in you. You had a desire to be free of that sin I wrote about. You were angry about it. You were afraid. You wanted to do something about it. In every way you did what you could to make it right. [12]I sent this. It was not written only because of the man who did the wrong or because of the one who suffered. [13]All this has given us comfort. More than this, we are happy for the joy Titus has. His spirit has been made stronger by all of you. [14]I told him how proud I was of you. You did not make me ashamed. What we said to Titus proved to be true. [15]He loves you all the more. He remembers how all of you were ready to obey and how you respected him. [16]I am happy that I can have complete trust in you.

The Christian Way To Give

8 Christian brothers, we want you to know how the loving-favor of God has been shown in the churches in the country of Macedonia. [2]They have been put to the test by much trouble, but they have much joy. They have given much even though they were very poor. [3]They gave as much as they could because they wanted to. [4]They asked from their hearts if they could help the Christians in Jerusalem. [5]It was more than we expected. They gave themselves to the Lord first. Then they gave themselves to us to be used as the Lord wanted. [6]We asked Titus to keep on helping you finish this act of love. He was the one to begin this. [7]You are rich in everything. You have faith. You can preach. You have much learning. You have a strong desire to help. And you have love for us. Now do what you should about giving also.

[8]I am not saying that you must do this, but I have told you how others have helped. This is a way to prove how true your love is. [9]You know of the loving-favor shown by our Lord Jesus Christ. He was very rich, but He became very poor for your good. In that way, because He became poor, you might become rich.

[10]This is what I think. You had better finish what you started a year ago. You were the first to want to give a gift of money. [11]Now do it with the same strong desires you had when you started. [12]If a man is ready and willing to give, he should give of what he has, not of what he does not have. [13]This does not mean that others do not have to give and you have to give much. You should share alike. [14]You have more than you need now. When you have need, then they can help you. You should share alike. [15]The Holy Writings say, "The man who gathered much did not have too much. The man who did not gather much had enough." (Exodus 16:18)

Titus Will Be Coming

[16]I thank God that He gave Titus the same desire to help you. [17]He was glad when we asked him to help you. He decided himself to go to you. [18]We are sending the Christian brother along. He is respected in the churches for his preaching. [19]Not only that, but he has been asked by the churches to travel with me to Jerusalem. He will help in giving them the gift. The Lord will be honored by it because it shows how we want to help each other.

[20]We want everyone to trust us with the way we take this large gift of money to them. [21]We want to do the right thing. We want God and men to know we are honest. [22]We are sending another Christian brother with them. We have tested him many times. His faith has proven to be true. He wants very much to help because he trusts you. [23]Titus works with me to help you. The other two Christian brothers have been sent by the churches. Their lives honor Christ. [24]Show these men you love them and let the churches see your love. Show them the reason I am proud of you.

Giving To Help Other Christians

9 I do not need to write to you about helping those who belong to Christ. [2]I know you want to do it. I have told the people in the country of Macedonia that you were ready to send money last year. Your desire has started most of them to give. [3]I am sending these Christian brothers so the words I said about you will prove to be true and you will be ready to help. [4]What if some of the people of Macedonia came with me and found you were not ready to send your gift of money? We would all be ashamed since we have talked of you so much. [5]That is why I asked these men to go ahead of me. They can see that the gift you promised is ready. In that way, it will be a true gift and not something you were made to do.

[6]Remember, the man who plants only a few seeds will not have much grain to gather. The man who plants many seeds will have much grain to gather. [7]Each man should give as he has decided in his heart. He should not give, wishing he could keep it. Or he should not give if he feels he has to give. God loves a man who gives

because he wants to give. [8]God can give you all you need. He will give you more than enough. You will have everything you need for yourselves. And you will have enough left over to give when there is a need. [9]The Holy Writings say, "He has given much to the poor. His acts of love last forever." (Psalm 112:9) [10]It is God Who gives seed to the man to plant. He also gives the bread to eat. Then we know He will give you more seed to plant and make it grow so you will have more to give away. [11]God will give you enough so you can always give to others. Then many will give thanks to God for sending gifts through us. [12]This gift you give not only helps those in need, it makes them give thanks to God also. [13]You are proving by this act of love what you are. They will give thanks to God for your gift to them and to others. This proves you obey the Good News of Christ. [14]They will pray for you with great love because God has given you His loving-favor. [15]Thank God for His great Gift.

Paul Proves He Is A Missionary

10 I, Paul, ask you this myself. I do it through Christ Who is so gentle and kind. Some people say that I am gentle and quiet when I am with you, but that I have no fear and that my language is strong when I am away from you. [2]Do not make me speak strong words to you when I come. Some people think we want the things of the world because of what we do and say. I have decided to talk to these people if I have to. [3]It is true, we live in a body of flesh. But we do not fight like people of the world. [4]We do not use those things to fight with that the world uses. We use the things God gives to fight with and they have power. Those things God gives to fight with destroy the strong places of the devil. [5]We break

down every thought and proud thing that puts itself up against the wisdom of God. We take hold of every thought and make it obey Christ. [6]We are ready to punish those who will not obey as soon as you obey in everything.

[7]You are seeing things only as men see them. If anyone feels sure he belongs to Christ, he should remember that we belong to Christ also. [8]I am not ashamed if I say this of myself. The Lord gave me the right and the power to help you become stronger, not to break you down. [9]I do not want you to think I am trying to make you afraid with my letters. [10]They say, "His letters are strong and they make us think. When he is here with us, he is weak and he is hard to listen to." [11]What we say in our letters we will do when we get there. They should understand this. [12]We do not compare ourselves with those who think they are very good. They compare themselves with themselves. They decide what they think is good or bad and compare themselves with those ideas. They are foolish. [13]But we will not talk with pride more than God allows us to. We will follow the plan of the work He has given us to do and you are a part of that work. [14]We did not go farther than we were supposed to go when we came to you. But we did come to you with the Good News of Christ. [15]We take no pride in the work others have done there. But we hope your faith will keep growing because of help from others. Then we will grow because of you. [16]We hope to preach the Good News in the countries on the other side of you. Then we would take no pride in work done by another person in another country. [17]If anyone wants to be proud, he should be proud of what the Lord has done. [18]It is not what a man thinks and says of himself that is important. It is what God thinks of him.

Paul - The True Missionary

11 I wish you would listen to a little foolish talk from me. Now listen. ²I am jealous for you with a God-like jealousy. I have given you, as a woman who has never had a man, to one Husband, Who is Christ. ³Eve was fooled by the snake in the garden of Eden. In the same way, I am afraid that you will be fooled and led away from your pure love for Christ. ⁴You listen when someone comes and preaches a different Jesus than the One we preached. You believe what you hear about a different spirit and different good news than that which we preached.

⁵I do not think I am less than those special missionaries who are coming to you. ⁶Even if it is hard for me to speak, I know what I am talking about. You know this by now. ⁷Did I do wrong? I did not ask you for anything when I preached the Good News to you. I made myself poor so you would be made rich. ⁸I did take money from other churches. I used it while I worked with you so you would not have to pay me. ⁹Some of the time I had no money when I was with you. But I did not ask you for money. The Christians from the country of Macedonia brought me what I needed. I did not ask you and I will not ask you for anything. ¹⁰As sure as the truth of Christ is in me, I will not stop telling those in the country of Greece that I am proud of this. ¹¹Does it mean I do not love you? God knows I do.

¹²What I am doing now, I will keep on doing. I will do it to stop those who say they work as we do. ¹³Those men are false missionaries. They lie about their work. But they make themselves look like true missionaries of Christ. ¹⁴It is no surprise! The devil makes himself look like an angel of light. ¹⁵And so it is no surprise if his servants also make themselves look like preachers of the Good News. They and their work will come to the same end.

What Paul Suffered As A Missionary

¹⁶Let me say it again. Do not think of me as a fool. But if you do, then let this foolish man speak a little about himself. ¹⁷The Lord has not told me to talk about myself. I am foolish when I do talk about myself like this. ¹⁸Since the other men tell you all about themselves, I will talk about myself also. ¹⁹You are so wise! You put up with fools! ²⁰You listen to anyone who tells you what to do or makes money off of you or sets a trap for you. You will listen to anyone who makes himself bigger than you or hits you in the face. ²¹I am ashamed to say that I am weak! But I do not do as they do. Whatever they say about themselves, I can say about myself also. (I know what I am saying sounds foolish.)

²²Are they Jews? So am I. Are they from the family of Israel? So am I. Are they from the family of Abraham? So am I. ²³Do they work for Christ? I have worked for Him much more than they have. (I speak as if I am crazy.) I have done much more work. I have been in prison more times. I cannot remember how many times I have been whipped. Many times I have been in danger of death. ²⁴Five different times the Jews whipped me across my back thirty-nine times. ²⁵Three times they beat me with sticks. One time they threw stones at me. Three times I was on ships that were wrecked. I spent a day and a night in the water. ²⁶I have made many hard trips. I have been in danger from high water on rivers. I have been in danger from robbers. I have been in danger from the Jews. I have been in danger from people who do not know God. I have been in danger in cities and in the desert. I have been in danger on the sea. I have been in danger among people

who say they belong to Christ but do not. 27I have worked very hard and have been tired and have had pain. I have gone many times without sleep. I have been hungry and thirsty. I have gone without food and clothes. I have been out in the cold. 28More than all these things that have happened to my body, the care of all the churches is heavy on me. 29When someone is weak, I feel weak also. When someone is led into sin, I have a strong desire to help him. 30If I must talk about myself, I will do it about the things that show how weak I am. 31The God and Father of our Lord Jesus Christ is to be honored and thanked forever. He knows I am telling the truth. 32In the city of Damascus the leader of the people under King Aretas put soldiers at the gates to take me. 33But I was let down in a basket through a window in the wall and I got away.

Paul Sees Something True In A Special Dream

12 I have to talk about myself, even if it does no good. But I will keep on telling about some things I saw in a special dream and that which the Lord has shown me. 2I know a man who belongs to Christ. Fourteen years ago he was taken up to the highest heaven. (I do not know if his body was taken up or just his spirit. Only God knows.) 3I say it again, I know this man was taken up. But I do not know if his body or just his spirit was taken up. Only God knows. 4When he was in the highest heaven, he heard things that cannot be told with words. No man is allowed to tell them. 5I will be proud about this man, but I will not be proud about myself except to say things which show how weak I am. 6Even if I talk about myself, I would not be a fool because it is the truth. But I will say no more because I want no one to think better of me than he

does when he sees or hears me.

7The things God showed me were so great. But to keep me from being too full of pride because of seeing these things, I have been given trouble in my body. It was sent from Satan to hurt me. It keeps me from being proud. 8I asked the Lord three times to take it away from me. 9He answered me, "I am all you need. I give you My loving-favor. My power works best in weak people." I am happy to be weak and have troubles so I can have Christ's power in me. 10I receive joy when I am weak. I receive joy when people talk against me and make it hard for me and try to hurt me and make trouble for me. I receive joy when all these things come to me because of Christ. For when I am weak, then I am strong.

11I have been making a fool of myself talking like this. But you made me do it. You should be telling what I have done. Even if I am nothing at all, I am not less important than those false missionaries of yours. 12When I was with you, I proved to you that I was a true missionary. I did powerful works and there were special things to see. These things were done in the strength and power from God. 13What makes you feel less important than the other churches? Is it because I did not let you give me food and clothing? Forgive me for this wrong!

14This is the third time I am ready to come to you. I want nothing from you. I want you, not your money. You are my children. Children should not have to help care for their parents. Parents should help their children. 15I am glad to give anything I have, even myself, to help you. When I love you more, it looks as if you love me less.

16It is true that I was not a heavy load to you. But some say I set a trap for you. 17How could I have done that? Did I get anything from you through the men I sent to you? 18I asked Titus and the other Christian brother to visit you. Did Titus get anything from you? Did we not do things that showed we had the same desires and followed the same plan? 19 It may look to you as if we had been trying to make everything look right for ourselves all this time. God knows and so does Christ that all this is done to help you. 20 I am afraid that when I visit you I will not find you as I would like you to be. And you will not find me as you would like me to be. I am afraid I will find you fighting and jealous and angry and arguing and talking about each other and thinking of yourselves as being too important and making trouble. 21 I am afraid when I get there God will take all the pride away from me that I had for you. I will not be happy about many who have lived in sin and done sex sins and have had a desire for such things and have not been sorry for their sins and turned from them.

13 This is my third visit to you. The Holy Writings tell us that when people think someone has done wrong, it must be proven by two or three people who saw the wrong being done. 2 During my second visit I talked to you who have been sinning and to all the others. While I am away, I tell you this again. The next time I come I will be hard on those who sin. 3 Since you want to know, I will prove to you that Christ speaks through me. Christ is not weak when He works in your hearts. He uses His power in you. 4 Christ's weak human body died on a cross. It is by God's power that Christ lives today. We are weak. We are as He was. But we will be alive with Christ through the power God has for us.

5 Put yourselves through a test. See if you belong to Christ. Then you will know you belong to Christ, unless you do not pass the test. 6 I trust you see that we belong to Him and have passed the test. 7 We pray to God that you do no wrong. We do not pray this to show that our teaching is so great, but that you will keep on doing what is right, even if it looks as if we have done much wrong. 8 We cannot work against the truth of God. We only work for it. 9 We are glad when we are weak and you are strong. We pray that you will become strong Christians. 10 This is why I am writing these things while I am away from you. Then when I get there, I will not have to use strong words or punish you to show you that the Lord gives me this power. This power is to be used to make you stronger Christians, not to make you weak by hurting your faith.

11 Last of all, Christian brothers, good-by. Do that which makes you complete. Be comforted. Work to get along with others. Live in peace. The God of love and peace will be with you. 12 Say hello to each other with a kiss of holy love. 13 All those here who belong to Christ say hello. 14 May you have loving-favor from our Lord Jesus Christ. May you have the love of God. May you be joined together by the Holy Spirit.

GALATIANS

1 This letter is from Paul. I am a missionary sent by Jesus Christ and God the Father Who raised Jesus from the dead. I am not sent by men or by any one man. ²All the Christians join me in writing to you who are in the churches in the country of Galatia. ³May you have loving-favor and peace from God our Father and from the Lord Jesus Christ. ⁴He gave Himself to die for our sins. He did this so we could be saved from this sinful world. This is what God wanted Him to do. ⁵May He have all the honor forever. Let it be so.

⁶I am surprised you are leaving Christ so soon. You were chosen through His loving-favor. But now you are turning and listening to another kind of good news. ⁷No! There is not another kind of good news. There are some who would like to lead you in the wrong way. They want to change the Good News about Christ. ⁸Even if we or an angel from heaven should preach another kind of good news to you that is not the one we preached, let him be cursed. ⁹As we said before, I will say it again. If any man is preaching another good news to you which is not the one you have received, let him be cursed.

This Good News Is From God

¹⁰Do you think I am trying to get the favor of men, or of God? If I were still trying to please men, I would not be a servant owned by Christ.

¹¹Christian brothers, I want you to know the Good News I preached to you was not made by man. ¹²I did not receive it from man. No one taught it to me. I received it from Jesus Christ as He showed it to me.

¹³You have heard of my old life when I followed the Jewish religion. I made it as hard as I could for the Christians and did everything I could to destroy the Christian church. ¹⁴I had learned more about the Jewish religion than many of the Jews my age. I had a much stronger desire than they to follow the ways of our early fathers. ¹⁵But God chose me before I was born. By His loving-favor He called me to work for Him. ¹⁶His Son was to be seen in me. He did this so I could preach about Christ to the people who are not Jews. When this happened, I did not talk to men. ¹⁷I did not even go to Jerusalem to talk to those who were missionaries before me. Instead, I went to the country of Arabia. Later I returned to the city of Damascus.

¹⁸Three years later I went to Jerusalem to meet Peter. I stayed with him fifteen days. ¹⁹I did not see any of the other missionaries except James, the Lord's brother. ²⁰I am writing the truth. God knows I am not lying.

²¹I went from Jerusalem to the countries of Syria and Cilicia. ²²None of the Christians in the churches in the country of Judea had ever seen me. ²³The only thing they heard was, "The one who tried to destroy the Christian church is now preaching the Good News!" ²⁴And they gave thanks to God because of me.

The Church Leaders In Jerusalem Say Paul Is A True Missionary

2 Fourteen years later I went again to Jerusalem. This time I took Barnabas. Titus went with us also. ²God showed me in a special way I should go. I spoke to them about the Good News that I preach among the people who are not Jews. First of all, I talked alone to the important church leaders. I wanted them to know what I was preaching. I did not want that which I was doing or would be doing to be wasted.

3 Titus was with me. Even being a Greek, he did not have to go through the religious act of becoming a Jew. 4 Some men who called themselves Christians asked about this. They got in our meeting without being asked. They came there to find out how free we are who belong to Christ. They tried to get us to be chained to the Law. 5 But we did not listen to them or do what they wanted us to do so the truth of the Good News might be yours.

6 Those who seemed to be important church leaders did not help me. They did not teach me anything new. What they were, I do not care. God looks on us all as being the same. 7 Anyway, they saw how I had been given the work of preaching the Good News to the people who are not Jews, as Peter had been given the work of preaching the Good News to the Jews. 8 For God helped Peter work with the Jews. He also helped me work with those who are not Jews. 9 James and Peter and John were thought of as being the head church leaders. They could see that God's loving-favor had been given to me. Barnabas and I were joined together with them by shaking hands. Then we were sent off to work with the people who are not Jews. They were to work with the Jews. 10 They asked us to do only one thing. We were to remember to help poor people. I think this is important also.

11 But when Peter came to Antioch, I had to stand up against him because he was guilty. 12 Peter had been eating with the people who are not Jews. But after some men came who had been with James, he kept away from them. He was afraid of those who believe in the religious act of becoming a Jew. 13 Then the rest of the Jews followed him because they were afraid to do what they knew they should do. Even Barnabas was fooled by those who pretended to be someone they were not. 14 When I saw they were not honest about the truth of the Good News, I spoke to Peter in front of them all. I said, "If you are a Jew, but live like the people who are not Jews, why do you make the people who are not Jews live like the Jews?" 15 You and I were born Jews. We were not sinners from among the people who are not Jews. 16 Even so, we know we cannot become right with God by obeying the Law. A man is made right with God by putting his trust in Jesus Christ. For that reason, we have put our trust in Jesus Christ also. We have been made right with God because of our faith in Christ and not by obeying the Law. No man can be made right with God by obeying the Law. 17 As we try to become right with God by what Christ has done for us, what if we find we are sinners also? Does that mean Christ makes us sinners? No! Never! 18 But if I work toward being made right with God by keeping the Law, then I make myself a sinner. 19 The Law has no power over me. I am dead to the Law. Now I can live for God. 20 I have been put up on the cross to die with Christ. I no longer live. Christ lives in me. The life I now live in this body, I live by putting my trust in the Son of God. He was the One Who loved me and gave Himself for me. 21 I say that we are not to put aside the loving-favor of God. If we could be made right with God by keeping the Law, then Christ died for nothing.

3 You foolish Galatians! What strange powers are trying to lead you from the way of faith in Christ? We made it plain for you to see that Jesus Christ was put on a cross to die. 2 There is one thing I want to know. Did you receive the

Holy Spirit by keeping the Law? Or did you receive Him by hearing about Christ? [3]How foolish can you be? You started the Christian life by the Holy Spirit. Do you think you are going to become better Christians by your old way of worship? [4]You suffered so much because of the Good News you received. Was this all of no use? [5]He gave you the Holy Spirit and did powerful works among you. Does He do it because you do what the Law says or because you hear and believe the truth?

[6]It was the same with Abraham. He put his trust in God. This made Abraham right with God. [7]Be sure to remember that all men who put their trust in God are the sons of Abraham. [8]The Holy Writings said long ago that God would save the people who are not Jews from the punishment of sin also. Before this time the Holy Writings gave the Good News to Abraham in these words, "All nations will be happy because of you." (Genesis 12:3) [9]So then, all those who have faith will be happy, along with Abraham who had faith.

[10]All those who expect the Law to save them from the punishment of sin will be punished. Because it is written, "Everyone who does not keep on doing all the things written in the Book of the Law will be punished." (Deuteronomy 26:27) [11]No one is made right with God by doing what the Law says. For, "The man right with God will live by faith." (Habakkuk 2:4) [12]The Law does not use faith. It says, "You must obey all the Law or you will die." (Leviticus 18:5) [13]Christ bought us with His blood and made us free from the Law. In that way, the Law could not punish us. Christ did this by carrying the load and by being punished instead of us. It is written, "Anyone who hangs on a cross is hated and punished." (Deuteronomy 21:23) [14]Because of the price Christ Jesus paid, the good things that came to Abraham might come to the

people who are not Jews. And by putting our trust in Christ, we receive the Holy Spirit He has promised.

[15]Christian brothers, let me show you what this means. If two men agree to something and sign their names on a paper promising to stay true to what they agree, it cannot be changed. [16]Now the promise was made to Abraham and to his son. He does not say, "And to sons," speaking of many. But instead, "And to your Son," which means Christ. [17]This is what I am saying: The Law which came 430 years later could not change the promise. The promise had already been made by God. The Law could not put that promise aside. [18]If it had been possible to be saved from the punishment of sin by obeying the Law, the promise God gave Abraham would be worth nothing. But since it is not possible to be saved by obeying the Law, the promise God gave Abraham is worth everything.

[19]Then why do we have the Law? It was given because of sin. It was to be used until Christ came. The promise had been made looking toward Christ. The Law was given by angels through Moses who stood between God and man. [20]But when the promise was given to Abraham, God gave it without anyone standing between them. [21]Is the Law against the promise of God? No! Never! If it had been possible to be saved from the punishment of sin by obeying the Law, then being right with God would have come by obeying the Law. [22]But the Holy Writings say that all men are guilty of sin. Then that which was promised might be given to those who put their trust in Christ. It will be because their faith is in Him.

[23]Before it was possible to be saved from the punishment of sin by putting our trust in Christ, we were held under the Law. It was as if we were being kept in prison. We were kept this way until Christ came. [24]The Law was used to lead us to

Christ. It was our teacher, and so we were made right with God by putting our trust in Christ. [25]Now that our faith is in Christ, we do not need the Law to lead us. [26]You are now children of God because you have put your trust in Christ Jesus. [27]All of you who have been baptized to show you belong to Christ have become like Christ. [28]God does not see you as a Jew or as a Greek. He does not see you as a person sold to work or as a person free to work. He does not see you as a man or as a woman. You are all one in Christ. [29]If you belong to Christ, then you have become the true children of Abraham. What God promised to him is now yours.

Sons Of God

4 Let me say this another way. A young child who will get all the riches of his family is not different from a servant who is owned by the family. And yet the young child owns everything. [2]While he is young, he is cared for by men his father trusts. These men tell the child what he can and cannot do. The child cannot do what he wants to do until he has become a certain age. [3]We were as children also held by the Law. We obeyed the Law in our religious worship. [4]But at the right time, God sent His Son. A woman gave birth to Him under the Law. [5]This all happened so He could buy with His blood and make free all those who were held by the Law. Then we might become the sons of God. [6]Because you are the sons of God, He has sent the Spirit of His Son into our hearts. The Spirit cries, "Father!" [7]So now you are no longer a servant who is owned by someone. You are a son. If you are a son, then you will receive what God has promised through Christ.

[8]During the time when you did not know God, you worshiped false gods. [9]But now that you know God, or should I say that you are known

by God, why do you turn back again to the weak old Law? Why do you want to do those religious acts of worship that will keep you from being free? Why do you want to be held under the power of the Law again? [10]You do special things on certain days and months and years and times of the year. [11]I am afraid my work with you was wasted.

Living By The Law Or Being Free

[12]I ask you, Christian brothers, stay free from the Law as I am. Even if I am a Jew, I became free from the Law, just as you who are not Jews. You did no wrong to me. [13]You know I preached the Good News to you the first time because of my sickness. [14]Even though I was hard to look at because of my sickness, you did not turn away from me. You took me in as an angel from God. You took me in as you would have taken in Christ Jesus Himself. [15]What has become of the happiness you once had? You would have taken out your own eyes if you could have and given them to me. [16]Do you hate me because I have told you the truth? [17]Those false teachers are trying to turn your eyes toward them. They do not want you to follow my teaching. What they are doing is not good. [18]It is good when people help you if they do not hope to get something from it. They should help you all the time, not only when I am with you. [19]My children, I am suffering birth pain for you again. I will suffer until Christ's life is in your life. [20]I wish I could be with you now. I wish I could speak to you in a more gentle voice, but I am troubled about you.

[21]Listen! If you want to be under the Law, why do you not listen to what it says? [22]The Holy Writings say that Abraham had two sons. One was born from a woman servant (Hagar) who was owned by someone. She had to do what she was told. The other son was born from a

woman (Sarah) who was free to work and live as she desired. (Genesis 16:15; 21:2-9) 23The son born from the woman servant who was owned by someone was like any other birth. The son born from the free woman was different. That son had been promised by God. 24Think of it like this: These two women show God's two ways of working with His people. The children born from Hagar are under the Law given on Mount Sinai. They will be servants who are owned by someone and will always be told what to do! 25Hagar is known as Mount Sinai in the country of Arabia. She is as Jerusalem is today, because she and her children are not free to do what they want to do. 26But the Jerusalem of heaven is the free woman, and she is our mother. 27The Holy Writings say, "Woman, be happy, you who have had no children. Cry for joy, you who have never had the pains of having a child, for you will have many children. Yes, you will have more children than the one who has a husband." (Isaiah 54:1) 28Christian brothers, we are like Isaac. We are the children God promised. 29At that time the son born as other children are born made it very hard for the son born by the Holy Spirit. It is the same way now. 30But what do the Holy Writings say? They say, "Put the woman servant who is owned by someone and her son out of your home. The son of that woman servant will never get any of the riches of the family. It will all be given to the son of the free woman." (Genesis 21:10) 31Christian brothers, we are not children of the woman servant who was owned by someone (Hagar). We are children of the free woman (Sarah).

Christ Made Us Free

5 Christ made us free. Stay that way. Do not get chained all over again in the Law and its kind of religious worship.

2Listen to me! I, Paul, tell you that if you have the religious act of becoming a Jew done on you, Christ will be of no use to you at all. 3I say it again. Every man who has the religious act of becoming a Jew done on him must obey every Law. 4If you expect to be made right with God by obeying the Law, then you have turned away from Christ and His loving-favor. 5We are waiting for the hope of being made right with God. This will come through the Holy Spirit and by faith. 6If we belong to Jesus Christ, it means nothing to have or not to have gone through the religious act of becoming a Jew. But faith working through love is important.

7You were doing well. Who stopped you from obeying the truth? 8Whatever he used did not come from the One Who chose you to have life. 9It only takes a little yeast to make the whole loaf of bread rise. 10I feel I can trust you because of what the Lord has done in your life. I believe you will not follow another way. Whoever is trying to lead you in the wrong way will suffer for it. 11Christian brothers, if I would still preach that people must go through the religious act of becoming a Jew to be a Christian, I would not be suffering from those who are making it hard for me. If I preached like that, the Jews would have no reason to be against the cross of Christ. 12I wish those who are so willing to cut your bodies would complete the job by cutting themselves off from you.

13Christian brother, you were chosen to be free. Be careful that you do not please your old selves by sinning because you are free. Live this free life by loving and helping others. 14You obey the whole Law when you do this one thing, "Love your neighbor as you love yourself." (Leviticus 19:18) 15But if you hurt and make it very hard for each other, watch out or you may be destroyed by each other.

¹⁶I say this to you: Let the Holy Spirit lead you in each step. Then you will not please your sinful old selves. ¹⁷The things our old selves want to do are against what the Holy Spirit wants. The Holy Spirit does not agree with what our sinful old selves want. These two are against each other. So you cannot do what you want to do. ¹⁸If you let the Holy Spirit lead you, the Law no longer has power over you. ¹⁹The things your sinful old self wants to do are: sex sins, sinful desires, wild living, ²⁰worshiping false gods, witchcraft, hating, fighting, being jealous, being angry, arguing, dividing into little groups and thinking the other groups are wrong, false teaching, ²¹wanting something someone else has, killing other people, using strong drink, wild parties, and all things like these. I told you before and I am telling you again that those who do these things will have no place in the holy nation of God. ²²But the fruit that comes from having the Holy Spirit in our lives is: love, joy, peace, not giving up, being kind, being good, having faith, ²³being gentle, and being the boss over our own desires. The Law is not against these things. ²⁴Those of us who belong to Christ have nailed our sinful old selves on His cross. Our sinful desires are now dead.

²⁵If the Holy Spirit is living in us, let us be led by Him in all things. ²⁶Let us not become proud in ways in which we should not. We must not make hard feelings among ourselves as Christians or make anyone jealous.

Help Other Christians

6 Christian brothers, if a person is found doing some sin, you who are stronger Christians should lead that one back into the right way. Do not be proud as you do it. Watch yourself, because you may be tempted also. ²Help each other in troubles and problems. This is the kind of law Christ asks us to obey. ³If anyone thinks he is important when he is nothing, he is fooling himself. ⁴Everyone should look at himself and see how he does his own work. Then he can be happy in what he has done. He should not compare himself with his neighbor. ⁵Everyone must do his own work.

⁶He who is taught God's Word should share the good things he has with his teacher. ⁷Do not be fooled. You cannot fool God. A man will get back whatever he plants! ⁸If a man does things to please his sinful old self, his soul will be lost. If a man does things to please the Holy Spirit, he will have life that lasts forever. ⁹Do not let yourselves get tired of doing good. If we do not give up, we will get what is coming to us at the right time. ¹⁰Because of this, we should do good to everyone. For sure, we should do good to those who belong to Christ.

The Christian's Pride Should Be In The Cross

¹¹See what big letters I make when I write to you with my own hand. ¹²Those men who say you must go through the religious act of becoming a Jew are doing it because they want to make a good show in front of the world. They do this so they will not have to suffer because of following the way of the cross of Christ. ¹³Those who have gone through the religious act of becoming a Jew do not even keep the Law themselves. But they want you to go through that religious act so they can be proud that you are their followers. ¹⁴I do not want to be proud of anything except in the cross of our Lord Jesus Christ. Because of the cross, the ways of this world are dead to me, and I am dead to them. ¹⁵If a person does or does not go through the religious act of becoming a Jew, it is worth nothing. The important thing is to become a new person. ¹⁶Those who

follow this way will have God's peace and loving-kindness. They are the people of God.

¹⁷Let no one make trouble for me from now on. For I have on my body the whip marks of one who has been a servant owned by Jesus. ¹⁸Christian brothers, may the loving-favor of our Lord Jesus Christ be with your spirit. Let it be so.

EPHESIANS

1 This letter is from Paul. I am a missionary for Jesus Christ. God wanted me to work for Him. This letter is to those who belong to Christ in the city of Ephesus and to you who are faithful followers of Christ Jesus. ²May you have loving-favor and peace from God our Father and from our Lord Jesus Christ.

³Let us honor and thank the God and Father of our Lord Jesus Christ. He has already given us a taste of what heaven is like. ⁴Even before the world was made, God chose us for Himself because of His love. He planned that we should be holy and without blame as He sees us. ⁵God already planned to have us as His own children. This was done by Jesus Christ. In His plan God wanted this done. ⁶We thank God for His loving-favor to us. He gave this loving-favor to us through His much-loved Son. ⁷Because of the blood of Christ, we are bought and made free from the punishment of sin. And because of His blood, our sins are forgiven. His loving-favor to us is so rich. ⁸He was so willing to give all of this to us. He did this with wisdom and understanding. ⁹God told us the secret of what He wanted to do. It is this: In loving thought He planned long ago to send Christ into the world. ¹⁰The plan was for Christ to gather us all together at the right time. If we are in heaven or still on earth, He will bring us together and will be head over all. ¹¹We were already chosen to be God's own children by Christ. This was done just like the plan He had. ¹²We who were the first to put our trust in Christ should thank Him for His greatness. ¹³The truth is the Good News. When you heard the truth, you put your trust in Christ. Then God marked you by giving you His Holy Spirit as a promise. ¹⁴The Holy Spirit was given to us as a promise that we will receive everything God has for us. God's Spirit will be with us until God finishes His work of making us complete. God does this to show His shining greatness.

Paul's Prayer For The Christians In Ephesus

¹⁵I have heard of your faith in the Lord Jesus and your love for all Christians. ¹⁶Since then, I have always given thanks for you and pray for you. ¹⁷I pray that the great God and Father of our Lord Jesus Christ may give you the wisdom of His Spirit. Then you will be able to understand the secrets about Him as you know Him better. ¹⁸I pray that your hearts will be able to understand. I pray that you will know about the hope given by God's call. I pray that you will see how great the things are that He has promised to those who belong to Him. ¹⁹I pray

that you will know how great His power is for those who have put their trust in Him. ²⁰It is the same power that raised Christ from the dead. This same power put Christ at God's right side in heaven. ²¹This place was given to Christ. It is much greater than any king or leader can have. No one else can have this place of honor and power. No one in this world or in the world to come can have such honor and power. ²²God has put all things under Christ's power and has made Him to be the head leader over all things of the church. ²³The church is the body of Christ. It is filled by Him Who fills all things everywhere with Himself.

God Saved Us From Sin

2 At one time you were dead because of your sins. ²You followed the sinful ways of the world and obeyed the leader of the power of darkness. He is the devil who is now working in the people who do not obey God. ³At one time all of us lived to please our old selves. We gave in to what our bodies and minds wanted. We were sinful from birth like all other people and would suffer from the anger of God.

⁴But God had so much loving-kindness. He loved us with such a great love. ⁵Even when we were dead because of our sins, He made us alive by what Christ did for us. You have been saved from the punishment of sin by His loving-favor. ⁶God raised us up from death when He raised up Christ Jesus. He has given us a place with Christ in the heavens. ⁷He did this to show us through all the time to come the great riches of His loving-favor. He has shown us His kindness through Christ Jesus.

⁸For by His loving-favor you have been saved from the punishment of sin through faith. It is not by anything you have done. It is a gift of God. ⁹It is not given to you because you worked for it. If you could work

for it, you would be proud. ¹⁰We are His work. He has made us to belong to Christ Jesus so we can work for Him. He planned that we should do this.

Followers Now Become The Body Of Christ

¹¹Do not forget that at one time you did not know God. The Jews, who had gone through the religious act of becoming a Jew by man's hands, said you were people who do not know God. ¹²You were living without Christ then. The Jewish people who belonged to God had nothing to do with you. The promises He gave to them were not for you. You had nothing in this world to hope for. You were without God. ¹³But now you belong to Christ Jesus. At one time you were far away from God. Now you have been brought close to Him. Christ did this for you when He gave His blood on the cross. ¹⁴We have peace because of Christ. He has made the Jews and those who are not Jews one people. He broke down the wall that divided them. ¹⁵He stopped the fighting between them by His death on the cross. He put an end to the Law. Then He made of the two peoples one new kind of people like Himself. In this way, He made peace. ¹⁶He brought both groups together to God. Christ finished the fighting between them by His death on the cross. ¹⁷Then Christ came and preached the Good News of peace to you who were far away from God. And He preached it to us who were near God. ¹⁸Now all of us can go to the Father through Christ by way of the one Holy Spirit. ¹⁹From now on you are not strangers and people who are not citizens. You are citizens together with those who belong to God. You belong in God's family. ²⁰This family is the part on which the building stands. It is built on the teachings of the missionaries and the

early preachers. Jesus Christ Himself is the cornerstone, which is the most important part of the building. ²¹Christ keeps this building together and it is growing into a holy building for the Lord. ²²You are also being put together as a part of this building because God lives in you by His Spirit.

3 I, Paul, am in prison because I am a missionary for Jesus Christ to you who are not Jews. ²I am sure you have heard that God trusted me with His loving-favor. ³I wrote a little about this to you before. In a special way, God showed me His secret plan. ⁴When you read this, you will understand how I know about the things that are not easy to understand about Christ. ⁵Long ago men did not know these things. But now they have been shown to His missionaries and to the early preachers by the Holy Spirit. ⁶Let me tell you that the Good News is for the people who are not Jews also. They are able to have life that lasts forever. They are to be a part of His church and family, together with the Jews. And together they are to receive all that God has promised through Christ.

⁷God asked me to preach this Good News. He gave me the gift of His loving-favor. He gave me His power to preach it. ⁸Of all those who belong to Christ, I am the least important. But this loving-favor was given me to preach to the people who are not Jews. I was to tell them of the great riches in Christ which do not come to an end. ⁹I was to make all men understand the meaning of this secret. God kept this secret to Himself from the beginning of the world. And He is the One Who made all things. ¹⁰This was done so the great wisdom of God might be shown now to the leaders and powers in the heavenly places. It is being done through the church. ¹¹This was the plan God had for all time. He did this through Christ Jesus our Lord. ¹²We

can come to God without fear because we have put our trust in Christ. ¹³So I ask you not to lose heart because of my suffering for you. It is to help you.

Paul's Prayer For The Church

¹⁴For this reason, I bow my knees and pray to the Father. ¹⁵It is from Him that every family in heaven and on earth has its name. ¹⁶I pray that because of the riches of His shining greatness, He will make you strong with power in your hearts through the Holy Spirit. ¹⁷I pray that Christ may live in your hearts by faith. I pray that you will be filled with love. ¹⁸I pray that you will be able to understand how wide and how long and how high and how deep His love is. ¹⁹I pray that you will know the love of Christ. His love goes beyond anything we can understand. I pray that you will be filled with God Himself.

²⁰God is able to do much more than we ask or think through His power working in us. ²¹May we see His shining greatness in the church. May all people in all time honor Christ Jesus. Let it be so.

Full-grown Christians

4 I am being held in prison because of working for the Lord. I ask you from my heart to live and work the way the Lord expected you to live and work. ²Live and work without pride. Be gentle and kind. Do not be hard on others. Let love keep you from doing that. ³Work hard to live together as one by the help of the Holy Spirit. Then there will be peace. ⁴There is one body and one Spirit. There is one hope in which you were called. ⁵There is one Lord and one faith and one baptism. ⁶There is one God. He is the Father of us all. He is over us all. He is the One working through us all. He is the One living in us all.

mother. This is the first Law given that had a promise. ³The promise is this: If you respect your father and mother, you will live a long time and your life will be full of many good things.

⁴Fathers, do not be too hard on your children so they will become angry. Teach them in their growing years with Christian teaching.

⁵You servants who are owned by someone must obey your owners. Work for them as hard as you can. Work for them the same as if you were working for Christ. ⁶Do not work hard only when your owner sees you. You would be doing this just to please men. Work as you would work for Christ. Do what God wants you to do with all your heart. ⁷Be happy as you work. Do your work as for the Lord, not for men. ⁸Remember this, whatever good thing you do, the Lord will pay you for it. It is the same to the Lord if you are a servant owned by someone or if you work for pay.

⁹Owners, do the right thing for those who work for you. Stop saying that you are going to be hard on them. Remember that your Owner and their Owner is in heaven. God does not respect one person more than another.

Things God Gives To The Christian

¹⁰This is the last thing I want to say: Be strong with the Lord's strength. ¹¹Put on the things God gives you to fight with. Then you will not fall into the traps of the devil. ¹²Our fight is not with people. It is against the leaders and the powers and the spirits of darkness in this world. It is against the demon world that works in the heavens.

¹³Because of this, put on all the things God gives you to fight with. Then you will be able to stand in that sinful day. When it is all over, you will still be standing. ¹⁴So stand up and do not be moved. Wear a belt of truth around your body. Wear a piece of iron over your chest which is being right with God. ¹⁵Wear shoes on your feet which are the Good News of peace. ¹⁶Most important of all, you need a covering of faith in front of you. This is to put out the fire-arrows of the devil. ¹⁷The covering for your head is that you have been saved from the punishment of sin. Take the sword of the Spirit which is the Word of God.

How And What To Pray For

¹⁸You must pray at all times as the Holy Spirit leads you to pray. Pray for the things that are needed. You must watch and keep on praying. Remember to pray for all Christians. ¹⁹Pray for me also. Pray that I might open my mouth without fear. Pray that I will use the right words to preach that which is hard to understand in the Good News. ²⁰This is the reason I was sent out. But now I am in chains for preaching the Good News. I want to keep on speaking for Christ without fear the way I should. ²¹Tychicus will tell you how I am getting along. He is a much-loved brother and a faithful preacher. ²²I have sent him to you because I want him to tell you about us. He will comfort you.

²³May all the Christian brothers have peace and love with faith from God the Father and the Lord Jesus Christ. ²⁴May God give loving-favor to all who love our Lord Jesus Christ with a love that never gets weak.

PHILIPPIANS

1 This letter is from Paul and Timothy. We are servants owned by Jesus Christ. This letter is to all who belong to Christ Jesus who are living in the city of Philippi and to the church leaders and their helpers also. ²May you have loving-favor and peace from God our Father and the Lord Jesus Christ.

Paul Gives Thanks For The True Christians

³I thank God for you whenever I think of you. ⁴I always have joy as I pray for all of you. ⁵It is because you have told others the Good News from the first day you heard it until now. ⁶I am sure that God Who began the good work in you will keep on working in you until the day Jesus Christ comes again. ⁷It is right for me to feel like this about all of you. It is because you are very dear to me. While I was in prison and when I was proving that the Good News is true, you all shared God's loving-favor with me. ⁸God knows what I am saying. He knows how much I love you all with a love that comes from Jesus Christ. ⁹And this is my prayer: I pray that your love will grow more and more. I pray that you will have better understanding and be wise in all things. ¹⁰I pray that you will know what is the very best. I pray that you will be true and without blame until the day Christ comes again. ¹¹And I pray that you will be filled with the fruits of right living. These come from Jesus Christ, with honor and thanks to God.

Paul's Being In Prison Has Turned Out To Be A Good Thing

¹²Christian brothers, I want you to know that what has happened to me has helped spread the Good News. ¹³Everyone around here knows why I am in prison. It is because I preached about Jesus Christ. All the soldiers who work for the leader of the country know why I am here. ¹⁴Because of this, most of my Christian brothers have had their faith in the Lord made stronger. They have more power to preach the Word of God without fear.

¹⁵Some are preaching because they are jealous and want to make trouble. Others are doing it for the right reason. ¹⁶These do it because of love. They know that I am put here to prove the Good News is true. ¹⁷The others preach about Christ for what they get out of it. Their hearts are not right. They want to make me suffer while I am in prison. ¹⁸What difference does it make if they pretend or if they are true? I am happy, yes, and I will keep on being happy that Christ is preached.

Living Means Having Christ

¹⁹Because of your prayers and the help the Holy Spirit gives me, all of this will turn out for good. ²⁰I hope very much that I will have no reason to be ashamed. I hope to honor Christ with my body if it be by my life or by my death. I want to honor Him without fear, now and always. ²¹To me, living means having Christ. To die means that I would have more of Him. ²²If I keep on living here in this body, it means that I can lead more people to Christ. I do not know which is better. ²³There is a strong pull from both sides. I have a desire to leave this world to be with Christ, which is much better. ²⁴But it is more important for you that I stay. ²⁵I am sure I will live to help you grow and

be happy in your faith. 26This will give you reason to give more thanks to Christ Jesus when I come to visit you again.

Fight For The Faith

27Live your lives as the Good News of Christ says you should. If I come to you or not, I want to hear that you are standing true as one. I want to hear that you are working together as one, preaching the Good News. 28Do not be afraid of those who hate you. Their hate for you proves they will be destroyed. It proves you have life from God that lasts forever. 29You are not only to put your trust in Him, but you are to suffer for Him also. 30You know what the fight is like. Now it is time for you to have a part in it as I have.

A Christian Should Not Be Proud

2 Are you strong because you belong to Christ? Does His love comfort you? Do you have joy by being as one in sharing the Holy Spirit? Do you have loving-kindness and pity for each other? 2Then give me true joy by thinking the same thoughts. Keep having the same love. Be as one in thoughts and actions. 3Nothing should be done because of pride or thinking about yourself. Think of other people as more important than yourself. 4Do not always be thinking about your own plans only. Be happy to know what other people are doing.

Christ Was Not Proud

5Think as Christ Jesus thought. 6Jesus has always been as God is. But He did not hold to His rights as God. 7He put aside everything that belonged to Him and made Himself the same as a servant who is owned by someone. He became human by being born as a man. 8After He became a man, He gave up His

important place and obeyed by dying on a cross. 9Because of this, God lifted Jesus high above everything else. He gave Him a name that is greater than any other name. 10So when the name of Jesus is spoken, everyone in heaven and on earth and under the earth will bow down in front of Him. 11And every tongue will say Jesus Christ is Lord. Everyone will give honor to God the Father.

12My Christian friends, you have obeyed me when I was with you. You have obeyed even more when I have been away. You must keep on working to show you have been saved from the punishment of sin. Be afraid that you may not please God. 13He is working in you. God is helping you obey Him. God is doing what He wants done in you. 14Be glad you can do the things you should be doing. Do all things without arguing and talking about how you wish you did not have to do them. 15In that way, you can prove yourselves to be without blame. You are God's children and no one can talk against you, even in a sin-loving and sin-sick world. You are to shine as lights among the sinful people of this world. 16Take a strong hold on the Word of Life. Then when Christ comes again, I will be happy that I did not work with you for nothing. 17Even if I give my life as a gift on the altar to God for you, I am glad and share this joy with you. 18You must be happy and share your joy with me also.

Timothy Is Being Sent To You

19I hope by the help of the Lord Jesus that I can send Timothy to you soon. It will comfort me when he brings news about you. 20I have no one else who is as interested in you as Timothy. 21Everyone else thinks of himself instead of Jesus Christ. 22You know how Timothy proved to be such a true friend to me when we preached the Good News. He was like a son helping his father. 23I hope to send Timothy as soon as I know what they are going to do to me. 24I hope by the help of the Lord that I can come soon also.

25I thought it was right that I send Epaphroditus back to you. You helped me by sending him to me. We have worked together like brothers. He was like a soldier fighting beside me. 26He has been wanting to see all of you and was troubled because you heard he was sick. 27It is true, he was sick. Yes, he almost died, but God showed loving-kindness to him and to me. If he had died, I would have had even more sorrow. 28This is all the more reason I have sent him to you. When you see him, you will be glad and I will have less sorrow. 29Take him into your church with joy. Show respect for men like him. 30He came close to death while working for Christ. He almost died doing things for me that you could not do.

It Is Christ Only - Not The Things You Do

3 So now, my Christian brothers, be happy because you belong to Christ. It is not hard for me to write the same things to you. It is good for you. 2Watch out for false teachers. Watch out for sinful men. They want you to depend on the religious act of becoming a Jew for your hope. 3The act of becoming a Jew has nothing to do with us becoming Christians. We worship God through His Spirit and are proud of Jesus Christ. We have no faith in what we ourselves can do. 4I could have reason to trust in the flesh. If anyone could feel that the flesh could do something for him, I could. 5I went through the religious act of becoming a Jew when I was eight days old. I was born a Jew and came from the family group of Benjamin. I was a Jewish son of

Jewish parents. I belonged to the group of the proud religious law-keepers. 6I followed my religion with all my heart and did everything I could to make it very hard for the church. No one could say anything against the way I obeyed the Law.

Christ Must Be Lord Of Our Lives

7But I gave up those things that were so important to me for Christ. 8Even more than that, I think of everything as worth nothing. It is so much better to know Christ Jesus my Lord. I have lost everything for Him. And I think of these things as worth nothing so that I can have Christ. 9I want to be as one with Him. I could not be right with God by what the Law said I must do. I was made right with God by faith in Christ. 10I want to know Him. I want to have the same power in my life that raised Jesus from the dead. I want to understand and have a share in His sufferings and be like Christ in His death. 11Then I may be raised up from among the dead.

12I do not say that I have received this or have already become perfect. But I keep going on to make that life my own as Christ Jesus made me His own. 13No, Christian brothers, I do not have that life yet. But I do one thing. I forget everything that is behind me and look forward to that which is ahead of me. 14My eyes are on the prize. I want to win the race and get the prize of God's call from heaven through Christ Jesus. 15All of us who are full-grown Christians should think this way. If you do not think this way, God will show it to you. 16So let us keep on obeying the same truth we have already been following.

17Christian brothers, live your lives as I have lived mine. Watch those who live as I have taught you to live. 18There are many whose lives show they hate the cross of Christ. I have told you this before. Now I tell you again with tears in my eyes. 19Their god is their stomach. They take pride in things they should be ashamed of. All they think about are the things of this world. In the end they will be destroyed. 20But we are citizens of heaven. Christ, the One Who saves from the punishment of sin, will be coming down from heaven again. We are waiting for Him to return. 21He will change these bodies of ours of the earth and make them new. He will make them like His body of shining greatness. He has the power to do this because He can make all things obey Him.

4 So, my dear Christian brothers, you are my joy and prize. I want to see you. Keep on staying true to the Lord, my dear friends.

2I ask Euodias and Syntyche to agree as Christians should. 3My true helper, I ask you to help these women who have worked with me so much in preaching the Good News to others. Clement helped also. There are others who worked with me. Their names are in the book of life.

4Be full of joy always because you belong to the Lord. Again I say, be full of joy! 5Let all people see how gentle you are. The Lord is coming again soon. 6Do not worry. Learn to pray about everything. Give thanks to God as you ask Him for what you need. 7The peace of God is much greater than the human mind can understand. This peace will keep your hearts and minds through Christ Jesus.

8Christian brothers, keep your minds thinking about whatever is true, whatever is respected, whatever is right, whatever is pure, whatever can be loved, and whatever is well thought of. If there is anything good and worth giving thanks for, think about these things. 9Keep on doing all the things you learned and received and heard from me. Do the things you saw me do. Then the God Who gives peace will be with you.

10The Lord gives me a reason to be full of joy. It is because you are able to care for me again. I know you wanted to before but you did not have a way to help me. 11I am not saying I need anything. I have learned to be happy with whatever I have. 12I know how to get along with very little and how to live when I have much. I have learned the secret of being happy at all times. If I am full of food and have all I need, I am happy. If I am hungry and need more, I am happy. 13I can do all things because Christ gives me the strength.

14It was kind of you to help me when I was in trouble. 15You Philippians also know that when I first preached the Good News, you were the only church that helped me. It was when I left for the country of Macedonia. 16Even while I was in the city of Thessalonica you helped me more than once. 17It is not that I want to receive the gift. I want you to get the pay that is coming to you later. 18I have everything I need and more than enough. I am taken care of because Epaphroditus brought your gift. It is a sweet gift. It is a gift that cost you something. It is the kind of gift God is so pleased with. 19And my God will give you everything you need because of His great riches in Christ Jesus. 20Now may our God and Father be honored forever. Let it be so.

21Say hello to all those who belong to Christ Jesus. The Christian brothers here with me say hello to you. 22All those who belong to Christ say hello, and most of all, those who live in Caesar's house. 23May your spirit have the loving-favor of the Lord Jesus Christ.

COLOSSIANS

Paul Gives Thanks For The Christians In Colossae

1 This letter is from Paul, a missionary for Jesus Christ. God wanted me to work for Him. This letter is from brother Timothy also. ²I am writing to you who belong to Christ in the city of Colossae. May all the Christian brothers there have loving-favor and peace from God our Father.

³We always pray and give thanks to God for you. He is the Father of our Lord Jesus Christ. ⁴We give thanks to God for you because we heard of your faith in Christ Jesus. We thank God for your love for all those who belong to Christ. ⁵We thank God for the hope that is being kept for you in heaven. You first heard about this hope through the Good News which is the Word of Truth. ⁶The Good News came to you the same as it is now going out to all the world. Lives are being changed, just as your life was changed the day you heard the Good News. You understood the truth about God's loving-kindness. ⁷You heard the Good News through our much-loved brother Epaphras who is taking my place. He is a faithful servant of Christ. ⁸He told us that the Holy Spirit had given you much love.

⁹This is why I have never stopped praying for you since I heard about you. I ask God that you may know what He wants you to do. I ask God to fill you with the wisdom and understanding the Holy Spirit gives. ¹⁰Then your lives will please the Lord. You will do every kind of good work, and you will know more about God. ¹¹I pray that God's great power will make you strong, and that you will have joy as you wait and do not give up. ¹²I pray that you will be giving thanks to the Father. He has made it so you could share the good things given to those who belong to Christ who are in the light. ¹³God took us out of a life of darkness. He has put us in the holy nation of His much-loved Son. ¹⁴We have been bought by His blood and made free. Our sins are forgiven through Him.

¹⁵Christ is as God is. God cannot be seen. Christ lived before anything was made. ¹⁶Christ made everything in the heavens and on the earth. He made everything that is seen and things that are not seen. He made all the powers of heaven. Everything was made by Him and for Him. ¹⁷Christ was before all things. All things are held together by Him. ¹⁸Christ is the head of the church which is His body. He is the beginning of all things. He is the first to be raised from the dead. He is to have first place in everything. ¹⁹God the Father was pleased to have everything made perfect by Christ, His Son. ²⁰Everything in heaven and on earth can come to God because of Christ's death on the cross. Christ's blood has made peace. ²¹At one time you were strangers to God and your minds were at war with Him. Your thoughts and actions were wrong. ²²But Christ has brought you back to God by His death on the cross. In this way, Christ can bring you to God, holy and pure and without blame. ²³This is for you if you keep the faith. You must not change from what you believe now. You must not leave the hope of the Good News you received. The Good News was preached to you and to all the world. And I, Paul, am one of Christ's missionaries.

Paul Is Sent By God To Preach

²⁴Now I am full of joy to be suffering for you. In my own body I am doing my share of what has to be done to make Christ's sufferings complete. This is for His body which is the Church. ²⁵I became a preacher in His church for your good. In the plan of God I am to preach the Good News. ²⁶This great secret was hidden to the people of times past, but it is now made known to those who belong to Christ. ²⁷God wants these great riches of the hidden truth to be made known to the people who are not Jews. The secret is this: Christ in you brings hope of all the great things to come. ²⁸We preach Christ. We tell every man how he must live. We use wisdom in teaching every man. We do this so every man will be complete in Christ. ²⁹This is the reason I am working. God's great power is working in me.

The Christian Is Complete In Christ

2 I want you to know how hard I have worked for you and for the Christians in the city of Laodicea and for those who have never seen me. ²May their hearts be given comfort. May they be brought close together in Christian love. May they be rich in understanding and know God's secret. It is Christ Himself. ³In Christ are hidden all the riches of wisdom and understanding. ⁴I tell you this so no one will try to change your mind with big sounding talk. ⁵Even if I am far away from you in body, I am with you in spirit. I am happy to learn how well you are getting along. It is good to hear that your faith is so strong in Christ.

⁶As you have put your trust in Christ Jesus the Lord to save you from the punishment of sin, now let Him lead you in every step. ⁷Have your roots planted deep in Christ. Grow in Him. Get your strength from Him. Let Him make you strong

in the faith as you have been taught. Your life should be full of thanks to Him.

Wisdom Of The World Is Empty

⁸Be careful that no one changes your mind and faith by much learning and big sounding ideas. Those things are what men dream up. They are always trying to make new religions. These leave out Christ. ⁹For Christ is not only God-like, He is God in human flesh. ¹⁰When you have Christ, you are complete. He is the head over all leaders and powers. ¹¹When you became a Christian, you were set free from the sinful things of the world. This was not done by human hands. You were set free from the sins of your old self by what was done in Christ's body. ¹²When you were baptized, you were buried as Christ was buried. When you were raised up in baptism, you were raised as Christ was raised. You were raised to a new life by putting your trust in God. It was God Who raised Jesus from the dead. ¹³When you were dead in your sins, you were not set free from the sinful things of the world. But God forgave your sins and gave you new life through Christ. ¹⁴We had broken the Law many ways. Those sins were held against us by the Law. That Law had writings which said we were sinners. But now He has destroyed that writing by nailing it to the cross. ¹⁵God took away the power of the leaders of this world and the powers of darkness. He showed them to the world. The battle was won over them through Christ.

Watch For Those Who Want To Keep The Law

¹⁶Do not let anyone tell you what you should or should not eat or drink. They have no right to say if it is right or wrong to eat certain foods

or if you are to go to religious suppers. They have no right to say what you are to do at the time of the new moon or on the Day of Rest. [17] These things are a picture of what is coming. The important thing is Christ Himself. [18] Do not let anyone rob you of your prize. They will try to get you to bow down in worship of angels. They think this shows you are not proud. They say they were told to do this in a dream. These people are proud because of their sinful minds. [19] Such people are not a part of Christ. Christ is the Head. We Christians make up His body. We are joined together as a body is held together. Our strength to grow comes from Christ.

[20] You have died with Christ and become dead to those old ways. Then why do you follow the old ways of worship? Why do you obey man-made rules? [21] These rules say, "You must not put your hand on this." "Do not put this into your mouth." "You must not put your finger on that." [22] All these things come to an end when they are used. You are following only man-made rules. [23] It looks as if it is wise to follow these rules in an act of worship, because they are hard on the body. It looks as if they are done without pride, but they are worth nothing. They do not take away a man's desire to sin.

The New Life Lived By The Power Of Christ

3 If then you have been raised with Christ, keep looking for the good things of heaven. This is where Christ is seated on the right side of God. [2] Keep your minds thinking about things in heaven. Do not think about things on the earth. [3] You are dead to the things of this world. Your new life is now hidden in God through Christ. [4] Christ is our life. When He comes again, you will also be with Him to share His shining greatness.

The Old Person Put Aside

[5] Destroy the desires to sin that are in you. These desires are: sex sins, anything that is not clean, a desire for sex sins, and wanting something someone else has. This is worshiping a god. [6] It is because of these sins that the anger of God comes down on those who do not obey Him. [7] You used to do these sins when you lived that kind of life. [8] Put out of your life these things also: anger, bad temper, bad feeling toward others, talk that hurts people, speaking against God, and dirty talk. [9] Do not lie to each other. You have put out of your life your old ways. [10] You have now become a new person and are always learning more about Christ. You are being made more like Christ. He is the One Who made you. [11] There is no difference in men in this new life. Greeks and Jews are the same. The man who has gone through the religious act of becoming a Jew and the one who has not are the same. There is no difference between nations. Men who are sold to work and those who are free are the same. Christ is everything. He is in all of us.

[12] God has chosen you. You are holy and loved by Him. Because of this, your new life should be full of loving-pity. You should be kind to others and have no pride. Be gentle and be willing to wait for others. [13] Try to understand other people. Forgive each other. If you have something against someone, forgive him. That is the way the Lord forgave you. [14] And to all these things, you must add love. Love holds everything and everybody together and makes all these good things perfect. [15] Let the peace of Christ have power over your hearts. You were chosen as a part of His body. Always be thankful.

[16] Let the teaching of Christ and His words keep on living in you. These make your lives rich and full of wisdom. Keep on teaching and

helping each other. Sing the Songs of David and the church songs and the songs of heaven with hearts full of thanks to God. [17]Whatever you say or do, do it in the name of the Lord Jesus. Give thanks to God the Father through the Lord Jesus.

How Families Should Live

[18]Wives, obey your husbands. This is what the Lord wants you to do. [19]Husbands, love your wives. Do not hold hard feelings against them. [20]Children, obey your parents in everything. The Lord is pleased when you do. [21]Fathers, do not be so hard on your children that they will give up trying to do what is right.

[22]You who are servants who are owned by someone, obey your owners. Work hard for them all the time, not just when they are watching you. Work for them as you would for the Lord because you honor God. [23]Whatever work you do, do it with all your heart. Do it for the Lord and not for men. [24]Remember that you will get your pay from the Lord. He will give you what you should receive. You are working for the Lord Christ. [25]If anyone does wrong, he will suffer for it. God does not respect one person more than another.

4 Owners, give your servants what is right. Do the same for all. Remember that your Owner is in heaven.

Some Things To Do

[2]You must keep praying. Keep watching! Be thankful always. [3]As you pray, be sure to pray for us also. Pray that God will open the door for us to preach the Word. We want to tell the secret of Christ. And this is the reason I am in prison. [4]Pray that I will be able to preach so everyone can understand. This is the way I should speak. [5]Be wise in the way

you live around those who are not Christians. Make good use of your time. [6]Speak with them in such a way they will want to listen to you. Do not let your talk sound foolish. Know how to give the right answer to anyone.

Paul's Helpers Say Hello

[7]Tychicus will tell you how I am getting along. He is a much-loved brother and faithful helper. Both of us are owned by the Lord. [8]This is the reason I have sent him to you. It is so you can know about us. He can also bring joy to your hearts. [9]Onesimus is going with Tychicus. He is one of your own people. He is faithful and we love him very much. They will tell you about everything here.

[10]One of the men here in prison with me is Aristarchus. He says hello. Mark, the cousin of Barnabas, says hello. (You have heard before that if he comes to you, you are to receive him and make him happy.) [11]Jesus Justus says hello also. These are the only Jewish workers helping me teach about the holy nation of God. What a help they have been to me!

[12]Epaphras says hello. He is one of your people and a servant of Jesus Christ. As he prays for you, he asks God to help you to be strong and to make you perfect. He prays that you will know what God wants you to do in all things. [13]I can tell you for sure that he works hard for you and for the Christians in the cities of Laodicea and Hierapolis. [14]Luke, the dear doctor, and Demas say hello. [15]Say hello to all the Christians in Laodicea. Say hello to Nympha and the Christians who gather for church in her house. [16]When this letter has been read to you, have it read in the church in Laodicea also. Be sure you read the letter that is coming from Laodicea. [17]Tell Archippus to be sure to finish the work the Lord called him to do.

¹⁸I, Paul, am writing this last part with my own hand. Do not forget that I am in prison. May you have God's loving-favor.

1 THESSALONIANS

Paul Gives Thanks For Their Faith

1 This letter is from Paul and Silas and Timothy. It is to you, the church, in the city of Thessalonica. You belong to God the Father and the Lord Jesus Christ. May you have His loving-favor and His peace. ²We thank God for you all the time and pray for you. ³While praying to God our Father, we always remember your work of faith and your acts of love and your hope that never gives up in our Lord Jesus Christ. ⁴Christian brothers, we know God loves you and that He has chosen you. ⁵The Good News did not come to you by word only, but with power and through the Holy Spirit. You knew it was true. You also knew how we lived among you. It was for your good. ⁶You followed our way of life and the life of the Lord. You suffered from others because of listening to us. But you had the joy that came from the Holy Spirit. ⁷Because of your good lives, you are showing all the Christians in the countries of Macedonia and Greece how to live. ⁸The Word of the Lord has been spoken by you in the countries of Macedonia and Greece. People everywhere know of your faith in God without our telling them. ⁹The people themselves tell us how you received us when we came to you. They talk of how you turned to God from worshiping false gods. Now you worship the true and living God. ¹⁰They tell us how you are waiting for His Son Jesus to come down from heaven. God raised Him from the dead. It is Jesus Who will save us from the anger of God that is coming.

2 Christian brothers, you know that my visit with you was not wasted. ²Just before we came to you, we had been in the city of Philippi. You know how they worked against us and made us suffer. But God helped us preach the Good News to you without fear, even while many people hated us and made it hard for us. ³You remember what we said to you was true. We had no wrong desire in teaching you. We did not try to fool you. ⁴God has allowed us to be trusted with the Good News. Because of this, we preach it to please God, not man. God tests and proves our hearts. ⁵You know we never used smooth-sounding words. God knows we never tried to get money from you by preaching. ⁶We never looked for thanks from men, not from you or from anyone else. But because we were missionaries of Christ, we could have asked you to do much for us. ⁷Instead, we were gentle when we came to you. We were like a mother caring for her children. ⁸We had such a strong desire to help you that we were happy to give you the Good News. Because we loved you so much, we were ready to give you our own lives also. ⁹You remember, Christian brothers, we worked night and day for our food and clothes while we preached the Good News to you. We did not want to make it hard for you. ¹⁰You know, and so does God, how pure and right and without blame we were among you who believe. ¹¹As a father helps his children, you know how we wanted to help you and give you comfort. We told you with strong words ¹²that you should live to please God. He is the One Who chose you to come into His holy nation and to share His shining greatness.

¹³We always thank God that when you heard the Word of God from us, you believed it. You did not receive it as from men, but you received it as the Word of God. That is what it is. It is at work in the lives of you who believe. ¹⁴Christian brothers, you became just like the churches in the country of Judea. You had to suffer from the men in your country as those churches had to suffer from the Jews. ¹⁵It was the Jews who killed the Lord Jesus and the early preachers. The Jews made it hard for us and made us leave. They do not please God and are working against all men. ¹⁶They tried to keep us from preaching the Good News to the people who are not Jews. The Jews do not want them saved from the punishment of sin. The lives of the Jews are full of more sin all the time. But now God's anger has come to them at last.

¹⁷Christian brothers, because we have not been able to be with you, our hearts have been with you. We have wanted very much to see you. ¹⁸We wanted to come to you. I, Paul, have tried to come to you more than once but Satan kept us from coming. ¹⁹Who is our hope or joy or prize of happiness? It is you, when you stand before our Lord Jesus Christ when He comes again. ²⁰You are our pride and joy.

3 When we could wait no longer, we decided it was best to stay in the city of Athens alone. ²And we sent Timothy to you. He works with us for God, teaching the Good News of Christ. We sent him to give strength and comfort to your faith. ³We do not want anyone to give up because of troubles. You know that we can expect troubles. ⁴Even when we were with you, we told you that much trouble would come to us. It has come as you can see. ⁵For this reason, I could wait no longer. I sent Timothy to find out about your faith. I was afraid the devil had tempted you. Then our work with you would be wasted.

⁶But Timothy has come to us from you. He brought good news about your faith and love. It is good to know that you think well of us and that you would like to see us. We would like to see you also. ⁷Christian brothers, word about your faith has made us happy even while we are suffering and are in much trouble. ⁸It is life to us to know that your faith in the Lord is strong. ⁹How can we give God enough thanks for you for all the joy you give us? ¹⁰We keep on praying night and day that we may see you again. We want to help your faith to be complete. ¹¹May our God and Father Himself and the Lord Jesus Christ take us on our way to you. ¹²May the Lord make you grow in love for each other and for everyone. We have this kind of love for you. ¹³May our God and Father make your hearts strong and without blame. May your hearts be without sin in God's sight when our Lord Jesus comes again with all those who belong to Him.

Paul Tells Them To Live Holy Lives

4 Christian brothers, we ask you, because of the Lord Jesus, to keep on living in a way that will please God. I have already told you how to grow in the Christian life. ²The Lord Jesus gave us the right and the power to tell you what to do. ³God wants you to be holy. You must keep away from sex sins. [4]God wants each of you to use his body in the right way by keeping it holy and by respecting it. [5]You should not use it to please your own desires like the people who do not know God. [6]No man should do wrong to his Christian brother in anything. The Lord will punish a person who does. I have told you this before. [7]For God has not called us to live in sin. He has called us to live a holy life. [8]The one who turns away from this teaching does not turn away from man, but from God. It is God Who has given us His Holy Spirit.

[9]You do not need anyone to write to you about loving your Christian brothers. God has taught you to love each other. [10]You love all the Christians in all the country of Macedonia. But we ask you to love them even more. [11]Do your best to live a quiet life. Learn to do your own work well. We told you about this before. [12]By doing this, you will be respected by those who are not Christians. Then you will not be in need and others will not have to help you.

The Lord Is Coming Again

[13]Christian brothers, we want you to know for sure about those who have died. You have no reason to have sorrow as those who have no hope. [14]We believe that Jesus died and then came to life again. Because we believe this, we know that God will bring to life again all those who belong to Jesus. [15]We tell you this as it came from the Lord. Those of us who are alive when the Lord comes again will not go ahead of those who have died. [16]For the Lord Himself will come down from heaven with a loud call. The head angel will speak with a loud voice. God's horn will give its sounds. First, those who belong to Christ will come out of their graves to meet the Lord. [17]Then, those of us who are still living here on earth will be gathered together with them in the clouds. We will meet the Lord in the sky and be with Him forever. [18]Because of this, comfort each other with these words.

Watch For The Lord To Come Again

5 You do not need anyone to write to tell you when and at what kind of times these things will happen. [2]You know for sure that the day the Lord comes back to earth will be as a robber coming in the night. [3]When they say, "Everything is fine and safe," then all at once they will be destroyed. It will be like pain that comes on a woman when a child is born. They will not be able to get away from it. [4]But you are not in darkness, Christian brothers. That day will not surprise you as a robber would. [5]For you are children of the light and of the day. We are not of darkness or of night. [6]Keep awake! Do not sleep like others. Watch and keep your minds awake to what is happening. [7]People sleep at night. Those who get drunk do it at night. [8]Because we are men of the day, let us keep our minds awake. Let us cover our chests with faith and love. Let us cover our heads with the hope of being saved. [9]God planned to save us from the punishment of sin through our Lord Jesus Christ. He did not plan for us to suffer from His anger. [10]He died for us so that, dead or alive, we will be with Him. [11]So comfort each other and make each other strong as you are already doing.

Christian Living

[12]We ask you, Christian brothers, to respect those who work among you. The Lord has placed them over you and they are your teachers. [13]You must think much of them and love them because of their work. Live in peace with each other.

[14]We ask you, Christian brothers, speak to those who do not want to

work. Comfort those who feel they cannot keep going on. Help the weak. Understand and be willing to wait for all men. ¹⁵Do not let anyone pay back for the bad he received. But look for ways to do good to each other and to all people.

¹⁶Be full of joy all the time. ¹⁷Never stop praying. ¹⁸In everything give thanks. This is what God wants you to do because of Christ Jesus. ¹⁹Do not try to stop the work of the Holy Spirit. ²⁰Do not laugh at those who speak for God. ²¹Test everything and do not let good things get away from you. ²²Keep away from everything that even looks like sin.

²³May the God of peace set you apart for Himself. May every part of you be set apart for God. May your spirit and your soul and your body be kept complete. May you be without blame when our Lord Jesus Christ comes again. ²⁴The One Who called you is faithful and will do what He promised. ²⁵Christian brothers, pray for us. ²⁶Say hello to all the Christians with a kiss of holy love. ²⁷I tell you to have this letter read to all the Christians. ²⁸May you have loving-favor from our Lord Jesus Christ.

2 THESSALONIANS

1 This letter is from Paul and Silas and Timothy. It is to the church in the city of Thessalonica that belongs to God the Father and the Lord Jesus Christ. ²May you have loving-favor and peace from God the Father and the Lord Jesus Christ.

³We must give thanks to God for you always, Christian brothers. It is the right thing to do because your faith is growing so much. Your love for each other is stronger all the time. ⁴We are proud of you and tell the other churches about you. We tell them how your faith stays so strong even when people make it very hard for you and make you suffer. ⁵God wants you to prove yourselves to be worth being in His holy nation by suffering for Him. ⁶He does what is right and will allow trouble to come to those who are making it hard for you. ⁷He will help you and us who are suffering. This will happen when the Lord Jesus comes down from heaven with His powerful angels in a bright fire. ⁸He will punish those who do not know God and those who do not obey the Good News of our Lord Jesus Christ. ⁹They will be punished forever and taken away from the Lord and from the shining greatness of His power. ¹⁰On the day He comes, His shining greatness will be seen in those who belong to Him. On that day, He will receive honor from all those who put their trust in Him. You believed what we had to say to you. ¹¹For this reason, we always pray for you. We pray that our God will make you worth being chosen. We pray that His power will help you do the good things you want to do. We pray that your work of faith will be complete. ¹²In this way, the name of the Lord Jesus Christ will be honored by you and you will be honored by Him. It is through the loving-favor of our God and of the Lord Jesus Christ.

Some People Will Believe A Lie

2 Our Lord Jesus Christ is coming again. We will be gathered together to meet Him. But we ask you, Christian brothers, ²do not be troubled in mind or worried by the talk you hear. Some say that the Lord has already come. People may say that I wrote this in a letter or that a spirit told them. ³Do not let anyone fool you. For the Lord will not come again until many people turn away from God. Then the leader of those who break the law will come. He is the man of sin. ⁴He works against and puts himself above every kind of god that is worshiped. He will take his seat in the house of God and say that he himself is God. ⁵Do you not remember that while I was with you, I told you this? ⁶You know the power that is keeping the man of sin back now. The man of sin will come only when his time is ready. ⁷For the secret power of breaking the law is already at work in the world. But that secret power can only do so much until the One Who keeps back the man of sin is taken out of the way. ⁸Then this man of sin will come. The Lord Jesus will kill him with the breath of His mouth. The coming of Christ will put an end to him. ⁹Satan will use this man of sin. He will have Satan's power. He will do strange things and many powerful works that will be false. ¹⁰Those who are lost in sin will be fooled by the things he can do. They are lost in sin because they did not love the truth that would save them. ¹¹For this reason, God will allow them to follow false teaching so they will believe a lie. ¹²They will all be guilty as they stand before God because they wanted to do what was wrong.

You Belong To Those Who Believe The Truth

¹³Christian brothers, the Lord loves you. We always thank God for you. It is because God has chosen you from the beginning to save you from the punishment of sin. He chose to make you holy by the Holy Spirit and to give you faith to believe the truth. ¹⁴It was by our preaching the Good News that you were chosen. He chose you to share the shining greatness of our Lord Jesus Christ. ¹⁵So then, Christian brothers, keep a strong hold on what we have taught you by what we have said and by what we have written.

¹⁶Our Lord Jesus Christ and God our Father loves us. Through His loving-favor He gives us comfort and hope that lasts forever. ¹⁷May He give your hearts comfort and strength to say and do every good thing.

Christian Brothers, Pray For Us

3 My last words to you, Christian brothers, are that you pray for us. Pray that the Word of the Lord will go out over all the land and prove its power just as it did with you. ²Pray that we will be kept from sinful men, because not all men are Christians. ³But the Lord is faithful. He will give you strength and keep you safe from the devil. ⁴We have faith in the Lord for you. We believe you are doing and will keep on doing the things we told you. ⁵May the Lord lead your hearts into the love of God. May He help you as you wait for Christ.

⁶Now this is what we tell you to do, Christian brothers. In the name of the Lord Jesus, keep away from any Christian who is lazy and who does not do what we taught you. ⁷You know you should follow the way of life we lived when we were with you. We worked hard while we were there. ⁸We did not eat anyone's food without paying for it. We worked hard night and day so none of you would have to give us anything. ⁹We could have asked you to give us food. But we did not so

that you might follow our way of living. [10]When we were with you, we told you that if a man does not work, he should not eat. [11]We hear that some are not working. But they are spending their time trying to see what others are doing. [12]Our words to such people are that they should be quiet and go to work. They should eat their own food. In the name of the Lord Jesus Christ we say this. [13]But you, Christian brothers, do not get tired of doing good. [14]If anyone does not want to listen to what we say in this letter, remember who he is and stay away from him. In that way, he will be put to shame. [15]Do not think of him as one who hates you. But talk to him as a Christian brother.

[16]May the Lord of peace give you His peace at all times. The Lord be with you all. [17]I, Paul, write this last part with my own hand. It is the way I finish all my letters. [18]May all of you have loving-favor from our Lord Jesus Christ.

1 TIMOTHY

1 This letter is from Paul, a missionary of Jesus Christ. I am sent by God, the One Who saves, and by our Lord Jesus Christ Who is our hope. [2]I write to you, Timothy. You are my son in the Christian faith. May God the Father and Jesus Christ our Lord give you His loving-favor and loving-kindness and peace.

Watch For False Teachers

[3]When I left for the country of Macedonia, I asked you to stay in the city of Ephesus. I wanted you to stay there so you could tell those who are teaching what is not true to stop. [4]They should not listen to stories that are not true. It is foolish for them to try to learn more about their early fathers. These only bring more questions to their minds and do not make their faith in God stronger. [5]We want to see our teaching help you have a true love that comes from a pure heart. Such love comes from a heart that says we are not guilty and from a faith that does not pretend. [6]But some have turned away from these things. They have turned to foolish talking. [7]Some of them want to be teachers of the Law. But they do not know what they are talking about even if they act as if they do.

The Law Is Good

[8]We know the Law is good when it is used the way God meant it to be used. [9]We must remember the Law is not for the person who is right with God. It is for those who do not obey anybody or anything. It is for the sinners who hate God and speak against Him. It is for those who kill their fathers and mothers and for those who kill other people. [10]It is for those who do sex sins and for people who do sex sins with their own sex. It is for people who steal other people and for those who lie and for those who promise not to lie, but do. It is for everything that is against right teaching. [11]The great Good News of our honored God is right teaching.

God has trusted me to preach this Good News.

Paul Gives Thanks To God

12I thank Christ Jesus our Lord for the power and strength He has given me. He trusted me and gave me His work to do. 13Before He chose me, I talked bad about Christ. I made His followers suffer. I hurt them every way I could. But God had loving-kindness for me. I did not understand what I was doing for I was not a Christian then. 14Then our Lord gave me much of His loving-favor and faith and love which are found in Christ Jesus.

15What I say is true and all the world should receive it. Christ Jesus came into the world to save sinners from their sin and I am the worst sinner. 16And yet God had loving-kindness for me. Jesus Christ used me to show how long He will wait for even the worst sinners. In that way, others will know they can have life that lasts forever also. 17We give honor and thanks to the King Who lives forever. He is the One Who never dies and Who is never seen. He is the One Who knows all things. He is the only God. Let it be so.

The Good Fight Of Faith

18Timothy, my son, here is my word to you. Fight well for the Lord! God's preachers told us you would. 19Keep a strong hold on your faith in Christ. May your heart always say you are right. Some people have not listened to what their hearts say. They have done what they knew was wrong. Because of this, their faith in Christ was wrecked. 20This happened to Hymenaeus and Alexander. I gave them over to Satan to teach them not to speak against God.

2 First of all, I ask you to pray much for all men and to give thanks for them. 2Pray for kings and all others who are in power over us so we might live quiet God-like lives in peace. 3It is good when you pray like this. It pleases God Who is the One Who saves. 4He wants all people to be saved from the punishment of sin. He wants them to come to know the truth. 5There is one God. There is one Man standing between God and men. That Man is Christ Jesus. 6He gave His life for all men so they could go free and not be held by the power of sin. God made this known to the world at the right time. 7This is why I was chosen to be a teacher and a missionary. I am to teach faith and truth to the people who do not know God. I am not lying but telling the truth.

Women In The Church

8I want men everywhere to pray. They should lift up holy hands as they pray. They should not be angry or argue. 9Christian women should not be dressed in the kind of clothes and their hair should not be combed in a way that will make people look at them. They should not wear much gold or pearls or clothes that cost much money. 10Instead of these things, Christian women should be known for doing good things and living good lives.

11Women should be quiet when they learn. They should listen to what men have to say. 12I never let women teach men or be leaders over men. They should be quiet. 13Adam was made first, then Eve. 14Adam was not fooled by Satan. But it was the woman who was fooled and sinned. 15God will keep them safe when their children are born if they put their trust in Him and live loving and good lives.

What A Church Leader Must Be Like

3 It is true that if a man wants to be a church leader, he wants to do a good work. 2A church leader must be a good man. His life must be so no one can say anything against him. He must have only one wife and must be respected for his good living. He must be willing to take people into his home. He must be willing to learn and able to teach the Word of God. [3]He must not get drunk or want to fight. Instead, he must be gentle. He must not have a love for money. [4]He should be a good leader in his own home. His children must obey and respect him. [5]If a man cannot be a good leader in his own home, how can he lead the church? [6]A church leader must not be a new Christian. A new Christian might become proud and fall into sin which is brought on by the devil. [7]A church leader must be respected by people who are not Christians so nothing can be said against him. In that way, he will not be trapped by the devil.

What The Church Helpers Must Be Like

[8]Church helpers must also be good men and act so people will respect them. They must speak the truth. They must not get drunk. They must not have a love for money. [9]They must have their faith in Christ and be His followers with a heart that says they are right. [10]They must first be tested to see if they are ready for the work as church helpers. Then if they do well, they may be chosen as church helpers. [11]The wives of church helpers must be careful how they act. They must not carry stories from one person to another. They must be wise and faithful in all they do. [12]Church helpers must have only one wife. They must lead their home well and their children must obey them. [13]Those who work well as church helpers will be respected by others and their own faith in Christ Jesus will grow.

[14]I hope to come to you soon. I am writing these things [15]because it may be awhile before I get there. I wanted

you to know how you should act among people in the church which is the house of the living God. The church holds up the truth. [16]It is important to know the secret of God-like living, which is: Christ came to earth as a Man. He was pure in His Spirit. He was seen by angels. The nations heard about Him. Men everywhere put their trust in Him. He was taken up into heaven.

False Teaching In The Last Days

4 The Holy Spirit tells us in plain words that in the last days some people will turn away from the faith. They will listen to what is said about spirits and follow the teaching about demons. [2]Those who teach this tell it as the truth when they know it is a lie. They do it so much that their own hearts no longer say it is wrong. [3]They will say, "Do not get married. Do not eat some kinds of food." But God gave these things to Christians who know the truth. We are to thank God for them. [4]Everything God made is good. We should not put anything aside if we can take it and thank God for it. [5]It is made holy by the Word of God and prayer.

Christians Are To Grow

[6]If you keep telling these things to the Christians, you will be a good worker for Jesus Christ. You will feed your own soul on these words of faith and on this good teaching which you have followed. [7]Have nothing to do with foolish stories old women tell. Keep yourself growing in God-like living. [8]Growing strong in body is all right but growing in God-like living is more important. It will not only help you in this life now but in the next life also. [9]These words are true and they can be trusted. [10]Because of this, we work hard and do our best because our hope is in the living God, the One Who would

save all men. He saves those who believe in Him.

Paul's Helpful Words To Young Timothy

[11] Tell people that this is what they must do. [12] Let no one show little respect for you because you are young. Show other Christians how to live by your life. They should be able to follow you in the way you talk and in what you do. Show them how to live in faith and in love and in holy living. [13] Until I come, read and preach and teach the Word of God to the church. [14] Be sure to use the gift God gave you. The leaders saw this in you when they laid their hands on you and said what you should do. [15] Think about all this. Work at it so everyone may see you are growing as a Christian. [16] Watch yourself how you act and what you teach. Stay true to what is right. If you do, you and those who hear you will be saved from the punishment of sin.

Teaching About Women Whose Husbands Have Died

5 Do not speak sharp words to an older man. Talk with him as if he were a father. Talk to younger men as brothers. [2] Talk to older women as mothers. Talk to younger women as sisters, keeping yourself pure. [3] Help women whose husbands have died. [4] If a woman whose husband has died has children or grandchildren, they are the ones to care for her. In that way, they can pay back to their parents the kindness that has been shown to them. God is pleased when this is done. [5] Women whose husbands have died are alone in this world. Their trust is in the Lord. They pray day and night. [6] But the one who lives only for the joy she can receive from this world is the same as dead even if she is alive.

[7] Teach these things so they will do what is right. [8] Anyone who does not take care of his family and those in his house has turned away from the faith. He is worse than a person who has never put his trust in Christ. [9] A woman over sixty years old whose husband has died may receive help from the church. To receive this help, she must have been the wife of one man. [10] She must be known for doing good things for people and for being a good mother. She must be known for taking strangers into her home and for washing the feet of Christians. She must be known for helping those who suffer and for showing kindness.

[11] Do not write the names of younger women whose husbands have died together with the names of others who need help. They will turn away from Christ because of wanting to get married again. [12] Then they would be thought of as guilty of breaking their first promise. [13] They will waste their time. They will go from house to house carrying stories. They will find fault with people and say things they should not talk about. [14] I think it is best for younger women whose husbands have died to get married. They should have children and care for their own homes. Then no one can speak against them. [15] Some of these women have already turned away to follow Satan. [16] If you have any women whose husbands have died in your family, you must care for them. The church should not have to help them. The church can help women whose husbands have died who are all alone in this world and have no one else to help them.

Teaching About Leaders

[17] Older leaders who do their work well should be given twice as much pay, and for sure, those who work hard preaching and teaching. [18] The Holy Writings say, "When a cow is walking on the grain to break it

open, do not stop it from eating some" (Deuteronomy 25:4), and "A person who works should be paid." (Matthew 10:10)

19Do not listen to what someone says against a church leader unless two or three persons say the same thing. 20Show those who keep on sinning where they are wrong in front of the whole church. Then others will be afraid of sinning. 21I tell you from my heart that you must follow these rules without deciding before the truth is known. God and Jesus Christ and the chosen angels know what I am saying. Show favors to no one. 22Do not be in a hurry about choosing a church leader. You do not want to have any part in other men's sins. Keep yourself pure.

23Do not drink water only. Use a little wine because of your stomach and because you are sick so often.

24The sins of some men can be seen. Their sins go before them and make them guilty. The sins of other men will be seen later. 25In the same way, good works are easy to see now. But some that are not easy to be seen cannot always be hid.

Teaching About Christians Who Were Sold To Work

6 All you Christians who are servants must respect your owners and work hard for them. Do not let the name of God and our teaching be spoken against because of poor work. 2Those who have Christian owners must respect their owners because they are Christian brothers. They should work hard for them because much-loved Christian brothers are being helped by their work. Teach and preach these things.

Live Like God Wants You To Live

3Someone may teach something else. He may not agree with the teaching of our Lord Jesus Christ. He may not teach you to live God-like lives. 4Such a person is full of pride and knows nothing. He wastes time on questions and argues about things that are not important. This makes those he teaches jealous and they want to fight. They talk bad and have bad ideas about others. 5Men who are not able to use their minds in the right way because of sin argue all the time. They do not have the truth. They think religion is a way to get much for themselves.

6A God-like life gives us much when we are happy for what we have. 7We came into this world with nothing. For sure, when we die, we will take nothing with us. 8If we have food and clothing, let us be happy. 9But men who want lots of money are tempted. They are trapped into doing all kinds of foolish things and things which hurt them. These things drag them into sin and will destroy them. 10The love of money is the beginning of all kinds of sin. Some people have turned from the faith because of their love for money. They have made much pain for themselves because of this.

Fight The Good Fight Of Faith

11But you, man of God, turn away from all these sinful things. Work at being right with God. Live a God-like life. Have faith and love. Be willing to wait. Have a kind heart. 12Fight the good fight of faith. Take hold of the life that lasts forever. You were chosen to receive it. You have spoken well about this life in front of many people. 13I tell you this before God Who gives life to all people and before Jesus Christ Who spoke well in front of Pontius Pilate. 14You must do all our Lord Jesus Christ said so no one can speak against you. Do this until He comes again. 15At the right time, we will be shown that God is the One Who has all power. He is the King of kings and Lord of lords. 16He can never die. He lives in a light so bright that no man can go near Him. No man has ever seen God or can see Him. Honor and power belong to Him forever. Let it be so.

Paul's Last Words To Timothy

17 Tell those who are rich in this world not to be proud and not to trust in their money. Money cannot be trusted. They should put their trust in God. He gives us all we need for our happiness. 18 Tell them to do good and be rich in good works. They should give much to those in need and be ready to share. 19 Then they will be gathering together riches for themselves. These good things are what they will build on for the future. Then they will have the only true life!

20 Timothy, keep safe what God has trusted you with. Turn away from foolish talk. Do not argue with those who think they know so much. They know less than they think they do. 21 Some people have gone after much learning. It has proved to be false and they have turned away from the faith. May you have God's loving-favor.

2 TIMOTHY

1 This letter is from Paul, a missionary of Jesus Christ. God has sent me to tell that He has promised life that lasts forever through Christ Jesus. 2 I am writing to you, Timothy. You are my much-loved son. May God the Father and Christ Jesus our Lord give you His loving-favor and loving-kindness and peace.

Timothy's Special Gift

3 I thank God for you. I pray for you night and day. I am working for God the way my early fathers worked. My heart says I am free from sin. 4 When I remember your tears, it makes me want to see you. That would fill me with joy. 5 I remember your true faith. It is the same faith your grandmother Lois had and your mother Eunice had. I am sure you have that same faith also.

6 For this reason, I ask you to keep using the gift God gave you. It came to you when I laid my hands on you and prayed that God would use you. 7 For God did not give us a spirit of fear. He gave us a spirit of power and of love and of a good mind. 8 Do not be ashamed to tell others about what our Lord said, or of me here in prison. I am here because of Jesus Christ. Be ready to suffer for preaching the Good News and God will give you the strength you need. 9 He is the One Who saved us from the punishment of sin. He is the One Who chose us to do His work. It is not because of anything we have done. But it was His plan from the beginning that He would give us His loving-favor through Christ Jesus. 10 We know about it now because of the coming of Jesus Christ, the One Who saves. He put a stop to the power of death and brought life that never dies which is seen through the Good News. 11 I have been chosen to be a missionary and a preacher and a

teacher of this Good News. 12For this reason, I am suffering. But I am not ashamed. I know the One in Whom I have put my trust. I am sure He is able to keep safe that which I have trusted to Him until the day He comes again. 13Keep all the things I taught you. They were given to you in the faith and love of Jesus Christ. 14Keep safe that which He has trusted you with by the Holy Spirit Who lives in us.

Onesiphorus Was Faithful

15I am sure you have heard that all the Christians in the countries of Asia have turned away from me. Phygelus and Hermogenes turned away also. 16Onesiphorus was not ashamed of me in prison. He came often to comfort me. May the Lord show loving-kindness to his family. 17When he came to Rome, he looked everywhere until he found me. 18You know what a help he was to me in Ephesus. When the Lord comes again, may He show loving-kindness to Onesiphorus.

Be A Good Soldier

2 So you, my son, be strong in the loving-favor of Christ Jesus. 2What you have heard me say in front of many people, you must teach to faithful men. Then they will be able to teach others also. 3Take your share of suffering as a good soldier of Jesus Christ. 4No soldier fighting in a war can take time to make a living. He must please the one who made him a soldier. 5Anyone who runs in a race must follow the rules to get the prize. 6A hard-working farmer should receive first some of what he gathers from the field. 7Think about these things and the Lord will help you understand them.

8Remember this! Jesus Christ, Who was born from the early family of David, was raised from the dead!

This is the Good News I preach. 9I suffer much and am in prison as one who has done something very bad. I am in chains, but the Word of God is not chained. 10I suffer all things so the people that God has chosen can be saved from the punishment of their sin through Jesus Christ. Then they will have God's shining greatness that lasts forever. 11These things are true. If we die with Him, we will live with Him also. 12If we suffer and stay true to Him, then we will be a leader with Him. If we say we do not know Him, He will say He does not know us. 13If we have no faith, He will still be faithful for He cannot go against what He is.

Foolish Talk

14Tell your people about these things again. In the name of the Lord, tell them not to argue over words that are not important. It helps no one and it hurts the faith of those who are listening. 15Do your best to know that God is pleased with you. Be as a workman who has nothing to be ashamed of. Teach the words of truth in the right way. 16Do not listen to foolish talk about things that mean nothing. It only leads people farther away from God. 17Such talk will spread like cancer. Hymenaeus and Philetus are like this. 18They have turned from the truth. They say the dead have already been raised. The faith of some people has been made weak because of such foolish talk. 19But the truth of God cannot be changed. It says, "The Lord knows those who are His." And, "Everyone who says he is a Christian must turn away from sin!"

20In a big house there are not only things made of gold and silver, but also of wood and clay. Some are of more use than others. Some are used every day. 21If a man lives a clean life, he will be like a dish made of gold. He will be respected and set apart for good use by the owner of the house.

²²Turn away from the sinful things young people want to do. Go after what is right. Have a desire for faith and love and peace. Do this with those who pray to God from a clean heart. ²³Let me say it again. Have nothing to do with foolish talk and those who want to argue. It can only lead to trouble. ²⁴A servant owned by God must not make trouble. He must be kind to everyone. He must be able to teach. He must be willing to suffer when hurt for doing good. ²⁵Be gentle when you try to teach those who are against what you say. God may change their hearts so they will turn to the truth. ²⁶Then they will know they had been held in a trap by the devil to do what he wanted them to do. But now they are able to get out of it.

Things That Will Happen In The Last Days

3 You must understand that in the last days there will come times of much trouble. ²People will love themselves and money. They will have pride and tell of all the things they have done. They will speak against God. Children and young people will not obey their parents. People will not be thankful and they will not be holy. ³They will not love each other. No one can get along with them. They will tell lies about others. They will not be able to keep from doing things they know they should not do. They will be wild and want to beat and hurt those who are good. ⁴They will not stay true to their friends. They will act without thinking. They will think too much of themselves. They will love fun instead of loving God. ⁵They will do things to make it look as if they are Christians. But they will not receive the power that is for a Christian. Keep away from such people.

⁶These are the kind of people who go from house to house. They talk to foolish women who are loaded down

with sins and all kinds of sinful desires. ⁷Such women are always listening to new teaching. But they are never able to understand the truth. ⁸Jannes and Jambres fought against Moses. So do these teachers fight against the truth today. Their minds think only of sinful things. They have turned against the Christian teaching. ⁹They will not get very far. Their foolish teaching will be seen by everyone. That was the way it was with the two who worked against Moses.

Teach The Truth

¹⁰But you know what I teach and how I live. You know what I want to do. You know about my faith and my love. You know how long I am willing to wait for something. You know how I keep on working for God even when it is hard for me. ¹¹You know about all the troubles and hard times I have had. You have seen how I suffered in the cities of Antioch and Iconium and Lystra. Yet the Lord brought me out of all those troubles. ¹²Yes! All who want to live a God-like life who belong to Christ Jesus will suffer from others. ¹³Sinful men and false teachers will go from bad to worse. They will lead others the wrong way and will be led the wrong way themselves.

¹⁴But as for you, hold on to what you have learned and know to be true. Remember where you learned them. ¹⁵You have known the Holy Writings since you were a child. They are able to give you wisdom that leads to being saved from the punishment of sin by putting your trust in Christ Jesus. ¹⁶All the Holy Writings are God-given and are made alive by Him. Man is helped when he is taught God's Word. It shows what is wrong. It changes the way of a man's life. It shows him how to be right with God. ¹⁷It gives the man who belongs to God everything he needs to work well for Him.

Paul's Work Is Finished - Timothy Must Carry On

4 These words are from my heart to you. I say this before God and Jesus Christ. Some day He will say who is guilty and who is not of those who are living and of those who are dead. It will be when Christ comes to bring His holy nation. ²Preach the Word of God. Preach it when it is easy and people want to listen and when it is hard and people do not want to listen. Preach it all the time. Use the Word of God to show people they are wrong. Use the Word of God to help them do right. You must be willing to wait for people to understand what you teach as you teach them.

³The time will come when people will not listen to the truth. They will look for teachers who will tell them only what they want to hear. ⁴They will not listen to the truth. Instead, they will listen to stories made up by men. ⁵You must watch for all these things. Do not be afraid to suffer for our Lord. Preach the Good News from place to place. Do all the work you are to do.

⁶It will soon be time for me to leave this life. ⁷I have fought a good fight. I have finished the work I was to do. I have kept the faith. ⁸There is a prize which comes from being right with God. The Lord, the One Who will say who is guilty, will give it to me on that great day when He comes again. I will not be the only one to receive a prize. All those who love to think of His coming and are looking for Him will receive one also.

⁹Come to me here as soon as you can. ¹⁰Demas left me. He loved the things of this world and has gone to the city of Thessalonica. Crescens has gone to the city of Galatia. Titus has gone to the city of Dalmatia. ¹¹Luke is the only one with me here. Bring Mark when you come. He is a help to me in this work. ¹²I sent Tychicus to the city of Ephesus. ¹³When you come, bring the coat I left with Carpus in the city of Troas. Bring the books and for sure do not forget the writings written on sheepskin. ¹⁴Alexander, the man who makes things out of copper, has worked hard against me. The Lord will give him the pay that is coming to him. ¹⁵Watch him! He fought against every word we preached.

¹⁶At my first trial no one helped me. Everyone left me. I hope this will not be held against them. ¹⁷But the Lord was with me. He gave me power to preach the Good News so all the people who do not know God might hear. I was taken from the mouth of the lion. ¹⁸The Lord will look after me and will keep me from every sinful plan they have. He will bring me safe into His holy nation of heaven. May He have all the shining greatness forever. Let it be so.

¹⁹Say hello to Prisca and Aquila for me and to all the family of Onesiphorus. ²⁰Erastus stayed in the city of Corinth. I left Trophimus sick in the city of Miletus. ²¹Try to come before winter. Eubulus, Pudens, Linus, Claudia, and all the Christian brothers say hello to you. ²²May the Lord Jesus Christ be with your spirit. May you have God's loving-favor.

TITUS

1 This letter is from Paul, a servant owned by God. And I am a missionary of Jesus Christ. I have been sent to those God has chosen for Himself. I am to teach them the truth that leads to God-like living. ²This truth also gives hope of life that lasts forever. God promised this before the world began. He cannot lie. ³He made this known at the right time through His Word. God, the One Who saves, told me I should preach it. ⁴I am writing to you, Titus. You are my true son in the faith which we both have. May you have loving-favor and peace from God the Father and Jesus Christ, the One Who saves.

What A Church Leader Must Be Like

⁵I left you on the island of Crete so you could do some things that needed to be done. I asked you to choose church leaders in every city. ⁶Their lives must be so that no one can talk against them. They must have only one wife. Their children must be Christians and known to be good. They must obey their parents. They must not be wild. ⁷A church leader is God's servant. His life must be so that no one can say anything against him. He should not try to please himself and not be quick to get angry over little things. He must not get drunk or want to fight. He must not always want more money for himself. ⁸He must like to take people into his home. He must love what is good. He must be able to think well and do all things in the right way. He must live a holy life and be the boss over his own desires. ⁹He must hold to the words of truth which he was taught. He must be able to teach the truth and show those who are against the truth that they are wrong.

False Teachers

¹⁰There are many men who will not listen or will not obey the truth. Their teaching is foolish and they lead people to believe a lie. Some Jews believe their lies. ¹¹This must be stopped. It turns whole families from the truth. They teach these things to make money. ¹²One of their own teachers said, "People of the island of Crete always lie. They are like wild animals. They are lazy. All they want to do is eat." ¹³This is true of them. Speak sharp words to them because it is true. Lead them in the right way so they will have strong faith. ¹⁴Do not let them listen to Jewish stories made up by men. Do not let them listen to man-made rules which lead them away from the truth. ¹⁵All things are pure to the man with a pure heart. But to sinful people nothing is pure. Both their minds and their hearts are bad. ¹⁶They say they know God, but by the way they act, they show that they do not. They are sinful people. They will not obey and are of no use for any good work.

Right Teaching

2 You must teach what is right and true. ²Older men are to be quiet and to be careful how they act. They are to be the boss over their own desires. Their faith and love are to stay strong and they are not to give up. ³Teach older women to be quiet and to be careful how they act also. They are not to go around speaking bad things about others or things that are not true. They are not to be chained by strong drink. They should teach what is good.

⁴Older women are to teach the young women to love their husbands and children. ⁵They are to teach them to think before they act, to be pure, to be workers at home, to be kind, and to obey their own husbands. In this way, the Word of God is honored. ⁶Also teach young men to be wise. ⁷In all things show them how to live by your life and by right teaching. ⁸You should be wise in what you say. Then the one who is against you will be ashamed and will not be able to say anything bad about you.

⁹Those who are servants owned by some one must obey their owners and please them in everything. They must not argue. ¹⁰They must not steal from their owners but prove they can be trusted in every way. In this way, their lives will honor the teaching of God Who saves us.

¹¹God's free gift of being saved is being given to everyone. ¹²We are taught to have nothing to do with that which is against God. We are to have nothing to do with the desires of this world. We are to be wise and to be right with God. We are to live God-like lives in this world. ¹³We are to be looking for the great hope and the coming of our great God and the One Who saves, Christ Jesus. ¹⁴He gave Himself for us. He did this by buying us with His blood and making us free from all sin. He gave Himself so His people could be clean and want to do good. ¹⁵Teach all these things and give words of help. Show them if they are wrong. You have the right and the power to do this. Do not let anyone think little of you.

The Work Of A Leader

3 Teach your people to obey the leaders of their country. They should be ready to do any good work. ²They must not speak bad of anyone, and they must not argue. They should be gentle and kind to all people.

God Saved Us From All These Things

³There was a time when we were foolish and did not obey. We were fooled in many ways. Strong desires held us in their power. We wanted only to please ourselves. We wanted what others had and were angry when we could not have them. We hated others and they hated us. ⁴But God, the One Who saves, showed how kind He was and how He loved us ⁵by saving us from the punishment of sin. It was not because we worked to be right with God. It was because of His loving-kindness that He washed our sins away. At the same time He gave us new life when the Holy Spirit came into our lives. ⁶God gave the Holy Spirit to fill our lives through Jesus Christ, the One Who saves. ⁷Because of this, we are made right with God by His loving-favor. Now we can have life that lasts forever as He has promised.

⁸What I have told you is true. Teach these things all the time so those who have put their trust in God will be careful to do good things. These things are good and will help all men.

Paul's Last Words To Titus

⁹Do not argue with people about foolish questions and about the Law. Do not spend time talking about all of your early fathers. This does not help anyone and it is of no use. ¹⁰Talk once or twice to a person who tries to divide people into groups against each other. If he does not stop, have nothing to do with him. ¹¹You can be sure he is going the wrong way. He is sinning and he knows it.

¹²I will send Artemas or Tychicus to you. As soon as one of them gets there, try to come to me in the city of Nicopolis. I have decided to spend

the winter there. [13]Zenas, the man who knows the law, and Apollos are going on a trip. Do everything you can to help them. [14]Our people must learn to work hard. They must work for what they need and be able to give to others who need help. Then their lives will not be wasted. [15]All those with me here say hello to you. Say hello to my Christian friends there. May you have God's loving-favor.

PHILEMON

1 This letter is from Paul. I am in prison because of Jesus Christ. Brother Timothy is also writing to you, Philemon. You are a much-loved workman together with us. [2]We are also writing to the church that meets in your home. This letter is also for our Christian sister Apphia and it is for Archippus who is a soldier together with us. [3]May God our Father and the Lord Jesus Christ give you His loving-favor and peace.

[4]I always thank God when I speak of you in my prayers. [5]It is because I hear of your love and trust in the Lord Jesus and in all the Christians. [6]I pray that our faith together will help you know all the good things you have through Christ Jesus. [7]Your love has given me much joy and comfort. The hearts of the Christians have been made happy by you, Christian brother.

[8]So now, through Christ, I am free to tell you what you must do. [9]But because I love you, I will only ask you. I am Paul, an old man, here in prison because of Jesus Christ. [10]I am asking you for my son, Onesimus. He has become my son in the Christian life while I have been here in prison. [11]At one time he was of no use to you. But now he is of use to you and to me. [12]I am sending him back to you. It is like sending you my own heart. [13]I would like to keep him with me. He could have helped me in your place while I am in prison for preaching the Good News. [14]But I did not want to keep him without word from you. I did not want you to be kind to me because you had to but because you wanted to. [15]He ran away from you for awhile. But now he is yours forever. [16]Do not think of him any longer as a servant you own. He is more than that to you. He is a much-loved Christian brother to you and to me.

[17]If you think of me as a true friend, take him back as you would take me. [18]If he has done anything wrong or owes you anything, send me the bill. [19]I will pay it. I, Paul, am writing this with my own hand. I will not talk about how much you owe me because you owe me your life. [20]Yes, Christian brother, I want you to be of use to me as a Christian. Give my heart new joy in Christ. [21]I write this letter knowing you will do what I ask and even more.

[22]Please have a room ready for me. I trust God will answer your prayers and let me come to you soon. [23]Epaphras says hello. He is a brother in Christ in prison with me. [24]Mark and Aristarchus and Demas and Luke who are workers with me say hello. [25]May the loving-favor of the Lord Jesus Christ be with your spirit.

HEBREWS

God Speaks Through His Son

1 Long ago God spoke to our early fathers in many different ways. He spoke through the early preachers. ²But in these last days He has spoken to us through His Son. God gave His Son everything. It was by His Son that God made the world. ³The Son shines with the shining greatness of the Father. The Son is as God is in every way. It is the Son Who holds up the whole world by the power of His Word. The Son gave His own life so we could be clean from all sin. After He had done that, He sat down on the right side of God in heaven.

The Son Was Greater Than The Angels

⁴The Son of God was made greater and better than the angels. God gave Him a greater name than theirs. ⁵God did not say to any of His angels, "You are My Son. Today I have become your Father." (Psalm 2:7) And He did not say to any angel, "I will be a Father to him. He will be a son to Me." (II Samuel 7:14) ⁶But when God brought His first-born Son, Jesus, into the world, He said, "Let all the angels of God worship Him." ⁷He said this about the angels, "He makes His angels to be winds. He makes His servants a burning fire." (Psalm 104:4) ⁸But about His Son, He says, "O God, Your place of power will last forever. Whatever You say in Your nation is right and good. ⁹You have loved what is right. You have hated what is wrong. That is why God, Your God, has chosen You. He has poured over You the oil of joy more than over anyone else." (Psalm 45:6-7) ¹⁰He said also, "Lord, You made the earth in the beginning. You made the heavens with Your hands. ¹¹They will be destroyed but You will always be here. They will all become old just as clothes become old. ¹²You will roll up the heavens like a coat. They will be changed. But You are always the same. You will never grow old." (Psalm 102:25-27) ¹³God never said to any angel, "Sit at My right side, until I make those who hate You a place to rest Your feet." (Psalm 110:1) ¹⁴Are not all the angels spirits who work for God? They are sent out to help those who are to be saved from the punishment of sin.

Do Not Wait To Be Saved From The Punishment Of Sin

2 That is why we must listen all the more to the truths we have been told. If we do not, we may slip away from them. ²These truths given by the angels proved to be true. People were punished when they did not obey them. ³God was so good to make a way for us to be saved from the punishment of sin. What makes us think we will not go to hell if we do not take the way to heaven that He has made for us. The Lord was the first to tell us of this. Then those who heard Him told it later. ⁴God proved what they said was true by showing us special things to see and by doing powerful works. He gave the gifts of the Holy Spirit as He wanted to.

Jesus, The Way To Heaven

⁵God did not make angels to be the leaders of that world to come which we have been speaking about. ⁶Instead, the Holy Writings say, "What is man that You think of him

and the son of man that You should remember him?" (Psalm 8:4) [7]"You made him so he took a place that was not as important as the angels for a little while. You gave him the prize of honor and shining greatness. [*]You made him the head over everything You have made. [8]You have put everything under his feet." (Psalm 8:4-6) There is nothing that does not obey him, but we do not see all things obey him yet. [9]But we do see Jesus. For a little while He took a place that was not as important as the angels. But God had loving-favor for everyone. He had Jesus suffer death on a cross for all of us. Then, because of Christ's death on a cross, God gave Him the prize of honor and shining greatness.

[10]God made all things. He made all things for Himself. It was right for God to make Jesus a perfect Leader by having Him suffer for men's sins. In this way, He is bringing many men to share His shining greatness. [11]Jesus makes men holy. He takes away their sins. Both Jesus and the ones being made holy have the same Father. That is why Jesus is not ashamed to call them His brothers. [12]Jesus is saying to His Father, "I will tell My brothers Your name. I will sing songs of thanks for You among the people." (Psalm 22:22) [13]And again He says, "I will put My trust in God." At another time He said, "Here I am with the children God gave Me." (Isaiah 8:17-18)

[14]It is true that we share the same Father with Jesus. And it is true that we share the same kind of flesh and blood because Jesus became a man like us. He died as we must die. Through His death He destroyed the power of the devil who has the power of death. [15]Jesus did this to make us free from the fear of death. We no longer need to be chained to this fear. [16]Jesus did not come to help angels. Instead, He came to help men who are of Abraham's family. [17]So Jesus had to become like His brothers in every way. He had to be one of us to be our Religious Leader to go between God and us. He had loving-pity on us and He was faithful. He gave Himself as a gift to die on a cross for our sins so that God would not hold these sins against us any longer. [18]Because Jesus was tempted as we are and suffered as we do, He understands us and He is able to help us when we are tempted.

Jesus Was Greater Than Moses

3 Christian brothers, you have been chosen and set apart by God. So let us think about Jesus. He is the One God sent and He is the Religious Leader of our Christian faith. [2]Jesus was faithful in God's house just as Moses was faithful in all of God's house. [3]The man who builds a house gets more honor than the house. That is why Jesus gets more honor than Moses. [4]Every house is built by someone. And God is the One Who has built everything. [5]Moses was a faithful servant owned by God in God's house. He spoke of the things that would be told about later on. [6]But Christ was faithful as a Son Who is Head of God's house. We are of God's house if we keep our trust in the Lord until the end. This is our hope. [7]The Holy Spirit says, "If you hear His voice today, [8]do not let your hearts become hard as your early fathers did when they turned against Me. It was at that time in the desert when they put Me to the test. [9]Your early fathers tempted Me and tried Me. They saw the work I did for forty years. [10]For this reason, I was angry with the people of this day. And I said to them, 'They always think wrong thoughts. They have never understood what I have tried to do for them.' [11]I was angry with them and said to Myself, 'They will never go into My rest.' " (Psalm 95:7-11)

[12]Christian brothers, be careful that not one of you has a heart so bad

that it will not believe and will turn away from the living God. ¹³Help each other. Speak day after day to each other while it is still today so your heart will not become hard by being fooled by sin. ¹⁴For we belong to Christ if we keep on trusting Him to the end just as we trusted Him at first. ¹⁵The Holy Writings say, "If you hear His voice today, do not let your hearts become hard as your early fathers did when they turned against Me." (Psalm 95:7-8)

¹⁶Who heard God's voice and turned against Him? Did not all those who were led out of the country of Egypt by Moses? ¹⁷Who made God angry for forty years? Was it not those people who had sinned in the desert? Was it not those who died and were buried there? ¹⁸Who did He say could never go into His rest? Was it not those who did not obey Him? ¹⁹So we can see that they were not able to go into His rest because they did not put their trust in Him.

The Christian's Rest

4 The same promise of going into God's rest is still for us. But we should be afraid that some of us may not be able to go in. ²We have heard the Good News even as they did, but it did them no good because it was not mixed with faith. ³We who have put our trust in God go into His rest. God said this of our early fathers, "I was angry and said, 'They will not go into My rest.' " (Psalm 95:11) And yet God's work was finished after He made the world.

God's Rest

⁴In the Holy Writings He said this about the seventh day when He made the whole world, "God rested on the seventh day from all He had made." (Genesis 2:2) ⁵But God said this about those who turned against Him, "They will not go into My rest." (Psalm 95:11) ⁶Those who heard the Good News first did not go into His rest. It was because they had not obeyed Him. But the promise is still good and some are going into His rest. ⁷God has again set a certain day for people to go into His rest. He says through David many years later as He had said before, "If you hear His voice today, do not let your hearts become hard." (Psalm 95:7-8)

⁸If Joshua had led those people into God's rest, He would not have told of another day after that. ⁹And so God's people have a complete rest waiting for them. ¹⁰The man who goes into God's rest, rests from his own work the same as God rested from His work. ¹¹Let us do our best to go into that rest or we will be like the people who did not go in.

¹²God's Word is living and powerful. It is sharper than a sword that cuts both ways. It cuts straight into where the soul and spirit meet and it divides them. It cuts into the joints and bones. It tells what the heart is thinking about and what it wants to do. ¹³No one can hide from God. His eyes see everything we do. We must give an answer to God for what we have done.

Jesus - Our Great Religious Leader

¹⁴We have a great Religious Leader Who has made the way for man to go to God. He is Jesus, the Son of God, Who has gone to heaven to be with God. Let us keep our trust in Jesus Christ. ¹⁵Our Religious Leader understands how weak we are. Christ was tempted in every way we are tempted, but He did not sin. ¹⁶Let us go with complete trust to the very place of God's loving-favor. We will receive His loving-kindness and have His loving-favor to help us whenever we need it.

The Job Of A Religious Leader

5 Every Jewish religious leader is chosen from among men. He is a helper standing between God and men. He gives gifts on the altar in worship to God from the people. He gives blood from animals for the sins of the people. ²A Jewish religious leader is weak in many ways because he is just a man himself. He knows how to be gentle with those who know little. He knows how to help those who are doing wrong. ³Because he is weak himself, he must give gifts to God for his own sins as well as for the sins of the people. ⁴A Jewish religious leader does not choose this honor for himself. God chooses a man for this work. Aaron was chosen this way.

Christ Is Our Religious Leader Who Has Made The Way For Man To Go To God

⁵It is the same way with Christ. He did not choose the honor of being a Religious Leader Who has made the way for man to go to God. Instead, God said to Christ, "You are My Son. Today I have become Your Father." (Psalm 2:7) ⁶God says in another part of His Word, "You will be a Religious Leader forever. You will be like Melchizedek." (Psalm 110:4) ⁷During the time Jesus lived on earth, He prayed and asked God with loud cries and tears. Jesus' prayer was to God Who was able to save Him from death. God heard Christ because Christ honored God. ⁸Even being God's Son, He learned to obey by the things He suffered. ⁹And having been made perfect, He planned and made it possible for all those who obey Him to be saved from the punishment of sin. ¹⁰In God's plan He was to be a Religious Leader Who made the way for man to go to God. He was like Melchizedek.

Do Not Fall Back Into Sin

¹¹There is much we could say about this, but it is hard to make you understand. It is because you do not want to hear well. ¹²By now you should be teachers. Instead, you need someone to teach you again the first things you need to know from God's Word. You still need milk instead of solid food. ¹³Anyone who lives on milk cannot understand the teaching about being right with God. He is a baby. ¹⁴Solid food is for full-grown men. They have learned to use their minds to tell the difference between good and bad.

Going Ahead

6 So let us leave the first things you need to know about Christ. Let us go on to the teaching that full-grown Christians should understand. We do not need to teach these first truths again. You already know that you must be sorry for your sins and turn from them. You know that you must have faith in God. ²You know about being baptized and about putting hands on people. You know about being raised from the dead and about being punished forever. ³We will go on, if God lets us.

⁴There are those who have known the truth. They have received the gift from heaven. They have shared the Holy Spirit. ⁵They know how good the Word of God is. They know of the powers of the world to come. ⁶But if they turn away, they cannot be sorry for their sins and turn from them again. It is because they are nailing the Son of God on a cross again. They are holding Him up in shame in front of all people. ⁷It is the same with a piece of ground that has had many rains fall on it. God makes it possible for that ground to give good fruits and vegetables. ⁸But if it gives nothing but weeds, it is worth nothing. It will be hated and destroyed by fire.

⁹Dear friends, even as we tell you this, we are sure of better things for you. These things go along with being saved from the punishment of

sin. [10]God always does what is right. He will not forget the work you did to help the Christians and the work you are still doing to help them. This shows your love for Christ. [11]We want each one of you to keep on working to the end. Then what you hope for, will happen. [12]Do not be lazy. Be like those who have faith and have not given up. They will receive what God has promised them.

God's Promise

[13]When God made a promise to Abraham, He made that promise in His own name because no one was greater. [14]He said, "I will make you happy in so many ways. For sure, I will give you many children." (Genesis 22:16-17) [15]Abraham was willing to wait and God gave to him what He had promised.

[16]When men make a promise, they use a name greater than themselves. They do this to make sure they will do what they promise. In this way, no one argues about it. [17]And so God made a promise. He wanted to show Abraham that He would never change His mind. So He made the promise in His own name. [18]God gave these two things that cannot be changed and God cannot lie. We who have turned to Him can have great comfort knowing that He will do what He has promised. [19]This hope is a safe anchor for our souls. It will never move. This hope goes into the Holiest Place of All behind the curtain of heaven. [20]Jesus has already gone there. He has become our Religious Leader forever and has made the way for man to go to God. He is like Melchizedek.

Melchizedek - Like Christ

7 Melchizedek was king of Salem. He was a religious leader for God. When Abraham was coming back from the war where many kings were killed, Melchizedek met Abraham and showed respect to him. [2]Abraham gave Melchizedek one-tenth part of all he had. Melchizedek's name means king of what is right. Salem means peace. So he is king of peace. [3]Melchizedek was without a father or mother or any family. He had no beginning of life or end of life. He is a religious leader forever like the Son of God.

[4]We can see how great Melchizedek was. Abraham gave him one-tenth part of all he had taken in the war. [5]The Law made the family of Levi the Jewish religious leaders. The Law said that the religious leaders were to take one-tenth part of everything from their own people. [6]Melchizedek was not even from the family group of Levi but Abraham paid him. Melchizedek showed respect to Abraham who was the one who had received God's promises. [7]The one who shows respect is always greater than the one who receives it. [8]Jewish religious leaders receive one-tenth part. They are men and they all die. But here Melchizedek received one-tenth part and is alive. [9]We might say that Levi, who receives one-tenth part, paid one-tenth part through Abraham. [10]Levi was not yet born. He was still inside Abraham's body when Abraham paid Melchizedek.

[11]The Law was given during the time when Levi and his sons were the religious leaders. If the work of those religious leaders had been perfect in taking away the sins of the people, there would have been no need for another religious leader. But one like Mechizedek was needed and not one from the family group of Aaron. [12]For when the family group of religious leaders changed, the Law had to be changed also. [13]These things speak of Christ Who is from another family group. That family group never had a religious leader who killed animals and gave gifts at

the altar for the sins of the people. [14]Our Lord came from the family group of Judah. Moses did not write anything about religious leaders coming from that family group.

A Different Religious Leader Has Come

[15]We can see that a different Religious Leader has come. This One is like Melchizedek. [16]Christ did not become a Religious Leader by coming from the family group of Levi as the Law said had to be. He became the Religious Leader by the power of a life that never ends. [17]The Holy Writings say this about Christ, "You are a Religious Leader forever like Melchizedek." (Psalm 110:4)

[18]God put the Law of Moses aside. It was weak and could not be used. [19]For the Law of Moses could not make men right with God. Now there is a better hope through which we can come near to God.

[20]God made a promise when Christ became the Religious Leader Who made the way for man to go to God. [21]God did not make such a promise when Levi's family group became religious leaders. But when Christ became a Religious Leader, this is the promise God made, "The Lord has made a promise. He will never change His mind. You will be a Religious Leader forever." (Psalm 110:4) [22]Christ makes this New Way of Worship sure for us because of God's promise. [23]There had to be many religious leaders during the time of the Old Way of Worship. They died and others had to keep on in their work. [24]But Jesus lives forever. He is the Religious Leader forever. It will never change. [25]And so Jesus is able, now and forever, to save from the punishment of sin all who come to God through Him because He lives forever to pray for them.

[26]We need such a Religious Leader Who made the way for man to go to

God. Jesus is holy and has no guilt. He has never sinned and is different from sinful men. He has the place of honor above the heavens. [27]Christ is not like other religious leaders. They had to give gifts every day on the altar in worship for their own sins first and then for the sins of the people. Christ did not have to do that. He gave one gift on the altar and that gift was Himself. It was done once and it was for all time. [28]The Law makes religious leaders of men. These men are not perfect. After the Law was given, God spoke with a promise. He made His Son a perfect Religious Leader forever.

8 Now the important thing is this: We have such a Religious Leader Who has made the way for man to go to God. He is the One Who sits at the right side of the All-powerful God in the heavens. [2]He is the Religious Leader of that holy place in heaven which is the true place of worship. It was built by the Lord and not by men's hands. [3]Every religious leader of the Old Way of Worship had the work of killing animals and of giving gifts on the altar to God. So Christ had to have something to give also. [4]If Christ were on the earth, He would not be a religious leader such as these. The religious leaders on earth give gifts like the Law says. [5]Their work shows us only a picture of the things in heaven. When Moses was putting up the tent to worship in, God told him, "Be sure you make the tent for worship like I showed you on Mount Sinai." (Exodus 25:40)

[6]But Christ has a more perfect work. He is the One Who goes between God and man in this new and better way. The New Way of Worship promises better things. [7]If the Old Way of Worship had been perfect, there would have been no need for another one. [8]God was not happy how the people lived by the Old Way of Worship. He said, "The

day will come when I will make a New Way of Worship for the Jews and those of the family group of Judah. ⁹The New Way of Worship will not be like the Old Way of Worship I gave to their early fathers. That was when I took them by the hand and led them out of Egypt. But they did not follow the Old Way of Worship. And so I turned away from them. ¹⁰This is the New Way of Worship that I will give to the Jews. When that day comes, says the Lord, I will put My Laws into their minds. And I will write them in their hearts. I will be their God, and they will be My people. ¹¹No one will need to teach his neighbor or his brother to know the Lord. All of them will already know Me from the least to the greatest. ¹²I will show loving-kindness to them because of their sins. I will remember their sins no more." (Jeremiah 31:31-34)

¹³When God spoke about a New Way of Worship, He showed that the Old Way of Worship was finished and of no use now. It will never be used again.

The New Way Of Worship Is Better

9 There were special ways of worship and a special holy place made by man for the Old Way of Worship. ²A big tent was built and set up. It was called the holy place. It had a light and a table, and the holy bread was on the table. ³Behind the second curtain there was another tent. This was called the Holiest Place of All. ⁴In the inside tent there was an altar where special perfume was burned. There was also a large box made of wood called the box of the Way of Worship. Both of these were covered with gold inside and out. Inside the box was a pot made of gold with the bread from heaven. It also had in it Aaron's stick that once started to grow. The stones on which the Law of Moses was written were in it. ⁵Above the box were the cherubim

of honor. Their wings were spread up and over and met in the center. On the top of the box and under the shadow of their wings was the mercy-seat. We cannot tell anymore about these things now.

⁶When everything was finished, the Jewish religious leaders went in and out of the outside tent to do the things which had to be done to worship God. ⁷Once each year the head religious leader would go into the inside tent alone. He would not go in without blood. He gave this blood to God as a gift in worship for his own sins and for the sins of all the people who sinned without knowing it.

⁸And so the Holy Spirit is teaching that, with the Old Way of Worship, the people could not go into the Holiest Place of All as long as the outside tent and its Old Way of Worship were being used. ⁹The outside tent is a picture of that day. With the Old Way of Worship, animals killed and gifts given in worship to God could not take away the guilty feeling of sin. ¹⁰The Old Way of Worship was made up of Laws about what to eat and drink. These Laws told how to wash and other things to do with the body. These things had to be done until Christ came to bring a better way of worship.

The New Way Of Worship Has A Better Gift

¹¹But Christ came as the Head Religious Leader of the good things God promised. He made the way for man to go to God. He was a greater and more perfect tent. He was not made by human hands and was not a part of this earth. ¹²Christ went into the Holiest Place of All one time for all people. He did not take the blood of goats and young cows to give to God as a gift in worship. He gave His own blood. By doing this, He bought us with His own blood and made us free

from sin forever. [13]With the Old Way of Worship, the blood and ashes of animals could make men clean after they had sinned. [14]How much more the blood of Christ will do! He gave Himself as a perfect gift to God through the Spirit that lives forever. Now your heart can be free from the guilty feeling of doing work that is worth nothing. Now you can work for the living God.

[15]Christ is the One Who gave us this New Way of Worship. All those who have been called by God may receive life that lasts forever just as He promised them. Christ bought us with His blood when He died for us. This made us free from our sins which we did under the Old Way of Worship.

[16]When a man wants to give his money to someone after he dies, he writes it all down on paper. But that paper is worth nothing until the man is dead. [17]That piece of paper means nothing as long as he is alive. It is good only when he dies. [18]The Old Way of Worship had to have a death to make it good. The blood of an animal was used. [19]Moses told the people all the things they had to obey in the Law. Then he took the blood of animals together with water and put it on the Book of the Law and on all the people. He used special branches and red wool as he put it on them. [20]Moses said, "This is the blood of the Way of Worship which God said you must obey." (Exodus 24:8) [21]In the same way, Moses put the blood on the tent and on all the things used in worship. [22]The Law says that almost everything is made clean by blood. Sins are not forgiven unless blood is given.

One Perfect Gift

[23]The tent to worship in and the things inside to worship with were like the things in heaven. They were made clean by putting blood on them. But the things in heaven were made clean by a much better gift of worship. [24]For Christ did not go into the Holiest Place of All that was made by men, even if it was like the true one in heaven. He went to heaven itself and He is before God for us. [25]Christ has not given Himself many times, as the head religious leader here on earth went into the Holiest Place of All each year with blood that was not his own. [26]For then Christ would have had to die many times since the world began. But He came once at the end of the Old Way of Worship. He gave Himself once for all time. He gave Himself to destroy sin. [27]It is in the plan that all men die once. After that, they will stand before God and He will say if they are guilty. [28]It is the same with Christ. He gave Himself once to take away the sins of many. When He comes the second time, He will not need to give Himself again for sin. He will save all those who are waiting for Him.

In The Old Way Of Worship Many Gifts Were Given

10 The Law is like a picture of the good things to come. The Jewish religious leaders gave gifts on the altar in worship to God all the time year after year. Those gifts could not make the people perfect who came to worship. [2]If those gifts given to God could take away sins, they would no longer feel guilty of sin. They would have given no more gifts. [3]When they gave the gifts year after year, it made them remember that they still had their sins. [4]The blood of animals cannot take away the sins of men.

In The New Way Of Worship One Gift Was Given

[5]When Christ came to the world, He said to God, "You do not want animals killed or gifts given in worship. You have made My body

ready to give as a gift. ⁶You are not pleased with animals that have been killed or burned and given as gifts on the altar to take away sin. ⁷Then I said, 'I have come to do what You want, O God. It is written in the Law that I would.' "

⁸Then Christ said, "You do not want animals killed or gifts given in worship to you for sin. You are not pleased with them." These things are done because the Law says they should be done. ⁹Then He said, "I have come to do what You want Me to do." And this is what He did when He died on a cross. God did away with the Old Way of Worship and made a New Way of Worship. ¹⁰Our sins are washed away and we are made clean because Christ gave His own body as a gift to God. He did this once for all time.

¹¹All Jewish religious leaders stand every day killing animals and giving gifts on the altar. They give the same gifts over and over again. These gifts cannot take away sins. ¹²But Christ gave Himself once for sins and that is good forever. After that He sat down at the right side of God. ¹³He is waiting there for God to make of those who have hated Him a place to rest His feet. ¹⁴And by one gift He has made perfect forever all those who are being set apart for God-like living.

¹⁵The Holy Spirit tells us this: First He says, ¹⁶"This is the New Way of Worship that I will give them. When that day comes, says the Lord, I will put My Laws in their hearts. And I will write them in their minds." Then He says, ¹⁷"I will not remember their sins and wrong-doings anymore." (Jeremiah 31:33-34) ¹⁸No more gifts on the altar in worship are needed when our sins are forgiven.

We Can Go To God Through Christ

¹⁹Christian brothers, now we know we can go into the Holiest Place of All because the blood of Jesus was given. ²⁰We now come to God by the new and living way. Christ made this way for us. He opened the curtain, which was His own body. ²¹We have a great Religious Leader over the house of God. ²²And so let us come near to God with a true heart full of faith. Our hearts must be made clean from guilty feelings and our bodies washed with pure water. ²³Let us hold on to the hope we say we have and not be changed. We can trust God that He will do what He promised. ²⁴Let us help each other to love others and to do good. ²⁵Let us not stay away from church meetings. Some people are doing this all the time. Comfort each other as you see the day of His return coming near.

Do Not Fall Back Into Sin

²⁶If we keep on sinning because we want to after we have received and know the truth, there is no gift that will take away sins then. ²⁷Instead, we will stand before God and on that day He will say we are guilty. And the hot fires of hell will burn up those who work against God. ²⁸Anyone who did not obey the Old Way of Worship died without loving-kindness when two or three men spoke against him. ²⁹How much more will a man have to be punished if he walks on and hates the Son of God? How much more will he be punished if he acts as if the blood of God's New Way of Worship is worth nothing? This New Way of Worship is God's way of making him holy. How much more will he be punished if he laughs at the Holy Spirit Who wanted to show him loving-favor? ³⁰For we know God said, "I will pay back what is coming to them." And, "The Lord will judge His people." (Deuteronomy 32:35-36) ³¹The very worst thing that can happen to a man is to fall into the hands of the living God!

³²Remember how it was in those

days after you heard the truth. You suffered much. [33]People laughed at you and beat you. When others suffered, you suffered with them. [34]You had loving-pity for those who were in prison. You had joy when your things were taken away from you. For you knew you would have something better in heaven which would last forever.

[35]Do not throw away your trust, for your pay will be great. [36]You must be willing to wait without giving up. After you have done what God wants you to do, God will give you what He promised you. [37]The Holy Writings say, "In a little while, the One you are looking for will come. It will not be a long time now. [38]For the one right with God lives by faith. If anyone turns back, I will not be pleased with him." (Habakkuk 2:3-4) [39]We are not of those people who turn back and are lost. Instead, we have faith to be saved from the punishment of sin.

Faith

11 Now faith is being sure we will get what we hope for. It is being sure of what we cannot see. [2]God was pleased with the men who had faith who lived long ago.

[3]Through faith we understand that the world was made by the Word of God. Things we see were made from what could not be seen.

[4]Because Abel had faith, he gave a better gift in worship to God than Cain. His gift pleased God. Abel was right with God. Abel died, but by faith he is still speaking to us.

[5]Because Enoch had faith, he was taken up from the earth without dying. He could not be found because God had taken him. The Holy Writings tell how he pleased God before he was taken up. [6]A man cannot please God unless he has faith. Anyone who comes to God must believe that He is. That one must also know that God gives what

is promised to the one who keeps on looking for Him.

[7]Because Noah had faith, he built a large boat for his family. God told him what was going to happen. His faith made him hear God speak and he obeyed. His family was saved from death because he built the boat. In this way, Noah showed the world how sinful it was. Noah became right with God because of his faith in God.

[8]Because Abraham had faith, he obeyed God when God called him to leave his home. He was to go to another country that God promised to give him. He left his home without knowing where he was going. [9]His faith in God kept him living as a stranger in the country God had promised to him. Isaac and Jacob had received the same promise. They all lived in tents together. [10]Abraham was looking to God and waiting for a city that could not be moved. It was a city planned and built by God.

[11]Because Sarah had faith, she was able to have a child long after she was past the age to have children. She had faith to believe that God would do what He promised. [12]Abraham was too old to have children. But from this one man came a family with as many in it as the stars in the sky and as many as the sand by the sea.

[13]These people all died having faith in God. They did not receive what God had promised to them. But they could see far ahead to all the things God promised and they were glad for them. They knew they were strangers here. This earth was not their home. [14]People who say these things show they are looking for a country of their own. [15]They did not think about the country they had come from. If they had, they might have gone back. [16]But they wanted a better country. And so God is not ashamed to be called their God. He has made a city for them.

[17]Because Abraham had faith, when he was tested, he gave his son

Isaac as a gift on the altar in worship. God had made a promise to Abraham that He would give him a son. And yet Abraham was willing to give his only son as a gift on the altar in worship. [18]God had said to Abraham, "Your family will come from Isaac." (Genesis 21:12) [19]Abraham believed God was able to bring Isaac back to life again. And so it may be said that Abraham did receive him back from death.

[20]Because Isaac had faith, he said that good would come to Jacob and Esau in the future. [21]Because Jacob had faith, he said that good would come to each of Joseph's sons as he was dying. He used his walking stick to hold him up as he prayed to God.

[22]Because Joseph had faith, he spoke of the Jews leaving the country of Egypt. He was going to die soon, and he told them to bury his body in the country where they were going.

[23]Because of faith, Moses, after he was born, was hidden by his parents for three months. They saw that he was a beautiful child. They were not afraid of the king when he said that all baby boys should be killed.

[24]Because Moses had faith, he would not be called the son of Pharaoh's daughter when he grew up. [25]He chose to suffer with God's people instead of having fun doing sinful things for awhile. [26]Any shame that he suffered for Christ was worth more than all the riches in Egypt. He kept his eyes on the pay God was going to give him.

[27]Because Moses had faith, he left Egypt. He was not afraid of the king's anger. Moses did not turn from the right way but kept seeing God in front of him. [28]Because Moses had faith, he told all the Jews to put blood over their doors. Then the angel of death would pass over their houses and not kill their oldest sons.

[29]Because the Jews had faith, they went through the Red Sea as if they were on dry ground. But when the people of Egypt tried to go through,

they were all killed by the water.

[30]Because the Jews had faith, the walls of the city of Jericho fell down after the Jews had walked around the city for seven days. [31]Because Rahab had faith, she was kept from being killed along with those who did not obey God. She was a woman who sold the use of her body. But she helped the men who had come in secret to look over the country.

There Were Many More Who Had Faith In God

[32]What more should I say? There is not enough time to tell of Gideon and of Barak and of Samson and of Jephthah and of David and of Samuel and of the early preachers. [33]It was because these people had faith that they won wars over other countries. They were good leaders. They received what God promised to them. They closed the mouths of lions [34]and stopped fire that was burning. They got away from being killed with swords. They were made strong again after they had been weak and sick. They were strong in war. They made fighting men from other countries run home. [35]It was because some women had faith that they received their dead back to life. Others chose to be beaten instead of being set free, because they would not turn against God. In this way, they would be raised to a better life. [36]Others were talked against. Some were beaten. Some were put in chains and in prison. [37]They were killed by stones being thrown at them. People were cut in pieces. They were tested. They were killed with swords. They wore skins of sheep and goats and had nothing they could call their own. They were hungry and sick. Everyone was bad to them. [38]They walked through places where no people live and over mountains. They looked for holes in the ground to live in. They were too good for this world. [39]It was because of their

faith that God was pleased with them. But they did not receive what God had promised. [40]God had planned something better for us. These men could not be made perfect without us.

Christ The Perfect One

12 All these many people who have had faith in God are now gathered around watching us. Let us put every thing out of our lives that keeps us from doing what we should. Let us keep running in the race that God has planned for us. [2]Let us keep looking to Jesus. Our faith comes from Him and He is the One Who makes it perfect. He did not give up when He had to suffer shame and die on a cross. He knew of the joy that would be His later. Now He is sitting at the right side of God.

[3]Sinful men spoke words of hate against Christ. He was willing to take such shame from sinners. Think of this so you will not get tired and give up. [4]In your fight against sin, you have not yet had to stand against sin with your blood. [5]Do you remember what God said to you when He called you His sons? "My son, listen when the Lord punishes you. Do not give up when He tells you what you must do. [6]The Lord punishes everyone He loves. He whips every son He receives." (Proverbs 3:11-12) [7]Do not give up when you are punished by God. Be willing to take it, knowing that God is teaching you as a son. Is there a father who does not punish his son sometimes? [8]If you are not punished as all sons are, it means that you are not a true son of God. You are not a part of His family and He is not your Father. [9]Remember that our fathers on earth punished us. We had respect for them. How much more should we obey our Father in heaven and live? [10]For a little while our fathers on earth punished us when they thought they should. But God punishes us for our good so we will

be holy as He is holy. [11]There is no joy while we are being punished. It is hard to take, but later we can see that good came from it. And it gives us the peace of being right with God.

[12]So lift up your hands that have been weak. Stand up on your weak legs. [13]Walk straight ahead so the weak leg will not be turned aside, but will be healed.

[14]Be at peace with all men. Live a holy life. No one will see the Lord without having that kind of life. [15]See that no one misses God's loving-favor. Do not let wrong thoughts about others get started among you. If you do, many people will be turned to a life of sin. [16]None of you should fall into sex sins or forget God like Esau did. He had a right to get all Isaac had because he was the oldest son. But for one plate of food he sold this right to his brother. [17]You know that later he would have received everything. But he did not get it even when he asked for it with tears. It was too late to make right the wrong he had done.

[18]For you have not come close to a mountain that you can touch. You have not come to worship where there is burning fire and darkness and storm and wind. [19]The sound of a horn was heard and God's voice spoke. The people cried out to Moses to have God stop speaking to them. [20]They could not stand to listen to His strong words, "Even if an animal comes to the mountain, it must be killed." (Exodus 19:12) [21]What Moses saw was so hard to look at that he said, "I am full of fear and am shaking." (Deuteronomy 9:19)

[22]But instead, you have come to the mountain of Jerusalem. It is the city of the living God. It is the Jerusalem of heaven with its thousands of angels. [23]You have gathered there with God's children who were born long ago. They are citizens of heaven. God is there. He will tell all men if they are guilty. The spirits of all those right with God are

there. They have been made perfect. [24]Jesus is there. He has made a way for man to go to God. He gave His blood that men might worship God the New Way. The blood of Jesus tells of better things than that which Abel used. [25]Be sure you listen to the One Who is speaking to you. The Jews did not obey when God's Law was given to them on earth. They did not go free. They were punished. We will be punished more if we do not listen to God as He speaks from heaven. [26]On Mount Sinai, God's voice shook the earth. But now He has promised, saying, "Once more I will shake the earth and the heavens." (Exodus 19:18) [27]When God says, "Once more," He means He will take away everything of this world that can be shaken so the things that cannot be shaken will be left. [28]Since we have received a holy nation that cannot be moved, let us be thankful. Let us please God and worship Him with honor and fear. [29]For our God is a fire that destroys everything.

Christian Living

13 Keep on loving each other as Christian brothers. [2]Do not forget to be kind to strangers and let them stay in your home. Some people have had angels in their homes without knowing it. [3]Remember those in prison. Think of them as if you were in prison with them. Remember those who are suffering because of what others have done to them. You may suffer in the same way.

[4]Marriage should be respected by everyone. God will punish those who do sex sins and are not faithful in marriage.

[5]Keep your lives free from the love of money. Be happy with what you have. God has said, "I will never leave you or let you be alone."

(Deuteronomy 31:6) [6]So we can say for sure, "The Lord is my Helper. I am not afraid of anything man can do to me." (Psalm 118:6)

[7]Remember your leaders who first spoke God's Word to you. Think of how they lived, and trust God as they did. [8]Jesus Christ is the same yesterday and today and forever.

[9]Do not let the many strange teachings lead you in the wrong way. Our hearts are made strong by God's loving-favor. Food does not make our hearts strong. Those who obey laws about eating certain foods are not helped by them. [10]We have an altar from which those who work in the place of worship have no right to eat.

[11]The head religious leader takes the blood of animals into the holy place to give it on the altar for sins. But the bodies of the animals are burned outside the city. [12]It was the same with Jesus. He suffered and died outside the city so His blood would make the people clean from sin. [13]So let us go to Him outside the city to share His shame. [14]For there is no city here on earth that will last forever. We are looking for the one that is coming. [15]Let us give thanks all the time to God through Jesus Christ. Our gift to Him is to give thanks. Our lips should always give thanks to His name. [16]Remember to do good and help each other. Gifts like this please God.

[17]Obey your leaders and do what they say. They keep watch over your souls. They have to tell God what they have done. They should have joy in this and not be sad. If they are sad, it is no help to you.

[18]Pray for us. Our hearts tell us we are right. We want to do the right thing always. [19]Pray for me all the more so that I will be able to come to you soon.

[20]God is a God of peace. He raised our Lord Jesus from the dead. Jesus is the Good Shepherd of the sheep. His blood made the New Way of Worship which will last forever.

²¹May God give you every good thing you need so you can do what He wants. May He do in us what pleases Him through Jesus Christ. May Christ have all the shining greatness forever! Let it be so.

²²Christian brothers, I beg of you to listen to these words that will help you. This has been a short letter. ²³I want you to know that Timothy is out of prison. If he comes soon, I will bring him with me when I come to see you. ²⁴Say hello to all of your leaders and to all those who belong to Christ. The Christians from the country of Italy say hello to you. ²⁵May all of you have God's loving-favor. Let it be so.

JAMES

1 This letter is from James. I am a servant owned by God and the Lord Jesus Christ. I say hello to the twelve family groups of the Jewish nation living in many parts of the world.

Take Hope When Tests Come

²My Christian brothers, you should be happy when you have all kinds of tests. ³You know these prove your faith. It helps you not to give up. ⁴Learn well how to wait so you will be strong and complete and in need of nothing.

⁵If you do not have wisdom, ask God for it. He is always ready to give it to you and will never say you are wrong for asking. ⁶You must have faith as you ask Him. You must not doubt. Anyone who doubts is like a wave which is pushed around by the sea. ⁷Such a man will get nothing from the Lord. ⁸The man who has two ways of thinking changes in everything he does.

⁹A Christian brother who has few riches of this world should be happy for what he has. He is great in the eyes of God. ¹⁰But a rich man should be happy even if he loses everything. He is like a flower that will die. ¹¹The sun comes up with burning heat. The grass dries up and the flower falls off. It is no longer beautiful. The rich man will die also and all his riches will be gone. ¹²The man who does not give up when tests come is happy. After the test is over, he will receive the prize of life. God has promised this to those who love Him.

God Does Not Tempt Us

¹³When you are tempted to do wrong, do not say, "God is tempting me." God cannot be tempted. He will never tempt anyone. ¹⁴A man is tempted to do wrong when he lets himself be led by what his bad thoughts tell him to do. ¹⁵When he does what his bad thoughts tell him to do, he sins. When sin completes its work, it brings death.

¹⁶My Christian brothers, do not be fooled about this. ¹⁷Whatever is good and perfect comes to us from God. He is the One Who made all light. He does not change. No shadow is made by His turning. ¹⁸He gave us our new lives through the truth of His Word only because He wanted to. We are the first children in His family.

¹⁹My Christian brothers, you know everyone should listen much

and speak little. He should be slow to become angry. 20A man's anger does not allow him to be right with God. 21Put out of your life all that is unclean and wrong. Receive with a gentle spirit the Word that was taught. It has the power to save your souls from the punishment of sin.

22Obey the Word of God. If you hear only and do not act, you are only fooling yourself. 23Anyone who hears the Word of God and does not obey is like a man looking at his face in a mirror. 24After he sees himself and goes away, he forgets what he looks like. 25But the one who keeps looking into God's perfect Law and does not forget it will do what it says and be happy as he does it. God's Word makes men free.

26If a person thinks he is religious, but does not keep his tongue from speaking bad things, he is fooling himself. His religion is worth nothing. 27Religion that is pure and good before God the Father is to help children who have no parents and to care for women whose husbands have died who have troubles. Pure religion is also to keep yourself clean from the sinful things of the world.

The Rich And The Poor

2 My Christian brothers, our Lord Jesus Christ is the Lord of shining greatness. Since your trust is in Him, do not look on one person as more important than another. 2What if a man comes into your church wearing a gold ring and good clothes? And at the same time a poor man comes wearing old clothes. 3What if you show respect to the man in good clothes and say, "Come and sit in this good place"? But if you say to the poor man, "Stand up over there," or "Sit on the floor by my feet," 4are you not thinking that one is more important than the other? This kind of thinking is sinful. 5Listen, my dear Christian brothers, God has chosen those who are poor in the things of this world to be rich in faith. The holy nation of heaven is theirs. That is what God promised to those who love Him. 6You have not shown respect to the poor man. Is it not the rich men who make it hard for you and take you to court? 7They speak against the name of Christ. And it was Christ Who called you. 8You do well when you obey the Holy Writings which say, "You must love your neighbor as you love yourself." 9But if you look on one man as more important than another, you are sinning. And the Law says you are sinning.

Keep The Whole Law

10If you obey all the Laws but one, you are as guilty as the one who has broken them all. 11The One Who said, "You must not do any sex sins," also said, "You must not kill another person." If you do no sex sins but kill someone, you are guilty of breaking the Law. 12Keep on talking and acting as people who will be told they are guilty or not by the Law that makes men free. 13Anyone who shows no loving-kindness will have no loving-kindness shown to him when he is told he is guilty. But if you show loving-kindness, God will show loving-kindness to you when you are told you are guilty.

Faith Without Works Is Dead

14My Christian brothers, what good does it do if you say you have faith but do not do things that prove you have faith? Can that kind of faith save you from the punishment of sin? 15What if a Christian does not have clothes or food? 16And one of you says to him, "Goodbye, keep yourself warm and eat well." But if you do not give him what he needs, how does that help him? 17A faith that does not do things is a dead faith.

18Someone may say, "You have

faith, and I do things. Prove to me you have faith when you are doing nothing. I will prove to you I have faith by doing things." 19You believe there is one God. That is good! But even the demons believe that, and because they do, they shake.

20You foolish man! Do I have to prove to you that faith without doing things is of no use? 21Was not our early father Abraham right with God by what he did? He obeyed God and put his son Isaac on the altar to die. 22You see his faith working by what he did and his faith was made perfect by what he did. 23It happened as the Holy Writings said it would happen. They say, "Abraham put his trust in God and he became right with God." He was called the friend of God. 24A man becomes right with God by what he does and not by faith only. 25The same was true with Rahab, the woman who sold the use of her body. She became right with God by what she did in helping the men who had been sent to look through the country and sent them away by another road. 26The body is dead when there is no spirit in it. It is the same with faith. Faith is dead when nothing is done.

The Power Of The Tongue

3 My Christian brothers, not many of you should become teachers. If we do wrong, it will be held against us more than other people who are not teachers. 2We all make many mistakes. If anyone does not make a mistake with his tongue by saying the wrong things, he is a perfect man. It shows he is able to make his body do what he wants it to do. 3We make a horse go wherever we want it to go by a small bit in its mouth. We turn its whole body by this. 4Sailing ships are driven by strong winds. But a small rudder turns a large ship whatever way the man at the wheel wants the ship to go.

5The tongue is also a small part of the body, but it can speak big things. See how a very small fire can set many trees on fire. 6The tongue is a fire. It is full of wrong. It poisons the whole body. The tongue sets our whole lives on fire with a fire that comes from hell. 7Men can make all kinds of animals and birds and fish and snakes do what they want them to do. 8But no man can make his tongue say what he wants it to say. It is sinful and does not rest. It is full of poison that kills. 9With our tongue we give thanks to our Father in heaven. And with our tongue we speak bad words against men who are made like God. 10Giving thanks and speaking bad words come from the same mouth. My Christian brothers, this is not right! 11Does a well of water give good water and bad water from the same place? 12Can a fig tree give olives or can a grapevine give figs? A well does not give both good water and bad water.

Wisdom From Above

13Who among you is wise and understands? Let that one show from a good life by the things he does that he is wise and gentle. 14If you have jealousy in your heart and fight to have many things, do not be proud of it. Do not lie against the truth. 15This is not the kind of wisdom that comes from God. But this wisdom comes from the world and from that which is not Christian and from the devil. 16Wherever you find jealousy and fighting, there will be trouble and every other kind of wrong-doing. 17But the wisdom that comes from heaven is first of all pure. Then it gives peace. It is gentle and willing to obey. It is full of loving-kindness and of doing good. It has no doubts and does not pretend to be something it is not. 18Those who plant seeds of peace will gather what is right and good.

4 What starts wars and fights among you? Is it not because you want many things and are fighting to have them? [2]You want something you do not have, so you kill. You want something but cannot get it, so you fight for it. You do not get things because you do not ask for them. [3]Or if you do ask, you do not receive because your reasons for asking are wrong. You want these things only to please yourselves.

[4]You are as wives and husbands who are not faithful in marriage and do sex sins. Do you not know that to love the sinful things of the world and to be a friend to them is to be against God? Yes, I say it again, if you are a friend of the world, you are against God. [5]Do you think the Holy Writings mean nothing when they said, "The Holy Spirit Whom God has given to live in us has a strong desire for us to be faithful to Him?"

[6]But He gives us more loving-favor. For the Holy Writings say, "God works against the proud but gives loving-favor to those who have no pride." (Proverbs 3:34) [7]So give yourselves to God. Stand against the devil and he will run away from you. [8]Come close to God and He will come close to you. Wash your hands, you sinners. Clean up your hearts, you who want to follow the sinful ways of the world and God at the same time. [9]Be sorry for your sins and cry because of them. Be sad and do not laugh. Let your joy be turned to sorrow. [10]Let yourself be brought low before the Lord. Then He will lift you up and help you.

Do Not Talk Against Each Other

[11]Christian brothers, do not talk against anyone or speak bad things about each other. If a person says bad things about his brother, he is speaking against him. And he will be speaking against God's Law. If you say the Law is wrong, and do not obey it, you are saying you are better than the Law. [12]Only God can say what is right or wrong. He made the Law. He can save or put to death. How can we say if our brother is right or wrong?

[13]Listen! You who say, "Today or tomorrow we will go to this city and stay a year and make money." [14]You do not know about tomorrow. What is your life? It is like fog. You see it and soon it is gone. [15]What you should say is, "If the Lord wants us to, we will live and do this or that." [16]But instead you are proud. You talk loud and big about yourselves. All such pride is sin. [17]If you know what is right to do but you do not do it, you sin.

5 Listen, you rich men! Cry about the troubles that will come to you. [2]Your riches are worth nothing. Your fine clothes are full of moth holes. [3]Your gold and silver have rusted. Their rust will speak against you and eat your flesh like fire. You have saved riches for yourselves for the last days. [4]See! The men working in your fields are crying against you because you have kept back part of their pay. Their cries have been heard by the Lord Who hears His people. [5]You have had everything while you lived on the earth and have enjoyed its fun. You have made your hearts fat and are ready to be killed as an animal is killed. [6]You have killed the One right with God. He does not try to stop you.

The Lord Will Come Again

[7]Christian brothers, be willing to wait for the Lord to come again. Learn from the farmer. He waits for the good fruit from the earth until the early and late rains come. [8]You must be willing to wait also. Be strong in your hearts because the Lord is coming again soon. [9]Do not complain about each other, Christian brothers. Then you will not be

guilty. See! The One Who says who is guilty is standing at the door. ¹⁰See how the early preachers spoke for the Lord by their suffering and by being willing to wait. ¹¹We think of those who stayed true to Him as happy even though they suffered. You have heard how long Job waited. You have seen what the Lord did for him in the end. The Lord is full of loving-kindness and pity.

Do Not Swear

¹²My Christian brothers, do not swear. Do not use heaven or earth or anything else to swear by. If you mean yes, say yes. If you mean no, say no. You will be guilty for saying anything more.

The Power Of Prayer In Healing

¹³Is anyone among you suffering? He should pray. Is anyone happy? He should sing songs of thanks to God. ¹⁴Is anyone among you sick? He should send for the church leaders and they should pray for him. They should pour oil on him in the name of the Lord. ¹⁵The prayer given in faith will heal the sick man, and the Lord will raise him up. If he has sinned, he will be forgiven. ¹⁶Tell your sins to each other. And pray for each other so you may be healed. The prayer from the heart of a man right with God has much power. ¹⁷Elijah was a man as we are. He prayed that it might not rain. It did not rain on the earth for three and one-half years. ¹⁸Then he prayed again that it would rain. It rained much and the fields of the earth gave fruit.

Bring Back Those Who Are Lost In Sin

¹⁹My Christian brothers, if any of you should be led away from the truth, let someone turn him back again. ²⁰That person should know that if he turns a sinner from the wrong way, he will save the sinner's soul from death and many sins will be forgiven.

1 PETER

The Living Hope

1 This letter is from Peter, a missionary of Jesus Christ. I am writing to those who were taken away from their homeland and are living in the countries of Pontus and Galatia and Cappadocia and Asia and Bithynia. ²You were chosen by God the Father long ago. He knew you were to become His children. You were set apart for holy living by the Holy Spirit. May you obey Jesus Christ and be made clean by His blood. May you be full of His loving-favor and peace.

³Let us thank the God and Father of our Lord Jesus Christ. It was through His loving-kindness that we were born again to a new life and have a hope that never dies. This hope is ours because Jesus was raised from the dead. ⁴We will receive the great things that we have been promised. They are being kept safe in heaven for us. They are pure and

will not pass away. They will never be lost. [5]You are being kept by the power of God because you put your trust in Him and you will be saved from the punishment of sin at the end of the world.

[6]With this hope you can be happy even if you need to have sorrow and all kinds of tests for awhile. [7]These tests have come to prove your faith and to show that it is good. Gold, which can be destroyed, is tested by fire. Your faith is worth much more than gold and it must be tested also. Then your faith will bring thanks and shining greatness and honor to Jesus Christ when He comes again. [8]You have never seen Him but you love Him. You cannot see Him now but you are putting your trust in Him. And you have joy so great that words cannot tell about it. [9]You will get what your faith is looking for, which is to be saved from the punishment of sin.

[10]The early preachers tried to find out how to be saved. They told of the loving-favor that would come to you. [11]The early preachers wondered at what time or to what person this would happen. The Spirit of Christ in them was talking to them and told them to write about how Christ would suffer and about His shining greatness later on. [12]They knew these things would not happen during the time they lived but while you are living many years later. These are the very things that were told to you by those who preached the Good News. The Holy Spirit Who was sent from heaven gave them power and they told of things that even the angels would like to know about.

Holy Living

[13]Get your minds ready for good use. Keep awake. Set your hope now and forever on the loving-favor to be given you when Jesus Christ comes again. [14]Be like children who obey. Do not desire to sin like you used to when you did not know any better. [15]Be holy in every part of your life. Be like the Holy One Who chose you. [16]The Holy Writings say, "You must be holy, for I am holy." (Leviticus 11:44-45) [17]The Father is the One Who says if you are guilty by what you do. He does not respect one person more than another. If you call Him Father, be sure you honor Him with love and fear all the days of your life here on earth. [18]You know you were not bought and made free from sin by paying gold or silver which comes to an end. And you know you were not saved from the punishment of sin by the way of life that you were given from your early fathers. That way of life was worth nothing. [19]The blood of Christ saved you. This blood is of great worth and no amount of money can buy it. Christ was given as a lamb without sin and without spot. [20]Long before the world was made, God chose Christ to be given to you in these last days. [21]Because of Christ, you have put your trust in God. He raised Christ from the dead and gave Him great honor. So now your faith and hope are in God.

The Living Word

[22]You have made your souls pure by obeying the truth through the Holy Spirit. This has given you a true love for the Christians. Let it be a true love from the heart. [23]You have been given a new birth. It was from a seed that cannot die. This new life is from the Word of God which lives forever. [24]All people are like grass. Their greatness is like the flowers. The grass dries up and the flowers fall off. [25]But the Word of the Lord will last forever. That Word is the Good News which was preached to you.

Food For Christians

2 Put out of your life hate and lying. Do not pretend to be someone you are not. Do not always want something someone else has. Do not say bad things about other people. ²As new babies want milk, you should want to drink the pure milk which is God's Word so you will grow up and be saved from the punishment of sin. ³If you have tasted of the Lord, you know how good He is.

The Living Stone

⁴Come to Christ as to a living stone. Men have put Him aside, but He was chosen by God and is of great worth in the sight of God. ⁵You are to be as living stones in the building God is making also. You are His religious leaders giving yourselves to God through Jesus Christ. This kind of gift pleases God. ⁶The Holy Writings say, "See, I lay down in Jerusalem a Stone of great worth, worth far more than any amount of money. Anyone who puts his trust in Him will not be ashamed." (Isaiah 28:16) ⁷This Stone is of great worth to you who have your trust in Him. But to those who have not put their trust in Him, the Holy Writings say, "The Stone which the workmen put aside has become the most important part of the building." (Psalm 118:22) ⁸The Holy Writings say, also, "Christ is the Stone that some men will trip over and the Rock over which they will fall." When they do not obey the Word of God, they trip over it. This is what happens to such men. ⁹But you are a chosen group of people. You are the King's religious leaders. You are a holy nation. You belong to God. He has done this for you so you can tell others how God has called you out of darkness into His great light. ¹⁰At one time you were a people of no use. Now you

are the people of God. At one time you did not have loving-kindness. Now you have God's loving-kindness.

Our Home Is Not Here On Earth

¹¹Dear friends, your real home is not here on earth. You are strangers here. I ask you to keep away from all the sinful desires of the flesh. These things fight to get hold of your soul. ¹²When you are around people who do not know God, be careful how you act. Even if they talk against you as wrong-doers, in the end they will give thanks to God for your good works when Christ comes again.

Obey The Leaders

¹³Obey the head leader of the country and all other leaders over you. This pleases the Lord. ¹⁴Obey the men who work for them. God sends them to punish those who do wrong and to show respect to those who do right. ¹⁵This is what God wants. When you do right, you stop foolish men from saying bad things. ¹⁶Obey as men who are free but do not use this to cover up sin. Live as servants owned by God at all times. ¹⁷Show respect to all men. Love the Christians. Honor God with love and fear. Respect the head leader of the country.

Servants

¹⁸Servants, you are to respect your owners and do what they say. Do this if you have a good and kind owner. You must do it even if your owner is hard to work for. ¹⁹This shows you have received loving-favor when you are even punished for doing what is right because of your trust in God. ²⁰What good is it if, when you are beaten for doing something wrong, you do not try to get out of it? But if you are beaten

when you have done what is right, and do not try to get out of it, God is pleased. 21These things are all a part of the Christian life to which you have been called. Christ suffered for us. This shows us we are to follow in His steps. 22He never sinned. No lie or bad talk ever came from His lips. 23When people spoke against Him, He never spoke back. When He suffered from what people did to Him, He did not try to pay them back. He left it in the hands of the One Who is always right in saying who is guilty. 24He carried our sins in His own body when He died on a cross. In doing this, we may be dead to sin and alive to all that is right and good. His wounds have healed you! 25You were like lost sheep. But now you have come back to Him Who is your Shepherd and the One Who cares for your soul.

Teaching For Married Christians

3 Wives, obey your own husbands. Some of your husbands may not obey the Word of God. By obeying your husbands, they may become Christians by the life you live without you saying anything. 2They will see how you love God and how your lives are pure. 3Do not let your beauty come from the outside. It should not be the way you comb your hair or the wearing of gold or the wearing of fine clothes. 4Your beauty should come from the inside. It should come from the heart. This is the kind that lasts. Your beauty should be a gentle and quiet spirit. In God's sight this is of great worth and no amount of money can buy it. 5This was the kind of beauty seen in the holy women who lived many years ago. They put their hope in God. They also obeyed their husbands. 6Sarah obeyed her husband Abraham. She respected him as the head of the house. You are her children if you do what is right and

do not have fear.
7In the same way, husbands should understand and respect their wives, because women are weaker than men. Remember, both husband and wife are to share together the gift of life that lasts forever. If this is not done, you will find it hard to pray.

Teaching For All Christians

8Last of all, you must share the same thoughts and the same feelings. Love each other with a kind heart and with a mind that has no pride. 9When someone does something bad to you, do not do the same thing to him. When someone talks about you, do not talk about him. Instead, pray that good will come to him. You were called to do this so you might receive good things from God. 10For "If you want joy in your life and have happy days, keep your tongue from saying bad things and your lips from talking bad about others. 11Turn away from what is sinful. Do what is good. Look for peace and go after it. 12The Lord watches over those who are right with Him. He hears their prayers. But the Lord is against those who sin." (Psalm 34:12-16) 13Who will hurt you if you do what is right? 14But even if you suffer for doing what is right, you will be happy. Do not be afraid or troubled by what they may do to make it hard for you. 15Your heart should be holy and set apart for the Lord God. Always be ready to tell everyone who asks you why you believe as you do. Be gentle as you speak and show respect. 16Keep your heart telling you that you have done what is right. If men speak against you, they will be ashamed when they see the good way you have lived as a Christian. 17If God wants you to suffer, it is better to suffer for doing what is right than for doing what is wrong.

Christ Suffered For Us

¹⁸Christ suffered and died for sins once for all. He never sinned and yet He died for us who have sinned. He died so He might bring us to God. His body died but His spirit was made alive. ¹⁹Christ went and preached to the spirits in prison. ²⁰Those were the spirits of the people who would not obey in the days of Noah. God waited a long time for them while Noah was building the big boat. But only eight people were saved from dying when the earth was covered with water. ²¹This is like baptism to us. Baptism does not mean we wash our bodies clean. It means we are saved from the punishment of sin and go to God in prayer with a heart that says we are right. This can be done because Christ was raised from the dead. ²²Christ has gone to heaven and is on the right side of God. Angels and powers of heaven are obeying Him.

Following Christ Will Mean Suffering

4 Since Christ has suffered in His body, we must be ready to suffer also. Suffering puts an end to sin. ²You should no longer spend the rest of your life giving in to the sinful desires of the flesh. But do what God wants as long as you live in this world. ³In the past you gave enough of your life over to living like the people who do not know God. You gave your life to sex sins and to sinful desires. You got drunk and went to wild parties and to drinking parties and you worshiped false gods. ⁴Those who do not know God are surprised you do not join them in the sinful things they do. They laugh at you and say bad things against you. ⁵Remember, they will give an answer to Him Who says who is guilty from all who are living or dead. ⁶For this reason, the Good News was preached to the dead. They stood in the flesh

before the One Who says who is guilty so they might live in the Spirit as God wants.

Love Each Other

⁷The end of the world is near. You must be the boss over your mind. Keep awake so you can pray. ⁸Most of all, have a true love for each other. Love covers many sins. ⁹Be happy to have people stay for the night and eat with you. ¹⁰God has given each of you a gift. Use it to help each other. This will show God's loving-favor. ¹¹If a man preaches, let him do it with God speaking through him. If a man helps others, let him do it with the strength God gives. So in all things God may be honored through Jesus Christ. Shining greatness and power belong to Him forever. Let it be so.

Stay True During Suffering

¹²Dear friends, your faith is going to be tested as if it were going through fire. Do not be surprised at this. ¹³Be happy that you are able to share some of the suffering of Christ. When His shining greatness is shown, you will be filled with much joy. ¹⁴If men speak bad of you because you are a Christian, you will be happy because the Holy Spirit is in you. ¹⁵None of you should suffer as one who kills another person or as one who steals or as one who makes trouble or as one who tries to be the boss of other peoples' lives. ¹⁶But if a man suffers as a Christian, he should not be ashamed. He should thank God that he is a Christian. ¹⁷The time has come for Christians to stand before God and He will say who is guilty. If this happens to us, what will happen to those who do not obey the Good News of God? ¹⁸If it is hard for a man who is right with God to be saved, what will happen to the sinner? ¹⁹So if God wants you

to suffer, give yourself to Him. He will do what is right for you. He made you and He is faithful.

5 I want to speak to the church leaders among you. I am a church leader also. I saw Christ suffer and die on a cross. I will also share His shining greatness when He comes again. ²Be good shepherds of the flock God has put in your care. Do not care for the flock as if you were made to. Do not care for the flock for money, but do it because you want to. ³Do not be bosses over the people you lead. Live as you would like to have them live. ⁴When the Head Shepherd comes again, you will get the prize of shining greatness that will not come to an end.

⁵In the same way, you younger men must obey the church leaders. Be gentle as you care for each other. God works against those who have pride. He gives His loving-favor to those who do not try to honor themselves. ⁶So put away all pride from yourselves. You are standing under the powerful hand of God. At the right time He will lift you up.

⁷Give all your worries to Him because He cares for you.

⁸Keep awake! Watch at all times. The devil is working against you. He is walking around like a hungry lion with his mouth open. He is looking for someone to eat. ⁹Stand against him and be strong in your faith. Remember, other Christians over all the world are suffering the same as you are. ¹⁰After you have suffered for awhile, God Himself will make you perfect. He will keep you in the right way. He will give you strength. He is the God of all loving-favor and has called you through Christ Jesus to share His shining greatness forever. ¹¹God has power over all things forever. Let it be so.

¹²I have known Silvanus as a faithful Christian brother and it is by him I have written this short letter to help you. It tells you of the true loving-favor of God. Stay true in His loving-favor. ¹³The church which is in the city of Babylon says hello. It has been chosen by God the same as you have been. My son, Mark, says hello also. ¹⁴Say hello to each other with a kiss of holy love. May all of you Christians have peace.

2 PETER

1 This letter is from Simon Peter. I am a missionary of Jesus Christ and a servant owned by Him. I am writing to those who have received the same faith as ours which is of great worth and which no amount of money can buy. This faith comes from our God and Jesus Christ, the One Who saves. ²May you have more and more of His loving-favor and peace as you come to know God and our Lord Jesus Christ better.

Christians Are To Grow

³He gives us everything we need for life and for holy living. He gives it through His great power. As we come to know Him better, we learn

that He called us to share His own shining greatness and perfect life. 4Through His shining greatness and perfect life, He has given us promises. These promises are of great worth and no amount of money can buy them. Through these promises you can have God's own life in you now that you have gotten away from the sinful things of the world which came from wrong desires of the flesh.

5Do your best to add holy living to your faith. Then add to this a better understanding. 6As you have a better understanding, be able to say no when you need to. Do not give up. And as you wait and do not give up, live God-like. 7As you live God-like, be kind to Christian brothers and love them. 8If you have all these things and keep growing in them, they will keep you from being of no use and from having no fruit when it comes to knowing our Lord Jesus Christ. 9But if you do not have these things, you are blind and cannot see far. You forget God saved you from your old life of sin.

10Christian brothers, make sure you are among those He has chosen and called out for His own. As long as you do these things, you will never trip and fall. 11In this way, the road will be made wide open for you. And you will go into the holy nation that lasts forever of our Lord Jesus Christ, the One Who saves.

12You already know about these things but I want to keep telling you about them. You are strong in the faith now. 13I think it is right as long as I am alive to keep you thinking about these things. 14I know that I will soon be leaving this body. Our Lord Jesus Christ has told me this. 15I will try to make a way for you to remember these things after I am gone.

16We had nothing to do with man-made stories when we told you about the power of our Lord Jesus Christ and of His coming again. We have seen His great power with our own eyes. 17When He received honor and shining greatness from God the Father, a voice came to Him from the All-powerful God, saying, "This is My much-loved Son. I am very happy with Him." 18We heard this voice come from heaven when we were with Christ on the holy mountain.

19All this helps us know that what the early preachers said was true. You will do well to listen to what they have said. Their words are as lights that shine in a dark place. Listen until you understand what they have said. Then it will be like the morning light which takes away the darkness. And the Morning Star (Christ) will rise to shine in your hearts.

20Understand this first: No part of the Holy Writings was ever made up by any man. 21No part of the Holy Writings came long ago because of what man wanted to write. But holy men who belonged to God spoke what the Holy Spirit told them.

Watch For False Teachers

2 But there were false teachers among the people. And there will be false teachers among you also. These people will work in secret ways to bring false teaching to you. They will turn against Christ Who bought them with His blood. They bring fast death on themselves. 2Many people will follow their wrong ways. Because of what they do, people will speak bad things against the way of truth. 3They will tell lies and false stories so they can use you to get things for themselves. But God said they were guilty long ago and their death is on the way.

4God did not hold back from punishing the angels who sinned, but sent them down to hell. They are to be kept there in the deep hole of darkness until they stand before Him Who tells them they are guilty.

⁵God did not hold back from punishing the people of the world who sinned long ago. He brought the flood on the world of sinners. But Noah was a preacher of right living. He and his family of seven were the only ones God saved. ⁶God said that the cities of Sodom and Gomorrah were guilty, and He destroyed them with fire. This was to show people who did not worship God what would happen to them. ⁷Lot was taken away from Sodom because he was right with God. He had been troubled by the sins that bad men did in wild living. ⁸He saw and heard how the people around him broke the Law. Everyday his own soul which was right with God was troubled because of their sinful ways. ⁹But the Lord knows how to help men who are right with God when they are tempted. He also knows how to keep the sinners suffering for their wrong-doing until the day they stand before God Who will say they are guilty. ¹⁰This is true about those who keep on wanting to please their own bodies in sinful desires and those who will not obey laws. They want to please themselves and are not afraid when they laugh and say bad things about the powers in heaven. ¹¹Angels are greater in strength and power than they. But angels do not speak against these powers before the Lord.

¹²Men like this are like animals who are not able to think but are born to be caught and killed. They speak bad words against that which they do not understand. They will die in their own sinful ways. ¹³This is the pay they will suffer for their sinful lives. They are not ashamed when they sin in the daylight. They are sores and dirty spots among you while they eat and drink big meals with you. ¹⁴Their eyes are full of sex sins. They never have enough sin. They get weak people to go along with them. Their hearts are always

wanting something. They are people who will end up in hell because ¹⁵they have left the right way and have gone the wrong way. They have followed the way of Balaam, who was the son of Beor. He loved the money he got for his sin. ¹⁶But he was stopped in his sin. A donkey spoke to him with a man's voice. It stopped this early preacher from going on in his crazy way.

¹⁷Such people are like wells without water. They are like clouds before a storm. The darkest place below has been kept for them. ¹⁸They speak big-sounding words which show they are proud. They get men who are trying to keep away from sinful men to give in to the sinful desires of the flesh. ¹⁹They promise that these men will be free. But they themselves are chained to sin. For a man is chained to anything that has power over him.

²⁰There are men who have been made free from the sins of the world by learning to know the Lord Jesus Christ, the One Who saves. But if they do these sins again, and are not able to keep from doing them, they are worse than they were before. ²¹After knowing the holy Law that was given to them, they turned from it. It would have been better for them if they had not known how to be right with God. ²²They are like the wise saying, "A dog turns back to what he has thrown up." (Proverbs 26:11) And, "A pig that has been washed goes back to roll in the mud."

The World Will Be Destroyed

3 Dear friends, this is the second letter I have written to you. In both of them I have tried to get you to remember some things. ²You should remember the words that were spoken before by the holy early preachers. Do not forget the teaching of the Lord, the One Who saves. This was given to you by your missionaries.

³First of all, I want you to know that in the last days men will laugh at the truth. They will follow their own sinful desires. ⁴They will say, "He promised to come again. Where is He? Since our early fathers died, everything is the same from the beginning of the world." ⁵But they want to forget that God spoke and the heavens were made long ago. The earth was made out of water and water was all around it. ⁶Long ago the earth was covered with water and it was destroyed. ⁷But the heaven we see now and the earth we live on now have been kept by His word. They will be kept until they are to be destroyed by fire. They will be kept until the day men stand before God and sinners will be destroyed.

⁸Dear friends, remember this one thing, with the Lord one day is as 1,000 years, and 1,000 years are as one day. ⁹The Lord is not slow about keeping His promise as some people think. He is waiting for you. The Lord does not want any person to be punished forever. He wants all people to be sorry for their sins and turn from them. ¹⁰The day of the Lord will come as a robber comes. The heavens will pass away with a loud noise. The sun and moon and stars will burn up. The earth and all that is in it will be burned up.

¹¹Since all these things are to be destroyed in this way, you should think about the kind of life you are living. It should be holy and God-like. ¹²You should look for the day of God to come. You should do what you can to make it come soon. At that time the heavens will be destroyed by fire. And the sun and moon and stars will melt away with much heat. ¹³We are looking for what God has promised, which are new heavens and a new earth. Only what is right and good will be there.

¹⁴Dear friends, since you are waiting for these things to happen, do all you can to be found by Him in peace. Be clean and free from sin. ¹⁵You can be sure the long waiting of our Lord is part of His plan to save men from the punishment of sin. God gave our dear brother Paul the wisdom to write about this also. ¹⁶He wrote about these things in all of his writings. Some of these things are hard to understand. People who do not have much understanding and some who are not strong in the faith change the meaning of his letters. They do this to the other parts of the Holy Writings also. They are destroying themselves as they do this.

¹⁷And so, dear friends, now that you know this, watch so you will not be led away by the mistakes of these sinful people. Do not be moved by them. ¹⁸Grow in the loving-favor that Christ gives you. Learn to know our Lord Jesus Christ better. He is the One Who saves. May He have all the shining greatness now and forever. Let it be so.

1 JOHN

Christ - The Word Of Life

1 Christ is the Word of Life. He was from the beginning. We have heard Him and have seen Him with our own eyes. We have looked at Him and put our hands on Him. 2 Christ Who is Life was shown to us. We saw Him. We tell you and preach about the Life that lasts forever. He was with the Father and He has come down to us. 3 We are preaching what we have heard and seen. We want you to share together with us what we have with the Father and with His Son, Jesus Christ. 4 We are writing this to you so our joy may be full.

Christians Are To Live In The Light

5 This is what we heard Him tell us. We are passing it on to you. God is light. There is no darkness in Him. 6 If we say we are joined together with Him but live in darkness, we are telling a lie. We are not living the truth. 7 If we live in the light as He is in the light, we share what we have in God with each other. And the blood of Jesus Christ, His Son, makes our lives clean from all sin. 8 If we say that we have no sin, we lie to ourselves and the truth is not in us. 9 If we tell Him our sins, He is faithful and we can depend on Him to forgive us of our sins. He will make our lives clean from all sin. 10 If we say we have not sinned, we make God a liar. And His Word is not in our hearts.

Christ Is Our Helper

2 My dear children, I am writing this to you so you will not sin. But if anyone does sin, there is One Who will go between him and the Father. He is Jesus Christ, the One Who is right with God. 2 He paid for our sins with His own blood. He did not pay for ours only, but for the sins of the whole world.

3 We can be sure that we know Him if we obey His teaching. 4 Anyone who says, "I know Him," but does not obey His teaching is a liar. There is no truth in him. 5 But whoever obeys His Word has the love of God made perfect in him. This is the way to know if you belong to Christ. 6 The one who says he belongs to Christ should live the same kind of life Christ lived.

7 Dear friends, I am not writing a new Law for you to obey. It is an old Law you have had from the beginning. The old Law is the Word that you have heard. 8 And yet it is a new Law that I am writing to you. It is truth. It was seen in Christ and it is seen in you also. The darkness is passing away and the true Light shines instead. 9 Whoever says he is in the light but hates his brother is still in darkness. 10 But whoever loves his brother is in the light. And there will be no reason to sin because of him. 11 Whoever hates his brother is not in the light but lives in darkness. He does not know where he is going because the darkness has blinded his eyes.

Do Not Love The World

12 I am writing to you, my children, for your sins have been forgiven because of Christ's name. 13 I am writing to you, fathers, because you know Him Who has been from the beginning. I am writing to you, young men, because you have power over the devil. I

have written to you, young boys and girls, because you have learned to know the Father. [14]I have written to you, fathers, because you know Him Who has been from the beginning. I have written to you, young men, because you are strong. You have kept God's Word in your hearts. You have power over the devil.

[15]Do not love the world or anything in the world. If anyone loves the world, the Father's love is not in him. [16]For everything that is in the world does not come from the Father. The desires of our flesh and the things our eyes see and want and the pride of this life come from the world. [17]The world and all its desires will pass away. But the man who obeys God and does what He wants done will live forever.

[18]My children, we are near the end of the world. You have heard that the false-christ is coming. Many false-christs have already come. This is how we know the end of the world is near. [19]These left us. But they never belonged to us. If they had been a part of us, they would have stayed with us. Because they left, it is known they did not belong to us. [20]The Holy Spirit has been given to you and you all know the truth. [21]I have not written to you because you do not know the truth. I have written because you do know the truth and you know that no lie comes from the truth.

[22]Who is a liar? He is a person who says that Jesus is not the Christ. The false-christ will have nothing to do with the Father and the Son and he will turn away from Them. [23]A person who will have nothing to do with the Son and turns against Him does not have the Father. The one who says he knows the Son has the Father also.

[24]Keep in your heart what you have heard from the beginning. Then you will belong to the Son and to the Father if what you have heard

from the beginning is in you. [25]And He has promised us life that lasts forever!

[26]I have written to you about those who are trying to lead you in the wrong way. [27]Christ gave you the Holy Spirit and He lives in you. You do not need anyone to teach you. The Holy Spirit is able to teach you all things. What He teaches you is truth and not a lie. Live by the help of Christ as the Holy Spirit has taught you. [28]And now, my children, live by the help of Him. Then when He comes again, we will be glad to see Him and not be ashamed. [29]You know that Christ is right with God. Then you should know that everyone who is right with God is a child of His.

We Are God's Children

3 See what great love the Father has for us that He would call us His children. And that is what we are. For this reason the people of the world do not know who we are because they did not know Him. [2]Dear friends, we are God's children now. But it has not yet been shown to us what we are going to be. We know that when He comes again, we will be like Him because we will see Him as He is. [3]The person who is looking for this to happen will keep himself pure because Christ is pure.

[4]The person who keeps on sinning is guilty of not obeying the Law of God. For sin is breaking the Law of God. [5]You know that Christ came to take away our sins. There is no sin in Him. [6]The person who lives by the help of Christ does not keep on sinning. The person who keeps on sinning has not seen Him or has not known Him. [7]My children, let no one lead you in the wrong way. The man who does what is right, is right with God in the same way as Christ is right with God. [8]The person who keeps on sinning belongs to the devil. The devil has sinned from the

beginning. But the Son of God came to destroy the works of the devil. [9]No person who has become a child of God keeps on sinning. This is because the Holy Spirit is in him. He cannot keep on sinning because God is his Father. [10]This is the way you can know who are the children of God and who are the children of the devil. The person who does not keep on doing what is right and does not love his brother does not belong to God. [11]This is what you have heard from the beginning, that we should love each other. [12]Do not be like Cain. He was a child of the devil and killed his brother. Why did he kill him? It was because he did what was sinful and his brother did what was right.

[13]Do not be surprised if the world hates you, Christian brothers. [14]We know we have passed from death into life. We know this because we love the Christians. The person who does not love has not passed from death into life. [15]A man who hates his brother is a killer in his heart. You know that life which lasts forever is not in one who kills.

[16]We know what love is because Christ gave His life for us. We should give our lives for our brothers. [17]What if a person has enough money to live on and sees his brother in need of food and clothing? If he does not help him, how can the love of God be in him? [18]My children, let us not love with words or in talk only. Let us love by what we do and in truth. [19]This is how we know we are Christians. It will give our heart comfort for sure when we stand before Him. [20]Our heart may say that we have done wrong. But remember, God is greater than our heart. He knows everything. [21]Dear friends, if our heart does not say that we are wrong, we will have no fear as we stand before Him. [22]We will receive from Him whatever we ask if we obey Him and do what He wants. [23]This is what He said we must do: Put your trust in the name of His Son, Jesus Christ, and love each other. Christ told us to do this. [24]The person who obeys Christ lives by the help of God and God lives in him. We know He lives in us by the Holy Spirit He has given us.

The Spirits Must Be Tested

4 Dear Christian friends, do not believe every spirit. But test the spirits to see if they are from God for there are many false preachers in the world. [2]You can tell if the spirit is from God in this way: Every spirit that says Jesus Christ has come in a human body is from God. [3]And every spirit that does not say Jesus has come in a human body is not from God. It is the teaching of the false-christ. You have heard that this teaching is coming. It is already here in the world. [4]My children, you are a part of God's family. You have stood against these false preachers and had power over them. You had power over them because the One Who lives in you is stronger than the one who is in the world. [5]Those false teachers are a part of the world. They speak about the things of the world. The world listens to them. [6]We are a part of God's family. The person who knows God will listen to us. The person who is not a part of God's family will not listen to us. In this way, we can tell what is the spirit of truth and what is the spirit of false teaching.

Loving God Makes Us Love Our Christian Brothers

[7]Dear friends, let us love each other, because love comes from God. Those who love are God's children and they know God. [8]Those who do not love do not know God because God is love. [9]God has

shown His love to us by sending His only Son into the world. God did this so we might have life through Christ. [10]This is love! It is not that we loved God but that He loved us. For God sent His Son to pay for our sins with His own blood.

[11]Dear friends, if God loved us that much, then we should love each other. [12]No person has ever seen God at any time. If we love each other, God lives in us. His love is made perfect in us. [13]He has given us His Spirit. This is how we live by His help and He lives in us.

Love Gives Us More Faith In Christ

[14]We have seen and are able to say that the Father sent His Son to save the world from the punishment of sin. [15]The person who tells of Him in front of men and says that Jesus is the Son of God, God is living in that one and that one is living by the help of God. [16]We have come to know and believe the love God has for us.. God is love. If you live in love, you live by the help of God and God lives in you.

The Love Of God Has Power Over Fear And Hate

[17]Love is made perfect in us when we are not ashamed as we stand before Him on the day He says who is guilty. For we know that our life in this world is His life lived in us. [18]There is no fear in love. Perfect love puts fear out of our hearts. People have fear when they are afraid of being punished. The man who is afraid does not have perfect love. [19]We love Him because He loved us first. [20]If a person says, "I love God," but hates his brother, he is a liar. If a person does not love his brother whom he has seen, how can he love God Whom he has not seen? [21]We have these words from Him. If you love God, love your brother also.

5 The person who believes that Jesus is the Christ is a child of God. The person who loves the Father loves His children also. [2]This is the way we know we love God's children. It is when we love God and obey His Word. [3]Loving God means to obey His Word, and His Word is not hard to obey. [4]Every child of God has power over the sins of the world. The way we have power over the sins of the world is by our faith. [5]Who could have power over the world except by believing that Jesus is the Son of God? [6]Jesus Christ came by water and blood. He did not come by water only, but by water and blood. The Holy Spirit speaks about this and He is truth. [7]There are three who speak of this in heaven: the Father and the Word and the Holy Spirit. These three are one. [8]There are three who speak of this on the earth: the Holy Spirit and the water and the blood. These three speak the same thing. [9]If we believe what men say, we can be sure what God says is more important. God has spoken as He has told us about His Son. [10]The person who puts his trust in God's Son knows in his own heart that Jesus is the Son of God. The person who does not have his trust in God's Son makes God a liar. It is because he has not believed the word God spoke about His Son. [11]This is the word He spoke: God gave us life that lasts forever, and this life is in His Son. [12]He that has the Son has life. He that does not have the Son of God does not have life.

[13]I have written these things to you who believe in the name of the Son of God. Now you can know you have life that lasts forever. [14]We are sure that if we ask anything that He wants us to have, He will hear us. [15]If we are sure He hears us when we ask, we can be sure He will give us what we ask for. [16]You may see a Christian brother sinning in a way that does not lead to death. You

should pray for him. God will give him life unless he has done that sin that leads to death. There is a sin that leads to death. There is no reason to pray for him if he has done that sin. [17]Every kind of wrong-doing is sin. But there is a sin that does not lead to death.

[18]We know that no child of God keeps on sinning. The Son of God watches over him and the devil cannot get near him. [19]We know that we belong to God, but the whole world is under the power of the devil. [20]We know God's Son has come. He has given us the understanding to know Him Who is the true God. We are joined together with the true God through His Son, Jesus Christ. He is the true God and the life that lasts forever. [21]My children, keep yourselves from false gods.

2 JOHN

1 The church leader writes to the chosen lady and to her children. I love you because of the truth. I am not the only one who loves you. All who know the truth love you. [2]It is because the truth is in us and will be with us forever. [3]Loving-favor and loving-kindness and peace are ours as we live in truth and love. These come from God the Father and from the Lord Jesus Christ, Who is the Son of the Father.

[4]I am happy to find some of your children living in the truth as the Father has said we should. [5]And now I ask you, lady, that we have love one for the other. I am not writing to you about a new Law but an old one we have had from the beginning. [6]Love means that we should live by obeying His Word. From the beginning He has said in His Word that our hearts should be full of love.

[7]There are many false teachers in the world. They do not say that Jesus Christ came in a human body. Such a person does not tell the truth. He is the false-christ. [8]Watch yourselves! You do not want to lose what we have worked for. You want to get what has been promised to you.

[9]Anyone who goes too far and does not live by the teachings of Christ does not have God. If you live by what Christ taught, you have both the Father and the Son. [10]If a person comes to you with some other kind of teaching, do not take him into your home. Do not even say hello to him. [11]The person who does has a share in his sins.

[12]I have many things to write to you. I do not want to write them in this letter. But I hope to come to you soon. Then we can talk about these things together that your joy may be full. [13]The children of your sister who was chosen by God say hello to you.

3 JOHN

1 The church leader writes to the much-loved Gaius. I love you because of the truth. ²Dear friend, I pray that you are doing well in every way. I pray that your body is strong and well even as your soul is. ³I was very happy when some Christians came and told me about how you are following the truth. ⁴I can have no greater joy than to hear that my children are following the truth.

⁵Dear friend, you are doing a good work by being kind to the Christians, and for sure, to the strangers. ⁶They have told the church about your love. It will be good for you to help them on their way as God would have you. ⁷These people are working for the Lord. They are taking nothing from the people who do not know God. ⁸So we should help such people. That way we will be working with them as they teach the truth.

⁹I wrote a letter to the church. But Diotrephes wants to be the leader and put himself first. He will have nothing to do with us. ¹⁰So if I come, I will show what he is doing by the bad things he is saying about us. Not only that, he will not take the Christian brothers into his home. He keeps others from doing it also. When they do, he puts them out of the church. ¹¹Dear friend, do not follow what is sinful, but follow what is good. The person who does what is good belongs to God. The person who does what is sinful has not seen God. ¹²Everyone speaks good things about Demetrius. The truth itself speaks for him. We say the same thing also and you know we are speaking the truth. ¹³I have much to write about but I do not want to write them in this letter. ¹⁴I hope to see you soon and then we can talk together. May you have peace. The friends here say hello to you. Say hello to each friend there by name.

JUDE

1 This letter is from Jude, a brother of James. I am a servant owned by Jesus Christ. I am writing to you who have been chosen by God the Father. You are kept for Jesus Christ. ²May you have much of God's loving-kindness and peace and love.

³Dear friends, I have been trying to write to you about what God did for us when He saved us from the punishment of sin. Now I must write to you and tell you to fight hard for the faith which was once and for all given to the holy people of God. ⁴Some sinful men have come into your church without anyone knowing it. They are living in sin and they speak of the loving-favor of God to cover up their sins. They

have turned against our only Leader and Lord, Jesus Christ. Long ago it was written that these people would die in their sins.

⁵You already know all this, but think about it again. The Lord saved His people out of the land of Egypt. Later He destroyed all those who did not put their trust in Him. ⁶Angels who did not stay in their place of power, but left the place where they were given to stay, are chained in a dark place. They will be there until the day they stand before God to be told they are guilty. ⁷Do you remember about the cities of Sodom and Gomorrah and the towns around them? The people in those cities did the same things. They were full of sex sins and strong desires for sinful acts of the body. Those cities were destroyed by fire. They still speak to us of the fire of hell that lasts forever.

What False Teachers Are Like

⁸In the same way, these men go on dreaming and sinning against their bodies. They respect no leaders. They speak bad against those who live in the heavens. ⁹Michael was one of the head angels. He argued with the devil about the body of Moses. But Michael would not speak sharp words to the devil, saying he was guilty. He said, "The Lord speak sharp words to you." ¹⁰But these men speak against things they do not understand. They are like animals in the way they act. By these things they destroy themselves. ¹¹It is bad for them! They have followed the way of Cain who killed his brother. They have chosen the way of Balaam and think only about making money. They were destroyed as Korah was destroyed who would not show respect to leaders. ¹²When you come together to eat the Christians' love suppers, these people are like hidden rocks that wreck a ship. They only think of themselves. They are like clouds without rain carried along by the wind and like trees without fruit in the fall of the year. They are pulled out by the roots and are dead now and never can live again. ¹³They are like the waves of a wild sea. Their sins are like the dirty water along the shore. They look like stars moving here and there. But the darkest place has been kept for them forever.

¹⁴Enoch was the head of the seventh family born after Adam. He said this about such people, "The Lord comes with many thousands of His holy ones. ¹⁵He comes to say that all are guilty for all the sin they have done and all the sinful things these sinners have spoken against God." ¹⁶These men complain and are never happy with anything. They let their desires lead them into sin. When they talk about themselves, they make it sound as if they are great people. They show respect to people only to get something out of them.

¹⁷Dear friends, you must remember the words spoken by the missionaries of our Lord Jesus Christ. ¹⁸They said, "In the last days there will be men who will laugh at the truth and will be led by their own sinful desires." ¹⁹They are men who will make trouble by dividing people into groups against each other. Their minds are on the things of the world because they do not have the Holy Spirit.

²⁰Dear friends, you must become strong in your most holy faith. Let the Holy Spirit lead you as you pray. ²¹Keep yourselves in the love of God. Wait for life that lasts forever through the loving-kindness of our Lord Jesus Christ. ²²Have loving-kindness for those who doubt. ²³Save some by pulling them out of the fire. Have loving-kindness for others but also fear them. Be afraid of being led into doing their sins. Hate even the clothes that have touched sinful bodies.

²⁴There is One Who can keep you from falling and can bring you before Himself free from all sin. He can give

you great joy as you stand before Him in His shining greatness. ²⁵He is the only God. He is the One Who saves from the punishment of sin through Jesus Christ our Lord. May He have shining greatness and honor and power and the right to do all things. He had this before the world began, He has it now, and He will have this forever. Let it be so.

REVELATION

1 The things that are written in the Book are made known by Jesus Christ. God gave these things to Christ so He could show them to the servants He owns. These are things which must happen very soon. Christ sent His angel to John who is a servant owned by Him. Christ made these things known to John. ²John tells that the Word of God is true. He tells of Jesus Christ and all that he saw and heard of Him. ³The man who reads this Book and listens to it being read and obeys what it says will be happy. For all these things will happen soon.

John Writes To The Seven Churches In Asia

⁴This is John writing to the seven churches in the countries of Asia. May you have loving-favor and peace from God Who was and Who is and Who is to come. May you have loving-favor and peace from the seven Spirits who are before the place where God sits. ⁵May you have loving-favor and peace from Jesus Christ Who is faithful in telling the truth. Jesus Christ is the first to be raised from the dead. He is the head over all the kings of the earth. He is the One Who loves us and has set us free from our sins by His blood. ⁶Christ has made us a holy nation of religious leaders who can go to His God and Father. He is the One to receive honor and power forever! Let it be so. ⁷See! He is coming in the clouds. Every eye will see Him. Even the men who killed Him will see Him. All the people on the earth will cry out in sorrow because of Him. Yes, let it be so.

⁸The Lord God says, "I am the First and the Last, the beginning and the end of all things. I am the All-powerful One Who was and Who is and Who is to come."

What God Wanted To Show John Of Christ

⁹I, John, am your Christian brother. I have shared with you in suffering because of Jesus Christ. I have also shared with you His holy nation and we have not given up. I was put on the island called Patmos because I preached the Word of God and told about Jesus Christ. ¹⁰I was worshiping on the Lord's Day when I heard a loud voice behind me like the loud sound of a horn. ¹¹It said, "*(I am the First and the Last.) Write in a book what you see and send it to the seven churches. They are in the cities of Ephesus and Smyrna and Pergamum and Thyatira and Sardis and Philadelphia and Laodicea."

¹²I turned around to see who was speaking to me. As I turned, I saw seven lights made of gold. ¹³Among

the lights stood One Who looked like the Son of Man. He had on a long coat that came to His feet. A belt of gold was around His chest. ¹⁴His head and His hair were white like white wool. They were as white as snow. His eyes were like fire. ¹⁵His feet were like shining brass as bright as if it were in a fire. His voice sounded like powerful rushing water. ¹⁶He held seven stars in His right hand. A sharp sword that cuts both ways came out of His mouth. His face was shining as bright as the sun shines at noon. ¹⁷When I saw Him, I fell down at His feet like a dead man. He laid His right hand on me and said, "Do not be afraid. I am the First and the Last. ¹⁸I am the Living One. I was dead, but look, I am alive forever. I have power over death and hell. ¹⁹So write the things you have seen and the things that are and the things that will happen later. ²⁰This is what the seven stars and the seven lights made of gold mean that you saw in My right hand. The seven stars are the angels of the seven churches. The seven lights are the seven churches.

Words To The Church In Ephesus

2 "Write this to the angel of the church in the city of Ephesus: 'The One Who holds the seven stars in His right hand and the One Who walks among the seven lights made of gold, says this: ²I know what you have done and how hard you have worked. I know how long you can wait and not give up. I know that you cannot put up with sinful men. I know that you have put men to the test who call themselves missionaries. You have found they are not missionaries but are false. ³You have waited long and have not given up. You have suffered because of Me. You have kept going on and have not become tired. ⁴But I have this one thing against you. You do not love Me as you did at first. ⁵Remember

how you once loved Me. Be sorry for your sin and love Me again as you did at first. If you do not, I will come to you and take your light out of its place. I will do this unless you are sorry for your sin and turn from it. ⁶But you have this: You hate what the Nicolaitans do. I hate what they do also. ⁷You have ears! Then listen to what the Spirit says to the churches. I will give the fruit of the tree of life in the garden of God to everyone who has power and wins.'

Words To The Church In Smyrna

⁸"Write this to the angel of the church in the city of Smyrna: 'The One Who is First and Last, the One Who died and came to life again, says this: ⁹I know of your troubles. I know you are poor. But still you are rich! I know the bad things spoken against you by those who say they are Jews. But they are not Jews. They belong to the devil. ¹⁰Do not be afraid of what you will suffer. Listen! The devil will throw some of you into prison to test you. You will be in trouble for ten days. Be faithful even to death. Then I will give you the prize of life. ¹¹You have ears! Then listen to what the Spirit says to the churches. The person who has power and wins will not be hurt by the second death!'

Words To The Church In Pergamum

¹²"Write this to the angel of the church in the city of Pergamum: 'The One Who has the sharp sword that cuts both ways, says this: ¹³I know where you live. It is the place where Satan sits. I know that you are true to Me. You did not give up and turn away from your faith in Me, even when Antipas was killed. He was faithful in speaking for Me. He was killed in front of you where Satan is. ¹⁴But I have a few things against you. You have some people who follow the teaching of Balaam. He taught

Balak to set a trap for the Jews. He taught them to eat food that had been given as a gift in worship to false gods and to do sex sins. [15]You also have some who follow the teaching of the Nicolaitans in the same way. [16]Be sorry for your sins and turn from them. If you do not, I will come to you right away. I will fight against them with the sword of My mouth. [17]You have ears! Then listen to what the Spirit says to the churches. I will give the hidden bread from heaven to everyone who has power and wins. I will give each of them a white stone also. A new name will be written on it. No one will know the name except the one who receives it!'

Words To The Church In Thyatira

[18]"Write this to the angel of the church in the city of Thyatira: 'The Son of God Who has eyes like fire and Whose feet are like shining brass, says this: [19]I know what you done doing. I know of your love and faith. I know how you have worked and how you have waited long and have not given up. I know that you are working harder now than you did at first. [20]But I have this against you: You are allowing Jezebel who calls herself a preacher to teach my servants. She is leading them in the wrong way and they are doing sex sins. And they are eating food that has been given as a gift in worship to false gods. [21]I gave her time to be sorry for her sins and turn from them. She does not want to turn from her sex sins. [22]See! I will throw her on a bed. Those who do sex sins with her will suffer much trouble and pain. I will let them suffer unless they are sorry for the sins they have done with her and turn from them. [23]And I will kill her children. All the churches will know that I am the One Who looks deep into the hearts and minds. I will give you whatever is coming to you because of your work. [24]But the rest of you there in the city of

Thyatira have not followed this false teaching. You have not learned what they call the secrets of Satan. So I will put no other load on you. [25]But hold on to what you have until I come. [26]To the one who has power and wins and does what I want him to do, I will give the right and the power over the nations. [27]He will be leader over them using a piece of iron. And they will be broken in pieces like pots of clay. My Father has given Me this right and power. [28]And I will give him the Morning Star. [29]You have ears! Then listen to what the Spirit says to the churches!'

Words To The Church In Sardis

3 "Write this to the angel of the church in the city of Sardis: The One Who has the seven Spirits of God and the seven stars, says this: I know what you are doing. I know people think you are alive, but you are dead. [2]Wake up! Make stronger what you have before it dies. I have not found your work complete in God's sight. [3]So remember what you have received and heard. Keep it. Be sorry for your sins and turn from them. If you will not wake up, I will come as a robber. You will not know at what time I will come. [4]But there are a few people in the church in the city of Sardis whose clothes are not dirty with sins. They will walk with Me wearing white clothes. They have done what they should. [5]Everyone who has power and wins will wear white clothes. I will not take his name from the book of life. I will speak of his name before My Father and His angels. [6]You have ears! Then listen to what the Spirit says to the churches.'

Words To The Church In Philadelphia

[7]"Write this to the angel of the church in the city of Philadelphia: 'He Who is holy and true, Who holds

the key of David, Who opens and no man can shut, Who shuts and no man can open, says this: [8]I know what you are doing. See! You do not have much power, but you have obeyed My Word. You have not turned against Me. So I have given you an open door that no man can shut. [9]See! There are some who belong to Satan. They say they are Jews, but they are not. They are liars. See! I will make them come to you and get down at your feet. Then they will know that I love you. [10]I will keep you from the time of trouble. The time to test everyone is about to come to the whole world. I will do this because you have listened to Me and have waited long and have not given up. [11]I am coming very soon. Hold on to what you have so no one can take your prize. [12]I will make the one who has power and wins an important part that holds up the house of God. He will never leave it again. I will write on him the name of My God and the name of the city of My God. It is the new Jerusalem. The new Jerusalem will come down from My God out of heaven. I will write My new name on him. [13]You have ears! Then listen to what the Spirit says to the churches.'

Words To The Church In Laodicea

[14]"Write this to the angel of the church in the city of Laodicea: 'The One Who says, Let it be so, the One Who is faithful, the One Who tells what is true, the One Who made everything in God's world, says this: [15]I know what you are doing. You are not cold or hot. I wish you were one or the other. [16]But because you are warm, and not hot or cold, I will spit you out of My mouth. [17]You say that you are rich and that you need nothing, but you do not know that you are so troubled in mind and heart. You are poor and blind and without clothes. [18]You should buy gold from Me that has been tested by fire that you may be rich. Buy white clothes to dress yourself so the shame of not wearing clothes will be taken away. Buy medicine to put on your eyes so you can see. [19]I speak strong words to those I love and I punish them. Have a strong desire to please the Lord. Be sorry for your sins and turn from them. [20]See! I stand at the door and knock. If anyone hears My voice and opens the door, I will come in to him and we will eat together. [21]I will allow the one who has power and wins to sit with me on the place where I sit. I had power and won also. Then I sat down beside My Father Who is sitting in His place of power. [22]You have ears! Then listen to what the Spirit says to the churches.' "

The King's Place Of Power In Heaven

4 After this, I looked and saw a door standing open in heaven. The first voice I heard was like the loud sound of a horn. It said, "Come up here. I will show you what must happen after these things." [2]At once I was under the Spirit's power. See! The throne was in heaven, and One was sitting on it. [3]The One Who sat there looked as bright as jasper and sardius stones. The colors like those of an emerald stone were all around the throne. [4]There were twenty-four smaller thrones around the throne. And on these thrones twenty-four leaders were sitting dressed in white clothes. They had crowns of gold on their heads. [5]Lightning and noise and thunder came from the throne. Seven lights of fire were burning before the throne. These were the seven Spirits of God.

[6]Before the throne there was what looked like a sea of glass, shining and clear. Around the throne and on each side there were four living beings that were full of eyes in front and in back. [7]The first living being was like a lion. The second one was like a young

cow. The third one had a face like a man. The fourth one was like a very large bird with its wings spread. [8]Each one of the four living beings had six wings. They had eyes all over them, inside and out. Day and night they never stop saying, "Holy, holy, holy is the Lord God, the All-powerful One. He is the One Who was and Who is and Who is to come."

[9]The four living beings speak of His shining greatness and give honor and thanks to Him Who sits on His throne as King. It is He Who lives forever. [10]The twenty-four leaders get down before Him and worship Him Who lives forever. They lay their crowns before Him and say, [11]"Our Lord and our God, it is right for You to have the shining greatness and the honor and the power. You made all things. They were made and have life because You wanted it that way."

The Book In Heaven

5 I saw a book in the right hand of the One Who sat on the throne. It had writing on the inside and on the back side. It was locked with seven locks. [2]I saw a powerful angel calling with a loud voice, "Who is able to open the book and to break its locks?" [3]No one in heaven or on the earth or under the earth was able to open the book or to look in it. [4]Then I began to cry with loud cries. I cried because no one was good enough to open the book or to look in it.

[5]One of the leaders said to me, "Stop crying. See! The Lion from the family group of Judah has power and has won. He can open the book and break its seven locks. He is of the family of David."

[6]I saw a Lamb standing in front of the twenty-four leaders. He was before the throne and in front of the four living beings. He looked as if He had been killed. He had seven horns

and seven eyes. These are the seven Spirits of God. They have been sent out into all the world. [7]The Lamb came and took the book from the right hand of the One Who sat on the throne. [8]When the Lamb had taken the book, the four living beings and the twenty-four leaders got down before Him. Each one had a music box with strings. They all had pots made of gold, full of special perfume, which are the prayers of the people who belong to God. [9]They sang a new song, saying, "It is right for You to take the book and break its locks. It is because You were killed. Your blood has bought men for God from every family and from every language and from every kind of people and from every nation. [10]You have made them to be a holy nation of religious leaders to work for our God. They will be the leaders on the earth."

[11]I looked again. I heard the voices of many thousands of angels. They stood around the throne and around the four living beings and the leaders. [12]They said with a loud voice, "The Lamb Who was killed has the right to receive power and riches and wisdom and strength and honor and shining greatness and thanks."

[13]Then I heard every living thing in heaven and on the earth and under the earth and in the sea and all that are in them. They were saying, "Thanks and honor and shining greatness and all power are to the One Who sits on the throne and to the Lamb forever." [14]The four living beings kept saying, "Let it be so!" And the twenty-four leaders got down and worshiped Him.

The Seven Locks [The First Lock] - Power To Win

6 I saw the Lamb break open the first of the seven locks. I heard one of the four living beings cry out like the sound of thunder, "Come and see!" [2]I looked and saw a white horse. The one who sat on it had a bow. A crown was given to him. He went out to win and he won.

The Second Lock - Fighting

³He broke open the second lock. Then I heard the second living being say, "Come and see!" ⁴Another horse came out. This one was red. The one who sat on it was given a long sword. He was given power to take peace from the earth so men would kill each other.

The Third Lock - No Food

⁵He broke open the third lock. Then I heard the third living being say, "Come and see!" I looked and saw a black horse. The one who sat on it had something in his hand with which to weigh things. ⁶I heard a voice from among the four living beings saying, "A small jar of wheat for a day's pay. Three small jars of barley for a day's pay. Do not hurt the olive oil and wine."

The Fourth Lock - Death

⁷He broke open the fourth lock. Then I heard the fourth living being say, "Come and see!" ⁸I looked and saw a light colored horse. The one who sat on it had the name of Death. Hell followed close behind him. They were given the right and the power to kill one-fourth part of everything on the earth. They were to kill with the sword and by people having no food and by sickness and by the wild animals of the earth.

The Fifth Lock - Killed For Telling Of Jesus

⁹He broke open the fifth lock. Then I saw under the altar all the souls of those who had been killed for telling the Word of God. They had also been killed for being faithful in telling about Christ. ¹⁰All those who had been killed cried out with a loud voice saying, "How long will it be yet before You will punish those on the earth for killing us? Lord, You are holy and true." ¹¹White clothes were given to each one of them. They were told to rest a little longer. They were to wait until all the other servants owned by God and their Christian brothers would be killed as they had been. Then the group would be complete.

The Sixth Lock - God's Anger On The Earth

¹²I looked as the Lamb broke the sixth lock. The earth shook as if it would break apart. The sun became black like dark cloth. The moon became like blood. ¹³The stars of the sky fell to the earth. They were like figs falling from a tree that is shaken by a strong wind. ¹⁴The sky passed away like paper being rolled up. Every mountain and island moved from its place. ¹⁵The kings and the leaders of the earth hid themselves in the holes and among the rocks of the mountains. All the head soldiers and rich men and strong men and men who were free and those who were owned by someone hid themselves also. ¹⁶They called to the mountains and to the rocks, "Fall on us! Hide us from the face of the One Who sits on the throne. Hide us from the anger of the Lamb, ¹⁷because the special day of Their anger has come! Who is able to stand against it?"

The Servants God Owns Are Marked

7 After this I saw four angels. They were standing at the four corners of the earth. They were holding back the four winds of the earth so no wind would blow on the earth or the sea or on any tree. ²I saw another angel coming from the east. He was carrying the mark of the living God. He called with a loud voice to the four angels who had been given power to hurt the earth and sea. ³The angel from the east said, "Do not hurt the earth or the sea or the trees until we have put the mark of God on the foreheads of the servants He owns."

⁴I heard how many there were who received the mark of God. There were 144,000 people of the twelve family groups of Israel. ⁵These received the mark of God: 12,000 from the family group of Judah, 12,000 from the family group of Reuben, 12,000 from the family group of Gad, ⁶12,000 from the family group of Asher, 12,000 from the family group of Naphtali, 12,000 from the family group of Manasseh, ⁷12,000 from the family group of Simeon, 12,000 from the family group of Levi, 12,000 from the family group of Issachar, ⁸12,000 from the family group of Zebulun, 12,000 from the family group of Joseph, and 12,000 from the family group of Benjamin.

The Many People Who Belonged To God

⁹After this I saw many people. No one could tell how many there were. They were from every nation and from every family and from every kind of people and from every language. They were standing before the throne and before the Lamb. They were wearing white clothes and they held branches in their hands. ¹⁰And they were crying out with a loud voice, "We are saved from the punishment of sin by our God Who sits on the throne and by the Lamb!" ¹¹Then all of the angels standing around the throne and around the leaders and the four living beings got down on their faces before God and worshiped Him. ¹²They said, "Let it be so! May our God have worship and shining greatness and wisdom and thanks and honor and power and strength forever. Let it be so!"

¹³Then one of the twenty-four leaders asked me, "Who are these people dressed in white clothes? Where did they come from?" ¹⁴I answered him, "Sir, you know." Then he said to me, "These are the ones who came out of the time of much trouble. They have washed their clothes and have made them white in the blood of the Lamb. ¹⁵For this reason they are before the throne of God. They help Him day and night in the house of God. And He Who sits on the throne will care for them as He is among them. ¹⁶They will never be hungry or thirsty again. The sun or any burning heat will not shine down on them. ¹⁷For the Lamb Who is in the center of the throne will be their Shepherd. He will lead them to wells of the water of life. God will take away all tears from their eyes."

The Seventh Lock - No Sound In Heaven

8 When the Lamb broke the seventh lock, there was not a sound in heaven for about one-half hour. ²Then I saw the seven angels standing before God. They were given seven horns.

³Another angel came and stood at the altar. He held a cup made of gold full of special perfume. He was given much perfume so he could mix it in with the prayers of those who belonged to God. Their prayers were put on the altar made of gold before the throne. ⁴Smoke from burning the special perfume and the prayers of those who belong to God went up before God out of the angel's hand. ⁵Then the angel took the cup of gold. He filled it with fire from the altar and threw it down on the earth. There was thunder and noise and lightning and the earth shook.

⁶The seven angels that had the seven horns got ready to blow them.

The First Horn - Hail And Fire

⁷So the first angel blew his horn. Hail and fire mixed with blood came

down on the earth. One-third part of the earth was burned up. One-third part of the trees was burned up. All the green grass was burned up.

The Second Horn - The Burning Mountain

⁸The second angel blew his horn. Something like a large mountain was burning with fire. It was thrown into the sea. One-third part of the sea turned into blood. ⁹One-third part of all sea life died. One-third part of all the ships was destroyed.

The Third Horn - The Star Of Poison

¹⁰The third angel blew his horn. A large star fell from heaven. It was burning with a fire that kept burning like a bright light. It fell on one-third part of the rivers and on the places where water comes out of the earth. ¹¹The name of the star is Wormwood. One-third part of the water became poison. Many men died from drinking the water because it had become poison.

The Fourth Horn - Not As Much Light

¹²The fourth angel blew his horn. One-third part of the sun and one-third part of the moon and one-third part of the stars were hurt. One-third part of them was made dark so that one-third part of the day and night had no light.
¹³Then I looked and saw a very large bird flying in the sky. It said with a loud voice, "It is bad! It is bad! It is bad for those who live on the earth when the sound comes from the horns that the other three angels will blow!"

The Fifth Horn - The Hole Without A Bottom

9 The fifth angel blew his horn. I saw a star from heaven which had fallen to earth. The key to the hole without a bottom was given to the angel. ²He opened the hole and smoke came out like the smoke from a place where there is much fire. The sun and the air became dark because of the smoke from the hole. ³Locusts came down to the earth out of the smoke. They were given power to hurt like small animals that sting. ⁴They were told not to hurt the grass or any green plant or any tree. They were to hurt only the men who did not have the mark of God on their foreheads. ⁵The locusts were not allowed to kill these men. They were to give them much pain for five months like the pain that comes from a small animal that stings. ⁶Men will look for ways to die during those days, but they will not find any way. They will want to die, but death will be kept from them. ⁷The locusts looked like horses ready for war. They had on their heads what looked like crowns of gold. Their faces were like men's faces. ⁸Their hair was like the hair of women. Their teeth were like the teeth of lions. ⁹Their chests were covered with what looked like pieces of iron. The sound their wings made was like the sound of many wagons rushing to war. ¹⁰They had tails like a small animal that stings. The sting came from their tails. They were given power to hurt men for five months. ¹¹These locusts have a king over them. He is the head angel of the hole that has no bottom. His name in the Hebrew language is Abbadon. In the Greek language it is Apollyon. (It means the one who destroys.)
¹²The first time of trouble is past. But see, there are two more times of trouble coming after this.

The Sixth Horn - The Killing Angels

¹³The sixth angel blew his horn. I heard a voice coming from the four corners of the altar made of gold that is before God. ¹⁴The voice said to the

sixth angel who had the horn, "Let the four angels loose that have been chained at the big river Euphrates." [15]They had been kept ready for that hour and day and month and year. They were let loose so they could kill one-third part of all men that were living. [16]The army had 200 million soldiers on horses. I heard them say how many there were.

[17]I saw, as God wanted to show me, the horses and the men on them. The men had pieces of iron over their chests. These were red like fire and blue like the sky and yellow like sulphur. The heads of the horses looked like the heads of lions. Fire and smoke and sulphur came out of their mouths. [18]One-third part of all men was killed by the fire and smoke and sulphur that came out of their mouths. [19]The power of the horses was in their mouths and in their tails. Their tails were like the heads of snakes and with them they could bite and kill. [20]The men that were still living after these troubles were past would not turn away from worshiping demons. They would not turn away from false gods made from gold and silver and brass and stone and wood. None of these false gods can see or hear or walk. [21]These men were not sorry for their sins and would not turn away from all their killing and their witchcraft. They would not stop their sex sins and their stealing.

The Angel And The Little Book

10 Then I saw another strong angel coming down from heaven covered with a cloud. He had many colors around his head. His face was like the sun. His feet were like long flames of fire. [2]He had in his hand a little book that was open. The angel put his right foot on the sea. He put his left foot on the land. [3]He cried with a loud voice like the sound of a lion. The seven thunders sounded. [4]I was ready to write when the seven thunders had spoken. Then I heard the voice from heaven saying, "Lock up the things which the seven thunders have spoken. Do not write them!"

[5]Then the strong angel that I saw standing on the sea and on the land lifted his right hand to heaven. [6]He made a promise in the name of God Who lives forever, Who made the heaven and the earth and the sea and everything in them. He promised that there will be no more waiting. [7]And when the seventh angel blows his horn, God will put His secret plan into action. It will be done just as He told it to the early preachers He owned.

[8]Then the voice I heard from heaven spoke to me again. It said, "Go and take the little book that is open. It is in the hand of the angel who is standing on the sea and on the land."

[9]I went to the angel and asked him to give me the little book. He said, "Take it and eat it. It will taste like honey in your mouth. But after you have eaten it, it will make your stomach sour." [10]Then I took it from the angel's hand and ate it. It was sweet as honey in my mouth, but it made my stomach sour after I had eaten it.

[11]Then they said to me, "You must tell what will happen again in front of many people and nations and families and kings."

The House Of God

11 I was given a stick that is used to see how big things are. Someone said, "Go up to the house of God and find out how big it is. Find out about the altar also. See how many people are worshiping. [2]Do not find out about the porch of the house of God. It has been given over to the nations who do not know God. They will walk over all the Holy City to wreck it for forty-two months. [3]I will give power to my two men who tell what they know. They will speak for God for 1,260 days (forty-two months). They will be dressed in clothes made from the hair of animals."

The Two Men Who Tell What They Know

4 These two men who tell what they know are the two olive trees and the two lights that stand before the Lord of the earth. 5 If anyone hates them and tries to hurt them, fire comes out of the mouths of these two men. The fire kills those who try to hurt them. 6 They have power to shut up the sky. During the time they speak for God, there will be no rain. They have power to change all waters into blood. They can send every kind of trouble to the earth whenever they want to.

The Death Of The Two Men Who Speak For God

7 When they have finished speaking for God, the wild animal will make war with them. It will come up out of the hole without a bottom. This wild animal will have power over them and kill them. 8 Their dead bodies will lie in the street of Jerusalem. It is where their Lord was nailed to a cross. The city is sometimes called Sodom and Egypt. 9 For three and one-half days those from every people and from every family and from every language and from every nation will look at their dead bodies. People will not allow the dead bodies of these two men to be put in a grave. 10 Those who are living on the earth will be happy because of the death of these two men. They will do things to show they are happy. They will send gifts to each other. They will do this because these two men brought much trouble and suffering to the people of the earth.

The Two Men Come To Life Again

11 After three and one-half days, life from God came into them again.

They stood on their feet. Those who saw them were very much afraid. 12 Then the two men who told what they knew heard a loud voice from heaven. It said, "Come up here." And they went up to heaven in a cloud. All those who hated them watched them go. 13 At the same time the earth shook. One-tenth part of the buildings of the city fell down. 7,000 people were killed. The rest of the people were afraid and gave honor to the God of heaven.

14 The second time of trouble is past. But look, the third time of trouble is coming soon.

The Seventh Horn - Worship In Heaven

15 The seventh angel blew his horn. There were loud voices in heaven saying, "The nations of the world have become the holy nation of our Lord and of His Christ. He will be the Leader forever." 16 Then the twenty-four leaders who sat on their thrones before God fell on their faces and worshiped God. 17 They said, "All-powerful Lord God, the One Who is and Who was and Who is to come, we thank You because You are using Your great power and have become Leader. 18 The people who do not know God have become angry with You. Now it is time for You to be angry with them. It is time for the dead to stand before You and to be told they are guilty. It is time for the servants You own who are the early preachers and those who belong to You to get the pay that is coming to them. It is time for the important people and those not important who honor Your name to get the pay that is coming to them. It is time to destroy those who have made every kind of trouble on the earth."

19 God's house in heaven was opened. The special box which held the Old Way of Worship was seen in the house of God. There was

lightning and thunder and noise. The earth shook and large hail stones fell.

The Woman And The Snake-Like Animal

12 Something very special was seen in heaven. A woman was there dressed with the sun. The moon was under her feet. A crown with twelve stars in it was on her head. ²She was about to become a mother. She cried out with pain waiting for the child to be born.

³Something else special was seen in heaven. A large snake-like animal was there. It was red and had seven heads and ten horns. There was a crown on each head. ⁴With his tail he pulled one-third part of the stars out of heaven. He threw them down to the earth. This snake-like animal stood in front of the woman as she was about to give birth to her child. He was waiting to eat her child as soon as it was born. ⁵Then the woman gave birth to a son. He is to be the leader of the world using a piece of iron. But this child was taken away to God and His throne. ⁶The woman ran away into the desert. God had made the place ready for her. He will care for her there 1,260 days.

War In Heaven

⁷Then there was war in heaven. Michael and his angels fought against this snake-like animal. This animal and his angels fought back. ⁸But the snake-like animal was not strong enough to win. There was no more room in heaven for them. ⁹The snake-like animal was thrown down to earth from heaven. This animal is the old snake. He is also called the Devil or Satan. He is the one who has fooled the whole world. He was thrown down to earth and his angels were thrown down with him. ¹⁰Then I heard a loud voice in heaven saying, "Now God has saved

from the punishment of sin! God's power as King has come! God's holy nation has come! God's Christ is here with power! The one who spoke against our Christian brothers has been thrown down to earth. He stood before God speaking against them day and night. ¹¹They had power over him and won because of the blood of the Lamb and by telling what He had done for them. They did not love their lives but were willing to die. ¹²For this reason, O heavens and you who are there, be full of joy. It is bad for you, O earth and sea. For the devil has come down to you. He is very angry because he knows he has only a short time."

War On Earth

¹³When the snake-like animal which is the devil saw that he had been thrown down to the earth, he began to hunt for the woman who had given birth to the boy baby. ¹⁴The woman was given two wings like the wings of a very large bird so she could fly to her place in the desert. She was to be cared for there and kept safe from the snake, which is the devil, for three and one-half years. ¹⁵Then the snake spit water from his mouth so the woman might be carried away with a flood. ¹⁶The earth helped the woman by opening its mouth. It drank in the flood of water that this snake-like animal spit from his mouth. ¹⁷This snake-like animal was very angry with the woman. He went off to fight with the rest of her children. They are the ones who obey the Laws of God and are faithful to the teachings of Jesus.

The Two Animals - The First One From The Sea

13 I stood on the sand by the seashore. There I saw a wild animal coming up out of the sea. It had seven heads and ten horns with a crown on each horn. There were names on each head that spoke bad words against God. ²The wild animal I saw was covered with spots. It had feet like those of a bear. It had a mouth like that of a lion. The snake-like animal gave this wild animal his own power and his own throne as king. The wild animal was given much power. ³One of the heads of the wild animal looked as if it had been killed. But the bad cut given to kill him was healed. The whole world was surprised and wondered about this, and they followed after the wild animal. ⁴They worshiped the snake-like animal for giving this wild animal such power. And they worshiped this wild animal. They said, "Who is like this wild animal? Who can fight against it?"

⁵The animal was given a mouth which spoke words full of pride and it spoke very bad things against the Lord. It was given much power for forty-two months. ⁶And it opened its mouth speaking very bad things against God. It spoke against God's name and His house and against those living in heaven. ⁷It was allowed to fight against the people who belong to God, and it had power to win over them. It had power over every family and every group of people and over people of every language and every nation. ⁸Every person on the earth from the beginning of the world whose name has not been written in the book of life of the Lamb Who was killed will worship this animal.

⁹You have ears! Then listen. ¹⁰Whoever is to be tied and held will be held. Whoever kills with a sword must himself be killed with a sword. Now is when God's people must have faith and not give up.

The Second Animal - From The Land

¹¹Then I saw another wild animal coming out of the earth. He had two horns like those of a lamb. His voice was like that of the snake-like animal. ¹²He used the power of the first wild animal who was there with him. He made all the people on earth worship the first wild animal who had received the bad cut to kill him but was healed. ¹³The second wild animal did great powerful works. It spoke and made those who did not worship the first wild animal to be killed. ¹⁴He fooled the men of the earth by doing powerful works. He did these things in front of the first wild animal. He told those who live on the earth to make a god that looks like the first wild animal. The first wild animal was the one that was cut by the sword but lived. ¹⁵The second wild animal was given power to give life to the false god. This false god was the one that was made to look like the first wild animal. It was given power to talk. All those who did not worship it would die. ¹⁶The second wild animal made every person have a mark on their right hand or on their forehead. It was given to important men and to those not important, to rich men and poor men, to those who are free and to those who are servants. ¹⁷No one could buy or sell anything unless he had the mark on him. This mark was the name of the first wild animal or another way to write his name. ¹⁸This is wisdom. Let the person who has good understanding learn the meaning of the other way to write the name of the first wild animal. This name is a man's name. It is 666.

The Lamb Stands In Jerusalem

14 Then I looked and saw the Lamb standing on Mount Zion. There were 144,000 people with Him. These people had His name and His Father's name written on their foreheads. ²I heard a voice coming from heaven. It was like the sound of rushing water and of loud thunder. The voice I heard was like people playing music from boxes with strings. ³This large group sang a new song. They sang before the throne and in front of the four living beings and the twenty-four leaders. Only the 144,000 could learn this song. They had been bought by the blood of Christ and made free from the earth. 4These are men who have kept themselves pure by not being married. They follow the Lamb wherever He goes. They have been bought by the blood of Christ and have been made free from among men. They are the first ones to be given to God and to the Lamb. 5No lie has come from their mouths. They are without blame.

The Three Angels

6Then I saw another angel flying in the heavens. He was carrying the Good News that lasts forever. He was preaching to every nation and to every family group and to the people of every language and to all the people of the earth. 7He said with a loud voice, "Honor God with love and fear. The time has come for Him to say who is guilty among men. Worship Him Who made heaven and earth and the sea and the places where water comes out of the earth."

8A second angel followed, saying, "Babylon has fallen! The great city Babylon has fallen! She made all the nations drink of the wine of her sinful sex life."

9A third angel followed, saying with a loud voice, "If anyone worships the wild animal and his false god and receives a mark on his forehead or hand, 10he will drink of the wine of the anger of God. It is mixed in full strength in the cup of God's anger. They will be punished with fire and burning sulphur in front of the holy angels and before the Lamb. 11The smoke of those who are being punished will go up forever. They have no rest day or night. It is because they have worshiped the wild animal and his false god and have received the mark of his name.

12This is why God's people need to keep true to God's Word and stay faithful to Jesus.

13Then I heard a voice from heaven, saying, "Write these words: 'From now on those who are dead who died belonging to the Lord will be happy.' " "Yes," says the Spirit, "they will have rest from all their work. All the good things they have done will follow them."

The War Of Armageddon

14I looked and saw a white cloud. Sitting on the cloud was One like the Son of Man. He had a crown of gold on His head. In His hand He had a sharp knife for cutting grain. 15Then another angel came out from the house of God and called to Him with a loud voice. He said, "Use Your knife and gather in the grain. The time has come to gather the grain because the earth is ready." 16He Who sat on the cloud raised His knife over the earth. And the grain was gathered in.

17Then another angel came out from the house of God in heaven. He had a sharp knife for cutting grain also. 18Another angel who has power over fire came out from the altar. He said with a loud voice to the angel who had the sharp knife, "Use your knife and gather in the grapes of the vine of the earth, for they are ready to gather." 19The angel used his sickle on the earth. He gathered from the vine of the earth and put the fruit into the large place for making wine. It was full of God's anger. 20They walked on it outside the city and blood came out of the place where wine is made. The blood ran as far as a man could walk in seven days. It came up as high as a horse's head.

Seven Angels With Seven Troubles

15 Then I saw something else special in heaven that was great and made me wonder. There were seven angels with the seven last kinds of trouble. With these, God's anger is finished. ²Then I saw something that looked like a sea of glass mixed with fire. I saw many standing on the sea of glass. They were those who had won their fight with the wild animal and his false god and with his mark. All of them were holding music boxes with strings that God had given to them. ³They were singing the song of Moses, who was a servant owned by God, and the song of the Lamb, saying, "The things You do are great and powerful. You are the All-powerful Lord God. You are always right and true in everything You do. You are King of all nations. ⁴Who will not honor You, Lord, with love and fear? Who will not tell of the greatness of Your name? For You are the only One Who is holy. All nations will come and worship before You. Everyone sees that You do the right things."

⁵After this I looked and saw that the Holiest Place of All in the house of God was opened. ⁶The seven angels who had the seven last kinds of trouble came out of the house of God. They were wearing clothes made of clean white linen. They were wearing belts made of gold around their chests. ⁷Then one of the four living beings gave to each of the seven angels a jar made of gold. These jars were filled with the anger of God Who lives forever. ⁸The house of God was filled with smoke from the shining greatness and power of God. No one was able to go into the house of God until the seven angels had completed the seven kinds of trouble.

The First Jar - Sinful Sores

16 Then I heard a loud voice coming from the house of God. The voice said to the seven angels, "Go and pour out the seven jars of God's anger onto the earth!"

²The first angel poured out his jar of God's anger onto the earth. Painful sores were given to everyone who had the mark of the wild animal and who worshiped his god.

The Second Jar - Death In The Sea

³The second angel poured out his jar of God's anger onto the sea. The water became like the blood of a dead man. Every living thing in the sea died.

The Third Jar - Water Turns To Blood

⁴The third angel poured out his jar of God's anger onto the rivers and places where water comes out of the earth. The water turned to blood. ⁵I heard the angel of the waters saying, "You are right in punishing by sending this trouble. You are the Holy One Who was and is and will be. ⁶They have poured out the blood of God's people and of the early preachers. You have given them blood to drink. They are getting the pay that is coming to them." ⁷I heard a voice from the altar saying, "Lord God, the All-powerful One! What You decide about people is right and true."

The Fourth Jar - Burning Heat

⁸The fourth angel poured out his jar of God's anger onto the sun. It was allowed to burn men with its fire. ⁹Men were burned with the heat of this fire and they called God bad names even when He had the power over these kinds of trouble. They were not sorry for their sins and did not turn from them and honor Him.

The Fifth Jar - Darkness

¹⁰The fifth angel poured out his jar of God's anger upon the throne of the wild animal. The whole nation of the wild animal was turned into

darkness. Those who worshiped him bit their tongues because of the pain. [11]They called the God of heaven bad names because of their pain and their sores. They were not sorry for what they had done.

The Sixth Jar - The Euphrates River Dries Up

[12]The sixth angel poured out his jar of God's anger onto the great Euphrates River. The water dried up. In this way, the kings of the countries of the east could cross over. [13]Then I saw three demons that looked like frogs. They came out of the mouths of the snake-like animal and the second wild animal and the false preacher. [14]These are demons that do powerful works. These demons go to all the kings of all the earth. They bring them together for the war of the great day of the All-powerful God. [15](See! I will come like a robber. The man is happy who stays awake and keeps his clothes ready. He will not be walking around without clothes and be ashamed.) [16]Then the demons brought the kings together in the place called Armageddon in the Hebrew language.

The Seventh Jar - The Earth Shakes And Hail Falls

[17]The seventh angel poured out his jar of God's anger into the air. A loud voice came from the throne in the house of God, saying, "It is all done!" [18]Then there were voices and lightning and thunder and the earth shook. The earth shook much more than it had ever shaken before. [19]The big and strong city of Babylon was split in three parts. The cities of other nations fell to the ground. Then God remembered the strong city of Babylon. He made her drink the wine from His cup of much anger. [20]Every island went down into the sea. No mountain could be found. [21]Large

pieces of hail fell from heaven on men. These pieces were about as heavy as a small man. But men called God bad names because of so much trouble from the hail.

The Sinful Woman

17 Then one of the seven angels who had the seven jars came to me. He said, "Come! I will show you how the powerful woman who sells the use of her body will be punished. She sits on the many waters of the world. [2]The kings of the earth have done sex sins with her. People of the world have been made drunk with the wine of her sex sins."

[3]My spirit was carried away by the angel to a desert. I saw a woman sitting on a red wild animal. It had seven heads and ten horns. All over the red wild animal was written bad names which spoke against God. [4]The woman was wearing purple and red clothes. She was wearing gold and pearls and stones worth much money. She had in her hand a gold cup full of sinful things from her sex sins. [5]There was a name written on her forehead which had a secret meaning. It said, "The big and powerful Babylon, mother of all women who sell the use of their bodies and mother of everything sinful of the earth." [6]I looked at the woman. She was drunk with the blood of God's people and those who had been killed for telling about Jesus. When I saw her, I wondered very much.

[7]The angel asked me, "Why do you wonder? I will tell you the secret about this woman and the red wild animal that carries her. It is the red wild animal with seven heads and ten horns. [8]The red wild animal you saw was alive but is now dead. It is about to come up from the hole without a bottom and be destroyed. The people of the earth, whose names have not been written in the book of life from the beginning of the world, will be

surprised as they look at the red wild animal. It was alive. Now it is dead, but it will come back again.

9"Here is where we need wisdom. The seven heads of the animal are mountains where the woman sits. 10They are seven kings also. Five of them are no longer kings. The sixth one is now king. The seventh one will be king, but only for a little while. 11The red wild animal that died is the eighth king. He belongs to the first seven kings, but he will be destroyed also.

12"The ten horns of the red wild animal which you saw are ten kings. They have not become leaders yet. But they will be given the right and the power to lead their nations for one hour with the red wild animal. 13They agree to give the right and the power to the red wild animal. 14These kings will fight and make war with the Lamb. But the Lamb will win the war because He is Lord of lords and King of kings. His people are the called and chosen and faithful ones."

15Then the angel said to me, "You saw the waters where the woman who sold the use of her body is sitting. The waters are people and large groups of people and nations and languages. 16The ten horns you saw and the red wild animal will hate the woman who sold the use of her body. They will take everything from her and even her clothes. They will eat her flesh and burn her with fire. 17God put in their minds a plan that would carry out His desire. They will agree to give their nation to the red wild animal until the words of God have been completed. 18The woman you saw is the big and powerful city that has power over the kings of the earth."

Babylon Is Destroyed

18 Then I saw another angel coming down from heaven. He had much power. The earth was made bright with his shining great-ness. 2He cried out with a loud voice, "The big and powerful city of Babylon is destroyed. Demons and every kind of unclean spirit live there. Unclean birds that are hated are there. 3For she gave her wine to the nations of the world. It was the wine of her desire for sex sins. The kings of the earth have done these sex sins with her. The men of the earth who buy and sell have become rich from the riches she received while living in sin."

4I heard another voice from heaven saying, "Come out from her, my people. Do not be a part of her sins so you will not share her troubles. 5For her sins are as high as heaven. God is ready to punish her for her sins. 6Pay her back for what she has paid you. Give back to her twice as much for what she has done. Give her in her own cup twice as much. Give back to her in her own cup twice as much as she gave you. 7Give her as much trouble and suffering as the fun and the rich living she chose for herself. In her heart she says, 'I sit here like a queen. I am not a woman whose husband has died. I will never have sorrow.' 8Because of this, troubles of death and sorrow and no food will come to her in one day. She will be burned with fire. For the Lord God is powerful. He is the One Who says she is guilty.

Kings Cry Because Of Babylon

9"Then the kings of the earth will cry for her and be sorry when they see the smoke of her burning. They are the ones who did sex sins with her and lived as rich people. 10They stand a long way from her because they are afraid of her sufferings. They say, 'It is bad! It is bad for the big and powerful city of Babylon. For in one hour she is destroyed.' 11The men of the earth who buy and sell are sorry for her and cry. They cry because there is no one to buy their things anymore. 12They sold gold and silver and stones worth much money and pearls. They sold fine linen and purple and red silk cloth. They sold all kinds of perfumed wood. They sold things made from the teeth of animals and things made from wood that cost much money. They sold brass and iron and stone. 13 They sold spices and perfumes of all kinds. They sold wine and olive oil and fine flour and wheat. They sold cows and sheep and horses and wagons. They sold men who are not free and they sold the lives of men. 14 They say to her, 'All the good things you wanted so much are gone from you. Your riches are gone. The things you liked so much are gone. You will never have them again.' 15 The men of the earth who became rich by buying and selling in that city will stand a long way back because they are afraid of her sufferings. They will cry and have sorrow. 16 They will say, 'It is bad! It is bad for that powerful city. She dressed in fine linen of purple and red. She covered herself with gold and pearls and stones worth much money. 17 For in one hour her riches are destroyed.' The captain of every ship and all who traveled on ships and all who worked on ships stood a long way back. 18 They cried out as they saw the smoke of her burning, saying, 'Has there ever been such a city as powerful as this one?' 19 They threw dirt on their heads. They cried out with much sorrow and said, 'It is bad! It is bad for the powerful city! She is the place where all those who owned ships on the sea became rich from all her riches. For in one hour everything is gone!'

20 "Be full of joy because of her, O heaven! Be full of joy, you who belong to God and missionaries and early preachers! For God has punished her for what she did to you."

21 Then a strong angel picked up a large stone like those used for grinding wheat. He threw it into the sea, saying, "The big and strong city of Babylon will be thrown down like this. It will never be found again. 22 The sound of those playing music on boxes with strings and on flutes and on horns will not be heard in you again. No workman doing any kind of work will be found in you again. The sound of the grinding stone will not be heard in you again. 23 No light will ever shine in you again. There will be no more happy voices from a wedding heard in you. Your men who bought and sold were the most powerful on earth. You fooled people over all the world by your witchcraft. 24 And in this city was found the blood of the early preachers and of those who belonged to God and of all those who had been killed on the earth."

Giving Thanks In Heaven

19 After this I heard what sounded like the voices of many people in heaven, saying, "Thanks to our God, the One Who saves. Honor and power belong to Him. 2 For the way He punishes people is right and true. He has punished the powerful woman who sold the use of her body. She was making the earth sinful with her sex sins. She killed those who worked for God. He has punished her for it." 3 Again they said, "Thanks to our God. The smoke from her burning goes up forever." 4 The twenty-four leaders and the four living beings got down and worshiped God Who was sitting on the throne. They said, "Let it be so. Thanks to our God!"

5 A voice came from the throne, saying, "Give thanks to our God, you servants who are owned by Him. Give thanks to our God, you who honor Him with love and fear, both small and great."

The Wedding Supper Of The Lamb

6 Then I heard what sounded like the voices of many people. It was like

the sound of powerful rushing water. And it was like loud thunder. It said, "Thanks to our God. For the Lord our God is King. He is the All-powerful One. 7Let us be full of joy and be glad. Let us honor Him, for the time has come for the wedding supper of the Lamb. His bride has made herself ready. 8She was given clean, white, fine linen clothes to wear. The fine linen is the right living of God's people."

9The angel said to me, "Write this: 'Those who are asked to the wedding supper of the Lamb are happy.'" And he said, "These are the true words of God." 10Then I got down at his feet to worship him. But he said to me, "No! Do not worship me. I am a workman together with you and your Christian brothers who tell of their trust in Christ. Worship God. For those who speak for Jesus are led in what to say as the early preachers were led.

The King Of Kings On The White Horse

11Then I saw heaven opened. A white horse was standing there. The One Who was sitting on the horse is called Faithful and True. He is the One Who punishes in the right way. He makes war. 12His eyes are a flame of fire. He has many crowns on His head. His name is written on Him but He is the only One Who knows what it says. 13The coat He wears has been put in blood. His name is The Word of God. 14The armies in heaven were dressed in clean, white, fine linen. They were following Him on white horses. 15Out of His mouth comes a sharp sword to punish the nations. He will be the Leader over them using a piece of iron. He walks on the grapes where wine is made, pressing out the anger of God, the All-powerful One. 16On His coat and on His leg is the name written, "KING OF KINGS AND LORD OF LORDS."

17Then I saw an angel standing in the sun. He cried out with a loud voice to all the birds flying in the sky, "Come and gather together for the great supper of God! 18Come and eat the flesh of kings and of captains of soldiers and of strong men and of the flesh of horses and of those sitting on them. Come and eat the flesh of all men, small and great. Some are free and some are not free."

19Then I saw the wild animal and the kings of the earth and their armies gather together. They were ready to fight against the One Who is sitting on the white horse and against His army. 20The wild animal was taken. The false preacher was taken with it. It was the false preacher who had done powerful works in front of the wild animal. In this way, he fooled those who had received the mark of the wild animal and those who worshiped his false god. These two were thrown alive into the lake of fire that burns with sulphur. 21The rest were killed with the sword that came out of the mouth of the One Who sat on the horse. All the birds were filled by eating the flesh of these who were killed.

Satan Is Chained For One Thousand Years

20 Then I saw an angel coming down from heaven. He had in his hand a key to the hole without a bottom. He also had a strong chain. 2He took hold of the snake-like animal, that old snake, who is the Devil, or Satan, and chained him for 1,000 years. 3The angel threw the devil into the hole without a bottom. He shut it and locked him in it. He could not fool the nations anymore until the 1,000 years were completed. After this he must be free for awhile.

4Then I saw thrones. Those who were sitting there were given the power to say who is guilty. I saw the souls of those who had been killed because they told about Jesus and preached the Word of God. They had not worshiped the wild animal or his false god. They had not received his mark on their foreheads or hands. They lived again and were leaders along with Christ for 1,000 years. 5 The rest of the dead did not come to life again until the 1,000 years were finished. This is the first time many people are raised from the dead at the same time. 6 Those who are raised from the dead during this first time are happy and holy. The second death has no power over them. They will be religious leaders of God and of Christ. They will be leaders with Him for 1,000 years.

Satan Is Destroyed Forever

7 When the 1,000 years are finished, Satan will be free to leave his prison. 8 He will go out and fool the nations who are over all the world. They are Gog and Magog. He will gather them all together for war. There will be as many as the sand along the seashore. 9 They will spread out over the earth and all around the place where God's people are and around the city that is loved. Fire will come down from God out of heaven and destroy them. 10 Then the devil who fooled them will be thrown into the lake of fire burning with sulphur. The wild animal and the false preacher are already there. They will all be punished day and night forever.

The Guilty Will Be Punished

11 Then I saw a great white throne. I saw the One Who sat on it. The earth and the heaven left Him in a hurry and they could be found no more. 12 I saw all the dead people standing before God. There were great people and small people. The books were opened. Then another book was opened. It was the book of life. The dead people were told they were guilty by what they had done as it was written in the books. 13 The sea gave up the dead people who were in it. Death and hell gave up the dead people who were in them. Each one was told he was guilty by what he had done. 14 Then death and hell were thrown into the lake of fire. The lake of fire is the second death. 15 If anyone's name was not written in the book of life, he was thrown into the lake of fire.

21 Then I saw a new heaven and a new earth. The first heaven and the first earth had passed away. There was no more sea. 2 I saw the Holy City, the new Jerusalem. It was coming down out of heaven from God. It was made ready like a bride is made ready for her husband. 3 I heard a loud voice coming from heaven. It said, "See! God's home is with men. He will live with them. They will be His people. God Himself will be with them. He will be their God. 4 God will take away all their tears. There will be no more death or sorrow or crying or pain. All the old things have passed away." 5 Then the One sitting on the throne said, "See! I am making all things new. Write, for these words are true and faithful." 6 Then He said to me, "These things have happened! I am the First and the Last. I am the beginning and the end. To anyone who is thirsty, I will give the water of life. It is a free gift. 7 He who has power and wins will receive these things. I will be his God and he will be My son. 8 But those who are afraid and those who do not have faith and the sinful-minded people and those who kill other people and those who do sex sins and those who follow witchcraft and those who worship false gods and all those who tell lies will be put into the lake of fire and sulphur. This is the second death."

The New Jerusalem

9 Then one of the seven angels who had the seven jars full of the seven

last troubles came to me and said, "Come! I will show you the bride, the wife of the Lamb." ¹⁰My spirit was carried away by the angel to a very high mountain. He showed me the Holy City of Jerusalem. It was coming out of heaven from God. ¹¹It was filled with the shining greatness of God. It shone like a stone worth much money, like a jasper stone. It was clear like glass. ¹²It had a very high wall, and there were twelve gates. Twelve angels stood by the gates. The names of the twelve family groups of the Jewish nation were written on the gates. ¹³There were three gates on each side. There were three on the east side and three on the north side and three on the south side and three on the west side. ¹⁴The walls were on twelve stones. The names of the twelve missionaries of the Lamb were written on the stones.

¹⁵The angel had a stick in his hand. It was used to find out how big the city and its gates and the walls were. ¹⁶He found out that the city was as wide as it was long and it was as high as it was wide. It was as long as a man could walk in fifty days. It was the same each way. ¹⁷The angel found out that the walls were the same as a man taking seventy-two long steps. The angel used the same way to find out about the city as a man would have used. ¹⁸The wall was made of jasper. The city was made of pure gold. This gold was as clear as glass. ¹⁹The city was built on every kind of stone that was worth much money. The first stone was jasper. The second was sapphire. The third was chalcedony. The fourth was emerald. ²⁰The fifth was sardonyx. The sixth was sardius. The seventh was chrysolite. The eighth was beryl. The ninth was topaz. The tenth was chrysoprase. The eleventh was jacinth and the twelfth was amethyst. ²¹The twelve gates were twelve pearls. Each gate was made from one pearl. The street of the city

was pure gold. It was as clear as glass.

²²I did not see a house of God in the city. The All-powerful Lord God and the Lamb are the house of God in this city. ²³There is no need for the sun and moon to shine in the city. The shining greatness of God makes it full of light. The Lamb is its light. ²⁴The nations will walk by its light. The kings of the earth will bring their greatness into it. ²⁵The gates are open all day. They will never be shut. There will be no night there. ²⁶The greatness and honor of all the nations will be brought into it. ²⁷Nothing sinful will go into the city. No one who is sinful-minded or tells lies can go in. Only those whose names are written in the Lamb's book of life can go in.

More About The New Jerusalem

22 Then the angel showed me the river of the water of life. It was as clear as glass and came from the throne of God and of the Lamb. ²It runs down the center of the street in the city. On each side of the river was the tree of life. It gives twelve different kinds of fruit. It gives this fruit twelve times a year, new fruit each month. Its leaves are used to heal the nations.

³There will be nothing in the city that is sinful. The place where God and the Lamb sit will be there. The servants He owns will work for Him. ⁴They will see His face and His name will be written on their foreheads. ⁵There will be no night there. There will be no need for a light or for the sun. Because the Lord God will be their light. They will be leaders forever.

Jesus Is Coming Soon

⁶Then the angel said to me, "These words are faithful and true. The Lord God of the early preachers has sent His angel to show the servants He

owns what must happen soon. [7]See! I am coming soon. The one who obeys what is written in this Book is happy!"

[8]It was I, John, who heard and saw these things. Then I got down at the feet of the angel who showed me these things. I was going to worship him. [9]But he said to me, "No! You must not do that. I am a servant together with you and with your Christian brothers and the early preachers and with all those who obey the words in this Book. You must worship God!" [10]Then he said to me, "Do not lock up the words of this Book. These things will happen soon. [11]And let the sinful people keep on being sinful. Let the dirty-minded people keep on being dirty-minded. And let those right with God keep on being right with God. Let the holy people keep on being holy.

[12]"See! I am coming soon. I am bringing with Me the pay I will give to everyone for what he has done. [13]I am the First and the Last. I am the beginning and the end. [14]Those who wash their clothes clean are happy (who are washed by the blood of the Lamb). They will have the right to go into the city through the gates. They will have the right to eat the fruit of the tree of life. [15]Outside the city are the dogs. They are people who follow witchcraft and those who do sex sins and those who kill other people and those who worship false gods and those who like lies and tell them.

[16]"I am Jesus. I have sent My angel to you with these words to the churches. I am the beginning of David and of his family. I am the bright Morning Star."

[17]The Holy Spirit and the Bride say, "Come!" Let the one who hears, say, "Come!" Let the one who is thirsty, come. Let the one who wants to drink of the water of life, drink it. It is a free gift.

[18]I am telling everyone who hears the words that are written in this book: If anyone adds anything to what is written in this book, God will add to him the kinds of trouble that this book tells about. [19]If anyone takes away any part of this book that tells what will happen in the future, God will take away his part from the tree of life and from the Holy City which are written in this book.

[20]He Who tells these things says, "Yes, I am coming soon!" Let it be so. Come, Lord Jesus. [21]May all of you have the loving-favor of the Lord Jesus Christ. Let it be so.

Topical Study

Outlines

*Teachings of the Christian
faith from the Word of God*

by Gleason H. Ledyard

CONTENTS

2

PART 1

WHAT THE WORD OF GOD TEACHES ABOUT GOD

[*Theology*]

THERE IS ONE TRUE GOD

There are five things that help men know there is a God. Not any one
of these truths proves in itself that there is a God. But by putting all five
together, we have proof of God's being, work and power. Each proof is
like one stick. It can be broken across a person's knee. But five sticks
are much stronger and cannot be broken.

The Bible does not try to prove that there is a God. Men everywhere
already know there is a God, One Who is head over all things. And
yet, many people wonder about Who this God is and would like to
know many things about Him.

1. MAN KNOWS THERE IS A GOD BECAUSE OF WHAT HE SEES AROUND HIM.

How did this world come into being? It could not come into being by
itself. Who made it? There is no secret about it. God's Word tells
Who made the world. "In the beginning God made from nothing the
heavens and the earth" (Genesis 1:1). The sky above man and the
earth around him prove that Someone made them. This did not just
happen. When man makes something, he uses things to make other
things. But God did not use anything to make the world. "Let them
praise the name of the Lord! For He spoke and they came into being"
(Psalm 148:5). These things around man do not tell him Who made
the world. But they do tell him that Whoever made it was very
great.

2. MAN KNOWS THERE IS A GOD BECAUSE ALL THINGS WORK AS THEY WERE PLANNED.

Think of the earth, sun, moon and stars. They do not run into each
other. They go year after year in the way they were planned to go!
Millions of stars were put in their places. Nights and days come and
go always as they were planned. Summers and winters come and go
always as they were planned. The One Who planned all this had
great wisdom. In Psalm 19:1 we read, "The heavens are telling of the
greatness of God and the great open spaces above show the work of
His hands." God's Word also says in Romans 1:20, "Men cannot say
they do not know about God. From the beginning of the world, men
could see what God is like through the things He has made. This
shows His power that lasts forever. It shows that He is God."

3. MAN KNOWS THERE IS A GOD BECAUSE OF THE WAY PEOPLE ARE MADE.

The One Who brought man into being had to be greater than man. Man can know and feel and act. Man has something inside him that tells him when he has done wrong. He is not only flesh, blood, and bones, man is able to know right from wrong. This makes him know there is an All-powerful God who made man and rules over him. "When I look up and think about Your heavens, the work of Your fingers, the moon and the stars, which You have set in their place, what is man, that You think of him, the son of man that You care for him? You made him a little less than the angels and gave him a crown of greatness and honor. You made him to rule over the works of Your hands. You put all things under his feet. All sheep and cattle, all the wild animals, the birds of the air, and fish of the sea, and all that pass through the sea. O Lord, our Lord, how great is Your name in all the earth" (Psalms 8:3-9)!

4. MAN KNOWS THERE IS A GOD BECAUSE OF WHAT THE PAST TELLS HIM.

Man knows the Bible is the Word of God. Early preachers said certain things would happen in the future, and they did happen. Christ came to the earth by a powerful work to do something special for men. The followers of Christ have taken the Good News around the world through the years. Men's lives have been changed as they have put their trust in Christ. Sinful men have never been able to destroy what God has made. These things could only be done through God's power and work. "The kings of the earth stand in a line ready to fight, and all the leaders are against the Lord and against His Chosen One. They say, 'Let us break their chains and throw them away from us.' He who sits in the heavens laughs. The Lord makes fun of them" (Psalm 2:2-4).

5. MAN KNOWS THERE IS A GOD BECAUSE ALL MEN KNOW THEY NEED A GOD.

Every person knows there is something wrong in his life. He may not call it sin, but he has a guilty feeling. Every person knows there must be One Who is perfect. He knows there must be Someone Who is head over all. Man needs a leader. The Word of God does not try to prove there is a God. It just tells us about God because men over all the world already know that He is. The Word of God tells us there is only one true God. "The Lord our God is one Lord" (Deuteronomy 6:4)! (Mark 12:29b) Isaiah 44:6b says, "...There is no God besides Me." God is the Head over all things. He is the one and only God.

THE NAMES OF GOD

In many parts of the world a name given to a person has a meaning. In
Bible times names had special meaning. They were given to certain
people for certain reasons. The names of God show what He is like.
They show how He acts and works among the people He made. Men
should know what they meant to the people long ago and what they
can mean today. Knowing the names of God can help man know God
better. His name is greater than any other name. The Old Testament
was written in the Hebrew language and the three most important
names for God are in that language. The names given below are the
names in English.

1. *THE THREE MOST IMPORTANT NAMES OF GOD IN THE
   OLD TESTAMENT.*

   A. God - This name means *The Power That Rules*. In the very first
      verse of the Bible this word is used. "In the beginning God made
      from nothing the heavens and the earth" (Genesis 1:1). This
      power made the world and rules over it.

   B. LORD - This name is written in big letters. It is not the same as
      Lord. It means *Life* or *The One Who Always Has Been, Is Now,
      And Always Will Be*. It also means *To Be* and *The One Who
      Needs Nothing* and *The Coming One*. In Exodus 3:14 God said to
      Moses, "I AM WHO I AM."

   C. Lord - This is the name which shows that God is Ruler over men
      and that men put themselves under God's rule and trust Him.
      (Genesis 15:2) It means *Owner* or *Husband*. John 13:13 says,
      "You call Me Teacher and Lord. You are right because that is
      what I am." And in II Corinthians 11:2-3 the same word means
      Husband. *Lord* can be used for a man, but then a small 'L' is
      used.

2. *THESE ARE THE OTHER IMPORTANT NAMES OF GOD IN
   THE BIBLE.*

   A. All-powerful God - means *The Strong One* and *The God Who Is
      Enough* and *The One Who Gives Strength* and *The Strong One
      Who Sees* and *The God Who Has Power Over All*. (Genesis
      16:13; 17:1-20)

   B. Most High God - means *The Highest* or *The One Who owns
      Heaven and Earth*. Isaiah 66:1a says, "The Lord says, 'Heaven is

My throne, and the earth is the place where I rest My feet.' "
(Deuteronomy 32:8; Psalm 83:18; Acts 7:48-50)

C. God Who Lasts Forever - means that God will never die. It also
means that He is the God Who is over *things* that last forever.
Psalm 90:2 says, "Before the mountains were born, before You
gave birth to the earth and world, forever and ever, You are
God." "You made the earth in the beginning. You made the
heavens with Your hands. They will be destroyed but You will
always live" (Psalm 102:25-26a).

D. LORD God is first used in Genesis 2:4. This name is used two
ways: (1) God as maker of man (Genesis 2:7); (2) God as leader
of Israel (Genesis 24:7; Exodus 3:15; Deuteronomy 12:1). It is
used as *Owner* and *Leader* and *The One Who Saves.* And then it
is also used when God talked or promised things to His chosen
people. Sometimes it is written *Lord God.* This means *Owner.*

E. LORD of ALL is a name of God showing His power and shining
greatness in war, and also in caring for others. (I Samuel 17:45;
Psalm 46:7, 11; Isaiah 47:4)

3. *OTHER NAMES OF GOD USED IN THE OLD TESTAMENT
WHICH TELL ABOUT HIM AND HOW HE WORKS.*

A. The LORD Who Will Give What Is Needed - This name means
The Lord Will Take Care Of Our Needs. This name was used
when Abraham was about to give his son as a gift on the altar to
God. (Genesis 22:13-14)

B. The LORD Who Heals - He is the One Who heals men's bodies
from sickness and disease. (Exodus 15:26)

C. The LORD Who Wins For Us - It is God Who fights against
Satan for man. (Exodus 17:8-15)

D. The LORD Our Peace - It is God Who gives peace. (Judges 6:24)

E. The LORD My Shepherd - God is the One Who leads men
through hard places. (See Psalm 23 which is given at the end of
this chapter.)

F. The Lord - God's Life In Us - This speaks of the day when Christ
will be King of the earth, but Christ's life is now in those who
have put their trust in Him. (Jeremiah 23:6; I Corinthians 1:30)

G. The LORD Is Here Now - This name also looks forward to the day Christ will be king of the earth. (Ezekiel 48:35; Revelation 11:15; 17:14; 20:4; 21:3)

H. The Lord Is The One Who Sets Us Apart and Makes Us Holy. (Exodus 31:13; Leviticus 20:26)

I. The Lord Is The One Who Makes Us Right With Himself. (Jeremiah 23:6)

J. God Is The One Who Will Pay Back or The Lord Will Punish And Pay Back. (Jeremiah 51:56; Ezekiel 7:9; Romans 12:19)

K. The names that bring all the others together and make them complete are Alpha and Omega. These are the first and last Greek letters and mean the *First and Last*, the *Beginning and End* of all things. These names of God are used in many different parts of God's Word. (Revelation 1:8) One part that uses many of these different names is Psalm 23.

Psalm 23

(1) The Lord is my Shepherd. I will have everything I need. (The Lord is my Shepherd)

(2) He lets me rest in fields of green grass. He leads me beside the quiet waters. (The Lord Who gives me what I want)

(3) He makes me strong again. He leads me in the way of living right with Himself which brings honor to His name. (The Lord Who makes me right with Himself)

(4) Yes, even if I walk through the valley of the shadow of death, I will not be afraid of anything, because You are with me. You have a walking stick with which to guide and one with which to help. These comfort me. (The Lord our peace)

(5) You are making a table of food ready for me in front of those who hate me. You have poured oil on my head. I have everything I need.

(6) For sure, You will give me goodness and loving-kindness all the days of my life. Then I will live with You in Your house forever. (The Lord is here now)

CERTAIN THINGS ABOUT GOD THAT HE DOES NOT SHARE WITH MAN

It is hard to understand the difference between who God is and what God is like. The next two chapters will help to show the difference.

There Are Certain Things About God That He Does Not Share With Man:

1. *GOD ALWAYS WAS AND ALWAYS WILL BE.* Because everything has a beginning and an end, it is hard to understand how God had no beginning. He always was. God is without beginning or end. He is the "I AM." He is always the same. In Revelation 1:8 it says, "The Lord God says, 'I am the First and the Last, the beginning and the end of all things. I am the All-powerful One Who was and Who is and Who is to come.' " And in Psalm 90:2 it says, "Before the mountains were born, before You gave birth to the earth and the world, forever and ever, You are God." (Isaiah 41:4b)

2. *GOD NEVER CHANGES.* Anytime something changes, it is for the better or for the worse. But God cannot change for the better because He is already perfect. He cannot change for the worse because He is God. Malachi 3:6 says, "For I, the Lord, do not change." James 1:17 says, "Whatever is good and perfect comes to us from God. He is the One Who made all light. He does not change. No shadow is made by His turning." (Psalm 33:11)

3. *GOD KNOWS ALL THINGS.* He knows Himself and He knows all other things. He knows everything that will happen to man. He knows if man will put his trust in His Son, or turn away from Him. (Genesis 15:13-15; Exodus 3:7-9; Ecclesiastes 12:14; Luke 12:2; I Corinthians 4:5; I Peter 1:10-12)

   A. God knows what a man is thinking about. I Chronicles 28:9 says, "...For the Lord looks into all hearts, and understands every plan and thought..." No thought can be kept from God. Job 42:2 says, "I know that You can do all things. Nothing can put a stop to Your plans." And in Psalm 139:2 it says, "You know when I sit down and when I get up. You understand my thoughts from far away."

   B. There is not a word that comes from the mouth of man without the Lord knowing it. Psalm 139:4 says, "Even before I speak a word, O Lord, You know it all."

C. We may not think of certain things that we should tell Him, but He knows all things. I John 3:20 says, "Our heart may say that we have done wrong. But remember, God is greater than our heart. He knows everything." "For the ways of a man are seen by the eyes of the Lord, and He watches all his paths" (Proverbs 5:21).

D. The plan God has for man to be saved from the punishment of sin is greater than anything man can think of. In Romans 11:33 it says, "God's riches are so great! The things He knows and His wisdom are so deep. No one can understand His thoughts. No one can understand His ways." (Isaiah 55:7; 64:4; I Corinthians 2:9)

E. God knows each person He has made and knows everything about them. In Matthew 10:29-30 it says, "Are not two small birds sold for a very small piece of money? And yet not one of the birds falls to the earth without your Father knowing it. God knows how many hairs you have on your head." (Psalm 33:13-15; Jeremiah 1:5)

F. God sees all things that happen in every place. In Hebrews 4:13 it says, "No one can hide from God. His eyes see everything we do. We must give an answer to God for what we have done." Proverbs 15:3 says, "The eyes of the Lord are in every place, watching the bad and the good." (Proverbs 5:21)

G. God knows all the sorrows of men. "The Lord said, 'I have seen the suffering of My people in Egypt. I have heard their cry because of the men who make them work. I know how they suffer' " (Exodus 3:7).

H. God knows all things that have happened in the past and all things that will happen in the future. (Isaiah 46:9-10; Acts 2:23; Romans 8:27-29).

Some other verses that show God knows all things:

Acts 1:24 "Then the followers prayed, saying, 'Lord, You know the hearts of all men. Show us which of these two men You have chosen.' " (I Samuel 16:7)

Acts 15:8 "God knows the hearts of all men. He showed them they were to have His loving-favor by giving them the Holy Spirit the same as He gave to us." God knew Pharoah would not let the Israelites go. (Exodus 3:19)

I Corinthians 3:20 "They also say, 'The Lord knows how the wise man thinks. His thinking is worth nothing.' " (Psalm 94:11)

II Timothy 2:19 "But the truth of God cannot be changed. It says, 'The Lord knows those who are His.' And, 'Everyone who says he is a Christian must turn away from sin!' "

Romans 8:29 "God knew from the beginning who would put their trust in Him. So He chose them and made them to be like His Son. Christ was first, and all those who belong to God are His brothers."

4. *GOD IS ALL-POWERFUL.* He can do everything He wants to do. His power has no end. Nothing can change or stop God's power. When God says He will do something, He will do it. (Numbers 23:19)

A. Men can do *some* things, but they cannot do *all* things. In Matthew 19:26 it says, "Jesus looked at them and said, 'This cannot be done by men. But with God all things can be done.' " (Job 42:2)

B. God can do things that are hard to believe. Luke 1:36-37 says, "See, your cousin Elizabeth, as old as she is, is going to give birth to a child. She was not able to have children before, but now she is in her sixth month. For God can do all things." (Genesis 18:14)

C. God does not only give life, but He can also bring a person back to life after death. Acts 26:8 says, "Why do you think it is hard to believe that God raises people from the dead?" John 11:43-44 says, "When He had said this, He called with a loud voice, 'Lazarus, come out!' The man who had been dead came out. His hands and feet were tied in grave clothes. A white cloth was tied around his face. Jesus said to the people, 'Take off the grave clothes and let him go!' " (I Kings 17:22; II Kings 4:32-34; John 11:1-44)

5. *GOD IS EVERYWHERE.* There is no place where God is not. Man must not think of God as having a body like his. Even if man reads of God having ears, eyes, feet, or a right side, it must be understood that this speaks of Him being *able* to see, hear, and feel everywhere at the same time. Man cannot understand how big God is. The heavens are not big enough for Him. II Chronicles 6:18b says, "...See, heaven and the highest heaven cannot hold You. How much less can this house hold You which I have built." Heaven, hell, every part of the sea, all darkness and all light are full of God. And God is not far from each one of those who are His children. Acts 17:27 says, "They were to look for God. Then they might feel after Him

and find Him because He is not far from each one of us." There is no place man can go without God being there. In Jeremiah 23:24 it says, " 'Can a man hide himself in secret places so that I cannot see him?' says the Lord. 'Do I not fill heaven and earth?' says the Lord." God is everywhere because He is Spirit. But there is a special place called heaven where God is. Matthew 5:34-35 tells where God is. "I tell you, do not use strong words when you make a promise. Do not promise by heaven. It is the place where God is. Do not promise by earth. It is where He rests His feet. Do not promise by Jerusalem. It is the city of the great King." While Stephen was being killed, he said in Acts 7:56, "See! I see heaven open and the Son of Man standing at the right side of God!" (Psalm 139:7-10)

CERTAIN THINGS ABOUT GOD THAT HE SHARES WITH MAN

The last chapter taught how God did not share certain things with man. In this chapter it can be seen how God has certain things that He desires to share with man. Man does not have these things himself. After he becomes a Christian and has a desire to live for Him, God shares these things.

1. *GOD IS HOLY.* The word "holy" means to be free from all sin, or to be pure. In I Peter 1:15 it says, "Be holy in every part of your life. Be like the Holy One Who chose you." God is holy and is willing to share this with man. When man is like God in this way, it means he is set apart for God-like living and set apart to work for God. In John 17:11b it says, "Holy Father, keep those You have given to Me in the power of Your name." God speaks of Himself as being holy in I Peter 1:16 when He says, "You must be holy, for I am holy." (Joshua 24:19; Psalm 99:5, 9)

Luke 1:49 "He Who is powerful has done great things for me. His name is holy." (Isaiah 57:15)

Revelation 4:8 "Each one of the four living beings had six wings. They had eyes all over them, inside and out. Day and night they never stop saying, 'Holy, holy, holy is the Lord, the All-powerful One. He is the One Who was and Who is and Who is to come.' " (Isaiah 6:3)

Revelation 6:10 "All those who had been killed cried out with a loud voice saying, 'How long will it be yet before You will punish those on the earth for killing us? Lord, You are holy and true.' " (Deuteronomy 32:43; Psalm 79:10)

Revelation 15:4 "Who will not honor You, Lord, with love and fear? Who will not tell of the greatness of Your name? For You are the only One Who is holy. All nations will come and worship before You. Everyone sees that You do the right things." (Psalm 86:9; Jeremiah 10:7)

2. *GOD IS ALWAYS RIGHT AND WHATEVER HE DOES IS GOOD.* God made a way for man to be right with Himself. God will forgive and receive the sinner who comes through Jesus' death on the cross. In I Corinthians 1:30 it says, "God Himself made the way so you can have new life through Christ Jesus. God gave us

Christ to be our wisdom. Christ made us right with God, and set us apart for God and made us holy. Christ bought us with His blood and made us free from our sins." (Psalm 19:9; Jeremiah 23:5)

3. *GOD IS ALWAYS FAITHFUL AND TRUE.* God can always be trusted. In I Corinthians 10:13 it tells how God is faithful to His children. "You have never been tempted to sin in any different way than other people. God is faithful. He will not allow you to be tempted more than you can take. But when you are tempted, He will make a way for you to keep from falling into sin." God is faithful in what He promised. In I Thessalonians 5:24 it says, "The One Who called you is faithful and will do what He promised." And in Hebrews 10:23 it says, "Let us hold on to the hope we say we have and not be changed. We can trust God that He will do what He promised." And He is faithful to Himself. In II Timothy 2:13 it says, "If we have no faith, He will still be faithful for He cannot go against what He is." (Deuteronomy 7:9; Isaiah 49:7)

4. *GOD IS A GOD OF LOVING-PITY AND LOVING-KINDNESS.* This is also seen in the Christian who desires to please God. In Romans 2:4 it says, "Do you forget about His loving-kindness to you? Do you forget how long He is waiting for you? You know that God is kind. He is trying to get you to be sorry for your sins and turn from them." In Romans 11:22 it says, "We see how kind God is. It shows how hard He is also. He is hard on those who fall away. But He is kind to you if you keep on trusting Him. If you do not, He will cut you off." (Psalm 89:24)

5. *GOD IS LOVE.* Most people think of God as a God of love. True love is from God and the Christian has love for others because God gives him love. The Christian way of worship is the only way of worship that says God is love. The gods of wood, stone, and other things that many people worship in many parts of the world are thought to be full of hate. These people think something must be given to these false gods all the time so the gods will not punish them. Those who put their trust in God's Son, Jesus Christ, are loved by God. (Deuteronomy 7:7-8; Jeremiah 31:3; II Corinthians 5:14a; 13:11b)

I John 4:8-16 "Those who do not love do not know God because God is love. God has shown His love to us by sending His only Son into the world. God did this so we might have life through Christ. This is love! It is not that we loved God but that He loved us. For God sent His Son to pay for our sins with His own blood. Dear friends, if God loved us that much, then we should love each other. No person has ever seen God at any time. If we love each other, God lives in us. His love is made perfect in us. He has given us His Spirit.

This is how we know we live by His help and He lives in us. We have seen and are able to say that the Father sent His Son to save the world from the punishment of sin. The person who tells of Him in front of men and says that Jesus is the Son of God, God is living in that one and that one is living by the help of God. We have come to know and believe the love God has for us. God is love. If you live in love, you live by the help of God and God lives in you."

John 14:21 "The one who loves Me is the one who has My teaching and obeys it. My Father will love whoever loves Me. I will love him and will show Myself to him." (Deuteronomy 10:12; Proverbs 8:17)

John 16:27 "...because the Father loves you. He loves you because you love Me and believe that I came from the Father."

John 17:23, 26 "I am in them and You are in Me so they may be one and be made perfect. Then the world may know that You sent Me and that You love them as You love Me." "I have made your name known to them and will make it known. So then the love You have for Me may be in them and I may be in them." God loves the world of men, even though they are sinful. John 3:16 says, "For God so loved the world that He gave His only Son. Whoever puts his trust in God's Son will not be lost, but will have life that lasts forever." Romans 5:8 says, "But God showed His love to us. While we were still sinners, Christ died for us." God took care of the sin problem by giving His Son. (Isaiah 53:5-6)

Romans 1:7 "So I write to all of you in the city of Rome. God loves you and has chosen you to be set apart for Himself. May God our Father and the Lord Jesus Christ give you His loving-favor and peace." (Psalm 91:14)

Romans 5:8 "But God showed His love to us. While we were still sinners, Christ died for us." (Isaiah 53:6)

Galatians 2:20 "I have been put up on the cross to die with Christ. I no longer live. Christ lives in me. The life I now live in this body, I live by putting my trust in the Son of God. He was the One Who loved me and gave Himself for Me."

Ephesians 2:4 "But God had so much loving-kindness. He loved us with such a great love." (Nehemiah 9:17b)

Hebrews 12:6 "The Lord punishes everyone He loves. He whips every son He receives." (Psalm 119:75; Proverbs 3:11-12)

I John 3:1 "See what great love the Father has for us that He would

call us His children. And that is what we are. For this reason the
people of the world do not know who we are because they did not
know Him."

These things God shares with men who have been saved from the
punishment of sin, and have a desire to live a God-like life.

WHAT GOD IS LIKE

Since God is Who He is, words are hard to find to tell about Him. The Word of God helps man know about Him and what He is like. It is not possible to tell Who God is without telling what He is like and what He does.

1. *GOD IS SPIRIT.* God does not have a body. Because of Who He is and how He works, He does not need a body like a human being. In John 4:24 it says, "God is Spirit. Those who worship Him must worship Him in Spirit and in truth." (Deuteronomy 4:15; Psalm 139:7)

2. *GOD IS LIGHT.* This tells what He is like and how He works. The first thing He did after He made the world was to make light. "And God said, 'Let there be light,' and there was light" (Genesis 1:3). In I John 1:5 it says, "This is what we heard Him tell us. We are passing it on to you. God is light. There is no darkness in Him." (Isaiah 60:19)

3. *GOD IS LOVE.* God is not only full of love, He is love. He is happy to share His love with man. In I John 4:16 it says, "We have come to know and believe the love God has for us. God is love. If you live in love, you live by the help of God and God lives in you." (God loves man but He hates sin. Proverbs 6:16-19) (Isaiah 43:4; Jeremiah 31:3)

4. *GOD IS A FIRE WHO DESTROYS WHAT IS SINFUL.* God is right in everything He does. He is holy and perfect. When silver and gold are made pure so that no other metal is mixed with them, a hot fire is used to burn away everything that is not good. Fire cleans. In Hebrews 12:29 it says, "For our God is a fire that destroys everything." (Deuteronomy 4:24; 9:3,19)

5. *GOD IS A PERSON.* The three things that make a person are: (1) The power of knowing, (2) The power of feeling, and (3) The power of choosing. God has these three things and He is a person. He does not have a body because He is Spirit. Spirits do not have bodies. We know He is a person because:

   A. *God has the power of knowing.* God knows Himself. When He called Moses from the burning bush, He said, "I AM WHO I AM." It could be said no stronger. God was sure of Himself. God knows all things. In Acts 15:18 it says, "God has made all His

works known from the beginning of time." And Hebrews 4:13
says, "No one can hide from God. His eyes see everything we
do." (II Chronicles 16:9; Psalm 33:13-15)

B. *God has the power of feeling.* The verse that shows this best is
John 3:16, "For God so loved the world..." And James 5:11b
says, "The Lord is full of loving-kindness and pity." (Psalm
103:8)

C. *God has the power of choosing.* Psalm 115:3 says, "But our God
is in the heavens. He does whatever He wants to do." (Psalm
103:19)

6. *GOD DOES NOT CHANGE.* Nothing can change Him or His
actions. He has no beginning and He will always be. God always has
been the same and always will be the same. In Malachi 3:6a it says,
"For I, the Lord, do not change." It also says in James 1:17a,
"Whatever is good and perfect comes to us from God. He is the One
Who made all light. He does not change." Hebrews 6:17-18 says,
"And so God made a promise. He wanted to show Abraham that He
would never change His mind. So He made the promise in His own
name. God gave these two things that cannot be changed and God
cannot lie. We who have turned to Him can have great comfort
knowing that He will do what He has promised." (I Samuel 15:29)

7. *GOD IS ALL WISDOM.* God is not only wise, but He knows all
things. He uses what He knows in a way that is right and good. In
Romans 11:33 it says, "God's riches are so great! The things He
knows and His wisdom are so deep! No one can understand His
thoughts. No one can understand His ways." (Psalm 104:24; Daniel
2:20)

8. *GOD IS ALL-POWERFUL.* There is nothing God cannot do.
Matthew 19:26 says, "But with God all things can be done."
(Jeremiah 32:17)

9. *GOD IS HOLY AND PERFECT.* Everything He does is right and
good. In I Peter 1:15-16 it says, "Be holy in every part of your life.
Be like the Holy One Who chose you. The Holy Writings say, 'You
must be holy, for I am holy.' " Also in John 17:11 it says, "I am no
longer in the world. I am coming to you. But these are still in the
world. Holy Father, keep those You have given to Me in the power
of Your Name. Then they will be one, even as We are One."
(Deuteronomy 32:4; Psalm 18:30a)

10. *GOD IS TRUTH.* In John 3:33 it says, "Whoever receives His
words proves that God is true." Part of Romans 3:4 says, "God is

always true even if every man lies." I John 5:6-7 says, "Jesus Christ came by water and blood. He did not come by water only, but by water and blood. The Holy Spirit speaks about this and He is truth. There are three who speak of this in heaven: the Father and the Word and the Holy Spirit. These three are one." (Isaiah 65:16)

11. *GOD IS THE ONE WHO BRINGS EVERYTHING INTO BEING, KEEPS IT, AND BRINGS IT TO ITS END.* Everything is under God's great power, and He is the One Who is head over all things. In Isaiah 45:5-7 it says, "I am the Lord, and there is no other. There is no God besides Me. I will give you strength, even though you have not known me. Then men may know from sunrise to sunset that there is no God besides Me. I am the Lord, and there is no other. I make the light, and I make darkness. I bring good and I make trouble. I am the Lord Who does all these things." Colossians 1:17b says, "All things are held together by Him."

12. *GOD IS THREE-IN-ONE.* (See the next chapter for this study.)

THE THREE-IN-ONE GOD

The Three-in-one God or *Trinity* means that there is one God in three persons as: Father, Son, and Holy Spirit. This is hard to understand, and yet the Word of God tells of one God in three persons. This may help. A large group of people meeting together is called *one* group. Some grapes grow together and are called *one bunch.* The husband and wife are *one.* Matthew 19:5 says, "For this reason a man will leave his father and his mother and will live with his wife. The two will become *one."*

Matthew 3:16-17 shows the three different persons. "When Jesus came out of the water, the heavens opened. He saw the Spirit of God coming down and resting on Jesus like a dove. A voice was heard from heaven. It said, 'This is My much-loved Son. I am very happy with Him.' " The *Father* speaks from heaven, the *Son* is baptized in the Jordan River, and the *Holy Spirit* comes down on the Son as a dove. In Matthew 28:19 Jesus tells His followers to baptize new Christians in the name of the Father, and the Son, and the Holy Spirit.

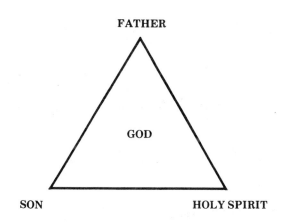

GOD IS ONE GOD IN THREE PERSONS.

Paul ends his letter to the Christians in the city of Corinth by saying in II Corinthians 13:14, "May you have loving-favor from our Lord Jesus Christ. May you have the love of God. May you be joined together by the Holy Spirit."

In John 14:16a Jesus says, "Then I will ask My Father and He will give you another helper." *Jesus* is asking the *Father* to give the *Holy Spirit*. In Romans 1:7 it speaks of the *Father* Who is God; in Hebrews 1:8 the *Son* Who is God; and in Acts 5:3-4 the *Holy Spirit* Who is God. Not one of the three Persons is greater or less than the others, and there can never be a division among them.

It may help to understand by thinking of it this way:

The Father is God, the part of the Three-in-one God Who is not seen. (John 1:18) The Son is God, the part of the Three-in-one God Who left heaven to live in human flesh among sinful men. (John 1:14-18) The Holy Spirit is God, the part of the Three-in-one God Who works in and through men. (I Corinthians 2:9-10)

THE WORKS OF GOD

The works of God are what He has done in the past, what He is doing
now, and what He will do in the future. In Romans 1:20 it says, "Men
cannot say they do not know about God. From the beginning of the
world, men could see what God is like through the things He has made.
This shows His power that lasts forever. It shows that He is God." They
see His works. But to know His works is not the same as knowing His
ways. His works may be known by those who know about Him. But
His ways are known by those who know Him as a person. "He made
known His ways to Moses, and His acts (works) to the children of
Israel." The works of God show His plan for all times. In I Timothy
1:17 it says, "We give honor and thanks to the King Who lives forever.
He is the One Who never dies and Who is never seen. He is the One
Who knows all things. He is the only God. Let it be so." In Ephesians
1:11 it says, "We were already chosen to be God's own children by
Christ. This was done just like the plan He had." It can be seen how
everything works as He planned it. God works just as He plans. This is
seen in Ephesians 3:11, "This was the plan God had for all time. He did
this through Christ Jesus our Lord."

1. GOD MADE [BROUGHT INTO BEING] EVERYTHING.

The word *creation* is used in most versions. It means the work of the
Three-in-one God by which in the beginning and for His own shining
greatness, He made, without the use of anything that was before, the
whole world that can be seen and that which cannot be seen.
(Genesis 1:1-2; John 1:1-3)

*2. IT CAN BE SEEN THAT EVERY WORK OF GOD IS DONE
BY THE THREE-IN-ONE GOD.*

A. God the Father was the One Who planned it and started it.
Ephesians 3:9 says, "I was to make all men understand the
meaning of this secret. God kept this secret to Himself from the
beginning of the world. And He is the One Who made all
things." (Genesis 1:1; Deuteronomy 4:39; I Corinthians 8:6; II
Corinthians 4:6)

B. God the Son brought it into being. Colossians 1:16 says, "Christ
made everything in the heavens and on the earth. He made
everything that is seen and things that are not seen. He made all
the powers of heaven. Everything was made by Him and for
Him." (John 1:1-3; I Corinthians 8:6; Hebrews 1:2; 11:3)

C. God the Holy Spirit finished it. (Genesis 1:2; Job 26:13; 33:4)

It can be thought of this way: When a house is built, one plans how it is to be built. Another builds the building, and another finishes the inside. Each had a part. This can be seen in Genesis 1:1-3: God the Father in verse 1, God the Spirit in verse 2, and God the Son in verse 3. God did not only make the world that is seen, He made things that are not seen. He made the angel world as seen in Colossians 1:16, which says, "Christ made everything in the heavens and on earth. He made everything that is seen and things that are not seen. He made all the powers of heaven. Everything was made by Him and for Him."

The Hebrew word for *created* is found three times in Genesis 1. In verse 1 - God *created* (made from nothing) the heavens and the earth. In verse 21 - He made animal life. In verse 26 - He made human life. Man has always had a desire to know how God did these things, but He chose to keep His ways a secret. Some people make the mistake of thinking the things God made are God Himself. God should not be worshiped in what He has made. These things prove that an All-powerful God made them, but men must not worship them. Man must worship the One Who made them. The question is asked, why did God *create* (make things from nothing)? There is only one answer. God made everything for His own shining greatness, just as He wanted them, and for His own use. This is seen in Revelation 4:11, "Our Lord and our God, it is right for you to have the shining greatness and the honor and power. You made all things. They were made and have life because you wanted it that way." (Nehemiah 9:6; Romans 11:36; Ephesians 1:5)

3. GOD KEEPS AND TAKES CARE OF THINGS HE MADE.

Colossians 1:17 says, "Christ was before all things. All things are held together by Him." Some people have made the mistake of thinking God has left the world to run by itself. Hebrews 1:3 says, "The Son shines with the shining greatness of the Father. The Son is as God is in every way. It is the Son Who holds up the whole world by the power of His Word. The Son gave His own life so we could be clean from all sin. After He had done that He sat down on the right side of God in heaven." This is the part Christ has in keeping things together and running well. Christ spoke of the birds of the sky and the flowers of the field as being cared for by God. If He cares for them, how much more does He care for man? (Matthew 5:45; 6:26; 10:29-31)

God shows in His Word that He has made and is keeping things as He wants them.

A. The earth, sun, moon, and stars stay as they were planned. (Psalm 119:89-91)

B. The nations of the world are where God put them or where He allows them to be. Acts 17:26 says, "He made from one blood all nations who live on the earth. He set the times and places where they should live." (Deuteronomy 32:8)

C. The length of human life is as God planned it. Job 14:5 says, "A man's days are numbered. You know the number of his months. He cannot live longer than the time You have set."

D. The acts of man, both good and bad, are allowed by God. Luke 22:22 says, "The Son of Man will be taken this way because it has been in God's plan. But it is bad for that man who hands Him over!" (Acts 2:23; 4:27-28; Ephesians 2:10; I Peter 2:8; Revelation 17:17)

E. The saving of men from the punishment of sin is by God's plan. (Isaiah 53:5; Romans 8:29-30; Ephesians 1:3, 10, 11)

PART 2

WHAT THE WORD OF GOD TEACHES ABOUT ITSELF

[*Bibliology*]

THE HOLY WRITINGS

1. THE HOLY WRITINGS CAME FROM GOD.

The Bible is the only written word God has for people. This greatest of all books *The Holy Bible* does not just have God's Word in it, it *IS* the Word of God. It is all of the Holy Writings of God in one Book. There are sixty-six different books in the Bible. Thirty-nine of these are in the Old Testament and twenty-seven are in the New Testament.

God used about 40 different men to write what He told them to write. The first books were written about 1,500 years before Christ and the last ones were written about 100 years after Christ's death. From the beginning to the end it was 1,600 years. II Peter 1:20-21 says, "Understand this first: No part of the Holy Writings was ever made up by man. No part of the Holy Writings came long ago because of what man wanted to write. But holy men who belonged to God spoke what the Holy Spirit told them."

The Holy Writings were written long ago. And yet they were written for all people and for all times. There has been no need for other writings to be given from God after the first ones because they were complete. God's Word has everything a person needs to know about God, about Jesus Christ, about the Holy Spirit, about the way for a sinful person to become a child of God, about how to have peace in this life, and about life after death. God has given us His Word in writing. It can never be destroyed. Matthew 24:35 says, "Heaven and earth will pass away, but My words will not pass away."

2. THE HOLY WRITINGS ARE IN TWO PARTS - THE OLD TESTAMENT AND THE NEW TESTAMENT.

The word *Testament* means that God agreed or promised to do certain things for His people. Later, this word came to mean the book which had these promises in it.

God has always wanted people to worship Him. The Old Testament can be called the *Old Way of Worship*. It is the same with the New Testament. It can be called the *New Way of Worship* because the two ways of worship are different. The first, or Old Way of Worship, was by a set of laws or rules and the giving of animals or other things on the altar as an act of worship. In the New Way of Worship, Christ was given. He was God's perfect gift. Christ was the only one Who was able to keep the old laws. When man puts his trust in Christ, he gives God his true worship. (Hebrews 9:1-14)

A. *The Old Testament* tells of the beginning of the world and all that God made on it and around it. It tells how He gave His laws or rules for living to His people. It tells how men lived in that day. Sometimes they pleased God and sometimes they fought against Him. It tells how certain men were able to tell what would happen in the future. And it tells how Christ, the Promised One, the Son of God, would come to save people from the punishment of their sins when they put their trust in Him.

B. *The New Testament* tells of the birth, life, and death of Christ, and this happened as it was told it would happen in the Old Testament by God's early preachers. It tells of the beginning of the church as it is known today. It tells of the problems of the new churches and what must be done to live in a way to please God. It tells what will happen before Christ comes to earth the second time and how it will happen.

3. THE BIBLE IS **THE** BOOK.

The English word *Bible* comes from the language in which the New Testament was written. Bible means *book*. About 500 years after the birth of Christ, the Holy Books came to be called *The Holy Bible.*

Sometimes the writings in the Bible are called the Scriptures which means the *Holy Writings.* The first Christians called the Word of God *The Scriptures.*

The Bible is not just a book. It is **THE** Book. It is the most important of all books because of the One Who caused It to be written, and what It has in It. The word *Holy* is in front of the word *Bible* and is used because the Word of God is truth and It is set apart from all other books as God's Word to people of all times.

Long ago God chose certain men to write down what He told them. There were many different men. They lived at different times and at different places. Their lives were different because of the places where they lived. Many of them never saw each other. Their families were different. God used men as men, not as *machines.* The writings that were written down all agree with each other and show that they came from the same Person. That Person was God.

HOW THE BIBLE CAME TO MAN

1. THE BIBLE CAME TO MAN IN A POWERFUL WAY.

God has kept His Writings over the many years. The Old Testament was written in the Hebrew language on animal skins. This was the way it was kept until books were printed. The New Testament books were written in the Greek language on writing paper made from *papyrus reed* that grew in Egypt. For many years the words of the Bible were written one word at a time by hand. The first Bible to be put into the English language was in the year 1382. The first Bible to be printed was in 1454. The King James Bible was *translated* from the Greek and Hebrew languages into the English language and printed in the year 1611. The Word of God has been put into many different languages so people over all the world can understand it. This was why The NEW LIFE Testament was put into easy-to-read English. In this way God's Word can mean even more because it is easy to read and understand.

NEW LIFE
Testament 1969
Bible 1986

Many other
Translations
from
1900-1970

Wycliffe
Bible
1320

First
Writings
in
Greek
&
Hebrew

Berkeley
Bible
1959

Tyndale
Bible
1525

Amplified
Bible
1958

King James
Bible
1611

Revised
Standard
Bible
1952

2. THERE ARE FALSE WRITINGS THAT SINFUL MEN TRY TO SAY ARE THE WORD OF GOD.

There are some writings that people have wanted to put in the Bible that are not God's Word. These false writings must not be taken for God's Word.

About 1,500 years ago the leaders of the church met to take a careful look at these books and test them for the truth. There are many false books that have been written that look like the Holy Writings. These false writings have words in them that talk about God, but they were not written by holy men God spoke through. The Holy Writings must not be added to or have words taken from them. Deuteronomy 4:2 says, "Do not add to the Word that I tell you, and do not take away from it. Keep the Laws of the Lord your God which I tell you." Revelation 22:18-19 says, "I am telling everyone who hears the words that are written in this book: If anyone adds anything to what is written in this book, God will add to him the kinds of trouble that this book tells about. If anyone takes away any part of this book that tells what will happen in the future, God will take away his part from the tree of life and from the Holy City which are written in this book."

3. *HOW IT WAS DECIDED WHICH WRITINGS WERE GOD-GIVEN AND MADE ALIVE BY HIM.*

There were certain men God chose to write His word. But there were other men who wrote other writings that looked much like God's Word, and some even tried to call these false writings *Holy* writings. Books that became part of the Bible had to pass certain tests.

A. The books in the Old Testament had to be written, put together, or spoken of as true, by an early preacher. The Writings in the New Testament had to be written by one of the twelve men Christ chose to follow Him, or one who lived and worked with one of the followers of these men.

B. Help had to come from these Writings so that people could grow in their Christian lives.

C. The Writings had to be already in use by the churches and had to have proved themselves.

D. The most important test was if the book showed that it was God-given and made alive by Him.

Every one of the 66 books in the Bible today have gone through many tests. The 66 books that are in the Bible passed the tests. The other writings that did not pass these same tests are not put - and should not be put - in the Bible.

WHY THE BIBLE WAS WRITTEN

1. *THE MOST IMPORTANT REASON FOR THE THE BIBLE BEING WRITTEN WAS FOR GOD TO TELL PEOPLE THE THINGS HE WANTED THEM TO KNOW. THE BIBLE IS GOD SPEAKING.*

A. God spoke in the Old Testament through special preachers who wrote down what He told them. Hebrews 1:1 says, "Long ago God spoke to our early fathers in many and different ways. He spoke through the early preachers." (Luke 1:70; Acts 3:21; Romans 1:2) In the Old Testament He tells how the world and everything in it was made and how He helped His people, the Jews. The Old Testament also tells the news that He would send His Son, Jesus, at a later time. (Jeremiah 36:2-3; Ezekiel 1:3)

B. God spoke in the New Testament through Jesus. In Hebrews 1:2a it says, "But in these last days He (God) has spoken to us through His Son."

The New Testament tells about the birth of Jesus and His work while on earth. God's Word says many things about people also. God wants man to know he is a sinner. Then God wants him to know what can be done to be saved from the punishment of sin. In Romans 6:20-23 it says, "When sin had power over your life, you were not right with God. What good did you get from the things you are ashamed of now? Those things bring death. But now you are free from the power of sin. You have become a servant for God. Your life is set apart for God-like living. The end is life that lasts forever. You get what is coming to you when you sin. It is death! But God's free gift is life that lasts forever. It is given to us by our Lord Jesus Christ."

Once a man sees this truth and puts his trust in Christ, he finds the Bible has much in it to help him live his life in the right way. In II Timothy 3:16-17 it says, "All the Holy Writings are God-given and are made alive by Him. Man is helped when he is taught God's Word. It shows what is wrong. It changes the way of a man's life. It shows him how to be right with God. It gives the man who belongs to God everything he needs to work well for Him."

When a man wonders what the answer is to problems he has in his life, he should read the Word of God. Great comfort can be found in God's Word, and it tells everything man needs to know to live for God.

2. THE BIBLE WAS WRITTEN FOR MAN TO LEARN ABOUT GOD.

Christians can learn something by reading the Bible again and again. The Holy Spirit helps man understand what God is saying to him through the Bible. The Bible will help Christians grow to become stronger Christians. It is hard for a man to read a book when the room is getting dark. It is hard to see what he is reading. When he turns on a light, it becomes easy to read. The same is true when the Bible seems hard to understand. When he asks the Holy Spirit to help him, it is like a light to his mind making it easier for him to know what he is reading.

The Bible is not God, but it is God speaking. God has spoken and the Bible is His Word in writing to man. II Peter 1:20-21 says, "No part of the Holy Writings was ever made up by any man. No part of the Holy Writings came long ago because of what man wanted to write. But holy men who belonged to God spoke (wrote) what the Holy Spirit told them."

THE HOLY WRITINGS ARE GOD-GIVEN AND MADE ALIVE BY HIM

How the Holy Writings were given is hard to understand. No one knows all the answers.

1. GOD GAVE HIS WORD TO MEN TO WRITE.

At different times during 1,600 years 40 different men were used of God to write the sixty-six books of the Bible, yet it is only one Book. It tells of the one and only way to be saved from sin, and the one way to heaven. No other religious book has such a plan. No other book has proven all it contains is true.

How the Holy Writings were given is hard to understand. A special power that is not known today was given to the holy men long ago who wrote down what God led them to write even to the very words they should use. They were kept from making a mistake and from leaving out anything that should have been written. It was power given by the Holy Spirit but we do not know how it worked. This power was given only to the men who wrote the Holy Writings. This means that no other books are God's Holy Writings. The Holy Spirit *led* or *guided* them in what they wrote and the words to use. This means that the first writings had no mistakes. (It is possible for Bibles written in the languages of today to have mistakes. Words in any language change in meaning over many years, and because of this some of the meanings are not the same today. It is important that people be sure the Bible they read is true to the languages the Bible was first written in.)

2. GOD GAVE HIS WORD TO MAN.

God is powerful, holy, pure, and full of love, and has loving-pity for the people He made. It can be seen everywhere that He has made things for man to use. He gives air to breathe. He makes the seeds grow and gives sunshine and rain. He has given man the understanding as to how to make these things give him what he needs. But man needs more than just these things. He has a sin problem! He feels guilty and knows something is wrong in his heart. None of the things that God made for man to use, or the understanding a man has can help him know what to do about the guilty feeling, or how to be right with God. Man knows there is something more after this life. He needs to be ready for life after death. God who gave man all the other things he needed, also made a way for him to know and understand how he can be right with God. He gave man His holy pure Word.

3. GOD'S WORD IS TO BE TRUSTED.

A. The Bible, God's Word, is more important than any other religious book. It tells what man must be like to be right with God. It tells how bad sin is and tells the sinner how to get right with God.

B. Two different times God's Word tells of the very words being written by God and Christ. In Exodus 31:18 it says, "When the Lord had finished speaking with Moses on Mount Sinai, He gave him the two stone writings of the Law, pieces of stone written on by the finger of God." And in John 8:6 it says, "Jesus got down and began to write in the dust with His finger." Both of these writings were soon destroyed. The pieces of stone with the written Law were broken in front of the children of Israel who were worshiping a false god, and it was not long before the people walked over what Jesus had written on the ground. But it pleased God to have His Law and the Good News of life that lasts forever written through men He chose for that special job.

C. It is important to know that Jesus trusted and taught the Old Testament Writings. Never once did He tell His followers they needed to watch out for mistakes in the Holy Writings. Jesus was quick to show the wrong-doings of the people of His day. (Matthew 23) In Luke 9:55 it says, "Jesus turned and spoke sharp words to them. He said, 'You do not know what kind of spirit you have. The Son of Man did not come to destroy men's lives. He came to save them from the punishment of sin.' " It was easy for Him to get them straight in their thinking about things so it would have been just as easy for Him to tell about certain mistakes that got into the early Holy Writings which were not given by His Spirit, if there had been any.

But instead of this, He always used the Holy Writings, making it plain to the people that every word could be trusted. Matthew 5:18 says, "I tell you, as long as heaven and earth last, not one small mark or part of a word will pass away of the Law of Moses until it has all been done." And in Luke 21:22 it says, "All things will happen as it is written." In Luke 24:44 it says, "All things written about Me in the Law of Moses and in the Books of the early preachers and in the Psalms must happen as they said they would happen." Jesus used the words *The Law of Moses and the Books of the early preachers and the Psalms* when speaking of the whole Old Testament. Such words would not be used by Jesus if any parts were not given by the Holy Spirit or were not true.

4. THE BIBLE IS GOD'S WORD - NOT MAN'S WORD.

And so, the Holy Writings were written by men God chose for that job. God's written Word was breathed upon and made alive by Him. As time went on, other men put these same words on other skins and on *papyrus reed* paper. The first ones were destroyed or lost. Some of the ones made later are in some of the large cities of the world and can be read by those who know the languages in which they were written. We still have with us today about 1,000 pieces of the Old Testament and about 4,000 pieces of the New Testament.

GOD'S WORD IS TRUE

1. THE BIBLE IS TRUE BECAUSE GOD SAYS IT IS TRUE.

The Bible is God's Word. God always tells the truth. So the Bible is true because it is God's Word. Psalm 119:89 says, "Forever, O Lord, Your Word will never change in heaven." Psalm 119:160 says, "All of Your Word is truth, and every one of Your laws, which are always right, will last forever." Isaiah 40:8 says, "The grass dries up. The flower loses its color. But the Word of our God stands forever."

2. THE BIBLE IS TRUE BECAUSE JESUS BELIEVED IT TO BE TRUE.

Jesus knew the Holy Writings, now called the Old Testament. He loved them, lived by them, preached them, built His teachings on them, called them *the Truth, God's Truth, and God's Word*. In Luke 4:4-12 when Jesus was tempted by the devil, He spoke words from the Holy Writings. In Luke 4:16-21 it says that Jesus read the Holy Writings at Nazareth. When praying to God the Father, Jesus said in John 17:17b, "Your Word is truth." Jesus says in Matthew 24:35, "Heaven and earth will pass away, but My words will not pass away."

Jesus said in John 10:35, "The Word of God cannot be put aside." Jesus taught from the Holy Writings because He believed them. These are some of the things Jesus believed happened that are told about in the Holy Writings:

A. God made man (Genesis 2:7; Matthew 19:4)

B. Marriage (Genesis 2:24; Matthew 19:5)

C. The burning bush (Exodus 3:4-6; Luke 20:37)

D. Moses (Exodus 20:1-21; Deuteronomy 25:5; Mark 7:10; 12:19-26)

E. The blood of Abel (Genesis 4:8; Luke 11:51)

F. Noah and the flood (Genesis 6:5-7; Matthew 24:37-39)

G. Solomon and the Queen of Sheba (I Kings 10:1; Matthew 12:42)

H. Abraham, Isaac, Jacob (Exodus 3:6; Mark 12:26)

I. Lot, his wife, and the city of Sodom were destroyed. (Genesis 19; Luke 17:28, 29, 32)

J. The food God sent from heaven to the people in the desert
   (Exodus 16:4-5; John 6:31, 32, 49)

K. The snake on a pole (Numbers 21:9; John 3:14)

L. Elijah and the long time everyone was without food. The woman
   whose husband had died at Zarepath. Naaman healed from a
   very bad skin disease. (I Kings 17:1-9; II Kings 5:1-14; Luke 4:25-
   27)

M. Jonah in the fish (Jonah 1:17; Matthew 12:39-41; 16:4)

Jesus began His time of preaching on earth with the words, "It is
written." (Matthew 4:4, 7, 10) "Jesus said, 'You foolish men.
How slow you are to believe what the early preachers have
said' " (Luke 24:25).

Jesus taught using words from 22 books of the Old Testament.
He taught from the Holy Writings as Words from God. Not once
did He take away from the words and from the truth of them.
He said that He did not come to do away with the Law of Moses
or the Writings of the early preachers. "I have not come to do
away with them but to complete them. I tell you, as long as
heaven and earth last, not one small mark or part of a word will
pass away of the Law of Moses until it has all been done"
(Matthew 5:17-18). Jesus knew that even the smallest letter used
in writing God's Word was important.

3. THE BIBLE IS TRUE BECAUSE THE WRITERS OF THE
   NEW TESTAMENT BELIEVED GOD'S WORD TO BE TRUE.

In Matthew there are about 55 verses used from the Old Testament

Mark	32
Luke	40
John	30
Acts	40
Romans	55
Corinthians	15
II Corinthians	8
Galatians	12
Ephesians	5
I Timothy	1
II Timothy	1
Hebrews	35 → (16 Old Testament books are
James	4 used in Hebrews. Many of them
I Peter	9 are used a number of times.)
II Peter	2
Jude	1

4. *THE BIBLE IS TRUE BECAUSE MANY OF THE THINGS IT SAID WOULD HAPPEN HAVE ALREADY HAPPENED.*

A. Things happened in the life of Jesus that the Bible told about many years before Jesus was born.

Number of years before Jesus' birth	Where it is found in the Old Testament	Where it happened in the New Testament in the life of Jesus	
1898 yrs.	Gen. 18:18	Born in Abraham's family	Acts 3:25
1898 yrs.	Gen. 17:19	Born in Isaac's family	Matt. 1:2
1452 yrs.	Num. 24:17	Born in Jacob's family	Luke 3:34
1689 yrs.	Gen. 49:10	Born in Judah's family	Luke 3:33
710 yrs.	Micah 5:2	Place of birth	Matt. 2:1
538 yrs.	Daniel 9:25	Time of birth	Luke 2:1-2
742 yrs.	Isaiah 7:14	Born of a woman who had never had a man	Matt. 1:18
487 yrs.	Zech. 11:12	Sold for 30 pieces of silver	Matt.26:15
712 yrs.	Isaiah 53:12	On the cross beside sinners	Matt.27:38
1050 yrs.	Psalm 109:4	Prays for enemies	Luke 23:34
1050 yrs.	Psalm 34:20	Not a bone broken	John 19:33,36
1050 yrs.	Psalm 16:10	Raised from the dead	Matt.28:9

B. God's Word also tells many things about the Jewish nation. Things that were told many years ago have come true.

5. *THE BIBLE IS TRUE BECAUSE THE WAY IT WAS WRITTEN SHOWS IT IS THE WORD OF GOD.*

Most of the men who wrote the books of the Bible had never seen each other. Some of the men even spoke different languages and lived in different countries. Some of the men were shepherds. Some were kings. One made tents. One was a doctor and one was a tax-collector. Yet every part of the Bible agrees with all other parts. Only the All-powerful God could have led all these men to write one Book.

6. *THE BIBLE IS TRUE BECAUSE OF THE WAY IT CHANGES LIVES.*

No other book has done the things the Bible has done. The Bible tells of the only way for man to have peace with God. It tells how man must be born again. God's great power can be seen changing lives when people read and obey what the Bible teaches. The Bible tells how man can come to God. Jesus says that He is the *Way* and the

Truth and the *Life*. He says that no one can go to the Father except by Him. (John 14:6)

7. THE BIBLE IS TRUE BECAUSE TRUTH NEVER CHANGES.

Books that have been written by men lose their meaning as the years go by. The Bible still has meaning and truth to all who read it today just as much as it did for those who first read it years ago.

8. THE BIBLE IS TRUE BECAUSE IT HAS NEVER BEEN OR NEVER CAN BE DESTROYED.

Some men have tried to destroy the Bible. Some men tried to burn all the copies of the Bible. People have been put to death with much pain for having a Bible. But the more men try to destroy the Bible, the more it is read and believed.

PART 3

WHAT THE WORD OF GOD TEACHES ABOUT CHRIST

[*Christology*]

CHRIST IS ONE OF THE THREE-IN-ONE GOD

1. CHRIST ALWAYS WAS, IS NOW, AND ALWAYS WILL BE.

The Word of God tells in many places that Christ was with the Father. There has never been a time when Christ was not. The first five verses in John tell of this. John 1:1-5 says, "The Word (Christ) was in the beginning. The Word was with God. The Word was God. He was with God in the beginning. He made all things. Nothing was made without Him making it. Life began by Him. His Life was the Light for men. The Light shines in the darkness. The darkness has never been able to put out the Light." The first verse of Genesis tells about when the world was made. But John tells us about the One Who was before the world was made. As there has never been a time when God the Father was not, so there has never been a time when Christ was not.

Some *translations* of the New Testament use the word *begotten* in John 3:16. This word in the English language means *brought into the world* or *given life* which would mean that Christ was not with the Father from the beginning, but began life in Bethlehem. The Greek word means *only* or *only one of a kind.*

In Philippians 2:6-7 it says, "Jesus has always been as God is. But He did not hold to His rights as God. He put aside everything that belonged to Him and made Himself the same as a servant who is owned by someone. He became human by being born as a man." Christ was with the Father before He came as a man to live among men. Certain things belong only to God. When Christ left heaven to come to this world, He (as God) did not lay these things aside, but He did not use them while He was on earth.

Hebrews 1:2-3 says, "But in these last days He has spoken to us through His Son. God gave His Son everything. It was by His Son that God made the world. The Son shines with the shining greatness of the Father. The Son is as God is in every way. It is the Son Who holds up the whole world by the power of His Word. The Son gave His own life so we could be clean from all sin. After He had done that, He sat down on the right side of God in Heaven." Christ brought the world into being and keeps it by His power. In Colossians 1:16 it says that all things are for Christ and by Him. Hebrews 10:5-7 tells why Christ came to earth. "When Christ came to the world, He said to God, 'You do not want animals killed or gifts given in worship. You have made My body ready to give as a gift. You are not pleased with animals that have been killed or burned and given as gifts on the altar to take away sin.' Then I said, 'I have come to do what You want, O God. It is written in the Law that I would.' "

Jesus said in John 8:58 that He was before Abraham. In John 17:5 He spoke of the shining greatness which He had with the Father before the world was. In John 17:24 He spoke of the Father's love for Him before the world was made. When Jesus talked with His followers in the room on the second floor before He gave His life, He said, "I came from the Father and have come into the world. I am leaving the world and going to the Father." Christ was before John the Baptist (John 1:15); before Abraham (John 8:58); and before the world was made. (John 1:1; 17:5, 24; Colossians 1:17; Hebrews 1:2)

Christ is One of the Three-in-one God. He is the One Who left heaven and lived in human flesh. I Timothy 3:16 says, "It is important to know the secret of God-like living, which is: Christ came to earth as a Man. He was pure in His spirit. He was seen by angels. The nations heard about Him. Men everywhere put their trust in Him. He was taken up into heaven." (Christ was the Lamb of God Who was killed for man like a lamb and given on the altar.) A good man who was full of loving-pity and loving-kindness would not have been good enough. Man needed the Lord of heaven, the Christ Who could pay for man's sins with His own blood and set him free. Man needed One Who has always been alive and always will be. (Isaiah 53:6)

Making the world from nothing was the work of Christ. John 1:3 says, "He made all things. Nothing was made without Him making it." Colossians 1:16 says, "Christ made everything in the heavens and on the earth. He made everything that is seen and things that are not seen. He made all the powers of heaven. Everything was made by Him and for Him." In Colossians 1:15 it says, "Christ is as God is. God cannot be seen. Christ lived before everything was made." It is true that He entered the human family to live as a man, but this was not the beginning of life for Him. He always was. All things were made by Christ and for Him. Nothing was made that He did not make. That is why Christ is the Head of all things.

2. *CHRIST IS SEEN IN THE OLD TESTAMENT.* He showed Himself in two ways:

A. In the Old Testament, Christ is seen in things or objects. Some of the things that Christ is seen in were in the Garden of Eden. Adam and Eve were allowed to see the shining greatness of the Lord and hear the voice of the LORD God. "Then they heard the sound of the Lord God walking in the garden in the evening. The man and his wife hid themselves from the Lord God among the trees of the garden" (Genesis 3:8). After sin entered into the hearts of the first two people, special cherubim stood east of the garden of Eden holding burning swords. "So He drove the man out. And He placed cherubim east of the garden of Eden with a sword of fire that turned every way. They kept watch over the path to the tree of life" (Genesis 3:24). These were the ones through which Christ made Himself known at that time. He showed Himself to Abraham before he moved to the land of Canaan. "Now the Lord said to Abram, 'Leave your country, your family and your father's house, and go to the land that I will show you. And I will make you a great nation. I will bring good to you. I will make your name great, so you will be honored. I will bring good to those who are good to you. And I will curse those who curse you. Good will come to all the families of the earth because of you' " (Genesis 12:1-3).

At the burning bush, Moses saw the fire and heard the voice of God. "Now Moses was taking care of the flock of his father-in-law Jethro, the religious leader of Midian. He led the flock to the west side of the desert, and came to Horeb, the mountain of God. There the Angel of the Lord showed Himself to Moses in a burning fire from inside a bush. Moses looked and saw that the bush was burning with fire, but it was not being burned up. So Moses said, 'I must step aside and see this great thing, why the bush is not being burned up.' The Lord saw him step aside to look. And God called to him from inside the bush, saying, 'Moses, Moses!' Moses answered, 'Here I am.' God said, 'Do not come near. Take your shoes off your feet. For the place where you are standing is holy ground.' He said also, 'I am the God of your father, the God of Abraham, the God of Isaac, and the God of Jacob.' Then Moses hid his face. For he was afraid to look at God" (Exodus 3:1-6).

God was able to lead the Jewish people with a cloud during the day and with a fire during the night. "The Lord went before them, in a pillar of cloud during the day to lead them on the way, and in a pillar of fire during the night to give them light. So they could travel day and night. The pillar of cloud during the day and the pillar of fire during the night did not leave the people" (Exodus 13:21-22). The shining greatness of God was seen when a cloud covered the place of worship. "Then the cloud covered the meeting tent. The shining greatness of the Lord filled the holy tent. Moses was not able to go into the meeting tent because the cloud had rested upon it and the shining greatness of the Lord filled the holy tent. When the cloud was lifted from the meeting tent, the people of Israel would go on their way through all their traveling days. But when the cloud was not lifted, they did not move on until the day when it was lifted. For the cloud of the Lord rested on the meeting tent during the day. And fire was in the cloud during the night. It was seen by all the house of Israel as they traveled" (Exodus 40:34-38).

It is in these things or objects that Christ was seen by the people in the Old Testament times. *The shining greatness of the Lord* is a name for Christ as He was *seen* by men. *The Word of the Lord* is a name for Christ as He was *heard* by men.

B. In the Old Testament, Christ is seen as a person. There is a being called the Angel of Jehovah. He has the right and the power to do things that others cannot or must not do. He has the right to be worshiped. The Bible speaks of One such Being or Angel. This One is also called the Son of God and the All-powerful God.

The work done by this Angel of Jehovah is said to be the work of Christ Himself. (Genesis 22:1, 11, 12, 16;32:24-32)

In Micah 5:2 it teaches that Christ showed Himself many times in the early days. These times when He was seen and heard in the Old Testament were as pictures of when He would come to earth in human flesh. His birth in the town of Bethlehem was not the beginning of Him, because He always was.

Each One of the Three-in-one God is God. Each One has a certain work and each works together with the Others. What Christ was like before the world was made is best seen in John 17:5, "Now, Father, honor Me with the honor I had with You before the world was made." And in John 17:24, "Father, I want My followers You gave Me to be with Me where I am. Then they may see My shining greatness which You gave Me because You loved Me before the world was made." Man does not know what that shining greatness was. When Christ left all the greatness and honor of heaven to come to the earth to live as a man among sinful men, He did not put His greatness aside. He and the Father were One even when He became as one who is owned by someone. (John 14:7-11) Philippians 2:6-7 says, "Jesus has always been as God is. But He did not hold to His rights as God. He put aside everything that belonged to Him and made Himself the same as a servant who is owned by someone. He became human by being born as a man."

CHRIST WAS BORN AS A MAN

The Holy Writings teach that Jehovah of the Old Testament became
flesh in the person of Jesus Who was born in the town of Bethlehem.
(Matthew 1:18-25; Luke 1:26-35; John 1:14; Acts 10:38; Romans 8:34;
Galatians 4:4; I Timothy 3:16; Hebrews 2:14)

The way Christ of heaven became flesh on earth is told in Luke 1:34-35.
This does not mean that men can understand how it happened.
Ephesians 3:19 says such things go beyond what can be understood.
Romans 11:33b says, "No one can understand His thoughts. No one can
understand His ways."

Why Christ left heaven to come to earth in human flesh:

1. *TO MAKE THE FATHER KNOWN.* John 1:18, "The much-loved
   Son is beside the Father. No man has ever seen God. But Christ has
   made God known to us."

2. *TO UNDERSTAND MAN.* Hebrews 2:18, "Because Jesus was
   tempted as we are and suffered as we do, He understands us and He
   is able to help us when we are tempted."

3. *TO TAKE AWAY SINS.* I JOHN 3:5, "You know that Christ
   came to take away our sins. There is no sin in Him."

4. *TO SHOW MAN HOW TO LIVE.* I Peter 2:21, "These things
   are all a part of the Christian life to which you have been called.
   Christ suffered for us. This shows us we are to follow in His steps."

5. *TO DESTROY THE WORKS OF THE DEVIL.* I John 3:8, "The
   person who keeps on sinning belongs to the devil. The devil has
   sinned from the beginning. But the Son of God came to destroy the
   works of the devil."

6. *TO WIN OVER DEATH.* Hebrews 2:14, "It is true that we share
   the same Father with Jesus. And it is true that we share the same
   kind of flesh and blood because Jesus became a man like us. He died
   as we must die. Through His death He destroyed the power of the
   devil who has the power of death."

7. *TO GET THINGS READY FOR HIS SECOND COMING.*
   Hebrews 9:28, "It is the same with Christ. He gave Himself once to
   take away the sins of many. When He comes the second time, He

will not need to give Himself again for sin. He will save all those
who are waiting for Him."

Christ came into this world the same as all other men BUT WITHOUT
SIN. Because He was without sin, He was able to give Himself for
man's sin. Without sin, He was able to take the punishment for man's
sins and set man free.

1. CHRIST WAS TRUE MAN.

A. He was born of a women and grew as other men. He looked like
a man and got tired like other men. John 4:6 says, "Jacob's well
was there. Jesus was tired from traveling so He sat down just as
He was by the well. It was about noon."

B. He became hungry. Matthew 4:2 says, "Jesus went without food
for forty days and forty nights. After that He was hungry."

C. He became thirsty. John 19:28 says, "Jesus knew that everything
was now finished. Everything happened as the Holy Writings
said it would happen. He said, 'I am thirsty.' "

D. He chose to call Himself the Son of Man. Matthew 26:64 says,
"Jesus said to him, 'What you said is true. I say to you, from now
on you will see the Son of Man seated on the right hand of the
All-powerful God. You will see Him coming on the clouds of the
sky.' "

2. CHRIST WAS ALSO TRUE GOD.

A. He wanted people to worship Him. Matthew 14:33 says, "Those
in the boat worshiped Jesus. They said, 'For sure, You are the
Son of God!' " Luke 24:52 says, "...they worshiped Him. Then
they went back to Jerusalem with great joy." John 20:28 says,
"Thomas said to Him, 'My Lord and my God!' " (Isaiah 40:3)

B. He is All-powerful. Matthew 28:18 says, "Jesus came and said to
them, 'All power has been given to Me in heaven and on earth.' "

C. He knows all things. John 16:30 says, "Now we are sure You
know everything. You do not need anyone to tell You anything.
Because of this we believe that You came from God."

D. He is everywhere by the Holy Spirit. Matthew 18:20 says, "For
where two or three are gathered together in My name, there I am
with them." Matthew 28:20 says, "Teach them to do all things I
have told you. And I am with you always, even to the end of the
world."

E. When Christ was on trial, He told the leaders that He was God.
Matthew 26:63-66 says, "Jesus said nothing. Then the head
religious leader said to Him, 'In the name of the living God, I tell
You to say the truth. Tell us if You are the Christ, the Son of
God.' Jesus said to him, 'What you said is true. I say to you from
now on you will see the Son of Man seated on the right hand of
the All-powerful God. You will see Him coming on the clouds of
the sky.' Then the head religious leader tore his clothes apart. He
said, 'He has spoken as if He were God! Do we need other people
to speak against Him yet? You have heard Him speak as if He
were God! What do you think?' They said, 'He is guilty of
death!' "

3. CHRIST WAS THE GOD-MAN.

He is true God and He is true Man. When He became human flesh,
He not only became a human person, He also became a part of the
whole human family. Yet, He was still one of the Three-in-one God
at the same time.

A. Christ is the Religious Leader Who made the way for man to go
to God. Hebrews 7:23-28 says, "There had to be many religious
leaders during the time of the Old Way of Worship. They died
and others had to keep on in their work. But Jesus lives forever.
He is the Religious Leader forever. It will never change. And so
Jesus is able, now and forever, to save from the punishment of
sin all who come to God through Him because He lives forever to
pray for them. We need such a Religious Leader Who made the
way for man to go to God. Jesus is holy and has no guilt. He has
never sinned and is different from sinful men. He has the place of
honor above the heavens. Christ is not like other religious
leaders. They had to give gifts every day on the altar in worship
for their own sins first and then for the sins of the people. Christ
did not have to do that. He gave one gift on the altar and that
gift was Himself. It was done once and it was for all time. The
Law makes religious leaders of men. These men are not perfect.
After the Law was given, God spoke with a promise. He made
His Son a perfect Religious Leader forever."

B. Christ is going to return to earth again. Acts 1:11 says, "They
said, 'You men of the country of Galilee, why do you stand
looking up into heaven? This same Jesus Who was taken from
you into heaven will return in the same way you saw Him go up
into heaven.' " (See Part 9)

CHRIST IS TRUE GOD AND TRUE MAN

It is important to understand that Jesus Christ was both God and man at the same time. He is called the God-Man. It must be remembered that He was perfect God and perfect man in one person. He put aside everything that belonged to Him and He became human by being born as a man, but in no way did He stop being God. (Philippians 2:6-7; Colossians 2:9)

1. IT IS TRUE THAT JESUS WAS GOD.

We read in John 1:1, "The Word (Christ) was in the beginning. The Word was with God. The Word was God." Here the Bible calls Jesus, God. Also in Hebrews 1:8 it says, "But about His Son, He says, 'O God, Your place of power will last forever. Whatever You say in Your nation is right and good.' " (Genesis 1:26)

Christ, as God, is called God, the Son of God, Lord, King of Kings and Lord of Lords. He has all power, knows all, is everywhere, and does not change. He makes things, keeps things going, forgives sins, gives life to the dead, and says who is guilty. He is honored by angels and men and one day all men will bow down before Him and say He is Lord.

Jesus left heaven and came to earth. Through the powerful work of God, Jesus was born in human flesh. This is called the *virgin birth* and it means that the baby to be born came to be inside the mother without a father like other children have. How was Jesus born? "The birth of Jesus Christ was like this: Mary His mother had been promised in marriage to Joseph. Before they were married, it was learned that she was to have a baby by the Holy Spirit" (Matthew 1:18). In Isaiah 7:14, long before Jesus was born, it says, "So the Lord Himself will give you a special thing to see: A young women, who had never had a man will give birth to a son. She will give Him the name Immanuel." Matthew 1:20-23 says, "While he was thinking about this, an angel of the Lord came to him in a dream. The angel said, 'Joseph, son of David, do not be afraid to take Mary as your wife. She is to become a mother by the Holy Spirit. A Son will be born to her. You will give Him the name of Jesus because He will save His people from the punishment of their sins.' This happened as the Lord said it would happen through the early preacher. He said, 'The young woman, who has never had a man, will give birth to a Son. They will give Him the name Immanuel. This means God with us' " (Isaiah 7:14). When Jesus was born, He was born like any baby is born. (Luke 2:6-7) But how He came to be inside Mary was a special powerful work of God by the Holy Spirit.

What was Mary, the Mother of Jesus, like? In Luke 1:26-38 we read of an angel telling Mary that God had chosen her from among many women to be the mother of Jesus by the Holy Spirit. She was chosen because of her faith in God. Mary was a woman of honor to be the mother of Jesus, but she was not without sin. Jesus was born without sin because the Holy Spirit was the One Who made Jesus come to be inside Mary. Jesus showed no special favor to His mother. When His mother and brothers came to see Jesus, He acted as if He did not know they were His own family. (Mark 3:31-35) He said, "Whoever does what My Father wants is My brother and My sister and My mother." The Bible tells us that Mary had other children, brothers and sisters of Jesus. Mark 6:3 says, "Is He not a Man Who makes things from wood? Is He not the Son of Mary and the brother of James and Joses and Judas and Simon? Do not His sisters live here with us?"

2. IT IS TRUE THAT JESUS WAS MAN.

The Bible proves to us that Jesus was human in every way.

A. He was born of a woman. (Galatians 4:4)
B. He grew as other people. (Luke 2:52)
C. He became hungry. (Matthew 4:2)
D. He became tired. (John 4:6)
E. He cried. (John 11:35)
F. He died. (Matthew 27:50)

In Philippians 2:6-7 it says, "Jesus has always been as God is. But He did not hold to His rights as God. He put aside everything that belonged to Him and made Himself the same as a servant who is owned by someone. He became human by being born as a man." He did this so He might show man God as well as teach man how to live. He also came to save man from the punishment of sin and to destroy the works of the devil. Because He came, He understands man and makes the way for him to go to God. He proved that God told the truth long ago when He promised that Christ would come.

Jesus Christ was human, a man just like men are today, but it must be understood that He never sinned. He was tempted like man is, but He did not sin. (Hebrews 4:15)

3. IT IS IMPORTANT TO UNDERSTAND THAT JESUS IS THE TRUE GOD-MAN.

There are false teachers who say that He did not come in a human body. (I John 4:2-3; 5:20-21) It is hard to understand how Christ was God and man at the same time. But in His life here on earth He was seen as both.

CHRIST THE GOD-MAN

As a man He was tired, and yet as God He called the tired to Himself for rest.

As a man He was hungry, and yet as God He was "The Bread of Life."

As a man He was thirsty, and yet as God He was "The Water of Life."

As a man He was in pain, and yet as God He healed those who were sick and in pain.

As a man He grew, and yet as God He was from the beginning.

As a man He was tempted, and yet as God He could not be tempted.

As a man He did not know everything, and yet as God He knew all things.

As a man He made Himself less important than the angels, and yet as God He was more important than they were.

As a man He said, "My Father is greater than I," and yet as God He said, "I and My Father are one."

As a man He prayed, and yet as God He answered prayer.

As a man He cried at the grave, and yet as God He called the dead to arise.

As a man He died, and yet as God He is life that lasts forever.

CHRIST'S NAMES

There are over 100 names given to Christ in God's Word. These names give Him honor and put Him high above everything. He is the *Holy One*, *Lord of All*, the *Beginning and the End*. He is *God's only Son*, the *Bright and Morning Star*, and *God's Greatest Gift*. He is called *Wonderful*, *One Who comes along side to help*, *The Father that lasts forever*, the *Prince of Peace*. He is also the *King of the Jews*, the *King of Kings*, the *Lord Strong and Powerful*, the *True God*, and *Lord powerful to save*.

1. THE NAMES AND MEANINGS:

A. Jesus - This name means *to save, to help, to make free*. Matthew 1:21b says, "...You will give Him the name of Jesus because He will save His people from the punishment of their sins."

B. Christ - The name *Christ* means *One Who was chosen to do a special job* or *Anointed One*. It is the same as *Messiah* in the Old Testament. *Anointing* means to pour oil on a person. In Old Testament times, men chosen for a special job had oil poured over them. At first He was called *Jesus the Christ* but later this was changed to *Jesus Christ*. Matthew 16:16 says, "Simon Peter said, 'You are the Christ, the Son of the living God.'"

C. Lord - Lord means that He is leader of the Church. John 9:38 says, "He said, 'I do put my trust in You, Lord.' Then he got down in front of Jesus and worshiped Him."

D. Son of Man - This was a name Jesus called Himself. It means He was God, and yet He became man. Luke 19:10 says, "For the Son of Man came to look for and to save from the punishment of sin those who are lost."

E. Son of David - This name means that God was telling the truth long ago when He promised Christ would come. Matthew 9:27 says, "Jesus went on from there. Two blind men followed Him. They called out, 'Take pity on us, Son of David.'" (Jeremiah 23:5)

F. Immanuel - This was the name given Christ when He was born. It means *God with us*. Matthew 1:23b says, "...They will give Him the name Immanuel. This means God with us." (Isaiah 7:14)

2. HE IS ALSO CALLED:

A. The Word - which means One Who helps men understand.

B. Teacher - As teacher He taught others.

C. Religious Leader (High Priest) - He goes to God for man. Because of Adam all men were born in sin, but Christ made the way for men's sins to be forgiven.

D. Lamb of God - He was perfect and the only one who could take away sins.

3. MANY NAMES TELL OF THE WORK CHRIST DID:

The *One Who cares for others*, the *One Who saves*, the *Head Shepherd*, and the *One Who helps us out of trouble or danger*.

He is *Faithful*, *True*, *Friend of Sinners*, *Gift of God*, the *Light of the World*, and the *One Who says what is right or wrong*.

He can be trusted because He is the *Rock* and *Corner Stone*, the *Way* and the *Door* to heaven. He is *Life*.

CHRIST'S DEATH

The Old Testament told about the death of Christ. In Genesis 3:15 it says that Satan, the snake, would hurt the Special Person to come. Isaiah 53 tells about Christ putting men's sins on Himself. It shows that the Special Person to come would die. Zechariah 13:6-7 says that the Shepherd would die and the sheep would run away. In John 10 Jesus says that He is that Good Shepherd.

The Old Testament showed in different ways how Christ would die. When Adam and Eve were put out of the garden of Eden, God made coats of skin for them which showed that blood had to be given to make a covering. Adam's son Abel killed a lamb as a gift on the altar in worship. This was a picture of how Christ would die for men. This same picture was shown in Exodus 12 where a lamb was killed and the blood put on the door in a special way to show that sins were covered. In Numbers 21, when Moses made a snake from brass and put it up on a pole for the Jews to see, it showed how Christ would be put up on a cross. Christ talked about that in John 3:14-15.

The New Testament teaches that when Christ died, He died in the place of those who had sinned. I Peter 3:18 teaches that Christ never sinned but God put men's sin on Him so men could be made right with God. II Corinthians 5:21 teaches that Christ let Himself be hated and punished instead of man. Galatians 3:13 teaches that Christ died. Christ had to die as man dies if He was to die in man's place for sin. And yet His death was planned before God made the world and man. Even though He died, His death was different. Matthew 27:50 says, "Jesus...gave up His Spirit and died." He wanted to die for men and He was free to do so. When the soldiers came to kill the men on the crosses, they did not break Jesus' legs as they did the other two who were hanging beside Him. They saw He was already dead, but they cut His side to be sure. When blood and water came out, they were sure He was already dead.

Christ died to give His life for men. He did not die because the court said He must be killed. The nails did not hold Jesus on the cross. He gave His life for others that they might have life. Hebrews 10:10-14 says that He gave Himself as a gift to God. Romans 5:6-9 says that He gave His life for all sinners and that His blood paid the punishment for sin. I John 2:2 says that He paid for the sins of the whole world.

Because Jesus died, men can be saved. (Romans 5:9) Men can be saved or set free from the power of sin over them. (John 8:32-36; Romans 6:10) Men can be saved from being guilty of sin. (Romans 5:16-17) He saved men from the fear of sin. (II Timothy 1:7) Christ saved men through love. (John 4:9-10) So His death paid for the punishment of the sins of all men from Adam to the end of the world.

**AS MOSES LIFTED UP THE SNAKE
IN THE DESERT, SO THE SON OF
MAN MUST BE LIFTED UP.**

CHRIST WAS RAISED FROM THE DEAD

The truth that Jesus was raised from the dead after He died on the cross to take the punishment for man's sins is one of the most important truths in the Word of God. Being made right with God depends on this. I Corinthians 15:17 says, "If Christ was not raised from the dead, your faith is worth nothing and you are still living in your sins." A person must believe that Christ was raised from the dead. It has been known for almost two thousand years that Jesus was raised from the dead.

1. *THE TRUTH THAT JESUS WAS RAISED FROM THE DEAD SHOWS MANY THINGS:*

   A. It shows that the Lord Jesus finished His work by dying in man's place taking the punishment for his sin. God received Jesus' death in our place.

   B. It proves and promises to man that some day Christ will come again. Christ's death on the cross to take the punishment for man's sins would be of no use unless He had been raised from the dead. (Romans 4:25; I Corinthians 15:14,17) We know that God received Christ's finished work, because God raised Christ and put Him in a place of power at God's own right side. (Philippians 2:8-10; Hebrews 1:3) If Christ had not been raised from the dead, He could not have gone to Heaven. And if He had not gone to heaven, He could not come again to take man to heaven with Him. (I Thessalonians 4:14-16; Acts 1:3,9-11) But He was raised from the dead!

   C. The truth that Christ was raised from the dead is the greatest truth of all times. (Acts 1:3)

      It is the greatest proof of the Christian way of worship. (Romans 1:4)

      It is the greatest show of God's power. (Ephesians 1:19-20)

      It is the greatest truth of the Good News. (I Corinthians 15:3-4; Romans 10:9-10)

      It is the greatest thing to make man believe and trust. (I Thessalonians 4:14)

      It is the greatest thing to make sure of man's coming pay for trusting in Christ. (I Corinthians 15:20)

It is the greatest thing to make man want to be holy. (Romans 6:9-12)

D. The truth that Jesus was raised from the dead was so proven to the followers of Christ that they did not have any doubt about it. They went out and preached it without being afraid. They preached this even to people who hated them. They were ready to be killed for preaching it. They told those who were listening that they were guilty of killing Jesus, the very One Whom God raised from the dead. (Acts 2:23-24, 36b; 3:13-15) Those people were very angry but they could not say that those things were not true.

E. After His suffering and death, Jesus showed Himself alive to many of His followers. He was seen by them during the 40 days He was on earth after He was raised from the dead. This is proof that He was raised from the dead.

He showed Himself to many people:

(1) To 500 people who saw Him at one time (I Corinthians 15:6)

(2) To Mary Magdalene (John 20:14-16)

(3) To the women returning from the tomb (Matthew 28:8-10)

(4) To Peter (Luke 24:34)

(5) To His followers toward evening (Luke 24:33-36)

(6) To the two followers on the road to Emmaus (Luke 24:13-31)

(7) To all the missionaries eight days later (John 20:26)

(8) To seven by the lake of Tiberias (John 21:1-23)

(9) To James (I Corinthians 15:7)

(10) To the eleven (Matthew 28:16-20)

(11) To Stephen outside Jerusalem (Acts 7:55)

(12) To Paul near the city of Damascus (Acts 9:3-6)

(13) In the House of God (Acts 22:17-21)

(14) To John on the Island of Patmos (Revelation 1:10-19)

2. *THESE PROVE JESUS WAS RAISED FROM THE DEAD:*

   A. The empty grave (Mark 16:5-6)

   B. The grave clothes had not been moved. (Luke 24:12)

   C. The way Christ acted after being raised from the dead. (Luke 24:36-40)

   D. The early church taught it. (Acts 13:29-31)

   E. The changed lives of the followers of Christ. (Acts 13:47)

   F. The change from sinner to Christian in Saul's life. (Acts 9:1-18)

   G. The New Testament proves it.

   H. The way Christ gives new life to a person proves this more than anything else.

3. *THE TRUTH THAT JESUS WAS RAISED FROM THE DEAD WAS TALKED ABOUT.*

   A. Years ago God showed His people what would happen in the future.

      (1) The Old Testament tells about it. (Job 19:25-26; Psalm 16:10)

      (2) Christ Himself tells about it. (Matthew 17:22-23; 20:17-19)

      (3) God completed what He promised in the Holy Writings. Acts 13:32-33a says, "We bring you the Good News about the promise made to our early fathers. God has finished this for us who are their children. He did this by raising Jesus from the dead." Psalm 2:7b says, "You are My Son. Today I have become Your Father." (Luke 24:45-46)

   B. Angels and those who hated Him talked about it. Matthew 28:5-6 says, "The angel said to the women, 'Do not be afraid. I know you are looking for Jesus Who was nailed to the cross. He is not here! He has risen from the dead as He said He would. Come and see the place where the Lord lay.' " (Matthew 28:11-15; Luke 24:1-4,7,23)

4. *SOME OF THE THINGS THAT ARE SHOWN BY CHRIST BEING RAISED FROM THE DEAD:*

A. It shows that God the Father was happy to receive Jesus.

B. It shows that Jesus is God's Only (Unique) Son.

C. It shows how Jesus has won over the devil and death.

D. It shows how Jesus can never be destroyed.

E. It shows how the one who has put his trust in Christ is as if he had never sinned.

F. It shows the power of Christ in the Christian.

G. It gives a living hope to the Christian.

H. It gives the Christian a Religious Leader.

I. It promises the Christian that some day he, too, will be raised from the dead to be with God in Heaven.

J. It shows the world His truth.

K. It tells the world that all men will be raised up some day. They will be told they are guilty and will be punished, or they will receive their pay for living for Christ.

L. It tells the world that someday it will be told it is guilty.

All other religions worship a dead god. Christians are the only people who worship a God Who has won over death and lives today.

CHRIST WAS TAKEN UP TO HEAVEN

1. *THE TRUTH THAT CHRIST HAS BEEN TAKEN UP INTO HEAVEN AND IS AT THE RIGHT SIDE OF THE FATHER AND HAS BEEN GIVEN POWER AND HONOR AND GREATNESS MEANS THAT GOD IS PLEASED WITH THE WORK CHRIST DID TO TAKE AWAY OUR SIN.* (Hebrews 9)

2. *CHRIST'S GOING TO HEAVEN WAS NEEDED.* The giving of power and honor and greatness to Christ was needed:

   A. To finish His work to make men free. (John 20:16-17)

   B. So His followers could do greater works. John 14:12 says, "For sure, I tell you, whoever puts his trust in Me can do the things I am doing. He will do even greater things than these because I am going to the Father."

   C. So the Holy Spirit could be given. John 7:39 says, "Jesus said this about the Holy Spirit Who would come to those who put their trust in Him. The Holy Spirit had not yet been given. Jesus had not yet been raised to the place of honor." (John 16:7)

   D. So what He did could be known over all the world. People over all the world could worship Him. Matthew 28:18-20 says, "Jesus came and said to them, 'All power has been given to Me in heaven and on earth. Go and make followers of all the nations. Baptize them in the name of the Father and of the Son and of the Holy Spirit. Teach them to do all the things I have told you. And I am with you always, even to the end of the world.' "

   E. So His followers, both then and now, would be able to tell others what happened to Jesus after He had died and had been raised from the dead. They saw Him taken up into heaven. Luke 24:50-51 says, "Jesus led them out as far as Bethany. Then He lifted up His hands and prayed that good would come to them. And while He was praying that good would come to them, He went from them and was taken up to heaven and they worshiped Him." (Mark 16:9; Acts 1:9)

3. *CHRIST'S WORK NOW IS PRAYING FOR MEN AS HE SITS AT THE RIGHT SIDE OF GOD IN HEAVEN.* Hebrews 10:12b says, "...He sat down at the right side of God." And Hebrews 7:25 says, "And so Jesus is able, now and forever, to save from the

punishment of sin all who come to God through Him because He lives forever to pray for them." (Isaiah 53:12b; Romans 8:26)

4. *THE TRUTH OF CHRIST BEING TAKEN UP INTO HEAVEN WAS TAUGHT BY:*

A. Peter - Acts 2:32-33 says, "Jesus is this One! God has raised Him up and we have all seen Him. This Jesus has been lifted up to God's right side. The Holy Spirit was promised by the Father. God has given Him to us. That is what you are seeing and hearing now!"

B. Paul - Hebrews 8:1 says, "Now the important thing is this: We have such a Religious Leader Who has made the way for man to go to God. He is the One Who sits at the right side of the All-powerful God in the heavens." (Ephesians 1:20-21; 4:8-10)

C. Stephen - who saw Jesus at God's right side. Acts 7:56 says, "He said, 'See! I see heaven open and the Son of Man standing at the right side of God!' "

D. The Revelation of Jesus Christ as given to John.

CHRIST RECEIVED GREAT HONOR AND A VERY IMPORTANT PLACE

1. *GOD'S WORD TELLS OF CHRIST BEING RAISED FROM THE DEAD AND BEING TAKEN UP TO BE WITH THE FATHER.* He also was raised up to receive great honor and was given a very important place.

   A. His followers, standing on the mountain of Olives, saw Him go up. (Luke 24:50-52) From that time on, they knew He had gone to be with the Father. At the prayer meeting as told in Acts 1, His followers did not expect Him to visit them as he had between the time of His being raised from the dead and going to the Father. They knew He was with the Father.

   B. Right after He went to be with the Father, two angels told His followers of His going. Acts 1:10-11 says, "They were still looking up to heaven, watching Him go. All at once two men dressed in white stood beside them. They said, 'You men of the country of Galilee, why do you stand looking up into heaven? This same Jesus Who was taken from you into heaven will return in the same way you saw Him go up into heaven.' "

   C. As Peter preached to the many people the day the Holy Spirit came on the church, he told of Christ being at the right side of God. Acts 2:33 says, "This Jesus has been lifted up to God's right side. The Holy Spirit was promised by the Father. God has given Him to us. That is what you are seeing and hearing now!"

   D. Just before Stephen was killed, he was allowed to look into heaven, and he said, "See! I see heaven open and the Son of Man standing at the right side of God!" (Acts 7:56)

   E. Paul tells of this. Ephesians 1:20-21 says, "It is the same power that raised Christ from the dead. This place was given to Christ. It is much greater than any king or leader can have. No one else can have this place of honor and power. No one in this world or in the world to come can have such honor and power."

2. *WHAT HAPPENED WHEN CHRIST WAS TAKEN UP TO BE WITH THE FATHER.*

   A. Christ returned to the same place of shining greatness He had before He left. John 17:5 says, "Now Father, honor Me with the honor I had with You before the world was made." (Hebrews 1:8-9; Revelation 5:11-12)

B. After Christ was taken back to heaven, the Holy Spirit came down upon the church. Jesus promised this would happen, and it was one reason He returned to the Father. The Holy Spirit was not given until Christ had been raised to the place of honor. John 16:7 says, "I tell you the truth. It is better for you that I go away. If I do not go, the Helper will not come to you. If I go, I will send Him to you."

C. A new and living way has been opened to man which Christ made possible. Hebrews 10:20-21 says, "We now come to God by the new and living way. Christ made this way for us. He opened the curtain, which was His own body. We have a great Religious Leader over the house of God."

D. Because Christ was raised to the place of honor, man has hope for His return. Acts 2:20-21 says, "The sun will turn dark and the moon will turn to blood before the day of the Lord. His coming will be a great and special day. It will be that whoever calls on the name of the Lord will be saved from the punishment of sin."

The first time He came it was to take care of man's sins. The second time He comes He will take all those who have put their trust in Him to be with Himself. Hebrews 9:28 says, "It is the same with Christ. He gave Himself once to take away the sins of many. When He comes the second time, He will not need to give Himself again for sin. He will save all those who are waiting for Him."

It is from this high place of honor in heaven that Christ will come again. Philippians 3:20-21 says, "But we are citizens of heaven. Christ, the One Who saves from the punishment of sin, will be coming down from heaven again. We are waiting for Him to return. He will change these bodies of ours of the earth and make them new. He will make them like His body of shining greatness. He has the power to do this because He can make all things obey Him."

3. THERE WERE SPECIAL REASONS CHRIST WAS TAKEN UP TO BE WITH THE FATHER.

A. To give great honor to God. John 17:1 says, "When Jesus had said these things, He looked up to heaven and said, 'Father, the time has come! Honor Your Son so Your Son may honor You.' "

B. To make it possible for men to put their trust in Him. I Timothy 3:16 says, "It is important to know the secret of God-like living, which is: Christ came to earth as a Man. He was pure in His Spirit. He was seen by angels. The nations heard about Him. Men everywhere put their trust in Him. He was taken up into heaven."

C. To give gifts to men. Ephesians 4:8 says, "The Holy Writings say, 'When Christ went up to heaven, He took those who were held with Him. He gave gifts to men.' "

D. To give the gift of the Holy Spirit. John 16:7 says, "I tell you the truth. It is better for you that I go away. If I do not go, the Helper will not come to you. If I go, I will send Him to you."

E. To make an end to the sin problem. Hebrews 1:3 says, "The Son shines with the shining greatness of the Father. The Son is as God is in every way. It is the Son Who holds up the whole world by the power of His Word. The Son gave His own life so we could be clean from all sin. After He had done that, He sat down on the right side of God in heaven."

F. So that men might go with complete trust to the very place of God's loving-favor. Hebrews 4:14-16 says, "We have a great Religious Leader Who has made the way for man to go to God. He is Jesus, the Son of God, Who has gone to heaven to be with God. Let us keep our trust in Jesus Christ. Our Religious Leader understands how weak we are. Christ was tempted in every way we are tempted, but He did not sin. Let us go with complete trust to the very place of God's loving-favor. We will receive His loving-kindness and have His loving-favor to help us whenever we need it."

G. To make the way ready for men to go to God. Hebrews 6:19-20 says, "This hope is a safe anchor for our souls. It will never move. This hope goes into the Holiest Place of All behind the curtain of heaven. Jesus has already gone there. He has become our Religious Leader forever and has made the way for man to go to God. He is like Melchizedek." (Genesis 14:18-20)

H. To save from sin. Hebrews 7:25 says, "And so Jesus is able, now and forever, to save from the punishment of sin all who come to God through Him because He lives forever to pray for them." (Romans 8:34; Hebrews 9:24)

I. To be man's Religious Leader. Hebrews 8:1 says, "Now the important thing is this: We have such a Religious Leader Who has made the way for man to go to God. He is the One Who sits at the right side of the All-powerful God in the heavens."

J. To answer anything anyone says against Christians. Romans 8:33-34 says, "Who can say anything against the people God has chosen? It is God Who says they are right with Himself. Who then can say we are guilty? It was Christ Jesus Who died. He was raised from the dead. He is on the right side of God praying to Him for us."

K. To give comfort to men by their coming near to God and holding on to the hope they have. Hebrews 10:22-23 says, "And so let us come near to God with a true heart full of faith. Our hearts must be made clean from guilty feelings and our bodies washed with pure water. Let us hold on to the hope we say we have and not be changed. We can trust God that He will do what He promised."

L. To make it possible for us to do greater things. John 14:12 says, "For sure, I tell you, whoever puts his trust in Me can do the things I am doing. He will do even greater things than these because I am going to the Father."

M. To give men a place with Christ in the heavens. Ephesians 2:6 says, "God raised us up from death when He raised up Christ Jesus. He has given us a place with Christ in the heavens." (John 14:1-3)

N. To give Jesus a name that is greater than any other name, so that everyone will give honor to God the Father. Philippians 2:8-9 says, "After He became a man, He gave up His important place and obeyed by dying on a cross. Because of this, God lifted Jesus high above everything else. He gave Him a name that is greater than any other name."

O. To fill all the world with Himself. Ephesians 4:10 says, "Christ Who went down into the deep also went up far above the heavens. He did this to fill all the world with Himself."

P. So that Christ may have the power to rule. Matthew 28:18 says, "Jesus came and said to them, 'All power has been given to Me in heaven and on earth.' " (Acts 3:20-21; Hebrews 10:12-13; I Peter 3:22)

Q. So that Christ could take His right place as head of the church. Colossians 1:18 says, "Christ is the head of the church which is His body. He is the beginning of all things. He is the first to be raised from the dead. He is to have first place in everything." (Ephesians 4:15-16; 5:30-32)

R. To clean the heavens where Satan worked against God. In Hebrews 9:23-24 it says that the blood of animals was used to clean the house of God which was a picture of the house of God in heaven. But heaven needed something better than the blood of animals. It had to have the blood of Christ.

CHRIST SPOKE FOR GOD

In Deuteronomy 18:18-19 it says, "I will give them a man who speaks for God like you from among their brothers. I will put My words in his mouth. And he will make known to them all that I tell him. He will speak in My name. And I will punish whoever will not listen to him." Long ago one of the early preachers said that Christ would be One Who spoke for God. (Acts 3:22)

The first and most important meaning of the word *prophet* is *one who brings things to light*. It also means *one who tells what will happen*. In the Old Testament the name meant: *one who sees*, or *one who sees what the eye does not see*. The New Testament meaning is, *one who spoke to the people must speak what God wanted spoken*. The meaning in both the Old and New Testaments show that Christ was One Who spoke for God.

1. EARLY PREACHERS SPOKE FOR GOD.

Many think that a prophet is one who tells only what is going to happen in the future. This is not true. The One who spoke for God during the time of Israel was interested in what *was happening* as well as what *was going to happen* in the future. Much of what those who spoke for God said to the people was about what was happening then. But they also said many things that had to do with the future. God used special men He chose in Old Testament times to speak to His people, but He used Christ to speak to His people in the times of the New Testament. Hebrews 1:1-2a says, "Long ago God spoke to our early fathers in many different ways. He spoke through the early preachers. But in these last days He has spoken to us through His Son."

2. CHRIST SPOKE FOR GOD.

Christ was One Who spoke for God from the time He was baptized at the Jordan River until He was nailed to the cross on Calvary. Acts 2:22 says, "Jewish men, listen to what I have to say! You knew Jesus of the town of Nazareth by the powerful works He did. God worked through Jesus while He was with you. You all know this." (Matthew 4:23-25; Luke 4:14-17; Hebrews 9:26-28)

During the time He was on earth, Christ spoke for God about important things in the future:

A. He spoke of His death and about His being raised from the dead. (Matthew 12:39-40; 26:1-2; John 2:19-22)

B. He told what would happen between the time of His death and the time Jerusalem would be destroyed. (Matthew 24:4-14; Mark 13:13; Luke 21:5-24)

C. He told that Jerusalem would be destroyed, and that the Christians would suffer and be killed and be sent everywhere. Also He told about a very sinful man-made god that would stand in the house of God in Jerusalem. (Matthew 24:15-22; Mark 13:14-23; Luke 21:20-28)

D. He told that the Good News would be preached over all the earth. (Matthew 24:14)

E. He told how He would come again to earth. (See Part 9)

3. *IN THE PAST THERE HAVE BEEN "FALSE PREACHERS," AND THERE ARE MANY TODAY. CERTAIN TESTS SHOW IF THEY ARE "FALSE PREACHERS."*

A. Christ gave a test that can be used today. "So you will know them by their fruit" (Matthew 7:20). They try to prove they are ones who speak for God by doing powerful things, but they are false.

B. If early preachers did not preach against sin and tell men to be sorry for their sin and turn from it, they were false. It is the same today.

C. False preachers can be tested by the Word of God. Even if they do all kinds of things that look like powerful works, if what they say is not true to what the Word of God says, they are false.

D. The spirits can be tested. I John 4:13 says, "Dear Christian friends, do not believe every spirit. But test the spirits to see if they are from God for there are many false preachers in the world. You can tell if the spirit is from God in this way: Every spirit that says Jesus Christ has come in a human body is from God. And every spirit that does not say Jesus has come in a human body is not from God. It is the teaching of the false-christ. You have heard that this teaching is coming. It is already here in the world."

CHRIST IS MAN'S RELIGIOUS LEADER WHO HAS MADE THE WAY FOR HIM TO GO TO GOD

A religious leader is one who stands between God and man, and prays to the perfect God for the guilty sinner. The Word of God tells that Christ is our Religious Leader. Hebrews 5:6; 6:20 say, "God says in another part of His Word, 'You will be a Religious Leader forever. You will be like Melchizedek.' " "Jesus has already gone there. He has become our Religious Leader forever and has made the way for man to go to God. He is like Melchizedek." (Psalm 110:4)

THIS IS HOW

THE

JEWISH HIGH PRIEST

DRESSED

1. *CHRIST WAS ALL THE THINGS A RELIGIOUS LEADER HAD TO BE.*

   A. In the Old Way of Worship there were special religious leaders for the Jewish people. These men were called *priests* and they were helpers standing between God and man. In Hebrews 5:1-4 it tells what a religious leader had to be:

      (1) He was chosen from among men.

      (2) He was a helper standing between God and man.

      (3) He gave gifts from the people on the altar in worship to God.

      (4) He gave blood from animals for the sins of the people.

      (5) A Jewish religious leader was just a man himself and weak in many ways. And because he was weak he had to give gifts to God for his own sins as well as for the sins of the people.

      (6) God chose the man for his work.

      (7) Under the Jewish Law, Levi and his sons were the religious leaders, and all religious leaders were to come through that family. (Hebrews 7:11)

B. Jesus Christ is man's Religious Leader Who has made the way for man to go to God. Christ could be man's Religious Leader because:

(1) He was chosen from among men. (Hebrews 5:4-6)

(2) He was more than a helper standing between God and men. He is man's Religious Leader Who made the way for him to go to God.

(3) Christ gave only one gift on the altar and that was Himself. He was a perfect gift and never again does a gift have to be given for man's sins. (Hebrews 9:25-26)

(4) Christ gave His own blood, not the blood of animals like the other religious leaders did.

(5) Jesus Christ, man's Religious Leader, is holy and has no guilt. He has never sinned and is different from sinful men. (Hebrews 7:26) That is why He could give Himself as a gift for all men and not have to give one for Himself like the other religious leaders did.

(6) God chose Christ to be man's Religious Leader. (Hebrews 5:6)

(7) Jesus did not come from the family of Levi but from the family of Judah. Those from the family of Levi were not able to give gifts which would last forever on the altar for the sins of the people. God changed this. Jesus was from another family, and He was the Gift which was perfect in every way. He then could be given for the sins of the people. (Hebrews 7:11-14)

2. CHRIST DID ALL THE THINGS A RELIGIOUS LEADER HAD TO DO.

   A. In the Old Way of Worship the religious leader did three special
      things:

      (1) He killed animals and gave them on the altar as a gift in →
          worship for the people.

      (2) He went inside the Holy Place to pray for the people. The →
          head religious leader went into the Holiest Place of All once a
          year taking the blood of an animal to give for his own sins
          and for the sins of all the people. (Hebrews 9:6-7)

      (3) After he gave the blood in the Holiest Place of All, he came →
          out. Then he gave thanks and prayed that good would come
          to the people.

B. As our great Religious Leader, Christ did all three things:

→
(1) He gave Himself as a gift on the altar. Hebrews 9:14 says, "How much more the blood of Christ will do! He gave Himself as a perfect gift to God through the Spirit that lives forever. Now your heart can be free from the guilty feeling of doing work that is worth nothing. Now you can work for the living God."

→
(2) Christ is now praying to God for man. Romans 8:34 says, "Who then can say we are guilty? It was Christ Jesus Who died. He was raised from the dead. He is on the right side of God praying to Him for us." Hebrews 7:25 says, "And so Jesus is able, now and forever, to save from the punishment of sin all who come to God through Him because He lives forever to pray for them."

→
(3) When Christ comes to earth the second time, He will take with Him all those who have put their trust in Him. Hebrews 9:28 says, "It is the same with Christ. He gave Himself once to take away the sins of many. When He comes the second time He will not need to give Himself again for sin. He will save all those who are waiting for Him." (I Thessalonians 4:16; I Peter 1:5; Revelation 20:4)

Hebrews 4:15-16 says, "Our Religious Leader understands how weak we are. Christ was tempted in every way we are tempted, but He did not sin. Let us go with complete trust to the very place of God's loving-favor. We will receive His loving-kindness and have His loving-favor to help us whenever we need it."

CHRIST'S DEATH IN MAN'S PLACE

The word *atonement* means the work of Christ when He gave Himself to pay for the sins of guilty sinners to satisfy God Who, being holy, hates sin. This was done by Christ's holy life, His death on the cross in place of the sinner, His being raised from the dead, and His receiving great honor in heaven.

The word *atonement* is not found in most translations of the Bible, but it is often used when speaking about the work of Christ. God gave what was needed to make peace between the sinner and Himself. Man did not make a way, God took care of it for man. Man could never work his way up to God. God came down to man to take care of his need.

1. THE TEACHING OF CHRIST'S DEATH IN OUR PLACE IS IMPORTANT BOTH IN HEAVEN AND ON EARTH.

A. It is one of the things the angels wanted to know about. I Peter 1:11-12 says, "The early preachers wondered at what time or to what person this would happen. The Spirit of Christ in them was talking to them and told them to write about how Christ would suffer and about His shining greatness later on. They knew these would not happen during the time they lived but while you are living many years later. These are the very things that were told to you by those who preached the Good News. The Holy Spirit Who was sent from heaven gave them power and they told of things that even the angels would like to know about."

B. Christ Himself said this was the most important part of His work. Mark 10:45 says, "For the Son of Man did not come to be cared for. He came to care for others. He came to give His life so that many could be bought by His blood and be made free from sin."

C. Christ knew this teaching would attract men to Him. John 12:32 says, "And when I am lifted up from the earth, I will attract all people toward me."

D. The Holy Writings tell much about Christ giving Himself for sinners. The death of Christ is spoken of more than 175 times in the New Testament. Paul speaks of it often, as do other New Testament writers.

God's loving-favor to man means love in action. Even before man knew what his need was, God took care of it. Romans 4:25; 5:6 say, "Jesus died for our sins. He was raised from the dead to make us right with God." "We were weak and could not help ourselves. Then Christ came at the right time and gave His life for all sinners."

There are many religions that tell men they can go to God after they become good. This is not true. God's Word says that He makes men know they are sinners and gives them a desire to be free from sin. False ways of worship try to take men to God. But men, being sinners, are not ready to stand before God. The true way of worship is possible because God became man, and in doing so, He made the way for men to go to Himself.

2. FOUR REASONS WHY CHRIST HAD TO DIE IN MAN'S PLACE:

A. God is holy. When man first sinned, this was not pleasing to God. God, being holy, hates sin. But God is not only holy, He is also love. He loved man, not because man had no sin, but while man was a sinner. Romans 5:8 says, "But God showed His love to us. While we were still sinners, Christ died for us."

Even if a sinner stopped doing bad things, it would not change his desires and thoughts. The sinner would still be at war with God. God is holy and He cannot forget these things. He cannot love the sin, but He does love the sinner. The answer to this problem was in the death of Christ, God's own Son. Christ took upon Himself the punishment that should have been given to the sinner. Because God is holy, something had to be done. His Son did something about it. He died in our place.

B. The Laws of God were broken so a gift had to be given to God. Only a perfect gift could be given on the altar in worship. Christ was that Perfect Gift. He is the only One Who could be a gift on the altar for the sinner.

C. When a man sins, his heart tells him that he is guilty. Peace and rest cannot come until the sinner knows that his sin is forgiven. When the sinner knows that Christ took his punishment upon Himself, peace and rest come to him. Romans 5:1 says, "Now that we have been made right with God by putting our trust in Him, we have peace with Him. It is because of what our Lord Jesus Christ did for us."

D. The lost sinner knows he is lost. His heart tells him that he is guilty. When the Holy Spirit speaks to him through the Word of God, he sees how much he has broken God's Law, and how lost he is. If man is to be saved from sin, the One Who never sinned must find him and save him. This is just what Christ did. Luke

19:10 says, "For the Son of Man came to look for and to save
from the punishment of sin those who are lost."

3. *WHAT CHRIST DID WHEN HE DIED IN OUR PLACE WAS*
   IMPORTANT BECAUSE:

   A. It was the most important reason for Christ being born. (Mat-
      thew 1:21)

   B. It has an important place in the first four books of the New
      Testament. Each of the four writers of these books told many
      things. But with great care they told about the life and death of
      Christ. Of the twenty-one chapters in the book of John, ten of
      them tell of the things leading to Christ's death and of His being
      raised from the dead.

   C. Christ came to earth to show that what God had promised to the
      early fathers was true. Through the Old Way of Worship, God at
      different times had promised to send His Son into the world.
      (Romans 15:8; II Timothy 1:9; II Peter 1:10-12)

   D. Christ became a man so He could make His Father known. "No
      man has ever seen God. But Christ has made God known to us"
      (John 1:18b). Jesus taught us many things about God the Father.
      He taught us that God the Father loves us. John 16:27 says,
      "...because the Father loves you. He loves you because you love
      Me and believe that I came from the Father."

   E. Christ came to be the Religious Leader Who made the way for
      man to go to God. In the book of Hebrews it teaches us that the
      head Jewish religious leaders were taken from among men so that
      they would act in the place of men. (Hebrews 5:1-2) In Hebrews
      5:4-5 it also tells us that in the same way, Christ was taken from
      among men so He could act in the place of men before God.

      Hebrews 2:17-18 says, "So Jesus had to become like His brothers
      in every way. He had to be one of us to be our Religious Leader
      to go between God and us. He had loving-pity on us and He was
      faithful. He gave Himself as a gift to die on a cross for our sins so
      that God would not hold these sins against us any longer.
      Because Jesus was tempted as we are and suffered as we do, He
      understands us and He is able to help us when we are tempted."

      I Corinthians 10:13 says, "You have never been tempted to sin in
      any different way than other people. God is faithful. He will not
      allow you to be tempted more than you can take. But when you
      are tempted, He will make a way for you to keep from falling
      into sin."

F. Christ died so that He could destroy sin. "He gave Himself to destroy sin" (Hebrews 9:26b). (Mark 10:45b; John 3-5; II Corinthians 5:21; Romans 5:21; 6:12-18; Hebrews 2:8)

G. Christ died to destroy the works of the devil. "But the Son of God came to destroy the works of the devil" (I John 3:8b). (John 12:31; Hebrews 2:14-15; Revelation 20:10a)

H. Christ died to make ready for the time He will come again. "...when He comes the second time, He will not need to give Himself again for sin" (Hebrews 9:28). (Romans 8:18-25; Revelation 21:27)

I. Christ died so those who have put their trust in Him might have life, "a great full life." (John 10:10b; Romans 5:1; 8:1-3; Hebrews 2:14-15; I John 4:10)

4. WHO DID CHRIST DIE FOR?

I Timothy 2:6 says, "He gave His life for all men so they could go free and not be held by the power of sin..." Hebrews 2:9 says, "But we do see Jesus. For a little while He took a place that was not as important as the angels. But God had loving-favor for everyone. He had Jesus suffer death on a cross, for all of us. Then, because of Christ's death on a cross, God gave Him the prize of honor and shining greatness." I John 2:2 says, "He paid for our sins with His own blood. He did not pay for ours only, but for the sins of the whole world."

But the *atonement* is good only for those who take God's Gift. God loves all sinners, but only those who put their trust in Him will be saved from sin. Romans 10:9 says, "If you say with your mouth that Jesus is Lord, and believe in your heart that God raised Him from the dead, you will be saved from the punishment of sin."

Christ divided time. All things before Christ were done looking forward to Christ's birth. All the things that happened after Christ's death look back to what He did when He died on the cross. Christ said, "No one can have greater love than to give his life for his friends" (John 15:13). Men have given their lives for their friends, but Christ had great love for those who were not even His friends.

Romans 5:8 says, "But God showed His love to us. While we were still sinners, Christ died for us." He came from heaven to the cross and bowed His head in a death of shame and pain. His was the greatest gift that was ever given to men. "For God so loved the world that He gave His only Son. Whoever puts his trust in God's Son will not be lost, but will have life that lasts forever" (John 3:16).

THERE IS SOMETHING MAN MUST DO

Man knows he is not right with God. He knows he is a sinner and is lost. There is nothing man can do in his own power to become right with God.

1. MAN MUST BELIEVE THERE IS A GOD

In Hebrews 11:6 it says, "...Anyone who comes to God must believe that He is..." When a man believes, he is sure of a truth and accepts it as truth. It is not only important that he believes God is, but also that he believes Christ died to save sinners, and was raised up from the grave to be the living One Who saves from the punishment of sin. (Isaiah 53:1-12; I Corinthians 15:3-4)

But believing, alone, is not enough. In James 2:19 it says, "You believe there is one God. That is good! But even the demons believe that, and because they do, they shake." The demons of Satan believe (that is, they know of the truth and accept it as truth) but they do no more than believe.

2. MAN MUST HAVE FAITH IN GOD.

Hebrews 11:6a says, "A man cannot please God unless he has faith." In Hebrews 11:1 it tells what faith is. "Now faith is being sure we will get what we hope for. It is being sure of what we cannot see." If a man only believes that there is a God, but does not have faith in Him, then he is not saved from the punishment of his sin.

3. MAN MUST TRUST CHRIST TO SAVE HIM FROM HIS SIN.

Trust is the action that goes along with believing and faith. Trust is different than believing or faith. This trust means to put one's self into the care of the One in Whom he has faith.

4. MAN MUST BE SORRY FOR HIS SINS AND TURN FROM THEM.

This is called *repentance*. It is a change of one's heart and mind that will lead to a change in what he will do.

It is possible to feel sorry because of sin, and yet have no desire to stop. The rich man in hell cried out for loving-kindness. He was full of sorrow but it was too late to be sorry for his sins and turn from them.

Luke 16:24-28 says, "He cried out and said, 'Father Abraham, take pity on me. Send Lazarus. Let him put the end of his finger in water and cool my tongue. I am in much pain in this fire.' Abraham said, 'My son, do not forget that when you were living you had your good things. Lazarus had bad things. Now he is well cared for. You are in pain. And more than all this, there is a big deep place between us. No one from here can go there even if he wanted to go. No one can come from there.' Then the rich man said, 'Father, then I beg you to send Lazarus to my father's house. I have five brothers. Let him tell them of these things, or they will come to this place of much pain also.' "

Those who are not sorry for their sins now and will not turn from them will some day cry and grind their teeth. They will have sorrow, but it is not the same as being sorry now.

5. *MAN MUST TELL HIS SINS TO GOD, AND TELL OF GOD TO OTHER MEN.*

   A. To God - God wants man to tell his sins to Him so He can forgive him. I John 1:9 says, "If we tell Him our sins, He is faithful and we can depend on Him to forgive our sins. He will make our lives clean from all sin."

   B. To men - Men who have put their trust in Christ as the One Who saves must tell other men what has been done in their lives. Romans 10:10b says, "...We tell with our mouth how we were saved from the punishment of sin."

THERE ARE SOME THINGS THAT HAPPEN WHEN A MAN PUTS HIS TRUST IN CHRIST

1. HE BECOMES A NEW PERSON.

II Corinthians 5:17 says, "For if a man belongs to Christ, he is a new person. The old life is gone. New life has begun."

2. HE IS GIVEN A NEW LIFE.

Titus 3:4-5 says, "But God, the One Who saves, showed how kind He was and how He loved us by saving us from the punishment of sin. It was not because we worked to be right with God. It was because of His loving-kindness that He washed our sins away. At the same time He gave us new life when the Holy Spirit came into our lives."

3. HE IS MADE RIGHT WITH GOD.

Romans 3:24 says, "Anyone can be made right with God by the free gift of His loving-favor. It is Jesus Christ Who bought them with His blood and made them free from their sins." (Romans 4:24)

4. HE IS SAVED FROM THE PUNISHMENT OF SIN, AND ITS GUILT AND BLAME.

Romans 5:9 says, "Now that we have been saved from the punishment of sin by the blood of Christ, He will save us from God's anger also." (Ephesians 2:5,8)

5. HE IS BOUGHT AND MADE FREE FROM SIN.

Ephesians 1:7 says, "Because of the blood of Christ, we are bought and made free from the punishment of sin. And because of His blood, our sins are forgiven. His loving-favor to us is so rich." (I Peter 1:19)

6. HE IS IN GOD'S FAMILY.

Ephesians 2:19 says, "From now on you are not strangers and people who are not citizens. You are citizens together with those who belong to God. You belong in God's family." (Romans 8:15, 23; 9:4; II Corinthians 6:17-18; Galatians 3:26; 4:4-7; Ephesians 1:4-11; I John 3:2)

7. HE IS BAPTIZED INTO THE BODY OF CHRIST BY THE HOLY SPIRIT.

I Corinthians 12:13 says, "It is the same way with us. Jews or those who are not Jews, men who are owned by someone or men who are free to do what they want to do, have all been baptized into the one body by the same Holy Spirit. We have all received the one Spirit."

8. HE IS A PART OF GOD'S BUILDING.

Ephesians 2:22 says, "You are also being put together as a part of this building because God lives in you by His Spirit."

9. HE IS GIVEN A PLACE WITH CHRIST IN HEAVEN.

Ephesians 2:6 says, "God raised us up from death when He raised up Christ Jesus. He has given us a place with Christ in the heavens."

10. HE IS MARKED FOR GOD BY THE HOLY SPIRIT.

Ephesians 1:13 says, "The truth is the Good News. When you heard the truth, you put your trust in Christ. Then God marked you by giving you His Holy Spirit as a promise."

11. HE IS SET APART FOR GOD-LIKE LIVING.

I Corinthians 6:11 says, "Some of you were like that. But now your sins are washed away. You were set apart for God-like living to do His work. You were made right with God through our Lord Jesus Christ by the Spirit of our God."

12. HE RECEIVES GIFTS FROM THE HOLY SPIRIT.

I Corinthians 12:4-11 says, "There are different kinds of gifts. But it is the same Holy Spirit Who gives them. There are different kinds of work to be done for Him. But the work is for the same Lord. There are different ways of doing His work. But it is the same God who uses all these ways in all people. The Holy Spirit works in each person in one way or another for the good of all. One person is given the gift of teaching words of wisdom. Another person is given the gift of teaching what he has learned and knows. These gifts are by the same Holy Spirit. One person receives the gift of faith. Another person receives the gifts of healing. These gifts are given by the same Holy Spirit. One person is given the gift of doing powerful works. Another person is given the gift of speaking God's Word. Another person is given the gift of speaking in special sounds. Another person is given the gift of telling what these special sounds mean. But it is the same Holy Spirit, the Spirit of God, Who does all these things. He gives to each person as He wants to give." (Romans 12:5-8; Ephesians 4:11-12)

PART 4

WHAT THE WORD OF GOD TEACHES ABOUT THE HOLY SPIRIT

[*Pneumatology*]

The Person Of The Holy Spirit

The Work Of The Holy Spirit

WHO THE HOLY SPIRIT IS

The Holy Spirit is part of the Three-in-one God.

1. THE HOLY SPIRIT IS GOD.

A. Acts 5:3-4 says, "Peter said to Ananias, 'Why did you let Satan fill your heart? He made you lie to the Holy Spirit...You have lied to God, not to men.' " (I Corinthians 3:16-17)

B. He is as God is.

(1) He has all power. Luke 1:35 says, "The Holy Spirit will come on you. The power of the Most High will cover you." (Romans 15:13-19)

(2) He knows all things. I Corinthians 2:10 says, "It is the Holy Spirit Who Looks into all things, even the secrets of God." (Luke 2:25-32)

(3) He is everywhere. Psalm 139:7-10 says, "Where can I go from Your Spirit? Or where can I run away from where You are? If I go up to heaven, You are there! If I make my bed in the place of the dead, You are there! If I take the wings of the morning or live in the farthest part of the sea, even there Your hand will lead me and Your right hand will hold me."

(4) He is alive forever. Hebrews 9:14b says, "...He gave Himself as a perfect gift to God through the Spirit that lives forever."

This is also shown by Christ when He told His followers to preach the Good News everywhere. He said to baptize in the name of all three of the Three-in-one God. Matthew 28:18-20 says, "Jesus came and said to them, 'All power has been given to Me in heaven and on earth. Go and make followers of all the nations. Baptize them in the name of the Father and of the Son and of the Holy Spirit. Teach them to do all the things I have told you. And I am with you always, even to the end of the world.' "

To end a letter, the missionaries would often write, "May you have loving-favor from our Lord Jesus Christ. May you have the love of God. May you be joined together by the Holy Spirit." The early missionaries spoke of Him as God.

The Revelation of Jesus Christ to John tells of the Holy Spirit as Someone Who should be listened to, "Then listen to what the Spirit says to the churches" Revelation 3:22b).

The work of the church is done by people through gifts given by the Holy Spirit. "There are different kinds of gifts. But it is the same Holy Spirit Who gives them...But it is the same God Who uses all these ways in all people" (I Corinthians 12:4-6). God and the Holy Spirit are spoken of as One in the Bible.

NAMES OF THE HOLY SPIRIT

It is hard for people to understand or learn about someone they cannot touch with their hands or see with their eyes. This is the way with the Holy Spirit. He is part of the Three-in-one God, but He cannot be touched or seen. The Holy Spirit should not be called *It*. The Holy Spirit is a person, and should be called *He* just as God the Father and Christ is a person, and should be called *He*. He has the power to know, the power to feel, and the power to choose. In John 14:16; 16:7 He is called the Helper, or *One called along side to help*. Such a name can be given only to a person. The Holy Spirit took Jesus' place when Jesus left the earth. Such a work as the Holy Spirit does can be done only by a person.

It is important to learn some of the names of the Holy Spirit and then He can be understood better.

1. NAMES OF THE HOLY SPIRIT:

A. The Holy Spirit - Matthew 4:1 says, "Jesus was led by the Holy Spirit to the desert. There He was tempted by the devil."

B. The Spirit of Truth - John 14:17 says, "He is the Spirit of Truth. The world cannot receive Him. It does not see Him or know Him. You know Him because He lives with you and will be in you."

C. The Helper - John 14:26 says, "The Helper is the Holy Spirit. The Father will send Him in My place. He will teach you everything and help you remember everything I have told you."

D. God's Spirit - Romans 8:9 says, "But you are not doing what your sinful old selves want you to do. You are doing what the Holy Spirit tells you to do, if you have God's Spirit living in you. No one belongs to Christ if he does not have Christ's Spirit in him."

E. Christ's Spirit - (Romans 8:9)

F. The Spirit of the Living God - II Corinthians 3:3 says, "You are as a letter from Christ written by us. You are not written as other letters are written with ink on pieces of stone. You are written in human hearts by the Spirit of the Living God."

G. His Holy Spirit of promise - Ephesians 1:13 says, "The truth is the Good News. When you heard the truth, you put your trust in Christ. Then God marked you by giving you His Holy Spirit as a promise."

H. His Spirit - Ephesians 1:17 says, "I pray that the great God and Father of our Lord Jesus Christ may give you the wisdom of His Spirit. Then you will be able to understand the secrets about Him as you know Him better."

I. God's Holy Spirit - Ephesians 4:30 says, "Do not make God's Holy Spirit have sorrow for the way you live. The Holy Spirit has put a mark on you for the day you will be set free.

J. The Spirit that lives forever - Hebrews 9:14 says, "How much more the blood of Christ will do! He gave Himself as a perfect gift to God through the Spirit that lives forever. Now your heart can be free from the guilty feeling of doing work that is worth nothing. Now you can work for the living God."

K. The Spirit - Revelation 2:7, 11, 29 say, "You have ears! Then listen to what the Spirit says to the churches. I will give the fruit of the tree of life in the garden of God to everyone who has power and wins." "You have ears! Then listen to what the Spirit says to the churches. The person who has power and wins will not be hurt by the second death!" "You have ears! Then listen to what the Spirit says to the churches!"

WHAT THE HOLY SPIRIT IS LIKE

Men cannot see the Holy Spirit as they saw Christ when He was on earth. Just as no one has seen God the Father at anytime, no one has seen the Holy Spirit. The Bible gives different pictures that show what the Holy Spirit is like.

1. WHAT THE HOLY SPIRIT IS LIKE:

A. He is like a dove. John 1:32 says, "I saw the Holy Spirit come down on Jesus as a dove from heaven. The Holy Spirit stayed on Him."

B. He is like water. In John 7:38 Jesus says, "The Holy Writings say that rivers of living water will flow from the heart of the one who puts his trust in Me." John 7:39 says, "Jesus said this about the Holy Spirit Who would come to those who put their trust in Him. The Holy Spirit had not yet been given. Jesus had not yet been raised to the place of honor." What water means to thirsty lips or rain to dry ground, the Holy Spirit means to a Christian. Nothing makes thirst end like water and nothing makes the heart as happy as the Holy Spirit.

C. He is like oil. I Samuel 16:13 says, "Then Samuel took the horn of oil and poured the oil on him in front of his brothers. The Spirit of the Lord came upon David with strength from that day on." When people poured oil over someone it was a way to show that God was covering them with Himself. When a person was being set apart to be a religious leader, oil was put first on his ear so he would always hear God's Word. Then oil was put on his thumb so everything he did would bring shining greatness to God. And then oil was put on his toe because he was to walk with God. These things are what the Holy Spirit does in the life of a Christian.

D. He is like wind. John 3:8 says, "The wind blows where it wants to and you hear its sound. You do not know where it comes from or where it goes. It is the same with everyone who is born of the Spirit of God." When the Holy Spirit came down upon the followers after Jesus went to heaven, it says in Acts 2:2, "All at once there was a sound from heaven like a powerful wind. It filled the house where they were sitting." You cannot see wind, yet you can feel it and can see its power. It is this way with the Holy Spirit.

E. He is like fire. Acts 2:3 says, "Then they saw tongues which were divided that looked like fire. These came down on each one of them." After Jesus went to heaven, the Holy Spirit was sent to come on His followers. Tongues of fire were seen above their heads. Fire burns away waste and makes things clean. Burning gives heat. It also gives light to see, and can give power and strength to things being made. All these are pictures of the Holy Spirit. He takes the bad out of men's lives and makes them clean. He makes their hearts hungry for God and gives them a desire to love God. He also tests them to see if they are faithful to God.

F. He is like clothing. Judges 6:34a says, "But the Spirit of the Lord came upon Gideon." The word *came* means *putting on clothes*. He covered Gideon. The Holy Spirit covers His people.

HOW THE HOLY SPIRIT CAN BE HURT

It must be remembered that the Holy Spirit is a person, just as the Son and the Father are persons. With this in mind, it is easier to understand that the Holy Spirit can be hurt. It is because of His loving-kindness that He can be hurt.

1. HOW THE HOLY SPIRIT CAN BE HURT BY THOSE WHO ARE NOT CHRISTIANS:

People who have not put their trust in Jesus Christ can hurt the Holy Spirit. He wants to work in their lives so they will put their trust in Jesus Christ. Here are three ways people who are not Christians can hurt the Holy Spirit when He tries to show them the truth about sin.

A. The Holy Spirit can be hurt by those who have hearts that will not listen to Him. Acts 7:51 says, "You have hard hearts and ears that will not listen to me! You are always working against the Holy Spirit. Your early fathers did. You do too." It is sad to see how the Holy Spirit is hurt when He is working in the lives of people to bring them to see their need of putting their trust in Jesus Christ.

B. The Holy Spirit is hurt when He is showing the sinner God's loving-favor, but is laughed at.

C. The Holy Spirit can be hurt if bad words are spoken against Him. The person who does this will not be forgiven. Matthew 12:31-32 says, "I tell you, every sin and every bad word men speak against God will be forgiven, but bad words spoken against the Holy Spirit will not be forgiven. Whoever speaks a word against the Son of Man will be forgiven, but whoever speaks against the Holy Spirit will not be forgiven in this life or in the life to come."

This *could* mean that anyone who says bad words against the special birth of Christ, or says that God's Word is not true, or says that God did not make the world is saying bad words against the Holy Spirit. The Holy Spirit is the One Who gave the words to the men of God who wrote them down. The Holy Spirit is the One Who came upon Mary so that she could give birth to Jesus. The Holy Spirit is the One Who made the world, as it is written in the first chapters of Genesis. To say things against what the Holy Spirit has done is hurting Him. The Bible says that a person who speaks against the Holy Spirit will never be forgiven.

2. HOW THE HOLY SPIRIT CAN BE HURT BY CHRISTIANS:

A. The Holy Spirit lives in the Christian to be his Helper. He wants to work in the Christian's life to make him free from his sinful old self. In Galatians 5:16-17 it says, "I say this to you: Let the Holy Spirit lead you in each step. Then you will not please your sinful old selves. The things our old selves want to do are against what the Holy Spirit wants. The Holy Spirit does not agree with what our sinful old selves want. These two are against each other. So you cannot do what you want to do." (Also read verses 19-21 because they tell what the old sinful self is like.)

B. In Ephesians 4:30 it shows how the Christian can hurt the Holy Spirit and cause Him to have sorrow for the way he lives. It says, "Do not make God's Holy Spirit have sorrow for the way you live. The Holy Spirit has put a mark on you for the day you will be set free."

C. The Christian can stop the work of the Holy Spirit in his life if he stops obeying Him. Acts 5:32b says, "...God gives His Spirit to those who obey Him." I Thessalonians 5:19 says, "Do not try to stop the work of the Holy Spirit."

THE HOLY SPIRIT'S WORK BEFORE THE CHURCH BEGAN

1. *THE HOLY SPIRIT, AS PART OF THE THREE-IN-ONE GOD, HAS ALWAYS BEEN AND ALWAYS WILL BE.*

2. *EACH OF THE THREE-IN-ONE GOD HAD A PART OF THE WORK IN MAKING THE WORLD AND IN KEEPING IT GOING.*

   A. The Father - Genesis 1:1 says, "In the beginning God made from nothing the heavens and the earth."

   B. Jesus Christ - Colossians 1:16 says, "Christ made everything in the heavens and on the earth. He made everything that is seen and things that are not seen. He made all the powers of heaven. Everything was made by Him and for Him."

   C. The Holy Spirit - Genesis 1:2b says, "And the Spirit of God was moving over the top of the waters." Job 33:4 says, "The Spirit of God has made me. And the breath of the All-powerful gives me life."

3. *THE WORK OF THE HOLY SPIRIT IS TO KEEP ALL LIVING THINGS GOING AS THEY WERE PLANNED.*

   He brings beauty to the world and keeps everything in its right place. Job 26:13a says, "By His breath the heavens are made beautiful." The Holy Spirit had a part in placing and keeping the heavens in their right place. The work of the Holy Spirit is to give life to man. The Holy Spirit has an important work in the whole world today.

   A. He keeps making the face of the earth new. (Psalm 104:30)

   B. He keeps plant life growing. (Psalm 104:10-13)

   C. He keeps animal and human life growing. (Job 33:4; Psalm 104:11, 12, 14, 21, 27)

4. *THE HOLY SPIRIT DID CERTAIN THINGS DURING THE OLD WAY OF WORSHIP.*

   A. He had a part in telling the early preachers where and what they should preach. (II Peter 1:19-21)

B. He had a part in telling the future. He was the One Who brought the Word of God to the minds of the early preachers who wrote about the future. (I Peter 1:10-12)

5. THE HOLY SPIRIT GAVE THE HOLY WRITINGS TO MAN.

(See Part 2, Chapter 11; II Samuel 23:2; Isaiah 1:2; Jeremiah 1:4; Ezekiel 1:3; II Peter 1:20-21)

6. THE HOLY SPIRIT IS THE ONE WHO TELLS WHAT THE HOLY WRITINGS MEAN.

In I Corinthians 2:9-14 it says, "The Holy Writings say, 'No eye has ever seen or no ear has ever heard or no mind has ever thought of the wonderful things God has made ready for those who love Him.' God has shown these things to us through His Holy Spirit. It is the Holy Spirit Who looks into all things, even the secrets of God, and shows them to us. Who can know the things about a man, except a man's own spirit that is in him? It is the same with God. Who can understand Him except the Holy Spirit? We have not received the spirit of the world. God has given us His Holy Spirit that we may know about the things given to us by Him. We speak about these things also. We do not use words of man's wisdom. We use words given to us by the Holy Spirit. We use these words to tell what the Holy Spirit wants to say to those who put their trust in Him. But the person who is not a Christian does not understand these words from the Holy Spirit. He thinks they are foolish. He cannot understand them because he does not have the Holy Spirit to help him understand." (John 16:13-15; Ephesians 1:17)

7. THERE ARE SOME SPECIAL THINGS THE HOLY SPIRIT DID WHILE CHRIST WAS ON EARTH.

A. He had an important part in bringing Christ to earth and in making Christ able to do His work here on earth. John 3:34b says, "God gives Him all of His Spirit." (Matthew 1:18b; Luke 1:35)

B. He was there when Jesus was baptized in the Jordan River, and He came down from heaven like a dove. (Luke 3:22; John 1:32)

C. He was with Christ when He was tested by the devil in the desert. (Luke 4:1-13)

D. He was there when God showed that He had put His hand on Christ and had chosen Him. (Isaiah 61:1; Luke 4:16-21)

E. He was the One Who taught men when Christ spoke to them. (John 3:3-6; 14:25-26)

F. His power was able to heal people. (Acts 10:38)

G. He showed His power in Christ's life. (Luke 4:14-15)

H. He had a part in raising Christ from the dead. Romans 8:11 says, "The Holy Spirit raised Jesus from the dead. If the same Holy Spirit lives in you, He will give life to your bodies in the same way."

I. He told men they were guilty of their sins. The followers of Jesus knew they were guilty of sins and they trusted Christ. The Holy Spirit must have told them this.

The most important thing to remember is that the Holy Spirit, as one part of the Three-in-one God, has always been and always will be. The Holy Spirit was doing things before Christ came in the flesh to this earth. The Holy Spirit did things during the time Christ was on earth. The Holy Spirit is doing things today, and the Holy Spirit will do things forever.

THE WORK OF THE HOLY SPIRIT IN PEOPLE

1. THE WORK OF THE HOLY SPIRIT IN SINNERS

A. He does not live in the sinner. (John 14:17)

B. He works with people to make them want to put their trust in Christ. (John 16:6-11) He will not always do this. John 6:44 says, "The Father sent Me. No man can come to Me unless the Father gives him the desire to come to Me. Then I will raise him to life on the last day."

C. He shows the world about sin. John 16:9 says, "He will show the world about sin, because they do not put their trust in Me."

D. He tells sinners not to turn away from God, but asks them to come to God. Hebrews 3:7-10 says, "The Holy Spirit says, 'If you hear His voice today, do not let your hearts become hard as your early fathers did when they turned against Me. It was at that time in the desert when they put Me to the test. Your early fathers tempted Me and tried Me. They saw the work I did for forty years. For this reason, I was angry with the people of this day. And I said to them, "They always think wrong thoughts. They have never understood what I have tried to do for them." ' "

E. He makes God's Word alive. John 6:63 says, "It is the Spirit that gives life. The flesh is of no help. The words I speak to you are spirit and life."

F. He tells sinners the truth that Jesus is the One Who saves from sin. Acts 5:30-32 says, "The God of our early fathers raised up Jesus, the One you killed and nailed to a cross. God raised this Man to His own right side as a leader and as the One Who saves. He makes it possible for the Jews to be sorry for their sins. Then they can turn from them and be forgiven. We have seen these things and are telling about them. The Holy Spirit makes these things known also. God gives His Spirit to those who obey Him."

G. He gives power to the Word of God as it is preached to sinners. I Corinthians 2:4, 13 says, "What I had to say when I preached was not in big sounding words of man's wisdom. But it was given in the power of the Holy Spirit." "We speak about these things also. We do not use words of man's wisdom. We use words given to us by the Holy Spirit. We use these words to tell what the Holy Spirit wants to say to those who put their trust in Him." (I Thessalonians 1:5)

H. He is the *Spirit of Life* making men free from the power of sin and death. Romans 8:2 says, "The power of the Holy Spirit has made me free from the power of sin and death. This power is mine because I belong to Christ Jesus."

I. He takes away sin and gives new life. Titus 3:5 says, "...by saving us from the punishment of sin. It was not because we worked to be right with God. It was because of His loving-kindness that He washed our sins away. At the same time He gave us new life when the Holy Spirit came into our lives."

2. THE WORK OF THE HOLY SPIRIT IN CHRISTIANS

A. The Holy Spirit gives new life. II Corinthians 5:17 says, "For if a man belongs to Christ, he is a new person. The old life is gone. New life has begun." (John 3:5-6; I Corinthians 6:11; Titus 3:5)

B. The Holy Spirit sets the believer free from sin and death. Romans 8:2 says, "The power of the Holy Spirit has made me free from the power of sin and death. This power is mine because I belong to Christ Jesus."

C. The Holy Spirit makes the Christian's heart strong. Ephesians 3:16 says, "I pray that because of the riches of His shining greatness, He will make you strong with power in your hearts through the Holy Spirit."

D. The Holy Spirit leads Christians to a life set apart for God. Romans 8:14 says, "All those who are led by the Holy Spirit are sons of God."

E. The Holy Spirit tells Christians that they are children of God. Romans 8:16 says, "For the Holy Spirit speaks to us and tells our spirit that we are children of God."

F. The Holy Spirit brings fruit in the life of the Christian. Galatians 5:22-23 says, "But the fruit that comes from having the Holy Spirit in our lives is: love, joy, peace, not giving up, being kind, being good, having faith, being gentle, and being the boss over our own desires. The Jewish Law is not against these things."

G. The Holy Spirit leads the Christian into all truth. John 16:13 says, "The Holy Spirit is coming. He will lead you into all truth.

He will not speak His own words. He will speak what He hears.
He will tell you of things to come." (I John 2:20)

H. The Holy Spirit helps the Christians to remember things Christ
said. John 14:26 says, "The Helper is the Holy Spirit. The Father
will send Him in My place. He will teach you everything and
help you remember everything I have told you."

I. The Holy Spirit shows Christians things about God and helps
them understand. I Corinthians 2:9-14 says, "The Holy Writings
say, 'No eye has ever seen or no ear has ever heard or no mind
has ever thought of the wonderful things God has made ready for
those who love Him.' God has shown these things to us through
His Holy Spirit. It is the Holy Spirit Who looks into all things,
even the secrets of God, and shows them to us. Who can know
the things about a man, except a man's own spirit that is in Him?
It is the same with God. Who can understand Him except the
Holy Spirit? We have not received the spirit of the world. God
has given us His Holy Spirit that we may know about the things
given to us by Him. We speak about these things also. We do not
use words of man's wisdom. We use words given to us by the
Holy Spirit. We use these words to tell what the Holy Spirit
wants to say to those who put their trust in Him. But the person
who is not a Christian does not understand these words from the
Holy Spirit. He thinks they are foolish. He cannot understand
them because he does not have the Holy Spirit to help him understand." (Isaiah 64:4; 65:17)

J. The Holy Spirit makes the Christian able to tell to others the
Good News in power. Acts 6:10 says, "Stephen spoke with
wisdom and power given by the Holy Spirit. They were not able
to say anything against what he said." I Corinthians 2:1-5 says,
"Christian brothers, when I came to you, I did not preach the
secrets of God with big sounding words or make it sound as if I
were so wise. I made up my mind that while I was with you I
would speak of nothing except Jesus Christ and of His death on
the cross. When I was with you, I was weak. I was afraid and I
shook. What I had to say when I preached was not in big
sounding words of man's wisdom. But it was given in the power
of the Holy Spirit. In this way, you do not have faith in Christ
because of the wisdom of men. You have faith in Christ because
of the power of God."

K. The Holy Spirit helps, leads, and gives power to the Christian in
prayer. Jude 20 says, "Dear friends, you must become strong in
your most holy faith. Let the Holy Spirit lead you as you pray."
(Romans 8:26-27; Ephesians 6:18)

L. The Holy Spirit leads the Christian to honor and give thanks to God. Ephesians 5:18-20 says, "Do not get drunk with wine. That leads to wild living. Instead, be filled with the Holy Spirit. Tell of your joy to each other by singing the Songs of David and church songs. Sing in your heart to the Lord. Always give thanks for all things to God the Father in the name of our Lord Jesus Christ."

M. The Holy Spirit helps the Christian to worship God in a good and true way. Philippians 3:3 says, "The act of becoming a Jew has nothing to do with us becoming Christians. We worship God through His Spirit and are proud of Jesus Christ. We have no faith in what we ourselves can do."

N. The Holy Spirit calls Christians and tells them to go and do special kinds of work. Acts 13:2,4 says, "While they were worshiping the Lord and eating no food so they could pray better, the Holy Spirit said, 'Let Barnabas and Saul be given to Me for the work I have called them to.' " "They were sent by the Holy Spirit to the city of Seluecia. From there they went by ship to the island of Cyprus."

O. The Holy Spirit leads the Christian even in the small things of life each day. (Where to go, what to do and what to say.) Acts 8:29 says, "The Holy Spirit said to Philip, 'Go over to that wagon and get on it.' " (Acts 16:6-7)

P. The Holy Spirit gives life to the body of the Christian. Romans 8:10-11 says, "If Christ is in you, your spirit lives because you are right with God, and yet your body is dead because of sin. The Holy Spirit raised Jesus from the dead. If the same Holy Spirit lives in you, He will give life to your bodies in the same way."

Q. The Holy Spirit gives gifts to Christians to help them work better for Him. (I Corinthians 12)

THE WORK OF THE HOLY SPIRIT IN THE CHURCH

The church is made up of all people who have put their trust in Christ. The Holy Spirit was given to the church fifty days after Jesus went up to heaven from the earth. Acts 2:1-4 says, "The followers of Jesus were all together in one place fifty days after the special religious gathering to remember how the Jews left Egypt. All at once there was a sound from heaven like a powerful wind. It filled the house where they were sitting. Then they saw tongues which were divided that looked like fire. These came down on each one of them. They were all filled with the Holy Spirit. Then they began to speak in other languages which the Holy Spirit made them able to speak."

The living church of Christ cannot be seen since it is not a building. It may be thought of as a body. Jesus Christ is the Head, and Christians are all parts of the body. Since Christ is the Head, He tells the body what to do. He does this by the Holy Spirit Who lives in the lives of Christians. The church, or all Christians, is the home of the Holy Spirit. He lives and moves in the church.

1. WHAT THE HOLY SPIRIT DOES THROUGH THE CHURCH.

A. The Holy Spirit started the church as we know it today. (Acts 2:1-4) He gave it power, and it is to show the power of the Holy Spirit to the whole world. The church is Christ's body and He is the Head. Ephesians 1:22-23 says, "God has put all things under Christ's power and has made Him to be the head leader over all things of the church. The church is the body of Christ. It is filled by Him Who fills all things everywhere with Himself."

B. The Holy Spirit lives in the lives of Christians and Christians make up the church. (Ephesians 2:19-22) What is true of each Christian must be true of all the church. I Corinthians 6:19-20 says, "Do you not know that your body is a house of God where the Holy Spirit lives? God gave you His Holy Spirit. Now you belong to God. You do not belong to yourselves. God bought you with a great price. So honor God with your body. You belong to Him." (II Corinthians 6:16)

C. The Holy Spirit rules over the church and leads it. (Acts 15:28)

D. The Holy Spirit is making the church complete by calling people to God. These are the people who put their trust in Christ to save them from sin. The church is to preach the Good News about

Christ to all people. The Holy Spirit then works in the hearts of the people they preach to. He calls them, but they must decide to follow or not to follow. Mark 16:15-16 says, "He said to them, 'You are to go to all the world and preach the Good News to every person. He who puts his trust in Me and is baptized will be saved from the punishment of sin. But he who does not put his trust in Me is guilty and will be punished forever.' "

2. WHAT THE HOLY SPIRIT GIVES THE CHURCH TO HELP IN ITS WORK

A. The *gifts* of the Spirit help in the work of the church. They give power. Ephesians 4:11-12 says, "Christ gave gifts to men. He gave to some the gift to be missionaries, some to be preachers, others to be preachers who go from town to town. He gave others the gift to be church leaders and teachers. These gifts help His people work well for Him. And then the church which is the body of Christ will be made strong." (Romans 12:6-8; I Corinthians 12:4-11)

B. The *fruit* of the Spirit shows the kind of work done for God. The fruit of the Spirit is love. Joy is love singing. Peace is love resting. Not giving up is love working. Being kind is showing love to others. Being good is allowing God's love to work. Having faith is love trusting. Being gentle is love with no pride. Being the boss over our own desires is love in action. (Galatians 5:22-23)

The gifts of the Spirit and the fruit of the Spirit are not the same, but work together.

PART 5

WHAT THE WORD OF GOD TEACHES ABOUT ANGELS AND DEMONS

[*Angelology*]

GOOD ANGELS

Angels are beings who do not have bodies. They receive their power from God but are not all-powerful as He is.

1. WHERE ANGELS COME FROM.

Angels were made (brought into being) by a powerful work of God. In Colossians 1:16 it says, "Christ made everything in the heavens and on the earth. He made everything that is seen and things that are not seen. He made all the powers of heaven. Everything was made by Him and for Him." They were made before men, but it is not known when they were made. Nehemiah 9:6 says, "You alone are the Lord. You made the heavens, the heaven of heavens with all their angels. You have made the earth and all that is on it, and the seas and all that is in them. You give life to all of them, and the angels of heaven bow down to You."

2. ANGELS HAVE AN IMPORTANT PLACE.

Angels are different from men and are better in all ways than men are (in this life). In Hebrews 2:7a it says, "You made him so he took a place that was not as important as the angels for a little while." Angels are not all-powerful, do not know all things, and are not everywhere at one time.

3. ANGELS ARE NOT LIKE PEOPLE.

A. They listen to God and do what He says. Psalm 103:20 says, "Praise the Lord, you powerful angels of His who do what He says, obeying His voice as He speaks!"

B. Angels are able to tell men what will happen and what they should do. Acts 27:23-24 says, "I belong to God and I work for Him. Last night an Angel of God stood by me and said, 'Do not be afraid, Paul. You must stand in front of Caesar. God has given you the lives of all the men on this ship.' " (Genesis 19:15-22; Matthew 2:13-14; Luke 2:9-14)

C. Angels desire to look into the secrets of how men can be saved from sin. I Peter 1:12b says, "The Holy Spirit Who was sent from heaven gave them power and they told of things that even the angels would like to know about."

D. Angels are God's helpers. In Hebrews 1:14 it says, "Are not all the angels spirits who work for God? They are sent out to help those who are to be saved from the punishment of sin."

E. When angels were brought into being, they had no sin. Some of the angels chose to fight against God and were thrown out of heaven along with Satan. But the angels who chose to stay holy as God made them are called *holy* angels. Jude 6 says, "Angels who did not stay in their place of power, but left the place where they were given to stay, are chained in a dark place. They will be there until the day they stand before God to be told they are guilty."

F. Angels are spirits but are able to do their work by using a body when they need to. Many times they can be seen by men and even look like men. John 20:12 says, "She saw two angels dressed in white clothes. They were sitting where the body of Jesus had lain. One angel was where His head had lain and one angel was where His feet had lain." (Genesis 19:1-11; 32:1-2; Matthew 1:20; Luke 1:26)

G. Angels are not held back by locked doors. In Acts 12:7-9 it says, "All at once an angel of the Lord was seen standing beside him. A light shone in the building. The angel hit Peter on the side and said, 'Get up!' Then the chains fell off his hands. The angel said, 'Put on your belt and shoes!' He did. The angel said to Peter, 'Put on your coat and follow me.' Peter followed him out. He was not sure what was happening as the angel helped him. He thought it was a dream."

H. Angels do not marry. Mark 12:35 says, "When people are raised from the dead, they do not marry and are not given in marriage. They are like angels in heaven."

I. Angels do not die. In Luke 20:36a it says, "They cannot die anymore. They are as the angels and are sons of God.

J. Angels are strong.

   (1) They have greater power and strength than men. II Peter 2:11 says, "Angels are greater in strength and power than they. But angels do not speak against these powers before the Lord." (II Kings 19:35)

   (2) John saw an angel having great power. Revelation 18:1 says, "Then I saw another angel coming down from heaven. He had much power. The earth was made bright with his shining greatness."

(3) An angel rolled the stone back from Christ's grave. Matthew 28:2-3 says, "At once the earth shook and an angel of the Lord came down from heaven. He came and pushed back the stone from the door and sat on it. His face was bright like lightning. His clothes were as white as snow."

THE WORK OF GOOD ANGELS

1. *ANGELS HAVE AN IMPORTANT WORK IN DOING WHAT GOD WANTS DONE FOR THE CHRISTIAN AND THE SINNER.*

   A. The Law of God was given through angels. Acts 7:53 says, "You had the Law given to you by angels. Yet you have not kept it." (Galatians 3:19; Hebrews 2:2)

   B. Angels lead things being done in the nations. "At that time the great angel Michael, who watches over your people, will rise up. And there will be a time of trouble, the worst since there was a nation. But at that time, every one whose name is written in the Book will be taken out of the trouble" (Daniel 12:1).

   C. Angels watch over people.

      (1) An angel helped Elijah. I Kings 19:5 says, "When he lay down and slept under the juniper tree, an angel touched him. The angel said to him, 'Get up and eat.' "

      (2) An angel shut the lions' mouths. Daniel 6:22a says, "My God sent His angel and shut the lions' mouths. They have not hurt me... ."

      (3) An angel led Peter out of prison. Acts 12:7-9 says, "All at once an angel of the Lord was seen standing beside him. A light shone in the building. The angel hit Peter on the side and said, 'Get up!' Then the chains fell off his hands. The angel said, 'Put on your belt and shoes!' He did. The angel said to Peter, 'Put on your coat and follow me.' Peter followed him out. He was not sure what was happening as the angel helped him. He thought it was a dream."

      (4) Angels have the job of watching over Christians. Psalm 34:7 says, "The angel of the Lord stays close around those who fear Him, and He takes them out of trouble." Psalm 91:11 says, "For He will have His angels care for you and keep you in all your ways." (II Kings 6:15-17)

   D. Angels take God's children to heaven. Luke 16:22 says, "He was taken by the angels into the arms of Abraham."

   E. When Christ returns, angels will be with Him. Matthew 25:31 says, "When the Son of Man comes in His shining greatness, He will sit down on His place of greatness. All the angels will be with Him." II Thessalonians 1:7 says, "He will help you and us who are suffering. This will happen when the Lord Jesus comes down from heaven with His powerful angels in a bright fire."

F. Angels will do what God wants done to sinful people who have not been saved from sin. Matthew 13:47-50 says, "The holy nation of heaven is like a big net which was let down into the sea. It gathered fish of every kind. When it was full, they took it to the shore. They sat down and put the good fish into pails. They threw the bad fish away. It will be like this in the end of the world. Angels will come and take the sinful people from among those who are right with God. They will put the sinful people into a stove of fire where there will be loud crying and grinding of teeth." (Matthew 13:39-42)

G. Angels hold back God's anger on men. Revelation 7:1-3 says, "After this I saw four angels. They were standing at the four corners of the earth. They were holding back the four winds of the earth so no wind would blow on the earth or the sea or on any tree. I saw another angel coming from the east. He was carrying the mark of the living God. He called with a loud voice to the four angels who had been given power to hurt the earth and sea. The angel from the east said, 'Do not hurt the earth or the sea or the trees until we have put the mark of God on the foreheads of the servants He owns.' "

H. Angels will gather God's people together. Matthew 24:31 says, "He will send His angels with the loud sound of a horn. They will gather God's people together from the four winds. They will come from one end of the heavens to the other."

I. Angels will not allow men to worship them but will have men worship God. Revelation 19:10 says, "Then I got down at his feet to worship him. But he said to me, 'No! Do not worship me. I am a workman together with you and your Christian brothers who tell of their trust in Christ. Worship God.' " (Revelation 22:8-9)

2. ANGELS CAN BE EVERYWHERE.

A. The place where angels are most of the time is in heaven, but they can do their work on earth. Mark 12:25b says, "...They are like angels *in heaven*." Matthew 28:2a says, "At once the earth shook and an angel of the Lord *came down from heaven*." Luke 1:11 says, "Zacharias saw an angel of the Lord *standing on the right side of the altar* where the special perfume was burning." (Numbers 22:22-31)

B. In Jacob's dream, he saw angels *coming and going from heaven.*
(Genesis 28:12)

3. THERE ARE MORE ANGELS THAN MAN IS ABLE TO UNDERSTAND.

A. Jesus could have called more than 70,000 angels before He was to
be put on the cross. Matthew 26:53 says, "Do you not think that
I can pray to My Father? At once He would send Me more than
70,000 angels."

4. THE BIBLE SPEAKS OF TWO ANGELS HAVING NAMES.

A. Michael - This name means *who is like God.* He is called a head
angel in Jude 9. In Revelation 12:7 it says that he will fight
against Satan. (Daniel 10:12-14)

B. Gabriel - This name means *the one who always wins for God.*
Luke 1:19, 26a says, "The angel said to him, 'My name is
Gabriel. I stand near God. He sent me to talk to you and bring to
you this good news.' " "Six months after Elizabeth knew she was
to become a mother, Gabriel was sent from God to Nazareth."
(Daniel 8:16-26; 9:21-22)

5. THREE SPECIAL GROUPS OF ANGEL-LIKE BEINGS.

A. Cherubim - special bodies of honor. (Genesis 3:24; Hebrews 9:5)

B. Seraphim - these are only mentioned once and that is in Isaiah
6:2.

C. Living beings - spoken of in Revelation 4 and 5. (Ezekiel 1:5-9)

DEMONS AND THEIR LEADER

1. DEMONS ARE SATAN'S HELPERS.

A. Demons are spirits without bodies. They are bad angels who work for Satan. (Matthew 12:26-27; 25:41; Mark 1:23; 32-34; Revelation 16:13-16)

B. Demons have the power to mix up men's minds. They can make men's bodies sick. (Matthew 12:22; 17:15-18; Luke 13:16)

C. Demons know that Jesus Christ is the Son of God. They even call Him "The Holy One of God," but they do not worship Him. There is no hope for them. One day they will be thrown *into the fire that lasts forever.* (Matthew 25:41; 8:28-32; Mark 1:22-24; Acts 19:15; James 2:19)

D. Demons have an important part in Satan's place of rule. Ephesians 6:12 says, "Our fight is not with people. It is against the leaders and the powers and the spirits of darkness in this world. It is against the demon world that works in the heavens."

E. Demons spread false teaching and fight against God's plan and His people. (Ephesians 6:12; I Timothy 4:1-3; I John 4:1-6) The Word of God tells in many places about demons and how men worship them. I Corinthians 10:20 says, "I am saying that the people who do not know God bring gifts of animals in worship. But they have given them to demons, not to God. You do not want to have any share with demons." Demons help in the work of witchdoctors, and witchcraft is done in all parts of the world today. (Deuteronomy 32:17; I Samuel 28:7-20; Psalm 106:36-37)

2. THERE ARE TWO DIFFERENT GROUPS OF DEMONS.

A. The demons who are now traveling the heavens and the earth. (Ephesians 6-12)

B. The demons who are now tied up but will be loose to hurt men in the last days during *The time of much trouble.* (Revelation 9:1-21; 16:13-16)

3. SATAN IS THEIR LEADER.

Satan, who is also known as *the Devil,* is the leader of the demons.

He is the great enemy of God and man. (Matthew 12:26-27; 25:41)
There are so many demons that no one can count them. (Mark 5:9)

4. WHAT SATAN IS LIKE.

He is a killer. He does not tell the truth because he is the father of
lies. Satan has the power of death, and he is the leader of the world
now. (John 8:44; 14:30; Hebrews 2:14; I John 3:8) Satan hates both
God and man. (Job 1:6-12; Zechariah 3:1; Matthew 13:19, 39; John
13:2; Acts 5:3; II Corinthians 11:3; Ephesians 6:11-12; I Peter 5:8)

5. SATAN'S NAMES:

A. devil (Revelation 12:9; 20:2)

B. snake (Revelation 12:3, 7; 13:2; 20:2)

C. Lucifer - the morning star - the one who carries light. (Isaiah
14:12)

D. man of sin (II Thessalonians 2:8)

E. the tempter (Matthew 4:3; I Thessalonians 3:5)

F. the god of this world (II Corinthians 4:4)

G. the leader of the powers of darkness (Ephesians 2:2)

H. the leader of this world (John 12:31; 14:30; 16:11)

I. liar and murderer (John 8:44)

J. Apollyon (Revelation 9:11)

K. Abaddon (Revelation 9:11)

THE WORK OF SATAN AND DEMONS

Looking into the way demons work is not a study that brings happiness. But for the Christian who is obeying the Word of God and living daily to please the Lord, there need be no fear. Demons can work on Christians, but most of their work is done in those who have never put their trust in Christ.

1. WHAT DEMONS ARE ABLE TO DO.

A. Demons are able to have power over the body of a man. Luke 4:35 says, "Jesus spoke sharp words to the demon and said, 'Do not talk! Come out of him!' When the demon had thrown the man down, he came out without hurting the man." (Luke 8:29; Acts 19:16)

B. Demons are able to leave and return to the body of a man. Matthew 12:43-45 says, "When a demon is gone out of a man, it goes through dry places to find rest. It finds none. Then it says, 'I will go back into my house from which I came.' When it goes back, it sees that it is empty. But it sees that the house has been cleaned and looks good. Then it goes out and comes back bringing with it seven demons more sinful than itself. They go in and live there. In the end that man is worse than at first. It will be like this with the sinful people of this day."

C. Demons are able to bring sickness to the body. Luke 13:16 says, "Should not this Jewish woman be made free from this trouble on the Day of Rest? She has been chained by Satan for eighteen years."

D. Demons are able to bring sickness to the mind. Mark 5:5 says, "Night and day he was among the graves and in the mountains. He would cry out and cut himself with stones."

2. HOW DEMONS START THEIR WORK.

A. Drugs are full of danger. These and strong drink make a person so that his mind is an easy place for demons to work. (I Corinthians 10:20-21)

B. Demons can take over a mind that has turned against God. (Matthew 12:43-45)

C. Through fear. (II Timothy 1:7; Romans 8:15)

D. Hating someone without wanting to forgive them is a way that lets demons work in a person. II Corinthians 2:10-11 says, "If you forgive a man, I forgive him also. If I have forgiven anything, I have done it because of you. Christ sees me as I forgive. We forgive so that Satan will not win. We know how he works!" Luke 11:4 says, "Forgive us our sins, as we forgive those who sin against us. Do not let us be tempted." (Matthew 5:43-48; 6:14-15; Mark 11:25-26; Luke 6:36-37; Hebrews 12:15; James 3:14-15)

WHAT THE CHRISTIAN IS TO DO ABOUT DEMONS

Christians should remember that they are at war at all times with the devil. They need always to be ready to stand up against Satan.

The Bible tells what should be done to keep demons from being able to work. In James 4:7 it says, "So give yourself to God. Stand against the devil and he will run away from you." Christians are to watch out for him. I Thessalonians 5:22 says, "Keep away from everything that even looks like sin." There is no place in the Bible that gives the idea that the Christian can stand against the devil. Christians have no Biblical grounds to talk with Satan or his demons, but turn him over to the power of the Holy Spirit in the name of Jesus Christ. (I Peter 5:8-11; Jude 9)

The Christian need not worry about demons using their power on him to take over his mind. They can - and do - work on a Christian, but their power is held back because the Christian belongs to God. The Christian can at any time call upon the blood of Christ to cover him from the power and actions of demons. (Revelation 12:11)

Ephesians 6:10-17 says, "This is the last thing I want to say: Be strong with the Lord's strength. Put on the things God gives you to fight with. Then you will not fall into the traps of the devil. Our fight is not with people. It is against the leaders and the powers and the spirits of darkness of this world. It is against the demon world that works in the heavens. Because of this, put on all the things God gives you to fight with. Then you will be able to stand in that sinful day. When it is all over, you will still be standing. So stand up and do not be moved. Wear a belt of truth around your body. Wear a piece of iron over your chest which is being right with God. Wear shoes on your feet which are the Good News of peace. Most important of all, you need a covering of faith in front of you. This is to put out the fire-arrows of the devil. The covering for your head is that you have been saved from the punishment of sin. Take the sword of the Spirit which is the Word of God."

POWERFUL WORKS (FALSE) DONE BY THE HELP OF SATAN

There have always been those who have done what looked to be powerful works (miracles), but it was done by the power of Satan and is called *magic*. Such things are spoken of in the Word of God as sinful. Deuteronomy 18:9-14 says, "When you go into the land the Lord your God gives you, do not learn to follow the hated and sinful ways of those nations. There must not be found among you anyone who makes his son or daughter pass through the fire, or uses secret ways, or does witchcraft, or tells the meaning of special things, or is a witch, or uses secret power on people, or helps people talk to spirits, or talks to spirits himself, or talks with the dead. For the Lord hates whoever does these things. And because of these hated things, the Lord your God will drive them out from in front of you. You must be without blame before the Lord your God. For these nations that you are about to take listen to those who do witchcraft and use secret ways. But the Lord your God has not allowed you to do so." (II Corinthians 6:17)

1. MAGIC IS DONE IN THESE WAYS:

    A. Telling what will happen in the future. (Genesis 44:5; Hosea 4:12)

    B. Telling what will happen in the future by talking with the spirits of dead people. (I Samuel 28:8; I Chronicles 10:13-14; II Chronicles 33:6)

    C. Telling what will happen in the future from certain things that happen. (Ezekiel 21:21)

    D. Fooling people (magic). (Genesis 41:8; Exodus 7:11; Daniel 4:7)

    E. Deciding what to do by drawing numbers.

    F. Black art (magic with a desire to hurt people)

PART 6

WHAT THE WORD OF GOD TEACHES ABOUT MAN

[Anthropology]

WHERE MAN CAME FROM

One question that has been asked through the years is, "Where did man come from?" Man has always wanted to know who made the first man and how he was made. There is no secret Who made him and what he was made from because the Bible tells all about it.

1. STORIES OF MAN

The Word of God is very plain in teaching that *man was made* by God, and that he was made a man *all at once by a powerful work of God.* God's Word says this, but still, people in different nations of the world have made up false stories about where man came from. Some sinful men who did not believe God's Word made up the story that man came from animals through a lot of changes. Birds, fish, and animals all have some things that are much alike. The way they breathe, their blood, their hearts, their stomachs, are alike in some ways. When some people, who do not believe God, look at these things, they say that one living thing grew to become a different living thing. Then that living thing grew to become a different living thing. This kept going on, these people say, until man came into being. These people do not teach that God made man, but that man became man through lots of changes that happened to animals over a long time. This is called *evolution* and should never be read or studied as truth.

Man is different from the animals. Man has been man since God made him from the dust. Would it not be just as easy for God to make a man as to make an animal? God's Word says that all living animals on the earth would give birth to animals of the same kind. (Genesis 1:24-25) Man cannot become one of these animals. None of the animals can become man. No one has ever proven that man came from any animal. People who do not believe in God or do not believe that His Word is true have made up false stories to try to take the power and greatness away from God.

2. WHAT GOD SAYS

In Genesis 2:7 it tells how man was made, and in Genesis 2:21-22 it tells how woman was made. The Word of God teaches that when the first man and woman were brought into being, they were the first of their kind and were made from nothing like them. The words used in the Hebrew language do not mean *to grow from* or *to be changed from.* Those who believe that man came from an animal like to teach that man *grew* from an animal or man *changed* from an animal. This is not what God's Word teaches! In Genesis 2:7 it teaches that the body of the first man was made from dust. Then God breathed into man the breath of life and man became a living soul. The Word of God tells that the first man and woman, Adam and Eve, were made by God at one time by a powerful work and were the beginning of the human family.

3. OTHER THINGS THAT SHOW GOD MADE MAN:

A. Words and writings have been handed down from the first people of nations and family groups which tell how man came from one place at one time in Central Asia. All people of the earth have the same kind of blood. In Acts 17:26 it says, "He made from one blood all nations who live on the earth. He set the times and places where they should live."

B. All the more important languages came from the same place.

C. All men everywhere in the world are much the same in the things they do and how they act.

D. People from different nations are able to have children with each other. The body of a person from one part of the world is just as warm as a person from another part of the world. The heart beat is the same with all people of the world. All people can get the same diseases. These things are not true with different animals. It is easy to see in the Word of God how the first man was made and when he was made. In Genesis 1:27 it says, "And God made man in His own likeness. In the likenss of God He made him." Man is different from animals because he was made like God.

WHAT MAN IS LIKE

1. MAN IS MADE OF THREE PARTS - BODY, SOUL, AND SPIRIT.

The Word of God teaches that man is made of three parts, one part is seen, and the other two parts are not seen. In I Thessalonians 5:23b it says, "May your *spirit* and your *soul* and your *body* be kept complete." This picture may help in understanding how each man has three parts.

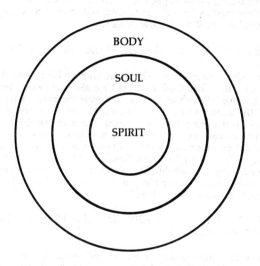

The body is made up of flesh, bones, fat and blood. The soul and the spirit cannot be seen. There is a soul and there is a spirit. Luke 1:46-47 speaks of the difference between soul and spirit. Hebrews 4:12 says, "It cuts straight into where the soul and spirit meet and it divides them."

A. The *body* of man is that which can be seen. God has made the body so that it has life. It can see, hear, smell, taste, and touch things.

B. The *soul* part of man is that which is often called the heart of man. It is not the heart of a man because the heart is flesh. The soul of man cannot be seen. In Luke 6:45 it says, "Good comes from a good man because of the riches he has in his heart. The mouth speaks of what the heart is full of." All of man's actions come from his heart. The soul does three things: it knows, it feels, and it chooses.

C. The *spirit* of the man is a part which cannot be seen. It is a very important part because it is by man's spirit that he can know God. In Romans 8:16 it says, "For the Holy Spirit speaks to us and tells our spirit that we are children of God." To begin with, man's spirit is at war with God. It needs to be at peace with God. But this can only happen when he puts his trust in Jesus Christ. When man's spirit belongs to God, only then can he know when the Holy Spirit is talking with his spirit.

2. WHEN GOD MADE MAN, HE MADE HIM LIKE HIMSELF.

In the Old Testament it tells about God making man. It says in Genesis 1:26, "Then God said, 'Let Us make man like Us and let him be head over the fish of the sea, and over the birds of the air, and over the cattle, and over all the earth, and over everything that moves on the ground.'" This means that man can think and have feelings and can live with other men. Sin changed man. He is not like God. But by putting his trust in Christ, man can again be like God through what Christ has done. Romans 8:29 says, "God knew from the beginning who would put their trust in Him. So He chose them and made them to be like His Son. Christ was first and all those who belong to God are His brothers."

3. MAN IS ABLE TO KNOW THE DIFFERENCE BETWEEN RIGHT AND WRONG.

A. The first man (Adam) knew the difference between right and wrong. The first man, Adam, knew God. Yet Adam chose to do wrong and not obey God. (Genesis 3:6-7)

B. Man today knows the difference betweeen right and wrong. Romans 2:15b says, "Their own hearts tell them if they are guilty." (Acts 24:16; I Corinthians 10:25, 27, 28; I Timothy 1:19; Hebrews 10:22; I Peter 3:16) Titus 1:15 says, "All things are pure to the man with a pure heart. But to sinful people nothing is pure. Both their minds and their hearts are bad." God's Word tells them they are wrong. (II Timothy 4:3) Man's heart is able to tell him what is right or wrong as the Holy Spirit speaks to him.

C. Man is able to choose. Every person has the power to choose. Ephesians 2:3a says, "At one time all of us lived to please our old selves. We gave in to what our bodies and minds wanted." (I Peter 4:3) Man can choose Christ as His Lord and the One Who saves from sin by putting his trust in Him, or he can turn away from Him. John 1:12-13 says, "He gave the right and the power to become children of God to those who received Him. He gave this to those who put their trust in His name. These children of God were not born of blood and of flesh and of man's desires, but they were born of God."

GOD TESTED MAN

God tested man long ago and He still tests men today. A test is a question or a problem given so that the one who is giving the test can find out something about the one being tested. After God made man, He gave him a choice. If Adam chose right, he would receive pay from God. If Adam chose wrong, he would be punished. God told Adam and Eve in Genesis 2:8-17 not to eat of one tree in the Garden. He did not give them a reason. God does not have to give men reasons for what He says to do or not to do. God just said, "Do not eat of that tree." Adam chose the wrong way. (Genesis 3:6-7)

1. WHY DID GOD TEST MAN?

A. God made man to be able to choose right from wrong and He wanted him to be able to choose not to sin. God made man to *honor* Him. God wants man today to love Him and serve Him because they want to.

B. God wanted to test man to see if he would obey or disobey Him. Since God made man, He had the right to test him.

C. It is sure that whatever God did, He did it for man's own good. If Adam had chosen not to sin, he could have had many great things from God. Since he did choose to sin, he led all men away from God. Men disobey God today just as Adam did long ago.

2. WHAT DID MAN DO WITH THIS TEST?

God let Satan tempt Adam and Eve to sin so that God could know if man would obey Him. Adam and Eve sinned (they followed Satan) and so God knew that Adam and Eve did not pass the test. God knew that all people are like Adam and Eve. All people have sin in them and do not pass God's test unless they put their trust in Jesus Christ Who is the One Who saves. Man needs God. Man needs God's loving-favor. Even when man sins, God still shows His loving-favor. Romans 5:20b and 21a say, "But where sin spread, God's loving-favor spread all the more. Sin had power that ended in death. Now, God's loving-favor has power to make men right with Himself."

MAN SINNED AGAINST GOD

1. SATAN IS THE ONE WHO TEMPTED MAN.

When man was made, Satan had already been put out of heaven. Satan's work was to make man sin against God. Satan had a way of fooling Eve by turning the truth of God into a lie. He made himself into a snake and came and talked to Eve. Satan tried to trap Eve and tempt her to sin. When she did sin, she tempted her husband Adam into sinning also. Since Adam was the head of all other people who would live after him, Satan was working hard to make him sin. (Genesis 1:26-28) Adam was the one God trusted to lead all other people. (Genesis 2:16) But his sin made sinners of all people. God's Word makes it clear that all people are sinners because of Adam's sin. Romans 5:12-14 says, "This is what happened: Sin came into the world by one man, Adam. Sin brought death with it. Death spread to all men because all have sinned. Sin was in the world before the Jewish Law was given. But sin is not held against a person when there is no Law. And yet death had power over men from the time of Adam until the time of Moses. Even the power of death was over those who had not sinned in the same way Adam sinned. Adam was like the One Who was to come." (Romans 5:15-19)

2. HOW SATAN TEMPTED EVE.

A. He made sin look good to the *body*. Eve saw that the tree was good for food. (Genesis 3:6a)

B. He made sin look good to the *mind*. She saw that the tree looked good to the eyes. (Genesis 3:6b) Eve's mind was tempted because she thought the fruit of the tree would make her wise. (Genesis 3:6c)

C. He made sin look good to the *spirit*. Adam and Eve shared with God through their spirits. Satan tempted Eve in her spirit by telling her that the fruit of the tree would make them *as gods knowing good from bad*. (Genesis 3:5) In this way, all of Eve, her body, soul, and spirit, was tempted.

3. SIN BROUGHT A CHANGE TO EVERYTHING THAT HAD BEEN PERFECT.

Because of the sin of Adam, many things changed:

A. Man could not share with God in the same way anymore. Before Adam's first sin, God and Adam walked and talked together. But after the first sin, Adam and Eve hid from God. They knew that God was no longer pleased with them because they did not obey God. Adam and Eve felt shame because of their sin. Their own hearts told them they were guilty. (Genesis 3:8-11; 22-24)

B. Men were no longer without sin or guilt. When God first made man, he was holy and without sin and guilt. Death came into the world because of Adam's sin. (Romans 5:12)

C. Men's bodies began to die. God had told men this would happen after they sinned. (Genesis 3:19) I Corinthians 15:22 teaches that sickness and the death of the body is part of the punishment for sin. (Genesis 2:17; 3:19; Job 2:6-7; Romans 6:23; II Timothy 1:10)

D. Even the ground changed because of Adam's sin. God allowed weeds to grow and men today cannot keep them from taking over the ground. When Jesus Christ comes back again to rule, the ground will be returned to the way it was when God first made the earth. (Genesis 3:17-19; Romans 8:20-22)

E. Because of their first sin, Adam and Eve were put out of the Garden of Eden, and man had to begin working for a living. (Genesis 3:23-24)

4. SIN CAME TO ALL MEN.

A. All men, everywhere, are sinners before God. Romans 3:9-11 says, "What about it then? Are we Jews better than the people who are not Jews? Not at all! I have already said that Jews and the people who are not Jews are all sinners. The Holy Writings say, 'There is not one person who is right with God. No, not even one! There is not one who understands. There is not one who tries to find God.' " (Psalm 14:2; Romans 5:12; 3:19b; Galatians 3:10; Ephesians 2:3)

B. Men are under the power of sin and Satan. Ephesians 2:3 says, "At one time all of us lived to please our old selves. We gave in to what our bodies and minds wanted. We were sinful from birth like all other people and would suffer from the anger of God." (Romans 7; John 8:31-36)

5. SIN BROUGHT DEATH.

In Genesis 2:17b it says, "For the day you eat from it you will die for sure." Adam did eat of the fruit of that tree and sin came into all the world and death came to all people. In Romans 5:12 it says, "This is want happened: Sin came into the world by one man, Adam. Sin brought death with it. Death spread to all men because all have sinned." There are three kinds of death. The Bible talks about all three and it is important to understand the difference.

A. Death of the body is when the heart and breath stops. The body no longer has life. In II Peter 1:14 it says, "I know that I will soon be leaving this body." (II Corinthians 5:1-5)

B. Death which divides the spirit from God came about because of Adam's sin. He was no longer able to share and talk with God. Because all people are children from Adam, all are born with their spirit divided from God and stay that way until they are saved. (Romans 5:12-19) Man can have new life through Jesus Christ and again share and talk with God. Then his spirit is no longer divided from God.

C. Death that lasts forever means being kept from God forever. It does not destroy the person, but he is kept away from God and he knows it. This death is for those who have never put their trust in Jesus Christ. (Revelation 20:6, 14, 15) Those who do not have their names written in the book of life will be put into the lake of fire forever. Those who have their names written in the book of life will have life that lasts forever. Luke 16:19-31 teaches that men die, with their soul and spirit divided from their bodies. Lazarus had been dead. His spirit was no longer in his body. But he had put his trust in Christ before he died and his spirit was with God. The rich man had not put his trust in Christ before he died, so his spirit was kept away from God forever.

PART 7

WHAT THE WORD OF GOD TEACHES ABOUT SIN

[*Hamartialogy*]

WHAT SIN IS

1. WHAT GOD'S WORD SAYS ABOUT SIN.

Sin is:

A. Doing anything that is not right. This means the desire to sin, and the acts of sin that men do. I John 5:17a says, "Every kind of wrong-doing is sin."

B. Not obeying God's Law. I John 3:4a says, "The person who keeps on sinning is guilty of not obeying the Law of God."

C. Not doing what should be done. James 4:17 says, "If you know what is right to do but you do not do it, you sin."

D. Not believing or trusting in Christ. John 16:8-9 says, "When the Helper comes, He will show the world the truth about sin. He will show the world about being right with God. And He will show the world what it is to be guilty. He will show the world about sin, because they do not put their trust in Me."

2. THE HOLY WRITINGS TELL WHAT SIN IS BY THE WORDS USED FOR SIN.

In the Old Testament three words are used for sin.

A. Sin - This word means *to miss the mark.* It also means *anything short of what God expects or wants done* or *falling short of what should be full or complete.* It is not only the acts of sin but the sinful thoughts and plans of the mind. (Genesis 4:7; Exodus 9:27; Psalm 51:2, 4; Proverbs 8:36)

B. Transgression - This word means *to turn against someone and not obey the one who is boss.* (Deuteronomy 9:12; Psalm 51:2-3)

C. Iniquity - This word means *not straight.* It is not so much the act of sin as it is the way people are sinful in their hearts. (Genesis 6:5; Psalm 32:5)

In the New Testament four words are used for sin.

A. Sin - This word means the same thing in the New Testament that it means in the Old Testament. It is used 174 times in the New Testament. It means both the act of sin and the way people are sinful in their hearts. (Romans 3:23)

B. Transgression - This means *not doing what has been told to be done*, or *not obeying God and His Laws*. (I Timothy 2:14)

C. Fault - This means *to fall instead of stand*, or *not being able to do what is known to be right and should be done*. (Galatians 6:1; James 4:17)

D. Error - This means *not to know what should have been learned and known*. (Hebrews 9:7)

3. WHAT SIN IS LIKE

Sin is like cancer. The sinful old self causes a person to do sinful acts. Every time a person pleases his sinful old self, more acts of sin come out in his life. When cancer starts in a person, if it is not taken care of, it spreads and takes over in his body. Cancer brings death. In the same way, if sin is not taken care of, it will spread. Then the person will have death that lasts forever. (Romans 6:23; James 1:14-15)

4. THERE IS A DIFFERENCE BETWEEN THE POWER OF SIN AND SINS.

Most of the time sins are thought of as stealing, lying, becoming angry and many things like that, and that is what these are for sure. But the power of SIN is what makes the person want to do such things. Sin is the *want to*, or *the desire for what is wrong*. A PERSON IS NOT A SINNER BECAUSE HE SINS. HE SINS BECAUSE HE IS A SINNER. It is easy to sin because man was born with a desire to sin. It is a power that works in him, and he can do nothing to get it out of him by himself.

When a man steals something from another man he is doing something wrong against the other man. It is sin. But the reason he stole was because of the power of SIN in his life. He did not only do something wrong against the other man, he sinned against God by doing what God said should not be done.

A man may think it is sin only if it is found out. But it was sin when he first thought about it.

When a person is saved, he must be saved from the power of SIN. The power that makes him want to do wrong must not be allowed to work in him.

A person may feel the need to be saved because of some sin he has done. He may feel sorry, and pray to be forgiven, but he may be doing this only because of that one sin. He must understand that he should ask to have the power of SIN taken out of his life. If this is not done, he will find himself doing the same sin again as well as other sins. He must understand that he has to be saved from the heart of the SIN problem.

WHERE SIN CAME FROM AND WHERE IT IS

1. WHERE SIN CAME FROM

A. The Bible says that sin came into the world by the devil who was the head leader of bad angels. (Isaiah 14:12-17; Revelation 12:7-9) This head leader of angels, called Lucifer, was a special angel. He lived in heaven with other angels who worked for God. Lucifer was a very beautiful angel. He became proud, and said he would be like the Most High God. He wanted to sit where God sits. Lucifer sinned by wanting his way and not God's way. Five times in Isaiah 14:13-14 Lucifer says, "I will." The fifth time in Isaiah 14:14b Lucifer says, "I will make myself like the Most High." The Bible does not say how this sin came to be in Lucifer. All it says is that Lucifer wanted to be like God. God had to punish Lucifer for this sin by putting him out of heaven. Ezekiel 28:15-17 says, "You were without blame in your ways from the day you were made until sin was found in you. Through all your trading you were filled with bad ways, and you sinned. So I have sent you away in shame from the mountain of God and I have destroyed you and driven you out from the stones of fire, O cherub who kept watch. Your heart was proud because of your beauty. You made your wisdom sinful because of your beauty. So I threw you to the ground. I laid you in front of kings for them to see you." God also said that the devil would be punished in hell.

Revelation 12:9 says that Lucifer, the old snake, tried to fight God, but he lost. He and his bad angels were thrown down to earth. He was then called the *devil* or *Satan*. Jesus said that the devil is the father of lies. It was the devil who brought sin into the world. (Genesis 3:1-7; John 8:44; I John 3:8)

2. WHERE SIN IS

A. In the heavens: Because of the fall of Satan and his angels, sin was in heaven and it was necessary that heaven be made pure. Christ did this with His blood. (Hebrews 9:23-24) The heavens (the sky) is where Satan and his demons work now. They make war with the Christian. Ephesians 6:11-12 says, "Put on the things God gives you to fight with. Then you will not fall into the traps of the devil. Our fight is not with people. It is against the leaders and powers and the spirits of darkness in this world. It is against the demon world that works in the heavens." But there is a day coming when he will be put out of the heavens and will be on the earth. (Revelation 12:7-12)

B. On the earth: Because of the sin of Adam and Eve, sin is on the earth.

(1) Plants suffer. (Genesis 3:17-18) Weeds grew then, and men have not been able to do away with them. (Revelation 22:3)

(2) Animals and men suffer. Since the flood men and animals have been afraid of each other. (Genesis 9:2) But during the time when Christ will return to rule the earth, they will be at peace with each other. (Isaiah 11:6-9) The day the new heavens and the new earth will appear all suffering will be gone forever. Things will be perfect again. (Romans 8:19-23; Revelation 21:1-5)

C. In man: Before Adam sinned, he was able to share together in a perfect way with God. After he sinned, he had nothing to share:

(1) With God. He lost the right to share with God. (John 3:3; I Corinthians 2:14; Ephesians 4:18)

(2) With God's Law. His soul became sin-sick. (Genesis 6:5-12; 8:21; Psalm 94:11; Jeremiah 17:9; Romans 1:19-31; 7:18; 8:7-8)

(3) With man. Sin changed man's feeling toward other people. (Genesis 4; Titus 3:3)

D. Sin is in all of man - spirit, soul, and body.

(1) Man's spirit has been divided from God because of sin. In Ephesians 4:18 it says, "Their minds are in darkness. They are strangers to the life of God. This is because they have closed their minds to Him and have turned their hearts away from Him." Sin brought man down to a place where his desires are to please himself. In I Corinthians 2:14 it says, "But the person who is not a Christian does not understand these words from the Holy Spirit. He thinks they are foolish. He cannot understand them because he does not have the Holy Spirit to help him understand." Man must be born again in order to know the things of God.

(2) Man's soul has been hurt by sin. Man's own heart is not truthful to himself. (Jeremiah 17:9) The thoughts of man's heart are sinful. (Genesis 6:5, 12; 8:21; Psalm 94:11; Romans

1:19-31) Man's sinful mind works against God. (Romans 8:7-8) Man's desire is to sin. (Romans 7:18)

(3) Man's body became weak and will die because of sin. Romans 8:13a says, "If you do what your sinful old selves want you to do, you will die in sin."

3. THINGS THAT SHOW SIN

A. God's Word tells the truth about sin.

Romans 3:23 tells that *all have sinned.*

Galatians 3:22 says *all men are guilty of sin.*

John 1:29 tells about *the sin of the world.*

(I Kings 8:46; Psalm 143:2; Proverbs 20:9; Ecclesiastes 7:20)

B. God's Word gives a word picture of the sin of the whole man.

Head - Isaiah 1:5, "...Your whole head is sick."

Eyes - II Peter 2:14, "Their eyes are full of sex sins."

Mouth - Romans 3:14, "Their mouths speak bad things against God. They say bad things about other people."

Lips - Romans 3:13, "Whatever they say is like the poison of snakes."

Tongue - Romans 3:13, "They tell lies with their tongues." James 3:6, "The tongue is a fire. It is full of wrong. It poisons the whole body."

Neck - Jeremiah 19:15b, "...because they have made their necks hard and would not listen to My Words."

Ears - Acts 7:51a, "You have hard hearts and ears that will not listen to me!"

Hands - Isaiah 1:15, "Your hands are full of blood."

Feet - Proverbs 1:16, "Their feet run to sin and hurry to kill."

From head to foot - Isaiah 1:6 "From the bottom of the foot even to the head, there is no good part."

Bones - Habakkuk 3:16, "My bones began to waste away."

Mind - Romans 1:28, "Their minds were sinful and they wanted only to do things they should not do."

Thoughts - Genesis 6:5, "Then the Lord saw that man was very sinful on the earth. Every plan and thought of the heart of man was sinful always."

C. The earth tells the truth about sin. Romans 8:22 says, "We know that everything on earth cries out with pain the same as a woman giving birth to a child."

D. God's Law tells the truth about sin. The Law shows men how sinful they are. (Romans 3:20) Even Paul thought he was free from sin until he looked into the mirror of God's Law. (Romans 7:7-8)

E. What men see in their own lives shows the truth about sin.

Moses, David, Peter, and John each saw in their own lives the truth of sin. I John 1:8 says, "If we say that we have no sin, we lie to ourselves and the truth is not in us." The truth of sin can be seen in laws made by men. Because of sin, we must have laws. False ways of worship show the truth of sin because men know there is a need for something to be done about their sin.

F. Men tell the truth about sin.

(1) Men of God tell it. Isaiah 6:5 says, "...It is bad for me, for I am destroyed! Because I am a man whose lips are unclean. And I live among a people whose lips are unclean. For my eyes have seen the King, the Lord of All." Paul said, "Christ Jesus came into the world to save sinners from their sin and I am the worst sinner" (I Timothy 1:15).

(2) Sinners tell it. Pharoah said, "I have sinned this time" (Exodus 9:27b). Achan's answer was, "It is true. I have sinned against the Lord, the God of Israel" (Joshua 7:20b). Balaam said, "...I have sinned " (Numbers 22:34a). Even Judas, who turned against Jesus, said, "...I have sinned..." (Matthew 27:4a)

All men know they are sinners, but men do not like to say so. Some try to get away from the guilt of sin by saying it is not there. Others try hard to forget it. Others try to make it sound as if it is not so bad by giving it different names. They may call it *mistakes* or *wrongs* or names like these. But that does not change the truth about sin.

THINGS THAT HAPPENED BECAUSE OF SIN

1. WHAT HAPPENED BECAUSE OF SIN.

A. When Adam and Eve sinned some changes took place. Before they sinned they did not wear clothes and they were not ashamed. But after they sinned they saw they were without clothes and became ashamed. (Genesis 3:7-10)

B. Before they sinned they had shared together with God and did not know what fear was. But after their sin they were afraid and hid themselves from God and were not able to share together with Him. (Genesis 3:10)

C. Before they sinned they lived in a beautiful garden where it was easy to grow fruits and vegetables. Adam had power over all the animals and they obeyed him. After they sinned Adam and Eve were not allowed to live in the beautiful garden. (Genesis 3:23-24) Many weeds, thorns, and thistles grew. Adam had to work very hard for their food, and he lost his power to rule over the animals. (Genesis 3:17-19)

D. Because of her part in their sin, Eve also suffered. In Genesis 3:16 it says that she would have sorrow and pain when she gave birth to children. It also says that her husband would rule over her.

E. The snake (the devil) that tricked Eve was also punished. In Genesis 3:14-15 it says that the snake would be below all other animals and would have to move around on its stomach.

F. Because of this first sin, all men through the years have suffered. Man's body, soul, and spirit changed from the way God made him. The *spirit* that once knew God is now in darkness. (Ephesians 4:18) Men are strangers to God. The *soul* does not want to do what is right. (Ephesians 4:19) The *body*, which was made perfect, can now get diseases, suffer pain, and will die. (Psalm 14:2-3; Romans 5:12; 8:6)

2. THE PUNISHMENT FOR SIN IS DEATH

A. Punishment is the pay one receives for the wrong that was done. Punishment for sin is the pain or suffering that comes to a man when he breaks God's Law. The reason for punishment is not to make a man good, but to punish a man because God says sin must be paid for. (Revelation 19:1-2)

B. Kinds of punishment - It takes only one word to tell of the punishment for sin. The Holy Writings call this death. There are three different deaths spoken of in God's Word:

   (1) Death of the body - This death is the dividing of the spirit from the body. It is when the body no longer has life or breath in it. It is shown in the Holy Writings to be part of the punishment for sin. (Genesis 2:17; 3:19; Numbers 16:29; 27:3; Psalm 90:7-11; Isaiah 38:17-18; John 8:44; Romans 4:24-25; 5:12, 14, 16, 17; I Peter 4:6)

   (2) Death which is the dividing of the spirit from God - The penalty placed upon man in the Garden of Eden is first of all a dividing of the spirit from God. (Ephesians 2:1-5) By this death man loses the right to be with God. (Luke 15:32; John 5:24; 8:51)

   (3) Death that lasts forever - Death that lasts forever is the dividing of the soul from God forever, and the soul will receive punishment forever. (Matthew 10:28; 25:41; Hebrews 10:31; Revelation 14:11; 20:11-15)

C. Who receives the punishment for sin?

   (1) The sinner will receive the pay that is promised to him in the Word of God. Romans 6:23 says, "You get what is coming to you when you sin. It is death! But God's free gift is life that lasts forever. It is given to us by our Lord Jesus Christ."

   Hebrews 9:27 says that after the body dies, the sinner will come before God to be told he is guilty and he will never be able then to put his trust in Christ.

   (2) Christ received the punishment for sin for those who will put their trust in Him. (Romans 5:1-2; 5:6)

PART 8

WHAT THE WORD OF GOD TEACHES ABOUT THE CHURCH

[*Ecclesiology*]

WHAT THE CHURCH IS

1. THE CHURCH IS MADE UP OF CHRISTIANS EVERY-WHERE.

All Christians, past, present, and future, make up what is called the *church*. These are people whose sins have been forgiven and in whom the Holy Spirit lives. (Romans 1:6-7; I Corinthians 1:2; Galatians 1:13; Ephesians 5:25)

The Greek word for *church* means being called out for a group meeting. It may help to think of the church as a body. Jesus Christ is the Head, and all Christians are a part of the body. (Ephesians 5:23-24; Colossians 1:18)

2. THE CHURCH IS A GROUP OF CHRISTIANS IN ONE PLACE.

Many places in the New Testament it tells of a church that worships together in a certain place, such as, *the church of Jerusalem.* Paul, the missionary, started many of these churches. It is possible for people who are not Christians to be part of this group. (Galatians 1:1-2; Ephesians 1:1; Philippians 1:1; Colossians 1:2)

3. THE WORD "CHURCH" HAS THREE OTHER MEANINGS.

A. The word *church* can mean those who are true Christians, but are from different groups.

B. The word *church* can mean a group of people who believe and worship in the same way. These groups are known as *denominations.* These people may have many church buildings in different places where they worship. But all the people in each of these church buildings believe the same way about what the Bible says, and they desire to worship in the same way.

C. The word *church* can mean a building. When people talk about going to church they mean the building where a group of Christians worship.

4. SOME IMPORTANT THINGS ABOUT THE CHURCH.

A. In Ephesians 4:15-16 it says that the church is a part of Christ. He is the Head and the church is the body.

B. In Colossians 1:18 it says that Christ was raised from the dead and will never die again. We know that if the Head cannot die, the body - the church which is a part of Christ - can never die.

C. In Ephesians 3:20-21 it says that the church was brought into being to show Christ and His shining greatness to the world.

D. In Ephesians 5:23-24 it says that the church has the work of obeying and carrying out the plan of its Head, Jesus Christ.

CHURCH GOVERNMENT

1. THERE ARE THREE KINDS OF CHURCH GOVERNMENT.

A. Government by *bishops*

B. Government by *elders*

C. Government by the *Christians* themselves

The first and second ways are seen in Acts 14:23; Acts 20:17,28;
Titus 1:5. But it can be seen how the third way was also used.

2. THESE THINGS CAN BE SEEN IN EACH KIND OF CHURCH GOVERNMENT.

A. Every church had the power to go to anyone of its group who
had done some wrong and try to get the wrong made right. If the
Christian would not turn from his sin, he would be put out of the
church. The reason for this was to keep the church pure and free
from sin. Matthew 18:15-17 says, "If your brother sins against
you, go and tell him what he did without other people hearing it.
If he listens to you, you have won your brother back again. But
if he will not listen to you, take one or two other people with
you. Every word may be remembered by the two or three who
heard. If he will not listen to them, tell the trouble to the church.
If he does not listen to the church, think of him as a person who
is as bad as the one who does not know God and a person who
gathers taxes." (I Corinthians 5:1-5; II Thessalonians 3:6)

B. Every church decided who should be its leaders. (Acts 1:26; 6:1-6)

CHURCH ORGANIZATION

The church is a group of Christians who have joined themselves
together to worship, to learn from the Word of God, to share what they
have in God with each other, and to tell the Good News to others. The
Bible teaches that churches should have leaders.

1. THERE ARE TWO DIFFERENT GROUPS OF CHURCH LEADERS FOR EACH CHURCH.

A. Church leaders (elders)

(1) *What church leaders must be.* I Timothy 3:1-7 says, "It is true that if a man wants to be a church leader, he wants to do a good work. A church leader must be a good man. His life must be so no one can say anything against him. He must have only one wife and must be respected for his good living. He must be willing to take people into his home. He must be willing to learn and able to teach the Word of God. He must not get drunk or want to fight. Instead, he must be gentle. He must not have a love for money. He should be a good leader in his own home. His children must obey and respect him. If a man cannot be a good leader in his own home, how can he lead the church? A church leader must not be a new Christian. A new Christian might become proud and fall into sin which is brought on by the devil. A church leader must be respected by people who are not Christians so nothing can be said against him. In that way, he will not be trapped by the devil."

(2) *What church leaders must do.* Titus 1:5-9 says, "I left you on the island of Crete so you could do some things that needed to be done. I asked you to choose church leaders in every city. Their lives must be so that no one can talk against them. They must have only one wife. Their children must be Christians and known to be good. They must obey their parents. They must not be wild. A church leader is God's servant. His life must be so that no one can say anything against him. He should not try to please himself and not be quick to get angry over little things. He must not get drunk or want to fight. He must not always want more money for himself. He must like to take people into his home. He must love what is good. He must be able to think well and do all things in the right way. He must live a holy life and be the boss over his own desires. He must hold to the words of truth which he was taught. He must be able to teach the truth and show those who are against the truth that they are wrong."

B. Church helpers (deacons)

(1) *What a church helper must be.* I Timothy 3:8-13 says, "Church helpers must also be good men and act so people will respect them. They must speak the truth. They must not get drunk. They must not have a love for money. They must have their faith in Christ and be His followers with a heart that says they are right. They must first be tested to see if

they are ready for the work as church helpers. Then if they do well, they may be chosen as church helpers. The wives of church helpers must be careful how they act. They must not carry stories from one person to another. They must be wise and faithful in all they do. Church helpers must have only one wife. They must lead their home well and their children must obey them. Those who work well as church helpers will be respected by others and their own faith in Christ Jesus will grow."

(2) *What a church helper must do.* Acts 6:1-6 says, "In those days the group of followers was getting larger. Greek-speaking Jews in the group complained against the Jews living in the country around Jerusalem. The Greek-speaking Jews said that their women whose husbands had died were not taken care of when the food was given out each day. So the twelve missionaries called a meeting of the many followers and said, 'It is not right that we should give up preaching the Word of God to hand out food. Brothers, choose from among you seven men who are respected and who are full of the Holy Spirit and wisdom. We will have them take care of this work. Then we will use all of our time to pray and to teach the Word of God.' These words pleased all of them. They chose Stephen who was a man full of faith and full of the Holy Spirit. They also chose Philip, Prochorus, Nicanor, Timon, Parmenas and Nicholas of Antioch who had become a Jew. These men were taken to the missionaries. After praying, the missionaries laid their hands on them."

I Corinthians 12:28 says, "God has chosen different ones in the church to do His work. First, there are missionaries. Second, there are preachers or those who speak for God. And third, there are teachers. He has also chosen those who do powerful works and those who have the gifts of healing. And He has chosen those who help others who are in need and those who are able to lead others in work and those who speak in special sounds."

C. Leaders who are over many churches (bishops)

Soon after the early church was started there were leaders over several or even many churches. They were called bishops. Later other names for such leaders were presidents, presbyters, district superintendents, etc.

CHURCH MEETINGS

When Christians met together to worship God in the early church they did certain things in their meetings:

1. THEY THANKED GOD AND TOLD HIM HOW GREAT HE WAS.

This was done by singing and speaking. Ephesians 5:19-20 says, "Tell of your joy to each other by singing the Songs of David and church songs. Sing in your heart to the Lord. Always give thanks for all things to God and the Father in the name of our Lord Jesus Christ."

2. THEY PRAYED TO GOD.

Acts 4:23-24 says, "As soon as the missionaries were free to go, they went back to their own group. They told them everything the religious leaders had said. When they heard it, they all prayed to God, saying, 'Lord God, You made the heaven and the earth and the sea and everything that is in them.' "

3. THEY SPOKE GOD'S WORD.

I Corinthians 14:3-4 says, "The man who speaks God's Word speaks to men. It helps them to learn and understand. It gives them comfort. The man who speaks in special sounds receives strength. The man who speaks God's Word gives strength to the church."

4. THEY TALKED ABOUT GOD'S WORD.

Acts 13:27 says, "The people of Jerusalem and their leaders did not know Him. They did not understand the words from the early preachers. These words were read to them every Day of Rest." (Acts 15:21)

5. THEY READ LETTERS TO THE CHURCH FROM THE MISSIONARIES, PAUL, JAMES, PETER, JOHN AND OTHERS.

6. THEY RECEIVED MONEY FOR OTHER CHRISTIANS WHO WERE IN NEED, AND HELPED IN SHARING THE GOOD NEWS WITH OTHERS.

Galatians 2:10 says, "They asked us to do only one thing. We were to remember to help poor people. I think this is important also."

Philippians 4:16-17 says, "Even while I was in the city of Thessalonica you helped me more than once. It is not that I want to receive the gift. I want you to get the pay that is coming to you later." (I Corinthians 16:1-4)

7. *THEY ATE THE LORD'S SUPPER TOGETHER.* (See Chapter 48)

8. *THEY BAPTIZED NEW CHRISTIANS.* (See Chapter 48)

Baptism in the early church took place soon after the person put his trust in Christ. It was done by one of the older Christians or church leaders. (Acts 2:38-41; 8:12, 36-38; 9:18; 10:47-48; 16:15, 33; 18:8; 19:3-5; 22:16)

A. It showed the new Christian belonged to Christ. Romans 6:3 says, "All of us were baptized to show we belong to Christ. We were baptized first of all to show His death."

B. It showed the new Christian had become a part of the body of Christ, the true church. Galatians 3:27-28 says, "All of you who have been baptized to show you belong to Christ have become like Christ. God does not see you as a Jew or as Greek. He does not see you as a person sold to work or as a person free to work. He does not see you as a man or as a woman. You are all one in Christ."

WATER BAPTISM

When a believer is baptized, he is telling the world he belongs to Christ. Water baptism does not make a person a Christian, it shows he has put his trust in Christ who died and was buried but arose from the grave. Romans 6:3-5 says, "All of us were baptized to show we belong to Christ. We were baptized first of all to show His death. We were buried in baptism as Christ was buried in death. As Christ was raised from the dead by the great power of God, so we will have new life also. If we have become one with Christ in His death, we will be one with Him in being raised from the dead to new life." Colossians 2:12 says, "When you were baptized you were buried as Christ was buried. When you were raised up in baptism you were raised as Christ was raised. You were raised to a new life by putting your trust in God. It was God Who raised Jesus from the dead." (Acts 2:41; Galatians 3:27)

The Word of God tells us we must be sorry for our sins and turn from them and put our trust in Jesus Christ before we are baptized. Acts 2:38 says, "...Be sorry for your sins and turn from them and be baptized in the name of Jesus Christ, and your sins will be forgiven..." Acts 2:41a says, "Those who believe what he said were baptized..." Acts 8:12b says, "Both men and women put their trust in Christ and were baptized."

Christ told His followers to teach and baptize all nations. Mark 16:15 says, "He (Christ) said to them, 'You are to go to all the world and preach the Good News to every person. He who puts his trust in Me and is baptized will be saved from the punishment of sin'..." Matthew 28:19 says, "Go and make followers of all the nations. Baptize them in the name of the Father and of the Son and of the Holy Spirit."

The word *baptism* means *to dip into, cover up,* or *go under.* Acts 8:38-39 says, "...Then both Philip and the man from Ethiopia went down into the water and Philip baptized him. When they *came up out of the water,* the Holy Spirit took Philip away..." (Matthew 3:6; Mark 1:9-10; John 3:23)

It is a picture of the believer being buried as Christ was buried, and being raised as Christ was raised. It shows the believer is putting away the old life as in death and being raised to new life with Christ. Only a person who has put his trust in Christ should be baptized.

Water baptism often takes place when a new Christian becomes a part of the church where he will worship. In many countries, a Christian is not talked against or hurt until he is baptized. Then his family and others often make it very hard for him and may even bring about his death.

THE LORD'S SUPPER

The Lord's Supper, often called *communion*, is an act of worship started by Christ before He died on the cross. It was done with His followers so they would remember what He was about to do. It showed His followers that the Old Way of Worship was finished and the New Way of Worship had begun.

Exodus 12 tells the story of how the Jews were told what to do so they could hurry from Egypt at night. At the supper that night, they had to do special things to get ready. To save their oldest son from death they had to kill a lamb and put its blood on the sides and top of the door and the death angel would pass over that house. Hebrews 11:28 says, "Because Moses had faith, he told all the Jews to put blood over their doors. Then the angel of death would pass over their houses and not kill their oldest sons." Later the Jews were told to remember how God helped them leave Egypt by a special religious gathering. It was called the *Passover*, meaning the angel of death passed over that house.

All the Jews took part in this special religious gathering to remember how the Jews left Egypt. Jesus had His followers make ready for this supper. (Matthew 26:17-30) In verse 19 it says, "The followers did as Jesus told them. They made things ready for this special supper." This was the *Last Supper*. As He went through each part of the supper, He showed how He Himself was that part bringing an end to the Old Way of Worship. Hebrews 10:10-12, 14, 18 says, "Our sins are washed away and we are made clean because Christ gave His own body as a gift to God. He did this once for all time. All Jewish religious leaders stand every day killing animals and giving gifts on the altar. They give the same gifts over and over again. These gifts cannot take away sins. But Christ gave Himself once for sins and that is good forever. After that He sat down at the right side of God." "And by one gift He has made perfect forever all those who are being set apart for God-like living." "No more gifts on the altar of worship are needed when our sins are forgiven." (Hebrews 9:14-15)

After Jesus went back to heaven, His followers called this act of worship *The Lord's Supper.*

1. THE PARTS OF THE LORD'S SUPPER

   A. First the bread is eaten to help Christians remember how Christ's

body was given for all. Luke 22:19 says, "Then Jesus took bread
and gave thanks and broke it in pieces. He gave it to them
saying, 'This is my body which is given for you. Do this to
remember Me.' "

B. Then the drink from the fruit of the vine is taken. This helps
Christians remember how Christ's blood was given to take away
sins. Luke 22:20b says, "This is My blood of the New Way of
Worship which is given for you." Some churches use wine and
some use grape juice. The Bible says *the fruit of the vine.* Mark
14:25 says, "For sure, I tell you, that I will not drink of the fruit
of the vine until that day when I drink it new in the holy nation
of God."

2. WHO SHOULD EAT THE LORD'S SUPPER

A. Only persons who have been saved from sin should eat the
Lord's Supper. A child should not take part in this worship unless
he has been saved and understands what it means. (I Corinthians
11:24-25)

B. There is danger for anyone eating the Lord's Supper if his spirit is
not right with the Lord. I Corinthians 11:29-30 says, "Anyone
who eats the bread and drinks from the cup, if his spirit is not
right with the Lord, will be guilty as he eats and drinks. He does
not understand the meaning of the Lord's body. This is why some
of you are sick and weak, and some have died." The important
thing is to get everything right with God, and then worship the
Lord.

Nowhere in God's Word does it say that eating the Lord's Supper
takes away sins.

HOW THE CHURCH TAKES CARE OF PROBLEMS AND TROUBLES

The church can be what it should be and do what it should do only when there is no sin, and when every Christian in the church does his part. If there are problems and trouble in the church, the work will be slowed down. If there is sin in the lives of the Christians, the work of the church will not be done. It is important to speak to anyone who is living in sin, and this is to be done by the church. (I Corinthians 5:1-5)

1. *THE WAY A SINNING CHRISTIAN SHOULD BE HELPED* (Matthew 18:15-17)

   A. A Christian is to go to the one who has sinned and talk to him.

   B. If he does not listen to the one Christian, one or two more Christians should go and talk to him.

   C. If he does not listen to these Christians, he should be taken in front of all the Christians of the church and the trouble should be told to them. When Paul thought Peter had done something wrong, he spoke to him about it in front of all the Christians in the church. (Galatians 2:14)

   D. If he does not listen to what the church has to say, he should be put out of the church. But even yet there is hope and forgiveness if the person turns from his sinful ways and asks to be forgiven. (II Corinthians 2:5-8)

2. *WAYS TO TAKE CARE OF PROBLEMS THAT COME TO A CHURCH:*

   A. Trouble between two or more people in the church. (Matthew 18:15-17)

   B. The Christian who sins. (I Corinthians 5:4-5, 11; II Corinthians 2:6-11; 13:2; I Timothy 1:19-20)

   C. The person who says he is a Christian but who teaches lies about God and His Word. (Romans 16:17; Galatians 5:10-12; II Thessalonians 3:6; I Timothy 6:3-5; Titus 1:10-11, 13; 3:10; II John 1:10-11)

D. The Christian who turns against the church and all that is said to him. (II Thessalonians 3:6, 14-15)

E. The weak Christian (Romans 14:1-23; 15:1; Galatians 6:1)

F. The church leader or helper who sins. (I Timothy 5:19-20)

G. The Christian who joins himself to a sinner. (I Corinthians 7:39; II Corinthians 6:14-15)

The Word of God tells how to take care of problems and trouble in the church. An important lesson is seen in Hebrews 12:6, "The Lord punishes everyone He loves. He whips every son He receives." The church must also show great love when a Christian who has sinned is punished.

THE WORK OF THE CHURCH

The church is not just a group of people who choose to worship together, but it is expected to do a work for God. No such work can be done unless the Christians are living God-like lives.

The Bible speaks of the Christians as:

1. THE SALT OF THE EARTH

In Matthew 5:13 it says, "You are the salt of the earth." Salt is used in two ways:

A. To keep things from spoiling. This means that the Christians are to make peace among people. Mark 9:50 says, "Salt is good, but if salt loses its taste, how can it be made to taste like salt again? Have salt in yourselves and be at peace with each other."

B. To make food taste better. The Christians are to always bring out the best in others and be a help whenever they can.

2. THE LIGHT OF THE WORLD

Matthew 5:14 says, "You are the light of the world." The Christian shines by allowing Christ, the great Light, to shine through him. Matthew 5:15 says, "Men do not light a lamp and put it under a basket. They put it on a table so it gives light to all in the house." The church is to shine in the world. Philippians 2:15-16 says, "In that way, you can prove yourselves to be without blame. You are God's children and no one can talk against you, even in a sin-loving and sin-sick world. Take a strong hold on the Word of Life. Then when Christ comes again, I will be happy that I did not work with you for nothing."

There are two important jobs of the church:

1. HELPING EVERY PERSON IN THE CHURCH TO BECOME A STRONG CHRISTIAN

A. After a person has become a Christian, he is to be taught the Word of God so there will be growth. (II Timothy 4:2b) I Peter 5:1-4 says, "I want to speak to the church leaders among you. I am a church leader also. I saw Christ suffer and die on a cross. I will also share His shining greatness when He comes again. Be good shepherds of the flock God has put in your care. Do not care for the flock as if you were made to. Do not care for the flock for money, but do it because you want to. Do not be bosses over the people you lead. Live as you would like to have them live. When the Head Shepherd comes again, you will get the prize of shining greatness that will not come to an end." (Colossians 3:16; Hebrews 4:12; I Peter 2:2)

B. Every Christian is to be filled with the Holy Spirit. Ephesians 5:18 says, "Do not get drunk with wine. That leads to wild living. Instead, be filled with the Holy Spirit." (Galatians 5:16)

C. The gifts of the Spirit were given to help the Christian. (Romans 12:6-8; I Corinthians 12:6-11; Ephesians 2:21-22)

The Christian is not only saved by God's loving-favor, but he is to keep on learning more about Christ, the One Who saved him. He becomes a new place for the Holy Spirit to live. Ephesians 2:21 says, "Christ keeps this building together and it is growing into a holy building of the Lord."

2. TELLING THE GOOD NEWS OF CHRIST

Jesus told His followers to preach the Good News. Mark 16:15-16 says, "He said to them, 'You are to go to all the world and preach the Good News to every person. He who puts his trust in Me and is baptized will be saved from the punishment of sin. But he who does not put his trust in Me is guilty and will be punished forever.' "

The Christian is not told to take the world to Christ, but to take Christ to the world. When Christ is taken to the world, the Good News of Christ being able to save becomes the power of God to everyone who believes. Romans 1:16 says, "I am not ashamed of the Good News. It is the power of God. It is the way He saves men from the punishment of their sins if they put their trust in Him. It is for the Jews first and for all other people also."

In each of the first four Books of the New Testament and in Acts, Christ gives the word to go and teach all people.

Matthew 28:18-20 says, "Jesus came and said to them, 'All power has been given to Me in heaven and on earth. Go and make followers of all the nations. Baptize them in the name of the Father and of the Son and of the Holy Spirit. Teach them to do all the things I have told you. And I am with you always, even to the end of the world.' "

Mark 16:15-16 says, "He said to them, 'You are to go to all the world and preach the Good News to every person. He who puts his trust in

Me and is baptized will be saved from the punishment of sin. But he who does not put his trust in Me is guilty and will be punished forever.' "

Luke 24:46-48 says, "He said to them, 'It is written that Christ should suffer and be raised from the dead after three days. It must be preached that men must be sorry for their sins and turn from them. Then they will be forgiven. This must be preached in His name to all nations beginning in Jerusalem. You are to tell what you have seen.' "

John 20:21 says, "Then Jesus said to them again, 'May you have peace. As the Father has sent Me, I also am sending you.' "

Acts 1:8 says, "But you will receive power when the Holy Spirit comes into your life. You will tell about Me in the city of Jerusalem and over all the countries of Judea and Samaria and to the ends of the earth."

We do not learn from Acts 1:8 that we are to tell the Good News only in Jerusalem until all have heard, then go on to the next places - Judea and Samaria. Then after all three places are covered, go to the rest of the world. The whole world is to hear as soon as possible.

PART 9

WHAT THE WORD OF GOD TEACHES ABOUT THE LAST THINGS

[*Eschatology*]

CHRIST'S SECOND COMING

It tells all through God's Word that Christ will come to earth again. Before Christ came to earth the first time, the early preachers told about it in many of the books of the Old Testament. In the first four books of the New Testament it tells of how Christ came to earth. It was all just as the early preachers wrote.

These same men of God wrote about how Christ will come to earth the second time. We have no reason to believe He will not come just as they told about it long ago.

1. THE BIBLE SPEAKS OF CHRIST'S SECOND COMING.

It tells of His second coming eight times more often than of His first coming. It speaks of it 318 times in the New Testament.

2. THE CHURCH LEADERS TAUGHT THAT CHRIST WOULD RETURN.

Acts 3:20 says, "He will send Jesus back to the world. He is the Christ Who long ago was chosen for you." II Thessalonians 1:7 says, "He will help you and us who are suffering. This will happen when the Lord Jesus comes down from heaven with His powerful angels in a bright fire." (James 5:8; II Peter 1:16; I John 2:28; Jude 14)

3. THE ANGELS TOLD OF CHRIST'S RETURN

Acts 1:11 says, "They said, 'You men of the country of Galilee, why do you stand looking up into heaven? This same Jesus Who was taken from you into heaven will return in the same way you saw Him go up into heaven.' "

4. JESUS TOLD OF HIS RETURN.

Matthew 24:27 says, "The Son of Man will come as fast as lightning goes across the sky from east to west." (Mark 13:26; Luke 21:27; John 14:3; 21:22)

The second coming of Christ is just what it says it is in plain language. Christ Himself is coming again as a person and will be seen by everyone. Revelation 1:7 says, "See! He is coming in the clouds. Every eye will see Him. Even the men who killed Him will see Him. All the people on the earth will cry out in sorrow because of Him. "

Some of the Old Testament early preachers wrote of Christ's first and second coming without telling of the many years in between. When a man looks at two mountains that are a long way off, he does not see the valley between them. They look to him as if they are close together.

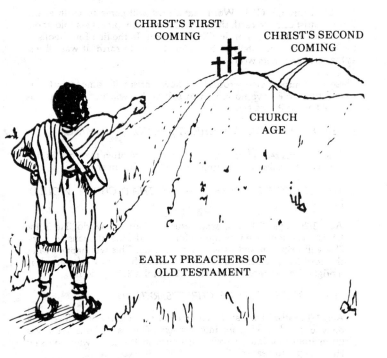

CHRIST'S FIRST COMING

CHRIST'S SECOND COMING

CHURCH AGE

EARLY PREACHERS OF OLD TESTAMENT

CHRIST'S SECOND COMING WILL BE AT TWO DIFFERENT TIMES

1. FOR THE CHRISTIANS (Rapture)

The first time Christ comes in the future, He will come *for* the Christians. During the first time He will come *in the air* (sky) and the Christians will meet him there. This is called the *rapture*. I Thessalonians 4:13-18 says, "Christian brothers, we want you to know for sure about those who have died. You have no reason to have sorrow as those who have no hope. We believe that Jesus died and then came to life again. Because we believe this, we know that

God will bring to life all those who belong to Jesus. We tell you this as it came from the Lord. Those of us who are alive when the Lord comes again will not go ahead of those who have died. For the Lord Himself will come down from heaven with a loud call. The head angel will speak with a loud voice. God's horn will give its sounds. First, those who belong to Christ will come out of their graves to meet the Lord. Then, those of us who are still living here on earth will be gathered together with them in the clouds. We will meet the Lord in the sky and be with Him forever. Because of this, comfort each other with these words."

2. WITH THE CHRISTIANS [Revelation]

The second time Christ comes in the future, He will come *with* the Christians. During this second time He will come *to the earth* where He and the church will rule the nations. This is called the *revelation*.

In Zechariah 14:4 it says, "On that day His feet will stand on the Mount of Olives, in front of Jerusalem on the east. And the Mount of Olives will be divided in two from east to west by a very large valley. Half the mountain will move toward the north and the other half toward the south."

THE TIME OF GREAT TROUBLE

1. THERE WILL BE SEVEN YEARS OF VERY MUCH TROUBLE ON EARTH. THIS IS KNOWN AS THE GREAT TRIBULATION.

Churches are divided as to what they believe about when Christ will return the first time.

A. The word *pre-tribulation* means that Christ will return before the seven years of much trouble.

B. The word *mid-tribulation* means that Christ will return in the middle of the seven years, or after three and one-half years of much trouble.

C. The word *post-tribulation* means that Christ will return after the seven years of much trouble.

SIGNS OF THE TIMES

Certain things show that Christ's return is in the near future. Luke 21:31 says, "In the same way, when you see these things happening, you will know the holy nation of God is near." The Word of God tells us that we should know about these things so we will not be surprised. (I Thessalonians 5:1-4) But we cannot know the day or the hour. Only God knows that. Matthew 24:36 says, "But no one knows the day or the hour. No! Not even the angels in heaven know. The Son does not know. Only the Father knows."

In Matthew 24:3-14 these signs are given:

1. *MANY PEOPLE WILL USE CHRIST'S NAME IN A FALSE WAY.* Verse 5 says, "Many people will come using My name. They will say, 'I am Christ.' They will fool many people and will turn them to the wrong way."

2. *THERE WILL BE WARS AND LOTS OF TALK ABOUT WARS.* Verses 6-7a says, "You will hear of wars and lots of talk about wars, but do not be afraid. These things must happen, but it is not the end yet. Nations will have wars with other nations. Countries will fight against countries."

3. *THERE WILL BE NO FOOD FOR PEOPLE.* Verse 7b says, "There will be no food for people."

4. *THE EARTH WILL SHAKE AND BREAK APART IN DIFFERENT PLACES.* Verse 7c says, "The earth will shake and break apart in different places."

5. *CHRISTIANS WILL BE HURT AND KILLED AND HATED.* Verse 9 says, "Then they will hand you over to be hurt. They will kill you. You will be hated by all the world because of My name."

6. *MANY PEOPLE WILL GIVE UP AND TURN AWAY.* Verse 10 says, "Many people will give up and turn away at this time. People will hand over each other. They will hate each other."

7. *MANY FALSE RELIGIOUS TEACHERS WILL START WORKING.* Verse 11 says, "Many false religious teachers will come. They will fool many people and will turn them to the wrong way."

8. *BECAUSE OF PEOPLE BREAKING THE LAWS AND SIN BEING EVERYWHERE, THE LOVE IN THE HEARTS OF MANY PEOPLE WILL BECOME COLD.* Verses 12-13 say, "Because of people breaking the laws and sin being everywhere, the love in the hearts of many people will become cold. But the one who stays true to the end will be saved."

These signs are given also:

9. *THERE WILL BE A LOT MORE SIN, BUT PEOPLE WILL SAY EVERYTHING IS FINE AND SAFE.* I Thessalonians 5:3 says, "When they say, 'Everything is fine and safe,' then all at once they will be destroyed. It will be like pain that comes on a woman when a child is born. They will not be able to get away from it."

10. *PEOPLE WILL LOVE THEMSELVES AND MONEY.* II Timothy 3:2a says, "People will love themselves and money. They will have pride and tell of all the things they have done. They will speak against God."

11. *CHILDREN AND YOUNG PEOPLE WILL NOT OBEY THEIR PARENTS.* II Timothy 3:2b says, "Children and young people will not obey their parents."

12. *PEOPLE WILL NOT BE THANKFUL AND THEY WILL NOT BE HOLY.* II Timothy 3:2c says, "People will not be thankful and they will not be holy."

13. *PEOPLE WILL NOT LOVE EACH OTHER. THEY WILL LOVE FUN INSTEAD OF LOVING GOD.* II Timothy 3:3-4 says, "They will not love each other. No one can get along with them. They will tell lies about others. They will not be able to keep from doing things they know they should not do. They will be wild and want to beat and hurt those who are good. They will not stay true to their friends. They will act without thinking. They will think too much of themselves. They will love fun instead of loving God."

14. *THE GOOD NEWS OF CHRIST WILL BE PREACHED OVER ALL THE WORLD.* Matthew 24:14 says, "This Good News about the holy nation of God must be preached over all the earth. It must be told to all nations and then the end will come."

15. *THE JEWS WILL RETURN TO THEIR HOMELAND.* Ezekiel 36:24 says, "For I will take you from the nations and gather you from all the lands, and bring you into your own land."

16. *THE JEWS WILL MAKE THE WASTE LAND BECOME LIKE A GARDEN.* Isaiah 35:1b says, "...The desert will be full of joy and become like a rose." The land of Israel is like this now, so different than it was even some years ago.

17. *PEOPLE WILL GO PLACES THEY HAVE NEVER GONE BEFORE, AND WILL KNOW MORE THAN THEY HAVE EVER KNOWN BEFORE.* Daniel 12:4b says, "...Many will travel here and there and knowledge will be more and more."

FALSE-CHRIST

Just before Christ returns to the earth with His Church, the false-christ or the person known as the *antichrist* or the *lawless one* will be given power to rule over all the earth. This time will be known as *the time of much trouble* or *the great tribulation*, and will last for seven years.

There will be much bad and wrong done in the world. This will be brought on by many false-christs. I John 2:18 says, "My children, we are near the end of the world. You have heard that the false-christ is coming. Many false-christs have already come. This is how we know the end of the world is near." Things will get worse because of the *real false-christ* taking over everything.

1. *THE FALSE-CHRIST WILL BE THE RULER OVER ALL RELIGIONS, GOVERNMENTS, AND MONEY OF THE WORLD.*

   Revelation 13:7, 15 says, "It was allowed to fight against the people who belong to God, and it had power to win over them. It had power over every family and every group of people and over people of every language and every nation." "The second wild animal was given power to give life to the false god. This false god was the one that was made to look like the first wild animal. It was given power to talk. All those who did not worship it would die."

   Satan will be his boss, and he is also called *the wild animal*. Revelation 13:2 says, "The wild animal I saw was covered with spots. It had feet like those of a bear. It had a mouth like that of a lion. The snake-like animal gave this wild animal his own power and his own throne as king. The wild animal was given much power." In II Thessalonians 2:3 he is called *the man of sin*.

2. *THE FALSE-CHRIST'S JOB WILL BE TO WORK AGAINST GOD, AND ALL THAT IS RIGHT AND GOOD.*

   He will put himself up as if he is God. He will have power over all the nations of the earth.

3. *NO ONE KNOWS WHEN THE FALSE-CHRIST WILL FIRST BE SEEN.*

   After the church is taken up to heaven and the Holy Spirit will no longer be working with people on earth, the false-christ will start his work right away. (II Thessalonians 2:6-8) But all Christians are given hope to look for *Christ*, *not* the false-Christ. (Luke 21:28, 36)

4. THE FALSE-CHRIST WILL BE ALLOWED TO COME TO PUNISH THOSE WHO TURNED AWAY FROM CHRIST AND CHOSE TO TURN AWAY FROM GOD'S WORD.

In II Thessalonians 2:11-12 it says, "For this reason God will allow them to follow false teachings so they will believe a lie. They will all be guilty as they stand before God because they wanted to do what was wrong."

THE 1,000 YEAR TIME

The word *millennium* means 1,000 years. In the first seven verses of Revelation 20, *1,000 years* is used six times.

Churches are divided in what they think the Holy Writings teach about the 1,000 year time. There are three different ideas:

1. PREMILLENNIUM

Premillennium means that Christ will return before the 1,000 years. It teaches that there is a 1,000 year time to come and that Christ will return to earth before the 1,000 years. When He comes He and the Christians will rule the world. For the first 300 years the early church taught this.

2. AMILLENNIUM

Amillennium means that the millennium started with the coming of Christ and goes through the whole New Testament time until the end of this age. It means that the Christians are now ruling with Christ and those who have died are ruling with Him up in heaven.

3. POSTMILLENNIUM

Postmillennium means that Christ will return to earth after the 1,000 year time is over.

Two important things will take place before the 1,000 year time:

1. THE BATTLE OF ARMAGEDDON

This will be a world war against God and the Jews. (Revelation 16:12-16) Christ will have power over those who make war against God because He will come down from the sky and destroy the sinful armies. (Psalm 2; Isaiah 29:1-8; Joel 3:9; Zechariah 14:1-5; 14:12-15; Revelation 19:17-21)

2. THE NATIONS ARE TOLD IF THEY ARE GUILTY.

After Christ wins the war of Armageddon, He will set up His holy nation on earth and gather the nations before Him to say if they are guilty. (Matthew 25:31-46)

Some other things will happen:

1. *SATAN WILL BE TIED AND THROWN INTO THE HOLE WITHOUT A BOTTOM DURING THIS 1,000 YEAR TIME.* (Revelation 20:1-3)

2. *THE CHRISTIANS WHO HAVE BEEN RAISED FROM THE GRAVES WILL HAVE THEIR NEW SINLESS BODIES AND WILL RULE WITH CHRIST ON EARTH.* (Revelation 20:4)

3. *THE SINFUL DEAD PEOPLE WILL NOT BE RAISED FROM THE DEAD UNTIL THE 1,000 YEAR TIME IS FINISHED.* (Revelation 20:5, 12)

4. *THE JEWISH NATION WILL BECOME A LEADING WORLD POWER DURING THIS 1,000 YEAR TIME.* (Zechariah 8:23; 14:8, 9, 16; Romans 11:23-32)

The 1,000 year time and what will happen to the church, the Jews, and the nations:

1. *THE CHRISTIANS WILL RULE WITH CHRIST.*

   This would also mean that those who suffered for Christ during the time of much trouble will rule with Christ. Revelation 20:4 says, "Then I saw thrones. Those who were sitting there were given the power to say who is guilty. I saw the souls of those who had been killed because they told about Jesus and preached the Word of God. They had not worshiped the wild animal or his false god. They had not received his mark on their foreheads or hands. They lived again and were leaders along with Christ for 1,000 years."

2. *GOD MADE A PROMISE TO DAVID WHICH HAS NEVER BEEN BROKEN.*

   God promised that the throne on which David sat to rule his nation would be kept forever, and that David would never want a man to sit on it. (II Samuel 7:11-17; Jeremiah 33:17) When Christ came to earth as a baby in the town of Bethlehem, He had the right to take that throne. (Luke 1:32) When Christ will return and rule on earth, He will use that same throne. (Isaiah 9:6-7) The house of God that David built will be built again. (Acts 15:16) The Jews will be a respected and honored people on the earth. (Zechariah 8:13)

3. *THE BATTLE OF ARMAGEDDON*

   This will take place before the 1,000 year time and will not kill all the people of the earth, but only those armies that are fighting in that battle. There will be people living in other parts of the world who will say Who Christ is. Romans 14:11 says, "The Holy Writings say, 'As I live, says the Lord, every knee will bow down before Me. And every tongue will say that I am God.' " If every knee does bow down before Christ, it does not mean that all these nations will put their trust in Christ. It is one thing to bow down before Him and another to put one's trust in Him. If any nation does keep on fighting against God and will not obey, that nation will be punished right away. (Zechariah 14:16-19) The important thing for that time will be holy living. (Zechariah 14:20-21)

The reason for the 1,000 year time:

1. THE 1,000 YEAR TIME WILL BE WHEN GOD WILL TEST MAN THE LAST TIME.

The 1,000 year time is not what the Christians are looking forward to. They are looking forward to the Holy City, the new Jerusalem. (Revelation 21:9-22) This 1,000 year time will be when God will test man the last time. Things will be better then because Satan will be tied and out of the way and Christ will be ruling.

2. THE 1,000 YEAR TIME WILL BE A GREAT TIME FOR THE JEWS.

Micah 4:6-7 says, " 'In that day,' says the Lord, 'I will gather together those who cannot walk and those who have been driven away, even those whom I have made to suffer. I will make a new beginning with those who cannot walk. I will make a strong nation of those who have been driven away. And the Lord will rule over them in Mount Zion from that day and forever.' " There will be peace over all the earth. (Isaiah 2:2-4; Micah 4:3-4) There will be lots of money, food, and things. (Isaiah 35) All animals will get along well together. (Isaiah 11:6-9) Christ will rule all things well. What He says and does will be right. (Isaiah 11:1-4)

After the 1,000 years Satan will be let loose for awhile. He will go around lying to the nations. Many people will follow him. Soon after he will be thrown into the lake of fire. (Revelation 20:10) The earth and the heaven will leave. In Revelation 20:11 it says, "Then I saw a great white throne. I saw the One Who sat on it. The earth and the heaven left Him in a hurry and they could be found no more." This is, no doubt, what Peter wrote about in II Peter 3:7-10. Then the great white throne where God sits will be seen, and those who have never put their trust in Christ will be told they are guilty. (Revelation 20:11-15) The One Who will sit on that great white throne is Christ Jesus. (John 5:22; Acts 17:31)

PEOPLE WILL BE RAISED FROM THE DEAD AND TOLD IF THEY ARE GUILTY

1. THE 1,000 YEAR TIME WILL NOT BE THE END OF THE WORLD.

Before the end of the world other things will happen:

A. The Christians will be raised from their graves when Christ comes for those who have put their trust in Him. I Corinthians 15:22-23 says, "All men will die as Adam died. But all those who belong to Christ will be raised to new life. This is the way it is: Christ was raised from the dead first. Then all those who belong to Christ will be raised from the dead when He comes again." (I Thessalonians 4:14-17) This will be before the 1,000 year time. It is called the *first resurrection*. Revelation 20:6 says, "Those who are raised from the dead during the first time are happy and holy. The second death has no power over them. They will be religious leaders of God and of Christ. They will be leaders with Him for 1,000 years."

B. Those who did not put their trust in Christ will be raised from their graves after the 1,000 year time is finished. In Revelation 20:12-13 it says, "I saw all the dead people standing before God. There were great people and small people. The books were opened. Then another book was opened. It was the book of life. The dead people were told they were guilty by what they had done as it was written in the books. The sea gave up the dead people who were in it. Death and hell gave up the dead people who were in them. Each one was told he was guilty by what he had done."

2. THE CHRISTIAN WILL STAND BEFORE GOD BEFORE THE 1,000 YEAR TIME. THIS IS KNOWN AS THE JUDGEMENT SEAT OF CHRIST.

The Christian is not told he is guilty because God has already put that guilt on His Son, Jesus Christ, on the cross. John 5:24 says, "For sure, I tell you, anyone who hears My Word and puts his trust in Him Who sent Me has life that lasts forever. He will not be guilty. He has already passed from death into life." His sins were taken care of at the cross, and by faith in that work, he is free from the punishment of sin. But all Christians must stand before Christ. In II Corinthians 5:10 it says, "For all of us must stand before Christ when

He says who is guilty or not guilty. Each one will receive pay for what he has done. He will be paid for the good or the bad done while he lived in this body." This will take place when the church is taken up to meet the Lord in the air. The reason Christians must stand before Christ at that time is to tell what they have done in their work for Christ. (Matthew 25:14-30; Luke 19:11-27)

The *works* of every Christian will be tested by fire. Some will be burned to ashes because they are only *wood, hay, and grass.* Other *works* will stand the test, and come out as *gold, silver, and stones worth much money.* Those whose works are burned up will be saved as if they were going through a fire. I Corinthians 3:12-15 says, "Now if a man builds on the Stone with gold or silver or beautiful stones, or if he builds with wood or grass or straw, each man's work will become known. There will be a day when it will be tested by fire. The fire will show what kind of work it is. If a man builds on work that lasts, he will receive his pay. If his work is burned up, he will lose it. Yet he himself will be saved as if he were going through a fire." This will be a time when the Christian receives the pay that is coming to him for his work.

Revelation 11:18b says, "...It is time for the servants You own who are the early preachers and those who belong to You to get the pay that is coming to them. It is time for the important people and those not important who honor Your name to get the pay that is coming to them. It is time to destroy those who have made every kind of trouble on the earth." Revelation 20:8b-9 says, "He will gather them all together for war. There will be as many as the sand along the seashore. They will spread out over the earth and all around the place where God's people are and around the city that is loved. Fire will come down from God out of heaven and destroy them."

3. *THE SINNER WILL STAND BEFORE GOD AFTER THE 1,000 YEAR TIME. THIS IS KNOWN AS THE GREAT WHITE THRONE JUDGEMENT.*

The person who is not a Christian will be told he is guilty because his name is not written in *The Book of Life.* In John 14:6 Jesus said, "I am the *Way* and the *Truth* and the *Life.* No one can go to the Father except by Me." (Acts 4:12; I John 5:12)

Those who are told they are guilty will suffer punishment for sin forever. There will never be an end to the suffering. (Matthew 25:46; Mark 9:43, 48; Revelation 14:9-11)

The place of that suffering is called the *lake of fire.* (Revelation 19:20; 20:10, 15)

It should be remembered that the *lake of fire* was made ready for *the devil and his angels,* not for man. (Matthew 25:41) But those who keep on in the way of sin must suffer the same punishment as the devil and his angels.

God wants all men to be saved from the punishment of sin. He said in Revelation 22:17b, "Let the one who wants to drink of the water of life, drink it. It is a free gift." And in II Peter 3:9b He says, "...The Lord does not want any person to be punished forever." II Corinthians 6:2b says, "Now is the right time! See! Now is the day to be saved." (Isaiah 49:8)

THE NEW HEAVEN AND THE NEW EARTH

After the heavens and earth are destroyed with fire (II Peter 3:10) there will be new heavens and a new earth. (II Peter 3:13) This will be called the *Holy City* or the *New Jerusalem.*

It will be a far better place than man can think of. Only what is right and good will be there. There will be no more death, or sorrow, or crying, or pain. Everyone will be worshiping God. There will be no night there. It will be the new home for all those who have put their trust in Christ and have been saved from the punishment of their sins. (Revelation 21; 22:5)

"He Who tells these things says, 'Yes, I am coming soon!' Let it be so. Come, Lord Jesus." (Revelation 22:20)

WORD LIST

Words Used In Other Translations	Words Used In This Translation

A

abominable	sinful-minded people
adultery	sex sins
	not faithful in marriage
almighty	All-Powerful
Amen	let it be so
anointed	chosen
anointed (with oil)	poured oil on
antichrist	false-christ
apostle	missionary
archangel	head angel
ark of the covenant	special box that held the Old Way of Worship
	box of the Way of Worship
armour	things God gives you to fight with
astonished	surprised and wondered
authority	the right and the power

B

beloved	much-loved
	dear friends
beseech	ask you from my heart
betray	hand Him over to them
bitterness	bad feelings about other people
blameless	without blame
blaspheme	speaks like he is God
	speaks against God
bless, blessed, blessing	respect and give thanks
	give honor to Him and thank God
bondwoman	woman who is owned by someone and who has to do what she is told
bottomless pit	hole without a bottom
bridegroom	man to be married soon

C

centurion	captain of the army
chariot	wagon
cheer	take hope
circumcise	religious act of becoming a Jew
command	told them with strong words

commandment	teaching
	Law
	God's Word
compassion	loving-pity
concupiscence	desire for sex sin
condemn	guilty and be punished forever
confess	told their sins
conscience	their own hearts tell them they are guilty
corruptible	that which dies
counsel (take)	talk about what to do
courage	strength of heart
Covenant (Testament)	New Way of Worship
	Old Way of Worship
covetousness	wanting something that belongs to someone
create	make from nothing
creation	the whole world
crown of life	prize of life
crucify	nail Him on a cross

D

day of judgment	the day men stand before God to be told they are guilty
deacons	church helpers
deceit	lying
deceive	fools you and turns you to the wrong way
deny, denied	lied and said he did not know Me
	act as if you never knew Him
despise	hate
disciple	follower
discipline	punish
divisions	dividing people into groups against each other
doctrine	teaching

E

ears to hear	if you have ears, then listen
effeminate	men who act like women
elders	church leaders
elect	the people of God
emulations	jealousy
enemy	one who hates
	one who works against you
endure	keeps on
enmity	fighting
envying	wanting something someone else has
escape	get away from it
eternal life	life that lasts forever

evangelist	a preacher who goes from town to town
everlasting fire	fire that never goes out
everlasting life	life that lasts forever
evil	bad
	sinful
evil speaking	bad talk
example	I have done this to show you

F

false witness	tell a lie about someone else
fasting	not eating so you can pray better
fear (of the Lord)	respect
	honor
feast	religious gathering
	religious supper
	special supper
fellowship	share together
	joined together
flesh (worldy)	old self
	sinful things of this life (world)
for My sake	because of Me
	because you trust in Me
fornication	sex sins
forsake	leave alone
foundation	the part on which the building stands
foundation of the world	before the world was made
fulfilled	it happened as the early preacher said it would happen

G

gain	use you to get things for themselves
generation	people of this day
	family
Gentiles	people who do not know God
	people who are not Jews
glory	shining greatness
	honor
glory, glorified	receive great honor
	honors
gnashing of teeth	grinding of teeth
godliness	God-like
	holy living
Gospel	Good News
grace	loving-favor
	God's love
greed	always wanting something

| groan | we cry inside ourselves with sounds that cannot be put into words |
| guile | speaking words of hate
talking bad about others |

H

hark	Listen!
harlot	a woman who sells the use of her body
harps	music boxes of strings
harvest	gathering time
heathen	people who do not know God
heresy	false teaching
high priest	head religious leader
homosexual	people who do sex sins with their own sex
Host (Lord of)	Lord of All
House (of David)	Family of David
humble	no pride
hypocrisy	saying one thing but thinking something else
hypocrite	you who pretend to be someone you are not

I

idol	a god
idolatry	worshiping false gods
immortality	life that never dies
imperishable	will never die
incense	special perfume
incorruptible	never dies
inn	place where people stay for the night
inordinate affection	a strong and bad desire to please the body
intercedes	prays to God for us

J

judge	punish says he is guilty or not
judged	told he is guilty told he is wrong
judgment	they will stand before God and He will say if they are guilty
justified	made right with God

K

kingdom	holy nation
kingdom of God	holy nation of God
kingdom of heaven	holy nation of heaven
knowledge	much learning

L

lasciviousness

desire for sex sins
desire for wrong things

law (God's Law) — Law
law (of the land) — law
lawyer (see scribe) — man who knew the law
leper — a man with a bad skin disease
longsuffering — being able to wait
lots (casting) — drawing names
lunatic — those who lose the use of their minds for awhile

lust — a desire for sex sins

M

majesty — great power
malice — bad talk which hurts other people
manifested — shown
manna — bread from heaven
market place — the center of town where people gather
marvelled — surprised and wondered
master

teacher
owner

meekness — not having pride
mercy — loving-kindness
messenger

man to carry news
helper

minister (serve) — care for
miracles — powerful works
mock — make fun of
mourn — have sorrow
multitude — many people
murder — kill other people
murmur

talk among themselves against Him
talk against

mystery

hidden truth
secret
great truth that is hidden

O

offend

ashamed of Me and leave Me
ashamed and turns away

oppression — bad power held over them
ordain — set apart
overcome

power over the devil
won the fight

overcomer — have power over

P

partiality	to respect one person more than another
Passover	a special religious gathering to remember how the Jews left Egypt
pastor	church leader
patience	not give up
	being willing to wait
Pentecost	fifty days after the special religious gathering to remember how the Jews left Egypt
	that special day to remember how the Holy Spirit came on the church
perish	lost
	lost from God forever
persecute	make it hard for them
perseverance	faith stays strong even when people make it very hard for you
Pharisee	proud religious law-keeper
plagues	troubles
precious	of great worth
	no amount of money can buy it
priests	religious leaders
(Christ as High Priest)	Religious Leader Who stands between God and man
	Religious Leader Who made the way for men to go to God
(High Priest)	head Jewish religious leader
prophecy	preach
	speaking God's Word
	tell what will happen in the future
prophet	special preacher
	early preacher
	one who speaks for God
	one who tells what is going to happen
propitiation	paid for our sins with His own blood

R

ransom	He gave His life so they could go free
rebuked	spoke sharp words
reconcile	turn from your sins and come to God
redeem (redemption)	bought by the blood of Christ and made free
regeneration	new life
reign	has power
reject	have nothing to do with
	turn away from
remission	forgiveness

rend	tear to pieces
repent	be sorry for your sins and turn from them
reproach	have no honor
	shame
reprobate	person in sin on his way to hell
reprove	speak strong words to
resist	stand against
resurrection	raised from the dead
	come up from the grave
revelation	some things the Lord has shown me
	some special words from God
revelings	wild parties
reverence	honor God with love and fear
reward	pay
righteousness	right with God

S

Sabbath	Day of rest
sackcloth	clothes made from hair
sacrifice (offering)	a gift given on the altar in worship
Sadducees	religious group of people who believe no one will be raised from the dead
saints	true Christians
	those who belong to Christ
sanctify	set apart
	made holy
	right with God
	set apart for God-like living and to do His work
Sanhedrin	religious leaders' court
scribe (see lawyer)	teacher of the Law
Scripture	Holy Writings
	God's Written Word
seditions	dividing into little groups and thinking the other group is wrong
self-control	being the boss over our own desires
sign	something special to see
	something to look for
slander	talk that hurts people
slave	one who is sold to work
sober	be careful how they act
	keep our minds awake
spiritual	full-grown Christians
	strong Christians
spiritual gifts	gifts of the Holy Spirit
steadfast	not to be moved by others
straightway	at once
swear	promise
sword (two-edged)	sword that cuts both ways

T

tabernacle	tent to worship in
temperance	the right use of what we have
temple	house of God
temptation	causes you to sin
tender	kind
Testament (Covenant)	New Way of Worship
	Old Way of Worship
tongues	languages
	special sounds
tradition	teaching that was given by our fathers (man-made)
trample	break them under their feet
treasures	riches
tribes	early families, family groups
tribulation	time of much trouble
triumph	win the fight
tumult (commotion)	making much noice

V

vain (not in vain)	that I did not work with you for nothing
verily	for sure
virgin	a woman who has never had a man
virtue	the power to stand against sin
vision	saw in a dream what God wanted him to see
	special dream

W

watch	look and listen
weeping	loud crying
welcome	receive him and make him happy
	say hello
wicked	sinful
widow	woman whose husband has died
will (God's will)	what God wants done
winepress	a place for making wine
withered	dried up
	dying
witness	tells what he knows
woe	it is bad for you
worthy	has the right to
	good enough
wrath	anger
	bad temper
	God's anger

THE NEW TESTAMENT

TOPICAL VERSE FINDER

Afraid
Matt. 14:25-27
John 14:27
Heb. 13:6
I John 4:18

Angels
Matt. 28:2-5
Acts 5:17-20; 8:26; 12:7-9;
27:21-26
I Cor. 6:3
Col. 2:18
Heb. 13:2

Anger
Eph. 4:26,31
Col. 3:5-8
James 1:20

Baptism
Matt. 3:13-17
Rom. 6:3-5
Col. 2:12
Eph. 4:5

Becoming Full-Grown Christians
Eph. 3:16-19
Col. 1:9-11; 3:12-17
I Tim. 4:11-16
II Tim. 2:14-19
I Peter 2:1-3
II Peter 1:5-9; 3:17-18

Being Pure
Phil. 2:13-15
I Tim. 5:22
James 3:16-18; 4:8
I John 3:3

Being The Boss Over Your Own Desires [*Self-Control*]
Rom. 13:14
I Cor. 9:24-25
I Tim. 6:11-12
II Tim. 2:3-5

Being Tempted
Matt. 26:41
I Cor. 10:11-13
Heb. 2:18; 4:14-16
James 1:14; 4:7
II Pet. 2:9

Christ: One Of The Three-In-One God
Matt. 26:62-64
John 1:1-4,18; 10:30; 14:8-10
Col. 1:15-19; 2:9
Titus 2:13
Heb. 1:3,8
I John 5:20

Church
Matt. 16:18; 18:15-17
Acts 2:42-47; 14:23; 16:4-5
Rom. 16:5
Eph. 1:21-22

Comfort and Help
Matt. 5:4; 11:28-30
Rom. 15:1-6
II Cor. 1:3-5
I Thess. 5:14
II Thess. 2:16-17

Death
Rom. 14:7-9
II Cor. 5:1-9

Phil. 1:21-22
I Thess. 5:9-10
II Tim. 4:6-8
Heb. 9:27
Rev. 21:1-4

Death Of A Loved One
John 5:28-29
I Cor. 15:12-57
I Thess. 4:13-18

Divorce
Matt. 5:31-32; 19:3-9
Mark 10:2-12
Luke 16:18
Rom. 7:1-3
I Cor. 7:10-16

Doubtful Things
Rom. 14:1-23
I Cor. 8:1-13
Phil. 2:12-15
Col. 3:1-10,17
I Thess. 5:21-22
Titus 2:12-14
James 4:4-5
I John 2:15-17

Doing The Right Things
Matt. 7:12
James 1:5-6; 4:17

Debts
Rom. 13:8

Faith
Rom. 10:17
Eph. 2:8
Heb. 11:1-40; 12:1-2
James 1:2-8
I Peter 1:7
I John 5:4

Fear
John 14:27

Rom. 8:28,31,35-39
II Tim. 1:7
Heb. 13:5-6
I John 4:18

**Feeling Bad Over Something
That Happened [*Disappointment*]**
John 14:27; 16:31-33
Rom. 8:28
I Thess. 5:18
Heb. 4:16
I Peter 1:3-9

Foolish Son [*Prodigal Son*]
Luke 15:11-32

Forgiveness Of Sin
Matt. 6:14-15
Col. 1:14
I John 1:7-9

Forgiving Others
Matt. 6:12,14-15; 18:15-17,21-22
Mark 11:25-26
Luke 17:3-4
Eph. 4:32
Col. 3:12-13

Free Because Of Christ [*Liberty*]
John 8:31-32,36
Rom. 6:6-11,15-23; 7:6; 8:1-2
Gal. 5:1,13-14

Friends, and Being Friendly
John 13:34-35; 15:12-14
Gal. 6:1-5,10

Fruit Of The Spirit
Gal. 5:22-23

Gifts Of The Holy Spirit
Rom. 12:6-8
I Cor. 12-14
Eph. 4:11-12
I Peter 4:10

Giving With A Heart Of Love
Matt. 5:42
Luke 6:38
Rom. 12:8
II Cor. 9:6-7

God Meets The Needs
Of His Children [*Provision*]
Matt. 6:25-34
II Cor. 9:8
Eph. 3:20
I Peter 1:4
II Peter 1:3-4

God's Care
Eph. 3:20
Phil. 4:14-19
Heb. 4:14-16; 13:5-6
I Peter 5:5-7
I John 4:14-16

God's Will
Eph. 5:15-21
Phil. 2:12-18
I Thess. 4:3
I Peter 3:17

Going Without Food [*Fasting*]
Matt. 6:16-18
Mark 9:28-29
Acts 14:23

God's Word
Col. 3:16
Heb. 4:12
I Peter 1:23;2:2-3

Golden Rule
Matt. 7:12
Luke 6:31

Good Samaritan
Luke 10:30-37

Hard Things That Come Your Way
Rom. 8:28
II Cor. 4:16-18
Heb. 5:8; 12:6-11
Rev. 3:19

Happiness
Matt. 5:2-12
Rom. 14:22
James 5:11
I Peter 3:14; 4:14

Having No Pride [*Humility*]
Acts 20:19
Rom. 12:3,16
Phil. 2:1-4
I Peter 5:5-7

Heaven
Acts 7:44-50
I Cor. 2:9
Heb. 8:1
I Peter 1:4
Rev. 21:3-4,27

Hell
Matt. 5:22; 18:8-9; 22:13; 25:41,46
Mark 9:48
II Thess. 1:8-9
Jude 6-7
Rev. 20:15

Helping Other Christians
Matt. 5:13-16; 10:37-42
Luke 3:10-14
Gal. 6:1-5,10
James 2:1-9
I John 3:17-18

Holy Spirit
John 14:15-18
Acts 2:1-4; 5:1-11
I Cor. 3:16-17; 6:18-20; 12:1-3
II Cor. 13:14
I Peter 1:2

Hope
Rom. 5:5; 8:24; 15:4,13
I Cor. 13:7
Gal. 5:5
II Thess. 2:16
Titus 1:2
Heb. 11:1
I Peter 1:3

How To Know You Are Saved
John 5:24; 6:37; 10:27-30; 20:31
Rom. 8:16-17; 10:8-13
I John 5:11-13

Husbands
I Cor. 7:1-4
Eph. 5:25-33
Col. 3:19
I Peter 3:7

Jesus' Teachings
On The Mountain [*Beatitudes*]
Matt. 5:3-12
Luke 6:20-26

Jesus: As Lord
Luke 4:40-41
Rom. 10:9
I Cor. 6:19-20
Phil. 2:5-11

Jesus: The One Who Saves
Matt. 1:21
Luke 19:10
John 3:16-17; 14:6
Acts 4:12
Rom. 5:8
Eph. 1:7
I John 5:12

Knowing All Is Well
Gal. 6:9
Eph. 3:12
Phil. 1:6
Heb. 10:35-36
I Peter 2:9-10

Living For Christ
II Cor. 5:17
Col. 2:6-7
II Tim. 2:19
I Peter 2:2-3

Living Water
John 4:7-14; 7:37-39
Rev. 7:17; 22:17

Lord's Day
Matt. 12:1-14
Mark 2:27-28
Luke 6:5; 13:14-17
John 7:23
Acts 20:7
I Cor. 16:2

Lord's Prayer
Matt. 6:9-13
Luke 11:2-4

Lord's Supper
Matt. 26:26-30
Acts 2:42; 20:7
I Cor. 11:23-32

Love
John 3:16; 13:34-35; 15:12-14
Rom. 5:8; 8:35-39
I Cor. 13
I John 3:1

Man's Need To Be Saved
Rom. 3:10-12,23; 5:12; 6:23
I John 1:9-10

Marriage
Matt. 19:3-9
I Cor. 7
Eph. 5:22-33
Heb. 13:4
I Peter 3:1-8

Never Alone
Matt. 18:20; 28:20

Acts 18:10
Heb. 13:5

New Heaven And Earth
Rev. 21-22

Obeying Christ And His Word
John 14:21
II Cor. 10:5-6
James 2:10
I John 3:22

Obeying The Laws And Leaders Of Your Nation
Matt. 5:16
Rom. 13:1-7
I Tim. 2:1-3
I Peter 2:13-17

Parents
Eph. 6:1-4
Col. 3:20-21
I Tim. 5:4

Pay For Doing Good [Rewards]
I Cor. 9:24-27; 15:58
Gal. 6:9
Eph. 6:8
II Tim. 4:6-8

Peace
John 14:27; 16:33
Rom. 5:1
II Cor. 1:3-5
Phil. 4:4-9
Col. 3:12-15

Poor
Matt. 26:11
II Cor. 8:9
Gal. 2:10
James 2:1-9

Power Over Satan
James 4:7
I John 4:4

Power Over Temptation [Overcoming]
Matt. 26:41
I Cor. 10:11-13
Phil. 1:6,10
I Thess. 3:2-3
James 4:7-10
II Peter 2:9
I John 4:4

Praise and Being Thankful
Eph. 5:15-20
Phil. 4:4-6
Col. 3:15-17
I Thess. 5:18
Heb. 13:15
I Peter 1:6-9

Prayer
Matt. 6:5-13; 7:7-11; 21:22
John 14:13-14; 15:7
Eph. 6:18-19
Phil. 4:6
Heb. 4:14-16
James 5:16-18
I John 5:14-15

Prize Of Life [Crown]
I Cor. 9:24-27
I Thess. 2:19-20
II Tim. 4:6-8
James 1:9-12
I Peter 5:1-4
Rev. 2:9-10

Satan
James 4:7
I John 4:4

Second Coming Of Christ
Matt. 24:35-44; 25:1-13
Luke 21:33-36
Acts 1:11
I Thess. 4:13-18
Titus 2:13

Heb. 10:25
II Peter 3:8-15
I John 3:2-3

Sex Sins
[*Adultery and Fornication*]
Matt. 5:27-28; 19:18
Gal. 5:19
I Thess. 4:1-8
Heb. 13:4

Sharing The Good News
[*Witnessing*]
Matt. 5:16; 28:18-20
Mark 5:18-20
Luke 24:48
John 17:18
Acts 1:8
Rom. 1:16-17
II Cor. 5:18-21
II Tim. 4:2
I Peter 3:15-17; 4:11

Sharing Together [*Fellowship*]
Matt. 18:20
John 13:34
Acts 2:42-47
I Cor. 1:9
II Cor. 13:14
Col. 1:12; 2:19
Heb. 10:24-25
I John 1:3,7

Sickness
Matt. 4:23
John 11:4
James 5:13-16

Sin
John 8:33-36
Rom. 3:23; 5:12; 6:23; 14:23b
Gal. 6:7-8

Sinful Desires
Matt. 5:27-30

Gal. 5:17-21

Sin That Cannot Be Forgiven
[*Unpardonable Sin*]
Matt. 12:30-32
Mark 3:22-30
Luke 12:10
Heb. 10:26-27
I John 5:16-17

Sorrow
Matt. 11:28-30
John 16:22
Rom. 8:26-28
II Cor. 1:3-5; 4:17-18; 6:10

Strength
II Cor. 12:7-10
Phil. 4:10-13

Studying and Teaching
Acts 17:11; 20:29-31
II Tim. 2:15; 3:14-17
Heb. 4:12-13
I Peter 2:2-3

Suffering
Rom. 8:18
II Cor. 1:3-5; 4:17; 12:7-10
Phil. 1:29; 3:10
II Tim. 2:12
Heb. 12:3-13
I Peter 3:14-17; 4:12-16; 5:8-11

Suffering For Christ
[*Persecution*]
Matt. 5:10-11; 10:22
Mark 10:30
Acts 5:40-42; 9:10-16
Rom. 8:17
II Tim. 3:10-13
Heb. 11:24-26
James 1:2-3

Tell The Good News To Those Who Have Not Heard
Matt. 28:18-20
Mark 16:15-16
Luke 24:47-49
John 20:21
Acts 1:8

The Way To Be Saved
John 3:3,16-17; 5:24; 14:6
Acts 16:31
Rom. 10:9-10,13
II Cor. 5:17
Eph. 2:8-9
Titus 3:4-7
I John 5:11-13

Things God Gives Christians To Stand Against Satan [*Armor*]
Eph. 6:10-18

Things That Will Happen Before Christ Comes Again
Matt. 24:3-14
Luke 21:25-28
I Thess. 4:13-18; 5:2-3
II Thess. 2:1-11
I Tim. 4:1
II Tim. 3:1-5
James 5:7-8
I Peter 4:7
II Peter 3:3-13

Time Of Much Trouble [*Tribulation*]
Matt. 24:21
Rev. 7:14; 11:2-3; 13:5

Trust
John 3:16-18; 20:30-31
Rom. 1:16; 3:22
Gal. 3:22

Way Of Life
Rom. 8:5-11
Eph. 5:18
II Tim. 3:10

I Peter 1:15
II Peter 3:11

Wedding Supper Of The Lamb
Rev. 19:7-10

When Guilty
Rom. 8:1-17
II Cor. 5:20-21
Col. 2:11-18

When Discouraged
Matt. 11:28-30
John 14:27; 16:33
Heb. 4:16
I Peter 1:3-9
I John 5:14-15

Winning The Battle Over Satan
Rom. 8:31-39
I Cor. 15:57
II Cor. 2:14
II Tim. 2:19
I John 5:4
Rev. 3:5; 21:7

Wives
I Cor. 11:2-16
Eph. 5:22-24
Col. 3:18
I Tim. 3:11
Titus 2:3-5
I Peter 3:1-6

Working For A Living
Rom. 12:11
Eph. 4:28
II Thess. 3:10-12

Worry
Matt. 6:25-34
Phil. 4:6
I Peter 5:7

Worship
Matt. 4:10
John 4:19-24
Rev. 19:10; 22:8-9

THINGS THAT HAPPENED WHILE JESUS WAS ON EARTH

	PLACE	MATTHEW	MARK	LUKE	JOHN
Luke Writes To Theophilus				1:1-4	
Before The Earth Was Made					1:1-14
The Family Of Jesus		1:1-17		3:23-38	
An Angel Tells Of The Birth Of John The Baptist	Jerusalem			1:5-25	
Mary Learns Of Jesus' Birth	Nazareth			1:26-38	
Mary Visits Elizabeth	A city of Judah			1:39-56	
Birth Of John The Baptist	A city of Judah			1:57-66	
Zacharias' Song	A city of Judah			1:67-80	
Birth Of Jesus	Bethlehem	1:18-25		2:1-7	
Shepherds Learn Of Jesus' Birth	Near Bethlehem			2:8-14	
Shepherds Go To Bethlehem	Near Bethlehem			2:15-20	
Jesus Taken To The House Of God	Jerusalem			2:21-38	
Visit Of The Men Who Learned From The Stars	Bethlehem	2:1-12			
Joseph Takes Mary And Jesus To Egypt	Bethlehem to Egypt	2:13-15			
Boys Killed By Herod	Bethlehem	2:16-18			
Joseph Takes Mary And Jesus To Nazareth	Egypt to Nazareth	2:19-23		2:39-40	
Jesus In The House Of God	Jerusalem			2:41-52	
John The Baptist Preaches	Judea	3:1-12	1:1-8	3:1-18	1:15-28
Jesus Was Baptized	Jordan	3:13-17	1:9-11	3:21-22	1:29-34
Jesus Was Tempted	Judea	4:1-11	1:12-13	4:1-13	
Call Of Andrew And Peter	Jordan				1:35-42
Call Of Philip And Nathanael	Galilee				1:43-51
First Powerful Work— Water Changed To Wine	Cana				2:1-12

Event	Location	Matthew	Mark	Luke	John
Nicodemus Visits Jesus At Night	Jerusalem				3:1-21
Jesus Preaches In Judea	Judea				3:22
John The Baptist Tells More About Jesus	Judea				3:23-36
Jesus Talks To The Woman At The Well	Samaria				4:1-42
Jesus Goes To Galilee	Galilee				4:43-45
Healing Of The Dying Boy	Galilee				4:46-54
John The Baptist Put Into Prison	Macherus	14:1-5	6:14-20		
Jesus Preaches In Galilee	Galilee	4:12-17	1:14-15		
In Nazareth They Do Not Believe In Jesus	Nazareth			4:16-30	
Call Of Simon, Andrew, James And John	Capernaum	4:18-22	1:16-20	5:1-11	
A Demon Put Out	Capernaum		1:21-28	4:31-37	
Peter's Mother-in-law Healed	Capernaum	8:14-15	1:29-31	4:38-39	
Many People Healed	Capernaum	8:16-17	1:32-34	4:40-41	
Jesus Keeps On Preaching In Galilee	Galilee	4:23-25	1:35-39	4:42-44	
Man With Skin Disease Healed	Galilee	8:1-4	1:40-45	5:12-16	
The Man Let Down Through The Roof	Capernaum	9:1-8	2:1-12	5:17-26	
Call Of Matthew	Capernaum	9:9-13	2:13-17	5:27-32	
Man Healed At Pool Of Bethesda	Jerusalem				5:1-47
Followers Ate Grain On Day Of Rest	Capernaum	12:1-8	2:23-28	6:1-5	
Jesus Heals On The Day Of Rest	Capernaum	12:9-14	3:1-6	6:6-11	
Jesus Heals By The Side Of The Lake	Capernaum	12:15-21	3:7-12	6:17-19	
Jesus Teaches On The Mountain	Capernaum	5:1-27		6:20-49	
Healing Of The Captain's Helper	Capernaum	8:5-13		7:1-10	
The Widow's Son Raised From The Dead	Nain			7:11-17	
John The Baptist Asks About Jesus	Capernaum	11:1-6		7:18-23	
Jesus Tells About John The Baptist	Capernaum	11:7-19		7:24-35	

		MATTHEW	MARK	LUKE	JOHN
Jesus Teaches In Galilee	Galilee			8:1-3	
A Nation That Cannot Stand	Capernaum	12:22-37	3:22-30	11:14-23	
When Bad Goes From A Person	Capernaum	12:43-45		11:24-26	
Jesus Tells About Jonah	Capernaum	12:38-42		11:29-32	
The New Kind Of Family	Capernaum			8:19-21	
It Will Be Bad For The Proud Religious Law-keepers	Capernaum	12:46-50	3:31-35	11:37-54	
Jesus Teaches His Followers	Capernaum			12:1-59	
Everyone Should Be Sorry For Their Sins And Turn From Them	Capernaum			13:1-5	
Picture-stories—Seed, Yeast, Pearl, Fish Net	Capernaum	12:1-52	4:1-34	8:4-18	
Testing Of Some Followers	Galilee	8:18-22	5:21-43	9:57-62	
The Wind And Waves Obey Jesus	Galilee	8:23-27	4:35-41	8:22-25	
Demons Ask To Live In Pigs	Galilee	8:28-34	5:1-20	8:26-39	
Jesus Teaches About Not Eating	Capernaum	9:14-17	2:18-22	5:33-35	
Two Healed Through Faith	Capernaum	9:18-26	5:21-43	8:40-56	
Two Blind Men Healed	Capernaum	9:27-31			
A Demon Put Out	Capernaum	9:32-34			
They Do Not Believe In Nazareth	Nazareth	13:53-58	6:1-6		
The Twelve Sent Out	Galilee	10:1-42	6:7-13	9:1-6	
John The Baptist Is Killed	Galilee	14:6-12	6:21-29	9:7-9	
Feeding Of Five Thousand	Galilee	14:13-21	6:30-44	9:10-17	6:1-14
Jesus Walks On Water	Galilee	14:22-33	6:45-52		6:15-21
People Are Healed At Gennesaret	Gennesaret	14:34-36	6:53-56		
Teaching On Bread Of Life	Capernaum				6:22-71
Jesus Speaks Sharp Words To Leaders	Capernaum	15:1-20	7:1-23		
Demon Put Out Of Girl	Tyre, Sidon	15:21-28	7:24-30		
Man Who Could Not Hear Or Speak Healed	Decapolis		7:31-37		

Event	Location				
Feeding Of The Four Thousand	Decapolis	15:32-39	8:1-9		
Jesus Speaks Sharp Words To Proud Religious Law-keepers	Magadan	16:1-4	8:10-13		
Jesus Teaches Against Proud Religious Law-keepers	Galilee	16:5-21	8:14-21		
A Blind Man Is Healed	Bethsaida		8:22-26		
Peter Says Jesus Is The Christ	Caesarea	16:13-20	8:27-30	9:18-20	
Jesus Tells Of His Death, First Time	Caesarea	16:21-28	8:31-38	9:21-27	
A Look At What Jesus Will Be Like	Caesarea	17:1-13	9:1-13	9:28-36	
A Boy Is Healed	Caesarea	17:14-21	9:14-29	9:37-42	
Jesus Tells Of His Death, Second Time	Galilee	17:22-23	9:30-32	9:43-45	
House Of God Tax	Capernaum	17:24-27			
Teaching About Faith As A Child	Capernaum	18:1-35	9:33-50	9:46-50	
Jesus And Followers Leave Galilee	Judea			9:51-56	
The Seventy Sent Out To Preach	Judea			10:1-24	
Jesus Teaches At Religious Gathering	Jerusalem				7:1-52
Jesus Talks To The Woman Found In Sin	Jerusalem				8:1-11
Jesus Talks To The Jews	Jerusalem				8:12-59
Picture-story Of Good Samaritan	Judea			10:25-37	
Jesus Visits Mary And Martha	Bethany			10:38-42	
The Followers Taught How To Pray	Judea			11:1-13	
The Blind Man Healed	Jerusalem				9:1-41
The Shepherd And The Door	Jerusalem				10:1-39
Many People Believe In Jesus	East of the Jordan River				10:40-42
Picture-story Of The Fig Tree	East of the Jordan River			13:6-9	
Woman Healed On The Day Of Rest	East of the Jordan River			13:10-17	
Jesus Teaches On Way To Jerusalem	East of the Jordan River			13:22-35	
Jesus Heals, Teaches, Picture-story Of Big Supper	East of the Jordan River			14:1-24	

Event	Location	MATTHEW	MARK	LUKE	JOHN
Giving Up Things Of This Earth	East of the Jordan River	10:37-39		14:25-35	
Picture-story Of Lost Sheep, Lost Money, Son Who Spent All His Money	East of the Jordan River			15:1-32	
Picture-story Of The Boss Who Stole	East of the Jordan River			16:1-13	
Jesus Teaches The Law Is Not Finished	East of the Jordan River			16:14-31	
Jesus Teaches About Forgiving	East of the Jordan River			17:1-10	
Ten Men With Skin Disease Healed	Samaria			17:11-19	
Jesus Tells Of His Second Coming	East of the Jordan River			17:20-37	
Picture-story Of The Woman Whose Husband Had Died	East of the Jordan River			18:1-8	
Picture-story Of The Proud Religious Law-keepers And Tax Gatherers	East of the Jordan River			18:9-14	
Lazarus Is Raised From The Dead	Bethany				11:1-44
Proud Religious Law-keepers Try To Kill Jesus	Jerusalem				11:45-54
Teaching On Divorce	East of the Jordan River	19:1-12	10:1-12		
Jesus Gives Thanks For Little Children	East of the Jordan River	19:13-15	10:13-16	18:15-17	
Jesus Teaches About Keeping The Law	East of the Jordan River	19:16-30	10:17-31	18:18-30	
Picture-story Of Workmen In Grape Field	East of the Jordan River	20:1-16			
Jesus Tells Of His Death, Third Time	East of the Jordan River	20:17-19	10:32-34	18:31-34	
James And John Ask Something Hard	East of the Jordan River	20:20-28	10:35-45		
Two Blind Men Healed Near Jericho	Jericho	20:29-34	10:46-52	18:35-43	
The Changed Life Of Zacchaeus	Jericho			19:1-10	
Picture-story Of Ten Workman And The Money	Jericho			19:11-28	
Proud Religious Law-keepers Look For Jesus	Jerusalem				11:55-57
Mary Of Bethany Puts Perfume On Jesus	Bethany	26:6-13	14:3-9		12:1-11
The Last Time Jesus Goes Into Jerusalem	Jerusalem	21:1-11	11:1-11	19:29-44	12:12-19

Jesus Stops The Buying In The House Of God	Jerusalem	21:12-17	11:15-19	19:45-48	2:13-17
The Fig Tree Dries Up	Jerusalem	21:18-22	11:20-26		
They Ask Jesus Who Gave Him Power	Jerusalem	21:23-32	11:27-33	20:1-8	
Picture-story Of The Grape Field	Jerusalem	21:33-46	12:1-12	20:9-18	
Picture-story Of The Marriage Supper	Jerusalem	22:1-14			
Proud Religious Law-keepers Try To Trap Jesus	Jerusalem	22:15-22	12:13-17	20:19-26	
They Ask About Being Raised From The Dead	Jerusalem	22:23-33	12:18-27	20:27-40	
The Great Law	Jerusalem	22:34-40	12:28-34		
Jesus Asks Proud Religious Law-keepers About The Christ	Jerusalem	22:41-46	12:35-37	20:41-44	
False Teachers	Jerusalem	23:1-36	12:38-40	20:45-47	
Jesus Sorrows Over Jerusalem	Jerusalem	23:37-39			
A Woman Whose Husband Had Died Gave All She Had	Jerusalem		12:41-44	21:1-4	
The Greek People Want To See Jesus	Jerusalem				12:20-50
Jesus Tells Of The House Of God	Mountain of Olives	24:1-51	13:1-37	21:5-36	
Picture-story Of The Ten Young Women	Mountain of Olives	25:1-13			
Picture-story Of The Ten Men And The Money	Mountain of Olives	25:14-30			
Sheep And Goats	Mountain of Olives	25:31-46			
They Try To Find A Way To Kill Jesus	Jerusalem	26:1-5	14:1-2	22:1-6	
Judas Hands Jesus Over To Be Killed	Jerusalem	26:14-16	14:10-11		13:21-35
Getting Ready For The Special Supper	Jerusalem	26:17-19	14:12-16	22:7-13	
The Last Special Supper	Jerusalem	26:20-25	14:17-21	22:14-18	
They Argue Who Is Greatest	Jerusalem			22:24-30	
Jesus Washes His Followers' Feet	Jerusalem				13:1-20
The First Lord's Supper	Jerusalem	26:26-30	14:22-26	22:19-20	
Jesus Tells How Peter Will Lie About Him	Jerusalem	26:31-35	14:27-31	22:31-34	13:36-38

	Location	MATTHEW	MARK	LUKE	JOHN
Jesus Comforts His Followers	Jerusalem				14:1-31
The Vine And The Branches	Jerusalem				15:1-27
The Work Of The Holy Spirit	Jerusalem				16:1-33
Jesus' Prayer	Jerusalem				17:1-26
Jesus Prays In Gethsemane	Mountain of Olives	26:36-46	14:32-42	22:39-46	
Jesus Handed Over To Sinners	Mountain of Olives	26:47-56	14:43-52	22:47-51	18:1-11
Jesus Stands In Front Of Caiaphas	Jerusalem	26:57-58	14:53-54	22:52-54	18:19-24
The Court Room	Jerusalem	26:59-68	14:55-65		
Peter Lies About Jesus	Jerusalem	26:69-75	14:66-72	22:55-62	18:15-18, 25-27
Jesus Stands In Front Of Pilate	Jerusalem	27:1-2, 11-14	15:1-5	23:1-5	18:28-37
Death Of Judas	Jerusalem	27:3-10			
Jesus Sent To Herod	Jerusalem			23:6-12	
Jesus Or Barabbas Is To Go Free	Jerusalem	27:15-26	15:6-14	23:17-25	18:38-40
The Headband Of Thorns	Jerusalem	27:27-32	15:15-21		19:1-5
Pilate Tries To Let Jesus Go Free	Jerusalem				19:6-16
Jesus On The Cross	Jerusalem	27:33-37	15:22-26	23:26-38	19:17-22
The Two Robbers	Jerusalem	27:38-44	15:27-32	23:39-43	
The Death Of Jesus	Jerusalem	27:45-50	15:33-36	23:44-49	19:28-37
The Powerful Works At His Death	Jerusalem	27:51-54	15:37-39		
The Women At The Cross	Jerusalem	27:55-56	15:40-41		19:25-27
Jesus' Grave	Jerusalem	27:57-66	15:42-47	23:50-56	19:38-42
Jesus Is Raised From The Dead	Jerusalem	28:1-10	16:1-8	24:1-12	20:1-18
The Jews Make Up A Story	Jerusalem	28:11-15			
Jesus' Followers Do Not Believe He Is Risen			16:9-14	24:13-43	20:24-29
Jesus Sends His Followers To Preach		28:16-20	16:15-18	24:44-49	20:21-23
Jesus Goes To Be Beside His Father			16:19-20	24:50-53	
The Risen Christ Talks To His Followers	Galilee				21:1-23